Understanding the
RELIGIONS
OF THE WORLD

Understanding the RELIGIONS OF THE WORLD

An Introduction

SECOND EDITION

Edited by
WILL DEMING

WILEY Blackwell

This edition first published 2025
© 2025 John Wiley & Sons Ltd

All rights reserved, including rights for text and data mining and training of artificial technologies or similar technologies. No part of this publication may be reproduced, stored in a retrieval system, or transmitted, in any form or by any means, electronic, mechanical, photocopying, recording or otherwise, except as permitted by law. Advice on how to obtain permission to reuse material from this title is available at http://www.wiley.com/go/permissions.

The right of Will Deming to be identified as the author of the editorial material in this work has been asserted in accordance with law.

Registered Office(s)
John Wiley & Sons, Inc., 111 River Street, Hoboken, NJ 07030, USA
John Wiley & Sons Ltd, New Era House, 8 Oldlands Way, Bognor Regis, West Sussex, PO22 8NQ, UK

For details of our global editorial offices, customer services, and more information about Wiley products visit us at www.wiley.com.

The manufacturer's authorized representative according to the EU General Product Safety Regulation is Wiley-VCH GmbH, Boschstr. 12, 69469 Weinheim, Germany, e-mail: Product_Safety@wiley.com.

Wiley also publishes its books in a variety of electronic formats and by print-on-demand. Some content that appears in standard print versions of this book may not be available in other formats.

Trademarks: Wiley and the Wiley logo are trademarks or registered trademarks of John Wiley & Sons, Inc. and/or its affiliates in the United States and other countries and may not be used without written permission. All other trademarks are the property of their respective owners. John Wiley & Sons, Inc. is not associated with any product or vendor mentioned in this book.

Limit of Liability/Disclaimer of Warranty
While the publisher and authors have used their best efforts in preparing this work, they make no representations or warranties with respect to the accuracy or completeness of the contents of this work and specifically disclaim all warranties, including without limitation any implied warranties of merchantability or fitness for a particular purpose. No warranty may be created or extended by sales representatives, written sales materials or promotional statements for this work. This work is sold with the understanding that the publisher is not engaged in rendering professional services. The advice and strategies contained herein may not be suitable for your situation. You should consult with a specialist where appropriate. The fact that an organization, website, or product is referred to in this work as a citation and/or potential source of further information does not mean that the publisher and authors endorse the information or services the organization, website, or product may provide or recommendations it may make. Further, readers should be aware that websites listed in this work may have changed or disappeared between when this work was written and when it is read. Neither the publisher nor authors shall be liable for any loss of profit or any other commercial damages, including but not limited to special, incidental, consequential, or other damages.

Library of Congress Cataloging-in-Publication Data Applied for:

Paperback: 9781119887478

Cover Design: Wiley
Cover Image: © Goldquest/Getty Images

Set in 10/13.5 pt Minion Pro by Straive, Pondicherry, India

CONTENTS

Authors and Major Contributors	vii
Preface to the Second Edition	ix
Preface for Teachers	x
Chapter Features	xiii
Introduction	1
1 Hinduism	9
2 Buddhism	60
3 Chinese Religion	114
4 Japan's Lived Religion	164
5 African Religions	204
6 Religions of Oceania	240
7 Indigenous Religions in the Americas	271
8 Judaism	337
9 Christianity	390
10 Islam	452
11 Change in Religions and New Religions	512
12 The Study of Religions	542
Glossary of Key Terms	577
Index	594

AUTHORS AND MAJOR CONTRIBUTORS

Gregory D. Alles, Professor Emeritus, Religious Studies, McDaniel College. (PhD University of Chicago)

Miguel Astor-Aguilera, Associate Professor, School of Historical, Philosophical and Religious Studies, Arizona State University. (PhD University at Albany, State University of New York)

David R. Bains, Professor of Biblical and Religious Studies, Samford University. (PhD Harvard University)

Thomas Borchert, Professor, Department of Religion, University of Vermont. (PhD University of Chicago)

Maria M. Dakake, Associate Professor, Religious Studies, George Mason University. (PhD Princeton University)

Will Deming, Professor Emeritus, Department of Theology, University of Portland. (PhD University of Chicago)

Gary L. Ebersole, Professor Emeritus of History and Religious Studies, University of Missouri–Kansas City. (PhD University of Chicago)

Anna M. Gade, Vilas Distinguished Achievement Professor, Center for South Asia, University of Wisconsin–Madison. (PhD University of Chicago)

Matthew B. Lynch, Instructor, School of History, Philosophy, and Religion, Oregon State University. (PhD University of North Carolina at Chapel Hill)

†Mary N. MacDonald, formerly Professor of Religious Studies and O'Connell Professor in Humanities, LeMoyne College. (PhD University of Chicago)

Jean-François Mayer, Director of the Religioscope Institute Fribourg, Switzerland. (PhD University of Lyon)

Jennifer Oldstone-Moore, Professor Emerita, Department of Religion, Wittenberg University. (PhD University of Chicago)

Paul R. Powers, Professor of Religious Studies, Lewis and Clark College. (PhD University of Chicago)

Joseph Schaller, Deputy Public Affairs Officer, U.S. Embassy Barbados. (PhD University of California at Berkeley)

Melvin Shaw, Aomori, Japan. (PhD University of Illinois in Chicago)

John W. Traphagan, Professor Emeritus, Department of Religious Studies, University of Texas at Austin. (PhD University of Pittsburgh)

Garry Trompf, Professor Emeritus in the History of Ideas, Department of Studies in Religion, University of Sydney, Australia. (PhD Australian National University)

Alan Unterman, former Honorary Research Fellow in Comparative Religion, University of Manchester. (PhD University of Delhi, India)

Mary Nyangweso Wangila, Professor and Peel Distinguished Chair of Religious Studies, East Carolina University. (PhD Drew University)

Robin M. Wright, Professor Emeritus, Department of Religion, University of Florida. (PhD Stanford University)

PREFACE TO THE SECOND EDITION

For this second edition of *Understanding the Religions of the World*, all the chapters from the first edition have been edited to remove mistakes, improve clarity, and treat important events that have taken place since 2015, when the first edition appeared. The one exception is the chapter on Japanese religion, which has been completely rewritten and renamed Japan's Lived Religion. This was necessitated by a growing consensus on the fundamental importance of the Meiji regime for the interpretation of Shinto. It also afforded an opportunity to expand the history section of this chapter and broaden and update the discussion of contemporary beliefs and practices.

Beyond this, three major additions have been made to the original text. First, a discussion of African-based religions in the American diaspora has been added to the chapter on African religions, providing an analysis of Candomblé, Umbanda, Vodou, and Santería. Second, a new chapter on the indigenous religions of the Americas has been added. This is a true innovation for texts of this kind, for not only does it cover North, Central, and South America, but it also moves away from an anecdotal approach of treating one or two widely practiced rituals by providing a comprehensive analysis of these religions—to the extent that this is possible in an introductory textbook. This chapter brings to light previously neglected religious traditions and completes the original design of the first edition, which at the time of its publication proved to be too ambitious. Third, a chapter on the study of religions has been added, with the goal of giving students a glimpse into this relatively new and heterogeneous discipline. It begins with the creation of the modern research university and ends with a consideration of the Cognitive Science of Religion, treating major figures, from Marx to Eliade along the way. It is concise and accessible to students in a manner that other treatments are not.

I would like to thank my wife, Lauren Wellford Deming, for her help with proofreading the drafts of this text, and my son, JD Deming, for his advice on clarity and style.

PREFACE FOR TEACHERS

Dear Colleague,

This text offers a new approach to the study of religions. Its goal is to help students understand how religions *work*—what makes them appealing, why they "make sense" to their adherents, and how we can study them as symbolic systems that orient people to things they regard as supremely important in their lives. As *systems*, each religion operates according to its own logic. This is simply another way of saying that religious people do not act at random. Yet a religion's particular logic can mystify outsiders, which is why members of one religion often find it difficult to empathize with members of another, and why students can experience unfamiliar religions as bizarre or confusing.

This book attempts to demystify religions for our students by first identifying each religion's own internal logic, and then explaining how this logic guides adherents into encounters and experiences with transcendent ideas, beings, relationships, and realities. This approach enables students to see why members of a given religion prefer *their* particular rituals, images, and beliefs over a multitude of alternatives, and why religions have developed so differently from one another. It also helps students understand why religious adherents invest so much of themselves and their resources into a religion.

What to Expect: The Specifics

Each chapter is written by or in partnership with an area specialist, and reviewed by other area specialists. This guarantees the latest scholarship and provides students a taste of the distinctive approaches that these specialists use in their respective fields. The study of Islam, for example, has developed quite differently than the study of Indigenous American religions.

The presentation of the material in Chapters 1–10 is guided by an understanding of each religion's particular logic. This is true not only for the sections on contemporary beliefs and practices, but also for the sections on history. The advantage for the historical sections is that each religion's past is organized with an emphasis on how it has changed over time as a dynamic system of meaning. The sections on contemporary beliefs and practices, in turn, move beyond the usual descriptive or thematic approaches by involving the reader in analysis. These sections are much longer than those of a typical textbook, in most cases comprising well over half the chapter.

Chapter Structure

Each chapter, with the exception of Chapters 11 and 12, has four principal sections: Overview, History, Contemporary Beliefs and Practices, and Conclusion.

- The *Overview* provides a brief description of how large the religion is, where it is practiced, something of its distinctive nature, and its major divisions or denominations.
- The *History* section summarizes past practices, doctrines, and organizational structures of a religion and gives an account of important developments and changes. The length of this section varies from chapter to chapter and sometimes includes an account of the western "discovery" of a religion. The chapter on the Religions of Oceania, for example, has a relatively short historical section and discusses the importance of European first contacts.
- *Contemporary Beliefs and Practices* is the heart of each chapter. This section begins with a thesis statement outlining a religion's basic premises and logical structures, and then explains what adherents do and why they do it in light of these premises and structures.
- The *Conclusion* provides a short summary with final insights.

Each chapter ends with questions for review and discussion, a list of key terms, and a short bibliography. The latter is divided into three parts: a good first book, further reading, and reference and research.

The Order of the Chapters

The first four chapters follow the rationale that Hinduism, which shares much of the worldview of Buddhism, prepares students for Buddhism; Buddhism, as a component of both Chinese and Japanese religions, prepares students for these two religions; and Chinese religion, both by its syncretistic nature and its early influence on Japan, prepares students for that religion.

Traditional and indigenous religions are often placed at the beginning of a text, giving the impression that they are more elemental (primitive) than other religions, or at the end, implying, perhaps, that they are not as important. To avoid this, African religions, the religions of Oceania, and indigenous religions in the Americas follow Japanese religion. The order of the last three religions, Judaism, Christianity, and Islam, follows the standard rationale that the religious worldview of Christianity presupposes that of Judaism, and the religious worldview of Islam presupposes that of both Judaism and Christianity. It also has the advantage of putting religions near the end that are already familiar to many students, but which they must now reassess in light of having studied other religions. The chapter entitled Change in Religion and New Religions follows these because it presupposes some knowledge of the religions discussed in the earlier chapters. Finally, the chapter on the study of religions is placed last, in the hope that the earlier chapters will have peaked the interest of some students to the point that they want to know more about the discipline.

Figures and End Matter

The photographs, diagrams, illustrations, and maps that accompany the text have been carefully chosen to further the discussion of the text, not simply to add ornamentation. At the end of the book, a combined glossary of key terms from all the chapters is assembled, as well as a comprehensive index.

A Personal Note

After teaching "world religions" to incoming first-year students for more than a decade, I began to formulate an analytical approach to the material, replacing the largely descriptive-chronological one I had been using. The result, three years later, was *Rethinking Religion* (2005), in which I outlined a model for making sense of religions. It was on the basis of that publication that I was asked to consider editing a textbook on religions, the first edition of which appeared in 2015. With this new edition, I am again pleased and excited to offer my colleagues what I consider to be a solid introductory text as well as a genuine pedagogical contribution to the study of religions in undergraduate courses.

Will Deming

CHAPTER FEATURES

Each chapter that presents a religious tradition (Chapters 1–10) is divided into four main sections: introduction, history, contemporary beliefs and practices, and conclusion. This is followed by questions for review and discussion, a glossary of key terms, and reading suggestions. In addition, these chapters contain feature boxes that highlight aspects of each religious tradition under discussion. There are five types of boxes:

A Closer Look offers an extra level of detail for topics mentioned in the text.

Rituals, Rites, Practices draws attention to distinctive activities performed by religious adherents.

Sacred Traditions and Scripture provides the reader with examples of the narratives, legal codes, and other compositions—both written and oral—that are authoritative for a religion.

Talking about Religion focuses on how adherents and scholars choose to express themselves when describing or explaining a religion.

Did You Know . . . makes connections between a religion and things that readers commonly know but had not associated with that religion.

Introduction

Understanding religions takes time.

Understanding the Religions of the World: An Introduction, Second Edition.
Edited by Will Deming.
© 2025 John Wiley & Sons Ltd. Published 2025 by John Wiley & Sons Ltd.

The Importance of Religion

Eighty-five percent of the world's population is religious—roughly 6.9 billion people. This means that religion shapes and justifies much of what goes on in the world. To understand religion is to understand people. To understand religion is to understand today's world.

When people go to war, when they make peace, when they buy and sell, when they start families, and when they honor their dead, they do so in ways influenced by religion. Here are some examples that have important political or economic implications: Almost one-fourth of the world's population (1.9 billion people) does not eat pork or drink alcohol for religious reasons. Another 1.4 billion people do not eat beef. Many countries have a national religion, display religious symbols or colors on their flags, or require their citizens to pay a religion tax. In the United States, sessions of Congress begin with prayer; the outcome of national elections is influenced by religious organizations; tens of thousands of churches, synagogues, mosques, and temples are exempted from paying taxes; and in the grocery store, many foods carry a religious mark or symbol (Figure I.1).

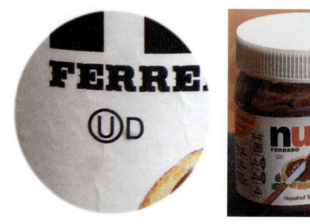

Figure I.1 Many foods at the grocery store bear a mark of religious certification. The "circle U" on this jar designates the approval of a Jewish organization called the Orthodox Union. The "D" signifies that the product contains dairy, and hence should not be eaten with meat. Source: Will Deming.

Knowledge of Religion

Despite religion's considerable presence and influence in the world (Figure I.2), most people know little about it. Maybe this is not so surprising. Most people know little about their own language. Religion, like language, is something people use but rarely think about—it is simply a given of their world. But even when people do ponder

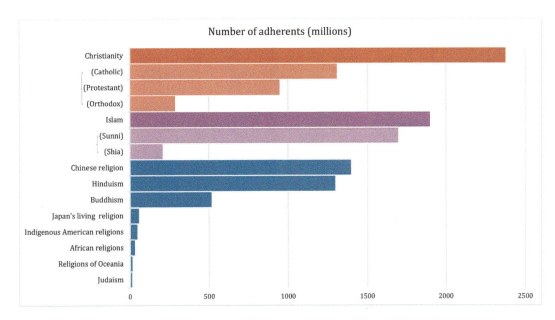

Figure I.2 Religion is a human activity practiced by about 85 percent of the world's population.

religion, it is usually their own religion that comes to mind. Most Roman Catholics, for example, know little about Islam or Hinduism. Most, in fact, know little about other forms of Christianity. And the same is true for Baptists and Methodists, and for different types of Muslims and Buddhists.

In the United States, several legal and social norms actually discourage people from learning about any religion beyond their own. The American principle of separation of church and state has limited the extent to which religion is studied in public schools, while the secular nature of American society promotes the idea that religion is a private matter, unsuited for public discussion. In the 1950s and 1960s, it was even popular to single out religion as one of two topics that people should avoid in polite conversation—the other being politics.

Beyond this, the absence of a national religion in the United States encourages religious diversity. Today, more religions are practiced in the United States than in any other country. But with so many smaller religious circles carrying on internal conversations of their own, a larger forum for the public discussion of religion has been slow to materialize. Historically, Christians and Jews have had little interaction with one another; Roman Catholics and Protestants have also kept to themselves; and the various Protestant denominations have more often than not established their identities by highlighting their differences. The unifying factors that now promote the public discussion of religion are fairly recent to the American scene. Ecumenical movements, the notions that most Americans practice an "Abrahamic religion" or share a common "Judeo-Christian" value system, and the adoption of the phrase "In God We Trust" as the national motto go back no further than the previous century.

Finally, the importance given to science in the United States often marginalizes religious perspectives on social and economic issues. In legislatures and boardrooms across the country, it is now a matter of course to demand that someone "do the science" before addressing an issue. By contrast, it is rarely appropriate to ask that someone consider the religious or spiritual dimensions of an issue—that is, "do the theology."

> **A Closer Look**
>
> ## Approaching Religion
>
> Not everyone interested in religion practices religion—some people are insiders and some are outsiders. *Religious adherents* and *theologians* are insiders. Those in the first group practice a religion; those in the second both practice a religion and seek to understand, explain, and articulate how that religion works. *Students of religion*, by contrast, engage in the academic study of both religion and religions from the outside, often by comparing several religions. They can practice a religion in their private lives as well, but they are rarely theologians.

Understanding Religions

The purpose of this book is to provide an objective approach to learning about and analyzing religions. It is one thing to know facts about a religion—its history, its size, its geographical distribution, and its principal beliefs and practices. It is quite another thing to understand a religion: to appreciate why a particular religion is so appealing to some people; why it makes sense to its adherents; and how it works as a system for defining and achieving human aspirations. This sort of understanding gives us insight into how religious people view the human condition and what motivates them to live as they do.

Defining Religion and Religions

There are many ways to define religion. Typical definitions include things like:

- a system of beliefs and moral behavior,
- faith in God, and
- the worship of supernatural beings.

While these definitions may be helpful in discussing certain religions or certain aspects of religions, they are not broad enough to cover all the religions we will study in this book. As a consequence, we must take a more inclusive approach, defining **religion** as *orientation to what is supreme or ultimate in one's life*.

A definition such as this is necessary because of the tremendous variation we find among the religions of the world. The word "orientation," for example, is flexible enough to account for the innumerable ways in which people practice their religions (pilgrimage, sacrifice, dancing, acts of kindness, storytelling, devotion, etc.). Likewise, the use of "what" in the phrase "what is supreme or ultimate" is necessary because the focal point of some religions, such as *brahman* in Hinduism or nirvana in Buddhism, is neither a thing nor a being. Indeed, according to some Buddhist teachings, nirvana may, in fact, neither exist nor not exist. For this reason, each of these is best designated as a "what." Finally, the phrase "supreme or ultimate" is needed because, while "ultimate" accurately describes the Muslim God and nirvana, it would distort African and Oceanian views of the divine world in a way that "supreme" does not. The difference is a subtle but indispensable distinction between what is most important and what is more important than anything else could ever be.

Given this definition of religion, we may define **religions** (the plural) as discrete systems or traditions of orientation to what is supreme or ultimate—for example, Buddhism and Islam (Figure I.2).

The goal of orienting oneself to what is supreme or ultimate is to make one's life more real, more true, and more meaningful, and in every religion this requires the use of **symbols**. While everyday English uses the word symbol to mean something that "represents" or "stands for" something else, it is important to think of *religious* symbols as tools. This is because religious symbols do not just represent something, they *do* something. They enable religious people to achieve their fullest potential in life by linking them to what is supreme or ultimate. Lighting a candle and placing it in front of the statue of a god does not simply represent wisdom or divine light. Rather, it nurtures a relationship with a divine being who is accessible through the symbols ("tools") of the candle and the statue. Likewise, prayer does not "stand" for anything. It is orientation to deities by speaking to them.

This raises an important question: what qualifies a candle, a statue, or a prayer as a religious symbol? As we will discover, many things serve as symbols: words, objects, images, sounds, motions, rituals, foods, animals, clothing, buildings, mountains, rivers, and much, much more. Even so, not just anything can be a symbol for a particular religion. Because each religion has its own understanding of what is supreme or ultimate, each will also have its own set of appropriate words, objects, images, etc. If what is supreme or ultimate comes through enlightenment, as in Buddhism, then meditation will be an appropriate tool for orientation. But if it comes through establishing balance and harmony in an ever-changing cosmos, as in Chinese religion, then acupuncture or eating bitter foods might be required.

This wide variation in symbols between different religions underscores a final important insight: each religion is a distinct, internally logical system. In this respect, religions may be compared to languages. Just as a word from one language may be meaningless or inappropriate in another language, most religious symbols are meaningless or inappropriate outside the context of their own religion. Praying in the direction of Mecca, as Muslims do, has no significance for Hindus and Buddhists. Removing one's shoes before entering a place of worship, as is practiced in Hinduism, Buddhism, and Islam, is normally quite inappropriate in Jewish and Christian worship. Even symbols that outwardly resemble one another are often appropriate in different religions for very different reasons. The Hindu practice of bathing in the Ganges River and Christian baptism are both methods of spiritual purification that use water. In Hinduism, however, bathing in the Ganges "makes sense" because the Ganges is a manifestation of the Great Goddess. For Christians, however, baptism is an effective tool because it connects them to God through the death of Jesus Christ. Likewise, while most Hindus do not eat beef and most Muslims do not eat pork, Hindus renounce beef because they consider the cow too god-like to harm, let alone eat, whereas Muslims forgo pork because they regard the pig as ritually and hygienically unfit for human consumption.

In the final analysis, what qualifies something as a symbol is its capacity to "work" in accordance with a religion's **internal logic**. Given a religion's understanding of what is supreme or ultimate, things that promise orientation to it have the potential to be effective symbols. When symbols lose this capacity, moreover, they become obsolete. This is why, for example, Roman Catholics no longer abstain from meat on Friday as a way to please God. Because of decisions made at the Second Vatican Council (1962–1965), abstaining from meat on Friday lost its effectiveness: it no longer "works" as a tool to draw close to God.

CONCLUSION

By defining religion and religious symbols, we have taken the first step in understanding the religions of the world. In the following chapters, we will examine 10 religions, each of which has its own view of what is supreme or ultimate, operates according to its own internal logic, and uses its own repertoire of symbols. Using this knowledge, we will consider each religion's beginning, its development over time, and its manifestation in today's world. In two final chapters we will explore the ways in which religions change over time, how new religions come into being, and how the study of religions became an academic discipline. For our efforts, we will gain valuable insight into how the people with whom we share the earth view themselves and others from a religious perspective.

For review

1. What is the role of symbols in a religion?
2. How is a religion's internal logic related to what it envisions as supreme or ultimate?
3. What is the difference between religion and *a* religion?
4. According to our definitions, do you consider yourself a religious adherent, a theologian, or a student of religion—or some combination of these?

For discussion

1. Can entire religions die out? Give some examples and explain why this happens.
2. Why, in an age of secularism and science, do people still find religion attractive?

Key Terms

internal logic	A system of meaning unique to a particular religion that determines how one orients oneself and others to what is supreme or ultimate.
religion	The human activity of orientation to what is supreme or ultimate.
religions	Symbolic systems by which people orient themselves to a particular vision of what is supreme or ultimate.
the supreme or ultimate	The focal point of religion and religions; that which is the most important, real, and true in someone's life.
symbol	The means by which people orient themselves to what is supreme or ultimate; depending on the religion, a symbol can be practically anything.

Bibliography

A good first book
Will Deming. *Rethinking Religion: A Concise Introduction*. New York: Oxford University Press, 2005.

Further reading
Peter L. Berger. *The Sacred Canopy: Elements of a Sociology of Religion*. New York: Anchor Books, 1967.
Thomas A. Tweed. *Religion: A Very Short Introduction*. New York: Oxford University Press, 2020.

Reference and research
Lindsay Jones, ed. *Encyclopedia of Religion*, 2nd edn, 15 vols. New York: Macmillan Reference USA, 2004.
Mark C. Taylor, ed. *Critical Terms for Religious Study*. Chicago: University of Chicago Press, 1998.

CHAPTER 1

Hinduism
The divine is in everyone

A *murti* (idol) of the Hindu god Ganesha, the elephant-headed son of the Great Goddess Devi. Source: Will Deming.

DID YOU KNOW …

The popular term avatar comes from Hinduism, where it has been used for hundreds of years to describe the 10 incarnations of the god Vishnu. In Hinduism an *avatar* is a form by which this god crosses over from his reality into ours.

Understanding the Religions of the World: An Introduction, Second Edition.
Edited by Will Deming.
© 2025 John Wiley & Sons Ltd. Published 2025 by John Wiley & Sons Ltd.

OVERVIEW

Hinduism is the predominant religion of India, the world's most populous nation. More than 80 percent of its population (around 1.4 billion people) identify themselves as Hindu. The next largest religion in India is Islam, at about 14 percent of the population, followed by Christianity and Sikhism, at about 2.3 and 1.7 percent, respectively. More than 50 million Hindus also live in countries surrounding India—Nepal, Bangladesh, Sri Lanka, Pakistan, and Myanmar—and significant populations can be found in Bali, Malaysia, the United States, Mauritius, Guyana, South Africa, and the United Kingdom (Figure 1.1).

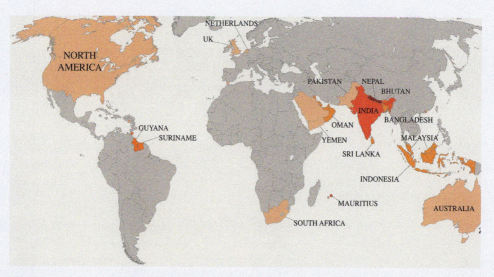

Figure 1.1 A map indicating the Hindu population of different countries as a percentage of each country's total population. Source: Wikimedia Commons.

Hindus have no single scripture that codifies their core beliefs, nor do they have a governing body that establishes a standard for religious practices. Instead, Hindus recognize a wide diversity within their religion. In India alone one finds innumerable regional differences, and outside the country this diversity is sometimes even greater. Indonesians, for example, practice forms of Hinduism that incorporate elements from Islam and local folk traditions.

Thus, it should come as no surprise to learn that the name Hinduism, which manages to gather this diversity neatly—perhaps too neatly—under a single designation, was not created by Hindus themselves. Rather, the ancient Persians used "Hindu" to designate their neighbors to the east, who lived along the banks of the Indus River. But even the

Persians did not intend to identify the religion of these people, just their geographical location. Only when India came under British colonial rule in the eighteenth century did Hinduism gain currency as an umbrella term for the religion. The British, who thought of religions as theological systems, and who governed India by taking into account the religious affiliation of their subjects, needed terms to distinguish Indians of this religion from Indians who were Sikhs, or Muslims, or something else. By contrast, Hindus had traditionally referred to their religious activities as *dharma* (duty), and distinguished themselves from others in various ways, such as calling themselves **Aryans** (noble people), or followers of **Brahmins** (Hindu priests), or devotees of a particular god in the Hindu pantheon. Today, many Hindus accept and use the names Hindu and Hinduism to speak of themselves and their religion, despite its unusual diversity.

To envision such a multiform religion, Julius Lipner has likened Hinduism to the famous banyan tree near Kolkata (Calcutta), in West Bengal. The banyan (Figure 1.2), India's national tree, sends out a profusion of aerial roots, which become new trunks, covering large areas and assimilating everything in their path. The Kolkata banyan covers approximately four acres. It has no central trunk or core segment, but is nonetheless a single tree. In a similar way, we can understand Hinduism as a single entity, but one whose diversity almost defies description. (Julius Lipner, "On Hinduism and Hinduisms: The Way of the Banyan," in *The Hindu World*, ed. Sushil Mittal and Gene Thursby (New York and London: Routledge, 2004).

Figure 1.2 Like the banyan tree, Hinduism has no center or main trunk.
Source: Wikimedia Commons.

History

Timeline	
2300–2000 BCE	The Indus Valley civilization is at its height.
2000–1500 BCE	The Indus Valley civilization is in decline.
1700–1500 BCE	Aryans migrate into the Indus Valley; the *Rig-Veda* is composed.
1200–900 BCE	The *Collections* are brought to completion.
900 BCE	Aryan peoples spread eastward to the Ganges River.
800–600 BCE	The *Brahmanas* are composed.
500–400 BCE	The first *Upanishads* are composed; Buddhism begins.
5th–4th century BCE	The caste system begins to take shape.
3rd century BCE	Ashoka becomes king of the Mauryan dynasty.
300 BCE–300 CE	The *Mahabharata* and the *Ramayana* are composed; the practice of *puja* begins.
1st century CE	The *Bhagavad Gita* is composed.
2nd century CE	The first evidence of Hindu temples.
3rd–4th century CE	Devotional practices (*bhakti*) become popular in south India among Tamils.
ca. 350 CE	The first *Puranas* are composed.
7th century CE	Devotional practices (*bhakti*) are used widely in Hinduism.
ca. 1000 CE	Muslims enter the Punjab.
1206–1526 CE	The Delhi Sultanate.
mid-13th century	Buddhism disappears from most of India.
15th century	Sikhism is founded.
1526–18th century	The Mughal Dynasty.
1600	The East India Company establishes offices in Kolkata.
1757	The beginning of British colonial domination.

(continued)

18th and 19th centuries	The Hindu Renaissance.
1869–1948	Mohandas Gandhi.
1872–1950	Aurobindo Ghosh.
1947	End of British rule; millions of Hindus and Muslims are uprooted and resettled during India's Partition, which creates the nation of Pakistan.
1950	The Indian Constitution guarantees certain civil liberties regardless of caste or religion.
1980s	The resurgence of Hindu Nationalism.

The Indus Valley

Hinduism began in the middle of the second millennium BCE in the Indus Valley, a fertile region fed by five tributaries of the Indus River. Today this area is known as the Punjab (five rivers) and is divided between the nations of India and Pakistan. From approximately 2300 to 2000 BCE, a complex, urban civilization flourished in the Indus Valley. It had two major cities, Harappa and Mohenjo-daro, a host of other towns and settlements, and a remarkably uniform culture spread out over 400 square miles.

Both the religion and the name of this civilization remain a mystery, since no one has been able to decipher what is left of its writing system—if, in fact, the curious shapes found there are a writing system. On the basis of archaeology, some scholars postulate connections between the religion of the Indus Valley civilization and later Hinduism. For example, there remain about 2000 soapstone seals from the Indus Valley civilization which were used to identify property, and some of these depict images of what might be incense burners or altars. One of the most celebrated images depicts a figure seated with his legs crossed in a yogic position, surrounded by various wild animals. It has been suggested that this is an early form of the Hindu god Shiva, who is master of yogic renunciation and sometimes carries the name Lord of the Animals. It has also been proposed that Hinduism's veneration of the Goddess may have roots in the worship of goddesses in the Indus Valley civilization.

Newcomers to the Indus Valley

Whether or not this earlier civilization influenced Hinduism, most of what constituted the first period of Hinduism came from a nomadic herding people who called themselves Aryans (noble ones). Scholars from the previous century believed that the Aryans had crossed over the Himalayas from central Asia and conquered or overwhelmed the Indus Valley's inhabitants. But archeological research has since cast doubt on this theory, leading most scholars to consider flooding, disease, or crop failure as the cause of the Indus Valley civilization's demise. The original homeland of the Aryans is now also debated, some scholars suggesting a location in what is now modern Turkey, or even another part of India.

> **A Closer Look**
>
> # The Swastika
>
> While westerners generally associate the swastika with the atrocities of Adolf Hitler's Nazi regime, this association is uniquely western and only goes back to the early twentieth century. As a religious symbol in India, the swastika is at least as old as the second millennium BCE, and has been used in Hinduism, Buddhism, and Jainism for many centuries (Figure 1.3).
>
>
>
> **Figure 1.3** This juxtaposition of swastikas and six-pointed stars on adjacent window screens might strike a westerner as jarring, as the former are usually associated with Nazi anti-Semitism and the latter with Judaism. In Hinduism, however, these symbols are often used together in the worship of the gods Ganesha and Skanda, sons of Devi and Shiva, respectively. Source: Reproduced by permission of H. Richard Rutherford, C.S.C.
>
> The word swastika derives from an ancient Sanskrit term for well-being. It later became associated with the pleasures of life and with spiritual truth. In Hinduism it often denotes the blessings that come from Ganesha, the god of good beginnings. In Buddhism it is an element in images of the Wheel of Law; and in Jainism it represents the endless process of birth and rebirth (*samsara*), in a diagram that depicts the tenets of that religion.

Regarding the further identity of the Aryans, it has been established that they belonged to a much larger group of nomadic peoples whom scholars call Indo-Europeans, and that their religious ideas appeared in the Indus Valley as early as 2000 BCE, around the time of the Indus Valley civilization's decline. "Indo-European" is actually a linguistic, rather than an ethnic designation, referring to the type of language these nomads spoke. Sanskrit (the sacred language of Hinduism), Greek, and Latin are members of the Indo-European language family, as are most of the local languages of northern India.

A Closer Look

Indo-European Languages

The discovery of ancient Sanskrit by westerners in the 1800s revolutionized the study of linguistics. One aspect of this discovery that especially fascinated scholars was the large number of cognates, or historically related words, that Sanskrit shared with Greek and Latin (as well as Persian, Hittite, German, Celtic, and others).

Latin	Greek	Sanskrit	English
est	*esti*	*asti*	is
mater	*mêtêr*	*matr*	mother/maternal
Jupiter	Zeus Patêr	Dyaus Pitar	Father Zeus
iugo	*zugê*	*yuga*	yoke
ignis (fire)	[none]	*agni*	ignite

Aryan scripture and religion

In contrast to the Indus Valley civilization, we are relatively well informed about the religion of the Aryans. This is because they composed a body of religious literature known as the **Veda** ("knowledge"). The earliest stratum of this literature was composed between 1700 and 900 BCE. Called the *Collections* (*Samhitas*), it consisted of thousands of hymns divided into four anthologies on the basis of their use in rituals around a sacrificial fire. The oldest and most important of these anthologies is the ***Rig-Veda***. It contains just over 1000 hymns that were chanted to honor the many gods of the Vedic pantheon. The other anthologies in the *Collections* contain similar material, as well as spells designed to achieve plentiful harvests, romantic success, and protection from curses and illness. Western scholars often refer to the *Collections* as the "four Vedas," but this is not a universally accepted Hindu usage.

Gods and sacrifices

The gods worshipped by the Aryans were thought to control the forces of order in society, nature, and the cosmos. They are opposed to another class of superhuman beings, the anti-gods, or demons, who promoted chaos. To receive blessings from the deities and protect society and the cosmos from demons, Brahmins (priests) used the Vedic hymns to praise and entertain the various gods and goddesses, while offering them sacrifices. One of these gods was Varuna, who had the task of enforcing divine law. He watched over the activities of mortals and punished those who did evil. Another Vedic god was **Indra**, the divine warrior-king. His most important function was to ensure the coming of the monsoon rains by annually killing Vritra, the demonic dragon who withheld these life-giving waters.

The ritual fire was the god **Agni**, who could be envisioned as an open mouth that consumed the Brahmins' offerings of grain, clarified butter (ghee), Soma (an intoxicating drink), and various animals (especially goats) who were killed by suffocation to avoid shedding their blood. In this way, Agni played a distinctive role as messenger to the other gods, for it was Agni who brought them the Brahmins' sacrifices by conveying them to heaven (*svarga*) on the updraft of his fire. Agni also served as Indra's weapon, in the form of lightning, when Indra battled Vritra; and he was responsible for the very important task of transporting souls to the afterlife through cremation.

Sacred Traditions and Scripture

The Great Deeds of Indra

This is one of many hymns from the *Rig-Veda* that praises the warrior and rain god Indra. It would have been chanted as a way to flatter Indra into attending a sacrifice held in his honor. The god's role as champion of truth and creator of the world are exalted in the second paragraph.

> I will tell the heroic deeds of Indra, those which the Wielder of the Thunderbolt first accomplished: He slew the dragon and released the waters. He split open the bellies of the mountain. He slew the dragon who lay upon the mountain. ...
>
> Rejoicing in his virility like a bull, he chose the Soma and drank the extract from the three bowls. The Generous One took up the thunderbolt as his weapon and killed the first-born of dragons. O Indra, when you killed the first-born of dragons and overcame the deluding lures of the wily, at that very moment you brought forth the sun, heaven, and dawn; since then you have found no overpowering enemy.

Wendy Doniger, *Hindu Myths: A Sourcebook Translated from the Sanskrit* (New York: Penguin Books, 1975), p. 74.

The end of the Veda

The complexity of the early Vedic rituals led to commentaries known as *Brahmanas* and *Aranyakas* (800–500 BCE). This literature offered philosophical remarks and folktales illustrating religious principles. The *Brahmanas* were particularly interested in human mortality, which it referred to as "recurrent death," and in the divine power, or *brahman*, inherent in the Vedic hymns and rituals. The final addition to the Veda was the *Upanishads*, the earliest of which may have been composed in the fifth century BCE. Known also as **Vedanta**, or "End of the Veda," they contain religious dialogues between various teachers, such as sages and fathers, and various students, including both men and women. Somewhat surprisingly, these dialogues take place in private settings without the supervision of the Brahmins, whose authority in religious matters had dominated the Aryan religion to this point.

Talking about Religion

Brahmin, *brahman*, Brahma, *Brahmanas*

There are several important words in Hinduism that all start with the letters *brahm*. This has been confusing for students, especially since many books distinguish between them using a technical system of accents and dots. In this chapter, we use the following system:

- **Brahmin** is used for the Hindu priest and the priestly class.
- ***brahman*** refers to ultimate reality in Hinduism.
- **Brahma** is the name of a creator god.
- ***Brahmanas*** are early commentaries on the meaning of the Vedic fire rituals.

The soul is *brahman*

A central issue for the *Upanishads* was the relation between *atman* (the soul of the individual), and *brahman* (divinity, ultimate reality). Assuming that the basis for our universe was the *brahman* that the priests experienced through Vedic hymns and ritual, the *Upanishads* speculated that if the existence of everything, including humans, was rooted in the universe, then everything, including humans, would have *brahman* as its foundation. Divinity, in other words, was not the exclusive possession of the gods, or accessible only by priests. Rather, it was a World Soul that pervaded the universe much like salt pervades water into which it has been dissolved. With regard to humans, the *Upanishads* taught that divinity was present in each person as a tiny speck of *brahman* that constituted the person's *atman*. Stated differently: a person's innermost, individual self was, at its truest and most profound level, identical with ultimate reality.

Reincarnation

In addition to identifying the human soul with *brahman*, the *Upanishads* articulated the core doctrines of reincarnation. One of the oldest *Upanishads*, the *Brihadaranyaka*, taught that upon death, a person's *atman* re-entered the life cycle through rebirth in another body. This could be the body of a rain drop, an insect, a human being, or one of a number of other bodies. Furthermore, the body that a particular *atman* received was determined by a person's morality during their previous life. Good people received good bodies, bad people received bad ones.

> **Did you know …**
>
> Missiles developed by the Indian military have been named after Hinduism's fire god, Agni. These include two intercontinental ballistic missiles, Agni V and Agni VI.

Reincarnation worked in this way because of something called **karma**. In earlier Vedic literature, *karma* had meant "action," especially the ritual actions that produced supernatural consequences. The Upanishadic sage Yajnavalkya, however, saw things differently. He contended that potentially *all* actions, not just ritual actions, created superhuman consequences for the doer, and that these consequences would be either beneficial or evil depending on the *moral intent* of the doer, not their ritual capability. It was not until a person died, however, that the good and bad karma (actions) of a person's life would be tallied. At that point, the combined consequences of one's karma forced their *atman* to be reborn in a body that was commensurate with the total good and evil of that person's life. In short, Yajnavalkya had postulated a law of karma, by which the morality of a person's life determined the form of their rebirth in the next.

While rebirth in a new body, supposing that one had lived a moderately good life, might sound desirable to a non-Hindu—one more go-round at life, if you will—the *Upanishads* saw rebirth as something to be avoided. This was because reincarnation not only involved rebirth, but also re-death. Furthermore, since the cycle of rebirth was never-ending (*not* just one more go-round), chances were good—in fact, certain—that sooner or later a person's next birth would turn out much worse than the one before.

Salvation as release

With the creation of the law of karma, the *Upanishads* also promoted a new religious goal: release, or **moksha**, meaning the release of one's *atman* from the endless cycle of reincarnation, now called **samsara** (flowing around). In practical terms, this required circumventing the law of karma by somehow living in a way that prevented the accumulation of any karma, whether bad *or* good. The starting point for such a life was knowing the Upanishadic truth that *atman* was *brahman*. Empowered with this knowledge, a person then engaged in renunciation. This is a practice, found in many religions, by which people deny themselves things in the human world—food, water, sexual intercourse, sleep. The expectation of renunciants is that by distancing themselves from the human world they draw near to the divine world. In the case of the *Upanishads*, the challenge was to distance oneself from the karmic world by renouncing desire, for actions performed without desire were, by definition, not motivated by good or bad intention, and thus created no karma. When the karma from one's former life exhausted itself in producing the circumstances of this life, and when no new karma took its place, the renunciant moved beyond simply understanding that *atman* was *brahman* to actually experiencing this truth. With the complete exhaustion of their karma, the renunciant entered the "worlds of *brahman*," never to be reborn.

Sacred Traditions and Scripture

The Self and the Sacred

In this famous text from the *Chandogya Upanishad*, the sage Uddalaka Aruni leads his son Shvetaketu into the deep truth that the self (*atman*) is identical with the sacred (*brahman*).

> "Bring me a piece of fruit from that banyan tree," said Uddalaka Aruni to his son.
> "Here it is, father."
> "Break it apart."
> "It's broken, father."
> "What do you see?"
> "Extremely tiny seeds, father."
> "Break one open."
> "It's broken, father."
> "Now what do you see?"
> "Nothing at all."

Then the sage said to his son, "What you don't see is the essence, but on that essence stands the existence of the whole banyan tree. Believe me, my son, all of existence has that essence for its self (*atman*). *That* is Real. *That* is the self (*atman*). *That* is you, Shvetaketu!"

Chandogya Upanishad 6.12.1-3.

Many gods or one divine essence

In contrast to earlier Vedic literature, the *Upanishads* understood ultimate reality as **monistic** rather than **theistic**. That is, they approached *brahman* as a single, divine essence that pervaded everything, not as a collection of gods with personalities and temperaments. The Veda, therefore, provided Hinduism with two distinct visions of ultimate reality: the earlier theism of the *Collections*, wherein deities were honored with praise and sacrifice, and the later monism of the *Upanishads*. This monistic perspective resonated profoundly throughout the subsequent history of Hinduism. The popularity of renunciation produced a vast tradition of Hindu ascetics, and the individual's pursuit of *moksha* became the highest priority for many Hindus. In its immediate context in the late Vedic period, moreover, the individualism of monism generated tensions between the Brahmins, who officiated over the sacrificial religion on behalf of Hindu society, and those who sought to escape the karmic world of society through renunciation.

Class and caste

Until about 900 BCE the Aryans were largely confined to the Punjab. Over the next 600 years they extended their political control eastward, into the fertile plains of the Ganges River, where they engaged in urbanization, political centralization, and expanded economic activity. These developments moved Hinduism toward a stratified society in which specific groups were identified with specific occupations. Prior to this, the Brahmins had envisioned society as a hierarchy of four classes. In order of importance, these were the Brahmins themselves, who were the religious authorities; the **Nobles**, who protected and governed society; the **Commoners**, who were the economic backbone of society—farmers, merchants, and skilled workers; and the **Servants**, whose assignment was to perform unskilled labor. Inherent in this social ranking was also a religious hierarchy which dictated that the higher one's class, the closer a person was to the gods and the more true and purposeful was their life.

Sometime during this same period (900–300 BCE), as the theologians of the *Upanishads* were exploring the religious implications of the law of karma and the identification of the *atman* with *brahman*, the Brahmins were investigating the concept of *dharma*. Initially they used this term to refer to the sacrificial duties of householders, including those done in public with Brahmins and those done at home, usually without a Brahmin. Eventually the Brahmins broadened the meaning of *dharma* to include *all* religious duties of *all* Hindus, especially those pertaining to what one could eat and with whom one could interact socially. In this way the Brahmins were able to extend their religious authority into the governance of social relations at a time when their animal sacrifices were losing public support due to the popularity of a new religious ideal called *ahimsa*, the non-destruction of life.

By about 300 BCE, the Brahmins began writing manuals on *dharma* that took into account the many occupational groups that had arisen in Hindu towns and cities near the Ganges River. Since a given occupation was usually associated with a particular family or clan, the Brahmins called the occupational groups **jatis** (births), which emphasized their hereditary nature. Thus, side by side with the four classes, there developed a hierarchical system of "castes"—the word Europeans would use to translate *jati*. Around 100 CE, the Brahmins began composing detailed analyses of the karmic consequences for good and bad actions according to one's caste. The most popular of these compositions was the *Code of Manu*, which also assigned each caste to one of the four classes.

Over time, the Brahmins defined thousands of occupational castes along hereditary lines, giving each a particular *dharma* and a particular value in Hindu society based on the presumed purity or impurity of each occupation. To maintain this caste system into future generations, the *dharma* of each caste prohibited marriage outside the caste and restricted social interaction. By enlisting the Upanishadic teachings about karma and rebirth, the Brahmins also taught that any attempt to change one's *dharma* or one's caste resulted in a great deal of bad karma and a worse birth in the next life, possibly in one of several hells. In this way, the Brahmins created a relatively inflexible social system in which one's prospects for social, economic, and religious advancement were largely determined at one's birth.

People left out of Hindu society

Below the four classes and the myriad castes, Hindus recognized yet another social group, the **Untouchables**. As the name implies, they were considered so distant from ultimate reality—so impure—that they could not participate in Hindu society. Having no class or caste, they were **outcastes** who were required to live in separate villages, drink from their own wells, and announce their presence in public lest contact with their persons (or even their shadows) pollute others. It is important to realize that in a religious system words like "impure" and "polluting" do not carry a hygienic meaning, for the ancient world knew nothing of microbes or modern hygienic practices. Untouchables were not, therefore, leper colonies or people with open wounds and communicable diseases. Rather "impurity," "pollution," and "uncleanness" are *religious* statements that designate a person's proximity to ultimate reality. The purer one is, the more closely they are oriented to what is real and meaningful in the world; the more *im*pure one is, the less meaningful and real is their life. As people who were so impure as to be untouchable, outcastes were thought to live existences largely bereft of meaning.

Like the castes, outcastes were endogamous, meaning they could only marry within their social groupings. Further, outcastes were not allowed to be educated in the Veda, participate in important Hindu rituals, or acquire any wealth. Their function in Hindu society was to handle things considered too impure for the four classes. This often meant taking jobs associated with death, such as handling corpses and working with leather. Their *dharma* was to absorb the inevitable pollutions of society on behalf of others.

Hinduism's epic tradition

In the fourth century BCE, Hindus had expanded south beyond the sub-continent, reaching the island of Sri Lanka; and near the end of that century, the Greek empire of Alexander the Great had reached the borders of India, making its military presence felt for a brief period. In the wake of Alexander's invasion and then retreat, a power vacuum was created, giving rise to a new Indian dynasty called the Mauryans. In the mid-third century BCE, its most famous king, Ashoka, brought much of India under his control through savage warfare. Yet, disturbed by his army's acts of carnage, he renounced these tactics once his kingdom was secure, and began to promote

Buddhism, which had begun in India in the fifth century. Through his patronage of monasteries he initiated a period of Buddhist expansion, both inside and outside of India. This led to centuries of interaction and competition between Hinduism and Buddhism as both religions vied for the hearts and minds of the Indian people.

Ashoka's reign coincided with the beginning of Hinduism's epic tradition its two great epics, the *Mahabharata* and the *Ramayana*, being composed sometime between 300 BCE and 300 CE and 200 BCE and 200 CE, respectively. As vast repositories of Hindu practices and beliefs (the *Mahabharata* is *15 times* the size of the Bible and the *Ramayana* is about a third that size), these epics provide a valuable window into this period of the religion's history. On the one hand, they portray a Hinduism that continued to develop along the lines set by late Vedic and early post-Vedic innovations. In them we see Vedic rituals, renunciants, discussions of karma and *moksha*, lengthy speeches on *dharma*, and developments in the caste system. But we also encounter several new practices, such as religious pilgrimages, worship called *puja*, in which fruit and flowers are offered to images of gods, the use of temples, and the formation of religious sects focused on a particular god or goddess.

The principal narrative of both epics describes a world threatened by evil, into which the god **Vishnu** intervenes to set things right. In the *Ramayana*, the ogre king Ravana has dethroned Indra, the king of the gods. Unable to withstand Ravana's power, the gods call on Vishnu for help, who responds by entering the human world as the man **Rama**. Growing to maturity by weathering several betrayals and other turns of plot (during which he periodically forgets he is a god), Rama becomes the embodiment of religious and social duty. When Ravana kidnaps Rama's wife Sita, Rama joins forces with Lakshman, his half-brother, and Hanuman, the ruler of monkeys (Figure 1.4). Together they storm Ravana's stronghold in Lanka, killing the ogre and rescuing Sita. In the end, Rama is crowned king,

Figure 1.4 Hanuman, the ruler of monkeys in the *Ramayana*, is a divine example of loyalty and devotion to Vishnu. Source: Will Deming.

restores order to the world, and governs India in a period of idealized rule. Sita, by contrast, is suspected of having been sexually violated by Ravana, and Rama must force her to undergo a series of tests to prove her purity, after which she vanishes.

In the *Mahabharata*, the royal throne is again usurped and the world order threatened, but this time by the Kauravas, the evil cousins of the rightful rulers, the Pandavas. After many betrayals, machinations, and turns of plot (including the simultaneous marriage of all five Pandava brothers to a single wife), Vishnu turns the tide in favor of the Pandavas. He does this, moreover, not as a king, but as the noncombatant **Krishna**, who serves as the rightful king's charioteer.

The *Song of the Lord*

This crucial and much celebrated scene from the *Mahabharata* is found in a section known as the **Bhagavad Gita**, or *Song of the Lord*, which may have been composed as early as the first century CE. It begins with two massive armies, poised for the decisive battle, staring each other down across a broad plain. **Arjuna**, the rightful king and commander of the Pandavas, suddenly has doubts about his course of action. Looking over at his cousins (albeit his *evil* cousins) and their forces, he cringes at the thought of killing so many former teachers, friends, and family members. He also realizes that the massive carnage about to take place (almost everyone in both armies is killed), will burden him with massive amounts of bad karma. Desperate for an exit strategy, Arjuna considers abandoning his status as a Noble (whose *dharma* is to fight for what is right) and pursue a life of renunciation in the jungle.

Sacred Traditions and Scripture

Arjuna Loses His Nerve Before the Great Battle

In the *Bhagavad Gita*, Arjuna expresses his misgivings to his charioteer with the following lines:

> "Shall we not, who see the evil of destruction, shall we not refrain from this terrible deed? The destruction of a family destroys its rituals of righteousness, and when the righteous rituals are no more, unrighteousness overcomes the whole family.
> When unrighteous disorder prevails, the women sin and are impure; and when women are not pure, O Krishna, there is disorder of castes, social confusion. This disorder carries down to hell the family and the destroyers of the family. The spirits of their dead suffer in pain when deprived of the ritual offerings.
> Those evil deeds of the destroyers of a family, which cause this social disorder, destroy the righteousness of birth and the ancestral rituals of righteousness.

(continued)

> And have we not heard that hell is waiting for those whose familial rituals of righteousness are no more?
> O day of darkness! What evil spirit moved our minds when, for the sake of an earthly kingdom, we came to this field of battle ready to kill our own people?..."
> Thus spoke Arjuna in the field of battle, and letting fall his bow and arrows, he sank down in his chariot, his soul overcome by despair and grief.
>
> *Bhagavad Gita* 1.39–45, 47, from Juan Mascaro, trans., *The Bhagavad Gita* (London: Penguin Books, 1962), 46–47.

With these misgivings, Arjuna brings to a head a theological quandary that goes back to late Vedic times: Should he remain and support the Hindu social order by fulfilling his *dharma*, or should he withdraw from society to pursue his own salvation? At this point, Arjuna begins a dialogue with his chariot driver, Krishna, who, as the reader knows, is an incarnation of Vishnu.

At first, Krishna admonishes Arjuna to do his duty. He reasons that since the law of karma metes out perfect justice on the basis of a person's actions, the combatants will only get what they deserve. Furthermore, since everyone's self, or *atman*, is immortal, the destruction wrought by war is only an *apparent* evil; yet Arjuna, he points out, stands to suffer punishment in many hells if he violates his *dharma* at this crucial moment. But since this is a rather flat-footed, doctrinaire explanation of the law of karma, Arjuna remains unconvinced, and Krishna must initiate him into a higher understanding of *dharma*. One must do one's duty, Krishna explains, but in a way that is detached from all motives of gain or loss. In this way a person avoids both good and bad karma and achieves release from the karmic world altogether.

By means of this explanation, Krishna combines duty *with* renunciation, offering Arjuna a way forward without having to choose one or the other. Even so, Arjuna is still repulsed by the atrocities of war, and so Krishna must teach him the path of divine knowledge, or *jnana*. Through the experience of *jnana*, which is acquired by discipline, renunciation, and meditation, Arjuna would be able to see beyond the illusion of the karmic world—beyond its apparent goodness and evil. With *jnana*, in other words, he can remain mentally firm and at peace, even in the midst of warfare. Then, as a gift to Arjuna, Krishna reveals a teaching even more profound than this. Instead of performing his duty with divine knowledge, Arjuna should go a step further and perform his duty out of devotion to God. Through self-surrender and service to God, his actions will result in union with God.

Following this revelation, Krishna gives Arjuna divine eyes to see the world as Krishna himself sees it. Krishna reveals himself to be the Great God Vishnu, a terrifying, universal being in whom all aspects of the creation exit. What Arjuna learns is that gods as well as demons, evil as well as good coexist in Krishna, and this leads him to the realization that even the evils of war are somehow part of God. Guided by this new insight, he now recognizes that the proper question is not *whether* a person should perform their *dharma*, but *how* a person should perform it. One can do it for personal benefit (good karma), or selflessly, or even with divine insight. But the highest path is to fulfill one's *dharma* out of wholehearted devotion to God. At this point in the epic, the *Song of the Lord* ends and Arjuna takes up his bow and leads his troops into battle.

The three ways The *Bhagavad Gita* was a watershed in the development of Hinduism, for it managed to synthesize the various Vedic and post-Vedic currents within the religion to a much greater degree than previous attempts. Instead of having to choose *either* ritual and social duties *or* the renunciation of society, individual Hindus could now select from among several mutually valid ways of achieving salvation. In the years following the writing of the *Gita*, Hindu theologians formulated these mutually valid ways as three religious paths: the path of action, which encompassed the duties of caste and ritual; the path of knowledge, which guided one beyond the karmic world through a divine understanding of human existence; and the path of devotion, which led to eternal union with God. Beyond this, by promoting the path of devotion as the highest practice of religion, the *Bhagavad Gita* became a powerful catalyst for the religious enfranchisement of all segments of Hindu society. As Krishna states explicitly in book nine of the *Gita*, even women and members of the Servant class, whose impurity had barred them from full access to Hinduism—even they could now attain *moksha* through devotion to God.

Three Great Gods

The *Bhagavad Gita*'s theism, which identified ultimate reality with the god Vishnu, was part of a broader development in Hinduism that envisioned several gods as all-powerful. Earlier, Hindus had believed that gods, like all other creatures, were under the edicts of the law of karma. These new, omnipotent gods, however, stood outside the karmic world and controlled it. Being themselves safe from the endless flow of *samsara*, they saved their devotees from karmic existence by granting them eternal life in their heavenly abodes, or complete union with themselves.

In time, three deities emerged as the principal expressions of the all-powerful, Great Gods: Vishnu, **Shiva**, and **Devi**. Vishnu was seen as a kindly overseer of the universe. He safeguarded the order of the world and entered human history in bodily form when humanity was threatened by the forces of evil and chaos. Vishnu's chief incarnations, known as **avatars**, were Krishna and Rama, the respective heroes of the *Mahabharata* and the *Ramayana*. Through numerous translations and retellings of the *Ramayana*, Rama in particular quickly developed a pan-Indian following. The list of Vishnu's *avatars* was eventually expanded to 10, which sometimes included the Buddha. Other *avatars* identified Vishnu with heroic figures from earlier mythologies, such as the Fish, the Boar (Figure 1.5), the Tortoise, and the Dwarf. In all these instances Vishnu's role was to come to the aid of human beings and lesser gods in times of cosmic crisis.

Figure 1.5 Vishnu, as the boar *avatar*, saves the world from drowning during the primeval flood. Source: Will Deming.

In contrast to Vishnu, Shiva was characterized by violence and power that was both destructive and creative. His worshippers praised him for this, as he used his power on their behalf to combat evil in their lives. The karmic world was a violent place, fed by an endless cycle of creation and destruction, birth, death, rebirth, and re-death. Yet those who approached Shiva with awe and reverence could appeal to the very god whose activities created their karmic reality. Sometimes Shiva's power was envisioned as male and female sexual energy. In his destructive mode, he renounced all sexual activity, producing death in the world. But Shiva also had an erotic side; and since sexual acts can be both violent and procreative, Shiva brought life to the world through erotic adventures.

A third possibility for envisioning an all-powerful deity was Devi. In Sanskrit, *devi* is the generic term for "goddess," and under this name worshippers identified many regional goddesses as the Great Goddess. Sometimes Devi was seen as the wife or sexual partner of Vishnu or Shiva. As such, she took on the characteristics of these gods: kindly and caring, or violent and erotic. As the Great Goddess in her own right, Devi was often pictured as a bloodthirsty warrior, using her horrific skills in battle to defend her followers, who sometimes slaughtered animals in her honor and offered her the blood.

Ancient Tales

Hinduism's new theism was vividly developed in a literature known as the **Puranas** (*Ancient Tales*), the earliest of which appeared around 350 CE (see Figure 1.6). According to tradition, there were 18 major *Puranas*, paired with 18 minor ones; but the actual number varied widely. The subject matter of the *Puranas* is vast, including the origin and structure of the universe, royal genealogies, and a cyclical theory of time. They also elaborated, in great detail, the theology, mythology, and rituals of various gods, including both the Great Gods and the lesser ones, the latter now being seen as mere helper gods. The *Puranas* filled out the divine families of the Great Gods; specified their weapons, their clothing, and the divine animals that transported them into our world; and associated each deity with important pilgrimage sites.

Devotional Hinduism

The practice of devoting oneself to a particular god, which Krishna had praised in the *Bhagavad Gita*, had originated around the turn of the millennium among a

Figure 1.6 Our earliest example of pages from a *Purana* (ca. eleventh century). Books in India were traditionally made from palm leaves, the letters being scratched into the shiny surface of a leaf and then wiped with ink, which would adhere only to the scratches. The holes in the middle of the leaves are for a string that held the book together.
Source: Wikimedia Commons.

non-Aryan people called the Tamils, who lived in the south of India. In the third and fourth centuries CE, two groups of poet-saints, the Nayanmars and the Alvars, began to express their passion and love for Shiva and Vishnu, respectively, through devotional songs. As they traveled north, they converted many Hindus, and by the seventh century CE, a devotional movement within Hinduism had developed, which, in the following centuries, spread throughout India.

Devotional worship, known as **bhakti**, encompassed many things, including sharing, service, hospitality, entertainment, and enjoyment. Devotees held festivals in honor of their gods, composed poems, songs, and responsive chants, and recited the gods' many names and attributes. As the *Puranas* became available, devotees could learn to love a god in detailed and intimate ways by memorizing, for example, the god's manner of dress, their mythological adventures, and their divine associates. The starting point of *bhakti* was the assumption that one could interact with a deity as a host might interact with a royal guest. A deity's temple came to be seen as a palace where they held audience through an image, such as a consecrated statue. A priest at the temple would act as mediator, tending to the needs of the god on behalf of the worshippers. He would awaken, bathe, and clothe the image in the course of the day, and present it with flowers and food offerings supplied by the worshippers. At night and at certain times of the day the priest would restrict visitation, allowing the deity to rest.

Islamic dynasties in India

Islamic incursions into India began in the early eleventh century CE under Mahmud, a Turko-Afghan ruler. Although Mahmud added the Punjab to his empire, his primary goal was not territorial expansion or religious mission. Rather, it was to enrich his treasury by sacking and looting the wealthy Buddhist monasteries and Hindu temples of northern India.

A permanent Islamic state in north India was only established in the late twelfth century, following the defeat of the Indian king Prithviraj by Muizzuddin Muhammad. By the early thirteenth century, a general from Muhammad's army had founded the Delhi Sultanate, which lasted from 1206 to 1526. In time, the Turko-Afghan dynasties of the Delhi Sultanate came to dominate the political life of north India, while several smaller Islamic kingdoms established themselves in central and south India. Hinduism, in turn, began to expand along trade routes into Indonesia.

In 1526 the Delhi Sultanate was succeeded by the Mughal Empire, which lasted into the eighteenth century and marked the height of Islamic rule in India. During these centuries of Turko-Afghan rule over India, Islam functioned on two levels. Politically, Islam's power was predominantly an urban phenomenon. Muslim clerics assisted rulers in implementing Islamic law from military garrisons in the cities they had conquered. Since Hindus were regarded as polytheists, their religious sites were occasionally defaced or destroyed. This violence was sporadic, however, and varied significantly from ruler to ruler.

On a popular level, missionaries from Islam's mystical branch, Sufism, became ambassadors of the religion to the general population. During the Delhi Sultanate, the Chishti and Suhrawardi orders established themselves throughout northern India, while later, under the Mughal Dynasty, the Naqshbandi and Qadiri orders spread Sufism into southern India. As Sufis were acculturated to the Indian worldview, they created new expressions of Islam that combined elements of Hinduism with Muslim practices. Tombs of Sufi saints were patronized by Hindus and Muslims alike, and in the fifteenth century a new religion altogether—Sikhism—arose from Sufi interaction with Hinduism.

By and large, however, Hinduism changed little through its contact with Islam. If anything, it retrenched itself more securely in its own traditions. Buddhism, by contrast, fared poorly in India under Muslim rule, although it is not entirely clear why. Many factors seem to have played a part, including economic and social factors, and most scholars see no simple correspondence between the spread of Islam in India and the decline of Buddhism there. By the mid-thirteenth century, Buddhism had all but vanished from the land of its origin, leaving behind only architectural remains in the form of reliquary shrines (*stupas*) and temples, as well as centuries of influence on Hinduism as the two religions had developed side-by-side.

British colonialism

The East India Company, chartered by British traders and established in Kolkata in 1600, would eventually supplant the Mughals as the main power on the subcontinent. The Mughal Empire nominally continued into the mid-1800s, but military losses in 1757 marked a decisive setback in its ability to rule. From that point onward, the East

India Company and the British government were the real overlords of India until its independence in 1947.

The British colonial presence in India challenged the religion and worldview of Hindus to an unprecedented degree. For educated Hindus, the greatest provocation actually came from Company officials who studied the history and languages of Hinduism. On the one hand, these officials tended to glorify Hinduism's ancient past to the detriment of its present, giving the impression that the Hinduism of their day was a shallow vestige of former times. On the other hand, they regarded Indian society and culture as inferior to their own. An example of this prejudice can be seen in James Mill's *History of British India*, written in the 1820s. In particular, Mill singled out Hinduism as the source of India's ostensible fall from greatness. The irrational, other worldliness of this religion, he claimed, had created a population unable to govern itself in the modern world (thereby justifying British rule). For decades, copies of Mill's work were distributed to Company officials departing for India to prepare them for their task and reinforce their sense of superiority over the indigenous populations. Yet Mill, a Company employee who lived in London, had written his book without ever having visited India!

The Hindu Renaissance and Indian independence

Colonial challenges like these engendered vigorous responses from Hindu leaders, resulting in what has been called the Hindu Renaissance. Somewhat ironically, several early Hindu activists based their demands for religious reform on the romanticized version of Hinduism that the British had created. For example, Raja Ram Mohan Roy, who founded the Society of God (Brahmo Samaj) in 1828, praised the *Upanishads* for their preservation of a pristine form of Hinduism which was devoid of fanciful myths and image worship, and whose monism compared favorably with Christianity's monotheism. Similarly, Swami Dayanand Sarasvati, who founded the Society of Noble Ones (Arya Samaj) in 1875, insisted that the *Rig-Veda*, which some European scholars had valorized as a religious masterpiece, contained infallible, eternal truth. On this basis, he insisted that all modern forms of Hinduism be measured against it, and that his followers call themselves Aryans rather than Hindus.

Yet Company officials, followed by the British Crown, to whom direct rule of India passed officially in 1858, also contributed in positive ways to the Hindu Renaissance. While they were reluctant to involve themselves directly in religious affairs, they did intervene in social practices rooted in Hindu culture. Because of this, Hindu reformers were able to use the British legal system to give women the right to study the Veda, encourage widows to remarry, and outlaw *suttee*, the practice whereby a widow mounted the funeral pyre of her late husband so as to accompany him into the afterlife.

A Closer Look

The Plight of Widows in Hinduism

Despite the rights that British law accorded Hindu widows in the nineteenth century, many still have no place or worth in the religion. According to tradition, women are "never independent of a man": daughters are dependent on their fathers, wives on their husbands, and widows on their sons. Consequently, widows without dutiful sons, or those with no sons at all, must take refuge in temples and ashrams, where they live on charity (Figure 1.7).

Figure 1.7 Disowned by their relatives, these widows in the city of Vrindavan, nicknamed City of Widows, wait in line for a meal. Source: © Salva Campillo/Alamy.

As the focus shifted to national independence in the late nineteenth and early twentieth centuries, reformers continued to rework elements of the Hindu tradition, but now toward political ends. Aurobindo Ghosh (1872–1950), who began his public career as a fiery political leader advocating militant nationalism, later turned to Hinduism, valorizing it as the eternal religion (*sanatana dharma*). This encouraged his followers to insist that the Veda was a trustworthy guide to modern social and political reform.

The most famous reformer of this period was Mohandas Gandhi (1869–1948), who became known as Mahatma, the "great-souled one." Having studied law in England, he practiced first in South Africa, where he litigated against racial prejudices aimed at the Hindu community there. (Many Hindus had moved to South Africa as indentured servants after the British Empire outlawed slavery.) This is where Gandhi developed his principle of "holding to truth," or *satyagraha*. Believing that God was truth, he encouraged others to address the forces of oppression with passive resistance, thereby exposing to one's oppressors the truth of their evil actions. After 17 years of legal practice in South Africa, Gandhi returned to India to work for social and political change there. While he supported the caste system (he himself was a Commoner), he regarded all occupations as being of equal value to society, believing that everyone was an integral part of the greater whole. He even extended a version of this perspective to other religions, claiming that each spoke truth to its own adherents. Gandhi also worked for the elimination of Untouchability, arguing that the institution had no place in true religion. To avoid using the name, he referred to Untouchables as "the Lord's children" (*harijan*).

In 1920 Gandhi became the head of the Indian National Congress and promoted *satyagraha* and passive resistance in India's fight for independence from England. As pressure for national independence increased, political groups formed around the interests of India's various religions, which included Islam. The result was the Partition, a division of the subcontinent in 1947 into a Hindu state and a Muslim state—India and Pakistan, respectively. The goal was to allow Hindus and Muslims to carve out their own political destinies. Tragically, the Partition, which resettled 10–12 million people, also brought about the death of some 500,000. One year after independence was achieved, Gandhi was killed by a Hindu nationalist extremist.

From the Partition to the present

The constitution of modern India became the law of the land in 1950. One of its primary authors was an Untouchable named Dr. Bhimrao Ambedkar. Although he converted to Buddhism to avoid discrimination (taking some 5 million Hindu followers with him), he left an important legacy to Hinduism in Part III of the Constitution, *Fundamental Rights*, which guaranteed basic civil liberties to all citizens of India, regardless of race, caste, religion, gender, or place of birth. Since that time, the Indian government has adopted several reform measures akin to affirmative action policies in the United States. The name **dalit** (oppressed people) has replaced "Untouchable," which is now prohibited by law; and dalits can legally enter temples and schools, and marry persons from the four social classes. The official government designation for dalits is the Scheduled Castes and Scheduled Tribes ("schedule" being a term from India's constitutional law).

Despite these changes, the caste system is still very much alive in India, especially in rural areas, where most of the population lives. Hindus are still able to distinguish between hundreds of castes, and while other religious communities, such as Muslims, Christians, and Sikhs, are avowedly anticaste, the pervasiveness of this ancient institution has even divided some groups within these communities along caste lines. Not surprisingly, dalits continue to convert to Buddhism to escape the stigma and limitations of their social status.

Hindu nationalism continues to play an important role in Indian politics, for even after the Partition, India retained a significant minority population of Muslims (currently estimated at 14 percent). The Indian People's Party (BJP) experienced a meteoric rise to prominence in the 1980s through a campaign that utilized Hindu religious symbols and espoused an ideology appealing to "essential Hindu identity," or *Hindutva*—an expression that had been used by Hindu nationalists in the 1920s. This show of political strength emboldened an anti-Muslim mob in 1992 to destroy the Babri Masjid, a mosque in the northern city of Ayodhya that had been built in the sixteenth century, because nationalists claimed it had been constructed over the birthplace of the god Rama. Eight years later, the legality of the destruction remained unresolved, provoking a riot in which more than 2000 people, mostly Muslims, were killed. Then, in 2019, India's Supreme Court ruled in favor of the nationalists. A groundbreaking ceremony for a magnificent temple took place in the following year, overseen by the leader of the BJP, India's prime minister Narendra Modi (Figure 1.8). In early 2024 the main *murti*, an image of Rama, was installed in the temple's innermost sanctuary; and although the temple was not yet finished, its inaugural opening, at which Modi was present, was timed just ahead of the 2024 parliamentary elections.

Figure 1.8 India's prime minister and leader of the Hindu nationalist party (BJP), Narendra Modi (left), presides over the 2020 groundbreaking of the Ram Mandir temple in Ayodya. The site was formerly the location of a sixteenth-century mosque that was destroyed by an anti-Muslim mob in 1992. Source: Wikimedia Commons.

Contemporary Beliefs and Practices

As we remarked at the beginning of this chapter, Hinduism embraces multiple theologies, rituals, and visions of ultimate reality. It is a striking example of religious pluralism within a single religion. One factor that has contributed to its diversity is Hinduism's cumulative nature, whereby older elements are easily joined with more recent ones, and little is ever completely discarded. Thus, Brahmins still chant Vedic hymns and conduct fire rituals; monism competes with theism; karma, *dharma*, and *moksha* rank among Hinduism's core beliefs; caste identity and renunciant traditions exist side-by-side; and the legends of the epics and the *Puranas* continue to inspire modern audiences.

Even in the face of such diversity, an overview of Hinduism can proceed on the basis of two observations. First, most Hindus believe that salvation, the final goal of religion, is to free oneself from the effects of karma, and that this freedom comes either by entering a heaven that is immune to karma, or by unifying one's *atman* with *brahman*. Second, the beliefs and practices of modern Hinduism function largely according to one of three patterns, or "logics." Some beliefs and practices depend mostly on the logic of karma, others on the logic of devotion, and still others on the logic of divine knowledge. In what follows we will examine each of these patterns, keeping in mind that they are not exclusive of one another, or even separate categories in the minds of most Hindus.

> #### Did you know …
>
> Even though leather is seen as polluting, most Hindus wear leather sandals or shoes. They consider the feet to be one of the most impure parts of the human body, and they avoid touching sandals and shoes with their hands. Some very strict Hindus wear wooden sandals, which stay on their feet by means of a wooden peg between the big toe and the other toes.

The logic of karma

Most Hindus believe that they possess an immortal soul, or *atman*, which has already experienced countless previous lives through reincarnation. Further, they believe that their current lives have been determined by past karma, and that each person's *atman* is now burdened with impurities from evil actions and contact with pollutants—urine, menstrual blood, a member of a lower caste, and corpses, to name just a few. And finally, they hold that performing one's religious duties (*dharma*) produces merit (good karma), which aids in cleansing the *atman* from these impurities (bad karma). This is the most basic understanding of the law of karma and the most basic motivation for Hindus to perform their *dharma*. Since the time of the *Upanishads*, however, it has also been popular to see the performance of *dharma* from another perspective. It is believed that when a person performs their *dharma* without any concern for personal gain, then liberation from rebirth, rather than merit, can result. Given these two perspectives on *dharma*, one can speak of both short- and long-range goals of living according to the logic of karma: to accumulate merit for a better rebirth, and to release oneself from the world of karma altogether.

Sources of *dharma*

The *dharma* of a particular individual is a combination of several factors. First, there is **class-and-life-stage *dharma***, which a person must perform based on their caste, gender, and time of life. Then there is **general *dharma***, which encompasses religious actions expected of all Hindus. Finally, there is personal *dharma*, which is defined by an individual's emotional temperament, talents, and physical make-up. Since this varies greatly from person to person, it will not be included in our discussion.

Class-and-life-stage *dharma* As an example of class-and-life-stage *dharma* we may consider the duties of a Brahmin man. These include prohibitions against eating meat and drinking alcohol, and on a typical day a Brahmin man is also expected to purify himself with water, recite a Vedic prayer to the Sun (usually several times), make offerings to various gods and forces of nature, read passages from the Veda out loud, and meditate. If he is a priest (not all males of the Brahmin class serve as priests), he has additional duties as well.

A second example of class-and-life-stage *dharma* is the performance of rituals designed to enhance a person's degree of purity as they grow older. These are known as *samskaras* (impressions). Traditionally there were 16 *samskaras*, but today, numbers one, three, and six (in italics below) are largely defunct. In the chronological order in which they are administered or undertaken, they are:

(1) *Impregnation.*
(2) Ensuring male offspring.
(3) *Parting of the mother's hair to ensure good luck for her and her infant.*
(4) Birthing rituals.
(5) Name-giving.
(6) *An infant's first outing.*
(7) The first eating of solid food.
(8) The first hair cutting (head shaving) for male babies.
(9) Ear piercing.
(10) Starting one's secular education.
(11) Investiture with the sacred thread.
(12) The beginning of Vedic study.
(13) The first shaving of facial hair for males.
(14) The formal end to the celibate, student stage of life.
(15) Marriage.
(16) Funerary rites.

Investiture with the sacred thread Of the 13 samskaras still practiced, three are considered central to the proper conduct of life: investiture with the sacred thread (11), marriage (15), and funerary rites (16). In most cases, an astrologer is called on to establish the most auspicious day, and sometimes hour, for these three. The investiture ritual is open only to male members of the highest three classes—Brahmins, Nobles, and Commoners—although today it is practiced mostly by Brahmins. It marks the beginning of a boy's obligation to fulfill all his adult social and religious duties. In a formal ceremony, the boy is given a cord consisting of three intertwined, single strands. This cord is placed on his left shoulder and falls across his chest and back, the ends being tied together on the right side near his lower abdomen. By putting on the "sacred thread," he undergoes a spiritual rebirth, receiving the designation "twice-born." The boy is also given a special chant, called the Gayatri mantra, that he will recite daily for the rest of his life.

A Closer Look

The Daily Prayer of the Twice-born

Gayatri Mantra

When spoken, the Gayatri *mantra* (Figure 1.9) is always preceded by Om and the "great utterance":

> Om. Earth, sky, heaven:
> May we attain to the surpassing
> glory of Savitar, the Sun,
> that he may inspire our prayers.

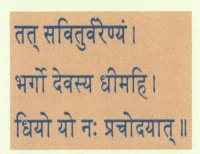

Figure 1.9 The Gayatri Mantra written in Sanskrit.

Marriage and children Unlike the investiture ceremony, the *samskara* of marriage is open to all classes (as well as both genders, of course). The *Rig-Veda* places great importance on this rite, since spouses are seen as "partners in dharma," performing many rituals as a team. Marriage also sanctifies the bearing of legitimate children, allowing for the continuation of the family's religious lineage and rituals. Many Hindus understand having children as the payment of a debt that a husband and wife owe to their parents and ancestors. A male child in particular is sought, not only because most Hindu groups trace their ancestry through the male line, but also because the oldest son plays a key role in his father's funeral rites. While the marriage ceremony consists of many activities, one of the most important is the groom leading his wife around the sacred fire (Agni) in seven steps while the couple recites verses from the *Rig-Veda*. This action, more than any other, aligns the new union with the divine world. As one of the most important of all Hindu *samskaras*, marriage is celebrated as lavishly as possible, often placing enormous financial burdens on poorer members of Hindu society.

Funeral rites The final *samskara* an individual undergoes is the funeral rites. These cleanse a family from the pollution caused by death and ensure that the deceased will be properly reincarnated in the next life. Other than the professionals who conduct the rites, only immediate relatives are permitted to participate. If something in the ritual were to go wrong, the soul of the deceased might become a troublesome wandering ghost.

Except for young children, persons who have died from certain illnesses, and renouncers who have forsaken society, the dead are always cremated, usually while hymns from the *Rig-Veda* are chanted. This is done to eliminate the pollution of the corpse by means of Agni, and to call upon Agni to transport the deceased to the next world on the updraft of his flames. Near the end of the cremation ceremony, the deceased's skull is shattered to release their *atman*, and any remaining bone

Figure 1.10 Hindu cremation in Nepal. After the body of the deceased is purified through cremation, the ashes are deposited in the river, which is thought to be a goddess.
Source: Reproduced by permission of Sue Ellen Christensen.

fragments are gathered into a jar. These will be submerged in a sacred river (Figure 1.10) or taken to a pilgrimage site or plot of ancestral land.

General duties

In contrast to the class-and-life-stage *dharma*, general *dharma* pertains equally to all Hindus. An especially common general duty is honoring divinity (*brahman*) wherever it is found. This includes showing deference to certain animals, such as cows, elephants, and particular species of birds and snakes. It also includes giving proper respect to holy persons, such as Brahmins, renunciants, and spiritual teachers (gurus), and honoring *brahman* as it manifests itself in shrines, temples, and the home.

Shrines and temples   Local shrines and temples allow ready access to the divine world. Typical Hindu villages have several shrines to local deities and guardian spirits, many of whom are fearsome goddesses bearing the title "mother." These shrines are frequented by lower caste Hindus, who bring small offerings and make pledges or oaths to the divinities in exchange for blessings. Sometimes village shrines are overseen by local, non-Brahmin priests, such as exorcists and shamans.

Larger villages and towns also have a temple, and cities usually have multiple temples. The Hindu temple is the residence of a deity and their divine entourage. The innermost sanctum, a shrine within a temple, contains an image of this god or goddess. Usually a sculpture, this image is consecrated with an installation ceremony in which the deity's animating spirit descends into the image. The image is also "given eyes," either by painting them on or by inserting ceramic eyeballs into the image's eye sockets. At this point the image can see and becomes a *murti*: a place of interaction between the divine and human worlds. At most temples, *murtis* of supporting deities, semi-divine beings, and auspicious persons are also consecrated in interior and exterior alcoves. Temple services are conducted by Brahmin priests who act as ritual specialists mediating between the divine world and the worshippers. They ensure that ritual purity is maintained; that interaction with the deities is done correctly; and that the proper *dharmic* protocol is observed by all castes of worshippers.

Domestic worship Hindus are not required to visit temples on a regular basis, and most religious practices take place in and around the home using domestic shrines. In the home of a poor family, this may be as simple as a recess in the wall in which an icon, lithograph, or simple drawing of the deity is placed. In wealthier homes, the shrine can take up an entire room and include elegant images as well as photographs of ancestors and spiritual teachers.

The performance of general *dharma* in domestic worship is overseen by the householders themselves. Occasionally a priest may be called in for his expertise or to give recitations of Vedic texts, but usually it is the senior woman and the other women of the household who assume the primary religious roles, for domestic rituals typically bear on issues of special importance to women. Domestic rituals that support a good marriage and healthy children are vital to a wife's social standing, and the ritual purity of her home is paramount, especially in matters involving food.

Pilgrimage to holy sites Honoring divinity at holy sites while on pilgrimage is also part of general *dharma*. These sites are places where gods and other manifestations of *brahman* have crossed over into our reality to make themselves accessible to humans. Holy sites, which are legion in India, are marked variously with elaborate structures, modest shrines, or even a splash of red pigment on a rock, or a small piece of cloth tied to a tree. Likewise, practices at these sites vary considerably, depending on localized traditions; and sites can offer healing, purification, material prosperity, religious merit, opportunities to appease various gods and spirits, and salvation itself. By far the most popular Hindu pilgrimage is the Kumbh Mela (Pitcher Gathering), which takes place about every three years in one of four locations, drawing tens of millions of people. The mythological basis for the pilgrimage is recounted in the *Mahabharata*. In a battle between the gods and the demons over a pitcher of divine nectar, four drops spill and fall to earth. The places where these drops landed are the four sites of the pilgrimage. Allahabad, in north central India, is regarded as the most powerful of the four, and it hosts a 42-day Great Kumbh Mela every twelfth year.

The logic of devotion

In most forms of religious devotion, or *bhakti*, Hindus establish a personal relationship with one of the Great Gods: Vishnu, Shiva, or Devi. Since each of these gods has distinctive traditions, emotions, and powers, and since Hindus vary with respect both to their *dharma* and to their accumulated karma, choosing one of these gods over the others often reflects one's spiritual needs and inclinations. The chosen god then becomes a person's *ishta-deva*, or cherished deity, but rarely does that lead to exclusive or monotheistic devotion to the god. The followers of Vishnu, Shiva, and Devi typically believe that their god encompasses all the others, implying that these gods, too, deserve worship. As a popular Hindu saying states, "God is one."

After choosing a god, a devotee becomes involved in the rituals and festivals associated with that god, learning to honor and love the way the deity dresses, the animals and lesser gods most closely associated with the deity, and the stories that recount the deity's adventures. Each deity has special scriptures containing this information, as well as information on proper temple construction, favorite offerings, important doctrines, and meditational techniques. For Vishnu and Shiva these scriptures are often called *Agamas*, while for Devi they are called either *Agamas* or *Tantras*.

Bhakti in the worship of images

Of the many ways to express devotion to Vishnu, Shiva, or Devi, one of the most popular is through the worship of images. At a private shrine in one's home, or at a temple dedicated to the deity, the god's *murti* is treated as an honored guest or visiting royalty. It is entertained with music and dance, offered incense and special food and drink, and generally afforded every consideration of hospitality and respect.

Hindus prepare themselves for devotional worship at a temple by ritual washing or bathing. They may also strike a large bell hanging at the entrance to the sanctum that houses the temple's primary *murti*. Its ring helps worshippers establish their spiritual focus and announces their presence to the deity. In a typical temple service, a priest begins by chanting praises to the deity, portions of which may also be chanted by the onlookers. Next the priest makes a variety of offerings to the deity. Common offerings are fruits, flowers, coconuts, rice, milk, yogurt, ghee, honey, sandalwood paste, confections, candles, and incense (Figure 1.11). On rarer occasions, worshippers have the priest offer an item of great value, perhaps in fulfillment of a vow. At the height of the ceremony the priest may shield the deity from the view of those attending by placing a curtain or other partition in front of the image. This is also the time when the priest utters *mantras* (sacred formulas) to render the ritual as a whole efficacious.

Following the recitation of *mantras*, the priest performs a ritual called *arati* by waving a lamp in a clockwise motion in front of the god. The lamp is then circulated among the worshippers, who cup their hands and wave the flame toward themselves to receive the deity's blessing and share in the merit generated by the ceremony. Next, worshippers receive *prasad*, a tangible gift from the deity. *Prasad* takes many forms, including ash or red powder that is applied by the priest to the area between one's eyebrows. It can also include some of the fruit that was offered to the deity, or water that has been sanctified by contact with the image. Once *prasad* has been received, it is common for worshippers to walk clockwise around the deity's *murti*, and then pay their respects to the temple's subsidiary deities. During this time, worshippers hope to receive *darshan* ("sight"). This refers to a visual exchange between a *murti* and the worshipper, for not only does the worshipper gaze reverently at the image, but the image may return the honor by looking back at the worshipper.

Figure 1.11 Merchants outside a temple in India sell various offerings to worshippers.
Source: Reproduced by permission of Jean-François Mayer.

Spiritual exercises

Bhakti is also practiced in a more disciplined manner under the guidance of a guru. Often called "father" or "mother," a guru oversees a devotee's progress as the latter develops an ever-deepening love for the deity. Early on, a devotee may chant a special name for the deity that the guru chooses especially for them. Devotees may also be encouraged to attend presentations and discussions about the deity; to imitate the deity's lifestyle by playing a flute or practicing austerities; to sing devotional songs for the deity; and to undertake memory exercises that keep the deity in mind throughout the day. As devotees grow in their devotion, they enter into a close relationship with the god or goddess. They can become the deity's son or daughter, a companion, or even a paramour. As is natural in such relationships, they also begin to experience profound emotions, such as rapture and ecstasy, or a sense of unworthiness and the desire to give oneself over to the deity as a slave.

Vishnu

Of the Great Gods, Vishnu is the most popular, followed by Shiva and then Devi. Vishnu is typically depicted as the "dark god," his skin being either blue or black. He has four arms, indicating great power, and often stands in front of his giant cobra, whose menacing hood is fully extended. In each of his four hands Vishnu holds a distinct object: a mace, a discus, a conch, and a lotus. The mace and the discus are the weapons with which he fights ignorance, sometimes depicted as demons, sometimes as the devotee's own ego. The conch is Vishnu's tool for creation. When he blows the conch, sound waves go forth to form the illusion that is our world. The lotus is symbolic of the salvation Vishnu grants: it is a plant that emerges from the mud (the karmic world) but opens into a pure and beautiful flower.

Vishnu's followers, called **Vaishnavas**, often identify themselves by painting his mark on their foreheads: three vertical lines connected at the bottom by a shorter line, which is said to be his footprint. They envision Vishnu as the Great God who supports the order of the world and protects and sustains all life. They also see him as the Supreme Soul, a cosmic being who suffuses all existence and oversees everything from the lives of insects to the destruction and creation of the world. The expansive, cyclical eras of Hindu time are but the alternating periods of Vishnu's activity and rest. At the dissolution of the world, Vishnu alone remains, sleeping at the bottom of the sea in the coils of his giant cobra. Then, awakened by the vibrations of the Vedic *mantra* "Om," Vishnu causes a lotus to sprout from his navel. In the flower of this lotus the Creator god Brahma appears, whom Vishnu commands to begin his work.

Vishnu's consort is Lakshmi, the goddess of wealth and domestic prosperity, and like Vishnu, she has four arms. She is often depicted standing on a lotus flower, richly dressed, flanked by royal elephants, and bestowing gold coins on her worshippers. She embodies Vishnu's creative power, and for this reason Vishnu sometimes has an emblem of her, the endless knot, painted on his chest, and wears a precious jewel in which she is said to reside. Both Vishnu and Lakshmi have animals that carry them to the human world. Lakshmi's mount is often an owl. Vishnu's is the brilliant sun bird Garuda, a divine eagle that once brought Soma down from heaven to be used by Brahmins in the Vedic sacrifices.

Vaishnavas can approach Vishnu directly, or through the praise and worship of Laksmi, Garuda, or Lakshmi's owl. More commonly, however, Vishnu's devotees approach him through one of his *avatars*. The stories associated with these *avatars* credit Vishnu with momentous deeds, such as slaughtering a band of Nobles who attempted to overthrow the Brahmins. In the story of the Dwarf, Vishnu comes to the rescue of the gods as the Dwarf *avatar* Vamana, after they had been bested in battle by the demons. In their arrogance, the demons decide that the gods should forever live in an area defined by one of the gods taking three steps. Through his illusory power, Vishnu appears as a dwarf and causes the demons to choose him. He then expands himself into a being of cosmic proportions and takes three strides, creating the earth, the sky, and the heaven. Finally, and for good measure, Vishnu ends his last step by crushing the leader of the demons. Vishnu is said to have 10 *avatars*, the last of which has not yet appeared but is expected at the end of time. This is Kalki, a warrior on a white horse (or sometimes the white horse itself), who arrives just before the dissolution of the world to defeat barbarian rulers in India and restore moral order one last time.

Vishnu's most popular *avatars* are Rama, the hero of the *Ramayana*, and Krishna, who counsels Arjuna in the *Gita*. Especially in northern India, Hindus celebrate Rama's victory over the ogre king Ravana in annual festivals called Ram-Lila (Rama-Play), and reenact the wedding between Rama and Sita (an incarnation of Lakshmi) using small devotional statues. The retelling of the *Ramayana* in Hindi, the main language of the region, has even been called the Bible of northern India; and when the *Ramayana* and the *Mahabharata* were serialized for Indian television, the country nearly came to a standstill every Sunday morning when the episodes were first broadcast (1987–1990).

Krishna's popularity as an *avatar* has spread throughout India, partly because of the inclusive nature of the *Bhagavad Gita*, and partly because Krishna's mythology has been extended far beyond his role in the *Gita*. An extensive literature recounts this *avatar*'s birth, childhood, and teenage years, making him attractive to a variety of worshippers. As a child, Krishna is depicted as sweet, clever, and mischievous. He steals the family's supply of clarified butter and defies his mother by eating mud. Yet his human mother is charmed by this naughtiness, which gives her sudden, astonishing glimpses of his true identity. A popular annual event is the celebration of Krishna's birthday.

As a teenager, Krishna is depicted as a cowherd who plays his flute, runs carefree with his teenage companions, and teases the milkmaids. Even though most of these milkmaids are married, Krishna's teasing usually takes an erotic turn. In one famous episode, Krishna sneaks up on them while they are bathing in the river and steals their clothes. As he sits perched on a tree limb looking down at them, he commands them to hold their arms above their heads in adoration of him to get their clothes back. Through his miraculous powers, Krishna also creates as many likenesses of himself as are necessary to lead each of these women to believe that she alone is with him. They dance, in pairs and collectively, and steal away later to engage in the arts of love throughout the night. Krishna's love for the milkmaids, and their love for him, is not literal, however. It is a model for the longing that is shared between the devotee and Vishnu. In the actions of these milkmaids, one senses the soul's desire for union with the Great God, regardless of the personal cost. One milkmaid in particular is the focus of Krishna's amorous adventures. This is Radha, who is seen both as the ideal devotee and as an incarnation of Lakshmi.

Sacred Traditions and Scripture

Radha's Love for Krishna

For centuries, devotees of Krishna have used love poetry filled with sensual language and erotic images to express the love between Krishna and Radha. Here is an example from the fifteenth-century poet Vidyapati:

> How beautiful the deliberate, sensuous union of the two; the girl Radha playing the active role this time, riding her Krishna's outstretched body in delight.
> Her smiling lips shine with drops of sweat: the god of love offering pearls to the moon.
> She of beautiful face hotly kisses the mouth of her beloved: the moon, with face bent down, drinks of the lotus.
> The garland hanging on her heavy breasts seems like a stream of milk from golden jars,
> The tinkling bells which decorate her hips sound the triumphal music of the god of love.

Through the *avatar* Krishna, devotees orient themselves to Vishnu in a variety of ways, depending on their personal inclinations. They can approach him as a child and love him as a mother would love her own little boy. Or their relationship to Krishna can be envisioned as that of a loyal teenage companion or an adoring girlfriend. Finally, one can worship Krishna as Lord Vishnu, as he reveals himself to Arjuna in the *Gita*. Like Vishnu, Krishna is depicted as blue or dark-skinned, and many Vaishnavas simply identify Krishna directly with Vishnu. For this reason, meditating on the playful and heroic deeds of Krishna's life or chanting his many divine names can lead to sudden visions of Vishnu.

Shiva

Hindus devoted to Shiva call themselves **Shaivas**. They number between 200 and 300 million, or about one-third to one-half the size of the Vaishnava movement, and are especially strong in southern India. In stark contrast to the kindly Vishnu, Shiva is envisioned as a fierce deity who destroys and creates through violent acts. He is a god who sometimes haunts cremation grounds, smeared with the ashes of the dead, which gives him a ghastly pallor. His hair is a mass of dark, coiled and matted locks; his throat is blue from having swallowed poison; he wears a snake around his neck and he girds his loins with a lion skin. His many names include the Howler and the Skull-Bearer, and sometimes he appears in his terrible form as Bhairava, a demonic-looking Untouchable accompanied by a dog (an impure creature).

As ultimate reality, or *brahman*, Shiva is a paradox beyond human comprehension. He is both life and death, loving and terrifying, approachable and fearsome, male and female, playful and destructive, erotic and ascetic. He is the fusion of opposites that cannot be unified in our world. Sometimes he is depicted as an androgyne, a man–woman whose left side is female and right side is male. Around his neck Shiva often wears a necklace made from the heads of past creator gods whom he decapitated. At other times he is the Lord of Animals, who both shepherds those under his care and slaughters them by the thousands. Another popular image depicts Shiva as the Lord of the Dance (Figure 1.12), enjoying himself as he crushes evil, quite nonchalantly, under his moving feet. Swaying and turning, he plays a toy drum whose sound waves create the insubstantial existence that is our karmic world.

At Shaiva temples, the most popular image of this god is the **lingam-yoni** (Figure 1.13), usually a black pillar (the *lingam*) set in a shallow dish with a spout on one side (the *yoni*). This is Shiva's creative and destructive energy envisioned as Shiva-Shakti, cosmic male and female sexual powers in eternal union with one another. Shaiva priests treat this image as a *murti*. In a daily liturgy, it is fed, bathed (hence the spout on the *yoni*), adorned in rich clothing, and entertained with music and dance. Sometimes the *lingam* has four faces carved near the top, indicating the Shiva's omniscience. More often, however, the pillar is smooth and uncarved, allowing devotees to experience Shiva's creative potential in its undifferentiated, unmanifest form. For this reason, "self-originating" *lingams*, such as those fashioned by nature from ice or rock, are considered especially powerful, sometimes drawing hundreds of thousands of pilgrims to their locations.

Hinduism 43

Figure 1.12 Enwrapped in the joy of his cosmic dance, Shiva effortlessly creates the universe and crushes demonic forces under his foot. Source: Wikimedia Commons.

Figure 1.13 The very popular *lingam-yoni* image. Shiva's *lingam* is set in a *yoni*, uniting cosmic male (Shiva) and female (Shakti) powers. The jewelry on the *lingam* bears Shiva's mark—the three horizontal lines—with his third eye (the ruby) in the center. Worshippers have left money as an offering to Shiva. Source: Will Deming.

The *lingam*, as the Universal Pillar, also figures in a popular Shaiva myth in which Shiva, rather than Vishnu or Brahma, is proclaimed creator and basis of the cosmos. According to this story, Vishnu and Brahma, who are regarded as creator gods by *their* devotees, meet while the world is still in a state of dissolution. As they argue over who is the actual creator god, the enormous Universal Pillar appears in a flash of blinding light before them, extending upward and downward beyond their field of vision. Filled with awe, they decide to discover the extent of this awe-inspiring pillar. Brahma ascends as a swan in search of its upper limit, while Vishnu descends as a boar in search of its lower limit. They return unsuccessful, however, for Shiva's *lingam* is infinite in height and depth. At this point Shiva emerges from his *lingam* as the true creator god, and Vishnu and Brahma are forced to concede his superiority and do obeisance to him.

Shiva also has a rich mythology as a god who rules the universe with his divine consort. Together they become Shiva-Shakti, the male and female energies that underlie the destruction and creation of our karmic world. The goddess has many names, depending on her role in a particular myth. Sometimes she is Parvati, a beautiful, serene goddess who rides either a goose or a mountain lion and keeps house with Shiva. They each have a son, Skanda and Ganesha. Skanda is Shiva's son, depicted with six heads and as many arms, being the consummate warrior god. His birth came about when the erotic activities of his parents were interrupted by the other gods, who feared that the violent sexual intercourse of Shiva and Parvati would rend the universe. As a result, Shiva spilled his semen. It became a drop of fire that none of the gods could contain. It was eventually deposited in the Ganges River, from which emerged the infant Skanda. Ganesha, by contrast, is a pot-bellied, elephant-headed boy (see the chapter-opening photo). According to one popular tradition, he was born from the filth of his mother during a bath. Shiva, becoming enraged that Ganesha would not allow him to barge in on Parvati as she continued to bathe, cut off his head, only to replace it later with the head of an elephant.

When Shiva is not at home being a family man, he becomes the great ascetic, renouncing all sexual activity. Roaming the world as an ominous drifter, he frequents cremation grounds and other lonely places, armed with a trident. If Parvati accompanies him, she does so as the ascetic goddess Uma. In this mode, Shiva is often depicted as seated beside his consort, deep in meditation, with a third eye set vertically in his forehead. This extra eye, which gives him inner vision and mystical insight, also enables him to destroy his enemies with a single, fiery glance.

Shiva's devotees accept the jarring paradox of his divine nature, believing that it forms the basis for the "stuff" of our world. This stuff, which they call *maya* (illusion) is seen by some as matter and by others as pure consciousness. Human beings, because of their ignorance and past karma, are caught in this *maya*, being born and reborn in the endless cycle of *samsara*. By devoting themselves to Shiva, however, they can move beyond the complexity and confusion of the world and experience the nonduality of the self (*atman*). They come to understand that Shiva's constant destruction and recreation of all things is intended to reveal the true, unified nature of existence. With this insight, they can achieve release through union with Shiva, whose fierceness ultimately gives way to grace and love.

Figure 1.14 With a snake around his neck, a trident, a drum, and three horizontal lines on his forehead, this *sadhu* (holy man) identifies himself with Shiva by imitating the Great God's ascetic practices. Source: Reproduced by permission of Nick Gier.

As with the devotees of Vishnu, Shaivas have several options for approaching their god. They can worship him directly through devotional songs filled with longing and abandon, or through dancing so passionate that it gives no thought to the safety of one's own person. They can also honor Shiva through imitation. Using the ashes from a cremation to mark their foreheads with three horizontal stripes (Shiva's *tilak*), many emulate Shiva's austerities. Taking in hand the trident, the snake, and the toy drum (Figure 1.14), they practice yogic techniques and meditation by the roadside, live in cremation grounds, or go on long pilgrimages to his many holy sites. Others imitate Shiva more simply by performing ritual bathing as an act of destruction and using meditation and the constant repetition of *mantras* as an act of creation. Finally, one can approach Shiva by honoring the bull Nandin, his loyal mount; or by worshipping his consort in her many forms; or by praising his sons Skanda and Ganesha and their mounts (the peacock and the bandicoot—a six-pound rodent). Skanda, who is believed never to have married, has become a divine model for sexual chastity, while Ganesha is much beloved as the god who removes obstacles and grants success in new undertakings, especially the undertakings of scholars and authors.

Devi

Visions of the divine as *female*—as goddesses or a cosmic principle—suffuse Hinduism. As Kathleen Erndl has observed, "Of all the world's religions, Hinduism has the most elaborate *living* goddess traditions" (Kathleen M. Erndl in *The Hindu World*, edited by Sushil Mittal and Gene Thursby, Routledge, 2004, p. 159, her emphasis). One of the most important goddesses in India is the River Ganges. Descending to earth through the Himalayas, she is said to be the Milky Way, her fall being softened by the mass of dreadlocks that cover Shiva's head. Through subterranean channels, her purifying powers are dispersed into all of India's rivers, which are, themselves, looked upon as the Ganges. Because of its many sacred rivers, ponds, lakes, and innumerable other holy sites, India itself is also considered a form of the goddess.

Devotees who choose the goddess Devi rather than Vishnu or Shiva call themselves **Shaktas**. Numbering around 50 million, they envision Devi as the creative power, or *shakti*, of the universe. She is seen as encompassing all the other goddesses, who express her many aspects. These partial manifestations of Devi include the consorts of Vishnu and Shiva, as well as several horrific goddesses such as Chamunda, Bhairavi, Candi, and Kali. For example, Chamunda, the goddess of famine, is the most prominent "mother" in a group known as the Seven Mothers. An emaciated hag, she abducts and eats infants and drinks blood from her begging bowl. Likewise, Kali ("dark one") wears a necklace of skulls and wields four savage weapons with her four arms to butcher her enemies before eating their flesh and drinking their blood on the field of battle.

The most popular manifestation of Devi, however, is the goddess Durga. A beautiful, richly clad goddess with 10 arms, she moves about the world astride a lion. Her most famous myth, told throughout India, begins with the defeat of the gods at the hands of the demons, and the subsequent rise of the Buffalo Demon to supreme power in the cosmos. Helpless in the face of this new ruler, Vishnu and Shiva become enraged, their combined anger producing the goddess Durga, a power far greater than either. After a prolonged battle in which the Buffalo Demon changes shape many times, Durga beheads him and restores order to the universe. In late September and early October, her victory is celebrated in the Durga-Puja, a nine-day festival in which almost all the inhabitants of Bengal take part. At the end of the festival, goats and buffalo are sacrificed in her honor, and the many temporary devotional images that her followers have used to worship her during the Puja—thousands upon thousands—are thrown into the Ganges after Durga's presence leaves them.

While it might seem that most of Devi's manifestations are fierce goddesses, her followers nonetheless see her as their loving mother. Her violence and great power are the attributes of a protective mother who cherishes and disciplines her children, while annihilating any who would threaten them. From a metaphysical perspective, moreover, Devi is understood as using her powers of annihilation to dispel the popular but false notion that the spirit is superior to matter, and that salvation is a process of liberating oneself from the material world through austerities and renunciation. Unlike the followers of Shiva, who identify their god with spirit and honor him as the great renouncer, Shaktas honor Devi as the basis for the world's physicality—its substance or matter. For Shaktas, therefore, the physical body is good, not evil, and the true path to salvation must unify the spirit with the body by subjecting the spirit to the body. In a striking reversal of the male-dominated relationship between Shiva and his consort that is envisioned by the Shaivas, a popular Shakta image depicts Devi, as Kali, dancing wildly on Shiva's pale, lifeless body. In subordinating Shiva's passive, austere energy to her active, creative energy, Devi can lead her devotees to salvation by joining physical enjoyment with release.

The devotional practices of Shaktas take two forms, often called exoteric, or public, and esoteric, or secretive. The former largely resemble the *bhakti* practices of Vaishnavas and Shaivas, but with Devi's *murti* as the object of devotion. The secretive practices, by contrast, include visualization techniques that use **yantras**, which are abstract images of the goddess; a form of Tantric discipline known as Kundalini Yoga; and the cultivation of magical powers called *siddhis*.

A *yantra* is a two-dimensional, geometric design. It typically consists of a square containing concentric circles, triangles (half of which are inverted), and arcs resembling the petals of a lotus flower (Figure 1.15). The upright triangles are

Figure 1.15 The Shri Chakra, a popular *yantra* design, with upward- and downward-pointing triangles.

spirit, the inverted ones are matter. The interior of the square is made accessible through entrances on the square's four sides, which are aligned to the cardinal points of the compass. These different features of the *yantra*, as well as the additional shapes formed by the intersection of the circles, triangles, and arcs, correspond to different aspects of the Goddess. At the very center of the *yantra* is a small area that gives access to the essence of the Goddess. The goal of her devotees is to reach this point by transmuting their own being into the Goddess herself. Metaphysically advancing though one of the entrances, devotees cross over into Devi's sacred world. They then chant *mantras* and use hand movements (*mudras*) to draw on Devi's creative energy. Since this process involves the manipulation of tremendous power, the *yantra* is an essential tool for controlling their progress and guiding them in the proper direction. While using a *yantra*, devotees also ingest certain substances, understood as divine aspects of the Goddess.

In Kundalini Yoga, Devi's *shakti* is envisioned as a snake sleeping in a coil at the base of the human spine. By using *mantras*, techniques of visualizing the deities and their attributes, and other yogic procedures such as breath control, the practitioner attempts to awaken this snake and guide it through six power centers in the human body (Figure 1.16). These are called **chakras** (disks) and are located along the spinal column and in the head. As *shakti* moves up through the *chakras*, the deities associated with each power center are activated and join the Goddess, such that she becomes all the deities, or *brahman*. Since the *chakras* in the body correspond to different parts of the *yantra* diagram, *yantric* techniques and Kundalini-Yoga often go hand in hand. If successful, a practitioner guides Kundalini from the *chakra* near the anus through *chakras* located in the sexual organs, the navel, the heart, and the throat, to a point at

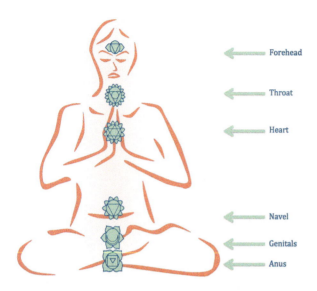

Figure 1.16 A diagram of the human body, showing the location of the six *chakras*.

the top of the nose between the eyebrows. This last *chakra* is the "thousand-petalled lotus," where *shakti* (as matter) joins Shiva (spirit). When this occurs, practitioners experience the eternal union and divine bliss of Shiva-Shakti in their own bodies.

Ritually and socially, esoteric Shaktism exists on the margins of Hinduism because it requires devotees to manipulate deities in order to gain *siddhis* (supernatural powers), which outsiders often suspect are used for nefarious purposes. Their misgivings are reinforced by the movement's protocols of secrecy, for its doctrines and practices are transmitted only to devotees, only in private interactions with spiritual mentors (gurus), and only after devotees have undergone a rigorous testing and purification process. Finally, the movement also endorses certain ritual practices known as left-handed Tantra which violate conventional Hindu notions of purity.

Among these left-handed practices, those that are particularly disturbing to outsiders are ones that involve self-immolation, the Five Ms, and (it is rumored) human sacrifice. The Five Ms are five things whose names in Sanskrit begin with the letter "m": fish, parched grain, meat, alcohol, and illicit sexual intercourse. These work according to a reversal of Hindu norms, which Tantric practitioners argue is necessary in this final, corrupt age of the world. Most Hindus consider the Five Ms to be powerful sources of impurity and bad karma. In Tantra, however, practitioners attempt to master and manipulate this dangerous power and use it in their quest to become gods. By ingesting one or more of the first four Ms in carefully planned rituals, they internalize and absorb this power. And in those branches of the tradition that practice illicit intercourse, the male seeks to absorb the *shakti* of the female, who is envisioned as the Great Goddess herself.

Hindu festivals

The practice of *bhakti* often cultivates a passionate, complex, and abiding relationship between the devotee and the deity, the intensity of which is most openly expressed in Hinduism's countless religious festivals. All Hindu temples have annual festivals, during which the *murti* of its main deity is brought out and paraded through the town or city. These festivals attract thousands of worshippers, many of whom arrive days beforehand to claim a place along the processional route. Local gurus and renunciants make an appearance, yoga practitioners display their feats of body control, and those with serious illnesses and disabilities come in hope of healing. The deity's image (which can be quite heavy) is carried

Figure 1.17 Topped with a red canopy, a cart for parading images of Krishna is pulled along by his devotees. These carts, which are sometimes as large as three-story houses, are dedicated to Krishna in his form as Jagannath, or Lord of the Universe. Europeans who first experienced them mispronounced this name as "juggernaut," which is now an English word meaning "an overwhelming, unstoppable force." Source: HT Digital Streams Limited.

on a wagon or chariot, the largest of which are 20–30 feet tall and require hundreds of worshippers to pull them (Figure 1.17). Throughout the festival, those present chant the names of the deity, sing devotional songs, and pray for absolution from sins and for final release. Festivals also provide the occasion for "unbroken readings" of epic and *Puranic* texts, and reenactments of a deity's mythology. Dramatic stagings of the *Ramayana*, for example, are performed annually throughout India, with month-long presentations taking place in and around the city of Ramnagar along the upper Ganges River. Puppet shows of episodes from the epics are also very popular.

The number of religious festivals in Hinduism, including local and regional celebrations, has been estimated at over 1000. What follows is a description of six of the most popular pan-Indian festivals, four of which are national holidays. Individually they can involve hundreds of millions of participants, and while each is associated with one of the principal three deities of *bhakti*, devotees of all the gods join in.

Maha-shiva-ratri The Grand Night of Shiva, or Maha-shiva-ratri, is a 24-hour festival whose center point is a moonless night in February or March. Early on the morning of the first day, devotees begin a fast (taking only fruit and liquids), take a ritual bath, apply ashes to their foreheads, and put on new clothes. They then collect leaves from the *bilva* tree, a plant sacred to Shiva, and go to a temple to offer them and perform other acts of *puja*. At the temple, the ritual bathing of Shiva's *lingam* by a priest takes place throughout the day and night, every three hours or so. On the morning of the second day, participants break their fast by accepting *prasad* from the deity.

While the festival is considered a special time for unmarried women to pray for a husband like Shiva, and for wives to pray for their husbands and sons, its fuller purpose is explained variously. Some see it as a celebration of Shiva's heroic drinking of poison at creation to save the other deities. Others say that it commemorates his marriage to Parvati, or the performance of his cosmic dance. And still others claim that the Maha-shiva-ratri celebrates Shiva's appearance to Vishnu and Brahma as the Universal Pillar.

Holi The festival of Holi also takes place in late February or early March and, depending on regional practices, can last 3 to 16 days. It is an end-of-winter festival that celebrates both the coming of spring and the divine love shared between Krishna and his favorite milkmaid, Radha. Leading up to the main day, devotees sing love ballads and recite stories of the romance between Krishna and Radha. On the evening before the main day, they light bonfires. In one account, this is to commemorate Vishnu's protection of a devoted follower named Prahlad, whose father, the powerful demon Hiranyakashipu, attempted to burn his son alive because of the latter's love of Vishnu (which is heresy for a demon). In another account, the bonfire recreates the deadly wrath of Shiva when he destroyed Kama, the god of love, after Kama had interrupted his meditation. On the main day of Holi, participants throw paint or colored power on each other just as Krishna is said to have done to Radha to make her skin as dark as his.

Holi is a time to revel in Krishna's playful and mischievous spirit. On the evening of the main day, and for an evening or two thereafter, risqué dance performances and poetry recitals are held. Caste rankings and other regulators of the social status are set aside, and family hierarchies are turned topsy-turvy. The women of a household playfully beat the male members, reversing the gender dominance that typically prevails; and members of the lower castes mock and ridicule Brahmins and Nobles for their ritual concerns and pompous ways. When the play of Holi is finished, however, people make the rounds of family and friends to express unbridled affection for those close to them. This is done to restore social order and to put an end to lingering grudges from the past year.

Janmastami A two-day celebration of Krishna's birth, Janmastami takes place sometime between mid-August and mid-September. On the first day, participants fast and women create small designs from rice powder resembling Krishna's baby feet, to lead him into their homes. At midnight, when this *avatar* of Vishnu is believed to have been born, an image of the baby Krishna is bathed in various precious substances and rocked in a cradle. A vigil of prayer and worship then continues until morning. Many devotees break their fast at midnight with *prasad*; others keep it until dawn of the next day; and a few refuse to drink any liquids during the fast.

Ganesh Chaturthi Ganesha's Fourth, or Ganesh Chaturthi, is celebrated on the fourth day of the moon's waxing phase in late August or early September. Ganesha, the elephant-headed son of Parvati who removes obstacles and gives success to those engaged in new undertakings, is arguably the most popular Hindu deity. Weeks before the festival begins, local artisans fashion clay images of Ganesha for sale. Smaller ones are purchased for domestic use during the festival, while larger ones are

Hinduism 51

Figure 1.18 Worshippers immerse a clay image of Ganesha at the conclusion of a Ganesh Chaturti festival. Source: Wikimedia Commons.

commissioned by various organizations and installed in public venues. The public images are sometimes flanked by clay images of Shiva and Parvati, whereas the household images are surrounded by small stones treated as Parvati. Once the clay images are in place and the breath of the deities has entered them, *puja* is performed: the images are bathed and anointed; food, drink, and flowers are presented; the deities are entertained with song and chant; and the fire blessing (*arati*) is waved before them. At the conclusion of the festival, all the clay images are taken to a lake, a river, or the sea to undergo the final immersion ceremony used for such temporary images (Figure 1.18). Expressing great emotional verve and sentiments of loss, participants bid the deities farewell and ask them to come again for next year's festival.

> **Did you know …**
>
> Although there are many theories, it is unknown why Hindus chose the cow to be a holy animal deserving reverence, and not to be eaten.

Dussehra Coming in late September and early October, Dussehra is celebrated with considerable regional variation in north and west India, Bengal, and south India, respectively. In all these locations, Dussehra is proceeded by the Navaratri (Nine Nights) festival, which accords three days each to the three principal manifestations of Devi, namely Durga, goddess of creative power, Lakshmi, goddess of wealth, and

Sarasvati, goddess of learning and the arts. These, in turn, are each worshipped in three manifestations under three further names. On the eighth day of Navaratri, a Vedic ritual is performed, and on the ninth day, nine young girls are presented and worshipped as manifestations of the Great Goddess. Their feet are washed and they are given new outfits to wear.

After the Nine Nights, Hindus in north and west India celebrate Dussehra with the Ram-Lila, or Rama Play. Actors present important scenes from the *Ramayana*: Rama is reunited with his brother Bharat (who wrongly came to power in his place); Rama's forces defeat the ogre Ravana and rescue his wife, Sita; and Rama takes his rightful place as king in the city of Ayodhya. Near the end of the Ram-Lila, huge effigies of Ravana and his evil allies are set ablaze. In south India, by contrast, women celebrate Dussehra by setting out small statues on miniature stages or steps. During the festival they feed these statues with a special dish made from chickpeas, and use them, rather than actors, to reenact scenes from the *Ramayana*. Finally, Bengali Hindus observe Dussehra by participating in the Durga-Puja, which, as we saw earlier, recounts and celebrates Durga's famous victory over the Buffalo Demon.

Diwali Also known as Deepavali, Diwali is the Festival of Lights, held in October and November. The core of the festival extends over three days, during which Hindus light small clay lamps filled with clarified butter or mustard seed oil, placing them along the walls and windowsills of their homes and in the surrounding pathways. These lamps serve two functions: they welcome the goddess Lakshmi, and they celebrate an individual's victory over evil. The first day of Diwali is said to commemorate either Krishna's triumph over the demon Narak (whose name refers to hell or the nether world), or Rama's return to Ayodhya after his many years of exile.

The second day, which is usually a new moon day, is dedicated to Rama's wife Lakshmi and Parvati's son Ganesha. In preparation for Lakshmi's visit, a kind of spring cleaning takes place, since Lakshmi only comes to homes that have been thoroughly cleaned. This day is especially dear to businesses, which consider it the beginning of their fiscal year. In the evening, worshippers don new clothes and visit friends and neighbors. Religious texts liken these guests to deities and recommend the sharing of food. It is also common for all adult members of a household to gamble, for one's luck at gambling indicates good or bad financial fortune in the coming year. The third day of Diwali marks Vishnu's defeat of Bali, a demon king who had gained great power and was planning to magnify this power still further by conducting one of the longest and most complex of all the Vedic rituals, the horse sacrifice. According to the Veda, this is when Vishnu appeared as the Dwarf *avatar*.

Diwali is preceded and followed by a host of other activities, all carried out in a highly festive spirit. Two days before the festival, in an event known as Dhanteras, Hindus commonly worship Lakshmi and purchase new cooking utensils, along with jewelry and coins made of precious metals. In the city of Varanasi, which is sacred to Shiva, Dhanteras is said to celebrate Shiva's return to the city after deposing king Divodasa through a clever ruse. Here the goddess Annapurna, patron of household bounty, is also worshipped, her devotees placing a seed of grain in their food supplies so that these supplies might never run empty. On the morning before Diwali, residents of Varanasi take a ritual bath in the Ganges River, and in the evening they place floating lamps in the river to guide wandering spirits to the next world.

The day after Diwali, many Hindus pause for rest. The festivities start to wind down and shopkeepers often close for the day. On this day or the next it is common for women to pray for good marriages and to create good luck designs in rice flour in the entryways to their homes. Geometric designs made of cow dung are also created in the area outside the home, and offerings are made. This is called Govardhan *puja*, and celebrates the boy Krishna's triumph over the storm god Indra. Following the Govardhan *puja*, women feed confections to their brothers, wave the sacred flame (*arati*) before them, and apply an auspicious mark (*tilak*) made from red *kumkum* powder to their foreheads. These ceremonies honor the bonds between siblings and promote their brothers' well-being.

The logic of jnana

Hindus explain the pursuit of *jnana* (divine knowledge) in many ways. It is a method to see beyond the illusion of our unsaved world, or a means to escape the consequences of karma. It unites and consolidates the spiritual energies in one's body, or frees the spirit from the world of matter. Likewise, its goal, *moksha*, which is said to be experienced in this life, is also described with a range of images. It is a stillness of mind that is one step beyond dreamless sleep, or the discovery of the real person (*atman*) as a radically free psychic faculty. It is eternal union with *brahman*, or the World Soul, or the supreme deity. It is the loss of all individual awareness and personal identity, as when a drop of water falls into the ocean. And it is the attainment of a boundless, universal consciousness, aware of everything but distracted and disturbed by nothing whatsoever. This variety of images arises, in part, from the conviction that those seeking *jnana* need to be guided by a guru, with the result that there are almost as many teaching traditions as there are famous gurus. Two of these teaching traditions that have come to North America are the International Society for Krishna Consciousness (ISKCON), and Transcendental Meditation (TM), which counted the Beatles among its early adherents. Still other teaching traditions are promoted by a loose international network of gurus called Satsang.

By contrast, the *practices* of *jnana*, as opposed to its teaching, are more uniform, due to their roots in the *Yoga-Sutras*, a treatise written by Patanjali around 150 BCE. Defining his approach as an alternative to the logic of karma, Patanjali outlined a method of salvation in eight "limbs," or disciplined courses of action designed to bring the mind and body under one's control. Over time, Patanjali's "limbs" became the core practices of many forms of yoga, including Hatha-Yoga (Force or Power Yoga), which emphasizes the importance of the physical body as a tool for attaining *moksha*; Mantra-Yoga, which relies especially on the repetition of sounds and sacred formulas (*mantras*); Tantric systems, such as the Kundalini Yoga that we discussed earlier; and Raja-Yoga (Royal Yoga), the form that most faithfully follows Patanjali's description. The pursuit of *jnana* is also one of these yogas, and is sometimes called **Jnana-Yoga**.

A Closer Look

Patanjali's Eight Limbs of Yoga

1. Abstention from violence, lying, sexuality, and greed.
2. Observance of purity, contentment, rigor, study, and love of god.
3. Body postures—lying, sitting, and standing positions.
4. Measured breathing.
5. Withdrawal from the use of sense organs.
6. Concentration developed by focusing on a single object.
7. Meditation.
8. Union with *brahman* (*samadhi*).

Sketched in the broadest terms, a person begins Jnana-Yoga by choosing a spiritual guide—a guru, a renunciant, or a holy person (*sant*)—who gives the new student several rules of conduct. These include prohibitions against deceit, theft, and the destruction of life, and obligations to practice good study habits, cleanliness, and mild austerities such as fasting and night vigils. On one level, these rules constitute a code of ethics. But on a deeper level, they are the entry into a structured way of life designed to detach a person from the world of karmic causality. A beginner interacts with the outside world based on mistaken inclinations and urgings of the mind and body, which are the product of ignorance, desire, and past karma, and only produce more karma. By training the body and mind to engage the world in an enlightened and disinterested fashion, the student can still act in the world, but without accumulating karma. It is especially important for a beginner to avoid the evils of greed, lust, and anger, which are understood to be the root causes of rebirth.

A spiritual guide also assigns practices that westerners associate with yoga classes, namely, sitting and standing postures and regulating one's breathing. While westerners generally see these as ways to reduce stress and promote physical well-being, Hindu practitioners rely on them to gain further detachment from *samsara*. The postures are intended to allow one's life forces to flow freely through the various ducts and veins in the body, while the breathing exercises reduce the activities of the body to a single, primary action: breathing. In this way, one's life forces can be consolidated and focused inward, toward the *atman*, rather than dispersed outward into the karmic world.

As students progress, they engage in activities designed to withdraw their senses—sight, smell, hearing, touch, taste—from the surrounding world. When this happens, they take less notice of the karmic world and eventually become indifferent to it.

Figure 1.19 "Om," the primal sound heard at the beginning of the creation of the cosmos.

One very popular exercise is the repetition of *mantras*, including sacred formulas, names of deities, and the sound "Om" (Figure 1.19). These orient the mind to *brahman* because in chanting them as part of a yogic regime, one can begin to hear and think *brahman*.

The chanting of *mantras* can be combined with practices that develop mental focus. Often a practitioner is instructed to concentrate on a single point or image, thereby learning to steady the mind and avoid worldly distractions. After concentration is mastered, meditation proper begins. When meditation is done correctly, the point or image that was the *object* of the previous exercise now fills the whole universe, leaving no room for the *subject*, the individual ego. Shortly after this, the practitioner slips into a state called *samadhi* and, completely oblivious to any distinction between object and subject, achieves *moksha*. The practitioner has now become a *jivan-mukta*, someone who is released (*mukta*) while still living (*jivan*) in this world. The life they now live is simply a product of unspent karma from this and previous lives; it produces no new karma. When one's old karma has been exhausted, the person dies, never to be reborn.

Even under the direction of a guru, it can take many years to attain *moksha* through Jnana-Yoga. Some schools of Jnana-Yoga, moreover, teach that nothing is guaranteed in the last stages of the journey, since it is only through the practitioner's determination and self-effort that passage out of *samsara* becomes possible. Others, following the *Yoga Sutras*, posit that the practitioner is helped by Ishvara (the Lord), an eternally pure spirit whose reality suddenly vanishes at the point of achieving *moksha*. Still others teach that the grace of one of the Great Gods is necessary, manifested in one's guru or through the deity directly. It is by adopting this last position that many Hindus find common ground between the logic of *jnana* and the logic of *bhakti*. Shaivas, as we have seen, honor Shiva as the foremost of renunciants and imitate him through meditation, while Shaktas often pursue salvation through Kundalini Yoga.

CONCLUSION

We began this chapter by reflecting on the bewildering complexity within Hinduism. We are now able to understand that this complexity has two sides. While it frequently perplexes outsiders in their efforts to gain even a general understanding of Hinduism, for Hindus themselves the complex nature of their religion is one of its strengths. Hindus believe that everyone has their own karma to work through in this life, and no single path to *brahman* can accommodate everyone. Some practice yoga, others are drawn to *puja*, and still others find salvation in a life of devotion to Vishnu—or Shiva, or Devi. And if one cannot approach Shiva directly, one can still worship Shiva through devotion to his consort Parvati or to one of their sons, Ganesha and Skanda, or their animal mounts. Likewise, if a person is drawn to the worship of Vishnu, they can choose from the *avatars* Rama and Krishna. The *avatar* Krishna, in turn, offers options suited to many combinations of gender, age, and personal inclinations. This might be Krishna the beautiful, vivacious baby; or Krishna the mischievous child; or Krishna the fun-loving teenager, exploring his adolescent sexuality; or Krishna the Lord of the *Bhagavad Gita*. Nor is there any necessity to choose just one. According to some texts, Hindus have 330 million gods, meaning that they have an infinite number of options open to them. As a popular Bengali saying goes, "We are all Vaishnavas in public, Shaivas at home, and Shaktas in secret."

For review

1. In what ways are *atman*, *samsara*, and *moksha* related to one another in Hindu theology?
2. Describe the Hindu notion of *dharma*. How is it related to rebirth and karma?
3. What role does the caste system play in Hinduism? How has this changed over time?
4. How are the gods of Hinduism related to *brahman*?
5. Who are the three Great Gods of Hinduism and what is the nature of their respective festivals?
6. How are images of gods (*murti*) used in Hinduism?
7. What is *puja* and how is it performed in a Hindu temple? How is this different than *bhakti*?
8. How is Patanjali related to Jnana-Yoga?

For discussion

1. How is sexual imagery used in Hinduism's vision of ultimate reality?
2. How does Hinduism account for people of other religions—e.g., Christians, Buddhists, Muslims?

Key Terms

Agni	The Hindu fire god.
arati	A Hindu blessing received from a ritual flame.
Arjuna	The righteous king to whom Krishna reveals his divinity in the *Bhagavad Gita*.

Aryans	Authors of the *Collections*; literally "Noble People."
atman	The imperishable soul in Hinduism.
avatar	One of 10 forms that Vishnu assumes in this world.
Bhagavad Gita	"Song of the Lord"; a Hindu poem from the *Mahabharata* proclaiming the greatness of Krishna.
bhakti	"Devotion"; acts of devotion to images of deities.
brahman	Ultimate reality in Hinduism.
Brahmin	A Hindu priest; the highest class in traditional Hindu society.
chakras	In Hindu schools of yoga, disks along the spine and in the head where divine power resides.
class-and-life-stage *dharma*	One of three sources of *dharma*; duties determined by one's birth and stage in life.
Commoners	The third-ranking class in traditional Hindu society.
dalit	The current name used in India for "outcaste."
darshan	A visual exchange between a *murti* and a Hindu worshipper.
Devi	One of the three great deities of Hinduism.
dharma	Hindu religious duty; religion.
general *dharma*	Religious duties incumbent upon all Hindus.
Indra	The king of the Hindu gods in the *Collections*.
ishta-deva	The Hindu deity chosen as the focus of one's religious devotion.
jati	"Birth"; the Hindu word translated into English as "caste."
jnana	Hindu divine knowledge.
Jnana-Yoga	A spiritual discipline in Hinduism for attaining divine knowledge (*jnana*).
karma	The good and bad consequences of one's actions.
Krishna	A popular *avatar* of the Hindu god Vishnu.
lingam-yoni	A popular *murti* of the Hindu god Shiva.
Mahabharata	The longest of India's two epic poems; composed ca. 300 BCE–300 CE
mantras	Sacred formulas chanted at rituals.
moksha	Release from the karmic world.
monism	The Hindu vision of ultimate reality as a single impersonal principle that pervades everything.
murti	A consecrated image used by Hindu gods to interact with worshippers.
Nobles	The second-ranking class in traditional Hindu society.
outcaste	An older term for *dalit*; impure persons excluded from traditional Hindu society.
prasad	A gift received from a *murti*.
puja	Worship in which such things as fruit and flowers are offered to a *murti*.

Puranas	A literature that first appeared in Hinduism ca. 350 CE; used as devotional texts for worshipping Hinduism's three great deities.
Rama	A popular *avatar* of the Hindu god Vishnu; the hero of the *Ramayana*.
Ramayana	One of India's two epic poems; composed ca. 200 BCE–200 CE.
Rig-Veda	The earliest and most authoritative part of the Hindu Veda.
samsara	"Flowing around." The beginningless, meaningless cycle of birth, death, and rebirth controlled by karma.
samskaras	Rituals performed at different stages of a person's life.
Servants	The lowest-ranking class in traditional Hindu society.
Shaivas	Devotees of the Hindu god Shiva.
Shaktas	Devotees of the Hindu goddess Devi.
shakti	The creative power of the universe; an aspect of the Hindu goddess Devi.
Shiva	One of three great deities in Hinduism.
theism	Ultimate reality envisioned as a god or gods.
Untouchable	An older Hindu term for *dalit*.
Upanishads	Late texts of the Hindu Veda that contain ideas about karma, rebirth, and renunciation.
Vaishnavas	Devotees of the Hindu god Vishnu.
Veda	The most authoritative collection of Hindu scripture, comprising the *Collections*, the *Brahmanas*, the *Aranyakas*, and the *Upanishads*.
Vedanta	Literally, "end of the Veda." A name for the *Upanishads,* the last scriptures to be added to the Vedic canon.
Vishnu	One of the three great deities of Hinduism.
yantra	A two-dimensional geometrical design used as an image of the Hindu goddess Devi.
yoga	A Hindu spiritual discipline using breath control and body posturing.

Bibliography

A good first book
Joyce B. Flueckiger. *Everyday Hinduism*. Chichester, West Sussex, UK: Wiley-Blackwell, 2015.

Further reading
Wendy Doniger. *The Hindus: An Alternative History*. New York: Penguin, 2009.
Wendy Doniger. *On Hinduism*. Oxford: Oxford University Press, 2014.
Hillary P. Rodrigues. *Introducing Hinduism*. London and New York: Routledge, 2016.
Eleanor Zelliot and Rohini Mokashi-Punekar. *Untouchable Saints: An Indian Phenomenon*. New Delhi: Manohar, 2005.

Reference and research
Gavin Flood, ed. *The Blackwell Companion to Hinduism*. Malden, MA: Blackwell, 2003.
Knut A. Jacobsen, ed. *Brill's Encyclopedia of Hinduism*, 6 vols. Leiden and Boston: Brill, 2009–2015.
Julius Lipner. *Hindus: Their Religious Beliefs and Practices*. London and New York: Routledge, 2002.
J. E. Llewellyn, ed. *Defining Hinduism: A Reader*. New York: Routledge, 2005.
Sushil Mittal and Gene Thursby, eds. *The Hindu World*. New York and London: Routledge, 2004.
Robin Rinehart, ed. *Contemporary Hinduism: Ritual, Culture, and Practice*. Santa Barbara, CA: ABC-CLIO, 2004.

CHAPTER 2

Buddhism
The alleviation of suffering

Veneration of the Buddha at a temple in Thailand. Source: Reproduced by permission of Chuck DeVoe.

DID YOU KNOW …

Buddhists regularly pray and make offerings to many gods and spirits. While they expect these beings to help them in a material sense, ultimate liberation (nirvana) comes not from the gods, but from human effort. Human beings are actually in a better position to attain this liberation than the gods.

Understanding the Religions of the World: An Introduction, Second Edition.
Edited by Will Deming.
© 2025 John Wiley & Sons Ltd. Published 2025 by John Wiley & Sons Ltd.

OVERVIEW

The religion we call Buddhism began some 2400 years ago in the northeast region of ancient India, in what is now the nation of Nepal. According to Buddhist tradition, **Siddhartha Gautama**, the son of a local king, undertook a six-year quest to overcome suffering. At the end of this quest he became the **Buddha**, the "Awakened One," and taught what he had discovered to an increasing number of disciples. Following his death, his teachings on the nature of the world and the suffering inherent in it spread across Asia. In the twentieth century they came to the west (Figure 2.1).

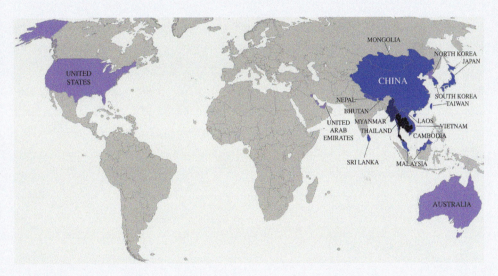

Figure 2.1 A map indicating the Buddhist population of different countries as a percentage of each country's total population.

Traditionally scholars of Buddhism have divided the religion into three branches or schools: **Mahayana**, "Great Vehicle," which is the largest; **Theravada**, "Teaching of the Elders," which is second in size; and **Vajrayana**, "Diamond or Thunderbolt Vehicle," which some scholars prefer to treat as a variation of Mahayana rather than a separate school in itself. Mahayana is practiced mostly in east Asia—China, Korea, Japan, and Vietnam. Theravada is practiced mostly in south and southeast Asia—southern India, Sri Lanka, Myanmar, Nepal, Thailand, Laos, Cambodia, Vietnam (again), and Singapore. And Vajrayana is practiced mostly in Tibet, Nepal (again), northern India, Bhutan, Mongolia, and Siberia.

Today, Buddhism is one of the world's four largest religions, Christianity being the largest. But whether Buddhism is the second, or third, or fourth largest is problematic and depends on how we identify who is Buddhist. As Buddhism initially spread across Asia, it did so in a manner that scholars often describe as practical or pragmatic. Then, as now, Buddhism's focus was on the alleviation of suffering. Things that did not pertain to this focus or distract from it were regarded as irrelevant, including the beliefs and practices of other religions. As a consequence, Buddhists and Buddhist institutions in Asia have generally coexisted and even partnered with other religions, serving particular needs in society while leaving other needs to these other religions. Until recently, for example, there were no Buddhist marriage ceremonies.

Because of this, many if not most Buddhists are not exclusively Buddhist—although exclusivity has gained ground in the last century. In other words, Buddhists often practice two or more religions. Japanese Buddhists, for example, often observe the New Year by going to both a Buddhist temple and a Shinto shrine; and in China, Buddhism is usually treated as just one component in a religious system that also draws on Confucianism and Daoism. Since there is no way to determine what percentage of Buddhism, over against other religions, one needs to practice to be considered a "full" Buddhist, the number of Buddhists in the world cannot be established with any precision, but only estimated within a broad range. Thus, while scholars estimate the number to be between 480 million and 530 million, Buddhism, in some measure, influences the lives of perhaps a fifth of the world's population.

History

Timeline	
5th century BCE	The life of the Buddha; the First Council meets after his death (ca. 400 BCE).
4th century BCE	The Second Council meets.
3rd century BCE	King Ashoka adopts Buddhism and holds the Third Council; Buddhism enters Sri Lanka and the Mahavihara is established.
1st century BCE–1st century CE	The Pali Canon is first written down.
1st century CE	Mahayana begins; Buddhism enters China.
2nd–3rd centuries CE	Nagarjuna develops the Madhyamaka teaching; the *Lotus Sutra* is composed.
2nd–4th centuries CE	Buddhism enters Vietnam, Burma (Myanmar), and Cambodia.
4th century	Yogacara schools appear; Buddhism enters Japan.
5th century	Buddhaghosa writes the *Path of Purification*.
6th century	Pure Land and Chan schools develop in China.
7th–8th centuries	Vajrayana develops in India, followed by the "First Dissemination" of Buddhism in Tibet.
early 9th century	The Borobudur complex is built in Indonesia; Saicho establishes Tendai Buddhism in Japan.
10th–13th centuries	Buddhism in India declines.
11th century	Anawratha unites Burma and adopts Theravada Buddhism, sending monks to Sri Lanka as well.
12th century	The Khmer empire in Cambodia adopts Buddhism.
12th–13th centuries	Zen and Pure Land are established in Japan.
14th century	Nichiren Buddhism is established in Japan.
early 17th century	The Tokugawa shogunate promotes Buddhism in Japan.
17th–18th centuries	Theravada Buddhism is reestablished in Sri Lanka from Thailand.
18th–19th centuries	Buddhist countries are colonized by European powers.

(continued)

1870s	The Meiji government disestablishes Buddhism in Japan.
1893	The World Parliament of Religions meets in Chicago at the World's Fair, introducing Buddhism to western audiences.
1920–1945	Zen Buddhism is used to support Japanese imperialism.
1950s	China invades Tibet, suppressing Buddhist practices and destroying monasteries.
1963	Thich Quang Duc immolates himself in Vietnam.
1989	The 14th Dalai Lama receives the Nobel Peace Prize.
2007	Buddhist monks lead protests against the Myanmar government; the Chinese government declares its authority to confer legitimacy on all high-ranking monks in Tibetan Buddhism.

The details of the Buddha's life were written down hundreds of years after his death, so it is not always possible to distinguish historical fact from later tradition. He seems to have been born around 480 BCE into the Gautama family of the Shakya clan, which held a small kingdom in the northeast region of ancient India. He was given the personal name Siddhartha and, at some point in early adulthood, he left home and became a wandering ascetic. It was during this time that he attained enlightenment and began his own religion. After many years of teaching, he died around 400 BCE, leaving behind an oral tradition of his beliefs and a group of monks and nuns who had reached enlightenment under his care.

The Buddha's life according to Buddhist traditions

Overtime, Buddhists developed much fuller accounts of the Buddha's life. According to several of these, there had been prophecies at the time of the Buddha's birth predicting that he would become either a great spiritual leader or a great king. His father, hoping that Siddhartha would choose the latter path, not only trained him in the arts of kingship, but also sheltered him from anything that might cause him to reflect on the human condition, including human suffering. Through a plan of the gods, however, Prince Siddhartha left the palace one day to inspect his father's kingdom and encountered people experiencing sickness, old age, and death. This disturbed him greatly, leading him to ponder human frailty, death, and the possibility of an afterlife. After this experience, Siddhartha encountered a destitute holy man by the side of the road who, despite his extreme poverty, was filled with contentment. Together, these **Four Sights,** as they are called, inspired the young prince to find such spiritual contentment for himself. Despite being married (and in some accounts having a newborn son), he left an opulent royal life and all its pleasures to spend the next six years following different teachers. Under their guidance he experimented with a number of ascetic practices, each more extreme than the one before. He restricted his intake of air to the absolute minimum and fasted until his backbone was visible through his stomach. In the end, however, he determined that all these practices were false paths to the peace that he sought.

> **Did you know …**
>
> Buddhist calendars in southeast Asia regard our year 2024 CE as 2566 BE (Buddhist Era), based on the tradition that the Buddha was born in the year 543 BCE. But historical research has recently inclined many scholars to date the Buddha's birth more than 60 years later, or around 480 BCE.

The Enlightenment

Giving up the practices of extreme asceticism, Siddhartha pursued what he would later call the Middle Way—a lifestyle that was disciplined, but rejected both asceticism and the luxuries of the world. After years of effort, he is said to have sat down under a fig tree, now referred to as the Bo or Bodhi Tree (enlightenment tree), resolving once and for all to attain the peace that had eluded him. Despite temptations and physical assaults by the great demon Mara, Siddhartha prevailed by dint of his own righteousness and with the aid of the Earth Spirit. Sitting through the night in meditation, he finally experienced enlightenment and became the Buddha, the Awakened or Enlightened One. In this moment, Siddhartha attained the wisdom to move beyond human suffering. He saw that all life was a series of ephemeral, ever-changing events that only *seemed* to have substance, reality, and meaning. Furthermore, while Hindu theologians were teaching that humans possessed an imperishable soul (*atman*), Siddhartha discovered that human beings have no permanent, unchanging core. They were *an-atman*, devoid of any stable self. What appeared to be the human self was, in fact, a collection of insubstantial phenomena that humans falsely interpreted to be their existence. These phenomena were conditioned by other phenomena, arising and dissipating according to patterns and forces that were quite beyond a person's control or even perception.

Because everything associated with human existence was in constant flux, insubstantial, and outside a person's control, life was filled with dissatisfaction and pain, a condition the Buddha called *dukkha*. Even those things that seemed good—close friends, health, good food—were temporary and momentary, and so desiring and enjoying them invariably led to a sense of loss. When a person died, they were reborn into a new life, but not because a soul was reincarnated into a new body. Rather, it was because the intentional actions of the person's life, called **karma** (also *kamma*), propelled each person into yet another existence characterized by *dukkha*. Karma was like a seed that germinated, ripened, and bore fruit in an endless and ultimately meaningless cycle of lives called *samsara*.

The Four Noble Truths

Initially the Buddha considered the depth and complexity of his enlightenment to be an impediment to teaching others. But through the pleading of the god Brahma, and out of compassion for the myriad beings still in the grip of *samsara*, he resolved to share his discoveries, which he called the **Dharma**, meaning saving truth. He thus began a long teaching career, turning first to those with whom he had practiced asceticism. In the Deer Park outside of Varanasi (Benares), he spoke to them in a sermon later known as the "Discourse on Setting the Wheel of Dharma in Motion." Its subject was the **Four Noble Truths,** by which the Buddha summarized his principal insights.

The first of the Buddha's Noble Truths was that *dukkha*—discomfort, disappointment, and suffering—was inherent in all things, no matter how pleasurable they might seem. The second Noble Truth was that *dukkha* is caused by *trishna*, one's desire or thirst for things, which led to attachment. The most obvious type of attachment was to physical things, such as an expensive house or nice clothes. A more subtle type was the attachment to ideas and beliefs, which occurs when one desires such things as heroism or holiness. The most subtle type—which was the crux of the Buddha's concern—was attachment to one's presumed self.

The third Noble Truth follows logically from the first two: one can put an end to *dukkha* by eliminating *trishna*. Yet this was no simple matter. Because it was so deeply engrained in every aspect of human existence, desire had to be cut off at its root, which was ignorance—namely, the ignorance of one's own impermanence and the absence of a self (*an-atman*). Only by ending this ignorance could one put a stop to desire. This led to the cessation of *dukkha*, a goal the Buddha called **nirvana** (also *nibbana*). It was an achievement that required multiple lifetimes, however, and the sheer complexity and subtlety involved was indicated by the Buddha's paradoxical insistence that the final desire to be eliminated was the desire for nirvana.

A Closer Look

The Teaching of No-self

The Buddha is remembered for having taught that humans have no permanent self. But this can be confusing, for the Buddha was not saying that a given person did not exist, but that no person existed in any *permanent* sense. In all likelihood, he was responding to the Hindu teaching that human souls were both eternal and so real that they were part of ultimate reality. For the Buddha, however, a person was a process: an arising and coming together of "aggregates" of physical and mental "moments," that came and went with great speed. Very much like the image that is created through the rapid succession of individual frames in a video, they were easily mistaken for something continuous, stable, and real (Figure 2.2).

Figure 2.2 For Buddhists, life is a series of disconnected, ephemeral moments, not anything substantial that exists over time. They teach that unenlightened people mistake these discrete moments for a unified reality in the same way that we mistake the individual frames of a video for fluid motion. Source: Will Deming.

The long and arduous path to nirvana was outlined by the Buddha in the fourth Noble Truth, which consisted of eight practices called the **Noble Eightfold Path**. These enabled people to overcome their ignorance by training them to live in the *right* way. One early version of the Path, which likens the eight practices to things needed by someone on a long journey, runs as follows:

1. *Right understanding* will be the torch to light the traveler's path.
2. *Right intentions* will be his guide.
3. *Right speech* will be the inn along the way.
4. *Right behavior* will be a balanced and measured stride.
5. *Right livelihood* will be his refreshment.
6. *Right efforts* will be his steps forward.
7. *Right meditation* will be his measured breathing.
8. *Right contemplation* will give him the peace that follows in the Buddha's footsteps.

What is envisioned here is a series of graded practices. The first two (right understanding and intentions) lead to an initial wisdom, while the next three (right speech, behavior, and livelihood) build on this wisdom and lead to proper ethics and moral behavior. Right efforts and right meditation, (6) and (7), then build on the previous five, resulting in proper concentration, which, if pursued correctly, will lead to nirvana. Yet this is a logical, not necessarily a chronological understanding of the Path, for all eight steps are mutually reinforcing. For example, beginners may start with the practice of right speech (3) without knowing why, but this will lead them to the practice of right intentions (2).

The practical nature of nirvana

Even though the Buddha identified the solution to suffering as nirvana, he said very little about what nirvana was, preferring to speak of it as the *cessation* of suffering, or the *extinguishing* of *samsara*. One early text famously compared human existence to the flame of a candle and recommended *eliminating* the flame by *depriving* it of its root causes, heat and fuel. Even in the teaching of the Noble Eightfold Path, where nirvana is reached by perfecting one's concentration, this perfection is no more than the *elimination* of delusional thinking, not the attainment of something better.

The Buddha's reluctance to discuss nirvana reflects his very practical approach to religion. If suffering (*dukkha*) was the problem of human existence, and its absence was the solution, then speculating about the nature of this absence was counterproductive, for it needlessly prolonged one's suffering. The Buddha is remembered as having equated such speculation to a foolish man who had been pierced by a poison arrow. Instead of asking for the arrow to be removed, which would have saved his life, he posed a series of questions about the nature of the arrow: its composition, its design, and the social rank of the archer, leading to his death. Thus, the Buddha's "negative" definition of nirvana—describing what it is *not*—should not be interpreted as a pessimistic or nihilistic view of life. Rather, it represents the teaching method of a thoroughgoing pragmatist. Like a doctor, the Buddha had no interest in delaying a cure to discuss a patient's future after recovery.

> **Talking about Religion**
>
> ### The Buddha's Practical Approach to Religion
>
> The Buddha always told his disciples not to waste their time and energy in metaphysical speculation. Whenever he was asked a metaphysical question, he remained silent. Instead, he directed his disciples toward practical efforts. Questioned one day about the problem of the infinity of the world, the Buddha said, "Whether the world is finite or infinite, limited or unlimited, the problem of your liberation remains the same." ... Life is so short. It must not be spent in endless metaphysical speculation that does not bring us any closer to the truth.
>
> From the Vietnamese monk Thich Nhat Hanh, *Zen Keys* (New York, Doubleday, 1974), p. 42.

The Buddhist community

Because the Buddha saw the Four Noble Truths as an advanced teaching, suitable only for those whose past lives had prepared them to undertake the Noble Eightfold Path, he admonished all others to improve their next birth through the accumulation of merit (good karma). They were to practice giving, or *dana*—especially to those who were ready for the more advanced teachings—and follow a few elementary moral precepts (*sila*). If they were able to master these simple practices, they were also encouraged to renounce sensual pleasures and engage in a type of meditation that would calm their minds. Altogether, there was not much distinctively Buddhist in this lesser path.

By contrast, those ready to undertake the Noble Eightfold Path were required to leave their homes and social obligations and live as celibate monks and nuns. They gave up their possessions, shaved their heads, put on monastic robes, and begged for their food. They were guided by rules that demanded simplicity and discipline and taught them how to interact with others, for all Buddhists, lay and monastic alike, were to be part of a supportive community, or **Sangha**.

Figure 2.3 A Cambodian reclining Buddha, depicting the Buddha's *maha-pari-nirvana* (entry into final nirvana). Source: Will Deming.

The Buddha's great final nirvana and the first Buddhist scriptures

When the Buddha died around 400 BCE, his death was described as the great final nirvana (*maha-pari-nirvana*) (Figure 2.3). Although the Buddha had attained nirvana some 40 years earlier, he had continued to live in a human body, which was the product of karma from his former lives. In Buddhist terminology, he had achieved nirvana "with remainder." At death, however, the Buddha left his human body, thereby achieving nirvana without remainder, also known as the "highest or final" nirvana. Because he was no longer part of *samsara*, it was now inappropriate to think of him as either dead or alive. Having moved completely beyond birth and rebirth, he defied description according to any category of existence or nonexistence.

Because the Buddha had urged that the monastic community be guided by the Dharma (saving truth), rather than a new leader after his death, the Sangha came together in what would later be known as the First Council, where they decided to preserve the Buddha's many teachings through continual recitation. The Council organized these teachings into two lengthy collections, one comprising the Buddha's sermons, known as the *Sutra-pitaka* (Basket of Discourses), the other comprising his rules for monastic discipline, known as the *Vinaya-pitaka* (Basket of Discipline). Together these constituted the Buddha's Dharma, and were transmitted to successive generations of Buddhists orally, even after they were written down in the first century BCE.

Early Buddhism in India

Although there are relatively few Buddhists in India today (only 8.5 million in a population of over 1.4 billion), Buddhism played an important role in the life of the subcontinent for more than 16 centuries. Without a designated successor to the Buddha, his followers formed into several monastic fraternities, or *nikayas*. These differed from one another on the basis of teaching lineages and with regard to how strictly each group of monastics interpreted the *vinaya* (disciplinary rules). Since new monks and nuns were required to be instructed by mentors, they developed loyalties to their teachers and their teachers' predecessors, identifying themselves as belonging to a "lineage" of teachers. The resulting *nikayas* nonetheless continued to dialogue and debate with one another.

Within a century of the Buddha's death, however, a Second Council became necessary because an argument developed between two *nikayas* over the importance of particular disciplinary rules. One group, called the Elders, argued that all the rules of the *vinaya* should be maintained. The other group, known as the Great Community, contended that certain rules could be considered minor, and were therefore optional. In the end, neither group would acknowledge the validity of the other's teaching lineage or authoritative writings.

The Higher Dharma movement

Beginning in the third century BCE, a new type of scholarship appeared in monastic communities. Known as the **Abhidharma**, or Higher Dharma teaching, it attempted to systematize and further elaborate the Buddha's discourses in the *Sutra-Pitaka*. It created lists of key teachings, which it then supplemented with commentary and analysis, often in the form of a question-and-answer exchange between the Buddha and his early disciples. As *Abhidharma* scholarship matured, it also formulated philosophically coherent explanations for all phenomena of life, calling these phenomena ***dharmas***, meaning the "facts" or "discrete truths" of the universe.

These *dharmas* constituted the building blocks of the existence, much like the elements of the periodic table used in western chemistry, except they accounted for both physical as well as psychological and spiritual facets of existence. *Dharmas* were thus the basis for the events, sensations, and processes that led to the illusion of a lasting and pleasurable life. They included such things as smell, faith, energy, motivation, anger, and duration. None of them had any permanence, however, for like the human soul, the *dharmas* were *an-atman*—devoid of any permanent core. They arose and dissipated almost instantaneously through a process called dependent co-arising. Beginning with ignorance, this process initially led to the formation of ideas that falsely attributed existence and permanence to an infinite number of fleeting phenomena. Some of these phenomena were mistaken for consciousness and sensory input, leading to the illusion of physical contact and emotions. Craving, grasping, and *becoming*—but no actual *being*—subsequently arose, leading to the illusion of birth, *dukkha*, and death, at which point the whole process began again, fueled by karma. This complicated sequencing of the dharmas, explored so meticulously in the Higher Dharma literature, was sometimes simplified in a very practical way, reminiscent of the second and third Noble Truths: "because *this* arises, *that* arises," and "if *this* does not arise, then *that* will not either."

Buddhism

King Ashoka's support of Buddhism

Around 250 BCE, a conflict arose between different factions within the Elders, and a Third Council was convened at the behest of the Mauryan King Ashoka, who ruled much of the Indian subcontinent. While the nature of the conflict remains uncertain, it seems to have resulted in Ashoka's support for a particular group known at the time as the Distinctionist School. This would be the only *nikaya* to survive from this early period (Figure 2.4).

In addition to convening the Third Council, King Ashoka is important in early Buddhist history for several other reasons. First, he was idealized as the *Dharma-Raja*, or Truth King for his endorsement of Buddhism. According to Buddhist chronicles, several years after becoming king, Ashoka defeated and killed a large number of his enemies. But feeling great remorse at this wholesale carnage, he became a patron of the Buddhist Sangha and promoted the Buddhist ideal of *ahimsa*, the nondestruction of life. He banned animal sacrifice, turned royal hunting excursions into religious pilgrimages, and converted the royal household to a vegetarian diet.

Second, Ashoka is credited with purifying the Sangha by removing corrupt monks, which established an important precedent for future Buddhist rulers.

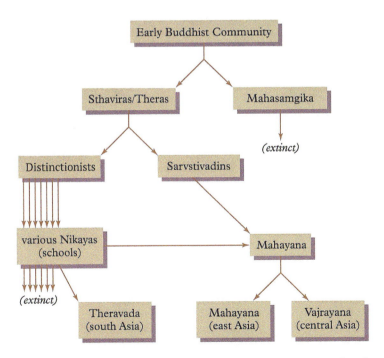

Figure 2.4 The Buddhist community developed in several directions over its long history, and the three variations practiced today are only indirectly connected with the original Sangha. The name Theravada, moreover, was rarely used before the early twentieth century. Followers of this branch of Buddhism usually referred to their religion simply as "the teachings of the Buddha."

Third, he energized Buddhist missions by sponsoring traveling Buddhist teachers. In particular, he is remembered for sending his son and daughter as monk and nun to Sri Lanka to spread Buddhism there. Finally, the reign of Ashoka provides a much-needed baseline for dating Buddhism, since the inscriptions on the stone pillars that he erected in support of Buddhism are the first artifacts of Buddhist history that we can date with any precision.

> **Did you know …**
>
> In the third century CE, Sri Lankan Buddhists acquired an important relic, a tooth of the Buddha, which was said to have come to the island nation on its own accord as a way of establishing an authentic branch of Buddhism there. It is now enshrined in the Temple of the Tooth in the city of Kandy.

Seeking refuge: the Buddha, the Dharma, and the Sangha

By the time of Ashoka, and probably before then, lay and monastic Buddhists had begun a regular practice of "taking refuge" in the **Three Jewels**, or Three Refuges. These were three precious things to which Buddhists could turn for help in the absence of the Buddha. They comprised the Buddha, the Dharma, and the Sangha. Even though the Buddha had moved quite beyond any communication with human beings when he attained final nirvana, one could still "take refuge in the Buddha" because the power of his enlightenment remained in the relics from his life. After his death, thousands of relics became objects of veneration, including the remains of his physical body after his cremation and items he had used during his stay on earth, such as his begging bowl (see Figure 2.5). To these relics were added simple images that memorialized teachings and events in his life: a wheel with eight spokes commemorated his discourse on the Noble Eightfold Path; an empty throne signified his universal majesty as well as his departure into final nirvana; a deer brought to mind his first sermon in the Deer Park; and natural depressions in large rocks and mountain ranges were seen as his footprint, which pointed to his absence, the mark he left on the world, and the path leading to nirvana. By seeking out these relics and images and leaving small gifts of flowers and fruit, Buddhists "brought the Buddha to mind," a ritual through which they drew encouragement and rededicated themselves to the task of salvation.

Taking refuge in the Dharma, on the other hand, meant copying, reciting, and studying Buddhist scriptures. These included the *Sutra-* and *Vinaya-pitakas*, which, having expanded over the years, now contained narrative examples of the *vinaya* and hundreds of stories about the Buddha's past lives, called *jataka* tales. In addition, the *Abhidharma* literature, which had also expanded in this way, was recognized as a third *pitaka*. Since the **Abhidharma-pitaka**, like the other two *pitakas*, was written in the Indian language of Pali, its inclusion led to Buddhist scriptures being called both the **Tri-pitaka** (*Three Baskets*), and the **Pali Canon**.

Figure 2.5 The tradition of venerating relics has been important throughout the history of Buddhism. Here, displayed in a golden lotus flower atop a jeweled pedestal, is a relic of the early fourteenth-century Tibetan teacher Longchenpa, widely regarded as a manifestation of the *bodhisattva* Manjusri. Source: Will Deming.

Sacred Traditions and Scripture

From the *Vinaya-pitaka*

An account of a conversation between the Buddha and his close disciple Ananda, regarding the ordination of women as nuns underscores the androcentric nature of this and most other religions:

A nun who has been ordained even for a century must greet respectfully, rise up from her seat, salute with joined palms and do proper homage to a monk ordained but that very day. A nun must not spend the rainy season in a residence where there is no monk…. A monk must not be abused or reviled in any way by a nun. From today, admonition of monks by nuns is forbidden, admonition of nuns by monks is not forbidden. Each of these rules is to be honored, respected, revered, venerated, and is never to be transgressed by a nun during her life.

Vinaya-pitaka 2. 253, in Edward Conze, ed., *Buddhist Texts Through the Ages* (New York, Harper and Row, 1964) pp. 24–25.

Finally, taking refuge in the Sangha meant seeking wisdom and encouragement from those in the monastic community. Monks and nuns, after all, were the heirs to the teaching lineages that went back to the Buddha, as well as the living practitioners of his wisdom. In reality, the majority of monastics were barely more enlightened than the laity, but those who had made significant progress toward nirvana were recognized as part of a hierarchy called the Four Noble Beings. To enter this hierarchy, monks and nuns had to develop the Dharma eye, which gave them their first fleeting glimpse of nirvana, as well as the ability to recognize the Dharma in others. When this occurred, they became stream winners, having entered the stream or current that led to nirvana. Stream winners could not be reborn into a hell or the realm of hungry ghosts, and they were guaranteed the attainment of full enlightenment within no more than seven lifetimes. Above the stream winners were the once returners, who were guaranteed nirvana in this or the next life, and above them were the nonreturners. Finally, at the very top were the *arhats*, who were considered very rare. Arhats were special beings who had completely conquered the five hindrances of sensual desire, anger, sloth, restlessness, and doubt; attained to the highest meditative states; and perfected the three teachings of higher morality, higher concentration, and higher wisdom. The last of these teachings was said to make them omniscient and give them the ability to fly, walk on water, pass through solid objects, and see into past and future lives. In the entire universe, the *arhat* was only superseded by the Buddha, and only because the Buddha had discovered the path to nirvana on his own, whereas the *arhat* had learned it through the Buddha's teachings.

The beginnings of Mahayana Buddhism

Sometime in the second or first century BCE, new *sutras* (discourses) began to circulate among the monastic communities. Unlike the earlier discourses of the Pali Canon, most of these were in Sanskrit and circulated in written form. The majority purported to be dialogues between the Buddha and his early disciples concerning a higher wisdom, or *prajna-paramita*—literally the "perfection of wisdom." It was said that these discourses had only now come to light because they were considerably more advanced than the Pali *sutras*. For this reason, the Buddha had entrusted them to serpent deities (*nagas*) until the Buddhist community had progressed to the point where it was able to receive them. Some proponents of these new sutras, moreover, argued that even if one doubted that they had originated with the Buddha, truth was truth, and so "whatever was well-spoken" was de facto the Dharma of the Buddha. Promising good karma to those who copied and taught them, these *sutras* became both popular and controversial.

Many of the important ideas in these new *sutras* had been part of Buddhism for centuries, but were now developed in novel ways. It was a new phase in Buddhist scholarship, much like the *Abhidharma* movement had been. The proponents of the new *sutras* initially lived and studied alongside other monastics, adhering to the same monastic rules (*vinaya*). In the late second or early third century CE, however, an influential teacher named Nagarjuna pioneered a school of thought called the Madhyamaka, which maintained that none of the *dharmas* (discrete truths), so carefully analyzed in the *Abhidharma-pitaka*, had any reality. Prior to this, Buddhist scholars had assumed that while life was an impermanent and ever-changing illusion, the *dharmas*, at least, had unique (although not abiding) qualities. On the molecular level, so to speak, there were real categories or distinctions that could be analyzed. Against this, however, Nagarjuna argued that the *dharmas* were only a conventional truth, not the highest truth that the Buddha had taught. Since every *dharma* arose from prior causes and conditions, none could be said to have a nature of its own: they were, in fact, empty (*sunya*) of any distinguishing features. From this analysis Nagarjuna drew two important conclusions: first, there was neither existence nor non-existence in the universe (and hence the name of his school, Madhyamaka, or "school in the middle"); and second, if one pursued this teaching of emptiness, or *sunyata*, to its logical conclusion, it was even impossible to make a meaningful distinction between *samsara* and nirvana, for ultimately they were both empty of any distinguishing qualities.

> **Talking about Religion**
>
> ## A Modern Reflection on Emptiness (*Sunyata*)
>
> *Sunyata* is an impish challenge to man's insistent desire to reify, to conceptualize, to classify, to discriminate. It refuses to give him an excuse to be lost in a sleep of fascination or limited awareness. It deprives him of any basis for his most gripping passions and his driving fears. Man's ego is alarmed by such a merciless foe, and declares its alarm to be a justifiable "fear of the void." But *sunyata* is not something in the first place, something that can be mistaken for something else, such as a "void." It is nothing—nothing to possess specific properties, nothing to be possessed, nothing to understand or to achieve. Its greatest impudence consists in telling man that he is nothing too.
>
> Tibetan lama Tarthang Tulku, *Sacred Art of Tibet*
(Berkeley, CA: Dharma Publishing, 1974), pp. 7–8.

The *Lotus Sutra*

Around the time Nagarjuna was active, the *Lotus Sutra of the True Dharma* appeared. More adversarial and critical of the older schools than earlier Sanskrit discourses, the *Lotus Sutra* declared that the Pali Canon represented a lower level of truth, which it labeled Hinayana, the "Lesser Vehicle." While still valid, its teachings were meant for inferior minds and led only to lower levels of enlightenment. Indeed, the Buddha had intended it as *upaya*, a "skillful means" to communicate with those who were not ready for the higher truths. The highest path to enlightenment, according to the *Lotus Sutra*, was the Mahayana, or Great Vehicle.

Designed for those who already perceived the emptiness of all phenomena, the Mahayana taught that one could acquire the Buddha's compassion (*karuna*) for all beings by moving beyond the notions of "self" and "other." Aspiring to the level of *arhat* was now criticized as a selfish act, for it focused on one's own salvation.

The goal of Mahayana practitioners, by contrast, was to become **bodhisattvas**. These were "beings dedicated to awakening" who passed through eons of rebirths in celestial buddha lands, tirelessly working for the salvation of all sentient beings before becoming buddhas themselves. In line with this teaching, the *Lotus Sutra* re-envisioned the cosmos as containing multiple buddhas, buddha lands, and *bodhisattvas*. All earlier schools of Buddhism, it claimed, had merely been instances of skillful teaching by these buddhas and *bodhisattvas*. Yet, because these schools had unknowingly taught the truth, their practitioners would eventually become buddhas as well.

Around the fourth century CE, Mahayanists began to organize the many teachings of the Sanskrit *sutras* into a coherent, new system and establish their own monasteries. Until this time, they had lived and practiced alongside monastics from other schools. This decision to separate from other Buddhists was hastened by the teachings of the Yogachara school, a tradition that may have developed as early as the first century CE, and which began to coalesce with Mahayana around this time. By proposing that consciousness (*vijnana*) was the only reality—that the world was "mind only"—the Yogachara gave added weight to Mahayana's insistence on the emptiness of all phenomena, the absence of any difference between *samsara* and nirvana, and the superiority of this school.

> ### Sacred Traditions and Scripture
>
> ## On the Non-difference Between *Samsara* and Nirvana
>
> In contrast to earlier forms of Buddhism, Mahayanists claimed that enlightenment entailed the complete dissolution of all distinctions, even those between *samsara*, the world of suffering, and nirvana, the cessation of suffering. The following parable from the *Perfection of Wisdom in Eight Thousand Lines* (*Astasahasrika Prajnaparamita*) attempts to impart this paradoxical teaching:
>
> > The enlightened one starts out in the Great Ferryboat, but there is nothing from which he starts out. He starts from the world, but he actually starts from nothingness. His boat is piloted by the Ten Perfections of the *bodhisattva*, but it really has no pilot. It is held afloat by nothing at all; it is held afloat by his experience of knowing everything, which acts as a non-support. Beyond this, no one has ever gone out in the Ferryboat, no one will ever go out in it, and no one is going out in it now. Why? Because neither the Ferryboat nor the traveler exists. So, who would be going out, where would he be headed, and why?

The emergence of Theravada Buddhism

At the beginning of the fifth century, the Indian scholar Buddhaghosa moved to Sri Lanka to study the Pali Canon. Not only is he credited with editing the Canon into its present form, but through his extensive commentary, the *Path of Purification*, he also organized the Canon's teachings into a unified system, arriving at an understanding of Buddhism quite distinct from Mahayana. The school to which he belonged, the only *nikaya* to survive from the early period, became known as Theravada, the Teaching of the Elders (see Figure 2.4). By the end of the fifth century, Buddhism was thus developing in two basic streams: Mahayana and Theravada.

Living up to its name, Theravadins preserved the older traditions and rejected the newer ones, even though its monastics continued to engage intellectually with Mahayana monastics well into the next millennium. Like earlier Buddhists, they insisted that the *arhat* was the highest goal of Buddhist practice, although they did not deny that one could become a *bodhisattva* or a buddha. Indeed, according to the Pali Canon, Siddhartha Gautama had done just that. In a previous life, as the wandering ascetic Sumedha, Siddhartha had had the good fortune to meet the Buddha who preceded him, Dipankara Buddha. Instead of training under Dipankara to become an *arhat*, however, Siddhartha chose to pursue the *bodhisattva* path and become a "perfect buddha." Theravadins, however, saw a repetition of this achievement as both unnecessary and impossible.

It was unnecessary because the difference between an *arhat* and a buddha was negligible. While a buddha was one who had established the Dharma after the Dharma of his predecessor had been forgotten by the world, an *arhat* was someone who learned the Dharma from a past or present buddha. Their enlightenment was the same, and at death both the *arhat* and the buddha equally attained to the highest nirvana. Becoming a *bodhisattva* or a buddha was impossible, moreover, because Theravada taught that only one buddha could be in the world at any given time, and that the next buddha could not appear until humans had completely forgotten the Dharma of his predecessor. But Gautama Buddha's Dharma was still in the world and, furthermore, a future buddha-in-waiting was already standing in the wings—the *bodhisattva* **Maitreya**, who now lived in the Tushita heaven, from whence all Buddhas entered the world.

With this traditional understanding of *arhats* and buddhas, Theravada kept within the intellectual confines of the Pali Canon. Educated monastics studied Buddhaghosa's *Path of Purification*, regarding it as an introspective masterpiece, and veneration of Maitreya as the future buddha increased among the laity. Since it was believed that Maitreya's appearance would make the Eightfold Path accessible to everyone, Theravadins encouraged all people to accumulate enough good karma to be reborn at the time of his coming. To this end, they sponsored festivals celebrating the Buddha's birth, enlightenment, and *maha-pari-nirvana*, and created ceremonies in which monks chanted the Pali Canon to remove moral defilements from the laity and protect them from dangers.

A cosmic Buddha and Buddhist cosmology

In contrast to Theravada's adherence to the Pali Canon, Mahayanist leaders used the newer Sanskrit texts to promote a cosmic understanding of the Buddha. From the *Lotus Sutra* they adopted the image of a resplendent Gautama Buddha preaching from Vulture Peak, a mountain of mythical proportions. Surrounded by crowds of buddhas and *bodhisattvas*, Gautama proclaimed that he had attained enlightenment many eons earlier and had appeared, time and time again, as various buddhas in the past. Beyond this, he revealed that *all* beings would eventually achieve buddhahood, and that those who already had were now active and accessible for the salvation of others. The Buddha's *maha-pari-nirvana* was thus not, as the Theravadins taught, his definitive exit into the final nirvana, but an example of his skill in means, which he had used to convince his early disciples to rely on themselves after his death.

> ## A Closer Look
>
> ### Partial Truths
>
> In a passage from the *Lotus Sutra*, the Buddha illustrates the technique of "skill in means" (*upaya*) with the following parable:
>
> A man comes home to find his house on fire and his children playing upstairs. Even though he pleads with them to leave the house, they continue playing with their toys. The man then tells them that he has wonderful toys for them to play with outside. Fooled by this, his children leave the house and escape the danger of the fire. When safely outside, the children receive some of the promised toys.
>
> The Buddha then explains that he is this man and the people of the world are his children. His first plea to them was the teaching of Mahayana, which, in their ignorance, they could not understand. He therefore resorted to Hinayana, the Lesser Vehicle (a derogatory name for Theravada), even though this was not the full truth. This was necessary and ethical, he concludes, because one must use all tactics available to alleviate the suffering of others.

Using two other *sutras*, the *Larger* and *Smaller Land of Bliss Sutras*, Mahayanists also developed teachings about a cosmic realm that **Amitabha**, the Buddha of Immeasurable Life and Light, had established for the salvation of others. According to these writings, Amitabha had accumulated merit well beyond what was necessary for his own salvation and, guided by his great compassion, used the excess to create a safe haven into which sinful people could be reborn. Once there, they could acquire wisdom for salvation with very little effort, for Amitabha's "land of bliss" was so thoroughly infused with truth that even its birds sang the Dharma. With this new possibility of salvation through Amitabha, an element of grace entered into Buddhism that does not seem to have been part of the earlier traditions, for one could now make significant progress along the path to nirvana on the basis of *another's* merit.

These and other developments within Mahayana inspired practices that went far beyond simply venerating Gautama Buddha as a model for one's life, for Mahayanists began petitioning an ever-increasing number celestial buddhas and *bodhisattvas* for their saving powers. To accommodate this multiplicity of enlightened beings, Mahayana thinkers developed the notion that there were three **buddha bodies**, which, in unenlightened terms, may be thought of as nirvanic realms or states (from an enlightened perspective, nirvanic realms and states neither exist nor do not exist).

Theravadins had long spoken of two buddha bodies: Gautama Buddha's earthly body, now extant only in relics, and his Dharma, understood as his body of teachings, which was contained in the Pali Canon and experienced through enlightenment. Mahayanists, however, viewed the buddhas bodies altogether differently. For them the first, or lowest, buddha body was the **body of transformation**, which enabled buddhas to appear in this world. Gautama Buddha, for example, is said to have taken on the body of transformation when he was born as Siddhartha. The next buddha body was the **body of bliss**, through which accomplished buddhas blessed and taught *bodhisattvas* and established their own buddha realms, or lands of bliss. This body was meant for the enjoyment of *bodhisattvas* as they traveled the path to buddha-hood. They could visit these lands through meditation or be reborn in them to learn the Dharma directly from their resident buddhas. Finally, the third and highest buddha body was the **Dharma body**, which Mahayanists likened to the luminous, nirvanic essence of the Buddha, which radiated truth throughout the universe.

> **Did you know …**
>
> A Buddhist tradition teaches that before the next Buddha comes into our world, Gautama Buddha's relics will come together, reconstitute his body, preach one last sermon, and then vanish.

It is hard to overstate the impact these teachings about the buddha bodies had on the subsequent development of Buddhist thought. Rather than understanding nirvana as a deathlessness achieved by extinguishing one's illusory karmic existence, Mahayanists envisioned it as a cosmic Buddha who extended compassion to all sentient beings through his bodies of bliss and transformation. In addition, since Mahayanists insisted that everything, including nirvana, was ultimately empty (*sunya*), they identified this cosmic Buddha, the Dharma-body, with the emptiness (*sunyata*) of human existence that Buddhist enlightenment revealed. In this way they arrived at a remarkable conclusion: attaining nirvana was nothing more and nothing less than uncovering the buddha that one *already was*. In their terminology, every sentient being already had the "buddha-womb."

The *bodhisattva* path

Just as the *arhat* had become the ideal figure in the Theravada community, the *bodhisattva* became the ideal for Mahayanists. A *bodhisattva*—who could even be a layperson, according to Mahayanists—is one who took a vow to work for the salvation of all beings for as long as they remained trapped in *samsara*. To become a *bodhisattva*, one had to master the six Perfections of giving, morality, patience, vigor, meditation, and wisdom. These inspired and transformed the person through virtues that the Buddha had cultivated during his many previous incarnations. At Perfection six, one obtained the nirvana of an *arhat*. When he died, however, the practitioner did not pass from this world into final nirvana, for, in contrast to *arhats*, Mahayana practitioners cultivated the Perfections without acknowledging them as Perfections or viewing themselves as virtuous beings. This allowed them to achieve the awakening mind (*bodhi-citta*), through which they could aspire to become a buddha solely for the salvation of others. Only at this point did they truly begin the *bodhisattva* path. By achieving the awakening mind, these fledgling *bodhisattvas* began to experience the true nature of the world, the emptiness beyond the *samsara*-nirvana duality. They cultivated the true compassion of the Buddha and, at death, entered into nonduality, which enabled them to remain active in the world out of compassion, without involvement in karma or *dukkha*.

Eventually, Mahayanists developed 10 discernible stages through which *bodhisattvas* passed on their road to buddhahood, coordinating them with Ten Perfections (adding four to the original six). In stages 7 through 9, according to this system, *bodhisattvas* were born into one of the buddha lands of the body of bliss (*sambhoga-kaya*) and advanced toward buddhahood under the tutelage of a celestial buddha. Then, in the tenth stage, they entered the Dharma Cloud in the Tushita heaven, where they became omniscient, being illumined by the wisdom of all previous buddhas.

The thunderbolt or diamond vehicle

As Mahayana continued into the seventh and eighth centuries, certain monks began advocating for techniques that promised to shorten the path of the *bodhisattva* dramatically. Influenced by practices of asceticism and visualization that had become popular among Hindu yogins, communities of Buddhist adepts (*siddhas*) experimented with the use of supernatural powers in their quest for buddhahood. Even though Mahayana had already accelerated and expanded one's prospects for developing merit and wisdom, the *bodhisattva* path still required three expansive eons to complete. By comparison, the proponents of these new methods insisted that no more than 17 lifetimes were necessary, and that it was even possible to gain buddhahood in one's present life. The name eventually given to this movement was Vajrayana, or the *vajra*-vehicle. The word *vajra*, which can mean either "thunderbolt" or "diamond," denoted power, supremacy, and achievement. As a thunderbolt, it was a divine weapon for breaking through spiritual obstructions, and as a diamond it signified a clear and indestructible authority. Sometimes taking the form of a hollow royal scepter, images of the *vajra* became the empty yet unyielding tool for destroying greed, hatred, and ignorance.

Doctrinally Vajrayana never made a radical break from Mahayana, although it often extended Mahayana ideas. Like Mahayana, it taught that laity did not need to enter a monastery to undertake the *bodhisattva* path, but added that the abilities of certain extraordinary lay Buddhists could even exceed those of accomplished monastics. Likewise, while Mahayana had proposed that the buddha-womb was inherent in every being, Vajrayana proclaimed that all beings were *already* fully buddhas, but that the vast majority did not realize it because they mistook nirvana for *samsara*. Finally, Vajrayana interpreted the Mahayana notions of *sunyata* (the emptiness of all phenomena) and *upaya* (skill in means) as justifications for using techniques that violated Buddhist norms of conduct. Under certain conditions, rules against eating forbidden foods, drinking alcohol, and engaging in sexual practices could be broken by advanced practitioners to help them move beyond the false dichotomies of good and evil.

The *Tantras*

Even though Vajrayana remained close to Mahayana in doctrine, it added several innovative practices, as when it expanded the use of *mantras*. These were short texts, phrases, or even individual words or syllables that Theravada and Mahayana monastics chanted during rituals, mostly for the purpose of recollecting the Buddha or focusing one's mind. Used by Vajrayana practitioners, however, *mantras* became magical formulas that could manipulate deities and gain entry into higher states of reality. In light of this novel use of *mantras*, Vajrayana was sometimes called Mantrayana, the *mantra*-vehicle.

Most of Vajrayana's new practices came from a literature called *Tantras*. Like the earlier Sanskrit *sutras*, *Tantras* claimed to be traditions that Gautama Buddha had imparted to his most advanced students, who had passed them down secretly through elite teaching lineages. But unlike *sutras*, *Tantras* were ritual manuals, not discourses. Sometimes giving only partial instructions for the execution of powerful, and therefore dangerous rituals, these manuals were intended to be used only with the guidance of an accomplished teacher, and only after a student had undergone elaborate initiation ceremonies.

The disappearance of Buddhism from India

By the eleventh century CE, Buddhism was clearly in decline throughout India, and some scholars see this process as having begun as early as the fourth century. Monastic communities had always relied on a combination of popular and royal support, and as these sources dried up in the face of competition from devotional Hinduism (*bhakti*), monasteries disappeared. Some forms of devotional Hinduism even co-opted the Buddha as an incarnation of the god Vishnu. In the sixth century, tribes from central Asia, including the White Huns, moved into north and northwest India, often looting and destroying the monasteries they encountered. Since a quorum of fully ordained monks was needed to ordain new monks and nuns, the fate of future generations of monastic leaders was often sealed when monks died in these raids. The invasions from central Asia were followed in the eleventh century by waves of Muslim forces from Turkey and Afghanistan. Unlike the earlier invaders, however, Muslim forces not only looted and destroyed monasteries, but also persecuted Buddhists as polytheists. Then, in 1198, Muslims sacked and burned Nalanda, the religion's last great university, thereby destroying centuries of Buddhist scholarship. By the middle of the thirteenth century, Buddhism survived only in south India and in small areas north of the Ganges, where it vanished altogether in the fifteenth century.

Buddhism outside of India

Even though Buddhism all but disappeared from the land of its origin, its zeal for alleviating the suffering of others had already taken it into areas south, east, and north of India. In the third century BCE, king Ashoka had sponsored missionaries to Sri Lanka, and is credited with sending a cutting from the original *Bo* tree to be planted there. These missionaries were so successful that the Sri Lankan king Tissa (307–267 BCE) established Buddhism as the state religion and constructed an enormous monastic complex, the Mahavihara, in the city of Anuradhapura, where the Pali Canon would later be written down for the first time.

Buddhism also traveled to Indonesia, perhaps as early as the second or first century BCE, and into China, Vietnam, Burma, and Cambodia in the first centuries CE. From China it was taken to Korea in the third century CE, and from there to Japan. Finally, in the seventh century, Vajrayana was taken north over the Himalayas into Tibet, eventually spreading into Mongolia, southern Russia, western China, Nepal, and Bhutan (Figure 2.6). The spread of Buddhism to these various lands not only accounts for its survival after the fifteenth century, but also for many surprising innovations,

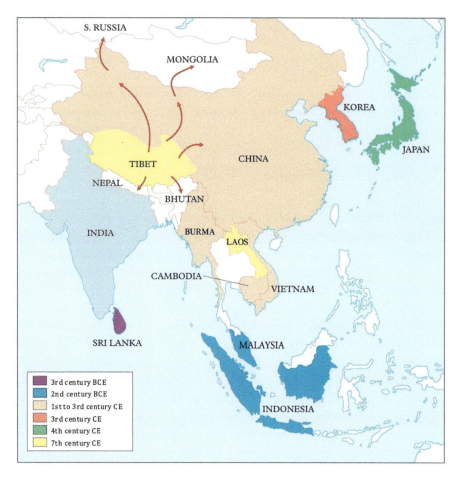

Figure 2.6 A map showing the spread of Buddhism from India into other parts of Asia by the seventh century CE.

for each of these areas developed its own *non-Indian* forms of Buddhism. In the next three sections we will explore the most distinctive and long lasting of these innovations to Buddhism that came about in Chinese, Japanese, and Tibetan Buddhism.

Chinese innovations

While Buddhism took on many new forms in China, two schools in particular stand out for their distinctiveness and longevity: **Pure Land** and **Chan**. Pure Land Buddhism appeared in China in the early sixth century CE, growing out of Chinese interest in the *Land of Bliss Sutras*. As we saw earlier, these *sutras* described a buddha realm created by Amitabha Buddha (Chinese: Amitofo). The Chinese called this Buddha realm either Pure Land or the Western Paradise, and taught that devotion to Amitabha led to rebirth there, even for laypersons (Figure 2.7). The benefit and urgency of this rebirth was explained with reference to the age of degenerate Dharma. According to this teaching, reliable knowledge of Gautama Buddha's Dharma was coming to an end. It had become convoluted through additions and misinterpretations to the point where its message of salvation was unintelligible. In these last times, people became terribly confused and a general moral break-down polluted human society, making it impossible to attain nirvana by earlier methods. Instead, Buddhists needed to rely on the compassion and intercession of Amitabha Buddha. While keeping the basic moral precepts of Buddhism, a practitioner could simply visualize the Buddha Amitabha, or even just repeat his name in a devotional formula, such as "Honor be to Amitabha Buddha." This secured their rebirth in Amitabha's Pure Land, where the *bodhisattva* path was readily accessible to all.

Chan Buddhism developed somewhat later in the sixth century. Said to have been brought from India in the late fifth century by the monk Bodhidharma, it claimed a teaching lineage that went back to Gautama Buddha. At its core, however, was an understanding of

Figure 2.7 Amitabha Buddha descends with his two attendant *bodhisattvas* to welcome devotees to his Pure Land. On Amitabha's right is Mahasthamaprapta, who embodies the great power of Amitabha's wisdom, and on his left is Guanyin, the very popular *bodhisattva* of his compassion. Source: Used by permission from the Corporate Body of the Buddha Educational Foundation.

nirvana that combined Yogacara notions of reality with native Chinese ideas about the Dao, the underlying Way of the universe. For Chan, nirvana became the buddha nature that was hidden behind all worldly phenomena, seen as the self and the natural world stripped of all ignorance and immorality. The goal of Chan was to "see into oneself" and "see into the moment," which happened primarily in meditation, or *chan*. For this reason, Chan monastics moved away from devotional practices and philosophical study and focused on meditation, which it defined in a number of new ways. Manual labor became an important form of meditation, as did pottery design, painting, and the martial arts. In using these activities for meditation, practitioners needed to proceed "mindfully," approaching every task with a "direct mind," detached from all else.

One of the school's most important scriptures was the *Platform Sutra of the Sixth Patriarch*, a document that described the experiences of the Chan master Hui-neng (638–713). It emphasized that while the buddha nature was revealed through meditation, meditation did not actually bring about enlightenment. Rather, because everyone already had the buddha nature, the challenge was not to achieve enlightenment, but to uncover and realize it. One could not *become* a buddha because, in some unrealized sense, one *was* a buddha. This opened up the possibility that buddhahood was within everyone's reach, which led to a heated debate among Chan masters as to whether enlightenment was best attained through sudden breakthroughs or through the gradual accumulation of wisdom. As a consequence, some schools of Chan emphasized *zazen*, or seated meditation, to develop calmness and focus of mind, while other schools employed sophisticated puzzles, called *gong-an*, designed to jolt a practitioner out of their normal frame of reference and into a sudden awareness of nirvana. Known later in Japan as *koans*, a famous collection of these puzzles, the *Transmission of the Lamp*, was compiled in 1004.

> ### Did you know …
>
> When Vajrayana first came to Tibet, it encountered stiff competition from established schools of Chinese Mahayana. Vajrayana got the upper hand, however, when Padmasambhava—a Vajrayana master later regarded as a second Buddha—defeated a Chinese monk in public debate.

Japanese innovations

Japan first received Buddhism from China by way of Korea, and then later directly from China itself. As a result, most Japan schools of Buddhism had antecedents in China. Japanese Tendai was a form of Chinese Tientai, **Zen** was a form of Chan, and Chinese Pure Land became Jodo. Each of these schools promoted Chinese traditions while adding distinctively Japanese features. For example, Zen continued Chan's practice of using *koans* while also developing tea ceremonies and theater (*noh* plays) as meditational techniques. Likewise, Jodo continued to emphasize the importance of calling on the name of **Amida Buddha** (the Japanese form of Amitabha), while a variation called Jodo Shinshu, or *True* Pure Land, questioned the efficacy of *any* human effort in the face of Amida's overpowering grace, and began to promote faith over action. In addition, Jodo Shinshu's founder, Shinran (1173–262), authorized the marriage of monks, a practice that eventually became the norm in Japan and spread to Korea through the later Japanese occupation of that country.

> ## Sacred Traditions and Scripture
>
> ### A Modern Explanation of Pure Land Buddhism
>
> According to the *Larger Sutra on the Buddha of Immeasurable Life*, which elaborates Amida Buddha in the greatest detail, and other related sutras, Pure Land Buddhism was intended to lead to Buddhahood even ordinary foolish people who, living at the bottom of society, had trouble doing good and were liable to commit wrongdoings. …
>
> Amida Buddha's teaching is the Buddhist path open equally to everybody and anybody, no matter how foolish and evil he may be. However, it is at the same time an extremely difficult, arduous path for the followers living in the secular world. …
>
> The path to Buddhahood … is exclusively centered on pronouncing the Name in daily life. No other religious practice is required. It is the path wherein we single-heartedly say the *nembutsu* (*Namo Amida Butsu*; "I entrust myself to Amida Buddha"), nothing more and nothing less. In this respect, this is an easy path which anybody can follow at any place and at any time, a path to Buddhahood suitable for all people.
>
> However, saying the *nembutsu* does not mean a mere oral utterance of the Name of the Buddha. It should be the act of final choice coming from a clear understanding that the *nembutsu* reveals to us the ultimate truth of life, the wisdom Buddhism points to. At the same time, it is the act of total negation of our mundane reality, based on the realization that this self-centered life of ours is false and unreal. …
>
> The true *nembutsu* totally jolts and upturns myself, mercilessly exposing my present reality before me and causing great pains to my inner self. While the *nembutsu* was my own choice in my earnest efforts toward Buddhahood, at the same time it begins to severely criticize and negate what I am. When this happens, the *nembutsu* as my own religious practice comes to be totally negated. And while I intently pronounce the Name, I am made to realize that this *nembutsu* is absolutely non-effectual. Then the *nembutsu* transcends myself to become the *nembutsu* of non-effort, and the *nembutsu* itself begins
>
> *(continued)*

> to say the *nembutsu*. This is the *nembutsu* of naturalness, no longer the *nembutsu* I say, but that which is only heard, coming from some place beyond myself. …
>
> In the true *nembutsu*, therefore, I choose to call the Buddha's Name, and yet at the very same time, the Buddha is calling me.
>
> Takamaro Shigaraki, *An Introduction to Shin Buddhism* (Hawaii, Buddhist Study Center Press, 1984), pp. 21–22.

An even more distinctively Japanese form of Buddhism appeared in the thirteenth century, taking its name from its founding monk, **Nichiren**. After studying Tendai Buddhism, which emphasized the *Lotus Sutra*, Nichiren came to believe that this *sutra* was the ultimate source of wisdom. Rejecting the claims of Zen and Pure Land Buddhism as mutually contradictory, he pointed to these two schools (especially Pure Land) as the cause of several natural disasters that has recently plagued Japan. According to Nichiren, instead of using the formula, "Honor to Amida Buddha," one should appeal directly to the saving power of the *Lotus Sutra* and chant the *daimoku*: "Honor to the *Lotus Sutra of the True Teaching*." This would not only concentrate the saving power of the Dharma on the speaker, but also protect the Japanese nation from foreign invasion and natural disasters.

Nichiren quickly perfected an antagonistic, confrontational preaching style, with which he harangued other Buddhists for their false teaching. He claimed that Pure Land's focus on chanting to Amida Buddha "led to Hell," while Zen was the invention of "tempter devils" (see Figure 2.8). To his mind, it was the task of Buddhists to transform Japan itself into a Pure Land by bringing about social and political reform. Near the end of his life Nichiren became convinced that he was an incarnation of Jogyo, the patron *bodhisattva* of the *Lotus Sutra*. For this reason, he created the Gohonzon, a **mandala**, or sacred diagram, that used Japanese calligraphy to depict a host of

Figure 2.8 A depiction from Sri Lanka of suffering in hell. Those sentenced to hell by their own karma vainly attempt to escape the fire of hell and the punishment of demons by climbing a tree covered with long, sharp thorns. Source: Reproduced by permission of Jerry Fish.

buddhas and other beings around the *daimoku*. Intended as a revelation of Nichiren's own enlightenment, the Gohonzon was used by his followers as a mirror that could reflect their inherent buddhahood.

Tibetan innovations

Buddhism in Tibet developed a distinctive form of Vajrayana, partly by incorporating elements of Bön, the region's rich tradition of shamans (tribal priests). Buddhas and *bodhisattvas* were understood by Tibetans as deities, and several local gods and goddess were added to this pantheon. The *bodhisattva* **Avalokiteshvara** (Tibetan: Chenrezig) became especially important, having been credited with taming and converting many of the region's demons, thereby establishing Tibet as his Pure Land. Tibetans sometimes even elevated Avalokiteshvara to full buddhahood, venerating his divine nature in both male and female forms.

Even though forms of Vajrayana also developed in China, Korea, and Japan, Tibet was where Vajrayana flowered after Buddhism's disappearance from India. Buddhist masters there became known as *lamas*, a title that approximates "spiritual teacher." Some were said to be able to choose their next incarnation, a doctrine called *tulku*, and the most renowned *lamas* were considered living buddhas. In the sixteenth century, the Yellow Hat Sect (Gelug school), began to refer to its leader as the Dalai Lama. Understanding this title to mean "limitless supreme being," or "ocean of wisdom," they regarded him as the incarnation of Avalokiteshvara. In the seventeenth century, aided by the Mongolian leader Gushi Khan, the fifth Dalai Lama was installed as both the spiritual and political leader of all Tibet, an office that each Dalai Lama since then held, until the communist Chinese invasion of Tibet in the 1950s.

Western imperialism and the rediscovery of Buddhism

European colonial rule over the Buddhist parts of Asia began with the Dutch colonization of Sri Lanka in the early sixteenth century and ended only in the twentieth century. During this time, the United Kingdom colonized India and eventually Burma and Sri Lanka. France colonized Vietnam, Laos, and Cambodia; and those areas not formally or fully colonized, such as Thailand and China, became the object of European and American ambitions.

In the eighteenth and nineteenth centuries, European and American intellectuals took an interest in Buddhism and began to study it as an academic discipline. With European diplomats, trade officials, and missionaries sending back field reports from all over Asia, scholars were able to collect and compare historical and ethnographic materials. Initially, however, they failed to see that the diverse materials they studied were related to a single religion. In part this was because the colonizers needed time to develop the language skills for reading Sanskrit, Pali, Tibetan, Chinese, Korean, and Japanese, to mention just the main languages.

> **Did you know ...**
>
> Hindu shrines and temples in Nepal often venerate both Buddhist and Hindu deities; and in Sri Lanka, the Hindu god Vishnu is revered as a guardian of the Dharma, and even a future Buddha.

Most Buddhists were also unaware of the historical and cultural similarities that linked the various forms of their religion, principally because Buddhism no longer had a unifying center. For more than half a millennium Buddhism had been largely absent from India, where it had originated and undergone some of its most important developments. Non-Indian Buddhists ceased to think of India as the religion's heartland, and the country's great temples and *stupas* became curiosities in a landscape now populated by Hindus, Muslims, Jains, and Sikhs. The great Buddhist centers of central Asia and Indonesia had also disappeared, and many of these regions had converted to Islam. Finally, where ties between Buddhist regions still existed, some tended to be political rather than religious, while others were unidirectional and aimed at conversion—for example, Tibetan missionaries traveling to China. Even the longstanding relations between the Sanghas of Sri Lanka, Burma, and Thailand were now only intermittently active; and under the Tokugawa shogunate (1603–1868), Japanese Buddhism was largely cut off from the rest of the world.

The resurgence of Buddhism as a global religion

By the late 1800s this situation began to change. The American Henry Steel Olcott, an ex-military man and one of the founders of the influential Theosophical Society, traveled to Sri Lanka, where he converted to Buddhism. Thereafter he focused his energies on reviving Sri Lankan Theravada. He founded Buddhist schools and wrote a *Buddhist Catechism* to help Sri Lankans learn the basic components of their religion. While Olcott's agenda was not always the same as that of the Sri Lankan monks, the two parties found common ground in building up Buddhist institutions that had been weakened by colonial rule.

Around the time of Olcott's engagement with Buddhism, western scholars had reached the point where a unified understanding of Buddhism was possible, although their tendency to privilege the earliest forms of Buddhism over later developments led them to discount Buddhism's living communities as corruptions of the original religion. But this prejudice was mitigated as Buddhist networks began to revive, due in no small measure to improved travel in Asia as a result of colonialism. Soon Buddhist leaders such as Sri Lanka's Anagarika Dharmapala and China's Taixu were promoting the religion's relevance for international politics and global trade, while others became eloquent spokespersons for the modern practice of Buddhism. Their efforts were greatly facilitated by the World Parliament of

Religions in Chicago in 1893, which gave Asians a venue to present Buddhism on a world stage, both to westerners and to other Buddhists. At this event, Buddhist leaders spoke not only as regional and national representatives, but also as members of a global religion.

> ## Talking about Religion
>
> ### Buddhism on the World Stage
>
> At the 1893 World Parliament of Religions in Chicago, the Buddhist spokesman Anagarika Dhamapala presented the case for Buddhism before an international audience. Born in Sri Lanka and educated in western schools, he introduced his religion in a way that appealed especially to western scientific minds at a time when many Christians felt their own religion had been undermined by Darwin's theory of evolution:
>
> > Speaking of deity in the sense of a Supreme Creator, Buddha says that there is no such being. Accepting the doctrine of evolution as the only true one, with its corollary, the law of cause and effect, he condemns the idea of a Creator and strictly forbids inquiry into it as being useless… . Buddhism is a scientific religion, in as much as it earnestly enjoins that nothing whatever be accepted on faith. Buddha has said that nothing should be believed merely because it is said. Buddhism is tantamount to a knowledge of other sciences.
> >
> > Anagarika Dharmapala, from his 1893 speech "The World's Debt to Buddha."

New leadership roles for the laity

Historically, meditation practices had been the domain of monks and nuns, not the laity—and not even all monastics meditated, for monasteries typically made a distinction between those who focused on study (the majority) and those who specialized in meditation. In the twentieth century, however, Buddhist revival movements in Asia encouraged meditation among the laity as a way of increasing lay support by engaging the laity in their Buddhist heritage. Meditation centers for lay people sprang up in Japan, Taiwan, Singapore, Myanmar, and Thailand, sometimes under the auspices of a monastery, and sometimes as freestanding, lay organizations. These proved especially popular among urban, middle-class populations, and large Asian businesses began using them for corporate retreats.

Westerners also took an interest in Buddhist meditational techniques, especially Zen meditation and Vipassana (insight meditation), which they used in prison reform programs, as relaxation exercises, and in combination with Christian meditation and western psychiatry. Because of this increase in lay meditation, the laity in both Asia and the west gained a greater leadership role in the Buddhist community, having assumed practices formerly reserved for monks and nuns. The distinction between lay and monastic, while still important, became much less pronounced.

Parallel to this development, both western Buddhists and westernized Asian Buddhists worked to reestablish monastic orders for nuns. Until the late twentieth century, full ordination for women was possible only in Mahayana communities in east Asia, not in Theravada, where the ordination lines had died out, or in Vajrayana, where higher ordination for women was never practiced. Women in these latter traditions had to settle for initiation as permanent novices, which typically meant that they shaved their heads, dressed in monastic robes, and lived celibate lives in community with other novices. Since they also kept three to five moral precepts beyond what was expected of laypersons, they were sometimes known as "precept keepers."

An international Buddhist women's organization, called Sakyadhita, took up the cause of full ordination for women in 1987, and several Buddhist leaders, including the Dalai Lama, supported it. In 1996, 11 female Theravadin novices traveled from Sri Lanka to India to receive full ordination. This was followed in the Vajrayana tradition by 10 ordinations in Tibet in 2014, and 142 in Bhutan in 2022. Even so, many Buddhist leaders continue to voice their opposition to the full ordination of women in the Theravada and Vajrayana traditions.

Engaged Buddhism

A final development in Buddhism in recent times has been its turn toward social activism. Often called engaged Buddhism, this new emphasis seeks to eliminate *dukkha* in human society through practical measures and social reform. Engaged Buddhism has taken many forms, and it is not always possible to distinguish it from Buddhism's long history of political involvement. Important early figures in the movement include:

- Dr. B.R. Ambedkar, who was born in India as a Hindu dalit (Untouchable) in the middle of the nineteenth century. Through his study of Buddhism and eventual conversion to the religion, he encouraged millions of India's dalits to gain greater social freedom by also converting to Buddhism.
- The fourteenth Dalai Lama, who received the 1989 Nobel Peace Prize for his humanitarian efforts on behalf of the Tibetan people after the Chinese invasion of his country in 1950.
- A.T. Ariyaratne, who founded the Sarvodaya Shramadana Movement in Sri Lanka to foster a Buddhist model of social development. Sarvodaya members live out the experience of *an-atman* (selflessness) by sharing with persons in need and using the Four Noble Truths to solve local problems.

- Thich Nhat Hanh, who founded a grassroots organization dedicated to rebuilding the lives of those who were victimized by the Vietnam War. More recently he has organized major walks for peace in Los Angeles in which participants are encouraged to practice Buddhist mindfulness in the cause of world peace.
- Sulak Sivaraksa, a Thai activist and persistent critic of military and democratic governments in Thailand. Founder of a variety of organizations for the promotion of Buddhist political and economic systems, he presents his ideology of Buddhism as an alternative to current systems.

> **Rituals, Rites, Practices**
>
> ### Walking and Eating Mindfully in the Park
>
> We shall walk in such a way that each step we make becomes a realization of peace; each step becomes a prayer for peace and harmony. Children will join us and we shall walk together in silence, with no banners and no pickets. The walk will not be a petition addressed to anyone, nor will it be a demonstration against anyone. The walk is to unite our heart, to nurture our togetherness, and to dissipate fear and separation … We shall learn together that wrong perceptions of self and other are at the foundation of separation, fear, hate, and violence; and that togetherness and collaboration is possible.
>
> Thich Nhat Hanh, from a newspaper advertisement for a peace walk that took place in MacArthur Park, Los Angeles in 2005.

Contemporary Beliefs and Practices

Although the schools of Buddhism differ in many ways, all Buddhists see the goal of religion as the alleviation of suffering, both for oneself and for others, and locate the source of human suffering in humanity's ignorance of Truth (Dharma). Blinded by this ignorance, human beings mistake the self and the world around them for fixed or permanent entities. The Dharma of the Buddha, however, teaches that everything changes constantly and is always in the state of becoming, never being. Because of this, every human action that is undertaken to acquire and hold on to things—wealth, love, honor, health, life—brings *dukkha* and rebirth in *samsara*, a cycle of suffering that has no beginning, no end, and no meaning. Nor is our world unique, for innumerable beings in countless other world-systems also suffer in *samsara*. Within this vast illusion of permanence, humans and other sentient beings are reborn in many ways—as animals, humans, hungry ghosts, and gods. In one popular explanation,

Buddhists speak of six realms of rebirth: two visible realms, dominated by humans and animals, respectively; three invisible realms containing gods, titans, and those suffering in hell; and a realm of ghosts that is sometimes visible and sometimes not (Figure 2.9).

Of all these, the human realm is seen as the most favorable because it is the only realm in which one can bring a halt to *samsara* by achieving nirvana. Animals, by contrast, never come to know the truth of their existence. They have limited powers of analysis and are driven mostly by instincts rooted in craving and pleasure-seeking. Gods, on the other hand, live in a realm that is *too* pleasurable: because their divine existence contains so little pain and discomfort, they are blind to the First Noble Truth, that suffering is inherent in everything. Even so, Buddhists respect the gods and make offerings to them, both out of compassion for them and in the hope of receiving boons from them, for gods are very powerful beings and not to be trifled with. Finally, hungry ghosts, titans, and hell-beings are engulfed in too much anger and greed, and experience too much pain to think clearly about anything. Hungry ghosts, for example, were extremely greedy and selfish beings in their former lives, and are often depicted as creatures with enormous, bloated stomachs but tiny mouths and narrow throats. As such, they experience little more than the pain that comes from constant hunger (Figure 2.10).

Birth into the human realm, therefore, is a precious thing, for humans have just enough intelligence, and encounter just enough pleasure and pain to be motivated to seek beyond their immediate circumstances in the visible world. But even for humans this is a considerable challenge, and it can take hundreds of lifetimes to make any significant progress toward the truth, let alone acquire the truth. This is why the vast majority of Buddhists—both lay and monastic—still live according to a mundane view of the world. While they might *know of* the Dharma, they do not *know* the Dharma, and so it plays little role in guiding their actions. For these Buddhists, the attainment of nirvana is sometimes spoken of as "a thousand lifetimes away." Until that day comes, they must settle for improving their karmic position in the human realm by accumulating merit.

In light of these observations, we may approach Buddhism as a religion that offers two complementary orientations to ultimate reality: an immediate karmic orientation, whose goal is to improve one's next rebirth; and a long-range orientation designed to achieve nirvana. The former, which is no less religious, focuses on the tasks of accumulating merit and alleviating suffering. Buddhists who follow this orientation acknowledge the presence of a self, saying things like, "*I* am hungry." This does not mean they are ignorant of the self's impermanence, however; rather, they are speaking on a mundane level, using "self" as a convenient fiction. As Buddhists, they know that this "I" is only conditional and not true at the deepest level of reality.

Buddhists can pursue karmic and nirvanic orientations either as laypersons or as monastics. While there are important differences between these two groups, it is not the case that monastics are thought to be superior to laypeople. Indeed, *all* differences between people, including the monastic-lay divide, are largely irrelevant in light of everyone's karmic past. Since each person has undergone an infinite

A Closer Look

The Wheel of Life

The Wheel of Life is a visual summary of the Buddha's teachings about our world, used by Vajrayana traditions. In the center of this wheel is the *mantra* "*Om mani padme hum*," which is said to encompass all of the Buddha's wisdom. Around this are the root causes of existence—greed, hatred, and delusion—pictured as a pig, a snake, and a rooster; and circling these, are the paths of salvation (left) and damnation (right). As we move outward from this, we pass through a band of lotus petals and a band of flames, and come to the six realms of becoming. Clockwise from the top these are the realms of the gods, humans, hungry ghosts (detail), hell-beings, animals, and demons. Further out on the wheel are the 12 elements in the causal chain of karmic existence, such as the distinction between self and others (pictured as a man being ferried across the ocean of life), and desire (depicted as a woman serving a man some tea). Around this is a second ring of flames; and the entirety is held in the grip of an evil being who personifies the fear of death and the futile clinging to life. Finally, in the top-right corner is a pure land and the hope of salvation.

Figures 2.9 and 2.10 The Buddhist Wheel of Life. Detail of hungry ghosts.
Source: Reproduced by permission of Sue Ellen Christensen.

number of rebirths, caused by an infinite amount of bad karma, there is nothing to be gained in dwelling on past mistakes—which, in any case, can only be fully known and comprehended by an omniscient buddha. Instead, people should use this life to think and act in ways oriented to the future and support one another to the extent they can.

> ### Rituals, Rites, Practices
>
> ## Monastic Ordination
>
> To become a monastic, a Buddhist must undergo two levels of formal ordination rituals—novice ordination and higher ordination. Novice ordination usually takes place between the ages of 10 and 20. Candidates for ordination are to be old enough to know what they are doing, which, in the Pali Canon, is described as "big enough to scare away crows." In Thailand, children need to have finished elementary school, and in Tibet, current law requires graduation from junior high school.
>
> To prepare for ordination, children have their heads shaved and are escorted to the temple—in a car, on a bicycle, on horseback, or carried on the backs of their relatives. At the temple, a monk preaches a sermon about their responsibilities, especially the Ten Precepts. These include the Five Precepts (*pancha sila*) that are sometimes required of laypersons, plus five more. Thus, in addition to refraining from killing, theft, sex, lying, and using intoxicants, novices are prohibited from taking food at inappropriate times (usually after noon), watching or taking part in musical or dance performances, wearing perfume or jewelry, sleeping on soft beds, and accepting money. The sermon prepares the novices to be proper examples and teachers for the laity, and it starts them down the Noble Eightfold Path of right understanding, right intentions, right speech, etc.
>
> It is worth pointing out that no one expects these children to behave properly at all times. While becoming a novice is about leaving home and beginning a life of discipline, they are still children, and in areas where temporary ordination is common, such as Laos and Thailand (see Figure 2.11), their commitment may only last a few weeks.
>
> In Theravada and Vajrayana, boys are allowed to undergo higher ordination when they turn 20. Higher ordination for girls, however, is quite limited in these traditions, and no official age has been established. In Mahayana, which offers higher ordination to both genders, the novice period is often extended and higher ordination takes place later in life. Candidates for higher ordination must learn and recite the 227 or more precepts called the *Pratimoksha*, which are arranged in categories and according to their importance. Breaking a minor

(continued)

precept can have little or no consequence, and even violating a major precept is not understood as a crime or sin. When someone breaks a precept, large or small, negative karma results, for which confession is usually sufficient. But four sins, which are known as "Defeat," are seen as so contrary to monastic life that they are punished with expulsion. These are first-degree murder, grand theft, knowingly and willingly having sexual intercourse, and falsely claiming to have the supernatural powers that the Buddha acquired when he attained enlightenment.

Figure 2.11 A novice with his parents in Thailand, just before he enters the monastery. Becoming a monk is an act of *dana*, a gift that produces merit. It is customary for sons to dedicate the merit gained by becoming a novice to their mothers, and that gained by taking higher ordination to their fathers.
Source: Reproduced by permission of Teerapatch Tachasirodom.

Karmic orientation

The practices associated with karmic orientation constitute most of what we call Buddhism. They consist of the practice of *sila* (precepts), *dana* (giving), and *puja* (veneration of images). The misconception that Buddhism is largely a matter of *nirvanic* orientation is recent, and mistakenly identifies the religion's scholarly tradition and meditative practices as Buddhism's truest expression.

Sila

Sila are moral precepts that can reduce the amount of *dukkha* in the world. Since morality is the gateway to truth and wisdom in Buddhism, a life guided by *sila* engenders the Four Immeasurables (kindness, compassion, sympathetic joy, and equanimity) and protects one from the Five Hindrances (desire, aversion, sloth, restlessness, and doubt). In the monastery, life is regulated by hundreds of precepts, collectively called the *Pratimoksha*, which monks and nuns recite in assemblies at full and new moon ceremonies. At the heart of the *Pratimoksha* are the Five Precepts, or *pancha sila*, which also apply to the laity. These prohibit killing, theft, sexual misconduct, lying, and intoxication. In current practice it is common for laity to keep one precept at a time, undertaking all five only during special periods of religious observance.

Because of their centrality to moral behavior, the *pancha sila* have had far-reaching consequences in Buddhist cultures. The prohibition of killing, for example, has encouraged various degrees of vegetarianism among Buddhists. Mahayanists often follow a strict vegetarian diet (although less so in Japan and Korea). While Theravada monks eat meat, they cannot accept meat if an animal has been killed specifically for them, and both monks and laity abstain from meat on certain occasions to accumulate good karma. Many Theravadins also abstain from beef in particular, as killing a cow, even when done by someone else, is thought to create an excessive amount of bad karma because the cow is such a large animal. In Tibetan Buddhist cultures, by contrast, Buddhists may both kill and eat animals, as meat is an essential source of protein in their diet. Yet even Tibetans will mark animals on the back or mane with red dye and ransom them from the butcher as a way of gaining merit.

Dana

Dana means "giving," and it is sometimes said to be the principal activity of Buddhism. As an action that produces merit, *dana* works in several ways. First, and most obviously, it alleviates suffering caused by hunger and poverty in the here and now, and, when practiced over time, it makes the giver a better, more compassionate person. Second, one can gain merit by rejoicing in another's act of giving. This is done by saying, "it is good" (*sadhu*) when someone else performs *dana*. Third, Theravada Buddhists hold *dana* ceremonies at temples, pilgrimage sites, and in homes for the purpose of giving all the resulting merit to all living beings. And fourth, *dana* is said to "plants seeds" that will produce merit in the future. In this case it is reasoned that giving can produce benefits quite unforeseen by the giver, especially when the

Figure 2.12 Laity perform *dana* outside a monastery in Laos. They hope that the progress and dedication of the monks will multiply the merit they receive. Source: Reproduced by permission of Greg Swanson.

recipient's life is guided by Dharma. Since wise people are thought to benefit many creatures, gifts to them produce good karma many times over.

This fourth understanding of *dana* has been critical for the interaction between monastics and laity, as it enables them to participate in a complementary, even symbiotic relationship, in which each provides what the other needs (Figure 2.12). Laymen and laywomen support monks and nuns by giving them the material things they need to survive (food, clothing, and places to live), as well as support for education, temples, and religious festivals. In return, monastics serve as teachers and ritual specialists, and as "fields of merit" into which the laity's seeds of *dana* are planted. Material support for monastics and their institutions is recognized as one of the best ways for laity to accumulate merit because the logic of *dana* dictates that the amount of merit one receives depends on the spiritual advancement of the recipient. Among the more promising fields of merit are spiritually advanced monks and nuns, those who have spent more "time in robes," and those who have superior educations or reputations as preachers or ritual specialists.

The religious importance of this *dana*-based relationship between monastics and laity can be gauged from a scandal that took place in 2022. When it was discovered that monks in a village monastery in Phetchabun province in northern Thailand had been using methamphetamines, the monastery was closed and the monks were defrocked and enrolled in rehab programs. While the villagers were surprised and disappointed that their monks had been using drugs, their main concern was that they had lost the ability to gain merit by supporting the monks through their gifts. They even invited monks from other villages to live at the monastery so that they could continue this form of *dana*.

Puja

Puja is the veneration of images—statues, pictures, and diagrams. Although it is seldom associated with Buddhism in the minds of westerners, it has many forms in the Asian context, and commonly involves bowing or prostrating oneself before an image, as well as chanting, praying, and making offerings on an altar (see the chapter-opening photo). Like *sila* and *dana*, it is practiced by most Buddhists as a way of gaining merit.

Puja takes place in the home, in one's place of business, at temples, and at shrines along pilgrimage routes. In businesses it is usually performed in front of a small altar on a raised shelf. The same is true for many homes, although some families choose to dedicate a corner of a room or even an entire room to their altars. In China and Japan, traditional family altars (*butsudan*) take the form of large, ornate armoires placed in special alcoves. Whether at home or at work, altars typically have a statue or picture of the Buddha, a place for offerings, and a stand or pot for burning incense. Depending on the region, altars may also have miniature *stupas*, images of *bodhisattvas*, and various other objects. Tibetan families often have images of the Three Jewels of Refuge on their altars: a statue of the Buddha, a portion of scripture for the Dharma, and a miniature *stupa* for the Sangha, as *stupas* are usually at the center of Tibetan monastic complexes.

At temples and large pilgrimage shrines, *puja* becomes considerably more elaborate. In Vajrayana traditions, one often begins by circumambulating the temple or shrine, chanting scriptures or *mantras*, and turning prayer wheels, which are cylinders containing written prayers and inscribed with prayers on the outside. These are thought to "say" (i.e., activate) these prayers with every turn. In other traditions, Buddhists offer incense or flowers at the entrance of a temple or shrine out of respect for the building's guardian spirits.

Rituals, Rites, Practices

Tibetan Prayer Wheels Containing the Jewel in the Lotus Mantra (*Om Mani Padme Hum*)

If you have a *mani* prayer wheel in your house, your house is the same as the Potala, the pure land of the Compassion Buddha. Simply touching a prayer wheel brings great purification of negative karma. Turning a prayer wheel containing 100 million *om mani padme hum* mantras accumulates the same merit as having recited 100 million *om mani padme hums*. Prayer wheels also stop disease. Anyone with a disease such as AIDS or cancer, whether or not they have any understanding of Dharma, can use the prayer wheel for meditation and healing.

The spiritual director of The Foundation for the Preservation of the Mahayana Tradition.

Upon entering a temple or shrine, visitors chant and make offerings again in a foyer. From there they proceed to the image hall, where they remove their shoes, enter, and bow or prostrate themselves in humility. Some Buddhists bow three times in honor of the Three Jewels. Following this, they approach the image or group of images and pray, chant, and present further offerings. Buddhist offerings include flowers, fruit, rice, nuts, tea, incense, candles, and many regional variations. In Thailand, one might see boxes of cigarettes on an altar, whereas Sri Lankan Buddhists bring betel nuts and leaves and scented water. Among the followers of Vajrayana Buddhism, clarified butter is offered (to be used in devotional lamps), and seven or more bowls of water or grain are often placed on the altar so that those in attendance can visualize additional offerings. Finally, in southeast Asia, Buddhists often venerate an image by applying thin sheets of gold leaf to its surface.

Prayers and chants during *puja* are typically begun with an invocation of the Buddha. A common invocation in Theravada is: "Honor to the Lord, O Arhat, completely and perfectly Enlightened One." More often than not, the private prayers of lay Buddhists include requests for everyday, practical things, such as success on exams or the health of a family member. If monastics are present, they may lead a group prayer for universal salvation, often while keeping cadence with a bell, drum, or symbols. They might also lead a group chant, which can involve several things—formulas for taking refuge in the Three Jewels or renewing one's commitment to the Five Precepts; reading and reciting Buddhist scriptures; and the repetition of *mantras*, using a string of beads (a rosary) to keep count. In Pure Land Buddhism, visitors repeat a devotional formula called the *nembutsu*, which gives praise and honor to Amitabha Buddha; and in Nichiren, they chant a formula that venerates their principal scripture, the *Lotus Sutra of the True Dharma*.

Images of the Buddha

Most *puja* is performed before an image of the Buddha, usually in his incarnation as Siddhartha Gautama. The most popular image of the Buddha shows him seated with legs crossed, deep in meditation. Another popular image depicts his *maha-pari-nirvana*, with the Buddha on his death bed. These reclining Buddhas bring to mind the truth of the impermanence of all things—even the Buddha himself. But they also make palpable the peace that comes with achieving nirvana, for they invariably show the dying Buddha as relaxed and serene even in the midst of pain (he is said to have died of botulism). Still other images portray the sermon to his first disciples in the Deer Park; the Buddha's unyielding determination to find enlightenment, as when he surpassed his fellow ascetics by surviving on a single grain of rice for six weeks; and his miraculous birth, during which he emerged from his mother's side without causing her pain, and then took seven steps and proclaimed that this would be his last life.

Almost all images of the Buddha include features that attest to the perfection of his body and his superhuman qualities. Some derive from the prodigious merit he accumulated in previous lifetimes. These include webbed fingers, toes of equal length, extended heels, and birthmarks on the soles of his feet (Figure 2.13). Other features come from his life as Siddhartha Gautama, such as the protuberance on the

Figure 2.13 The feet of a large reclining Buddha in Bangkok, Thailand, showing the birthmarks on his soles and the even length of his toes. Source: Reproduced by permission of Nick Gier.

top of his head and his elongated earlobes. The former is said to be a product of his enlightenment, which both expanded his mind and caused it to detach itself from his body. The latter was caused by the elaborate and costly earrings he wore in his days as a wealthy prince, a lifestyle he renounced for the sake of enlightenment, setting the example for others.

Other objects of veneration

Images of beings other than the Buddha, as well as many objects, also play a role in *puja*. In Theravada temples one frequently sees miniature *stupas*, Bo trees, and an image of the Earth Goddess. Miniature *stupas* are small versions of reliquaries, and sometimes enshrine a precious object representative of an event in Buddhism's history. The Bo tree and the Earth Goddess, in turn, help visitors bring to mind the Buddha's enlightenment, for he is said to have attained nirvana under a Bo tree, aided by the Earth Goddess. According to one popular tradition, when Siddhartha was on the verge of finding enlightenment, he was attacked by the demon Mara and his minions, who attempted to disrupt Siddhartha's concentration. Before that could happen, however, the Earth Goddess came to his rescue, first by bearing witness to Siddhartha's moral perfections, and then by wringing water from her hair to create a wave that washed Mara away.

Compared with Theravada, *puja* in Mahayana and Vajrayana temples uses considerably more images. Both these schools frequently use images of *bodhisattvas*, the most popular of which is Avalokiteshvara. Understood as the personification of compassion, he is often venerated in the image of an imposing male figure with multiple arms and heads. In China and Japan, however, Avalokiteshvara was said to have manifested himself as the female *bodhisattva* **Guanyin** (or Kannon), resulting in images of him as a young woman holding a baby or pouring out compassion on the world from a small flask (see Figure 2.7). In Japan, the *bodhisattva* Jizo is especially revered, his image taking either the form of a kindly old man or an infant with a large head and red apron or bib. Jizo is the *bodhisattva* of compassion for travelers, women, and children, and recently he has become popular as the patron *bodhisattva* of women who have had miscarriages or abortions. In Tibet, images of the celestial Buddha Shakyamuni (Sage of the Shaky clan) are widely used in *puja*, as are those of the *bodhisattva* Manjusri (Sweet Glory), who is the embodiment of Buddha Shakyamuni's wisdom. Manjusri is frequently depicted holding a book or a sword. The book signifies wisdom, while the sword is used to fight ignorance, wisdom's enemy. Manjusri can also be depicted as fighting ignorance in his wrathful form, the buddha Yamantaka.

Finally, beyond even these buddhas and *bodhisattvas*, images of many other beings are the object of *puja*. These include *arhats*, celestial protectors (including world protectors and Dharma protectors), deities, *lamas*, important teachers, famous monks, and certain Tibetan beings who defy any precise classification, such as **Tara**, a female being who appears in many forms and colors, especially green and white. Green Tara, for example, is the patron of Tibet and friend of all sentient beings, having been born from a tear shed by Avalokiteshvara as he expressed his compassion for the suffering of the world. Like many Tibetan buddhas and *bodhisattvas*, Tara also has a wrathful form, known as Kurkulla, who is sometimes a Dharma protector and sometimes a *yidam*. *Yidams* are said to be manifestations of the buddha body of bliss and reflect a person's consciousness and moral disposition. They serve as guides, instructors, and protectors for those who have been initiated into the higher truths, appearing in wrathful, peaceful, and intermediate forms.

Festivals and holy days at temples

Buddhists can visit a temple on any day of the week, and when they do, it is typically in the morning or evening. Lay Buddhists of all traditions visit temples on the first and fifteenth days of the lunar calendar (the full and new moons), and for festivals and special holy days. Temple festivals can be joyful, somber, or both. In Theravada, they open with an invocation of the Buddha, followed by the ceremony of taking refuge in the Three Jewels and a reaffirmation of the Five Precepts. In Mahayana and Vajrayana, they open with an invocation of many buddhas and *bodhisattvas*, a recitation of the Three Jewels, and a ritual in which the laity are encouraged to take the *bodhisattva* vow of working for the salvation of all beings.

Festivals that are common to all three schools are the celebration of the New Year (but on different dates), the Buddha's birthday, his enlightenment, and his *maha-parinirvana*. In Mahayana and Vajrayana, the last three are observed on separate days, whereas in Theravada they are combined in a single festival known as Vesak Day. Other variations between the schools include several Vajrayana additions to the New Year festival, and a ritual bathing of the Buddha on his birthday practiced by both Mahayana and Vajrayana traditions. For the New Year celebration, Vajrayanists burn effigies containing the evil of the previous year and stage elaborate dance performances and ritualized debates on Dharma to create a receptive environment for truth and enlightenment (Figure 2.14). In the birthday ritual of bathing the Buddha, Mahayana and Vajrayana Buddhists reenact the miracle of the nine dragons, who showered the infant Buddha with water immediately after his birth. Participants pour water over a small statue of the infant Buddha, who stands victoriously with his right hand pointing toward heaven and his left hand pointing toward earth.

Aside from these common festivals, each school has its own, distinct celebrations. In Theravada, when the rainy season begins in July, monks follow the ancient tradition of spending the next three months in and around the monastery rather than traveling. At the beginning of this retreat, they give sermons to the lay community, which responds with offerings of food. At the end of the retreat, the monks hold the Invitation Ceremony to extend a collective blessing to the laity, and the laity provide the monks with new robes. The giving of robes is an especially efficacious act of *dana* because after three months of confinement, the monks have built up a good deal of

Figure 2.14 Tibetan monks engaging in ritualized debates. As they question one another on issues they have been studying, they use body movements for emphasis and clap their hands at the one being quizzed. Source: Reproduced by permission of Sue Ellen Christensen.

spiritual power, making them particularly promising fields of merit. In Mahayana, Buddhists honor the birth (and sometimes the death) of the *bodhisattva* Guanyin; celebrate the Worshipping of All Buddhas festival; and hold ceremonies to express compassion for hungry ghosts. Major observances particular to Vajrayana include the commemoration of the death of Tsong Khapa (1340–1383), scholar, reformer, and founder of the Yellow Hat sect, and the Great Vow, which is a five-day event marking the defeat of rival teachers and evil forces.

Finally, Buddhists observe many auspicious days, on which one's chances of obtaining merit are increased. For Theravadins and Mahayanists, these occur on full moons and new moons, whereas Vajrayanists recognize these and many more days, including the eighth, tenth, fourteenth, fifteenth, twenty-fifth, and thirtieth of each lunar month. On auspicious days, pious Buddhists attend special classes on the Dharma, provide food offerings for the monastics, and stay overnight at the monastery. In Mahayana and Vajrayana, the laity may also participate in the monastics' twice-monthly recitation of the *Pratimoksha*, whereas in Theravada and Vajrayana, those who spend the night in the monastery adhere scrupulously to the Five Precepts. Finally, because auspicious days in Vajrayana can honor a great number of deities, buddhas, *bodhisattvas*, and lamas, the laity are careful to purify themselves by performing prostrations and by circumambulating the local temple or lama's residence in the early morning and late evening while chanting mantras and turning prayer wheels.

Monastics as ritual specialists

At festivals and on auspicious days, monastics give sermons called Dharma teachings and are active as ritual specialists. One of the most important rituals they perform on these occasions is chanting, either alone or with the laity. Through chanting, monastics actualize the Dharma and send it out into the world, and since the Dharma reveals the true nature of the universe, chanting changes the world for the better. Chanting also serves to protect the laity against evil and convey material blessings to the mundane world, such as successful harvests, a good business year, or a healthy family. In this case, chanting is thought to disperse a magical or transcendent power that is inherent in the Dharma. Additionally, some Buddhist communities practice a merit-transfer ceremony in which chanting is used to draw merit from an image of the Buddha. In this ceremony, a string is tied to the image and held by both monastics and laity. As the chanting proceeds, merit leaves the image via the string, travels through the monastics, and settles on the laity. At the conclusion of the ceremony, the string is cut and given in short pieces to the lay participants, who tie them around their wrists and wear them until they fall off. Finally, we should not overlook chanting's role in community-building and community entertainment. In mainland southeast Asia, for example, it is common to hear recitations of the *Vessantara Jataka*, which recounts the Buddha's life as Vessantara, which preceded his final birth as Siddhartha. Chanting this story not only teaches the value of generosity, but it is also highly entertaining—indeed, monks have become famous for their performance of certain roles in the narrative.

> **Sacred Traditions and Scripture**
>
> ### The Generosity of Vessantara
>
> The *Vessantara Jataka*, also known as the *Maha-Chat* ("Great Life"), introduces Vessantara as the prince of a kingdom whose citizens are happy and wealthy because they have a white, rain-producing elephant. But when the population of a neighboring kingdom suffers drought, Vessantara gives them the elephant. This infuriates the citizens of Vessantara's kingdom, and they force the king (his father) to send him into exile. There he meets up with a wicked Brahmin who asks the prince for his two children, and surprisingly Vessantara hands them over. Finally, he is approached by the god Indra in disguise, who asks for Vessantara's wife, and once again the prince obliges. At this point, Indra restores Vessantara's wife and children, and Vessantara's father and fellow citizens ask him to return from exile. Through this story, Vessantara (soon to be the Buddha) illustrates the perfection of generosity as a cure for greed and attachment.

Outside of festivals and auspicious days, the laity rely on monks and nuns for a variety of protective blessings—against illness, at the birth of a child, for a new home or car, and for success in new undertakings. Monastics also provide protection against the ill omens of divination and astrological predictions; and in Thailand, they bless small images of the Buddha and famous monks that the laity wear as protective charms. Finally, Buddhist laypersons are especially in need of the monastics' ritual expertise when someone dies, for rituals performed at a funeral service can help the deceased attain a better rebirth, or, in China and Japan, a better fate in the realm of the dead.

During Theravada funerals, the body is put in a coffin on or near an altar that has flowers, candles, incense, an image of the Buddha, and a picture of the deceased. For a week, visitors pay their respects and monks chant from the *Abhidharma-pitaka*, which the Buddha is said to have done at his mother's funeral to lead her to salvation. At the end of this week, the body is cremated and the laity feed the monks for seven days to create merit for the deceased. On the sixth day, the monks give a Dharma teaching; and on the seventh they perform a *dana* ceremony to provide merit for all beings.

> **A Closer Look**
>
> ### The Power of Chanting
>
> From an advertisement for a chanting CD:
>
> > This CD contains recitations by Lama Zopa Rinpoche of mantras and texts that are especially suitable for humans or animals to hear at the time of death. Hearing each mantra and text puts an imprint and blessing in

(continued)

> the mind that brings the result of good rebirths, liberation from *samsara*, and ultimately, full enlightenment. Lama Zopa Rinpoche advises that playing this CD for any human or animal will bring immense benefit. While particularly valuable at the time of death, there will be great benefit to anyone at any time who hears these mantras and texts.
>
> *"This is such an easy way to benefit animals and to bring them closer to enlightenment, so we must do it. We must attempt in every single way to benefit them. We must quickly liberate them from samsara, ... which has no beginning, which is continuous."*
>
> (Lama Zopa Rinpoche)

Among Tibetan Buddhists, the funeral ceremony can last up to 49 days. When someone dies, their soul is believed to fall into a trance and enter a period called *bardo*. At first the soul experiences a brilliant light, which is enlightenment radiating from Amitabha Buddha. On extremely rare occasions, a soul achieves nirvana at this point, but the vast majority are confused by the light because of their karma and turn away from it. As they regain their senses, they experience the presence of both wrathful and peaceful deities for several days. These are the emanations of the buddha body of bliss. While the soul, still in *bardo*, experiences these deities, monks chant from the *Book of the Dead* to enable it to make good decisions as it interacts with the deities. When *bardo* ends, the soul's disembodied journey comes to a close, and the Dharma-king Yama (Death) intervenes to determine its next incarnation.

In China and Japan, where belief in reincarnation exists alongside other notions of afterlife—either in a divine bureaucracy or in some manner of continuity with one's family line—it is often hoped that post-mortem rituals will enable the dead to work toward buddhahood. Chinese and Japanese monastics help the laity memorialize the dead in funerary tablets, which become part of a family shrine or altar, or are sometimes kept at a temple.

Nirvanic orientation

Unlike karmic orientation, *nirvanic* orientation is practiced by relatively few Buddhists, and even for most of these it occupies only a portion of their time. Before *nirvanic* orientation is even possible, a person must be quite advanced in Buddhist discipline and training, which usually requires many hundreds of lifetimes. As a shortcut, several Buddhist teaching lineages offer accelerated or expedited paths, but most Buddhists see these as ineffective or dangerous, unless one has the good fortune to study under an experienced and powerful master.

Since the purpose of *nirvanic* orientation is to extinguish the illusion that is our world, practitioners no longer focus on gaining merit, but strive to experience the world through Dharma. As one advances through *nirvanic* orientation, the illusion of the self and others disappears; the thirst for existence subsides; and compassion, insight, and wisdom begin to expand exponentially.

Rituals, Rites, Practices

The Public Creation of a *Mandala*

Tibetan monks sometimes invite the public to watch them create a *mandala* from colored sand. Holding a tapered copper tube filled with fine sand, they rub another tube against its ridged spine to control the amount of sand they apply to the *mandala* (Figure 2.15). When the *mandala* is complete, the monks give a Dharma talk, and then destroy it, sometimes handing out small bags of sand as souvenirs. *Mandalas* are spiritual and psychological maps that guide people to salvation, and so the destruction of such a splendid *mandala* so soon after its creation underscores an important truth: although it is a map, it is nonetheless the map of an illusion caused by ignorance, and therefore has no permanent value.

Figure 2.15 An inquisitive child looks on as a Tibetan monk begins to fill in the outermost border of a *mandala*. Source: Will Deming.

Study and meditation

Nirvanic orientation requires both study and meditation, for study cultivates a person's wisdom concerning the true nature of things, and meditation actualizes this wisdom in one's life. Novices are instructed to study the authoritative teachings of the Buddha (his *sutras*), accounts of his life and sometimes previous lives (*jatakas*), and the disciplinary codes (*vinaya*). In the Tibetan context, where a course of study may take 15 years and culminate in the *geshe* degree, compared at times to a PhD, monks also study Mahayana philosophers who elaborated on the nature of *sunyata* and how it becomes manifest in the world.

Study in Buddhism initially takes the form of an apprenticeship between a novice and a senior monk or a nun, and occurs whenever the two parties interact. The senior monk or nun, often referred to as a preceptor, is responsible for the novice's development. They model appropriate behavior and show the novice how to chant and perform rituals. This may be augmented by lectures from visiting Buddhist masters, who travel from place to place and speak on specific texts. A more formal course of study can take place in school classrooms. In Thailand, for example, the government has established a network of secondary schools for novices; and in Thailand and elsewhere, some Buddhist schools of higher education are accredited as four-year universities. These monastic schools run parallel to the public school system or exist in lieu of it. Novices studying there learn not only Buddhist subjects but nonreligious subjects as well, such as math, literature, English as a second language, and even computer science. While not all novices undertake the formal study Buddhism in a school, they all apprentice themselves to a preceptor.

Although study is *necessary* for the attainment of nirvana, it is not *sufficient*. Study must be actualized in one's life, which happens only in meditation. There are three basic methods of meditation. One is calming meditation, through which a practitioner expands the mind's ability to concentrate. By repeating certain exercises, such as following the breath as it goes in and out of the body, and by paying close attention to various physical and mental sensations, a person can discipline the mind. This discipline acts to calm the mind, which empowers it to concentrate and gain awareness of different levels of reality.

A second type of meditation is called insight meditation. It is used to "analyze" the world in the full sense of that word—that is, *break it down* into ever smaller bits and pieces. For example, a practitioner might analyze a car. Using insight meditation, they first strip away the car's outward shell, removing the tires, the fenders, the doors, the hood, and the windshield. This reveals the inner workings of the car—a level of truth normally hidden from view. Next the practitioner applies insight meditation to the floorboards, the engine, the drivetrain, and the chassis, revealing an additional level of truth, hidden deep within the car. The application of insight meditation continues in this way until every composite part of the car has been removed and dismantled, deconstructing them down to the screws and bolts and gaskets. In the mind of the practitioner, the car now lies in minute pieces, exposed as an illusion. It was never a single entity, it only appeared to be so. It had no core, no integrity, no essential being. By repeating this process on other entities, such as weapons, food, and the human body, the practitioner comes to understand that everything in life is insubstantial and ephemeral, and begins to catch glimpses of the truth that all existence is *an-atman* and *sunyata*.

While most monastic communities practice both calming and insight meditation, they differ in giving priority to one or the other. The third type of meditation, however, is largely confined to Vajrayana Buddhism. Called visualization meditation, it requires a person to focus the mind on an image that embodies the Dharma, such as a celestial buddha, a *bodhisattva*, or a Tara, which is often placed in the center of a *mandala*. Over the course of many sessions, during which the practitioner also has recourse to the techniques of calming meditation, they attain to a such a high level of concentration that the reality of the image becomes stronger as their own reality begins to pale by comparison. In the end, the reality of the image will overwhelm the reality of the practitioner and they will see the image as a mirror of their true self, thereby uncovering their buddha nature.

CONCLUSION

From time to time, western intellectuals have attempted to characterize Buddhism as a philosophy or a way of life rather than a religion. As we have seen, however, Buddhist practices presuppose the ultimate truth and reality of the Buddha's Dharma. From this starting point, lay Buddhists and monastics seek to conform their lives to the Dharma through giving (*dana*), adherence to moral precepts (*sila*), image veneration (*puja*), study, and meditation. These and other activities are thought to reduce universal suffering (*dukkha*), the final cessation of which is understood as salvation.

Part of the confusion as to whether Buddhism is a religion or simply a philosophy or way of life, stems from Buddhism's preeminently practical nature. It is quite accurate to describe the goal of Buddhism as the alleviation of suffering—in oneself, in others, and through all means possible. Due to this singular focus, Buddhists have often shown little interest in the sorts of things that many people associate with religion, such as existence in an afterlife or the sanctifying of human institutions such as marriage. Nonetheless, if we ignore or minimize the religious basis of Buddhism, we risk misunderstanding the motivations and aspirations of hundreds of millions of people in the world.

For review

1. What are the Four Sights that the Buddha saw, and what wisdom did he learn from them?
2. What are some of the principal differences between Theravada and Mahayana forms of Buddhism? Where are these forms of Buddhism practiced today?
3. How is Vajrayana Buddhism related to Mahayana?
4. How do Buddhists envision human salvation—that is, the escape from *samsara* and attainment of nirvana—given their doctrine of *an-atman*?
5. What are the three buddha bodies?
6. Why is compassion (*karuna*) so important in Buddhism?
7. How do Buddhists envision the beginning of existence in our world?
8. In what ways does "engaged Buddhism" express the ideals of Buddhism in today's world?
9. Explain the role of meditation in Buddhism: If meditation is necessary to attain nirvana, why do most Buddhists practice little or no meditation?

For discussion

1. Why would a Buddhist not commit suicide to attain release from *samsara*?
2. To what extent might Buddhists honor the gods and doctrines of other religions?

Key Terms

Abhidharma — "Higher Dharma"; teachings that synthesize and elaborate the Buddha's teachings.

Abhidharma-pitaka	The third and last division of early Buddhist scripture (see *Tri-pitaka*), which contains the "higher Dharma" teachings.
ahimsa	The religious principle of not destroying life.
Amida Buddha	The Japanese form of Amitabha Buddha. A Buddha who used his enormous store of merit to create a Pure Land for those in need of salvation.
Amitabha Buddha	See Amida Buddha.
an-atman	A term meaning devoid of any stable core or self.
arhat	"One worthy of honor"; a monastic who attains enlightenment through the teachings of the Buddha.
atman	The imperishable soul (whose existence Buddhist teachings deny).
Avalokiteshvara	The *bodhisattva* of compassion; see Guanyin.
bardo	A journey the soul experiences after death in Tibetan Buddhism.
bodhisattva	A "being dedicated to awakening"; a compassionate, enlightened being who postpones buddhahood to work for the salvation of others.
body of bliss	The buddha body that enables buddhas to create their own lands of bliss and teach *bodhisattvas* who are on their way to buddhahood.
body of transformation	The buddha body that enables *bodhisattvas* and new buddhas to come into the karmic world.
Buddha	The Enlightened one, the Awakened one; the founder of Buddhism. An enlightened being who brings Buddhist salvation to a world.
buddha bodies	Three realms or states that *bodhisattvas* can attain after death: the body of transformation, and the body of bliss, and the Dharma body.
Chan	"Meditation"; a Chinese school that emphasizes meditation as a way to see the buddha nature in oneself.
dana	The Buddhist practice of giving to gain merit (good karma).
Dharma	The message of the Buddha, the truth of the universe.
Dharma body	In Theravada, the teachings of the Buddha; in Mahayana, the highest of the buddha bodies, being the essence of the Buddha's *nirvana*.
dharmas	In *Abhidharma* teachings, the individual "facts" or "truths" of existence in this world.
dukkha	The dissatisfaction and suffering that Buddhism teaches is inherent in all life.
Four Noble Truths	A summary of the Buddha's teaching that comprises four foundational truths about the world.
Four Sights	An old man, a sick man, a corpse, and an impoverished holy man; the four things Siddhartha Gautama (later the Buddha) saw that began his search for truth.

Guanyin	A female form of the *bodhisattva* of compassion, Avalokiteshvara, popular in China.
Hinayana	"Lesser Vehicle"; a demeaning name used in the *Lotus Sutra* to describe the Buddhism of the Pali Canon.
karma	The good and bad consequences of one's actions.
lama	An accomplished spiritual leader in Tibetan Buddhism.
Mahayana	"Great Vehicle"; one of the three branches of contemporary Buddhism.
Maitreya	The Buddha that is to come into the world when people have forgotten Gautama Buddha's Dharma.
mandala	A diagram used in Buddhism as a spiritual and psychological map to salvation.
mantras	Sacred formulas chanted at rituals in Buddhism.
Nichiren	The thirteenth-century founder of Nichiren Buddhism, which stresses the importance of the *Lotus Sutra* above all else.
nirvana	The Buddhist goal of extinguishing this life; liberation from *samsara*.
Noble Eightfold Path	Eight actions and attitudes in Buddhism that one must practice to attain release from *samsara*.
Pali Canon	The early threefold Buddhist scripture written in Pali, consisting of the *Sutra-*, *Vinaya-*, and *Abhidharma-pitakas*; see *Tri-pitaka*.
puja	The veneration of images.
Pure Land Buddhism	A school of Buddhism that teaches that one can be reborn into Amitabha's Western Paradise (Pure Land) by practicing devotion to him.
samsara	"Flowing around"; the beginningless, meaningless cycle of birth, death, and rebirth.
Sangha	The Buddhist community, composed of men and women, monastics and laypersons.
Siddhartha Gautama	The name of the man who became the Buddha; the founder of Buddhism.
sila	The Buddhist practice of keeping ethical precepts.
stupa	A building or model of a building (especially on altars) containing a relic or precious object.
sunyata	"Emptiness"; an understanding of nirvana developed by Mahayana Buddhism.
Sutra-pitaka	"Basket of Discourses"; a collection of the Buddha's teachings, being the first division of the early Buddhist scriptures (see *Tri-pitaka* and Pali Canon).
Tantras	Practices of asceticism and meditation in Buddhism; texts that contain information about these practices.
Tara	A female divinity in Tibetan Buddhism.

Theravada	"Teaching of the Elders"; one of the three branches of contemporary Buddhism.
Three Jewels	Also known as the Three Refuges: the Buddha, the Dharma, and the Sangha.
Tri-pitaka	"Three Baskets"; the early threefold Buddhist scripture, consisting of the *Sutra-*, *Vinaya-*, and *Abhidharma-pitakas* (see Pali Canon).
Vajrayana	"Thunderbolt/Diamond Vehicle"; one of the three branches of contemporary Buddhism; sometimes treated as a form of Mahayana.
Vinaya-pitaka	"Basket of Discipline"; the Buddha's teachings on monastic discipline, being the second division of the early Buddhist scriptures (see *Tri-pitaka*).
Zen	The Japanese form of Chan Buddhism.

Bibliography

A good first book

Dale S. Wright. *Buddhism: What Everyone Needs to Know*. New York: Oxford University Press, 2020.

Further reading

Matthew T. Kapstein. *Tibetan Buddhism: A Very Short Introduction*. Oxford and New York: Oxford University Press, 2014.

Donald K. Swearer. *The Buddhist World of Southeast Asia*, 2nd edn. Albany, NY: SUNY Press, 2010.

Reference and research

Paula Arai and Kevin Trainor, eds. *The Oxford Handbook of Buddhist Practice*. New York: Oxford University Press, 2022.

Roderick S. Bucknell. *Reconstructing Early Buddhism*. Cambridge: Cambridge University Press, 2023.

Steve Collins. *Nirvana: Concept, Imagery, Narrative*. Cambridge: Cambridge University Press, 2010.

Stephen F. Teiser and Jacqueline I. Stone, eds. *Readings of the Lotus Sutra*. New York: Columbia University Press, 2009.

Karma L. Tsomo, ed. *Innovative Buddhist Women: Swimming Against the Stream*. Richmond: Curzon, 2000.

CHAPTER 3
Chinese Religion
Finding balance in the midst of change

The *luo pan*, or fengshui compass. The magnetized needle in the middle is surrounded by concentric circles that indicate the cardinal directions, the Eight Trigrams, the Ten Heavenly Stems, the Twelve Earthly branches, the Twenty-four heavenly breaths, family relationships, and still other aspects of the many patterns and powers in the heavens, time, and space. Source: Reproduced by permission of Lyn McCurdy.

DID YOU KNOW …

In Chinese religion the gods are envisioned as a governmental organization with a royal family, state officials, and petty bureaucrats. To gain access to the higher echelons of this spirit government, one must curry favor with gods in the lower ranks, even, in some cases, by bribing them.

Understanding the Religions of the World: An Introduction, Second Edition.
Edited by Will Deming.
© 2025 John Wiley & Sons Ltd. Published 2025 by John Wiley & Sons Ltd.

OVERVIEW

Chinese religion is the religion of the dominant ethnic group of China, the **Han**. While there are some 56 ethnicities in the People's Republic of China (PRC), the Han comprise over 90 percent of its mainland population and most of the population of Taiwan, an island province of China with an independent government. The Han also make up sizable portions of the populations of Singapore and Malaysia, and are found in cultural enclaves in the Americas, Europe, Africa, and Oceania. In all, there are more than 1.4 billion Han Chinese worldwide. Yet Chinese religion is interwoven into the Han culture in such a way that it presents several challenges to those who would estimate the religion's size or characterize its practices with any precision.

To begin with, because the Han approach religion as one of several aspects of their larger culture, different groups within the Han culture practice the religion selectively and to varying degrees. Just as some Americans prefer the American sport of football, while others prefer the equally American sport of baseball, some Han practice only certain elements of Chinese religion and neglect others altogether. For instance, a central tenet of Chinese religion is that the younger generation show respect and deference to the older generation. This can take several forms, including burial rites, the daily burning of incense at the family's home altar, and bending oneself to the will of parents or grandparents. But Han Chinese may observe all or none of these practices.

Second, it is not always possible to distinguish neatly between Han culture, on the one hand, and Chinese religion, on the other. While many Han practices are clearly "religious" by any definition—such as praying to the buddha Omituo Fo for a good rebirth in his heavenly Pure Land—others are not. Some practices that aim for success and good fortune only in this life are ambiguous, as when a person consults a fortuneteller; and others seem to skirt the category "religion" altogether, as when students submit assignments to a teacher by holding out their work with both hands and respectfully lowering their heads.

Rituals, Rites, Practices

Calligraphy and Talismans

Calligraphy has always been powerful, and even magical in China. Chinese calligraphy characters are found everywhere, on doors and entryways, on foods, and on wall hangings. According to legend, these characters originated 4000 years ago when the sage Cang Jie observed the marks made by the feet of animals and reasoned that there was a parallel between these marks and cosmic patterns. The Chinese word for literature and culture, *wen*, originally referred to patterns seen on animal hides and fish scales.

The art of calligraphy is not so much concerned with conveying information as with re-presenting cosmic patterns that have been "digested" by an individual through extensive training and self-cultivation. A calligrapher's skill, concentration, and response to inner states and outer realities makes calligraphy an art of self-expression. Chinese value calligraphy, in part, because they read the personality and character of a calligrapher in their writing, and for this reason it is typical to see examples of calligraphy by political leaders.

The Chinese tradition of calligraphy teaches that each character must be created with a specific number and order of strokes. The density of the ink, the type of brush, and the quality of paper must also be selected with care, and the proper modes of sitting and holding the calligraphy brush must be adhered to strictly. In the act of writing, the calligrapher varies the speed of the brush, the pressure of the brush on the paper, and the ratio, placement, and interplay of black ink and white paper. Preparation for writing includes entering into a calm, meditative state, often while preparing the ink from a dried ink block by rubbing it with water on a special stone.

A complementary art form is the creation of talismans, which are calligraphic conventions that provide blessings, protection from danger, and relief from illnesses. For instance, a common talisman among Daoist priests consists of inscribing a piece of paper with calligraphy, burning it, mixing its ashes with water, and giving it to a client to drink.

One scholar describes talismans as "a passport to the higher spheres." In ancient China, talismans were often tablets that were broken into two pieces and given to military envoys or spies sent out separately. If they happened to cross paths, the two halves of the broken talisman would confirm their joint mission. Daoists teach that talismans still have this function today: the gods have one half of a talisman and have sent the other half to Earth in anticipation of human-divine interaction.

A third complicating factor in understanding Chinese religion is that Han culture, like many cultures, has incorporated *several* religions into its cultural landscape. For more than two millennia, China has been home to Confucianism and Daoism; and for most of that time it has been an adopted home for Buddhism, which came from India. China also boasts a rich history of smaller sectarian groups, each with its own scriptures, practices, and beliefs, as well as a widespread popular tradition and a thriving, localized folk religion. In addition, Catholic and Protestant Christianity and Islam are active in some areas of the country; and Judaism, Manichaeism, and Nestorian Christianity, which are now gone from China, have made important contributions to China's religious heritage. Yet, these religious traditions have not so much competed with Chinese religion as they have coexisted with it and widened its scope. Christian elements, for example, such as Christmas trees, carols, and pictures of Mary with the baby Jesus are now part of the wider Han culture, and therefore potentially or indirectly an expression of Chinese religion; and this has taken place, not for religious reasons, but because Chinese are attracted to the lively, festive spirit of the Christmas holiday.

A Closer Look

Christians and Muslims in the PRC

In the PRC, Roman Catholicism, Protestantism, and Islam continue to struggle with government regulations on religion and grapple with questions of loyalty to a foreign authority. Catholics have faced the dilemma of loyalty to Rome versus loyalty to the Chinese government. Many belong to an official Chinese Roman Catholic church, whose bishops are appointed by the Chinese government rather than by the pope. But there is also an illegal Roman Catholic church with close ties to the Roman See. In 2018, in a gesture of reconciliation, Pope Francis recognized eight bishops who had been appointed by the Chinese government. Nonetheless, he declared that ultimate authority to appoint bishops must remain with Rome, and so conflicts continue.

Many Protestant groups, by contrast, have developed the so-called Three Self Principles of self-administration, self-support, and self-propagation to remain independent of any non-Chinese church hierarchy. Others, however, participate in a growing house church movement, meeting in members' homes to avoid government scrutiny.

Muslims in China comprise two distinct populations. One group is the Hui, who are well integrated into Chinese society in many parts of the country, being indistinguishable from the majority Han population except by dress and dietary practices. The other group, the Uighurs, live mostly in western China and often differ radically from Han Chinese in culture and appearance. Their language and ancestry tend to be Turkic, and they maintain connections with Muslims in Central Asia.

It is thus the nature of Han culture and Chinese religion to draw inspiration from other religions and, in particular, combine elements of the popular and folk traditions with the **Three Teachings**—Confucianism, Daoism, and Buddhism—without giving much preference to any of these. For this reason, Han Chinese do not call themselves Confucians or Daoists or Buddhists, but speak of "the three teachings becoming one" (Figure 3.1). In fact, "Confucianism" is not the Chinese name for that religious tradition, but refers to an intellectual movement called the "School of the Scholars," and it would be quite arrogant for a person to identify themselves as a scholar. That is a distinction bestowed by someone else. Likewise, calling oneself a Daoist or a Buddhist usually means that a person has been ordained in these religions as a priest, monk, or nun. Furthermore, it is not even the role of scholars, priests, monks, or nuns to educate the laity in religious doctrine. Their job is to perform rituals on the laity's behalf, whether or not the laity understand them or even participate. The average layperson simply does whatever "makes sense" according to individual needs, family practices, and regional variations.

Figure 3.1 An elderly Confucius presents the baby Gautama Buddha to a middle-aged Laozi. This famous image illustrates the harmony between the Three Traditions, as well as their respective ages in Chinese religious history. Source: Wikimedia Commons.

In sum, the religion of the Han Chinese draws on a great wealth of beliefs and practices but is nonetheless a *single* religion. It is this religion that we are calling Chinese religion.

History

Timeline	
1500–1045 BCE	The Shang dynasty; divination is used.
1045–256 BCE	The Zhou dynasty; the origin of the Five Classics and such ideas as *qi*, *yin*, *yang*, and the Mandate from Heaven.
551–479 BCE	Life of Confucius.
550–350 BCE	Core Daoist ideas appear, along with the *Daode Jing*.
370–286 BCE	Life of Zhuangzi.
206 BCE–220 CE	The Han dynasty, the development of the Han synthesis, and the appearance of the Celestial Masters.
50 CE	The arrival of Buddhism.
221–581 CE	Period of Disunity; religious Daoism develops.
581–906 CE	The Sui and Tang dynasties; Islam comes to China.
960–1279 CE	The Song dynasty; Neo-Confucianism, monastic Daoism, and "the Three Teachings" doctrine appear.
16th century	Matteo Ricci and Jesuit missions are active in China.
19th century	European and North American colonialists and missionaries arrive in China.
20th century	Chinese civil war; the establishment of the Republic of China and the People's Republic of China.
1966–1976	The Cultural Revolution is implemented on the mainland. Religion is targeted for eradication and many places of worship are destroyed and religious leaders persecuted.
1979	The PRC grants restricted religious freedoms.

Our earliest documents from China are records of divination rituals performed for the royal families of the Shang dynasty (ca. 1500–1045 BCE). These rituals used oracle bones—shoulder blades (scapulae) of sheep and cattle or underbellies (plastrons) of turtles—to gain information from ancestors, nature spirits, and sometimes a remote high god called Shang Di (an entirely different Chinese character than the one used for "Shang" dynasty). After a bone was inscribed with statements in both affirmative and negative forms (for instance, "it will rain; it will not rain"), a ritual specialist placed a heated poker on the bone, resulting in cracks spreading across the inscribed area. The specialist then interpreted the cracks to predict the future and determine the best course of action. Using this method, the unseen world was consulted on all manner of questions: whether enemies would attack, whether a pregnant queen would give birth to a boy or a girl, what spirit was causing the king's toothache, or when a sacrifice should be conducted.

The surviving documents indicate that oracle bones were probably only used for the Shang royal family. This presumes both a special connection between dynastic rulers and powerful cosmic forces, and an obligation on the part of these rulers to consult the spirit world before making important decisions. The documents also make clear that the spirit world was understood to function much like the world of the living: families (including ancestors) continued to unite around common interests, and older relatives needed to discipline younger family members, who, in turn, were expected to fulfill certain obligations. An exception was Shang Di. While he commanded the wind and the rain, he was seen as remote and far more unpredictable than nature spirits or ancestors.

The Shang assumed that deceased family members had a vested interest in their descendants' well-being. Yet the ancestors could become angry on occasion, perhaps because the royal family had forgotten to give certain offerings or perform important rituals. To bring a wayward descendant into line, the ancestral spirits might cause physical pain, like a toothache, or refuse to support a king's endeavors. Ritual offerings and sacrifices to appease the ancestors and other spirits were thus also part of the Shang royal religion. These included wine, grain, animals, and humans, while beautiful cast bronzes were used to honor the recipients when these were presented. Because the Shang interacted with their ancestors, they undoubtedly envisioned an afterlife, at least for the royal family. This is confirmed, moreover, by the elaborate burial sites that have been unearthed from this period. Horses, chariots, and other goods were buried in Shang royal tombs for a king's use in the next life (see Figure 3.2). Even people were buried with the king—some, perhaps, by their own choice, to remain in service to their king after his death; others because they were slaves or sacrificial victims.

A religious mandate for kingship and five early scriptures

The Zhou dynasty (1045–256 BCE) not only continued the Shang practices of divination and sacrifice, but also introduced some important innovations. Instead of appealing to the remote high god Shang Di, the Zhou appealed to Heaven. This was not a place of reward after death, but a divine force on the order of "nature" that was concerned for the human realm. According to the Zhou, Heaven had punished the Shang by taking away its kingdom because the Shang had neglected the welfare of the common people. By Zhou reckoning, Heaven had now designated the righteous Zhou to take charge of the human realm and rule wisely on behalf of the people, a notion they called the **Mandate of Heaven**.

A second innovation of the Zhou was to recognize a body of scripture that came to be called the **Five Classics**. These were: the *Classic of Documents* (also called the *Classic of History*), the *Classic of Change* (sometimes published as the *I Ching* or *Yijing*), the *Classic of Poetry*, the *Record of Ritual*, and the *Spring and Autumn Annals*. Their function was to provide advice and models that, when followed by those in power, created leaders who were civilized and refined, and,

Figure 3.2 Chinese emperors continued the elaborate burial practices of the Shang long after the Shang dynasty's demise. One of the most spectacular examples is the 1974 discovery of an entire underground necropolis built for the burial of the emperor Qin Shi Huang around the beginning of the second century BCE. It is estimated that this grave contains over 8000 terracotta foot soldiers (like those pictured here), along with chariots and horses, to protect the emperor in the afterlife. Source: Reproduced by permission of David Deming.

through a ripple effect, led to social peace and harmony. Thus, the *Record of Ritual* prescribed appropriate civil behavior, from the most mundane, daily habits to protocols for government celebrations. The *Classic of Documents* and the *Spring and Autumn Annals* contained stories of worthy and powerful figures whose successes and failures taught lessons on good government and moral virtue. The *Classic of Poetry* expressed the concerns and joys of the common people and provided solemn hymns for state affairs. These were considered vital to a government that wanted to keep the Mandate of Heaven by treating its subjects properly and performing its ritual duties. The *Classic of Change*, finally, was a book of divination, but of a different sort than the divination of the Shang royal religion.

> **Sacred Traditions and Scripture**
>
> ### A Model Duke
>
> An important text from the *Classic of Documents* tells the story of the Duke of Zhou, the younger brother of King Wen Wang. When the King became seriously ill, the Duke speculated that ancestors were angry, or perhaps wanted a descendant to join them in the spirit world to serve them. Performing the appropriate ritual, the Duke pleaded with the ancestors not to let the Mandate of Heaven depart from the Zhou family. He even offered himself in place of his brother. After the Duke performed this ritual, the king recovered.
>
> Chinese tradition holds up the Duke of Zhou as exemplary in many ways. He was a loyal minister to the king, offering himself so that his king might continue to fulfill the Mandate of Heaven; he was a dutiful son, offering his life so that he could serve the royal ancestors and the dynasty they had established; and he was a model younger brother, not seeking his older brother's throne, but humbling himself in his subordinate social position.

Under the Zhou, divination was a way to anticipate the future by determining the shifting patterns of place, time, and events that have already shaped a person's present situation in life. This was thought to give insight into how a person's ambitions might fare when confronted with these dynamic forces down the road. At the heart of Zhou divination were the concepts of **qi** (pronounced "chee" and sometimes written *ch'i*), **yin** and **yang**, and the **Five Phases** (also called the Five Elements or Five Agents). Together these were thought to explain all structures and movements within the cosmos, including nature and human society, physical properties, and spiritual and psychological phenomena. *Qi* was the "stuff" of the universe. *Yin* and *yang* were complementary states of *qi*, and the Five Phases were the basic modes into which "*yin qi*" and "*yang qi*" changed and alternated—water, metal, fire, wood, and earth. The Phases, in turn, combined in different proportions to create all the things of the universe, determining all their patterns of interaction with one another.

Early intellectuals and theorists

The Zhou dynasty produced many important religious figures. The most famous of these was **Confucius** (Chinese: *Kongzi*), who lived from 551 to 479 BCE, a period of political and social upheaval. Deeply committed to what he envisioned as China's remote, golden age of peace and harmony, Confucius described himself as a transmitter of the ideals and practices from that early period. These, he believed, would reestablish correct human relationships, beginning with the family, and restore balance to society. He held that an individual could become a **junzi**, a "superior person" or "gentleman," through education and personal effort. This was a revolutionary notion, for in Confucius' time the designation *junzi* referred only to those of noble birth. But Confucius insisted that *junzi* had originally indicated a person's noble *character*, and argued that rulers should return society to the golden past by concerning themselves with virtue rather than power.

> **Did you know …**
>
> The Chinese character for "humaneness" or "benevolence" is ren. It is composed of two elements: 人 "person," and 二 "two." In other words, being humane is what one does in relationship with other people:
>
> 仁

While Confucius' ideas were never adopted by Zhou rulers, they were recorded by his disciples in the **Analects**, which became such an important writing after his death that today he is remembered as the First Teacher. One of the earliest interpreters of the *Analects* was **Mencius**, (Chinese: Mengzi or Meng-tzu, ca. 370–300 BCE), who not only restated Confucius' teachings for a new generation, but also formulated two new insights. First, he reasoned that humans were naturally good, something Confucius had only hinted at. This underscored the tradition's reverence for learning, for just as plants needed careful tending to encourage their natural vitality, human beings needed education for their innate goodness to flourish. Second, he came to the conclusion that if a king's rule did not benefit the people, not only could Heaven retract its mandate, but the people themselves had the right to rebel against a tyrant.

Sacred Traditions and Scripture

The *Analects*

The *Analects* are the records Confucius' disciples made of their master's words and actions during his lifetime. They paint a picture of a man who met with friends to discuss moral and intellectual issues and loved the company of cultivated persons. Confucius believed that education, especially moral education, nurtured a certainty regarding values, enabling a person to perform rituals with a sincerity that came from the human heart and will.

Analects 1.1

Confucius said: "To study, and to practice what has been learned, is this not pleasurable? To have friends from far away come to visit, is this not happiness? To be unruffled when others aren't appreciative of one's accomplishments, isn't this the mark of a well-bred person?"

(continued)

> *Analects 2.7*
>
> Confucius' pupil Ziyou asked about filial piety. Confucius said, "Today filial piety means being about the task of nourishing one's parents. But that is what we do for dogs and horses. If there is no respect, how do these actions differ?"

Other intellectuals in the late Zhou also made contributions to Chinese religion—so many, in fact, that the Chinese refer to this as the Hundred Schools period. Some disagreed with part or all of Confucius' teachings, and some proposed completely unrelated theories. Mozi (ca. 470–380 BCE) criticized Confucius' love of ritual as a waste of the people's resources and argued that Confucianism promoted family obligations and friendship at the expense of love and support for *all* people. Yang Zhu (ca. 440–360 BCE) taught that each person should take care of their own concerns and needs, "not even plucking a hair to benefit the world." And a century and a half later, Xunzi (ca. 310–220 BCE) opposed Mencius' interpretation of Confucius by insisting that humans were naturally evil. In addition to protocol, ritual, and education, he insisted that strict laws with state enforcement were necessary to maintain order and meaning in human society.

The universal way

In contrast to Confucianism, most of the Hundred Schools faded in popularity after the Zhou. The great exception was a teaching called **Daoism**. Even though most Daoist rituals and practices came into being only after the Zhou, two key Daoist texts emerged during this period, sometime between the sixth and fourth centuries BCE. These were the **Daode Jing** and the **Zhuangzi**, which gave new expression to themes that had long existed in China, namely, self-cultivation, the quest for longevity, and the identification of a powerful, creative force called the **Dao**.

The *Daode Jing* (also written *Tao Te Ching*) translates into English as *The Classic of the Way and Its Power*. It proposed that behind everything there was a subtle yet relentless process by which chaos unfolded into creation and then returned to chaos. Despite its enormous power, this process had the unassuming name of the Dao, or Way. The Dao was said to exist before being and nonbeing. It was invisible, intangible, scentless, and inaudible, and yet, unnoticed, it influenced all things. Like water flowing quietly over a stone, wearing it down little by little, the Dao shaped all things. Like an uncarved block of wood, it had no particular manifestation or purpose, and thus could become anything. It was pure potentiality, the source of everything. People needed to conform to the Dao rather than work against it. In this way they would harmonize their lives with the eternal ebb and flow of becoming and decay, of being and nonbeing. They would align themselves with the natural rhythm of the cosmos, become a part of the universal pattern, and maximize their potential and life energy. To "go with the flow" of the Dao instead of swimming against the current required *wu wei* (pronounced "woo way"), or nonaction. But rather than indicating some sort of sedentary state, *wu wei* was "doing without ado," and ultimately "not taking any action contrary to nature (see Figure 3.3)."

> ### Sacred Traditions and Scripture
>
> #### Images of the Dao
>
> The *Daode Jing* uses many images to illustrate the Dao's quiet, apparently passive, and yet ultimately powerful nature. Some of the most striking images relate the Dao to water, empty space, and an uncarved block of wood.
>
> > Water benefits all creation but does not compete with it.
> > It resides in places people dislike;
> > Therefore it is like the Dao.
> > (from Chapter 8)
>
> > Dao is empty. Therefore it is useful, but its usefulness never exhausted.
> > An abyss, it seems as if it were the ancestor of all things.
> > (from Chapter 4)
>
> > In the world there is nothing softer and weaker than water,
> > But there is nothing so able to overcome strong and hard objects.
> > (from Chapter 78)
>
> > The things that are softest in the world overtake the hardest.
> > That which has no being penetrates places without space.
> > Thus I know the benefit of *wu wei*, taking no action.
> > (from Chapter 43)

The second text, the *Zhuangzi*, was named for its author. Zhuangzi (or Zhuang Zhou, ca. 370–286 BCE) not only praised the Dao, but delighted in all its manifestations, including those that seemed ugly, malformed, or useless to humans. He took the reader on flights of fantasy, questioning what people considered valuable, and speculating on the meaning and reality of dreams, life, and death. He pointed out that when humans call something valuable or good, they really mean that it is valuable or good *for themselves*. By contrast, the Dao never takes sides. Being the source of all things, it includes everything in its irresistible pattern. According to Zhuangzi, if humans could know and evaluate things as the Dao does, each with its place in the cosmic pattern, their sensitivity and alignment to the Dao would free them from all worries, and enable them to savor all life's moments and manifestations. Zhuangzi even spoke of achieving immortality, either in an organic way, by which one would carry on in some future manifestation as a "grasshopper's leg or rat's liver," or as a *true* human, who, by perfecting the movement of the Dao in their own life, lived a miraculous length of time.

Figure 3.3 One of China's most famous landscape paintings, Fan Kuan's *Travellers Among Mountains and Streams*, gives expression to both the dominance of the Dao and its harmonizing aspects in the natural world. The massive rock face (*yang*) is softened by a thin cascade of water (*yin*), as two human beings (barely visible in the detail on the right) accompany a small caravan of donkeys. Minuscule by comparison, these tiny creatures are completely integrated into, and at ease with, the vastness of nature. Source: Wikimedia Commons.

Confucianism and Daoism under the Han Dynasty

Although the principal figures and ideas of Confucianism had emerged during the Zhou, it was under the Han dynasty (206 BCE–220 CE) that they were shaped into formal religious traditions. As in earlier dynasties, religious and governmental concerns were seen as two sides of the same coin, for the Han emperor ruled by the Mandate of Heaven and was supported by his royal ancestors. Early on, Han royal families chose Confucian ideals as the means to monitor the emperor's own action and establish virtuous behavior among his officials. The Five Classics were adopted as the basis of statecraft, and the emperor founded a university dedicated to the Five Classics and Confucian principles to train men from around the country for service in the imperial bureaucracy. Virtually from the time of the Han until the twentieth century, Confucianism remained at the heart of imperial ethics, morality, and political theory.

> **Did you know …**
>
> Even though "Dao" is sometimes written "Tao," it is always pronounced with a "d" sound. The spelling with a "t" comes from an older system of transliteration in which our "t" sound would have been indicated by writing the word as T'ao.

The teachings and ideas of Daoism were also embellished and systematized during the Han. The Chinese call this the development of *religious* Daoism to distinguish it from teachings of the *Daode Jing* and the *Zhuangzi*, which they classify as *philosophical* Daoism. Religious Daoism had priests, temples, rituals, and sacred texts, and took shape as a revealed religion. That is, gods imparted or revealed special messages to humans, which became the basis for teachings, ritual, and scripture. One of the most important sects of religious Daoism was the Celestial Masters, which in later centuries came to be called the Orthodox Unity School (Zhengyi). In 142 CE, during a period of turmoil and intrigue in the royal court, the sect's founder, Zhang Daoling, had a revelation from **Lord Lao**, a deified form of the sage Laozi, the presumed author of the *Daode Jing*. As Lord Lao's representative on Earth, Zhang became the Celestial Master. He was told by Lord Lao that the end of the world was coming and that he and others needed to form a community organized around a strict moral code. In this community they would purify themselves in anticipation of becoming the core of a new society. Sin was thought to cause illness, and its remedy required rituals of confession and penance, as well as the supplication of Lord Lao and other deities.

The synthesis of religion under the Han and the arrival of a new religion

The attention Han scholars gave to Confucianism and Daoism, as well as to *yin-yang* theory, resulted in the **Han synthesis**. This worldview proposed that the cosmos was complete and self-sustaining, and that virtue governed both human

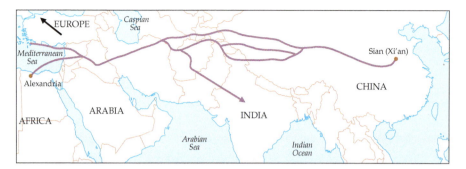

Figure 3.4 The Silk Road was actually a series of roads through central, south, and east Asia. It connected Europe, the Middle East, and India to the far east. In addition to material goods (including, of course, silk), the Silk Road spread culture, language, and religion throughout these regions.

relationships and natural processes. Heaven, Earth, and humans moved in concert with one another according to the same metaphysical patterns, and good emerged from their harmonious and balanced interplay. The emperor stood at the center of these patterns, as his actions were the pivot around which Heaven, Earth, and human beings turned, interacted, and intertwined. A bad emperor not only lost Heaven's Mandate, but his dynasty's demise would be heralded by grave disruptions in the natural order such as earthquakes and flooding.

In addition, the Han witnessed the coming of a new religion to China: Buddhism. Originating in India, it arrived primarily via the Silk Road, a name given to the network of trade routes through the vast deserts of central Asia and western China (Figure 3.4). Although Buddhism was originally promoted by a Han emperor who had a dream about the coming of this new religion, it did not take hold in China until after the Han, during the Period of Disunity (221 CE–581 CE), and only became firmly entrenched in Chinese culture under the Sui and Tang dynasties (581 CE–906 CE). With its ideas of reincarnation, enlightenment, and nirvana, which contrasted sharply with native Chinese ways of thinking, Buddhism proved to be an exciting catalyst for religious innovations and intellectual discoveries. This encouraged a continual flow of Buddhist missionaries from India into China, and many Chinese traveled to India to learn about Buddhism in the land of its origin. Monasteries housing both Indian and Chinese Buddhists sprang up in oasis towns along the Silk Road, and hundreds of volumes from the Buddhist canon were translated from Pali and Sanskrit into Chinese.

Buddhism reached the pinnacle of its popularity and influence in China in the seventh and eighth centuries under the early Tang dynasty. Rulers patronized Buddhist scholars and sects, and monasteries grew in prestige and wealth. This good fortune ended abruptly, however, with a change in government policy and an orchestrated backlash against the religion. During a three-year purge that began in 842, hundreds of thousands of monks and nuns were forced to return to secular life, and their temples and landholdings were confiscated by the government.

This severely crippled Buddhism, and although it continued to be an integral part of Chinese religion, it took centuries for it to recover its former prestige.

Neo-Confucianism, the Three Teachings, and popular religion

Under the Tang, Confucianism served as an ideology of the state but held little interest as a living religion, even among Confucian scholars. During the Song dynasty (960–1279), however, a new form of Confucianism emerged that joined Daoist and Buddhist ideas of the cosmos with the Confucian emphasis on cultivating relationships. The Confucian practice of self-cultivation, which had earlier encompassed education, scholarship, and the performance of rituals, now added a form of meditation whose goal was to uncover the mind's unity with the cosmos. Called Neo-Confucianism by western scholars, its essence was famously captured in the eleventh century in the opening lines of Zhang Zai's *Western Inscription*: "Heaven is my father and earth is my mother, and even so small a creature as I have a place in their midst (see Figure 3.3)." Daoism also moved toward synthesizing religious traditions. In imitation of Buddhism, it established its own monasteries, and its monks undertook spiritual exercises that combined visualization, gymnastics, sexual practices, and dietary restrictions in an effort to achieve immortality.

This melding of Confucian, Daoist, and Buddhist traditions under the Song was captured in a saying from the time, "the Three Teachings merge to be One." It encouraged a further synthesis of religious traditions in everyday life, which added elements from popular and folk religion. Soon, all manner of practices, including ancestor veneration, exorcism, divination, and sacrifices to gods, were adopted by ordinary Chinese as they also sought (Daoist) immortality, worried about (Buddhist) karma, and conformed to (Confucian) ideals of propriety and respect, especially in the family. This novel eclecticism spread unsystematically in homes and communities among ordinary people, taking shape in an elastic and fluid way that still characterizes Chinese religion today.

Additional developments

The complexity of Chinese religion was enriched still further by two developments in the following centuries. First, under the Yuan (1279–1368), a sectarian pattern of religion became more common. Laypeople, as *individuals*, joined independent religious organizations, thereby clearly separating religion from family and society. Second, the Neo-Confucian thinker Wang Yangming (1472–1529) proposed that moral knowledge, which was essential for virtuous living, was ultimately not something that could be gained through intensive study and scholarship. Rather, it was innate in all human beings. This meant that even uneducated people could become sages if they joined their innate moral knowledge with appropriate actions. Aside from these two developments, however, Chinese religion remained relatively stable until the nineteenth century.

The impact of European imperialism

While some Europeans had come to China as merchants and missionaries as early as the thirteenth century, with few exceptions they remained cultural outsiders. In the sixteenth century, Jesuit priests made a bold attempt to convert the entire country to Catholicism by taking on the trappings of Chinese scholars. Led by Matteo Ricci, their intention was to gain access to the royal court and in this way win over the imperial family as well as scholar–officials of the highest level. Yet their efforts were unsuccessful, and for the next two centuries there was little interaction between Chinese and Europeans.

The situation changed radically in the nineteenth century when Christian missionaries arrived in the wake of European and American imperialists and their militaries. Much of this century was humiliating for the Chinese as they lost war after war provoked by foreigners and were forced to sign disadvantageous treaties. Before this, westerners, who had not been allowed to travel in China's interior, had been duly impressed with Chinese culture. But missionaries and other foreigners now gained wide and largely unregulated access to China, and became highly critical of Chinese ways.

As their government, traditions, and country fell victim to ever increasing foreign incursion, Chinese themselves began to wonder what was wrong with their cultural heritage. The late nineteenth and early twentieth centuries thus became a period of profound self-doubt for Chinese. Many blamed religion as the principal cause of their weakness. Educational reformers identified Confucianism in particular as the source of China's conservative, backward, and unscientific society. Daoism and Buddhism were denigrated as superstitions, while popular and folk traditions were reviled as an even lower, more confused tangle of myths and practices. Others countered that Confucianism was essential to being Chinese, but needed to be updated to remain relevant; and still others embraced western political systems like democracy, socialism, and communism.

Chinese religion in Taiwan and the PRC

As the twentieth century advanced, two strategies were put into practice, with very different outcomes. In the 1930s, Chiang Kai-shek, a leader in the Chinese Nationalist Party, made Confucianism central to his social reforms. When he and his supporters lost a civil war to Chinese communists in 1949, Chiang left the mainland and established the Republic of China on the island province of Taiwan as a government in exile and protector of Chinese culture (Figure 3.5). Under Chiang and his successors, both the Chinese economy and religion flourished in Taiwan. Daoist and Buddhist leaders built temples and established monastic communities across the island, and the government funded Confucian studies at universities and promoted Confucian ideals among its citizenry.

On the mainland, the PRC came into being in 1949, promoting Marxist materialism and atheism. Even though its constitution granted freedom of religion,

Figure 3.5 The political history of modern China is complex. In the twentieth century, control of China was contested by Chinese Nationalists (Guomindang) and Chinese Communists. In 1949, the Nationalists fled the mainland for the island province of Taiwan, where they established a provisional government. By the 1980s their economy was booming and they spoke of becoming an independent nation. Yet the Communist government on the mainland (the PRC) remains adamant that Taiwan is a renegade province that must be brought under its control.

the government officially condemned religion and at different times permitted, discouraged, and punished its practice. The most severe persecutions came during a disastrous government initiative called the Cultural Revolution, which lasted from 1966 to 1976. Temples were destroyed and religious leaders were harassed, tortured, and killed. Even so, many elements of Chinese religion were preserved and adopted by the regime for the worship of the Chinese president Mao Zedong. His words were regarded as sacred, and he was eventually addressed with the same language and gestures used to address Chinese gods.

In 1979, three years after Mao's death, political and religious reforms heralded a new era. While retaining the power to determine what constitutes a religion, the government reaffirmed the religious rights of citizens, as long as religion did not undermine the stability of society or the state. Buddhist and Daoist temples were restored and reopened, and the surviving priests, monks, and nuns from both traditions began to repopulate their professional ranks—although ordination now included indoctrination into a state-endorsed political ideology. Confucius' hometown of Qufu received funding to promote tourism and pilgrimage, and Confucian ideals were again held in high esteem, especially those that fostered obedience to superiors and social harmony. The freedom to engage in popular and folk religious traditions, on the other hand, was not guaranteed under Chinese law, but the government tended to be lenient, especially in rural areas.

When official attitudes began to shift toward more religious tolerance, Chinese were initially cautious about how they described their religious activities. What they said in public frequently did not match their actions in private. At the same time, with the Cultural Revolution behind them, many Han Chinese moved to urban areas and focused on financial well-being, leaving behind the religious traditions of their parents. But increased wealth did little to address questions of meaning, identity, and purpose, and during the first decades of the twenty-first century China witnessed an astounding spiritual revival. Thousands of new temples, churches, and mosques opened each year, accommodating tens of millions of worshippers, and figures like Yu Dan, a university professor who became a household name for lecturing and writing on the relevance of the *Analects*, have once again made Confucianism a source of national identity and popular morality.

This explosion of interest in religion has been carefully monitored by the government. The religions of minority cultures, such as Tibetan Buddhists and Uighur Muslims, continue to be persecuted, sometimes violently, as has the popular Falun Gong sect. Other groups have been coerced into complying with government guidelines for religion, and the activities of global religions with foreign connections, such as Christianity, Islam, and Buddhism, are sometimes curbed or crushed.

At present, five religions are officially recognized by the PRC, each of which is affiliated with a government organization and subject to regulation by China's Bureau of Religious Affairs. These are Buddhism, Islam, Protestantism, Roman Catholicism, and certain schools of Daoism. All other traditions are regarded as either philosophy, as in the case of Confucianism, or superstition, which is censored as an obstruction to progress and social stability. Overall, however, the PRC prefers to co-opt religious groups rather than destroy them. This approach can be seen, for example, in the PRC's policy that it alone has the authority to ordain Tibetan Buddhist lamas and appoint bishops in the Chinese Roman Catholic Church.

Chinese religion outside the mainland

Chinese religion continues to thrive in Taiwan, Hong Kong, Singapore, Malaysia, and various Chinese communities across the globe. A new phenomenon has also emerged: the Three Teachings—Confucianism, Daoism, and Chinese forms Buddhism—have been appropriated from Han culture and practiced independently of one other. The so-called Third Wave of Confucianism, for example, includes modern Confucian scholars who live in Hawaii, Toronto, and Boston, who are not of Chinese or Asian origin. These educators often promote Confucianism ideals for western religious sensibilities, or apply its teachings as a self-contained resource for popular concerns such as ecology and globalism. The same can be said of Confucius Institutes, sponsored worldwide by the Chinese government to win support for its social policies. Similarly, Daoism and Chinese forms of Buddhism are practiced and studied as separate religions by organizations in Europe, North America, and Oceania. While some of these organizations are directed by Han Chinese, the majority are quite detached from the synthesis and cultural context of Chinese religion, and as such promote novel and essentialist perspectives and approaches.

Contemporary Beliefs and Practices

In Chinese religion, ultimate reality is not a place, like heaven, or a god who is the center of one's devotions. Rather, it is the universe, the source and sum of all existence, as guided by the divine Way, or Dao. It is by virtue of the Dao that life is meaningful and worth living, for the Dao supplies all aspects of the universe with distinct, natural patterns. This makes the world intelligible and good, and gives each element its form, intelligence, or life force, characteristics that determine an element's relation to all other elements.

Finding balance and harmony

The various patterns engendered by the Dao thus affect all levels of existence, including the functioning of the human body, the structure of society, and the intricacies and beauty of nature. They are at work in the ingredients of a medical prescription, the location of a gravesite, and even the items offered on a lunch menu. Furthermore, because these patterns are both interrelated and dynamic, the entire universe is characterized by constant movement.

Proper orientation in Chinese religion requires living in the universe in harmony and balance vis-à-vis the dynamic patterns of the Dao. It is an ongoing and demanding task, made all the more challenging by the fact that human beings have free will and are tempted to act immorally. For this reason, it is vital that humans practice the discipline and self-cultivation prescribed by the Three Teachings (Confucianism, Daoism, and Buddhism) and by China's popular and folk traditions, and at times seek the assistance or intervention of a ritual specialist. Only in this way can a person develop strong and harmonious ties with others and be blessed with a healthy body, an extensive and cohesive family, a long and prosperous life, and a favorable rebirth. If we switch to the language of ethics and morality, we can say that "good" in Chinese religion refers to states of harmony in the universe with respect to the shifting patterns of the Dao, whereas "evil" refers to states of disharmony with respect to these patterns.

Qi, yin and yang, and the Five Phases

Chinese today accept the idea of a universe made up of atoms, chemical reactions, and laws of physics. But alongside and coexisting with these western scientific notions, Chinese recognize another system governing the universe, based on traditional theories of harmony, change, relationship, and interrelatedness, all enlivened by the Dao. Although formless and invisible, the Dao becomes manifest in the "stuff" of the universe through *qi*, which can be translated as "vital matter," or "material life force." From the Chinese perspective, everything is composed of *qi*—from rocks to animals, and from apples to souls.

Beginning as a chaotic, unformed mass, *qi* inevitably divides in two. A traditional description of the process states that "at the beginning there is movement, then settling." This movement and settling is the first of many complementary pairs by which *qi* is analyzed, the most fundamental of which is the pair *yin* and *yang*, whereby everything becomes either *yin qi* or *yang qi*. *Yin* denotes the dark, settling, turbid, moist, gestating, female aspects of *qi*; *yang* denotes its light, rising, active, dry, growing, male aspects. As the 10,000 things (the creation) unfold according to the Dao, *yin* and *yang* take part in all things, being mixed in innumerable, subtle, and complex combinations.

Since *yin* and *yang* are complimentary, they ebb and flow in an eternal cycle, the one growing as the other diminishes. This dynamic relationship between *yin* and *yang* is illustrated in the diagram of the **Great Ultimate**, which depicts both a fluid mass of *yin* with a little *yang*, and a fluid mass of *yang* with a little *yin*, ever flowing into and out of each other (Figure 3.11). As *yang qi* and *yin qi* interact, they bring about the Five Phases, which are water, metal, fire, wood, and earth. These are more subtle forms of *qi*: water is greater *yin qi*, metal is lesser; fire is greater *yang qi*, wood is lesser; and earth is a neutral medium.

Because they are dependent on *yin* and *yang*, the Five Phases also change constantly, turning into each other through cycles of mutual engendering and mutual destruction (Figure 3.6). In the mutually engendering cycle, water creates wood (in the form of vegetation), wood brings about fire, fire creates earth (ashes), earth engenders metal (mined from the earth), and metal produces water (as it condenses on metal). In the mutually destructive cycle, water destroys fire, fire overcomes metal (melting it), metal overpowers wood (chopping it), wood destroys earth (covering or containing it), and earth overcomes water (in, say, the creation of dams). By taking these engendering and destructive cycles into account, Chinese construct theories of how things in the universe relate to one another. Then, abstracting and applying these theories more broadly, they determine how *qi*, *yin* and *yang*, and the Five Phases underlie relationships between all manner of things, including tastes, sounds, the seasons, the cardinal directions, colors, animals, governmental posts, and family relationships (Figure 3.7).

Despite the interrelatedness of the many patterns of the Dao, Chinese tend to divide them into three basic categories, each with its own internal logic and coherence. The first category relates to patterns in the physical world; the second, to patterns in human society, especially within the family; and the third encompasses

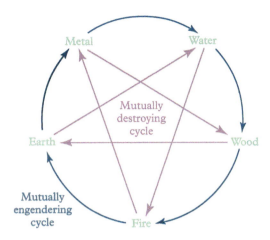

Figure 3.6 An image showing the mutually engendering and mutually destroying pairs of the Five Phases.

The Five Phases and their correspondences in the world

PHASE:	wood	fire	earth	metal	water
ANIMALS:	sheep	bird	ox	dog	pig
ORGANS:	spleen	lungs	heart	liver	kidneys
NUMBERS:	eight	seven	five	nine	six
COLORS:	green	red	yellow	white	black
TASTES:	sour	bitter	sweet	acidic	salty
SMELLS:	goatish	burnt	fragrant	rank	spoiled
VIRTUES:	humaneness	wisdom	trust	rightness	ritual protocol

Figure 3.7 A table showing how the Five Phases are reflected in our physical world.

patterns in the spirit world, envisioned as a divine bureaucracy overseen by gods. In what follows we will examine the nature of each of these categories.

Patterns in the physical world

The proper flow of *qi*

One important application of *qi* theory is called **fengshui**, which literally means "wind and water." This is the art of arranging objects and space—office furniture, houses, graves—with an awareness of the movement of *qi* through a certain area. For instance, it is believed that a burial site should ideally face south, with a mountain behind it to the north. This ensures that noxious *qi* is blocked and auspicious *qi* flows to the grave and collects there, benefitting the ancestors and thus the entire family. Fengshui masters are routinely hired for guidance in buying or situating homes, or arranging office space. These masters assess the presence and the nature of *qi* at a site, and determine the channels through which *qi* might flow, such as windows and streets. They also identify significant obstacles that might block its flow, such as hills and cul-de-sacs. With this information they give advice on how to design a building or arrange office furniture so that the flow of *qi* benefits the people using the site.

In medicine, a similar theory of *qi* is applied to flows of energy that travel through the human body. Just as fengshui masters must identify the movement of *qi* around a building or an office, doctors of traditional Chinese medicine monitor their patients' channels of *qi*, called **meridians**. Daoist practitioners even suggest that the body can be treated as a landscape, and use images like mountains and rivers to describe the body's internal components and structures. In all, the body is thought to have 12 meridians that carry *qi*, and illness is linked to a blockage or pooling of *qi* in one of the five main organs. For this reason, traditional doctors diagnose illnesses by taking a patient's pulse at different pulse points and depths, for it is commonly believed that when *qi* moves properly, blood also flows normally, promoting good health.

Standard therapies for the regulation of *qi* in the body are **acupuncture**, **moxibustion**, and **cupping**. Through acupuncture a specialist manipulates the flow of *qi* using pressure and needles that are inserted at specific nodes along the meridians (Figure 3.8). Moxibustion, which can be used in conjunction with acupuncture, is a corollary practice that employs heat from burning moxa (mugwort). This is a pungent herb commonly hung on the doors of homes and on clothing to fend off evil during certain times of the year. For moxibustion, the herb is fashioned into cigar-shaped rolls or ground into a powder and shaped into small cones. Then it is lit and allowed

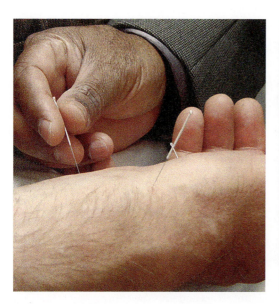 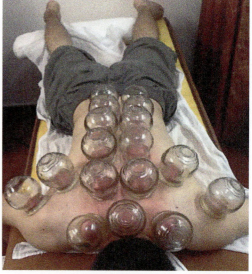

Figures 3.8 and 3.9 On the left (Figure 3.8), acupuncture needles are inserted into nodes of a patient's hand to treat arthritis. This quickens the flow of *qi* and promotes healing. On the right (Figure 3.9), cupping is used to draw fluids into particular areas of a patient's back. Sources: Wikimedia Commons (Figure 3.8) and Reproduced by permission of David Cai (Figure 3.9).

to smolder near critical areas or on the end of acupuncture needles inserted into the patient. The heat from the burning moxa is believed to dry out and warm the affected organs, which increases their *yang* and stimulates the proper flow of *qi*. Cupping, by contrast, is used to relieve the stagnation of *qi* by drawing fluids into an area (Figure 3.9). The air within a "cup" (a small glass jar) is heated and the cup is placed on an affected area. When the air within the cup cools, a vacuum is created, pulling in liquids from adjacent areas of the body.

Medicines are also used to recalibrate a patient's internal flow of *qi* by fortifying or replenishing certain types of *qi*. These medicines, which are either *yin* or *yang* in nature, are believed to cause one's *qi* to move in various ways (up, down, in, or out) through the body's meridians. Since doctors must consider the environmental particularities of a disease's time and place, as well as the specific profile of every patient (based on age, gender, horoscope, temperament, and numerous other factors), prescriptions are unique to each person. Chinese medical practitioners use all kinds of organic and inorganic ingredients, including herbs, insects, dried animal parts, and minerals, and most pharmacies have 100 to 200 ingredients on hand that can be mixed into the needed powders, tinctures, and infusions. Sometimes a medicine requires up to 20 ingredients, each measured out precisely for the individual patient. If the disease is chronic, the proportions and ingredients of a prescription are altered as the patient's condition improves or declines, and as seasonal and climatic variables change.

Diet and exercise

Medicine is considered part of **yangsheng**, or the practice of nurturing life, and needs to be practiced alongside other therapies, such as diet and physical exercise. The seventh-century Chinese physician Sun Simiao stated that a good doctor, having made a diagnosis, tries to cure the problem first with food. The medical benefits of food are assessed with regard to the Five Phases and the **Five Flavors**—sour, bitter, sweet, acrid, and salty—each flavor being assigned a *yin* or *yang* effect. Bitter, for instance, is the most *yin* flavor, and foods classified as bitter are used to reduce fevers and inflammation, as the nature of *yin* is cooling and settling. In nonmedical settings, Chinese cuisine practices a similar moderation in flavor and potency. Care is taken to offer foods that suit people's individual dispositions, as well as the particularities of weather and season. For instance, crab, which is seen as a very *yin*, or "cold" food, should be served in summer to offset the summer's heat. Venison, on the other hand, is a good winter food, because it is considered warming. It is common for restaurants to advertise seasonal menus (Figure 3.10).

Certain physical exercises also contribute to one's balance of *yin qi* and *yang qi*. Early in the morning at parks and other open spaces in Chinese communities, one can see large numbers of people moving in unison with one another. Many are performing **taiji quan** (also spelled *t'ai-chi ch'uan*), which has been called China's national exercise. It consists of breath control and fluid movements designed to circulate *qi* in the body, thereby increasing both one's energy level and one's mental acuity. Morning

Figure 3.10 This Taiwanese restaurant advertises a warming entrée—goat (or mutton) hotpot—which is considered a *yang* food, best eaten in winter. During the summer, this same restaurant will offer a lavish menu of cooling, *yin* foods (usually seafood) to counteract the heat of that season. Source: Reproduced by permission of Jennifer Oldstone-Moore.

is chosen because fresh *qi* is thought to permeate the morning air. The various movements of *taiji quan* are modeled after the more assertive and aggressive actions of the martial arts as practiced by certain Buddhist and Daoist monks, such as Shaolin and Wudang Quan. These, in turn, are thought to be abstractions of cosmic patterns of change, now reduced to the scale of the human body. By alternating between quick and slow, up and down, and pushing and pulling movements, practitioners of *taiji quan* are able to imitate and harmonize themselves with the workings of the universe. Beginning with "movement and settling," they perform and develop several modes of motion and stillness (e.g., stretching and contracting). They end with a final movement and settling that returns them to their original places and postures. The entire exercise is said to trace out a map of the Dao.

As an alternative to *taiji quan*, some Chinese have taken up *qigong*, a therapeutic practice that heals and strengthens through concentration and movements that stimulate *qi*. This is actually a recent development, first promoted by the PRC in the 1960s as a way to deemphasize the religious connotations inherent in *taiji quan*. But even though the language of *qigong* avoids images from Chinese metaphysics, its overall purpose is still to harmonize practitioners with larger cosmic patterns.

Rituals, Rites, Practices

Daoist Internal Alchemy

Daoist internal alchemy uses meditation and visualization, sexual practices, breathing, diet, and hygiene to cultivate long life. Historically it derives from the ancient search for elixirs that would transform the body into an immortal vessel, or "embryo of immortality." Over time, virtual practices developed, enacted in the interior of the body. These relied on materials from the body—saliva, blood, sexual fluids—rather than externally created elixirs.

(continued)

> Through meditation and visualization, the modern practitioner of internal alchemy takes a journey into the body, coordinating its interior landscape with the outside world. One might visualize ascending Spine Ridge (a pathway up the back) to Kunlun Mountain (located in the head). There they would find a lake (the base of the mouth) and a bridge (the tongue) that leads to a 12-story tower (the trachea). This interplay of microcosm and macrocosm works in the other direction as well. The remote regions of the world, said to be inhabited by Daoist immortals, are described and named with language referring to the human body. A tight passage in a cave, for example, might be designated Birth Canal.

The patterns of time

To remain oriented to the ever-changing cosmos, it is especially important for a person to understand patterns of time, for the passage of time is at the heart of change. Not surprisingly, Chinese divisions of time are highly complex, using a number of interlocking systems. For annual cycles of time, two calendars are used, one lunar and one solar. The lunar calendar divides the year into 12 months, with a thirteenth month added every two or three years to keep the months roughly aligned with the seasons. The first day of each month is a new moon; the fifteenth day is the full moon. As a month progresses, the phases of the moon indicate rising and falling levels of *yin* and *yang*. Likewise, days and years are divided to mark this ebb and flow: morning, noon, and night; solstices and equinoxes. The solar calendar, which is used simultaneously with the lunar calendar, divides the year into 24 half-months, called "breaths." These, in turn, have names that mark pivotal events in the year (such as equinoxes), or names descriptive of nature and the weather in northern China, where they were devised. For instance, the half-month Cold Dew comes in late fall, while Insects Awaken comes in the spring.

Using the lunar system, Chinese also measure longer periods of cosmic change in 60-year segments, called sexagenary cycles (i.e., rather than 100-year cycles, or centuries). Each of these sexagenary cycles consists of two smaller cycles called the Twelve Earthly Branches and the Ten Heavenly Stems. The Twelve Earthly Branches, more commonly known as the 12 Chinese zodiac animals and often found on placemats in Chinese restaurants, are given animal names: rat, ox, tiger, horse, dragon, rabbit, snake, pig, dog, monkey, sheep, and rooster. The Ten Heavenly Stems, by contrast, were originally names for the days in a 10-day week. Grouped in pairs with a color from one of the Five Colors and a phase from one of the Five Phases, these pairs are then individually assigned to one of the Twelve Earthly Branches to produce 5 cycles of *12* in a 60-year cycle of uniquely named years, each with its own zodiac animal, color, and phase (see the chapter-opening photo). To find one's place in this cycle of time, a person need only determine the year of their birth. Birthdays that occur at multiples of 12 years in the cycle are considered exceptionally fortunate, as they complete one of the Earthly Branches, and a birthday in the sixtieth year is even more so, as it completes the entire sexagenary cycle.

When a person's birth year is then combined with the particular month, hour, and minute of one's birth, one's place in the cosmic order is further clarified. This is accomplished by assigning two Chinese characters to each of these four elements (year, month, hour, and minute), one character designating an Earthly Branch and one designating one of the Five Phases. As a result, a person is identified with four pairs of two characters, or eight characters altogether, called *bazi*, which are used in Chinese horoscopes. In former times, parents took the Eight Characters of a prospective bride and groom to an astrologer to ensure the compatibility of the couple. Today's couples still use the Eight Characters in this way, some in fun, others quite seriously.

Assessing the future

Situating people in a predictable pattern of time not only yields information about their present situation and opportunities, but also raises the possibility of discerning their futures as that pattern unfolds. One way to do this is by using a Chinese almanac. Among the first books ever published in China, the almanac tracks the ebb and flow of *yin* and *yang* over the course of a year and explains what this might mean with regard to one's personal information, such as one's zodiac animal or *bazi*. On this basis, it then specifies times that burials or marriages should or should not take place, and identifies what days are "lucky" for buying clothes or getting a haircut, etc.

Another method, which is provided by many temples, involves a canister filled with numbered sticks. To determine their fortune, a person picks up the canister, tilts it sideways, and shakes it until a stick emerges. After looking at the number on the stick, the person takes this information to a temple attendant in a kiosk to receive a corresponding piece of paper that contains divinatory words, usually from the *Yijing*, the ancient *Classic of Change*. Finally, to get an even more detailed picture of future changes and likely events, many Chinese consult professional fortunetellers. Some of these can be found at community temples, while others operate from kiosks in markets or on the street.

A Closer Look

Trigrams and Hexagrams

The *Yijing* (the *Classic of Change*) investigates the patterns of change underlying trigrams and hexagrams. These symbols were said to have been discovered by Fuxi, a mythic ruler who created the **Eight Trigrams** based on his observations of patterns in the heavens and earth (Figure 3.11). In the *Yijing*, *yin* is designated by a broken line, *yang* by an unbroken line. *Yin* and *yang* lines are organized into trigrams, composed of different combinations and orders of three *yin* and *yang* lines. The trigrams are further grouped into pairs to make hexagrams. In all, there are 64 possible hexagrams used for *Yijing* divination, each indicating the flow and change of *yin* and *yang*.

(continued)

Figure 3.11 A traditional depiction of the eight trigrams circling the Great Ultimate, a fluid and balanced image of *yin* and *yang*.

Annual religious festivals

In addition to situating individuals in cosmic patterns of time, attention to patterns can also orient entire households and communities with a moment or a season. This sort of communal orientation to the shifting universe takes place especially at religious festivals, where entire groups can reap the benefits offered by a particular point in time or guard against dangers inherent in a growing imbalance of *yin* and *yang*.

The Lunar New Year Also called the Spring Festival, the Lunar New Year is the most widely celebrated festival in Chinese religion. Usually falling somewhere between January 21 and February 19, it celebrates the advent of spring and the return of *yang qi*. Preparation for the New Year is elaborate, and people go to great effort to make sure the old year is properly and fully concluded. They clean their homes, wrap up old obligations and debts, buy new clothes, and prepare large quantities of foods so that no chopping or cooking needs to be done on the first days of the New Year. Businesses close their ledgers, throw end-of-year parties, and hand out yearly bonuses.

Preparation for the New Year also includes wrapping up one's business with the spirit world. On the 23rd day of the last lunar month, families send their **Kitchen God** to Heaven. Each family is assigned a Kitchen God, which is usually a colorful image of the god printed on paper and placed over the stove. Since the kitchen is the best place to observe small family dramas and listen in on gossip, the role of the Kitchen God is to keep watch over a family's activities and report back to the **Jade Emperor**, the celestial bureaucrat who oversees Heaven. Since the Emperor uses this information to determine a family's fortune in the coming year, it is traditional to smear the Kitchen God's lips with something sticky and sweet before sending him to heaven. This ensures that he will either say sweet things in his report, or his lips will stick together so he can only mumble any criticisms he might have. The printed image of the Kitchen God is burned in the family hearth so that he may ascend in the smoke. He is then replaced with a new paper image for the coming year.

Ideally, scattered members of a family come together for the New Year to renew family bonds. Train tickets and hotels are sold out and the whole country is on the move as everyone tries to return home for this holiday. On New Year's Eve families eat a special meal and play games into the night. Ancestors are honored as well. They are invited to partake in the New Year's Eve feast, and they receive gestures of respect at the family altar. Children show respect to their parents, often with a formal bow called a *kowtow*, kneeling on the ground and bowing until the head touches the floor. Today the *kowtow* may be done with a more lighthearted air than in past centuries. Parents and elders also show affection for their children and give them red envelopes (*hong bao*) that contain a gift of money for the coming year. This is the family's way to align itself to the seasonal change: to celebrate while waiting together for the powerful, fresh *yang qi* of the New Year. When the moment finally comes, the family opens the front door to welcome the rejuvenating breath of the rising *yang*.

Through their behavior during the first days of the New Year, family members continue their efforts to foster good luck in the coming year. All talk must be amiable and pleasant, since bickering is a bad omen, and there is no cooking or cleaning, so that no one cuts or sweeps away this good luck. Beyond this, festive decorations are displayed to promote wealth, childbirth, social status, and good health; people wear new red clothes as a way to participate in the ascending *yang* of the season; and firecrackers are used to make things festive and lively, and to scare away ghosts.

> ### A Closer Look
>
> ## New Year's Dumplings
>
> Dumplings are a favorite food of northern Chinese. Typically, they are made with pork minced with green onion, cabbage, garlic, and ginger, but they can have almost any filling. Some dumpling masters make exotic fillings such as walnut paste or lotus seed. The mixture is placed onto a flour skin that is then pinched shut in a distinctive shape. Dumplings may be boiled (*jiaozi*) or fried (*guotie*, "potstickers").

(continued)

> At New Year's, a dumpling's ingredients and form convey good wishes for the coming year. Peanuts and seeds (whose pronunciation sounds like the Chinese word for "children") indicate the hope for offspring. Likewise, the traditional shape for dumplings resembles an old-fashioned Chinese gold ingot, and so having an abundance of dumplings is like having an abundance of wealth—a good omen for financial success in the coming year. Since each dumpling must be formed by hand, and since New Year's gatherings are typically very large, dumpling making becomes a communal activity—especially since many families also eat dumplings on Guo Nian, or New Year's Eve. Groups of people often make large mountains of dumplings.

Lion and dragon dances New Year's festivities continue for two weeks, ending on the full moon of the first month with the Lantern Festival. Cheerful and cleverly designed lanterns in all shapes and sizes create a festive atmosphere, and the roundness and brightness of the moon is seen as an omen of good luck for the completeness of the family and its bright prospects for the future. During the two weeks before the Lantern Festival, the days are filled with visits to friends and relatives (which allows children to collect more red envelopes), and eating special foods that impart blessings for wealth, long life, and many children. Particular days are designated for visiting various family members and for propitiating particular gods. Large public celebrations and spectacles also take place, two of the most striking being the lion dance and the dragon dance.

The lion is a powerful, protective beast whose dance exorcizes evil spirits and brings good luck to the community. The dance, which is highly gymnastic, is performed by two dancers, one managing the head and front legs, the other, the rest of the body (Figure 3.12). As with many theatrical offerings in China, its primary audience is the spirit world, although the dance draws large crowds from the human community as well. Typically, the lion dancers canvass neighborhood businesses, whose owners tempt the beast with food such as greens or cabbages. When the lion catches these morsels in its mouth, the owner gives it (through its huge mouth) a red envelope with money in exchange for good luck. All this is done to the incessant popping of firecrackers that scare away ghosts and to make things festive.

Dragons, who are even more powerful omens of good fortune and fertility, are seen as the consummate *yang* creatures. For the dragon dances, long, serpentine costumes are constructed. These consist of a head, a tail, and several sections of snakelike body in between, each carried by a separate dancer, and all connected by a fabric canopy. From head to tail, typical dragons can be 20 feet long. The daunting task of preparing a dragon and learning to work with others in the complicated dragon dance is a chance to pass on skills, strengthen relationships between family members, and demonstrate clan solidarity. An extended family may create an especially long dragon, with each family group contributing a section of the dragon. In smaller communities, several clans may band together, and in urban areas, dragon clubs organize work units or neighborhood groups. The dance itself is very demanding, with intricate, coordinated moves that require tremendous stamina. As a dragon master beats a

Figure 3.12 A tradition at New Year's celebrations, the lion dance is performed by two skilled gymnast-dancers who often climb ladders and leap from pedestal to pedestal. Lion dances can be commissioned for other happy occasions as well. Source: Reproduced by permission of Chow Shu-ka.

large drum and shouts, the dragon spins and jumps, led by a dancer who tempts the dragon with a large golden pearl. This pearl is said to be the sun or a pill that gives immortality. At the New Year's celebration in 2000, a giant dragon, extending almost 2 miles along China's Great Wall, was animated by 5000 dancers from Hong Kong, the PRC, and Chinese communities overseas.

Double Five Taking place at the height of summer, on the fifth day of the fifth lunar month, Double Five (*Duanwu*) marks the summer solstice, which is considered a critical point in the movement of *yin* and *yang*. The festival's focus is to protect people from the dangers of too much *yang* while preparing for the return of *yin*. Since a chief danger associated with the zenith of *yang* energy is epidemics, people mix aromatic, protective herbs during Double Five and carry them in small sachets or hang them on their doors. The particular herbs that are chosen are thought to ward off noxious vapors and must be gathered at their peak of potency—namely, shortly before the peak of *yang*. Some of these protective plants resemble weapons, like the herb known as sweet flag, which has the appearance of daggers and swords. Others are pungent herbs such as mugwort. People also wear the Five Colors (red, blue, yellow, black, and white), which are associated with the Five Phases and the Five Poisons: scorpion, centipede, spider, lizard, and toad. When brought together like this, these creatures are considered a powerful tool to navigate the dangers of surplus *yang* energy and thereby thwart the forces of illness and disorder.

Double Five is also the occasion for racing dragon boats. These are long, thin vessels, some with 60 or more rowers, whose rowing rhythm is regulated by a loud drumbeat. The boats get their name from their bows, or figureheads, which are carved in the shape of a dragon's head. Dragon boat races are considered appropriate during Double Five for several, somewhat unrelated reasons. On the one hand, dragons are associated with fire and heat, and therefore gravitate to the extreme *yang* of the summer solstice. But this solstice also brings the summer rains, when the rivers are full and suited for racing, and this is fitting because dragons are creatures of the water—Dragon Kings make their home in the seas. Finally, Double Five is a time to remember Qu Yuan, a poet, statesman, and exemplary human being who lived in the time of the ancient Zhou dynasty. A worthy and virtuous civil servant, Qu bemoaned his king's disregard for his advice. He became depressed, and after writing a long lament, flung himself into a river and drowned. In an attempt to save his corpse from being devoured by the fish, people raced about in boats, looking for his body among the river plants. They also put rice in the water as an offering to Qu's spirit. The dragon boat race thus recalls the frantic search for Qu Yuan, while a favorite food of Double Five festivals, a glutinous rice wrapped in lotus leaves (*zongzi*), recalls the water plants and the rice of the story.

The Feast of the Hungry Ghosts   Pudu, or the Feast of the Hungry Ghosts, draws extensively on Buddhist traditions. It is observed on the full moon of the seventh lunar month, which is when the gates of hell open, releasing the malevolent and uncared-for dead, who are suffering for sins committed in previous lifetimes. Even though the community is put in danger by their release, it also has the opportunity to help free them from their torments. Temples hire Daoist and Buddhist priests to chant liturgies that urge the ghosts to repent. **Spirit money**, the currency of the spirit world, is purchased at kiosks near the temples and sent to the spirit world by burning it. This provides spirits with the financial means to navigate the underworld by bribing corrupt spirit officials and bullies. Spirit money typically looks like currency used by the living, sometimes closely resembling American dollars.

Chinese also put out food for ghosts, who are thought to suffer from chronic hunger. Typically, the food is placed at the back door of homes, which prevents the ghosts from loitering around the front door or mistaking the food for an invitation to come inside. Food is also arranged quite elaborately in public areas to draw ghosts away from homes, and sometimes on boats for those spirits who are bound to the water, perhaps because of drowning. Once the spirits have eaten the food's spirit essence, the living can enjoy its material remains. Finally, ghosts are treated to operatic performances during Pudu, for both their entertainment and their edification. One very popular opera is based on a scripture from India that describes the effort and determination of Mulian, a Buddhist monk and devoted son who saved his evil mother from the torments of hell through a harrowing adventure in the underworld. This is a powerful and attractive story for Chinese, for it emphasizes the solidarity of family and the duties of a child to a parent, even after the child has chosen to leave home and pursue the individualistic life of a celibate monk.

The Mid-autumn Festival The last major festival of the lunar cycle is the Mid-autumn Festival. Timed to coincide with the fall equinox, it is celebrated on the full moon of the eighth month (near the end of September). This has traditionally been a harvest celebration, the full moon emulating the roundness and completion of the growing season and the togetherness of family. At this festival, the *yang* seasons of growing and harvesting are brought to an end, and *yin* begins to predominate. The Mid-autumn Festival also celebrates Chinese traditions and ideas of immortality. Festival goers remember the story of the Lady in the Moon, Chang E, who drank an elixir of immortality intended for her husband and floated off to the moon. The harvest moon itself is said to be inhabited by a toad or rabbit (stories vary) who prepares potent medicines for longevity by pounding together their ingredients; and a favorite food at this time is mooncakes, which are round pastries with sweet fillings. People go out in groups at night, ideally on boats, to see the moon's reflections in the water, tell moon stories, and recite traditional poems about the moon. Whatever the mix of people, the harmony and balance of the season should be reflected in the harmony of the festival goers.

A Closer Look

Moon Poems

Poetry became an important medium in China for expressing deep concerns of family, connections with nature, and the value placed on education and culture as a means of self-improvement. Li Bai (701–762 CE) is one of the most famous of all Chinese poets. He wrote during the Tang dynasty, a golden age of poetry, and is credited with over a thousand poems, a third of which express reverence and love for the moon. Many are playful, and one famous moon poem recounts drinking and dancing alone in the moonlight. The moon poem below, however, expresses a longing for home, a sentiment often inspired by the moon in Chinese poetry since friends and family who are far away can nonetheless gaze at the same moon. It is a poem known by most Chinese and frequently recited at the Moon Festival.

> The bright moonbeams shine before my bed;
> They seem like frost on the ground.
> I lift my head and gaze at the bright moon;
> Lowering my head, I dream of my old home.

床前明月光
疑是地上霜
舉頭望明月
低頭思故鄉

A community rite of cosmic renewal

In contrast to annual festivals, the Jiao, which means offering ritual, is sponsored by communities at varying intervals, such as every 3, 5, 10, or 60 years. Lasting several days, a Jiao includes offerings, music, opera, theater, gymnastic displays, and parades, all of which contribute to a grand liturgy whose goal is to bless and renew the entire community by calling down the primal energies of the universe. After community members have purified themselves by abstaining from meat, a Daoist priest creates a universe in miniature in the ritual space of the community temple. The ritual he performs for the community is simultaneously a ritual of self-cultivation, by which he internalizes primal Dao. Working behind the scenes with a retinue of ritual specialists, the priest envisions the patterns of the cosmos as a series of concentric circles. This allows him to break down the distinction between his body and the wider cosmos, and align the microcosm of his body with the macrocosm of the universe. His body becomes a chamber for cosmic rejuvenation: the external liturgy of the community is transformed through the internal alchemy in his body, and from there reverberates out into the universe. A particularly lavish Jiao, which lasted 12 days, was offered in Hong Kong in 2007. Liturgies overseen by more than 500 Daoist priests from several countries were conducted to bring about world peace, the harmony of *yin* and *yang*, and an end to cataclysmic natural disasters. The 2007 Jiao also gave thanks for the PRC's successful rule of Hong Kong since 1997, and especially for the continued prosperity of Hong Kong businesses.

Patterns in human society

The second fundamental category of patterns that must be mastered in Chinese religion governs the structures and changes within human society. One way to understand these patterns is to examine the notions of **li** and **ren**, two concepts emphasized by Confucius and the School of Scholars (Confucianism). *Li* can mean "etiquette," "protocol," or "ritual," and it is assumed that all human relationships have a specific *li*. This becomes complicated, however, because relationships change over time and from one context to the next. A daughter does not have the same social interactions (*li*) with her mother at age 3 as she does when she is 30. Likewise, a person must be guided by a different demeanor (*li*), respectively, at a family dinner, a concert, and while shopping in a store. Indeed, everyone present at the dinner, or the concert, or in the store assumes particular social obligations (*li*): the host must act differently than the dinner guest, the performer differently than the audience, and the produce manager differently than the cashier or the customer.

Ren, in turn, means "human heartedness," "benevolence," and "humaneness." It is the sentiment and attitude that makes the etiquette aspect of *li* come alive—the warmth that makes the ritual component of *li* effective. When social rituals are performed with *ren*, relationships are appropriate, fulfilling, and harmonious, enabling humans to contribute to the harmony of the family, the community, the state, and finally the universe.

Five essential human relationships

A second approach to the patterns within human society, which complements the first, begins with the **Five Relationships**, which are the human relationships that Confucius saw as the basis for all the others. They comprise the relationship between:

- a parent and a child,
- a ruler and a subordinate,
- an eldest brother and a younger brother,
- a husband and a wife, and
- a friend and a friend.

In social situations, Chinese are careful to call people by their correct social titles. This is part of a practice that Confucius had referred to as the rectification of names, and it assumes that a name, when matched with its appropriate social behaviors, can become a powerful means for bringing about harmony. Thus, there is no single word for "sister" in Chinese, only words that designate "older sister" and "younger sister." Likewise, there is no one word for "uncle," but a number of words that denote specifically the older or younger brother or brother-in-law of one's mother or father.

What becomes clear from this model is that people are expected to function within webs of relationships that are governed by distinct assumptions. Its complexity, moreover, becomes apparent when one realizes that every person necessarily plays a variety of social roles. As contexts change, a woman might fill the role of mother, daughter, daughter-in-law, wife, and friend in a single day, each role requiring different behaviors. Thus, while the process of learning proper human relationships follows basic principles, it is the work of a lifetime, demanding attentive study. Not surprisingly, there are also safety valves for this complex system of social relations, so that it does not become oppressive. One of these is a collection of stories describing the outrageous behavior of the Buddhist saint Jigong, whose antisocial antics have made him a champion of impropriety (Figure 3.13).

The parent and child relationship By far the most important social relationship in Chinese religion is the one between a parent and a child. As the first interaction a human being encounters, it frames the basic components of all future relationships in life. Ideally, a parent provides a child with care and sustenance, and takes responsibility for the child's moral and intellectual formation. Regarding a child's education, which can bring prestige to the whole clan (including the ancestors), it is typical for parents to register children for tutorials and extracurricular courses on school evenings and weekends. Many children take supplemental courses in language, music, and art, since these are seen as especially valuable in nurturing a child's intellectual capacity. While Chinese children are as overscheduled as their American counterparts, the difference is that most of their activities are not for leisure or entertainment, but academic in nature and designed to improve their chances for success at the university. Because education is still the road to social advancement, prestige, and wealth in China, Taiwan, and Singapore, parents keep a sharp eye on a child's daily efforts. A mother may bring little snacks to her child throughout the evening, checking on their progress in completing school lessons.

Figure 3.13 The horseshoe-shaped gravesite is common in Taiwan and southern regions of China. The shape of the grave maximizes the effect of good *fengshui* by trapping and collecting any auspicious *qi* that flows toward it. Source: Reproduced by permission of Shelley W. Chan.

Because Chinese education also includes a moral component, parents expect teachers to exert moral influence on students, not simply provide knowledge. They value teachers who are very strict and who give unsolicited advice to students about boyfriends and girlfriends, smoking and drinking, and diligence in schoolwork. Popular folklore envisions a special place in hell for lenient teachers, for if teachers fail to do their job, moral chaos will result, destroying any hope for social harmony.

A Closer Look

Sons, Little Emperors, and Little Empresses

Many Chinese couples believe it is necessary to have a son. Since families trace descent through the male line, one of the most important marks of a child's obedience is producing a male heir to continue the family. Furthermore, when a Chinese woman marries, she usually leaves her birth family and joins her husband's family, accepting his ancestors as her own. In this situation, her closest and most important blood relation is her son. He and his descendants will care for her in her old age and remember her in acts of veneration after her death.

The PRC's former policy of allowing couples to have only one child challenged this traditional preference for a son, but did not displace it entirely. China's one-child policy (1980–2015) was implemented after demographic

(continued)

> studies indicated the PRC would face grave difficulties in providing for its exploding population unless extreme measures were taken. An unforeseen consequence was the disruption it caused to the Confucian ideal of parent–child relationships, for under this policy a typical child had six doting adults: two parents and two sets of grandparents. This created "little emperors" and "little empresses," undermining traditional norms of obedience and submission to parental authority. After 2015, couples were allowed to have two children and since 2021, there have been no restrictions on family size.

For their part, children must show concern, deference, and respect to a parent, and eventually provide care to an elderly parent. This relationship is translated into English as **filial piety**, indicating its considerable—indeed, religious—significance. It is generally held that the obligation of a child to a parent is a debt that can never be repaid. Just as parents tend to a child's every need, especially in the first three years of life, so too must children grow up with the expectation that they will return this gift by caring for the needs of aging parents. Stemming from the very gift of life itself, this obligation is what one scholar has called a "velvet bond": soft but unyielding. Popular stories of exemplary filial piety in earlier times even describe extreme measures of care and self-sacrifice, such as using one's own flesh to feed and cure a sick parent.

Ancestors

Human society, according to Chinese religion, extends into the afterlife. The dead are an extension of the living community, and ancestors are treated as part of the family. Offspring show gratitude and affection to the departed, and ancestors bless their progeny with fertility and good fortune. Funeral rituals are an important means to care for the souls of the departed so that they continue to be a source of blessing for a family. Although Chinese ideas about the human soul are not systematic—there is, for example, no universally agreed upon number of souls per person—each person is said to have two kinds of souls: **hun souls**, which are *yang* and the rational aspect of consciousness, and **po souls**, which are *yin* and the source of one's bodily strength and physical awareness. While a person is alive, these souls are joined together to provide both rational capacity and animal vigor. At death they separate, the *hun* rising and the *po* settling into the earth.

Funeral rituals, which are presided over by both Buddhist and Daoist clergy, are intended to help these souls in their ascent and decent, respectively. Since most *po* souls are thought to go to an underworld where they are judged and punished, the attending priest performs rituals designed to speed them through their sentences. To provide some comfort during this ordeal, families send them spirit money and paper renditions of mansions, cars with chauffeurs, dishwashers, CD players, and other such amenities. Families may also select auspicious gravesites. In Taiwan and south China, it is typical to see horseshoe shaped graves with the opening facing south, so as to benefit from flows of auspicious *qi* in the landscape (Figure 3.14).

After the burial, it is important for a family to return to the grave annually to reaffirm its solidarity with the dead. This visit takes place in early April on Grave Sweeping Day, a season of new life and renewal. Also known as the "Clear and Bright Festival" (*Qingming*), it is a bittersweet time: family members remember the dead—some fondly, some with tears, depending on the freshness and poignancy of their bereavement—and together they clear away debris that may have accumulated on the grave during the year. They also take cold foods for a family picnic, offering some to the ancestors.

In addition to caring for *po* souls, funeral rites must also situate the ascending *hun* souls in a **spirit tablet**. This is a small placard that is placed on the family altar alongside images of deities worshipped by the family. Often located in the living room, this altar provides a setting for small gifts of incense, fruit, water, tea, or wine to be offered the *hun* souls enshrined there. A spirit tablet remains on a family's altar while the ancestor it enshrines is more or less within the memory of the living—no more than three to five generations. When an ancestor becomes more remote, their tablet is moved to a shrine shared by all the families of a clan. Here rites of respect and supplication are performed annually for the entire group.

Figure 3.14 Jigong is a disruptive Buddhist saint who eats meat, drinks alcohol, and once somersaulted in front of the empress without any underwear beneath his robes. Often called the "meat-eating monk," he is beloved precisely because he flouts bureaucracy and codes of propriety. He is especially concerned with the socially powerless, who often benefit least—and suffer most—from official rules. Several coins have been placed on this carving by worshippers making specific petitions. Source: Reproduced by permission of Jennifer Oldstone-Moore.

Ghosts

If the departed are not treated properly, they become ghosts rather than ancestors—dispossessed spirits that are lonely, hungry, and disgruntled. Although they typically have rather limited powers, ghosts can show their displeasure by haunting or cursing people. If this happens, individuals and families seek the help of a priest, diviner, or exorcist and attempt to appease a ghost with offerings of spirit money, food, drink, and incense. The dead can also become ghosts for unavoidable reasons, such as a violent or tragic death. These sorts of ghosts are said to haunt the places where they died, hoping to lure someone into sharing their same fate. When family lines die out, or infants or the unmarried die, it can become difficult to placate angry ghosts because the Chinese family structure, with its emphasis on filial piety, assumes that there will be children to venerate and sustain the forebears. Rituals focusing on the souls of stillborn or aborted fetuses are designed to prevent them from haunting their parents as ghosts or possessing siblings and causing bad behavior, while related rituals attempt to assuage a parent's sorrow or feelings of guilt. Many Chinese believe that if the fetus ghost finds rest it can be reincarnated, sometimes as a child of the bereaved parents.

Immortals

In a class all by themselves are those who never die: the immortals. The quest for immortality in China employs all the practices of bodily and spiritual self-cultivation, including eating according to the theories of *yin* and *yang*, physical exercise, meditation, and developing the qualities of the *junzi* (gentleman). The immortals are those who have perfected these practices, thereby harmonizing their bodies and souls with the Dao to such a degree that they slip the bonds of mortal existence. Freed from the toils of both humans and gods, and avoiding the hardships of the dead, they are looked upon with awe and admiration. Some of those who have obtained immortality are believed to inhabit the space between Heaven and Earth, having the ability to fly. Others live as hermits in remote places, such as mountains or distant islands, and occasionally appear to travelers as tattered beggars, ready to disclose secrets of immortality or share elixirs of longevity with those who treat them kindly.

Patterns in the spirit government

The third and final grouping of cosmic patterns in Chinese religion pertains to relationships that connect humans with gods. Most gods were once illustrious humans who were given a divine status at death, rather than becoming ancestors. Worshippers, either individually or corporately, make offerings to the gods, and the gods reciprocate with gifts of health, prosperity, status, and progeny. To benefit from this system, gods must continually give proof that they are spiritually powerful, or **ling**. Otherwise, worshippers direct their petitions and offerings to other gods, impoverishing and dishonoring the ineffective ones. In practical terms, since it is expected that family members will support their own ancestors, one could say that the act of *non*-family members making offerings to a spirit is what creates and sustains gods.

Most Chinese gods are envisioned as the royalty and civil servants of a vast spirit government modeled on the bureaucratic ideals of premodern, imperial China. They are not all-knowing or all-powerful beings, but figures of varying authority who keep order in the human and spirit communities and provide services. Just as human bureaucrats are called by their titles, such as "fire chief" or "district attorney," gods are typically known by titles rather than personal names. Each has a jurisdiction and sphere of influence, and most can be petitioned for favors and special requests. A god connected with commerce, for example, may be particularly effective at bolstering one's business, whereas a god in charge of education or health care services might be able to provide success in school or the cure for an illness. A well-positioned god—and a timely gift—can even gain the petitioner a hearing in higher circles of bureaucratic authority. As in human governments, bureaucratic positions in the divine government remain constant, while the gods who occupy these positions are periodically evaluated for promotion or demotion. If a god is deemed ineffective and human support dwindles, they are removed and another takes the position.

Temples

Since the logic of bureaucracy is the dominant model for interacting with the gods, Chinese temples resemble a palace or magistrate's office. They are funded and operated by laypeople in the community, who use them as centers for accessing the spiritual world. Community members provide for their upkeep and personnel, such as groundskeepers, and bear the expense of community rituals, which often require hiring a Daoist or Buddhist priest and his entourage. Although a tourist to China or Taiwan may find guidebooks describing any number of "Daoist" temples, very few temples are specifically Daoist, or Confucian, or Buddhist. In most cases, gods from all three traditions, as well as gods from no particular tradition at all, are honored at these community temples. For those who worship there, the religious tradition of a god is irrelevant; what is important is the god's accessibility and power.

A Closer Look

Chinese Temples

In China, "temple" usually refers to a complex of buildings surrounded by a high wall. The gates to a temple open into a courtyard where the main buildings are arranged symmetrically. Courtyards often have one or more incense braziers and places to offer candles and prayers, and a decorative stele—a large, carved stone slab bearing a poem, a story, a dedication, or the biography of a famous person. After lighting incense and bowing in the courtyard, worshippers climb steps to a sanctuary to pray to the god or gods housed there, often kneeling reverently. A table in front of the deity is for candles, food and drink, and other offerings. Many temples include offices or quarters for attendants, a kitchen, a gift shop, storage areas, and meeting places. The courtyards of large temples may be used by the community as a place to spread and dry harvested grain on mats.

Worship at a temple is usually done privately, motivated by personal concerns, and people visit the temple as frequently or as seldom as they like. Some worshippers come daily, as when praying for someone who is suffering from an illness, while others come only when their astrological birth year completes a 12-year cycle, so they can make an offering for success and health in the next cycle. Worshippers typically bring incense and spirit money, and after lighting the former in the temple courtyard, they stand facing the entrance of the sanctuary holding the incense in front of them and bow to the four directions. They then place the incense in a large brazier and put the spirit money in a special furnace. Worshippers may also bring food or drink as offerings. These are usually raw, or at least unprocessed, and include bottles of wine and cooking oil, whole fruit, and whole animals, such as a chicken or a pig. Unlike offerings to ancestors that consist of family-style meals, one does not presume to share a meal with a god. Even so, once the gods have consumed the spirit essence of the food, the worshippers can share what remains among themselves, which, when eaten, is thought to have beneficial qualities. After these offerings, worshippers proceed to the sanctuary where they voice their petitions on their knees, with prayerful hands and a bowed head.

At certain temples, worshippers can interact with the gods through divination and mediums. Divination practices at temples employ two moon blocks, which are crescent-shaped pieces of wood, often painted red, each with a flat and a round side. The worshipper asks the gods a question and throws the blocks. If the blocks land in a "balanced" arrangement, one in the *yin* position (its flat side down), the other in the *yang* position (its round side down), then the answer is "yes." Otherwise, the answer is "no."

Mediums are persons chosen by a god or gods, sometimes through a chronic illness, to be spokespersons for the unseen world. They generally cannot escape their callings, and many assume that they are fated to have short lives as a consequence of this service. Some act as vessels through which a god speaks, while others receive messages from the gods through spirit writing. In this practice a medium holds the legs of a small chair, which functions as the god's throne. When the god is seated, the legs of the chair dip and trace shapes resembling Chinese writing, either in a pan of sand or in the air, which the medium then interprets.

If Daoist priests are present at a temple, they can wield their powers to summon or even control many of the gods. These priests are generally divided into two sorts, called "black headed" and "red headed," in reference to the headgear they wear when performing rituals. Red-headed priests generally serve one god and are shamans capable of curing illnesses and performing exorcisms. Black-headed priests come equipped with copies of sacred texts, lavish vestments, and ritual implements that may have been passed down in their families for centuries. They usually inherit their positions, receive training from their fathers, and become ordained in the Orthodox Unity School. Black-headed priests typically specialize in certain scriptures from the Daoist canon, which encompasses well over a thousand volumes. Some black-headed priests even hire themselves out as sorcerers, using their knowledge of the Dao to hurt or threaten people on behalf of a client.

The variety of gods in Chinese religion

Gods in Chinese religion vary greatly. Some come from the folk tradition and some are associated with the Three Teachings. Many are manifestations of nature—gods of mountains, rivers, stars, thunder, and lightning—and three, known as the **Gods of**

Good Fortune, are identified with the life goals of longevity, prosperity, and progeny. Their images are found in most temples and are common in decorations for the home and places of business. Also found in most temples are the Three Pure Ones, a trio of Daoist gods who provide access to highly abstract cosmic principles and figure into rituals led by black-headed priests.

As mentioned earlier, most Chinese gods are thought to have begun their careers as human beings. By living exemplary lives, they are promoted at death to serve in the divine bureaucracy rather than becoming ancestors. Biographies of gods usually indicate that they died without progeny, because this makes their spiritual power (*ling*) accessible to nonfamily members rather than descendants. **Buddhas** and *bodhisattvas* are also part of the Chinese pantheon of gods. As elsewhere in Mahayana Buddhism, buddhas are enlightened beings who teach Buddhist law (the Dharma), and bodhisattvas are enlightened beings who have decided not to enter final nirvana at death, but reenter the world to help others achieve enlightenment. Identifying enlightened beings as gods actually contradicts Buddhist teachings, which hold that gods are *not* enlightened; but Chinese religion does not make this distinction.

By far the most important of these Buddhist figures is **Guanyin Pusa**, a *bodhisattva* whose name means "Hearer of Cries." Concerned especially with the troubles of women and children, Guanyin is the Chinese version of the Indian *bodhisattva* of compassion, Avalokiteshvara. Guanyin is also a good example of the way in which foreign figures can be transformed to fit Han Chinese culture. In China, this *bodhisattva* became linked with the story of Princess Miaoshan, who was the devout third daughter of a king. Because she wanted to devote herself wholly to Buddhism, she refused to marry and instead became a nun. This unfilial behavior infuriated her father, and he ordered that her convent be burnt down with her inside. The gods of the underworld were so shocked at this that they asked the Buddha to carry her to Mt. Putuo, where the Buddha rejoined her body with her soul. When the king was later afflicted with a terrible disease as punishment for his sins, Miaoshan appeared to him in disguise, offering him her own eyes and arms as medicine for the cure. When he thanked this selfless woman, she revealed herself as both his dutiful daughter and as a manifestation of Guanyin, thereby demonstrating that the Chinese ideal of filial piety is compatible with the Buddhist goal of renouncing the world. Today groups of pilgrims, especially women, travel to the city of Hangzhou and nearby Mt. Putuo to keep vigil on Miaoshan's birthday.

Other buddhas and *bodhisattvas* commonly seen in Chinese temples include:

- Shijia Fo, the historical Buddha who, as the man Siddhartha Gautama, discovered the way to enlightenment
- Omituo Fo, the buddha who presides over the Western Paradise of Pure Land Buddhism, China's most popular school of Buddhism
- Dizang Pusa, the *bodhisattva* who helps those troubled by ghosts of stillborn or aborted fetuses, shows compassion to children, and takes care of them in the spirit world
- Milo Fo, the future buddha.

Surprisingly, Confucius was never institutionalized as a god in Chinese religion, despite his exemplary life. Instead, he was honored by the imperial government (and now by the governments of the PRC, Singapore, and Taiwan) as the First Teacher and a worthy sage. Even so, it is typical for high school and college students to burn incense to Confucius at exam time in the hope of receiving guidance.

Many Chinese have drawn attention to the offerings and veneration given to the late Chairman Mao Zedong (1893–1976) by those outside his family, indicating his status as a god rather than an ancestor. His popularity as a deity, despite the firm atheism of both his regime and the present Chinese government, can be seen in such things as protective Mao amulets used by taxis drivers to keep them safe from accidents.

The Jade Emperor and the King of Hell Two gods who serve at the very highest levels of the spirit bureaucracy are the Jade Emperor and the King of Hell. The Jade Emperor oversees the entire spirit government through a multitude of cabinet members, civil servants, and clerks, but because he is so powerful, he is largely inaccessible to the average Chinese. Offerings are given to him on the ninth day of the New Year, and as stated earlier, the Kitchen Gods of all Chinese households report to him in the last week of each year. The King of Hell supervises a labyrinth of subterranean bureaus, each addressing a particular sin and meting out fitting punishments (Figure 3.15). In popular literature these bureaus are rendered quite vividly, and many people are anxious about the suffering of loved ones there. The bailiffs, jailors, and minions of hell behave in much the same way as lesser officials might in any bureaucracy: they work according to rules but are not above accepting bribes. Thus, the temples that give access to the gods of hell are full of petitioners making pleas and offering spirit money on behalf of deceased kin. Sometimes petitioners fill out the equivalent of bureaucratic paperwork, making requests on ribbons or small prayer boards that have spaces for the name and address of the incarcerated party, the date, and the petition.

The Lord of the Earth Since the Jade Emperor and the King of Hell are too remote for most Chinese to approach directly, people give much more attention to lesser gods, especially if a god has a reputation for being compassionate and is powerful in ways that match a specific need. One of the most popular of these lesser gods is **Tudi Gong**, the Lord of the Earth. There are thousands upon thousands of Tudi Gong gods, each responsible for a small jurisdiction, such as a village or a neighborhood. Just as a police officer has responsibility over a beat, each Tudi Gong patrols the area assigned to him, largely to protect people from unruly ghosts. In villages, Tudi Gong temples consist of an open-air altar and a small worship space, reflecting his localized power and low rank in the spiritual hierarchy. Even so, just as a police officer may be vital to a community but of no consequence beyond their jurisdiction, a Tudi Gong can be very important within his locality. Villagers greet Tudi Gong regularly, burning incense, making small token offerings, and bowing respectfully. They might also inform him of travel plans, births, deaths, and other important local news, just as a police station is used to register changes in local households. In cities, many neighborhood Tudi Gong gods are organized under the administration of a higher-ranking City God, giving residents access to a more powerful municipal deity (Figure 3.16).

Figure 3.15 The Eastern Peak Temple (Dongyue Miao), includes 76 replicas of Hell's chambers of judgment and punishment beneath the eastern summit of Mount Tai. Each chamber illustrates a specific punishment, which is administered by the jailors of Hell. This chamber shows the fate of those who have lied. Visitors hang prayer boards near the chambers they deem most appropriate for their deceased relatives in order to speed them through their punishment. Source: Reproduced by permission of Jennifer Oldstone‐Moore.

Guandi In contrast to the Tudi Gong, some gods are thought to have so much compassion and spiritual efficacy (*ling*) that their jurisdiction has no boundaries. One of these is **Guandi**, who is sometimes also called Guan Gong or Guan Yu. A righteous and loyal man, he was one of three brothers who swore to defend the Han dynasty during its collapse in the third century CE. Although he was captured and executed, he died at the height of his powers, with an abundance of *ling*. Because of his tremendous life force and noble character, he became a god to whom thousands of temples are dedicated. Given his martial prowess and strength, he is a welcome ally against unruly and dangerous spirits, and his many shrines in Hong Kong police stations attest to his appeal as a patron of law enforcement. Ironically, his proficiency in the martial arts also makes him a patron of gangs and organized crime. His story, which is told in the *Romance of the Three Kingdoms*, is still one of the most popular martial arts stories in China. Since Guandi was also a just and honest person, he has been given additional roles as a god of merchants and as the patron god of tofu sellers, which was one of his early occupations.

Figure 3.16 A man burns incense and bows at the entrance to a temple dedicated to the City God of Shanghai. The City God, like a city mayor, is a relatively high-ranking official who can be petitioned for a variety of needs. Source: Reproduced by permission of Jennifer Oldstone-Moore.

Empress of Heaven Many gods have birthdays that are celebrated by their worshippers. One of the most colorful birthday celebrations is for Mazu, whose name means "Granny," and who reigns as the Empress of Heaven. Much of her popularity stems from this dual identity: as a grandmother she is gentle and accessible and as Empress of Heaven she has the ear of the Jade Emperor. During her life as a human, Mazu was known as Lin Moniang, a good and pious fisherman's daughter in southern China. Beginning at a young age, she often went into trances that took her on spirit journeys. In one famous episode, she demonstrated her tremendous spiritual power by saving her father and brothers from a terrible storm that had capsized their fishing boat—only to drop her father at the last minute, having been roused from the trance at that critical moment by her mother.

When she died at a young age, Miss Lin was venerated by the fishing families in her home village and surrounding areas. Her marvelous spiritual powers were enhanced by the fact that she died a virgin. Credited with the ability to quell rising waves and warn fishermen of changing weather conditions, her temples spread throughout southern China and beyond. Under the Song, Yuan, and Ming dynasties, she received royal titles such as Princess of Supernatural Favor and Venerable Mother of Heaven Above, and was finally promoted to Empress of Heaven by an emperor of the Qing dynasty.

Today there are Mazu temples across the globe, and her birthday is celebrated each year on the twenty-third day of the third lunar month, perhaps most lavishly in the Taiwanese city of Pei-kang. Attending Mazu at her birthday festival and throughout the year are mediums called *jitong*. These are periodically possessed by a deity and undertake self-mortification under the deity's protection, inflicting pain on themselves with maces, skewers, daggers, and burning incense (Figure 3.17). Since Pei-kang is home to Taiwan's first Mazu temple, it is also the final destination of an annual pilgrimage on her birthday. Among the pilgrims are representatives of some 300 other Mazu temples in Taiwan, who bring images of Mazu from their temples to extend birthday greetings to the Pei-kang Mazu and replenish the spiritual energy of their images by interaction with their "mother."

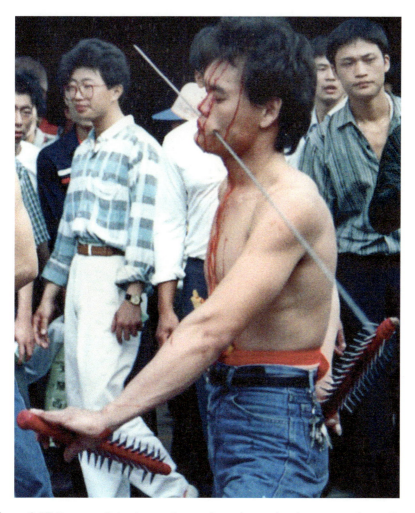

Figure 3.17 Jitong, or divination youths, are chosen by a god to demonstrate that god's protective power. They wield fearsome weapons and injure themselves under divine possession, but the blood stops quickly and they feel little or no pain because of the god's care. This jitong is at the Pei-kang Mazu festival in Taiwan. Source: Reproduced by permission of Michael Oldstone.

CONCLUSION

Chinese religion draws its inspiration from a range of sources—most prominently the Three Teachings (Confucianism, Daoism, and Chinese forms of Buddhism) and China's widespread popular tradition and localized folk traditions. From these, which espouse such disparate notions as filial piety, *yin* and *yang*, nirvana, and gods who act as petty bureaucrats, it forms a unified religious tradition that envisions ultimate reality as a balanced and harmonious universe. It is a universe that continually changes, however, balancing and rebalancing itself through a multitude of patterns that ebb and flow and intertwine with one another. Human beings derive meaning and purpose in life by finding their proper place within the ever-shifting dynamics of these patterns and harmonizing their lives with the all-embracing cosmic Way, or Dao. To achieve this, they must cultivate their minds, bodies, and actions with respect to the metaphysical, social, and bureaucratic patterns of cosmic interaction. Chinese religion is thus the labor of a lifetime, requiring diligence, practice, and the help of religious specialists. At the same time, however, it is so deeply embedded in the larger Han culture that it is also simply a part of being Chinese. There is no need to be initiated into Chinese religion or make a conscious commitment to its practices, as participation is largely a matter of habit or inclination, being one of several elements in the world of Chinese cultural expression.

For review

1. How is the Chinese understanding of religion informed by Confucianism, Daoism, Buddhism?
2. What are the three categories of cosmic patterns that make up the worldview of Chinese religion?
3. How is cosmic balance and harmony understood in terms of the Dao and *yin* and *yang*?
4. How are *qi*, *yin*, and *yang* manipulated through the practices of acupuncture, moxibustion, and cupping?
5. In what ways are diet and exercise a part of Chinese religion?
6. How are annual festivals related to *yin* and *yang*?
7. Describe the nature of the spirit government.
8. What is spirit money?
9. What are the Five Relations, and how are they governed by *ren* and *li*?
10. Who has *hun* and *po* souls, and what is the difference between them?
11. Describe the practices of worship at a Chinese temple.

For discussion

1. In what ways could an outsider convert to Chinese religion?
2. How might one reconcile a Chinese understanding of the forces in the universe to the teachings of modern western science?

Key Terms

acupuncture	The practice of inserting slender needles into various points along the body's meridians to improve a person's flow of *qi*.
Analects	The teachings of Confucius as recorded by his disciples.
bodhisattva	A "being dedicated to awakening"; a compassionate, enlightened being who postpones buddhahood to work for the salvation of others.
Buddha	The Enlightened one, the Awakened one; the founder of Buddhism. An enlightened being who brings Buddhist salvation to a world.
Confucius	Founder of Confucianism (551–479 BCE).
cupping	The practice of applying small, heated glass jars to parts of the body to manipulate the flow of *qi*.
Dao	The Chinese universal Way, understood as a cosmic force that influences everyone and everything.
Daode Jing	An early writing of Daoism.
Daoism	A philosophical and religious tradition that sees the Dao (Way) as the reality behind our world.
Eight Trigrams	The eight possible combinations of three *yin* lines and three *yang* lines, used in the *Classic of Change* for divination.
fengshui	The Chinese art of arranging things and space to achieve the optimal flow of *qi*.
filial piety	The most important virtue in Confucianism, the obligation of a child to a parent.
Five Classics	An early body of scripture that included five traditional writings: the *Classics of Documents*, *Change*, and *Poetry*, the *Record of Ritual*, and the *Spring and Autumn Annals*.
Five Flavors	The Chinese flavors associated with the Five Phases: sour, bitter, sweet, acrid, salty.
Five Phases	Five basic Chinese modes of *qi* under the influence of *yin* and *yang*: water, metal, fire, wood, earth.
Five Relationships	Five human relationships that Confucius held to be essential for all human interaction.
Gods of Good Fortune	The gods of longevity, prosperity, and progeny; found in most temples.
Great Ultimate	The universal ebb, flow, and balance of *yin* and *yang*.
Guandi	A Chinese god of great spiritual power (*ling*) and a patron of many professions, including law enforcement.
Guanyin Pusa	"Hearer of Cries," a popular female *bodhisattva* concerned especially with women and children.
Han	The predominate ethnic group of China, which practices Chinese religion; also, a dynasty that reigned from 206 BCE to 220 CE.

Han synthesis	A synthesis of Confucianism, Daoism, and *yin–yang* theory under the Han dynasty.
hun souls	The rational, or *yang*, aspect of human consciousness; one of two types of human souls found in each person.
Jade Emperor	The highest deity in the Chinese celestial bureaucracy.
junzi	"Gentleman," the word chosen by Confucius to designate the superior person.
Kitchen God	A minor deity who reports to the Jade Emperor after observing a family's interaction in the kitchen for a year.
li	The etiquette or protocol that governs each human relation.
ling	The state of being spiritually powerful.
Lord Lao	The deified sage Laozi, the putative author of the *Daode Jing*.
Mandate of Heaven	The belief in early China that a ruler's right to govern required Heaven's approval.
Mencius	An important early interpreter of Confucian principles.
meridians	In Chinese religion and medicine, channels by which *qi* moves throughout the human body.
moxibustion	The practice of heating various parts of the body with smoldering mugwort to manipulate a person's flow of *qi*.
po souls	The source of bodily strength and movement, characterized by *yin*; one of two types of human souls found in each person.
qi	The most basic "stuff" of the universe.
ren	The virtue of humaneness or "human heartedness."
spirit money	Currency sent to the spirit world to help the deceased garner favors or bribe minor gods.
spirit tablet	The final resting place of *hun* souls; placed on a family altar or in the clan's ancestral shrine.
taiji quan	Exercises of patterned breathing and fluid movement of the body that bring one into harmony with cosmic patterns.
Three Teachings	Confucianism, Daoism, Buddhism, each of which contributes to Chinese religion.
Tudi Gong	"Lord of the Earth," a popular, minor god who watches over villages and neighborhoods.
wu wei	The Daoist principle of not taking any action contrary to the Dao; "doing without ado."
yang	One of the two states of *qi*, characterized by bright, active, male attributes; the opposite of *yin*.
yangsheng	Chinese regimes of exercise and diet that nurture life.
yin	One of the two states of *qi*, characterized by dark, passive, female attributes; the opposite of *yang*.
Zhuangzi	An early writing of Daoism.

Bibliography

A good first book
Joseph Adler. *Chinese Religious Traditions*. New Jersey: Prentice Hall, 2002.

Further reading
Mario Poceski. *Introducing Chinese Religions*. New York: Routledge, 2009.

Reference and research
Ian Johnson. *The Souls of China: The Return of Religion After Mao*. New York: Pantheon, 2017.

Lindsay Jones, Mircea Eliade, and Charles J. Adams. *Encyclopedia of Religion*, 2nd edn, 15 vols. Detroit: Macmillan Reference USA, 2005.

David A. Palmer, Glenn Shive, and Philip L. Wickeri, eds. *Chinese Religious Life*. New York: Oxford University Press, 2011.

CHAPTER 4

Japan's Lived Religion

Turn to the deity in times of distress

Buddhist statues flank an ancient tree marked off as sacred space by a Shinto straw festoon—an example of the regular integration of these two traditions in Japan's lived religion.
Source: Reproduced by permission of John Traphagan.

DID YOU KNOW …

The Japanese word for god is *kami*. In the thirteenth century, Hachiman, a god of protection, was credited with destroying Mongol fleets that were attacking the islands of Japan. He did this by sending "divine winds," or *kami-kaze*, against them. This was also the unofficial name of suicidal units that the Japanese air force deployed during World War II.

Understanding the Religions of the World: An Introduction, Second Edition.
Edited by Will Deming.
© 2025 John Wiley & Sons Ltd. Published 2025 by John Wiley & Sons Ltd.

OVERVIEW

Japan is home to around 80,000 Buddhist temples and 100,000 Shinto shrines. Yet most Japanese who visit these temples and shrines do not identify themselves as Buddhists or "Shintoists"—a term for which there is not even a good Japanese translation. Instead, they go there to engage in a set of traditions that scholars call Japan's "common" or "lived religion," or simply "Japanese religion." It is this religion, rather than Buddhism or Shinto, that is the focus of this chapter.

The term "lived religion," which we will use here, refers to what religious people actually do, as opposed to what their religion teaches them to do. Of course, some slippage between practice and doctrine is inherent in all religions. In Japan's lived religion, however, the slippage is especially pronounced, for it involves two religions as well religious practitioners who, strictly speaking, are affiliated with neither religion. Thus, when Japanese visit Buddhist temples and Shinto shrines, their goal is to acquire benefits from the divine beings enshrined there. They show no interest in Buddhist teachings about reincarnation, and they all but ignore the distinctions many scholars make between buddhas and Shinto gods.

History

Timeline	
35,000 BCE	Peoples from the Asian mainland and Oceania settle in the Japanese archipelago.
5000 CE	Communities form around the worship of localized gods.
300–550 CE	Small chiefdoms form; *kofun* memorials are built for powerful leaders; foreign workers from China and Korea practice Buddhism in Japan.
4th century CE	The ruling classes are introduced to Buddhism, Confucianism, and Daoism.
5th century CE	The Yamato court is established.
6th century CE	The Soga clan gains political power; religious scholars use Chinese intellectual traditions to conceptualize the worship of gods.
7th century	An imperial ideology develops; Buddhism gains support from the royal court; Japanese gods are understood as karmic beings in need of Buddhist salvation, resulting in temples and shrines being built next to one another.
8th century	A new capital city is built at Nara on a Chinese imperial model. State support of Buddhism expands; diverse forms of Buddhism are practiced among commoners; earlier Japanese traditions are selectively edited as the *Kojiki*, *Nihonshoki*, and *Manyoshu*. In 794 the imperial capital is moved from Nara to Heian-kyo (Kyoto).
9th century	Emissaries to China return with Buddhist images, ritual paraphernalia, and scriptures. Shingon and Tendai Buddhist lineages are brought from China; the "true form and trace manifestation" theory becomes influential.
10th–11th centuries	Provincial temples become centers of power due to land grants by aristocrats. The wealthy undertake pilgrimages as pastimes and engage in the spiritual practices of poetry and music.
12th–13th centuries	Various *daimyo* rise to power; soldier-monks appear; the imperial capital of Heian-kyo is overrun and set ablaze. The shogunate form of government comes to power. Schools of Pure Land Buddhism are founded, as well as Soto and Rinzai Zen, and Nichiren.
14th century	An attempted coup fails to reinstate the emperor, instead bringing the Ashikaga clan to power.

(continued)

15th century	Independent schools of "Shinto" develop.
16th century	Catholic missionaries arrive.
17th–18th centuries	The imperial capital moves to Edo (Tokyo); the state bans Christianity, implements the *danka* system of citizen registration, and puts isolationist policies in place; the National Learning movement begins.
early to mid-19th century	Charismatic syncretistic movements begin to appear.
1853–1854	Japan's isolationist policies come to an end through the incursion of US warships.
1868	The Japanese emperor is brought back to power under the Meiji Restoration.
late 19th–early 20th centuries	The Meiji regime removes all Buddhist influences from shrines and defines religion as private practice and belief; the industrialization of Japan begins; the Japanese empire expands into surrounding areas.
1945–1952	World War II ends and Japan is occupied by Allied forces who demand a separation of religion and state; the emperor renounces his claims to divine status.
1952–1990	The Japanese economy grows exponentially.
1991-present	Younger generations move from rural areas to cities; many religious traditions in rural areas die out; new religious traditions develop in urban areas.

The nation of Japan is not a solid landmass, but an archipelago consisting of four large islands (Hokkaido, Honshu, Shikoku, and Kyushu) and thousands of smaller islands. Around 35,000 BCE, peoples from Oceania and mainland Asia began to settle on these islands, at first living in isolated homesteads and villages. Perhaps as early as 5000 BCE, larger communities formed around the worship of localized deities (*ujigami*). There was no religious uniformity in the archipelago, however. As archeological findings indicate, religious practices differed from place to place and ranged from goddess worship and fertility rituals, to shamanic trance, spirit possession, and divination.

By the first century CE, alliances began to form around warlords and their clans, and in the following centuries these alliances grew into chiefdoms that controlled large areas of land and the people who lived there. The wealth and resources amassed by chiefdoms on the islands of Honshu, Shikoku, and Kyushu can be seen in the more than 20,000 elaborate burial mounds constructed for the ruling families in between ca. 300 and 550 CE. Called *kofun*, these monumental earthworks took the form of raised circles, squares, rectangles, and keyholes, and were sometimes surrounded by moats (Figure 4.1). Many *kofun* are as large as a football field, and a few measure over a quarter of a mile in length.

As early as the third century CE, various forms of Buddhism entered "Wa"—an early Chinese designation for Kyushu and southern Honshu—through foreign workers.

Figure 4.1 Two large, keyhole shaped *kofun* in southeastern Honshu. Note the surrounding moats. Source: © Xinhua/Alamy.

It was not until the fourth century, however, when the sprawling Chinese empire and the three kingdoms on the Korean peninsula were vying for political influence, that Buddhism, as well as Daoism and Confucianism, were introduced to the elite members of the Japanese clans. Initially, the Japanese understood these religions as providing new technologies. Buddhist rituals emphasizing the recitation of **sutras** (sacred writings) and the manipulation of ritual implements were performed, for example, to cure physical and mental illnesses and to protect against fire. Similarly, Japanese rulers employed Daoist practices of divination to make plans for the future.

The Yamato court

By the fifth century, the Yamato clan had established control over northern Kyushu and southern Honshu. Through warfare, marriage, and diplomacy it also created a loose confederacy that included many of the other clans. Known by scholars as the **Yamato court**, it provided a forum for competing clans to work out differences and agree on major issues. In the sixth century, another clan, the Soga, emerged as one of the most influential groups within the Yamato court. It was an extended clan that included many immigrants from the Korean peninsula who worshipped Buddhist and Daoist gods. Its principal god was Yakushi, the Medicine Buddha, who, after some controversy, was worshipped at the Yamato court along with the indigenous gods of the other clans.

Also during the sixth century, Japanese theologians began to reimagine their own gods by drawing on the intellectual traditions of Confucianism, Daoism, and yin–yang theory. By the end of the century, many clan gods had been given human characteristics and mythologies, and were enshrined in buildings modeled after those used by Buddhists to house images of the Buddha. In the seventh century, an imperial ideology patterned on a Chinese model developed in the Yamato court. The leader of the court's most powerful clan took the title *tenno* (a Chinese loanword meaning "heavenly sovereign"), and the Chinese designation Wa, which meant "dwarf" and "submissive," was changed to Nippon, meaning "place of the Sun's origin." In 639 CE a temple was constructed so that Buddhist rituals could be performed for the benefit of the *tenno* and his family; and by 645 CE, as many as 50 Buddhist temples had been built for the royal family and other aristocracy in and around Kinai (Figure 4.2). Yet this royal patronage was by no means a conversion of the ruling classes to Buddhism. Rather, it was the integration of Buddhist ideas and rituals into the earlier worship of clan gods.

Figure 4.2 A map showing the four main islands of the Japanese archipelago and the early centers of religious and political power. Map outline source: Japan Map by Vemaps.com

Such integration posed no difficulty for Buddhism, which had always recognized the importance of gods and promoted reverence toward them. While gods could not lead humans to enlightenment, they could keep them healthy and out of poverty, and provide them with good teachers along the path to nirvana. Of course, from the perspective of enlightened beings—Buddhas and *bodhisattvas*—gods had no more substance or reality than anything else in our world, since all of existence was an illusion called *samsara*. But for the vast majority of humanity, who were not yet enlightened, disregarding the gods was the equivalent of ignoring food and shelter.

Beyond simply welcoming the worship of Japanese gods into Buddhism, Buddhist theologians in Japan sought to explain the nature of these new gods by drawing on theories that Chinese Buddhists had developed with regard to Chinese gods. One of their proposals identified Japanese gods as beings who had committed karmic offenses in earlier lives. This accounted for their present incarnation as gods, understood as karmic punishment. Like all other beings in the karmic world, Japanese gods, who became known as **kami**, needed the saving truth of Buddhism to attain nirvana. To help them toward this goal, Buddhists located shrines for these gods near their temples and placed images of the Buddha near established shrines so that the gods could benefit from Buddhist teachings and rituals (see the chapter-opening photo).

The Nara period (710–794)

In 710 CE the Yamato court established a permanent capital in the city of Nara. Previously, capitals had been moved to a new location every time a ruler died to avoid the ritual pollution caused by his death. Nara was a planned city patterned after the Chinese imperial capital: Buddhist temples guarded the cardinal entrances to the city, while the ruler's palace dominated its central district. To emphasize the new capital's religious importance, temples built elsewhere were moved to Nara. In addition, over 60 provincial temples were put under the authority of the city's Todai Temple, which housed an enormous bronze statue of Vairocana Buddha, the transcendent Buddha of Wisdom. Within a few generations, Buddhism, with its many Japanese gods, was transformed into the official state religion.

Yet efforts to regulate or standardize religion outside the capital were largely ineffective. Monks from different schools and teaching lineages lived in the same monasteries and chanted *sutras* together, while folk versions of Buddhism proliferated through the activities of traveling preachers, many of whom were not ordained and had only partial knowledge of Buddhism. By the eighth century, diverse forms of Buddhism had spread throughout Kyushu, Shikoku, and Honshu, and into all classes of society. Hokkaido, by contrast, remained an outlier, being inhabited by a distinct ethnic group known as the Ainu.

Buddhist memorial rites, in particular, were popular among commoners. The mixing of Buddhism with the worship of *kami* also continued unabated. Since *kami* worship had never been understood as a religion with exclusive doctrines and practices, priests who had traditionally overseen the worship of *kami* felt free to worship Buddhas and *bodhisattvas*, take Buddhist vows, and receive Buddhist funerary rites. Similarly, Buddhist monks and nuns prayed to *kami* and made offerings to them at Buddhist temples. Even at the imperial court, a *kami* named Yahata, who had earlier been identified with the deified spirit of an early ruler, took on a new existence as the *bodhisattva* Hachiman, a Buddhist deity of protection.

The Nara period also saw the creation of three important documents, the *Accounts of Ancient Things* (*Kojiki*), *A Chronicle of Japan* (*Nihonshoki*), and the *Anthology of Ten Thousand Leaves* (*Manyoshu*). While these documents purported to record history and mythology derived from earlier oral traditions, they were actually commissioned by powerful clan leaders as instruments of political propaganda. Employing earlier traditions selectively, and shaping them to meet their needs, the creators of these texts fashioned divine origins and royal lineages for the ruling families. The *Kojiki*, for example, traced the Yamato line back to the legendary first emperor (ostensibly in the seventh century BCE), and from him to the sun goddess, **Amaterasu-Omikami**. It was, in other words, an attempt to promote the legitimacy of the Yamato royal family while subordinating other families to them. On this basis, moreover, Yamato rulers legitimated their standing as divine sovereigns.

> **Did you know …**
>
> The official name that Japanese use for their nation is Nippon, pronounced "Nihon" in everyday speech. This name was brought to Europe by Portuguese merchants who had encountered the Chinese and Malay pronunciations "Chipangu" and "Japang," respectively, which is the origin of the English pronunciation, "Japan."

The Heian period (794–1185)

Near the end of the eighth century, the capital was moved 20 miles north to Heian-kyo (present-day Kyoto); and in the early ninth century, the self-styled Emperor of Japan sent official emissaries to China to bring back the latest knowledge and "technologies"—such as rainmaking, meditation, and visualization techniques. On their return, these emissaries also brought Buddhist statues, ritual paraphernalia, *sutras*, commentaries, and *mandalas* (sacred diagrams). In addition, two of those who returned, Kukai (774–835) and Saicho (767–822), brought teachings of esoteric Buddhism from China to Japan. These taught that enlightenment was potentially within the reach of everyone, by means of secret teachings and rituals that were passed directly from teacher to student in private meetings.

With the patronage of the emperor, Kukai founded a new school of Buddhism, called Shingon, building his school's headquarters in steep mountains far from the capital city. Drawing primarily from the teachings of the Chinese Zhenyan school, Shingon taught the efficacy of tantric rituals, *mantras* (ritual chants) and *mandalas*. Kukai is also credited with identifying Amaterasu-Omikami, the Japanese sun goddess, with Mahavairocana, the Great Sun Buddha and personification of wisdom. Saicho, in turn, transferred the lineage of the Tendai school, situating his headquarters on Mount Hiei, just northeast of the capital. He selected this location on the basis of Daoist theories so that his sect would protect the state by warding off disease, misfortune, and unrest. Tendai Buddhism emphasized, among other things, the saving power inherent in the *Lotus Sutra*.

By the end of the ninth century, a new theory had developed regarding the place of *kami* within Buddhism. Called "true form and trace manifestation" (*honji suijaku*) it proposed that *kami* were earthly, localized manifestations of transcendent, universal buddhas. They were, in other words, avatars (*gongen*) of important buddhas, assigned to various regions in Japan. In comparison to the earlier theory that had defined *kami* as suffering from the effects of karma and needing Buddhist teachings to escape their present condition, this new theory raised the status of *kami* to near equality with buddhas, paving the way for a full synthesis of *kami* worship with Buddhism. For the next 1000 years, with few exceptions, *kami* and buddhas were worshipped in the same places and served by the same priests, priestesses, and laypersons. At some religious sites, known as temple-shrines (*shaji*), a particular buddha was the main object of veneration, but *kami* were also worshipped. At other sites, known as shrine-temples (*jisha*), a particular *kami* was the central figure, but buddhas were worshiped as well.

The imperial court flourished during the Heian period, and Tendai and Shingon grew extremely wealthy and powerful under it. Both in the capital city and in the provinces, wealthy elites donated vast tracts of land, along with the commoners who lived on them, to these and other religious sects. They did this, in part, out of piety and for philanthropic reasons, but there was a practical, economic motive as well. Because landholdings, if donated in this way, were taken off the tax registers, religious sects became tax havens for the rich. Not surprisingly, the upper echelons of administrators for the major temple-shrine and shrine-temple complexes were quickly filled with their sons and daughters, and aristocrats often took ordination in retirement. Soon the leadership positions at these complexes were routinely passed down within elite families.

The ritual pageantry and splendor that the wealthy developed for themselves at temples and shrines contrasted sharply with the simple practices that itinerant and local clergy offered the common people. The economic disparity between rich and poor was particularly on display in a new religious activity: pilgrimage. For the wealthy, religious pilgrimage was an opportunity to visit storied sites in distant locations (see Figure 4.3). While they went on pilgrimages to offer prayers for themselves and others and as a form of religious retreat, they also went to see the world and be seen by it. Traveling in style, usually with an entourage of servants, they visited relatives who oversaw famous temples and shrines, and spent their days engaged in aesthetic pursuits such as poetry and music. Many of these religious sites took on mythical proportions and were celebrated in painted scrolls and woven tapestries that were displayed in temples back home. At the popular level, itinerate preachers and healers began to carry more modest depictions of these religious centers, making them known to the wider population and extolling the miraculous powers of their gods.

Figure 4.3 During the Heian period, Buddhist sects enjoyed the patronage of powerful aristocrats, enabling them to expand and embellish their temple complexes with beautiful architecture. This, in turn, encouraged members of the upper class to undertake religious pilgrimages to these sites. Pictured here is the Amida-do Hall, which was added in 1053 to the Byodo-in temple in Uji, a city just south of Kyoto. Source: Wikimedia Commons.

During the twelfth century, the authority and military power of the imperial family declined. Because so much land had been donated to religious centers, tax revenue flowing to the imperial coffers had been reduced considerably. Some religious centers, by contrast, became wealthy from the produce of their vast landholdings; and many of these were controlled by provincial aristocrats. At the same time, new, semiautonomous power centers appeared outside the capital led by *daimyo* (samurai lords). Once in service to the imperial family, these military leaders now filled the power vacuum created by its diminished authority. As armed conflict arose between individual *daimyo*, and between *daimyo* and the capital, religious centers began to train their own militias for self-defense. The sprawling Tendai headquarters on Mount Hiei, for example, trained hundreds of monk-soldiers (*sohei*). This was a major departure from earlier Buddhist practices that regarded occupations which took life, such as butchering, fishing, and military service, as sinful. In 1177, Heian-kyo, the Heian dynasty's once sacrosanct capital, was attacked and set ablaze, leading to the end of Heian rule eight years later.

The Kamakura period (1185–1333)

While violence and unrest continued throughout Japan for the next several centuries, a measure of stability was achieved when a new administrative capital was established in Kamakura, near present-day Tokyo. The emperor and imperial palace remained in Heian-kyo (Kyoto), but played only a symbolic role. The real power during this period was wielded by prominent religious centers and military dictators called **shoguns**, under whom the *daimyo* and their samurai served.

During the Kamakura period, many new schools of Buddhism appeared, three of these being founded by monks who had trained in the Tendai headquarters on Mount Hiei. Interpreting the chaotic state of the country as evidence that the world had entered the Age of Declining Dharma (*mappo*), they questioned the effectiveness of current religious practices. Believing that people's mental and spiritual capacities were rapidly diminishing during this age, they sought simplified methods for attaining nirvana, especially for laypersons. As a result, Honen (1133–1212) founded the Pure Land School (*Jodo-shu*); his former disciple Shinran (1173–1263) founded the New Pure Land School (*Jodo Shinshu*, also known as Shin Buddhism); and Ippen (1234–1289) founded the Time School (*Ji-shu*). All three schools taught that calling on **Amida Buddha** by using a short phrase known as the *nembutsu* guaranteed one's rebirth in Amida's **Pure Land**. Amida, also known as the Buddha of Immeasurable Light, had established this realm as a refuge from all evil and impurity, and so once there, his devotees would find nirvana within their grasp. While Honen and Shinran emphasized the need for faith in the saving power of Amida, Ippen's Time School stressed the importance of reciting the *nembutsu* at specific times of the day. Eventually, Ippen became convinced that even a single utterance of the *nembutsu* could bring salvation—or even accepting a prayer slip on which the *nembutsu* had been written out.

Sacred Traditions and Scriptures

A World in Chaos

Poet and essayist Kamo no Chomei was born into an aristocratic family around 1155 CE. As a young man, he assumed a hereditary position in the great imperial shrine-temple complex of Kamo, although he spent most of his time participating in poetry contests and other literary pursuits. When he lost his position at the Kamo Shrine by publicly humiliating a senior member of his extended family, Chomei took up residence in a "grass hut" retreat, located on a hill overlooking the imperial capital Heian-kyo. In his short essay "Hojoki" (An Account of My Hut), one of the most famous works of classical Japanese literature, Chomei recorded the devastation wrought on the capital city by war, famine, disease, fire, and natural disasters. He took these events to be evidence for the truth of the Buddhist teaching of emptiness (*mujo*): all things in this phenomenal world are characterized by constant change; everything is impermanent. The opening lines of this essay are known to practically all Japanese:

> The flowing river never stops and yet the water never stays the same. Foam floats upon the pools, scattering, re-forming, never lingering long. So it is with man and all his dwelling places here on earth. In our glorious capital the roof tops of the houses of the high and lowly stand in line and seem to jostle for prominence. They appear to have endured for generations but look more closely—those that have stood for long are few indeed. One year they burn down and the next are raised again. Great houses fade away, to be replaced by lesser ones.

Yasuhiko Moriguchi and David Jenkins, trans., *Hojoki: Visions of a Torn World* (Berkeley: Stone Bridge Press, 1996), pp. 31–32.

By contrast, Nichiren (1222–1282), a monk who trained with several schools in Japan, founded a school that focused on a *sutra* rather than on Amida Buddha. Dismissing all other schools as misguided and harmful, he insisted that by reciting the phrase *namu myoho renge kyo*, "Devotion to the mystic law of the *Lotus Sutra*," a person could not only uncover their own buddha-nature, but also transform the present world into a Buddhist Pure Land.

Finally, two schools of Zen were begun by monks who had studied Chan Buddhism in China: Dogen (1200–1253) founded Soto Zen, and Eisai (1141–1215) founded Rinzai Zen. The Soto school rejected all these "easy paths" to salvation, arguing that enlightenment came gradually through discipline and hard work, and was only available to fully ordained monks and nuns. In the final stages, the way to enlightenment required rigorous and prolonged seated meditation, or *zazen*. Soto Zen also pushed back against misogynistic arguments that women were inherently polluted because of their menses and had to be reborn as men in order to achieve salvation.

The Rinzai School, on the other hand, taught that enlightenment could come suddenly and unexpectedly. It practiced both seated meditation and walking meditation, and became known for its use of *koans* (conundrums that defy ordinary logic). In addition, Rinzai promoted *samu,* which is the performance of ordinary tasks with "mindfulness." By focusing one's attention entirely and exclusively on the work at hand, even raking leaves or tending a garden could lead to enlightenment. Rinzai's advocacy of mindfulness led to other important developments as well. One was the creation of esthetically oriented religious activities known as *michi* ("path, discipline"). These included writing and reciting poetry mindfully, and participating in a highly choreographed tea ceremony. A second development was the application of mindfulness to the martial arts, such as swordsmanship and archery. Not surprisingly, the samurai class quickly embraced the Rinzai school and endowed many new temples.

The Ashikaga period and the Warring states period (1333–1603)

The Kamakura period ended in 1333 with a failed coup to restore the imperial family to power. The coup was thwarted by the Ashikaga clan, whose shogunate subsequently ruled from 1336–1573. Under the Ashikaga, however, the influence and wealth of provincial *daimyo* continued to grow, resulting in almost a century and a half of infighting known as the Warring States period (1467–1603). *Daimyo* fought with one another, the shogunate, and the imperial family (who lived in exile in southern Japan); and leagues of peasants loyal to Nichiren and Pure Land sects overwhelmed and occupied entire cities.

During the Ashikaga period and the Warring States period, two developments took place that led to the emergence of a new, or newly defined, religion. In the fourteenth century, priests devoted to *kami* worship began to develop their own teaching lineages, after the manner of Buddhist teaching lineages. Then, in the fifteenth century, certain theologians began to single out the importance of *kami* in the mixed *kami*-Buddha worship. One of these theologians was the high-ranking bureaucrat Yoshida

Kanetomo (1435–1511), who proposed that "the way of the *kami*," or **Shinto**, was actually the foundation of both Confucianism and Buddhism. In his view, *kami* veneration was the root, Confucianism the branch, and Buddhism the flower of religion. The religious sect he created, which he called "one-and-only Shinto," spread to thousands of shrines. While it owed an indirect debt to esoteric Buddhism and contained some elements of Daoism, it was the first religious tradition in Japan since the sixth century to distinguish itself clearly from Buddhism. Kanetomo's one-and-only Shinto accorded new prestige to *kami* worship and gave impetus to later nationalistic movements that called for returning to what they imagined was a "pure and original" religion that was separate from and more authentically Japanese than Buddhism.

In the latter half of the sixteenth century, Roman Catholic missionaries arrived from Portugal and Spain. On the surface, these missionaries seem to have been quite successful—200,000 converts by the end of the century. But the rapid spread of Christianity was partly due to political calculations. While a few *daimyo* genuinely converted to Christianity, others did so as a means to gain European technology, firearms, and access to international markets; and in both cases the populations under their control were brought into Christianity with them. Nevertheless, many commoners truly embraced the new religion, understanding Jesus along the lines of a Buddhist *bodhisattva*, an enlightened being who came to earth to save the masses.

In this and the following centuries, however, the political and religious direction of Japan was ultimately determined by the *daimyo* Oda Nobunaga (1534–1582) and his immediate successors, Toyotomi Hideyoshi (1537–1598) and Tokugawa Ieyasu (1543–1616). During the 1570s and 1580s, Nobunaga gained control over a broad swath of the country, becoming known as the Great Unifier. Yet he was ruthless and calculating, and the unity he established was achieved by playing off his enemies against one other. In 1571 he attacked and razed the powerful Tendai Buddhist headquarters on Mount Hiei, killing tens of thousands of men, women, and children; and in 1573 he defeated the Ashikaga regime and claimed the title of shogun.

Nobunaga was succeeded by Hideyoshi, who consolidated his predecessor's gains through a series of edicts against Christianity that undercut the power of the Christian *daimyo* and limited their access to armaments. His military aspirations, however, overreached his abilities when he attempted to conquer the Korean peninsula. Having depleted his forces and his treasury, he died 1598, and within two years, his most senior general, Tokugawa Ieyasu, came to power.

The Tokugawa period (1600–1868)

Tokugawa Ieyasu established the Tokugawa shogunate, which ruled Japan in relative peace for the next 260 years from a new capital in Edo (present-day Tokyo). From the start, his shogunate took measures to consolidate its power and strengthen its grip on the country. Being suspicious of both Catholic missionaries and Japanese converts loyal to a pope in Rome, it prohibited the practice of Christianity on pain of death, and publicly crucified those who refused to comply. Many Christian communities went underground, especially in Kyushu (see Figure 4.4). The shogunate also barred foreigners from the country and minimized foreign influences by implementing a broad policy of isolationism. Japanese were prohibited from traveling outside the country, and trade was restricted to a handful of ports that welcomed only Dutch, Chinese, and Korean merchants.

To create what was essentially a centralized police state, the Tokugawa shogunate required all members of an extended family to register as a single entity, a *danka*, at a nearby Buddhist temple. The temples, in turn, were grouped by Buddhist school or sect into a hierarchical system that placed branch temples under the control of head temples, which were ultimately overseen by the government's Office of Temples and Shrines. Going forward, Buddhist temples were required to report all major rites of passage for their parishioners—births, deaths, marriages, divorces, adoptions—supplying the government with accurate census information for tax and planning purposes. The Buddhist establishment willingly participated in this *danka* system because most temples had been stripped of land and wealth during the Warring States period, and this guaranteed them a regular income, since their parishioners had to pay for these services.

During this period, commoners increasingly traveled on pilgrimages to temples and shrines, with the result that both institutions benefited from the sale of amulets (personal good luck charms). When pilgrims returned home with these and other souvenirs, they used them to create family altars, or *kamidana* ("god-shelves"). Along with *butsudan*, a type of Buddhist altar from China used to venerate a family's ancestors, *kamidana* became a standard feature in most Japanese households.

Figure 4.4 When Christianity was suppressed under the Tokugawa regime, statues of Mary and the baby Jesus began to appear in the guise of Kannon, the *bodhisattva* who provides safety for women and their babies during pregnancy and childbirth. This enabled Christians to venerate Mary without detection. Pictured is a statue in the so-called Maria Kannon tradition from the Tokugawa period. Source: Will Deming.

A further religious innovation during the Tokugawa period came in the mid-nineteenth century with the appearance of several charismatic movements. Typically founded by figures who claimed to have received a new revelation from a god, or to have discovered an overlooked teaching in a *sutra*, these religions were often hybrid forms of *kami*-Buddha worship, mixed with varying amounts of neo-Confucianism, shamanism, spirit possession, and localized folk traditions. Initially meeting as small groups in homes, some took on the characteristics of secretive cults. While many ended with the death of their founders, a few evolved into complex organizations with administrators, meeting halls, charitable operations, and hundreds or thousands of followers.

An example of a highly successful movement from this period is Tenrikyo, founded by Nakayama Miki (1798–1887). Miki was born into a well-off, extended family of farmers, registered at a local Jodo Shinshu temple. As a young woman, she contemplated becoming a Buddhist nun, but her family had other plans. In 1810 she acceded to her family's wishes and married into the prominent Nakayama family. But in 1837 Miki's oldest son developed a severe leg pain that the local doctor was unable to cure. The family turned to a *yamabushi*, a holy man living an ascetic life in the nearby mountains, and his assistant, a female medium. On one occasion, the medium was unable to attend and Miki was asked to take her place. When she did, she went into a trance and was possessed by a god who demanded that Miki "become his shrine." The Nakayama family eventually agreed to this demand, allowing Miki to sever all family ties and establish the Religion of Divine Wisdom, or Tenrikyo. According to her official biography, the god who possessed her gave her powers to heal the sick and produce the religion's sacred writings using the technique of automatic writing, whereby the god guided a brush in her hand.

While each of these innovations—the restructuring of Buddhism as a regulatory arm of the government, the participation of commoners in religious pilgrimage, and the appearance of charismatic movements—were all major religious developments during the Tokugawa period, an equally important innovation emerged in Tokugawa academic circles. In the latter part of the seventeenth century, a loosely affiliated group of scholars set about to define and articulate a "Japanese national character" through an investigation of Japan's most ancient documents. Influenced by neo-Confucian principles and motivated by a growing resentment for the dominance of Chinese culture, this new line of academic inquiry soon blossomed into an intellectual movement known as National Learning (*kokugau*), which sought to purge Japan of all foreign influences and reestablish Japanese culture in what was deemed its "pure and original form."

As we noted earlier, however, the Japanese archipelago was settled by peoples from many different places, and major advances in religion, culture, and technology had come about through interaction with China and Korea. A unified Japanese nation with a distinct, shared culture, only began to emerge in the late sixteenth century, and did not come to fruition until several centuries later. In other words, the National Learning movement's attempt to recover a pure and original Japanese way of life was an ideological undertaking, not a historical one. Precisely as an ideology, however, National Learning would have a profound impact on religious practices in Japan.

In 1853, the Tokugawa regime suffered a major setback that ultimately led to its downfall. Warships under the command of U.S. commodore Matthew Perry appeared off the coast of Japan near its capital city, Edo. Perry's mission, by order of President Millard Fillmore, was to end Japan's isolationism. Returning with additional gunboats in 1854, Perry secured agreements that would open Japan to the commercial interests of the United States and to Christian missionaries. Other western nations soon forced Japan into similar agreements. An internal political crisis ensued, fueled by anti-western sentiment, an ailing economy, and *daimyo* loyal to the emperor. Within a dozen years the shogun was forced to resign and the Tokugawa shogunate came to an end.

The Meiji period to the end of World War II (1868–1945)

Since the time of the Kamakura (twelfth century), emperors had played only a ceremonial role in government, with no real power. For the most part, they and the royal families had lived quietly in the imperial palace in Kyoto. In the summer of 1867, however, Japan's last shogun, Prince Tokugawa Yoshinobu, ceded power to Emperor Mutsuhito (posthumously known as Emperor Meiji). The shogunate capital of Edo was renamed Tokyo, or "Eastern Capital," and within three years it was transformed into the imperial capital.

The **Meiji period**, which coincided with Emperor Mutsuhito's reign (1868–1912), became a time for Japan to emerge from its medieval, feudal world and meet the industrial and technological challenge of modern western nations, especially in the area of military might. It was Japan's industrial revolution. Roads and railways were built to connect important cities and move raw materials; modern factories produced industrial machinery and consumer goods; educational exchanges with western nations promoted science and technology; and Japan's economy adopted the practices of western capitalism.

Cultural and religious changes during the Meiji period were equally dramatic. Guided by the ideology of the National Learning movement, public intellectuals and government policymakers promoted a nativism based on an idealized past. They relied especially on the *Accounts of Ancient Things* (*Kojiki*) and the *Anthology of Ten Thousand Leaves* (*Manyoshu*), ancient documents that had for centuries gathered dust in obscurity. Written in the early eighth century to further the interests of powerful clans, the *Accounts* and the *Anthology* were now used uncritically as depictions of Japan's earliest history. The imperial line was traced back to Amaterasu-Omikami, the sun goddess and daughter of the creator god Izanagi. This invested the emperor and his family with an elevated religious status and identified him as the 122nd emperor of Japan, grounding his authority in a continuous tradition of rulers that stretched back to the beginning of time. The identity of the Japanese people was also re-envisioned according to this nativistic ideology. Even though their ancestors had come to Japan from various homelands over multiple centuries, they were now described as the descendants of a single, indigenous people, born on the Japanese islands from the union of various lesser gods.

The Meiji regime initially encountered opposition to its policies from Buddhist institutions, which had acquired considerable wealth and political power under the *danka* system during the Tokugawa shogunate. As a result, the regime revoked the laws that had mandated the *danka* system and ordered the complete separation of temple and shrine worship (*shinbutsu-bunri*). Buddhist priests who conducted rituals at shrines were defrocked and given the choice of joining the laity or becoming shrine priests, and all Buddhist buildings, gods, and statues were removed from shrines. These actions by the government sparked a popular anti-Buddhist uprising, rooted in a widespread resentment for Buddhism's role in the *danka* system and the belief that Buddhism was un-Japanese, a notion championed by National Learning. Commoners seized Buddhist lands; destroyed texts, images, and ritual paraphernalia; and decapitated statues of the Buddha. Within a decade, tens of thousands of temples were torn down or closed (Figure 4.5).

Figure 4.5 A depiction of Japanese workers melting down bronze bells looted from temples during anti-Buddhist uprisings under the Meiji regime. Source: Wikimedia Commons.

While some in the Meiji government had favored adopting *kami* worship as the state's official religion, this idea was abandoned early on for several reasons. First, *kami* worship was not a unified entity. Different practices and beliefs prevailed at different shrines throughout Japan, making it unusable as an apparatus for promoting national solidarity. Some variants did not even support the emperor's claim to be a descendant of Amaterasu-Omikami. Second, it was reasoned that Japan could not be unified if Buddhist leaders were excluded from the state religion. Third, western nations were pressuring Japan to grant its citizens freedom of religion, including the right to become Christian, which would be impossible if a national religion was put in place. And fourth, some members of the imperial court were attracted to the western model of keeping government separate from religion, as this would free them from the political intrigue of religious disputes and sectarian infighting.

Defining government as free from religion eventually became the way forward for the Meiji regime. But there were two obstacles that needed to be surmounted. On the one hand, the ideology of National Learning, which the government promoted, maintained that the legitimacy of Meiji rule depended on the emperor's ability to trace his family line back to Amaterasu-Omikami. On the other hand, Japan had no tradition of state ceremonies or national memorials apart from religious rituals and shrines, for religious beliefs had been the mainstay of political ideologies throughout Japanese history. The solution, ultimately, was to appropriate shrines for government use, and define religion in such a way that the ceremonies conducted at these shrines could be seen as civil expressions of patriotism, not religious acts.

During the 1880s and 1890s, through a flurry of legislation, the regime put as many as 100,000 shrines under government oversight and at the same time defined religion as belief that was practiced in private. This meant that all *public* rituals and affirmations now qualified as nonreligious state ceremonies. Shrine priests were retrained and assigned to important shrines as representatives of the emperor. The rituals they conducted included national observances honoring the state, petitions for imperial blessings, and memorial services for national figures, soldiers killed in battle, and imperial ancestors. They also oversaw the performance of *kagura*, which were plays that emphasized the emperor's descent from the gods. Shrines that refused to cooperate with the state were classified as *kyoha shinto*, or "sect Shinto," marking them as religious institutions. Their priests were prohibited from teaching and conducting public rituals, and from engaging in politics. As the government consolidated its network of shrines to create regional ceremonial centers, shrines were merged with other shrines, and many smaller shrines were closed or abandoned, resulting in the loss of nearly 80,000 shrines by 1914.

While this was taking place at home, the Japanese military was expanding into East Asia and the South Pacific. Hokkaido, present-day Japan's northernmost large island, was inhabited by the Ainu, one of the earliest peoples to settle the archipelago. Colonization of this island had begun under the Tokugawa shogunate, and it was officially annexed by the Meiji regime in 1869. This was followed by the annexation of Okinawa, the Kuril Islands, Taiwan, part of Sakhalin Island, and the Korean peninsula. During World War I, in which Japan fought with the allied forces against Germany, it took control of German colonies in the South Pacific and German territories in China. After the war, it made further incursions into China, and during World War II, in which it joined the axis powers, the empire annexed the Philippines, the Dutch East Indies (Malaysia, Indonesia, and Papua New Guinea), French Indochina (Laos, Vietnam, and Cambodia), Thailand, and Burma. As it expanded, it built over 1,500 shrines to promote reverence for the emperor among the conquered peoples. In Taiwan, for example, the imperial court commissioned 66 shrines, and in Korea it supported the construction of more than 400.

Talking about Religion

Shukyo, "Religion"

Rather than forming a truly secular government, the Meiji constitution of 1889 put into place a "sacred and inviolable" emperor and an imperial cult. The legitimacy and authority of the emperor rested on his divine ancestry and on the unbroken imperial line that stretched back, mythologically, to the time of creation. Yet, by officially defining "religion" as private belief and practice, the Meiji regime was able to convince western powers that public devotion to the emperor was an expression of patriotism, not emperor worship, and that Japan was a nation whose people enjoyed freedom of religion.

To achieve this political sleight of hand, the regime employed the word *shukyo* to translate the western notion of "religion," which had no precise counterpart in

(continued)

> Japanese and was typically understood as "allegiance to a particular theology." Christianity, Buddhism, and thirteen types of "Sect Shinto" (*kyoha shinto*), which included some charismatic movements, were then classified as forms of *shukyo*, giving them legal status. All other religious traditions were banned as detrimental to the nation's well-being. The freedom to practice these forms of *shukyo* was not absolute, however. It was confined to private devotions that did not interfere with one's allegiance to the state, which included participation in the emperor cult, understood as an act of patriotism.

Post-War Japan (1945–present)

With its defeat in World War II, Japan relinquished control of its expanded empire, with the exception of Hokkaido and Okinawa. Under the terms of its surrender, the Emperor Hirohito renounced his claim to divine status, and the government relinquished its control over the nation's shrines. A new constitution came into effect in 1947 that guaranteed unconditional religious freedom. The use of shrines and priests for national ceremonies and patriotic observances was forbidden, as was all government funding of religion.

Following the Allied occupation, one of the most significant religious developments came about as a result of Japan's rapid industrialization after the war. Between 1952 and 1990, Japan rose from the devastation of World War II to become the world's second largest economy, after the United States. This encouraged large numbers of young people to move from the countryside into cities for work, making Japan's rural areas increasingly older and less populated. As a consequence, many temples and shrines in these areas closed due to lack of support, and religious traditions that had been maintained for generations within extended families were often discontinued. For example, between 1991 and 2005 the number of households that still had either a Buddhist altar (*butsudan*) or a god-shelf (*kamidana*) fell by more than 50 percent.

In the cities, where smaller households and nuclear families became the norm, and where social interactions often revolved around work-related events, new expressions of religion developed. A second wave of charismatic movements blossomed. Sometimes called "new religions" (*shinshukyo*), these movements attracted followers through large public spectacles, marketing campaigns, and the promise of community. Traditional temples and shrines in urban areas also benefited from Japan's growing economy. A prosperous middle class began frequenting these places of worship, and the parent organizations with which these places were affiliated received generous tax benefits to encourage tourism. In addition, Japan's many new corporations began to underwrite the cost of temple and shrine rituals. Like retailers and businesses in the past, these corporations sought the help of the gods for warding off failure, increasing their odds of success, and protecting themselves from the actions of competitors. Corporations also addressed the changed social context of their employees by offering opportunities for religious community-building in the workplace. Buddhist priests were hired to officiate over the funeral services of valued employees, and some corporations built on-site shrines for conducting the annual cycle of shrine rituals, which employees were encouraged to attend. Finally, in their desire to be good corporate neighbors, companies joined in sponsoring religious events such as New Year's celebrations and festivals called *matsuri* (see below), which cities and other municipalities could no longer underwrite due to strict laws on the separation of religion and government.

Contemporary Beliefs and Practices

Japan's lived religion is a coherent body of practices and ideas that incorporates many aspects of Japanese culture and is, for most practitioners, an integral part of what it means to be Japanese. Even so, there is no expectation of regular participation, only the traditional wisdom that one should "turn to the deity in times of distress." The goal of those who practice this religion is to receive practical, this-worldly benefits, or *genze riyaku*, by petitioning the gods at temples and shrines. These benefits include job security, safety while traveling, recovery from an illness, freedom from drug or alcohol addiction, success in gambling, finding romance or a life partner, high achievement in high school and university exams, and the avoidance of senility. While this emphasis on *genze riyaku* may, at first glance, seem materialistic or self-serving, several considerations should caution us against coming to such a conclusion.

First, Japanese seek these benefits not only for themselves, but also for family members and close friends, and for their communities and nation. In addition, even requests seemingly made for the benefit of oneself often have the well-being of others in mind. For example, petitioning a god for protection against senility in old age may stem from a fear of losing one's dignity, but it is equally grounded in the desire to avoid becoming a burden to others. Second, the benefit a person requests must be life-enhancing and morally positive. Benefits, in other words, must be *beneficial*, not simply expedient or advantageous. One comes before a god to express a heartfelt concern over some pressing matter, not greed. Third, to receive a benefit, a petitioner must be both worthy and earnest. Success at gambling, for example, is said to require dedication and hard work, for winning does not come to those who are lazy. In some instances, being worthy and earnest depends on having good karma, which can often be obtained by actions undertaken at a temple or shrine. In other cases, a petitioner can pledge to fulfill a moral obligation. Finally, while the gods expect, and even encourage humans to petition them for benefits, humans must do so with sincerity and respect. Honoring the gods for their power and generosity is essential, as is thanking them later for the benefits one receives.

Rather than simply materialistic or self-serving, therefore, we may understand Japan's lived religion as life-affirming and based on the conviction that life's meaning and purpose are to be found in this world rather than in an afterlife. Practitioners of this religion bring needs and apprehensions before the gods in the conviction that human beings are meant to be content, prosperous, and free from anxiety, and that the role of the gods is to grant them these blessings.

Temples and shrines

Japanese practice their lived religion at both Buddhist temples and Shinto shrines. A temple is a building or group of buildings in an area that has been marked off as sacred. At minimum, there is an **image hall**, where the statue of a buddha or *bodhisattva* is enshrined. These halls are dimly lit, and traditional ones do not have windows, creating a sense of otherworldliness. Larger temples may have, in addition: subsidiary halls for statues of other buddhas and *bodhisattvas*, shrines for various gods, public lecture halls, a founder's hall with an image of the sect's founder, pagodas, meditation gardens, offices, overnight accommodations for pilgrims, and dining facilities for monks and visitors.

The entrance to a temple's grounds is usually marked by a gateway with a tiled roof, often with enclosures on either side that house images of guardian deities (Figure 4.6). On a typical visit to the image hall, worshippers pass through the gateway, purify themselves with smoke from an incense brazier, and ring a bell to announce their presence to the spiritual beings there. They then enter the image hall, light a candle or incense, approach the statue of the buddha or *bodhisattva*, make an offering—often a few coins or a can of soda—and say a brief prayer.

> ### A Closer Look
>
> ### Japanese Temples
>
> Before I first went to Japan I studied Zen Buddhist thought, but it did not take long living in and visiting Zen temples, talking to the people at them and watching what went on there, for me to realize that there was a profound difference between the ideals and theories espoused by Buddhism and what actually went on at Zen (and other) Buddhist temples.
>
> Ian Reader, *Religion in Contemporary Japan* (Honolulu: University of Hawai'i Press, 1991), p. xi.
>
> There are approximately 80,000 Buddhist temples in Japan. While some of these are very large, with busy ritual calendars, the majority are more modest affairs, run by a single priest and his family. Unlike Buddhist monks elsewhere, Japanese monks are allowed to marry and raise a family, and the majority of temple priests inherit their positions from their fathers. At small temples, a priest may have to take a second job to make ends meet, and it is estimated that some 20,000 temples have no resident priest, but rely on occasional visits from priests who serve multiple temples.
>
> Normally a priest receives his formal training at a monastery associated with the sect to which his temple belongs. Even though this training includes doctrinal studies and meditation, his primary duties at the temple are conducting funerals for the families of parishioners and rituals for their ancestors. He may never again study or practice meditation after he leaves the monastery.

Figure 4.6 On the left, a torii with a *shimenawa* (straw festoon) and *shide* (white paper streamers folded in a zig-zag) marks the entrance to a Shinto shrine. On the right, a gateway flanked by celestial guardians marks the entrance to a Buddhist temple. Source: Wikimedia Commons.

Shrines, by contrast, consist of a sacred area that contains a *shintai*. This is a material body through which a god has agreed to "manifest," so as to be accessible to worshippers. *Shintai* can be objects, such mirrors or swords, or elements of nature, such as mountains, waterfalls, or distinctive rock formations. If the *shintai* is an object, it is enshrined in a structure called a *honden*. This can be a miniature house or a building big enough for people to enter. In either case, only priests are permitted to enter or reach inside. *Honden* are customarily identified by elevating them above their surroundings and by hanging an elaborately braided length of rope, called a *shimenawa*, over their entrances. *Shimenawa* are made from rice straw and sometimes have white paper streamers folded in zigzag patterns, called *shide*, attached to them.

All but the smallest shrines also have *haiden* ("oratories"), which are ritual halls where gods come to hear the prayers of worshippers and be honored by ceremonies. In addition, many shrines have a hall or passageway where offerings are stored, an office, a raised platform for ceremonial dancing, and multiple subsidiary *honden*. The entrance to a shrine is marked by a *torii*, which is a gateway constructed of two upright columns joined by one or two horizontal beams (Figure 4.6). If there are multiple *torii* at the entrance to a shrine, this indicates the increasing holiness of the site as one passes through the successive gateways toward the *honden*. Either just outside or just inside the *torii*, worshippers purify themselves by rinsing their hands and mouths with water from a small pool, basin, or fountain. Following this, they walk to the front of the *haiden* (or *honden* if there is no *haiden*) drop a coin in a collection box (*saisen-bako*), clap their hands twice to gain the god's attention, bow, and pray.

The gods

In Japan's lived religion, worshippers rarely identify themselves as "Buddhist" or "Shinto," but regard both traditions as valid resources for their religious practices. They treat buddhas, *bodhisattvas*, and gods alike (although this is contrary to

Buddhist teaching), and choose a particular temple or shrine based on convenience and on the reputation of the god enshrined there. They can appeal to several gods, either for different *genze riyaku* or for the same *genze riyaku*, for there is no sense that gods demand exclusive worship or that a particular god has a monopoly on any one benefit. The priests at temples and shrines welcome all visitors, without giving preference to those who may have formal ties to their places of worship.

While all gods grant *genze riyaku*, most are thought to have a specialty, and some are reputed to be particularly good at what they do. Inari, for example, is famous for success in business, and when businessmen and women visit Inari shrines they often leave business cards when making requests. Other examples include Tenjin, who specializes in academic success; the *bodhisattva* **Jizo**, who protects travelers and children; and Kannon, the *bodhisattva* of compassion who provides safety for women and their babies during pregnancy and childbirth. Temples and shrines that are famous for particular *genze riyaku* are usually known by the name of the god who grants them, even if they are not the principal god enshrined there. A striking example is the Myogonji Temple in the city of Toyokawa, Aichi Prefecture. Although it is owned by the Soto sect of Zen Buddhism, its popular name is Toyokawa Inari because its primary attraction is the (Shinto) shrine of Inari.

Traditionally it is said that there are 8 million gods, meaning an incalculable number. They inhabit the same world as humans, not a separate heaven or underworld, and they are understood as having a special relation to Japan and the Japanese people. They are not all-knowing, all-powerful, or omnipresent, but localized in the natural world—rivers, forests, mountains—and in shrines and amulets. At times they can become angry, moody, or fickle, and they can experience pain. Some gods, moreover, are impersonal forces, like the power of wind or rain or fire, and some are beautiful aspects of nature, such as waterfalls and autumn colors.

Talking about Religion

The Meaning of "Shinto"

"Shinto" has been used to designate the religion of Japan's many shrines only since World War II. Before that, it had several other meanings.

The origin of the term *shinto* is Chinese, not Japanese. Formed by combining the Chinese characters for "gods" (*shin*) and "way" (*to*), it means "way of the gods." The word first appeared in China in the third century CE as a designation for "foreign religions," mostly with reference to Buddhism. By the fourth century, it had been appropriated by Daoist theologians as a name for their religion. When and precisely how it came to Japan is a matter of speculation. It is first documented there in the eighth century and was used infrequently in the following seven centuries to refer to Buddhist traditions of venerating Japanese gods. In the fifteenth century, however, the term *shinto* gained currency among nativist theologians as a name for religious traditions that emphasized the superiority of Japanese gods.

(continued)

> The next major use of *shinto* appears at the beginning of the twentieth century during the Meiji period. In defining what constituted a lawful religion, the regime placed 13 religious traditions under the category *kyoha shinto*, meaning "sectarian religion." These included charismatic movements and groups of shrines that had be "cleansed" of Buddhist influence. The traditions thus classified as *kyoha shinto* rarely used this name, however, preferring the term *jinja*, meaning "shrine/place of *kami*." By contrast, shrines that were put under government control and used in the imperial cult were called *taikyo*, "great religion."
>
> After World War II, the occupying forces in Japan banned the imperial cult, which it named "State Shinto," and a non-governmental organization called the National Association of Shrines came into being. Currently, the NAS serves as an umbrella organization for around 80 percent of Japan's shrines. Another 3 percent are affiliated with the Fushimi Inari shrine in Kyoto, and the rest are more or less independent. Most shrines in Japan today accept the designation Shinto, although only a small percentage of worshippers who visit these shrines consider themselves members of a Shinto sect.

Outings, festivals, and pilgrimage

It is especially popular in Japan to visit temples and shrines on the weekends. Since the grounds of temples and shrines are often quite beautiful, families and friends go there for picnics, short hikes, and to enjoy nature. Many sites have trails that lead through woods, across streams, and open out onto dramatic scenery. While on these trails, visitors encounter images of gods, often marked with small plaques that indicate their special *genze riyaku*. They may also find rocks, trees, and grottos hung with *shimenawa* and *shide*, indicating the presence of gods. Worship on these occasions is usually lighthearted and spontaneous.

Temples and shrines, if they have the financial means, hold special events and celebrations throughout the year to attract additional visitors. Each god at a site has days of the year on which they offer special access to *genze riyaku*, and the main god enshrined there may offer special access on a monthly or biweekly basis. There are also yearly festivals to honor the founder of the sect with which a temple or shrine is affiliated, and seasonal festivals to pray for rain, bless the planting of a crop, and give thanks for harvests. Celebrations at small and midsized sites draw local and regional worshippers, while grander places of worship can attract national audiences and foreign tourists, sometimes by the millions.

Temples (as distinct from shrines) regularly commemorate milestones in the life of the Buddha, such as his birth (April 8) or his attainment of final nirvana (*mahaparinirvana*, February 15). They also organize gatherings to bring the power of the Buddha into newly installed statues, as well as occasions on which access is given to rarely-seen images. Called "opening of the curtain" (*kaicho*), these take place on designated years in repeating cycles of years, and are anticipated by worshippers as an opportunity to gain uncommon benefits. During all these events, priests recite portions of *sutras*, the sounds of which are popularly understood as magical incantations that call forth the compassion of buddhas and *bodhisattvas*. One of these is the *Heart Sutra*, which closes with a *mantra* (ritual chant) that is held to be a particularly powerful incantation. Another is the *Lotus Sutra*, which glorifies the Dharma (the saving truth of Buddhism) as a repository of this-worldly benefits.

> ### Rituals, Rites, Practices
>
> ## The Primacy of Ritual
>
> Belief, whether understood as belief in the gods or belief in religious doctrine, plays only a minor role in Japan's lived religion. When asked if they believe in the existence of the gods, practitioners sometimes answer that they are unsure; and if asked why they buy amulets for success in business or recovery from an illness, they might reply, "It can't hurt, and it might help." This guarded agnosticism stems from the religion's emphasis on performing ritual actions for the benefit of oneself and others. As expressions of concern, these actions are grounded in psychological, emotional, and visceral motivations. While belief may also be a motivating factor, it is not required.

Ritual gatherings at shrines, by contrast, are occasions to strengthen relations between worshippers and the gods enshrined there. Priests present the gods with costly gifts and offerings from the local community, and young women, called *miko*, entertain them with ceremonial dances to the sound of chanting and the music of flutes, drums, and stringed instruments. To bring *genze riyaku* to an entire community, shrines may also organize festivals called **matsuri**, during which the shrine's *shintai* is carried through the streets of a town or neighborhood in a joyful procession. To begin a *matsuri*, community leaders must first be purified by a priest, who waves a ceremonial wand over their heads. The wand is usually a shaft made from the wood of a sakaki, an evergreen tree, with *shide* tied to its tip. The leaders then present themselves before the shrine's *honden* and formally invite the god to participate in the procession. After this, the priest removes the *shintai* and places it in a portable shrine, called a **mikoshi**, which young men and women carry or wheel through the streets of the community as they rhythmically shout something like "heave ho!" (*wasshoi, wasshoi*), moving the *mikoshi* up and down to honor the god and spread its blessing (Figure 4.7). At times they may stop along the parade route to entertain the god with dance and theater performances, and feats of archery.

There are many regional variations of *matsuri*, some involving multiple *mikoshi* and colorful floats. Many include an element of competition between rival neighborhood groups and clubs, such as a choreographed mock fight, a contest for the best float, or a demonstration of strength, such as carrying a heavy *mikoshi* back to the shrine after hours of celebration and drinking. Participants and onlookers often dress in festive clothing, such as *happi* coats, enjoy snacks from food carts, and watch

Figure 4.7 Men and women in happi coats carry a *mikoshi* through the streets of their neighborhood. Source: © Jarmo Piironen/Alamy.

their children play carnival games. While many of these activities, which involve merrymaking, entertainment, and amusement, might seem more secular than religious, we should remember that Japan's lived religion regards opportunities to enjoy life as gifts from the gods.

Pilgrimages provide additional occasions for visiting temples and shrines. Information on thousands of religious sites can be obtained from guidebooks, either online or in print. These are organized either geographically, indicating which temples and shrines are located in the various regions of Japan, or by the *genze riyaku* for which pilgrims visit each site. Many guides are aimed at specific demographic groups, such as retired people or young adults. Those for young adults, for example, emphasize sites whose gods grant benefits for success at school or work, and help with romantic relationships. In describing a particular temple or shrine, guidebooks often quote remarks made by famous visitors, relate miracles that took place there, and show pictures of charms and souvenirs that each site has for sale.

It is common for temples and shrines to join together to create pilgrimage routes, and rural sites often do this out of economic necessity. Pilgrims hike, drive, or take tour busses between stops along the route, and it is not uncommon for them to combine pilgrimage with sightseeing when they pass near towns or buildings of historic interest. They frequently carry a booklet or scroll that they present to an official at each site who stamps it with the name of the site or writes the name in calligraphy. These serve as a record of one's progress along the route.

Two of the most famous routes are composed entirely of Buddhist temples: the Saigoku Kannon pilgrimage, which has 33 temples and focuses on the *bodhisattva* Kannon, and the Shikoku pilgrimage, which has 88 temples and focuses on Kobo Daishi, the posthumous name of Kukai, who founded Shingon Buddhism. The latter is a circular route 750 miles long, confined to the island of Shikoku. It is known for its many waterfalls, which are home to water gods. Pilgrims on both these routes usually complete only a section at a time. There are also multiple pilgrimage routes in urban areas consisting of seven temples and shrines, each dedicated to one of the seven Gods of Good Fortune. Three of these are historically Indian gods, two are Chinese (Daoist), one is Buddhist, and one, Ebisu, is likely of Japanese in origin.

Services offered by priests

Worshippers often request the services of Buddhist and Shinto priests at critical times in their lives. One such time is when a beloved pet dies or an object that has enriched one's life, such as a doll, a sewing needle, or a pair of eyeglasses, becomes worn out or broken. When pets or objects are regarded by their owners as having been especially important to their happiness, they may ask a priest to memorialize them as a way of expressing their thanks. This can take several forms. The memorialization of pets, for example—primarily cats, dogs, rabbits, and hamsters—may include the recitation of prayers or *sutras* over the pet's corpse at a family gathering, the burning of incense and candles, the creation of a memorial plaque or home altar, and cremation and the subsequent placement of a pet's ashes in a pet cemetery or columbarium. The memorialization of objects is usually much simpler. On a date specified for a particular object—e.g., dolls or needles—worshippers bring that object to the shrine or temple. There it is displayed during a service of prayer and thanksgiving conducted by a priest, and then returned to its owner, stored at the temple or shrine for safe keeping, or burned in a ceremonial fire.

The "calamitous years," or *yakudoshi*, is another critical time when many Japanese request the services of priests. It is widely believed that these years are particularly unlucky or dangerous and require special precautions. *Yakudoshi* for women are the years when they turn 19, 33, and 37, and for men, when they turn 25, 42, and 61. The years 33 and 42, moreover, are known as "great calamitous years," and are considered especially hazardous. To ward off evil, many attend a *yakudoshi* ceremony at a temple or shrine. In shrines this can take the form of a prayer service offered on January 18 and 19, at the end of which the priest purifies those attending using a ceremonial wand. There are plenty of regional variations, however. Some services, for example, take place in the middle, rather than at the beginning, of calamitous years and require purification by bathing in the ocean. At temples, by contrast, protection from *yakudoshi* is often achieved through exorcism.

Rituals, Rites, Practices

Naked Festivals

The annual festival known as *Somin-sai*, performed at the Buddhist mountain temple Kokuseiki-ji in northern Japan includes an unusual variation of a *yakudoshi*. This is a harvest festival in early February in which people pray to the local gods for a good harvest, health, and protection from disaster. It starts

(continued)

Figure 4.8 During a *hadaka matsuri*, two men use wands made of pine branches to purify the path for a procession of "naked men." Source: Reproduced by permission of John Traphagan.

around 10:00 p.m. and continues through the night, attracting hundreds of participants and spectators (Figure 4.8). It is one of the many *hadaka matsuri*, or "naked festivals," that take place throughout Japan, involving dozens or hundreds of entirely naked men, or men wearing only a Japanese loin cloth and split-toed socks (*tabi*). These men throw tangerines, rice cakes, and coins to the onlookers to promote life and renewal. They also engage in several physically demanding activities, such as immersing themselves in cold water. The heart of the festival is a ritualized battle between two groups over a bag of small amulets made of pine. Participating in this battle, which at times looks like a rugby scrum, is a way to come into close contact with the amulets and the gods connected with them, who will protect these men against the calamitous years.

Caring for the dead

Because Buddhist priests are regarded as experts in end-of-life rituals, their services are usually called for when there is a death in the family. If a family has not done so already, it must affiliate itself with a specific temple. Since many Japanese today live in nuclear families rather than the extended families of previous generations, and since temple affiliation is needed only for funeral services, this is a common occurrence. Their choice of a temple depends on such factors as convenience, the advice of friends, interactions with a priest on previous visits, and the esthetics of temple's buildings and grounds. The sect of Buddhism to which the temple belongs is rarely a consideration, and most families know little of the sect or its teachings even after the funeral.

The souls of the dead, somewhat like gods, are expected to provide benefits for the living, although mostly for family members. The purpose of a funeral, therefore, is to settle a soul in the afterlife in a manner that shows respect and concern, and enables the soul to find peace. To accomplish this, the priest leads family members and close friends in prayers for the Buddha's help, and chants *sutras* during the cremation and when the ashes are taken to the gravesite. In the popular understanding, this chanting begins the soul's journey to enlightenment.

Seven days after death, the deceased is given a new name, or *kaimyo*, to secure their status as a member of the community of non-physical beings. This posthumous name is inscribed on two temporary memorial tablets called *ihai*. One of these is placed at the gravesite, the other given to the family. It is sometimes held that these serve as an intermediate home for the soul. At the end of 49 days, the soul finally settles into the afterlife. The temporary *ihai* are retrieved and discarded, and a much nicer, permanent one is made and given to the family. Traditionally this was placed on the family altar, or *butsudan*, and attended to daily with prayer and simple offerings. Most families, however, no longer own a *butsudan*, and so the permanent *ihai* is either given to a family member for safe keeping or entrusted to the temple.

For the next 33 or 50 years, depending on a family's traditions, family members will show respect for the dead by performing rituals of memorialization. These include visiting the gravesite, lighting incense, and squatting or kneeling before the grave with hands pressed together in front of one's face (Figure 4.9). While there, family

Figure 4.9 A man performs *omairi*, a ritual of memorialization, in front of his family grave site during a religious observance marking the spring and fall equinoxes. Source: Reproduced by permission of John Traphagan.

members may also clean the site by pouring water over the gravestone and removing any accumulated brush, wilted flowers, or offerings left from previous visits. They then arrange fresh flowers and make new offerings.

Family members can visit a gravesite at any time, although it is customary to do so at the spring and autumn equinoxes, and during a three-day observance in August known as *obon*. This is when souls of the dead are welcomed into their former homes and entertained at festivals held in public parks, community centers, and temples. These festivals include games, dancing in traditional dress, and eating foods such as corn dogs and fried noodles (*yakisoba*). They are occasions for fun and amusement, and include a significant amount of drinking, particularly for men. *Obon* is one of the few times in the year—another being the New Year holiday—when extended families are able to celebrate and spend time together. After three days, *obon* comes to an end with a display of fireworks and, in some regions, small "parting fires," which participants float downriver on tiny rafts as they bid their ancestors farewell.

Mizuko kuyo   When death involves a fetus, either one that has died in the womb or has been aborted, a family or an individual may request a ritual called *mizuko kuyo*. This is especially common for single women, who do not speak publicly about their experiences but nonetheless feel the need to mourn. *Mizuko kuyo* are frequently performed at the spring and autumn equinoxes and during *obon*, but they are not limited to these occasions. Some temples hold monthly *mizuko kuyo*, and families can request simpler versions of the ritual at other times.

To prepare for a *mizuko kuyo*, the priest displays a large statue of the *bodhisattva* Jizo holding an infant in a public area at the temple. As mentioned earlier, Jizo is the patron god of travelers and children. A pot for burning incense is placed to the right of the statue, and red flowers are displayed on either side, as red is the color that fosters good luck. Those participating in the ceremony may choose to exhibit an *ihai* bearing the posthumous name of a fetus, or dress one of several small Jizo figures arranged on a display nearby. These are given bibs, aprons, and knit caps as a way for the bereaved to express their fetuses' individual identities and keep them warm on their journey to the afterlife. Participants may also give the little Jizos colorful flowers or small toys such as pinwheels (Figure 4.10). During the actual service, the priest recites *sutras* and prayers for the benefit of the fetuses. He may also recite the *Sai no kawara Jizo wasan*, or "Hymn to Jizo of the River Beach of Sai," which describes children gathered at the shore, longing for their parents and asking the Buddha for help in finding the path to his heavenly Pure Land.

Rituals of life and renewal

Shinto gods are closely tied to the everyday vigor of the natural world, and natural areas that inspire awe are identified as their special handiwork. It is common, for example, to find a very old and large tree in Japan marked off with *shide* and a *shimenawa* to acknowledge the presence of the god responsible for the tree's grandeur and longevity. For this reason, while Japanese associate Buddhist priests with services

Figure 4.10 In preparation for a *mizuko kuyo*, small statues of the *bodhisattva* Jizo are clothed with red knit hats and bibs and given flowers and pinwheels by women whose fetuses have died. Source: © domonabikejapan/Alamy.

that care for the dead, they typically rely on Shinto priests for services that celebrate and promote life. Since Shinto gods abhor any form of pollution, one of a priest's most important obligations is to purify the people and places that need the god's life-giving benefits.

The first shrine visit Shortly after birth, babies are taken to a Shinto priest for the ceremony of *miyamairi* ("shrine visit"). This introduces them to a shrine's god, so they may receive the benefit of vigorous and healthy development. On these occasions, the priest gives thanks for the baby's birth, recites a prayer, and waves a *tamagushi* over the baby's body to purify it. *Tamagushi* are freshly-cut branches of a sakaki tied with *shide*. Following the purification, the priest announces the baby's name to the god, along with the names of the parents and, sometimes, their street address. Afterwards, it is customary for the parents and grandparents to present the god with a *tamagushi*. At some shrines, the parents are given several small items designed to keep their baby safe by means of the god's power.

The seven, five, three ceremony As children grow, they return to the shrine with their parents to reaffirm their relationship with the god. This ceremony is called *shichigosan*—literally "seven, five, three"—and it takes place on the Sunday closest to November 15 after boys have reached the age of five and girls have reached the ages of three and seven. The children are dressed in formalwear, either traditional kimonos or nice dresses and suits, and sit with their parents while a priest chants prayers and purifies them with a wand called a *nusa*, which has multiple narrow streamers

Figure 4.11 A Shinto priest uses a *nusa* wand to purify a car and bless it with safety. Source: Wikimedia Commons.

attached to one end, resembling a pom-pom (see Figure 4.11). After the ceremony, the children are given "one-thousand-year candy" (*chitose ame*), a hard, stick candy, for longevity and growth.

Groundbreaking ceremonies When a new building is planned, either a home or a place of business, a Shinto priest can be hired to conduct a groundbreaking ceremony (*jichinsai*). This ensures that the construction of the building goes smoothly and safely, and that the family or business that moves into the building thrives. In preparation for the ceremony, a small, square section of the construction site is marked off using four upright poles of green bamboo or sakaki, connected at their tops with a rope to which *shide* are attached. After purifying this space, the priest constructs an altar on which he places food and drink offerings. Next, the attendees—the property owner or home buyer, the architect, and the contractor—wash their hands and mouths with water provided from a basin and enter the space, where the priest purifies them with a pom-pom style wand like the *nusa* used in the seven, five, three ceremony. Since groundbreakings do not take place at shrines, the priest must now invite gods to attend, tempting them with the food and drink offerings. These gods are thought of as the site's landlords, or simply as gods who live in the vicinity and watch over the neighborhood.

After the gods arrive, the priest informs them of the proposed building and its purpose, and requests their help during the construction process and later during the use of the building. The construction area is then purified by sprinkling salt, rice, and sake at its corners; the ground is ceremonially broken with a special spade or hoe; and a sacred object is buried on the site. Finally, one or more of the attendees places a *tamagushi* on the altar, offers a prayer, bows, and withdraws.

Benefits from religious objects

Religious objects and other small items sold at temples and shrines play a major part in Japan's lived religion. Some temples and shrines offer small packets of earth from their grounds that can be taken home and sprinkled around one's house for well-being or in a field to aid in crop production. If a temple or shrine has a stream or waterfall, it may sell bottles of water as a way of making the wisdom or healing powers of a god available to those who cannot visit the site. Worshippers can also purchase pillowcases that foster better sleep, hand towels for clearing one's complexion, and a great variety of other curative items that convey practical benefits from a god. In most cases, these come with a short prayer or *mantra* that is to be pronounced before their use.

Divination slips

Omikuji, or divination slips, are also widely available, although nowadays these are mostly bought for fun and amusement. At some temples and shrines, visitors select them from a display, where they are folded or rolled up and placed in tiny compartments. At others, visitors obtain a slip by shaking a box filled with numbered sticks until one pops out of a hole in the top of the box. They then take the stick to a kiosk where an attendant matches it to a corresponding divination slip. If the prediction on the slip is positive, the recipient takes it home or attaches it to a tree or wire fence at the site so that the good luck can spread out into the world. If it is negative, the recipient usually leaves it behind by attaching it to another wire fence provided for the purpose, so the misfortune does not follow them home (Figure 4.12).

Figure 4.12 A woman ties a divination slip to a fence so that its ill fortune will not follow her home. Source: © Mei Yi/Shutterstock.

Fuda and *omamori*

Certain objects from temples and shrines actually allow worshippers to take a god home with them. These are called *fuda* and *omamori*, often translated as talismans and amulets, respectively, and come in a variety of sizes and styles. *Fuda* are slips, cards, or small wooden tablets inscribed or stamped with names of one or more gods, the name of the temple or shrine where it was obtained, a *genze riyaku*, or any combination of these. *Omamori*, by contrast, are usually pouches or sachets of brocaded silk that close with a draw string. They contain a slip of paper with a prayer or sacred text, as well as names of gods, temples and shrines, and *genze riyaku*. The sachet is normally embroidered with an image identifying the particular *genze riyaku* it contains. As a general rule, *fuda* provide benefits for a place, whereas *omamori* are to be carried on one's person.

In preparing *fuda* and *omamori*, priests "sacralize" them in front of an image or *shintai*, which enables the god to dwell in them. This does not mean, however, that the god ceases to dwell in the image or *shintai*, or that the *fuda* or *omamori* has been infused with part of the god or the god's power. Rather, the ritual of sacralization enables the entire god both to remain in the image or *shintai* and dwell in the *fuda* or *omamori*. This phenomenon is known as "dividing the body" of the god. For this reason, it is not proper to speak of buying a *fuda* or *omamori*. Rather, one "receives" a *fuda* or *omamori* for a "donation," which is often said to produce good karma, making the recipient worthy of receiving the object.

Both *fuda* and *omamori* can come with instructions to keep them in a pure place, as well as directions for use, including such things as admonitions to work hard and treat others with sincerity. *Fuda*, for example, are to be placed on a family altar, if the family has one, and greeted with respect. Similarly, an *omamori*, if placed in one's car for safety while traveling, should be honored before each trip. The accompanying directions may also explain that *fuda* and *omamori* must be replaced annually by returning them to a temple or shrine and receiving a new one. This is typically done during the first three days of January to coincide with the New Year's celebration (*hatsumode*). They are returned as a way of thanking the god and to ensure that they are disposed of properly, often in a ritual fire so as to destroy any bad luck they may have absorbed. Their replacement is thought to be necessary because their benefit has been accomplished or exhausted in a year's time.

Receiving a *fuda* or an *omamori*, like petitioning a god, can be an expression of concern for others. Thus, grandparents commonly receive an *omamori* for a grandchild's first day at school, tying it to the child's backpack to ease their anxiety; and students commonly receive multiple *omamori* from family members and friends before taking college entrance exams. Family members typically receive a *fuda* during *obon* to place at the gravesite for the benefit of their ancestors; and when a woman is expecting, her relatives and friends often present her with *fuda* or *omamori* for the benefits of easing her pain in delivery and a safe birth.

Fuda and *omamori* are available for literally thousands of different benefits, and new benefits develop as new concerns enter into daily life. Some of the newest *fuda* and *omamori* are received for benefits related to malware, messaging, artificial intelligence, and climate change. The manufacturers of *fuda* and *omamori* have a hand in this, for they market new products to temples and shrines on a regular basis. One innovation has been the introduction of *omamori* in new shapes. Thus, in place of the traditional brocade sachet, *omamori* for safety in automobile travel can be received in the shape of a key chain, a rear-view mirror pendant, a bumper sticker, a dashboard figure, or a seatbelt patch. Likewise, a *fuda* or *omamori* for financial success can be received in the shape of a credit card.

Votive tablets

The final aspect of Japan's lived religion that we will examine is the purchase and use of votive tablets. Like *fuda* and *omamori*, votive tablets come already inscribed with *genze riyaku*, although they also allow worshippers to make a personal appeal. Unlike *fuda* and *omamori*, however, votive tablets are not sacralized and do not contain a god.

Two types of votive tablets are widely available from temples and shrines, *ema* and *gomagi*. *Ema* are thin tablets of wood with a hole drilled near one edge, through which a string is looped for hanging (Figure 4.13). Most are about the size of a 4 × 6 index card and take the form of an irregular pentagon. There are plenty of other shapes and sizes, however, including *ema* in the shape of animals. One side of the tablet is printed with calligraphy, an image, or a red stamp, indicating the general category of its *genze riyaku*—for example, relationships, safety, or health. The other side is left blank so worshippers can explain the specific nature of their concerns. Popular concerns include success on an examination, the curing of a disease, relief from an alcohol or drug

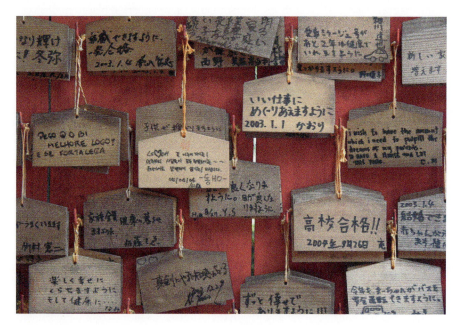

Figure 4.13 Wooden votive tablets (*ema*) with written requests hang on a display board at a shrine. Most are in Japanese, but one is in Portuguese and another is in English. Source: © Filter East/Alamy.

addiction, and finding a new love or breaking up with an old one. If an *ema* is used in connection with *mizuko kuyo*, the personal message may be an apology to the fetus for its abortion, an explanation why it was necessary, or a prayer that the soul of the fetus will soon be reborn in another child. After worshippers have written on the back of *ema*, they hang them on a rack at the temple or shrine provided for the purpose. The public display of *ema* is explained variously as revealing one's needs to others, posting a letter to the god, or making one's request known to a priest.

Gomagi, the second type of votive tablet, are also made of wood, although they are more stick-like in shape. One side of a *gomagi* is inscribed with calligraphy indicating its benefit, sometimes expressed as an imprecation or curse against an enemy; the other side is left blank for the worshipper's words. Unlike *ema*, however, *gomagi* are not displayed publicly but collected by priests and sent to the gods by burning. Depending on the popularity of a temple or shrine, burning rituals may be offered weekly or even daily.

CONCLUSION

The subject of this chapter has been Japan's lived religion. As we have seen, the practitioners of this religion pray to buddhas, *bodhisattvas*, and gods without making any significant distinction between them, and they make use of Buddhist temples and Shinto shrines. While formal religious organizations and affiliation exist in Japan—in Christianity, sectarian Buddhism, and charismatic movements—those who engage in Japan's lived religion show a distinct lack of interest in the typical trappings of religion, including group membership, theological speculation, and adherence to doctrine. Their priority, rather, is to secure vitality, health, and success for themselves and others. In this manner, Japan's lived religion locates the meaning and purpose of life in this world, not in the hope of a future existence in another world.

For review

1. What is meant by a "lived religion"?
2. What do the gods in Japan's lived religion want from human beings?
3. What do those who practice Japan's lived religion want from the gods?
4. Why does belief, either in the gods or in religious doctrines, play such a small role in this religion?
5. How do temples and shrines differ in respect to their physical appearance?
6. What sorts of services are offered at temples and shrines?

For discussion

1. Is it possible to speak of conversion to Japan's lived religion, and if so, how does this conversion differ from conversion to Judaism, Christianity, or Islam?
2. What constitutes good and evil in Japan's lived religion?

Key Terms

Amaterasu-Omikami	The sun goddess, identified with Mahavairocana, the Great Sun Buddha; considered the ancestor of the imperial family.
Amida Buddha	A Buddha who used his enormous store of merit to create a Pure Land for those in need of salvation.
butsudan	Traditionally, a large piece of furniture that serves as a Buddhist altar in China and Japan for memorializing a family's ancestors.
daimyo	Samurai lords, originally in service to the emperor. Beginning in the twelfth century they established military dictatorships throughout Japan.
danka	The members of an extended family registered at a Japanese temple during the Tokugawa shogunate.

fuda	Prayer slips or talismans available for purchase at Japanese temples and shrines.
genze riyaku	Practical benefits given by gods to human beings to enhance their lives in this world. Central to Japan's lived religion.
haiden	A worship hall at a Shinto shrine where gods come to hear prayers and be honored by ceremonies.
honden	The structure in which a Japanese god's *shintai* is kept; the focal point of a shrine.
ihai	A Japanese memorial tablet on which the posthumous name of a deceased person is inscribed.
image hall	The structure at a Buddhist temple in which the image of a Buddha or *bodhisattva* is displayed; the focal point of a temple.
Jizo	A popular *bodhisattva* known for protecting travelers and children.
kami	A Shinto god or divine force.
kamidana	Literally a "god-shelf"; a home altar used to worship family and household gods.
kofun	Large earthen memorials constructed in Japan for rulers between 300–550 CE.
matsuri	A festival in which a god is carried through a town or neighborhood in a portable shrine to bless the people of the area.
Meiji period	The reign of Emperor Mutsuhito (1868–1912), which brought the imperial family back to power and made important changes to religion in Japan.
mikoshi	A portable shrine used in Japanese festivals called *matsuri*.
mizuko kuyo	A funeral service for fetuses who die in childbirth or through abortion.
obon	A three-day Japanese Buddhist festival in August that welcomes and entertains the souls of the dead.
omamori	Traditionally, small pouches available for purchase at temples and shrines that contain a request for a *genze riyaku*.
Pure Land	A paradise created by Amida Buddha for the salvation of his devotees.
shide	Slips of white paper folded in a zigzag pattern, indicating the presence of deities.
shimenawa	A festoon, or length of rope, marking off sacred space.
shintai	An aspect of nature or a manufactured object that embodies a Japanese god. Often a sword or mirror.
Shinto	Literally, "the way of the gods." The current name for religious traditions associated with Japanese shrines.

shogun	A military dictator who commands *daimyo*. The shogunate form of government first appeared during the Kamakura period (1185–1333).
sutra	A Buddhist sacred writing chanted at temple rituals. Popularly understood as containing magical incantations.
tamagushi	Fresh branches of sakaki tied with *shide* and used in Shinto rituals as a purifying wand and as an offering to the god.
torii	The gateway that marks the entrance to a Japanese shrine, consisting of two upright posts joined by one or two horizontal beams.
yakudoshi	"Calamitous years." The years in a person's life considered particularly dangerous and requiring the protective services of a Buddhist or Shinto priest.

Bibliography

A good first book
Paul L. Swanson and Clark Chilson, eds. *Nanzan Guide to Japanese Religions*. Honolulu: University of Hawai'i Press, 2005.

Further reading
John Breen and Mark Teeuwen. *A New History of Shinto*. Oxford: Wiley-Blackwell, 2010.
Michiko Yusa. *Japanese Religions*. New York: Routledge, 2002.

Reference and research
Barbara R. Ambros. *Women in Japanese Religions*. New York: New York University Press, 2015.
Stephen G. Covell. *Japanese Temple Buddhism*. Honolulu: University of Hawai'i Press, 2006.
Helen Hardacre. *Shinto: A History*. New York: Oxford University Press, 2016.
John K. Nelson. *Enduring Identities: The Guise of Shinto in Contemporary Japan*. Honolulu: University of Hawai'i Press, 2000.
Inken Prohl and John Nelson, eds. *Handbook of Contemporary Japanese Religions*. Leiden: Brill, 2012.
Fabio Rambelli, Erica Baffelli, and Andrea Castiglioni, eds. *The Bloomsbury Handbook of Japanese Religions*. New York: Bloomsbury Academic, 2021.

CHAPTER 5

African Religions
An interconnected world

A Dogon ritual dancer in west Africa prepares to communicate with the unseen world by using a ritual mask.
Source: © larum stock/Alamy.

DID YOU KNOW …

In western cultures people are encouraged to think of themselves as individuals, but practitioners of African religions envision the human person as an integral part of a network of life. Each person draws on a universal life force, whose source is God, and each participates in an unseen, cosmic hierarchy, not as an individual, but as a representative of a community.

Understanding the Religions of the World: An Introduction, Second Edition.
Edited by Will Deming.
© 2025 John Wiley & Sons Ltd. Published 2025 by John Wiley & Sons Ltd.

OVERVIEW

The term African religions refers to a group of related indigenous religions practiced by indigenous African groups in the sub-Saharan region of the continent. These religions offer orientation to a highly integrated universe, the creator and ruler of which is known as the **Supreme Being**. The power, or **vital force**, of the Supreme Being is expressed through a hierarchy of spiritual and earthly beings, all of whom share in this divine, life-giving power via networks of dependency and support. The goal of human existence is to support life in all its forms by helping to maintain harmony in the universe.

The diversity found in African religions reflects not only the size of sub-Saharan Africa, but also the diversity of its cultures. Sub-Saharan Africa occupies about 9 million square miles and has a population of over 1.2 billion people. Of these, approximately 30 million people, who belong to literally thousands of distinct ethnolinguistic groups, practice some form of African religion. Beyond this, there are an estimated 200 million persons of indigenous African descent living outside the continent—in the Americas, Europe, the Middle East, Asia, and Australia—many of whom practice a religion that has been influenced by African religions, such as Vodou and Candomblé.

History

Timeline	
100,000 BCE	Ritual graves in east Africa.
25,000 BCE	The beginning of religious rock paintings in southern Africa.
8000 BCE	The beginning of divination practices in east Africa.
1500 BCE	Religious practices are localized in stable agricultural communities.
500 BCE–200 CE	Terra cotta Nok sculptures of humans and animals are made in northern Nigeria.
ca. 200 BCE	Slave trade begins.
5th–6th centuries CE	Religious groups venerate culture heroes.
7th century CE	The beginning of Muslim interaction with African communities in the north of the continent.
9th century CE	Muslim missionaries travel into sub-Saharan Africa.
11th–15th centuries	The appearance of sacred kingship.
15th–20th centuries	European colonization of the African continent begins; slave trade increases.
1700s	A renewal of Sufi missions begins.
1800s	Christian missions arrive.
beginning of 20th century	African Initiated Churches (AICs) appear.
1957–1994	European colonial rule ends; African nations gain independence.

Much of the religion practiced by indigenous African communities in premodern times is unknown because these communities left few written records. On the other hand, these communities did leave behind isolated instances of rock art, sculpture, burial sites, and monuments, the meaning of which archeologists and anthropologists continue to assess. Thus, a full and continuous history of African religions in the premodern period is beyond our reach, and so we must settle for an impressionistic account, dotted throughout with speculation and periods of silence.

From the earliest artifacts to the fifteenth century

As far back as 100,000 BCE, some east African communities appear to have buried their dead in religiously suggestive ways. Bodies were deliberately oriented in important directions, such as east or downstream, and there is evidence for the use of a red dye called ochre, perhaps to represent an individual's life force, envisioned as blood. From as early as 25,000 BCE to the beginning of the CE period, paintings on rock faces survive in southern Africa, and those that date from around 8000 BCE clearly depict both humans and game animals. While there can be no certainty on the matter, these images may portray religious leaders called shamans in states of trance, interacting with the spirit world to bring about success in hunting for the benefit of their communities (Figure 5.1). At this same time (8000 BCE), evidence appears in east Africa that communities were using divination practices in burial rituals to discern the nature of a person's fate in the afterlife.

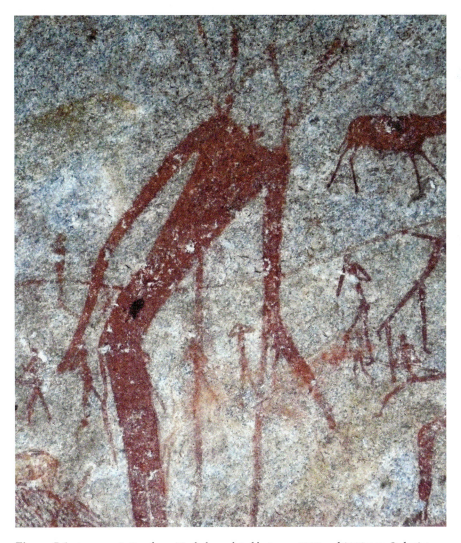

Figure 5.1 A cave painting from Zimbabwe, dated between 8000 and 3000 BCE. It depicts a shaman with an enormous body and a tiny head (perhaps in a state of trance), towering over various other beings. Source: Reproduced by permission of Michael C. FitzGerald, Professor of Fine Arts, Trinity College in Hartford, Connecticut.

By 1500 BCE, agricultural techniques had been introduced into sub-Saharan communities, and these began to replace the earlier practices of hunting and gathering. With this development came a localization of religious traditions in stable agricultural communities, as well as attempts to use religion to promote success in the annual cycle of planting, growing, and harvesting. In the period between 500 BCE and 200 CE, people in the area that is now central Nigeria produced vast numbers of terra cotta **Nok sculptures**, named for the site of their first discovery. These depict both humans and animals, and may have been a means to interact with spirits, forces in nature, and culture heroes. Sometime in the latter half of this period, slave traders entered sub-Saharan Africa from the north and from the Indian Ocean, subjecting large numbers of Africans to slavery in foreign lands. This caused a disruption of religious institutions in many areas, as well as religious borrowing and innovation, although the precise nature and extent of these changes is hard to discern.

During the fifth and sixth centuries CE, iron working was introduced into regions south of the Sahara. In sub-Saharan west Africa,. this resulted in the creation of religious cults that venerated ancestor spirits and envisioned culture heroes as supernatural blacksmiths and warriors. By the seventh century, Muslims had made contact with African communities in Ethiopia, and by the tenth century Islam began to spread in other areas south of the Sahara. The ensuing interaction between Muslim missionaries and the indigenous peoples led to religious borrowing and, in some cases, conversion to Islam.

Between the eleventh and the fifteenth centuries, religion entered into politics in the form of sacred kingship and royal cults. The governments of the larger cities acquired their own religious specialists, both men and women, who organized religious ceremonies, led community prayers and rituals, built temples, and had a hand in governing various kingdoms. In Zimbabwe, for example, monumental stone enclosures served as both temples and residential quarters for rulers. In the southwest Nigerian kingdom of Ife, royal families commissioned bronze heads of important government officials, perhaps as a way to enshrine the life force of these individuals, which was thought to reside in the skull.

The fifteenth century to the early twentieth century

The beginning of the modern history of African religions coincides with a period of enormous political and cultural upheaval in Africa. Toward the middle of the fifteenth century, Portuguese explorers ventured into Africa along its west coast. By the end of that century, European slave trade to the Americas had begun, capturing and removing millions from their homelands. It is estimated that between 1480 and 1900, some 12 million Africans were enslaved and shipped west, taking elements of African religions with them. In Africa, these European incursions inspired a new, or renewed, emphasis on an all-knowing creator god who ruled over the seen and unseen worlds. There was also a rise in the incidence of spirit possession, accompanied by an increase in spiritual healing.

> ### Talking about Religion
>
> ## African Religions and Western Scholarship
>
> The modern study of African religions has had to free itself from several misconceptions popularized by the earliest scholars of religion. The anthropologist E.B. Tylor (1832–1917) and the classicist James Frazer (1854–1941) were both influenced by the work of Charles Darwin. They argued that Hinduism, Islam, and Christianity were advanced stages in the evolution of religion, whereas African religions were "survivals" from a much earlier stage.
>
> Most western scholars also assumed that Christian theology was the standard by which other religions should be measured. From their perspective Christianity was a highly evolved form of "ethical monotheism," whereas African religions were still mired in polytheism, "fetishism," and "nature worship."

Beginning in the 1700s, Sufi missionaries were active in spreading forms of Islamic mysticism throughout Africa, and in the 1800s, Christian missionaries of various denominations established outposts in many areas. Also beginning in the 1800s, and continuing into the next century, European powers began a concerted effort to divide and stake claim to the African continent for commercial gain. This paved the way for colonialism on a large scale, as well as the conversion of many Africans to Christianity. Bent on civilizing Africans to their standards, Europeans replaced indigenous social, economic, and political structures with their own; established European-style schools and hospitals; and denigrated indigenous ways of education and healing as simply folklore and superstition.

African resistance to western imperialism took several religious forms. In eastern and southern Africa—Sudan, Uganda, Kenya, Tanzania, and Zimbabwe—political movements led by indigenous prophets developed. In Sudan and parts of west Africa, apocalyptic forms of Islam (Mahdism) and the Ahmadiyyah movement, a universalist form of Islam, became popular. These areas also saw the appearance of distinctively African forms of Sufi Islam, often manifesting themselves as militant neo-Sufism. Beginning in the twentieth century, **African Initiated Churches** (**AICs**) began to appear in Ethiopia, Nigeria, South Africa, and the Democratic Republic of the Congo. Emphasizing spiritual, psychological, and physical healing, these organizations were often radical transformations of both Christianity and African religions, having little to do with established Christian denominations. AICs were typically founded by prophets, some of whom became politically active in African nation-building in the last half of the century.

The middle of the twentieth century to the present

In the mid-twentieth century, when colonial powers began to withdraw from the African continent, a truer picture of African religions began to emerge. Scholars trained in modern anthropology began to study the many oral traditions of indigenous Africans. These had been ignored by earlier scholars, and provided a much-needed *African* perspective on religion.

The end of colonial rule, however, also coincided with a sharp decline in the practice of African religions. Looking for ways to forge modern national identities and visibility on the world stage, many of the newly independent African governments welcomed the assistance of Muslim and Christian NGOs. As a result, not only did the conversion of Africans to Islam and Christianity increase, but Muslim cultural and educational centers (*madrasas*) in the north promoted Islamic values and the use of Arabic, while Christian missions and humanitarian efforts in the south advanced western concepts of individualism, eroding communal aspects of religious life (Figure 5.2). Today it is estimated that less than 20 percent of Africans still practice African religions—even as the worldview of these religions continues to inform the national ethos of many African countries.

Some authority figures in African religions have adapted to these new circumstances by harmonizing foreign influences with indigenous beliefs. African healers, for example, sometimes use modern medical instruments while continuing to rely on palmistry, astrology, and herbal medicines. To gain credibility in the larger society, they take on titles like Doctor, Professor, and Sheikh, and work alongside physicians and registered nurses in hospitals and clinics.

In the realm of theology, it became fashionable to incorporate elements from Christianity and Islam into indigenous belief systems, including the belief in a bodily resurrection from the dead, and doctrines about end-time rewards and punishments in a literal heaven and hell. In addition, African concepts of the Supreme Being have been favorably compared to Christian and Islamic monotheism. The Kenyan-born Anglican priest John S. Mbiti (1931–2019) held that many Christian understandings of God were fully compatible with African notions of the divine, and the Nigerian scholar and Methodist minister E. Bolaji Idowu (1913–1993) argued that the Supreme Being and the invisible world of the spirits were a type of "diffused monotheism." Indeed, in parts of Africa where Christian and Islamic influences were the strongest, the Supreme Being could be worshipped as though the Christian or Muslim God and the indigenous Supreme Being were simply different names for the same deity.

Contemporary Beliefs and Practices

African religions envision the universe as a highly interconnected network of beings that is permeated by a powerful, vital force. This force flows throughout the universe in all directions, and is concentrated in beings according to their place in the hierarchy of existence. For humans, the vital force is the source of their life principle—the

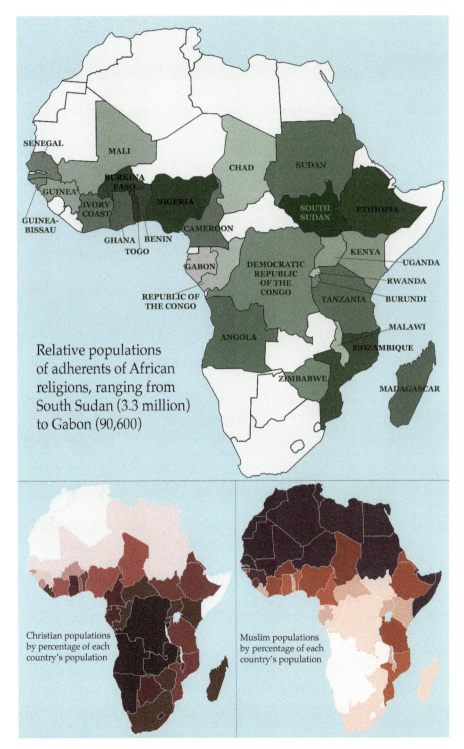

Figure 5.2 The upper map shows the relative numbers of those who practice African religions in each country. The lower two maps, by contrast, show the percentage of the population in each country that practices Christianity and Islam, respectively. Source: Wikimedia Commons.

biological, spiritual, and psychological energy of men and women. To find meaning as a human, to be real, to be alive, is to participate in this vital force by performing one's proper role in the world.

Since all beings depend on and are interconnected through this vital force, they have the ability to influence one another for good and bad. Moreover, as they interact with one another, they transform themselves. They can strengthen and renew each other or they can harm each other, thereby strengthening or harming the whole, of which they are a part. For this reason, it is a basic premise of African religions that the vital force of life should always be enhanced, never destroyed, since its destruction, ultimately, means the destruction of oneself.

Human beings are thought to play a special role in this system, not only because human life is considered precious, but also because human action, by its nature, can be particularly beneficial or detrimental to the whole. Humans can bring about cosmic harmony by achieving social harmony, or social harmony by advancing cosmic harmony. They can also be a source of chaos and destruction.

Invisible beings

The African hierarchy of existence places invisible beings above visible beings. Invisible beings include the Supreme Being, various nonhuman spirits, Ancestors, ghosts, and others. Visible beings include humans, animals, plants, and objects, both natural and human-made. Depending on its place in this hierarchy, each being possesses more or less of the vital force. Even inanimate objects can participate in the vital force if they are closely associated with a spirit.

The Supreme Being

African religions understand the Supreme Being to be the origin and ultimate source of life's vital force, as well as the being who controls the universe. As creators, they may simply initiate the creation, leaving the rest to lesser gods. A Supreme Being stands at the very top of the hierarchy of existence as one who is eternal, self-existent, all-knowing, and all-righteous. The Asante of Ghana, for example, use the expression **Gye Nyame** to honor the Supreme Being. Literally meaning "Except God!," it is a statement that some things are known to no one, except God, and that nothing infuses everything and is present in every event, except God. The relation between the Supreme Being and all other beings is one of dependence, the latter depending on the Supreme Being to sustain and renew their lives. Many also believe that the Supreme Being controls a person's fate. When beings die, the Supreme Being assesses the moral uprightness of each life and determines its destiny: the vital force that made each being's life possible returns to the Supreme Being and is reincarnated into new beings according to divine justice.

Personal being or impersonal power Often simply called God, the Supreme Being can be a personal being or an impersonal power—or both—depending on each ethnic group's perceptions. As an impersonal power, God is usually thought of as spirit, often associated with wind or air. Among the Dinka of Sudan, for example, God is known as Nhialic, the Spirit of the Sky and controller of the universe, while the Shilluk, who live along the Upper Nile, call God Juok, a name that describes a spirit that appears in many mysterious forms.

As a personal being, God takes on the characteristics of a human person, mostly male, but sometimes female. Among the Ijaw of Nigeria (also written Ijo), the Supreme Being is referred to as the Great Mother. Also known as Woyengi or Tamaru, she gives life to humans by breathing on them. In places where God is male, he is often portrayed as having a goddess as a consort, whereas other traditions report that the Supreme Being was once a goddess, but was overpowered and replaced by a god.

Yet God can also be completely without gender, as among the Ewe of Ghana, or even **androgynous**—that is, *both* male and female. Among the Fon of Benin and Dahomey, God is portrayed as Mawu Lisa, having both female (*mawu*) and male (*lisa*) features. Elsewhere, God may be described as "father and mother," manifesting the male attributes of the sun and the female attributes of the moon. Among the Batammaliba of Togo and Benin, the Supreme Being has a female right side and a male left side. Known as Kuiye, and commonly referred to as "The Sun, our Father and Mother," the dual nature of this god serves as a model by which the Batammaliba construct their houses. In a traditional house there is a "female" (right) and a "male" (left) side. The female side has a shrine to the god of women's initiation, skins of game animals, and "female" crops. The male side has the ancestral shrine, shrines for the war god and the god of men's initiation, the men's granary, "male" crops, and shrines to wild animals killed by men. In the middle of the house is a meeting place where both women and men can assemble to worship Kuiye.

Where the Supreme Being is presented as an impersonal power, this is often a statement of the incomprehensible nature of ultimate reality. By contrast, communities that experience God as a personal being with human attributes orient themselves to the Supreme Being on the model of family interactions. This is especially true when God is seen as the head of a divine family, living and interacting with wives, sons, and other relations. The Supreme Being of the Kikuyu in Kenya is something of an in between figure. While he is a personal being, he also stands by himself as a solitary god with no relations. This image seems to express the extraordinary and singular nature of his personality.

Far off or near at hand   African religions present the Supreme Being as both far off, or **transcendent**, and near at hand, or **immanent**. When Supreme Beings are perceived to be immanent, they are usually said to be active in the everyday aspects of nature. Thus Jok, the Supreme Being of the Lango in central Uganda, is accessible in the wind, the trees, and the mountains through prayer, while Nhialic, among the Dinka in Sudan, manifests his power in good harvests, abundant cattle, and the birth of children. But even Supreme Beings who are closely associated with natural phenomena are rarely identified with them. Most Africans believe that God is beyond nature. God may infuse nature, but is not synonymous with it.

When God is understood to be transcendent, or far away from the world, they dwell far off in the sky and are experienced through such remote phenomena as lightning and thunder. This vision of a Supreme Being who is withdrawn from the world explains why most Africans do not focus their worship on God, for it is rare to find temples, shrines, cults, or priests that are dedicated to worshipping God. Indeed, the Dangaleat-speakers among the Hadjarai of Chad neither call on God or speak his name.

Among the Barotse of Zambia, the Supreme Being Nyambi is said to have withdrawn into the sky to flee from one of his stubborn and destructive creatures, Kamonu, who represents human beings. The Yoruba of Nigeria have similar stories, explaining that the separation between the earth and sky resulted from a conflict between human beings and the Supreme Being. In such cases, God can be portrayed as practically indifferent to the universe, having withdrawn from regular participation in human affairs. Even so, God may still intervene as necessary, as when people find themselves in times of crisis.

> ### Sacred Traditions and Scripture
>
> ## A Creation Story
>
> African religions often understand the separation of God and human beings as the result of some human transgression that took place at the beginning of the world. An example of this belief can be seen in the creation story from the Barotse of Zambia:
>
> > In the beginning, Nyambi made all things. He made animals, fishes, birds. At the time he lived on earth with his wife, Nasilele. One of Nyambi's creatures was different from all the others. His name was Kamonu. Kamonu imitated Nyambi in everything Nyambi did. When Nyambi worked in wood, Kamonu worked in wood; when Nyambi forged iron, Kamonu forged iron. After a while, Nyambi began to fear Kamonu.
> >
> > Then one day Kamonu forged a spear and killed a male antelope, and he went on killing. Nyambi grew very angry at this. "Man, you are acting badly," he said to Kamonu. "These are your brothers. Do not kill them." Nyambi drove Kamonu out into another land. But after a while Kamonu returned. Nyambi allowed him to stay and gave him a garden to cultivate.
> >
> > It happened that at night buffaloes wandered into Kamonu's garden and he speared them. After that, he speared some elands and killed one. After some time Kamonu's dog died; then his pot broke; then his children died. When Kamonu went to Nyambi to tell him what had happened, he found his dog and his pot and his child at Nyambi's. Then Kamonu said to Nyambi, "Give me medicine so that I may keep my things." But Nyambi refused to give him medicine. After this, Nyambi met with his two counselors and said, "How shall we live since Kamonu knows too well the road hither?"

(continued)

> Nyambi tried various means to flee Kamonu. He removed himself and his court to an island across the river. But Kamonu made a raft of reeds and crossed over to Nyambi's island. Then Nyambi piled up a huge mountain and went to live on its peak. Still Nyambi could not get away from man. Kamonu found his way to him. In the meantime men were multiplying and spreading all over the earth.
>
> Finally, Nyambi sent birds to go look for a place for Litoma—God's town. But the birds failed to find a place. Nyambi sought council from a diviner. The diviner said "Your life depends on Spider." And Spider went and found an abode for Nyambi and his court in the sky. Then Spider spun a thread from earth to the sky and Nyambi climbed up on the thread. Then the diviner advised Nyambi to put out Spider's eyes so that he could never see the way to heaven again, and Nyambi did so. After Nyambi disappeared into the sky, Kamonu gathered some men around him and said, "Let us build a high tower and climb up to Nyambi." They cut down trees and put log on log, higher and higher toward the sky. But the weight was too great and the tower collapsed. Kamonu never found his way to Nyambi's home.
>
> But every morning when the sun appeared, Kamonu greeted it, saying, "Here is our King. He has come." And all the other people greeted him shouting and clapping. At the time of the new moon men call on Nasilele, Nyambi's wife.
>
> Susan Feldmann, ed., *African Myths and Tales* (New York: Dell, 1963), pp. 36–37.

Nonhuman spirits

Below the Supreme Being in the hierarchy of existence, most communities envision a world of invisible, nonhuman spirits. These spirits are believed to have been created by the Supreme Being to serve as mediators and envoys between God and the human community. The Yoruba, for example, specifically state that God called these spirits into existence to manifest God's vital force in the daily lives of people. Some groups give the spirits names that are similar to that of their Supreme Being; and the Nuer of Sudan even refer to them as Kwoth, which is also their name for God. In cases like this, the name emphasizes that the spirits are not independent entities, but rely on the Supreme Being for their authority.

Like the Supreme Being, nonhuman spirits are readily associated with nature—the sun, the rain, lightning, thunder, wind, and other natural events. They are commonly referred to as the spirit of the water, the spirit of the river, or the snake spirit. In east Africa, the spirits are also associated with mountains such as Kilimanjaro in Tanzania, Kirinyaga in Kenya, and Ruwenzori in Uganda. Yet unlike the Supreme Being, who can be transcendent and sometimes quite withdrawn, the spirits deal with the ongoing affairs of life, assisting or frustrating the fulfillment of human destinies on earth. The task of the spirits is thus to express the immanent side of ultimate reality. Quite often they will assume roles associated with specific social experiences, such as war, peace, fertility, and revenge, serving as points of orientation through which humans can access the vital energy of the universe.

Gods and goddesses Some African communities further divide nonhuman spirits into spirits, gods and goddesses. Gods and goddesses are spirits whose ranking in the hierarchy of existence has been elevated above other spirits due to their importance and influence in human society. The number of gods and goddesses in a given community is often difficult to ascertain. A single community may have several views on this, given that their traditional stories are told in several versions. Yoruban stories, for example, place the number of gods and goddesses between 201 and 1700. In many cases these deities are thought to relate to both human beings and the Supreme Being in terms of human family relations. Among the Ibo of Nigeria, the goddess Ani (or Ala) is believed to be the wife or sister of the Supreme Being Chukwu, as well as the mother of other deities. Moreover, as the queen of the underworld, she upholds morality among her people and controls their productivity and fertility.

The association of goddesses with fertility is not accidental, for deities are often assigned functions according to gender. Among the Yoruba, there are numerous goddesses associated with fertility, and since fertility is closely linked with water, all bodies of water in Yorubaland are connected with goddesses. Yemoja is a water goddess especially associated with the ocean; Olosa is the goddess of lagoons; and the three wives of the Sky Father Shango are the goddesses of the Niger, Oshun, and Oba rivers, respectively.

Gods and goddesses have shrines, temples, and priests, and in response to the rituals performed there, they confer blessings on the community or on certain individuals. While the Supreme Being is recognized by most as the highest reality, it is common for worshippers to direct their attention to a particular god or goddess. Among the Yoruba it is typical to see worshippers devoted to the goddess **Oshun** as the "provider of everything." Similarly, among the Akan of Ghana and the Igbo of Nigeria, the earth spirit goddess Asase is so popular that she is ranked immediately after the Supreme Being. In such cases a god or goddess has become the individual's principal connection with ultimate reality.

Playful and foolish pranksters Most African communities also have a **trickster** figure—a spirit or god who is known for mental dexterity, playfulness, and a good deal of foolishness. A trickster is able to foresee and address conflict and paradox in relationships and act as a mediator between different classes of beings. In crossing these boundaries, however, tricksters can also upset the normal order of things and instigate perversity. This is especially true in African accounts of the creation, which often blame a trickster for the strained or broken relations between humans and the Supreme Being. Tricksters generally prey on human weaknesses, such as greed or lust, and animal tricksters who tell lies and break rules are frequent actors in stories told to children as part of their moral education.

A good example of a trickster is the Yoruban god Eshu (Figure 5.3). Believed to be the most powerful of the deities because of his ability to bring resolution to conflict, Eshu appeals to the spirits on behalf of

Figure 5.3 Eshu, deity of the crossroads and spirit of trickery and chaos. Source: Wikimedia Commons.

human beings. Like an impartial judge, he mediates between the two parties by calling for sacrificial offerings. Yet there is also a sly and mischievous side to Eshu, for he will both deceive humans and garble their messages to the spirits. Having the ability to change his appearance at will, Eshu can assume 256 different shapes. He can be a giant in the morning and a dwarf in the evening. Contacting this "god of the crossroads" without first offering a sacrifice is unwise, since getting his help usually hinges on providing him with the proper gifts.

> ### Sacred Traditions and Scripture
>
> #### The Trickster Who Stole Fire
>
> Ture arose to go to his maternal uncles, who were the Abare peoples, and he met them under their forge, beating out their iron. They greeted him. Ture began to work their bellows for them. With deceit, he came and took fire for everybody, for once upon a time people did not have fire. Ture went on blowing the fire, then he left, telling them, "I will return tomorrow to dance for you." When the next day came, Ture gathered worn-out barkcloth around him at his home, a big stretch of it, and came and blew fire for a long time, then he arose and put his foot over the fire on one side, and his barkcloth glowed, catching fire. The people put it out. Then he jumped over the fire and dropped on the other side, and the fire caught his old barkcloth, and they put it out again. But it was not extinguished; they tried in vain to put it out. It glowed on Ture's barkcloth. The Abare gathered together to put out the fire on Ture; they tried in vain to put it out. Ture ran away with this fire and went with it into the dry grass, and the fire spread everywhere in the dry grass in Ture's tracks. He went on running. Because of Ture, people have fire.
>
> A summary of a Zande trickster myth from Sudan and the Democratic Republic of the Congo. From "Legba Crosses the Boundaries," *A Dictionary of African Mythology*, Harold Scheub, ed. (New York: Oxford University Press, 2000). Oxford Reference, https://www-oxfordreference-com.uportland.idm.oclc.org/display/10.1093/acref/9780195124569.001.0001/acref-9780195124569-e-163?rskey=6gJXV9&result=161, accessed 01/02/2024.

Ancestors

Below the gods and goddesses, and above human beings, there is an extremely important category of beings called the **Ancestors**. This term refers to the spirits of past community members who attained to exceptionally high moral standards. They are often spirits of important leaders of a community, or of the founders of a clan or ethnic group. Rather than reincarnate their vital force back into their human communities, the Supreme Being is said to promote them to this elevated status.

The importance of Ancestors to African religions—really, their *centrality*—cannot be overstated. It lies in the fact that the Ancestors are *human* spirits who have passed over into the world of invisible beings. As such, they provide the most immediate and potent contact that humans have with the Supreme Being and the nonhuman spirits of the invisible world. Indeed, keeping the Ancestors happy is the goal of much of African morality.

On the one hand, the Ancestors are powerful members of the unseen world. Together with the Supreme Being, the gods, and the goddesses, they institute and sanction the moral order that regulates all interaction between the visible and invisible worlds. In some communities, influential Ancestors may even assume roles normally associated with gods and goddesses. Such is the case of Ogun, an extraordinary Yoruban Ancestor who became the patron of those who work with iron. He is even referred to as "the god of iron and war," although this is something of an overstatement, for Ancestors are essentially different from gods, goddesses, and the other nonhuman spirits. It is this difference, in fact—their human origin and continued solidarity with the human world—that makes them so fundamental to religion in Africa.

Hence, on the other hand, Ancestors remain very much a part of the human world. They are considered ongoing members of the families and communities from which they came, owning land and cattle, and continuing in their roles as parents or grandparents. In the context of the clan, Ancestors are regarded as leaders, elders, or kings, continuing to exert influence on the living from their place in the invisible world.

Ancestors make regular inquiries and issue warnings to protect family members from danger; and when a community is in crisis, the Ancestors are invoked for help. They respond through signs in nature or in the organs of sacrificed animals, or directly through dreams and visions. As guardians of a group's morality, they watch over the behavior of individuals, families, the clan, and the entire society, reminding the living of their social and ritual obligations. In this way, they provide the individual with a sense of group identity, the family with a sense of unity and stability, and the entire society with a sense of cohesion in the cosmic order of things.

In spite of their role as the guardians of morality, there are times when Ancestors display human emotions, such as irrationality and jealousy, giving evidence of their abiding human traits and leanings. When this happens, community members will reprimand and scold them to remind them of what is right. If the Ancestors become unhappy, however, they can cause human misfortunes like childlessness, sickness, and death, and natural disasters like famine, drought, and earthquakes. It is believed that they do this only when it is necessary to remind the community of certain important obligations. To appease them, the community must correct its ways and give the Ancestors food offerings and animal sacrifices.

Ancestorhood is a great honor and the highest hope of the individual in indigenous communities. It is the reward for men and women who have lived long, exemplary lives and are acknowledged by their communities for their great wisdom. To become an Ancestor, however, one must also die a good death. This excludes those who die from leprosy or in unusual ways, such as being struck by lightning. In addition, for a man to become an Ancestor, it is often the case that he must be married and have two or more children, one of whom must be a son. Finally, to achieve the status of

Ancestor, one must be buried in the proper way, with a traditional, and sometimes quite elaborate, funeral. Among the Luo of Kenya, for example, if a man is thought to be truly exceptional, his funeral requires killing a bull and raiding cattle from a neighboring community in his honor.

In some traditions, the Ancestors are commemorated in annual ceremonies, during which they make appearances through masked performers (see the chapter-opening photo). In others, they are held in such high regard that they are venerated on a continual basis. Among the Fon of the Republic of Benin, for instance, a metal sculpture called **Asen** is usually placed in a house or in a traditional shrine in the community's compound to remind the community of their dependence on the Ancestors. An Asen also serves as a memorial altar, bringing the visible and invisible worlds together through offerings and sacrifices. At special times of veneration, Ancestors may be consulted about political conflicts and military battles, about the birth of a child, or about the agricultural season, after which the first portion of the harvest is offered to them as a thanksgiving.

Visible beings

Human society stands at an important nexus in the cosmic hierarchy. Not only is human life seen as the most valuable and ideal life that Supreme Beings have bestowed on their creatures, but humans also have unique opportunities for strengthening the whole. As part of the visible world, they interact directly with animals, plants, objects, and other humans. As those who have close ties with the Ancestors, they can also interact with and influence the invisible world of God and the nonhuman spirits. But with these opportunities come responsibilities, for the stability of human society, the natural world, and even the invisible world depends on human beings fulfilling their obligations and undertaking important tasks. Neglect by humans, or disobedience and evil deeds can bring great harm to the universe.

The human community

Africans traditionally understand human beings as members of a community, not isolated individuals. This is because every person is rooted in and nurtured by the vital force, which comes to them at birth through Ancestors, family members, and the clan. As John Mbiti has put the matter:

> Only in terms of other people does the individual become conscious of his own being, his own duties, his privileges and responsibilities … When he suffers, he does not suffer alone…; when he rejoices, he rejoices not alone but with his kinsmen, his neighbors and his relatives, whether dead or living … The individual can only say, 'I am because we are; and since we are, therefore I am'.
>
> John S. Mbiti, *African Religions and Philosophy*, 2nd ed. (Oxford: Heinemann, 1990), p. 106.

Similarly, the philosopher Kwasi Wiredu explains that among the Akan people of Ghana, everyone is thought to possess a life principle (*okra*), blood (*mogya*), and personality (*sumsum*). To become a "complete person," however, one must situate all three of these elements in a network of kinship and social relations (Kwasi Wiredu, *Cultural Universals and Particulars* [Bloomington, IN: Indiana University Press, 1996], p. 27). Individuality, in the African sense, is achieved by fulfilling one's role in a community, not through personal accomplishment.

This corporate role of the individual, as well as their place in the universal network of life, has three important consequences for African religions. First, it means that every life in the community must be respected, nurtured, and lived into old age, since each person shares in and contributes to the larger mystery whose source is God. Second, it means that humans participate in the cosmic hierarchy, not as self-sufficient individuals, but as members of communities. Human beings must work, *as members of human communities*, to maintain proper relations with the other beings of the universe, including plants, animals, nonhuman spirits, and God. And third, as an extension of this, it means that cosmic harmony depends, in part, on social harmony. Just as the interrelatedness of the universe defines the individual and shapes the human community, orderliness within the human community undergirds the order of the universe. For this reason, it is essential that all members of the community—humans and Ancestors alike—do their part. Anyone who does not share in this task interferes with the vital force, weakens the community, and threatens the whole.

Honoring spirits in the unseen world

Indigenous Africans make a clear distinction between worship, which is interaction with the Supreme Being and the spirits of the nonhuman world, and veneration, which is interaction with the Ancestors, who are human spirits. Africans do not worship Ancestors. Both activities, however, require a community to identify certain locations as special places where interaction between the visible and invisible worlds can occur. These places include natural formations like caves, springs, mountain peaks or the area around a particular tree, as well as human-made structures like shrines and temples.

Before approaching a place of worship or veneration, it is common for community members to engage in rituals of cleansing. Since the visible world contains impurities that can contaminate beings in the invisible world, participants must purify themselves by washing, sweating, or sometimes fasting. The ritual tools that are used in worship or veneration must also be cleansed. Drums, masks, headdresses, amulets, hunting trophies, instruments for divination, animal carvings, and even colors and numbers must all be cleansed through prayer and the application of herbs. Without this sort of preparation, it is considered dangerous to encounter the invisible world in one these special places.

Rituals, Rites, Practices

Masks

Religious masks allow invisible spirits to interact directly with the human world (Figure 5.4). During initiation rites and seasonal festivals, spirits associated with a particular mask enter into the body of a person wearing that mask to bless the community or intervene in cases of misfortune, such as drought and infertility.

Figure 5.4 Wearing masks that embody the spirits of the Woman and the Young Woman, these dancers teach onlookers about the potential of womanhood and pass on other tribal traditions. Source: Eye Ubiquitous/SuperStock.

Masks often have human features, since spirits are thought to possess human-like personalities and behave like human beings. The colors with which they are sometimes painted are also significant. White can indicate wisdom, innocence, or the presence of spirits. Black is usually associated with the visible world, and especially with social evils such as witchcraft, sorcery, or war. Red can indicate the danger inherent in rites of passage (see below) and transitional rituals.

Ways of communicating with the unseen world

An important part of indigenous worship is prayer, by which participants express their desires to God and the spirits closest to God. In the home, the oldest member of the family, whether male or female, is expected to offer prayer for the others on a daily basis. Although the expressions used in prayer vary from community to community, most prayers are offered for blessings, good health, and the general welfare of everyone.

These can be simple requests, in which case the family or clan members may join in, or they may be more complex petitions for special needs. Here is an example of a Dogon prayer, said for an ailing mother and her son:

> God, creator, head of this place, who changes a bowl of leaves into food, who changes a bowl of millet into leaves. God, creator, who changes everything … God of my mother, the evening has come. The sickness of my mother thickens. Diminish her illness. Give her a healthy body. Let her stand up. Let the illness disappear; do away with all evil things for the children. Thanks to the morning. Thanks to the evening. Her child is in the bush; bring him back from there. Thanks to you. There are some words [that threaten him]; protect him in those words. Thanks to you. Give him good words. Save him from the world. Diminish the illness. Do not mix the words. This is the chicken for purification. For the mistakes. For the failures. Forgive us. Forgive us. All the mistakes of the mouth, do not listen to those. Let our heart be pure, and accept our chicken.
>
> Walter E. A. Van Beek, "Sacrifices in Two African Cultures," *Nederlands Theologisch Tijdschrift* 37 (1983), pp, 191–197.

A different sort of communication is required between community members and the Ancestors. Because Ancestors are venerated rather than worshipped, most Africans do not regard speaking with them as prayer, but as a conversation or chat that one is having with their forebears. The goal is to honor the Ancestors as respected members of the community and keep them connected with ongoing concerns that might require their wisdom or their influence with the gods and goddesses.

Sacrifices and offerings

As the Dogon prayer above indicates, another important element of a community's interaction with the invisible world is the making of sacrifices and offerings to God and the spirits. While both deliver gifts in recognition of the community's dependence on these beings, sacrifices involve the shedding of blood while offerings do not. Sheep, oxen, goats, and birds are common animals of sacrifice, although preferences vary from community to community. Since blood is seen as a substance through which the vital force of life is transmitted, sacrifice is a means of returning to the invisible world the divine gift of life on which the human community so depends. It is also a ritual affirmation that *real* life can never be destroyed. Rather, it all belongs to God, who gives and takes in accordance with divine wisdom. Offerings include food stuffs like beer, milk, palm wine, cereals, tubers, tobacco, and the first fruits of harvests. These first fruits are thought to hold the vital force of the plant species from which they came, and in offering them, the community thanks the invisible world for all the foods and harvests that make human life possible.

Both sacrifices and offerings ensure that mutually beneficial relations continue between the seen and the unseen worlds. They convey the community's willingness to participate in a relationship of giving and receiving, and they can mend broken relationships by appeasing angered spirits. Sacrifices, moreover, bring the two worlds together for a common meal of succulent meat dishes. In consuming these meats, the participants are reenergized by the vital force in the victim's blood. All of these functions of sacrifice and offering are present, for instance, in the annual Yoruban festival for Ogun. During this festival, Ogun is invited to a feast in which he is given game meat to ensure good hunting, snails and palm oil to calm his wrath, and dogs and pigeons to secure his protection.

Seasonal festivals

Since the unseen world is more accessible at certain times of the year, and its support of the human community more apparent during these times, Africans hold several seasonal festivals. During the hunting, planting, and harvesting seasons, for example, whole communities entertain both themselves and the unseen world through singing, drumming, dancing, and sacrificial feasting.

The Gelede festival

Among the Yoruba, one of the most popular of these celebrations is the **Gelede festival**. This is held after the harvest to honor the Great Mother for granting a bountiful harvest, good health, and many children. Aside from providing entertainment, the Gelede festival promotes social harmony in gender relations. It gives honor to the maternal principle, which is responsible for the origin and continuation of life, and which resides in the goddess, the earth, and the female element of society.

The Gelede festival takes place in the market area, a space of female activity and where spirits are known to gather, usually at night. At the start of the festival, which is called Efe, the community is treated to a night performance of poetry and satire. The entertainer, known as the Efe masker, is also responsible for commenting on social behavior, through which he redirects the moral conscience of the community to promote harmony. The Great Mother is then invoked and invited to bless the event. She arrives dressed in a white robe, usually with a long white train, and wears a white mask that depicts either a bird or a bearded woman. Special members of the Gelede society then offer an official greeting, gathering around her and singing her praises as she engages in warding off evil forces in the marketplace.

The night performance is usually followed by dancing, often on the next day. The dance is carried out by male dancers dressed in costumes honoring the maternal principle. They wear large breasts of wood, bustles, and headdress masks that depict the beauty of a woman. These masks are sometimes carved with images of fighting birds, indicating the social conflict that arises if pregnancy and motherhood are not properly "managed." By contrast, images of snakes on the masks underscore the goal of the dance, which is to mollify—literally, "cool down"—the mothers of the community, who might otherwise internalize enough heat to direct powerful witchcraft against the men.

The Egungun festival

The Yoruba also have an annual festival that honors the yearly return of Ancestors from the spirit world. Often held at ancestral shrines, it begins with the arrival of masked dancers called Egungun, who collectively embody numerous Ancestors. They are usually dressed in brightly colored costumes that cover them from head to toe, concealing their entire bodies from human eyes. On their arrival at the ceremony, they are met by villagers who honor them with gifts. In return, the Egungun offer their blessings to the community. Those not initiated into the rites of the Egungun festival, which include women, are prohibited from approaching the dancers.

> **A Closer Look**
>
> ## African-based Religions in the Americas
>
> Because so many Africans came to the Americas through the slave trade, their religious traditions inspired several new religions outside their homelands. Collectively, these are called African-based religions or African Diaspora religions. They are also known as Black Atlantic religions, because of the Atlantic slave trade, and Yoruba-derived religions, since many of their features come from the religions of Yorubaland, an area encompassing parts of Nigeria, Togo, and Benin. The largest of these religions are Candomblé, Umbanda, Vodou, and Santería (which is also known as Regla de Ocha, or Lucumi). Brazil, which received almost half of the slaves from Africa, is home to the first two, while Vodou and Santería are mostly practiced in Haiti and Cuba, respectively.
>
> There is considerable variation within all four religions because their places of worship (often private homes) operate independently from one another and are led by locally taught priests and mediums. Nonetheless, they also share a number of common features because the different African traditions in which they are rooted have all been shaped by Catholicism, the experience of slavery, and a European practice of communicating with the unseen world called Spiritism. Practitioners of all four religions, for example, believe in a transcendent Supreme Being and a class of gods who serve as intermediaries to both lower spirits and human beings. These intermediary gods are modeled on West African spirits called *orishas* and *lwa*, but named after Catholic saints and honored on Catholic feast days.
>
> The goal of all four religions is for practitioners to receive guidance and healing from the spirit world. This is achieved through initiation, divine possession, and divination. In Candomblé, Santería, and Vodou, initiation is a process by which a god is seated in one's head, thereby becoming the initiate's guardian, or "master of the head." In Vodou, the gods are said to replace one of
>
> *(continued)*

a person's two "shadow souls." Since each god has a distinct personality, as well as likes and dislikes, initiates must learn what foods, colors, days of the week, songs, and dances make their particular gods happy; and they will eventually take on the personality traits of their gods.

All of these religions emphasize divine possession, which takes place during ceremonies in which offerings and sacrifices, as well as dancing, singing, and drumming are used to attract the gods. Offerings include liquor, fruit, and flowers, while chickens and goats are common sacrifices. In Vodou, a central column or pole, called a *poto mitan*, is provided to enable the gods to come down to earth, and line drawings made of cornmeal, called *vèvè*, are created to invite a particular god (Figure 5.5). When the gods arrive, they take possession of one or more of the dancers, who then lose consciousness and begin to sway and twist in ways characteristic of a particular god. In both Vodou and Santería the gods are said to mount the dancers and ride them like horses. Other participants approach those who are possessed and touch them to receive healing power or to ask them for advice regarding family relationships, money problems, and work-related issues.

Figure 5.5 The vèvè (line drawing) of Papa Legba, the lwa of communication and speech who is invoked at the beginning of Vodou ceremonies. He is often pictured as an old man with a dog, smoking a pipe or drinking rum. The crutch he uses to walk is depicted on the right side of the drawing. Source: Wikimedia Commons.

(continued)

In Umbanda, which is more heavily influenced by Spiritism than the other three, only those who are trained as mediums can dance and become possessed. These are predominantly women. In addition, Umbandists believe that the gods who serve the Supreme Being as intermediaries are too evolved and powerful to enter into human beings. As a result, a group of gods subservient to them, called *guias*, take possession of the dancers. These are said to be the spirits of people who lived in colonial times: wise old slaves, cowboys, indigenous Americans, and heroes who resisted the Portuguese. Evil or troublesome *guias* also exist. These include prostitutes, hustlers, and drifters, who must be avoided. When a particular *guia* possesses a medium, the latter is taken to a private area to be dressed in the characteristic attire of that *guia*. The Umbandists attending these ceremonies as onlookers, known as "clients," are then paired with a medium for short consultations with the *guia*.

Lastly, both Candomblé and Santería practice forms of divination in which small objects, such as palm nuts or cowrie shells, are thrown to create patterns that can be interpreted by priests. This technique is used to determine the cause of an illness, learn the characteristics of one's guardian deity, or gain information about the near future.

African-based religions continue to grow in the Americas, and since the 1960s they have spread into major cities in the United States and Canada. Since there are, however, no central organizations to keep membership tallies, and since members often identify themselves as Catholic, there is no reliable way to determine how many people practice these religions, although they likely number in the millions, if not tens of millions.

Spiritual transitions in the life of the individual

Just as certain times of the year provide both the opportunity and the necessity for heightened interaction with the vital force, certain times in an individual's life do so as well. Nor is this a coincidence, for it is believed that the seasonal patterns of the natural world, as well as seasonal events like hunting, planting, and harvesting, have counterparts in the lifespan of the individual. For this reason, ceremonies known to western scholars as **rites of passage** are common in African communities. These provide the means for individuals to transition from one stage of life to another in accord with the much larger structures of the cosmos. Many of these ceremonies take an individual through three stages, which are characterized by **seclusion**, **transition**, and **reincorporation**. During the seclusion stage, individuals are distanced from both the human world and their former identity in it, in preparation to receive a new identity. In the transition stage, they undergo an in between, or **liminal** experience, which can involve exposure to new knowledge and spiritual encounters, as well as a good deal of disorientation. Finally, in the reincorporation stage, an individual is returned to the human world, having a new identity and a new place in the community and the universe.

Pregnancy and birth

Rites of passage for a community member begin at conception. During pregnancy, prohibitions against certain foods and behaviors are strictly observed to protect the child and the mother. In some communities an expectant mother is prohibited from engaging in sexual intercourse; and among the Akamba of Kenya, an expectant mother cannot eat fat or beans, and must avoid the meat of game animals, lest the poison used in killing them harm the baby.

At birth, different rituals are performed depending on the baby's gender. Among the Gikuyu of Kenya, for example, the birth of a boy is met by five screams and five days of seclusion for the mother and baby. Also, five sugarcanes are cut and their juices given to the mother, while the sugarcane scrap is deposited on the *left* side of the house. The birth of a girl, by contrast, is met by four of everything: four screams, four days of seclusion, and four sugarcanes, the scraps of which are deposited on the *right* side of the house. After the seclusion, the father must offer a sacrifice to the Supreme Being and the Ancestors to secure blessings for the child and protection from danger and disease. The birth mother's hair is then shaved in preparation for her reincorporation into the community as a new mother among her people.

Preference for the birth of a boy or a girl varies from community to community. While boys are valued among the Gikuyu, the Akan of Ghana favor the birth of a girl because of the importance of females as the source of family and clan lineage. Twins, by contrast, can be sources of good or evil. Communities that see in twins the potential for evil sometimes separate them from their mother, or send both mother and twins away, or put the twins to death.

Naming

In a baby's rite of passage, the reincorporation is accomplished by a naming ceremony, either immediately after the seclusion or a full week after the birth. The delay is meant to ensure that the baby is not an evil spirit, or Abiku, whose mischievous intentions are to torment infertile women. Ghanaians believe that an Abiku lives no longer than a week. The naming ceremony itself is a public event that officially welcomes babies into the community, introducing them to the network of social and cosmic relationships on which human life depends. A baby becomes acquainted with relatives and neighbors; and prayers, conversations, sacrifices, and offerings on a baby's behalf are directed to God, the gods and goddess, and the Ancestors. Typically, a baby is named after an Ancestor, thereby further incorporating the baby into the clan lineage. This name is usually selected with the aid of a village elder or diviner. In some places, it is believed that Ancestors communicate the baby's name in a dream or through the baby's persistent cry. In the latter case, the name is determined by calling out the names of different Ancestors until the baby stops crying.

A variation on these practices can be seen among the Wolof of Senegal. Here, when a baby is born, a fire is lit in the house and kept burning day and night to mark the arrival of new life. A goat is also sacrificed, which communicates to the Ancestors that a new life has come to the clan. The mother and child are then secluded for a week until the naming ceremony, at which time the fire is extinguished, the house is cleaned, and the baby is bathed in medicinal herbs. The naming ceremony is led by an elderly person; invited guests bring gifts, and the baby is named according to the day of the week. A sheep or a second goat is then slaughtered, and the ceremony ends in feasting and dancing.

Adulthood

When children reach puberty, they must undergo elaborate rituals to be initiated into adulthood. The length of these rituals varies considerably from community to community, lasting anywhere from a few days to several years. In most communities these rituals are the precondition for taking on adult responsibilities such as marriage, and for gaining respect and acceptance in society. One important objective of these rituals is to ensure that girls and boys are educated in the history, lore, and spirituality of their community. They are instructed in social skills, cooking, hunting, healing, and domestic care. They learn important stories, songs, and dances; encounter the community's wisdom through proverbs, riddles, and sayings; and are exposed to ritual objects such as drums, rainmaking stones, and carvings of spirits, the knowledge of which is otherwise kept secret.

Sacred Traditions and Scripture

Examples of African Proverbs

The leaf that the big goat has eaten will be eaten by his kids.
If you take a knife from a child, give him a stick.
The dry stick kindles the green ones.
We can't eat the world on both sides.

Cited in Timothy Reagan, *Non-Western Educational Traditions*, 3rd ed. (Mahwah, NJ: Lawrence Erlbaum, 2005), pp. 65–66.

During the seclusion phase of these rituals, initiates are isolated from their communities and live in special huts or in shelters constructed in the forest. Here their childhood identity undergoes death, they internalize the central proverbs and stories of their peoples, and they experience physical and emotional challenges intended to bring about their transformation to adulthood. The latter include ritual markings made with a knife or other sharp object on the body or face, and sometimes the circumcision of boys and girls. Both painful and artistic, ritual markings are a test of courage as well as a procedure to beautify the initiate in preparation for marriage (see Figure 5.6). They also give boys and girls a tangible mark of belonging to a particular community. Near the end of the seclusion, initiates are adorned and painted in white, red, and black clay. Finally, they are reincorporated into the community at a ceremony where they assume the status of adults.

> ### Rituals, Rites, Practices
>
> ### Female Circumcision
>
> In some traditions, girls must undergo circumcision to become adults. This practice involves pricking, piercing, stretching, or burning the tissue around a girl's vagina. It can also involve cutting or removing the clitoris, or stitching together the outer lips of the vulva in order to narrow the vaginal opening. Over the last half century, feminists have rejected female circumcision as an androcentric practice designed to control the power of women, and all of these practices have been challenged as violations of basic human rights or for health reasons.

Marriage

Marriage has two important functions in African religions. It renews the vital force in human society through procreation, and it promotes new connections between the visible and invisible worlds by joining two families and their respective Ancestors. Although ceremonies vary from community to community, marriages, like other initiation rituals, take the participants through the stages of seclusion, transition, and reincorporation.

Among the Batoro of Zimbabwe, for example, the marriage ritual begins when the bride elopes with the help of nine men organized by the groom. In the process, the groom meets them, wielding a spear, which attests to his manhood. The groom then takes his bride to his home, where they undergo rebirth into their new status. They do this by "sitting" four times on the laps of his parents. The following day they take a cold bath together as "new children" of the home, the water acting as a binding agent between them. The bride is then secluded for two days, after which she rejoins her husband and receives her relatives, who by now have been informed of the marriage. Her relatives bring a smoking pipe and coffee berries, as well as gifts of food and drink to be shared with the groom's relatives. If the bride is a virgin, her aunt and mother are given a cow in gratitude for instilling uprightness in the girl.

Figure 5.6 A woman of the Suri tribe in Ethiopia displays the ritual markings on her forehead and cheeks she received in her passage from child to adult. Source: Photo by Rod Waddington.

> **Did you know ...**
>
> For a boy to become a Moran warrior among the Maasai of Kenya, he is expected to dedicate up to eight years to hunting, and to kill a lion. If his community's cattle are lost to lions or cattle rustlers, it is his responsibility to restock the herds through cattle raids on neighboring peoples.

In most African communities, traditional marriages are arranged in view of a couple's prospects for giving birth to healthy children. While some communities expect the couple to remain virgins before marriage, others encourage a trial marriage to ensure that a couple can have children before the marriage is officially sanctioned. Procreation is emphasized in this way because the more children a couple have, the more blessings and respect they will receive for their contribution to the renewal of the community. Childlessness, in turn, is considered a misfortune, and a couple who encounters infertility will seek help from a diviner. If it is determined that the woman is barren, the man is advised to take a second wife. If it is determined that the man is impotent, the woman is encouraged to procreate with her husband's relatives—usually his brothers or cousins.

Divorce, though permitted, is very rare. Before any divorce is finalized, members of the extended family and even the clan are invited to counsel the couple to find a resolution to their marital problems. This strategy resolves most marital conflicts because it brings the holistic and corporate view of society to bear on the situation. Thus family, clan, and indeed the whole village have a say in an individual's marriage. Even when divorce is granted, however, it does not always take place. This is because it may require that the wife's family return the bride-wealth that they received from the husband and his family, which significantly complicates the process.

A Closer Look

A Clash of Cultures: The Case of Silvano Melea Otieno

Silvano Melea Otieno was a practicing lawyer, a member of Kenya's parliament, and a resident of its capital city Nairobi, where he owned land and led a modern lifestyle. But he was also an elder in the Luo religion and presided over the affairs of his clan on a regular basis. When Otieno died in 1986, he left behind no written statement as to where he wanted to be buried. Among the Luo, an individual must be buried on ancestral land. His widow, however, Virginia Wambui Waiyaki, a prominent member of the National Council of the Women of Kenya, claimed that her husband wanted to be buried on his property in Nairobi.

(continued)

> After an intervention of the Kenyan president, a Nairobi court overruled Waiyaki's petitions to honor her late husband's wishes. The president then praised the winning lawyer in the case for "defending our culture," and rewarded him with an appointment to the Kenyan appeals court. In an interview with the *Washington Post*, the winning lawyer had this to say:
>
> A woman cannot be head of a family. There are things she cannot do: she cannot preside over negotiations for the marriage of her daughter. There is traditional regalia for attending burials, which she cannot wear. She cannot sit on her husband's traditional stool. She cannot organize a beer party. Women accept this. Not a single Luo woman, I repeat, not a single Luo woman has ever gone to court over these matters ever since the world began.
>
> Blaine Haden, Africa: Dispatches from a Fragile Continent
(Boston, MA: Houghton Mifflin, 1991), p. 121.

Death

Death is the passing of an individual from this world to the very real world of the spirits. It is an invitation to enter the invisible world, whereby the vital force of an individual's life returns to the Supreme Being, either to live on as an Ancestor or to be reincarnated back into one's clan. Although family members feel sorrow at the loss of a parent or a child, they accept death as a necessary transition, for it further connects the community, through this individual, to the larger network of existence. Villages often have communal shrines for the departed, which act as a point of contact between the living and the "living dead."

Even so, in African religions all deaths must be explained, and family members are not allowed to go into the unseen world without a fight. During a serious illness, a family investigates the possible causes of a disease and performs various rituals to stave off death. Among the Ndebele of Zimbabwe, for instance, when someone becomes extremely ill and is in great pain, relatives sacrifice an ox or a goat as a way of requesting that the Ancestors heal the person. If death does occur, attempts are made to revive the person by forcing the body to inhale smoke from certain herbs, or by pouring cold water on the body. If this proves ineffective, then all rumors of sorcery, witchcraft, or foul play must be investigated to exonerate the spirits and Ancestors who might otherwise be implicated in such a deed.

To bury the dead, the body must exit the house and yard through newly-made openings in the wall and the fence, which are then sealed up again. Because departure into the invisible world is extraordinary, an extraordinary path must be taken. It is also important that the deceased do not find their way back before the burial and become troublesome ghosts.

> ### A Closer Look
>
> ## The Realm of the Dead
>
> According to many African communities, the spirits of the dead are to be found everywhere, sleeping during the day and roaming around in the darkness of night. Other communities designate specific areas as spiritual realms. For example, the Banyarwanda and the Luhya of east Africa hold that the spirits of the deceased live underground. By contrast, the Luo of Kenya situate them out in the natural world: in the air, the woods, the rivers, and the mountains. Typically, human spirits are of two sorts: those that can be remembered, and those that are beyond memory. Those that can be remembered belonged to people who led morally upright lives. They are welcomed back into the family during certain rituals because they bring blessings to the community. Spirits that are beyond memory belonged to people who led immoral lives or who died without fulfilling life's expectations. They are often blamed for causing mischief or harm, manifesting themselves as unhappy ghosts or wicked spirits.
>
> Most burials are relatively simple, with the dead being wrapped in a blanket before interment. When a clan or community leader dies, however, funeral rites can become quite elaborate, involving stages of seclusion during sickness, transition by way of burial rites, and final incorporation into the unseen world. It is common to bury leaders with foodstuffs, personal belongings, weapons, and money to ensure their safety and well-being during the journey to the next world. After any burial, the participants must cleanse themselves in a river before returning home. Since death is associated with impurities often believed to be contagious, cleansing prevents these impurities from being brought home, where they would likely cause disorientation and more death.

Religious specialists

For communities to carry out their seasonal festivals, perform rites of passage, and manage various other interactions with the unseen world, Africans employ a host of religious specialists. These individuals, both men and women, rank above ordinary humans in the African spiritual hierarchy. In them the vital force is concentrated to a high degree, which combined with the necessary skills and knowledge, gives them the ability to mediate between society and the invisible world.

In their capacity as mediators, these specialists appease the Supreme Being with sacrifices and offerings, diagnose and heal the sick, hand down sacred traditions to the next generation, invite beings from the invisible world to partake in social functions, and perform any number of other rituals. Although each type of specialist has a particular area of expertise, depending on their training, a given person may play more than one role in a community. It is not unusual, for example, for the same individual to take on the responsibilities of both a healer and a medium. The number and variety of religious specialists varies considerably from community to community. Those described below are some of the most common.

Kings

Several nations in sub-Saharan Africa have one or more indigenous kingdoms within their borders. These include Ghana, Nigeria, Sudan, Ethiopia, and Tanzania. Within each kingdom, the prosperity and vitality of the people and the land are embodied in the person of the king. In some traditions it is believed that a king's emotional state can alter the weather. For this reason, kings are protected by many taboos. They are not to be addressed directly; no one is to see them eating food or suffering from an illness; they may not come into contact with death; and their own deaths are not announced publicly. A king derives his authority from the Supreme Being, gods, goddesses, and the Ancestors, and serves as their representative in the visible world. When a king dies, his soul leaves his body and lodges itself in his royal stool, a low wooden bench, which is placed in a shrine alongside the stools of other former kings. In this way, kings continue to guide their people, communicating with them through mediums.

Priests and priestesses

Priests and priestesses are individuals who oversee and perform rituals during worship. They are well versed in their communities' traditions of myths, legends, proverbs, and ritual practice. Guided by an extensive knowledge of the protocols of the unseen world, they lead prayers and singing and see that sacrifices and offerings are done properly. They also have the responsibility for the upkeep of temples and shrines, and for receiving gifts that humans present to the gods and goddesses.

Mediums

A **medium** is a specialist who mediates between the human and the spirit worlds by way of spirit possession, sometimes called **trance**. When possessed, mediums lose control over their own personalities and take on the characteristics and the authority of a spirit. Mediums work with clients by probing the possible sources of their problems. Quite often mediums will interrogate clients about their family situations to establish whether an illness is rooted in guilt, witchcraft, or natural disease.

A medium can only be possessed if a spirit is willing. This means that the spirit is largely in control, and the medium serves as the spirit's mouthpiece. The spirit is usually thought to "ride" the medium, either on the medium's head or back. When interrogated by a possessed medium, clients are often convinced that they are communicating directly with the god, goddess, or spirit. In this manner, a medium can command divine authority during a trance, compelling a client to a confess any and all wrongdoings.

Mediums sometimes work in conjunction with a healer or diviner to give proper counsel, and the solutions they prescribe for a client's problem typically involve herbal treatments and sacrifices. But prescriptions can also require social reconciliation to restore spiritual harmony. For this reason, some scholars have likened the role of a medium in African communities to that of a counselor or psychotherapist in western societies.

Diviners

Sometimes when a message is delivered from the spirit world, either through a medium, a dream, or an oracle, it requires interpretation. This is the expertise of the diviner. Like mediums, diviners also seek the cause of misfortunes such as infertility, illness, and death. Most often, however, diviners help people make decisions at critical junctures in their lives: at the birth of a child, in the midst of a social conflict, or in preparation for an important sacrifice.

Diviners can be chosen on the basis of birth into a certain family, or they can be specially appointed by a god or spirit. Divine appointment is often said to manifest itself in mysterious illnesses, often accompanied by epileptic fits. The process of training and initiating a diviner can take years, for diviners must memorize poems, incantations, and other oral traditions, and learn the power of herbs and the use various instruments of divination. They must master techniques for interpreting animal intestines and movement in pools of water, as well as methods for casting small objects such as nut or cowrie shells and deciphering the patterns into which they fall. Since diviners become experts in medicines and herbal treatments, it is sometimes difficult to distinguish them clearly from mediums and healers.

Figure 5.7 An Ashanti fertility doll, portraying the Ashanti ideal of female beauty. Ashanti women who wish to become pregnant often carry these dolls with them, tucked into their clothes.
Source: © Sabena Jane Blackbird/Alamy.

Healers

It is the job of healers to determine the nature of an illness, identify the agent responsible, and prescribe a remedy. If a healer learns that the problem stems from a spiritual cause, they must undertake a spiritual healing. Among the Acholi of Uganda, for instance, evil spirits known as *jok* can possess a person and cause illness. When this happens, a healer, known as *jwaka*, must exorcize them. The Asante of Ghana, in turn, cure infertility among women by using a small doll, known as Akuaba (Figure 5.7). Usually carved from a piece of sacred wood known as Odii and shaped in the image of a child, the doll imparts potent forces that aid conception. Depicted with a large forehead, a small mouth, and a long neck with creases of fat, Akuaba is also the model of female beauty, which should be emulated by Asante women.

Quite often the healer instructs a patient to make a public confession of any wrongs. This confession is then followed by a sacrifice or offering to appease the unseen world. A reaffirmation of the community's moral values thus becomes an intrinsic feature of healings. After this, herbs and minerals are applied to the patient, and future occurrences of the sickness are prevented through charms that the individual is instructed to wear. Finally, a patient may also be told to perform certain rituals at home to counteract any spells that might still be in effect.

The ability to heal, like divination, can be hereditary or revealed to an individual by the spirits or Ancestors during a vision or dream, especially when the individual is in the throes of a serious illness. The training process for a healer involves instruction in the causes, preventions, and cures of diseases and social disorders, as well as the medicinal properties of plants, herbs, minerals, bones, and insects. A trainee will also receive knowledge about witchcraft, sorcery, and magic in order to counteract them, although healers have been known to abuse this knowledge to harm others. Like most religious specialists, healers often work in conjunction with other experts. It is not unusual for a traditional healing center to have a healer, a medium, and a diviner; and counseling services, which are a significant component of African holistic healing, may also be provided.

Prophets

A prophet's vocation is to settle disputes and guide people in their daily affairs by interpreting the will of God and the spirits for the community. They also give oracles and foretell the future, and are experts in medicine and herbs. In the last century and a half, during times of colonial rule and nation-building, prophets have even organized movements for social change. In fact, most African resistance movements in the modern period have been led by these religious specialists. In Tanzania, for instance, the Maji Maji rebellion of 1905–1907 was inspired by the message of the prophet Kinjikitile. This resistance movement, named after an indigenous water medicine called *maji*, fought against forced labor on German cotton plantations. Likewise, in Senegal in the early 1940s, the prophetess Alinesitoue called for her people to boycott the economic system imposed on that country by French colonial rule. In more recent times, African prophets have adopted the custom of naming a successor to carry on their work, a trend that is attributed to the influence of Christian and Islamic millennialist teachings.

Witches and sorcerers

In African religions, human misfortune is ultimately assigned to one of three underlying causes. First, misfortunes that are the common plight of all humans, such as disability in old age, death, and being susceptible to illness, are traced to a mishap at the time of creation that permanently disrupted the original harmonious relationship between humans and the Supreme Being. Second, individuals can suffer misfortune as a result of their own misdeeds and transgressions, as when they fail to honor the Ancestors. And third, individuals can be afflicted by the malevolent designs of a witch or a sorcerer.

Witches are those who inherit the power to harm others, sometimes without realizing it themselves, while sorcerers are trained specialists who prepare herbal potions and wield magical objects to gain access to this power. In both cases, however, these religious specialists inflict evil on other human beings because they have chosen to live their lives in opposition to the cosmic and social order of things. Unlike orderly members of society, witches and sorcerers act at night, and witches are said to move about by flying or by walking upside down on their hands or heads. Many witches and sorcerers are also said to engage in antisocial behaviors such as eating the flesh of corpses, dancing naked, and murdering their relatives. Some witches are even thought to eat a person's soul or steal someone's blood as a way to augment their power, thereby destroying their victim's inner self. In line with this, the Azande of the Congo believe that a witch's power is located in their stomach.

Despite these beliefs, it is an oversimplification to associate a witch or sorcerer's power *only* with evil. While it is true that most are thought to act on evil intentions, any given individual may choose to use these powers to do good. Moreover, in the interconnected worldview of African religions, the evil that is attributed to these individuals, such as crop failure, infertility, and premature death, while unwelcome and widely condemned, is nonetheless accepted as an integral part of the universe. Thus, rather than condemning all witches and sorcerers, or witchcraft and sorcery itself, African communities rely on the services of other religious specialists to counteract the evil they contrive—specialists who often wield the same powers as the witches and sorcerers themselves. Finally, the distinction between a witch and a sorcerer is not always hard and fast, and some individuals perform both roles. In most communities, however, women are accused of witchcraft, while men are typically accused of sorcery.

CONCLUSION

The spiritual hierarchy envisioned by African religions stretches from the self-existent, all-knowing Supreme Being down to the insects and plants of the visible world, and all things are connected through their participation in the Supreme Being's vital force. As a result, gods and goddesses, Ancestors, forces of nature, and human beings depend on the Supreme Being and on each other. For humans, existence is suffused with moral and religious concerns to promote life in all its forms. Honor must be given to those beings who are higher up in the hierarchy; community members must be guided through life and assigned important duties toward the invisible world; and religious specialists must be trained to mediate between that world and the human community. Since multiple causes stand behind all important events and happenings, humans must work to sustain and strengthen the harmony of the whole in multiple ways.

For review

1. How have Africans integrated their religious beliefs and practices into modern western science?
2. What are some of the different ways in which Africans envision the Supreme Being?
3. Explain the relation between the Supreme Being, the vital force, and human society.
4. What do African creation stories tell us about the present relationship between human life and the invisible world?
5. Why are the Ancestors so very important in African religions? How does one become an Ancestor?
6. What is the function of the liminal experience in rites of passage?
7. Name some of the religious specialists of African religions and describe their activities and social roles.

For discussion

1. Are African Initiated Churches (AICs) and Umbanda legitimate forms of African religions, or something else?
2. What are the expectations for the afterlife in African religions? Do you find them appealing? How do they compare to your expectations of an afterlife?

Key Terms

African Initiated Churches (AICs)	Churches that are independent of European church authorities and combine African traditions with Christianity.
Ancestors	The spirits of exemplary human beings who have passed into the unseen world; central to African religions.

androgynous	A being who is both male and female, a quality sometimes attributed to Supreme Beings.
Asen	A metal sculpture used by the Fon (Republic of Benin) as an altar and to remind people of their dependence on the Ancestors.
Gelede festival	The harvest festival for the Great Mother in Yoruba.
Gye Nyame	"Except God!"; a phrase used by the Asante to honor the Supreme Being, expressing the notion that some things are unknowable or undoable except by God.
immanent	"Close by"; used to describe gods that dwell near human communities and are active in human affairs.
liminal	In rites of passage, the experience of being in between what one was and what one will be.
medium	A religious specialist who conveys messages from the unseen world when possessed by a spirit.
Nok sculptures	Terra cotta figurines from archaeological finds in central Nigeria depicting humans and animals; perhaps used to communicate with the spirit world, forces of nature, and culture heroes.
Oshun	A powerful goddess among the Yoruban.
reincorporation	The third and final part of a rite of passage, when someone emerges from the seclusion (liminal) stage with a new identity and is integrated back into society.
rites of passage	Rituals undertaken by individuals at important junctures in life to reaffirm their connection to their community and its gods and spirit beings.
seclusion	The first part of a rite of passage, when initiates are separated from their previous roles in society.
Supreme Being	The creator and source of all life in most African communities.
trance	Spirit possession, especially by mediums, leading to communication from the spirit world.
transcendent	"Far off" or "far above"; used to describe the Supreme Being's remoteness from humans.
transition	The second part of a rite of passage, when initiates leave their former identities behind in preparation for receiving a new identities.
trickster	A clever, mischievous god or spirit who mediates between the human and spirit worlds, often causing confusion or worse.
vital force	The life-giving power of the universe, distributed according to a hierarchy of beings and returned to the Supreme Being after death.

Bibliography

A good first book

Jacob Olupona. *African Religions: A Very Short Introduction*. Oxford: Oxford University Press, 2014.

Further reading

Benezet Bujo. *Foundations of an African Ethics*. New York: Herder & Herder, 2001.

Afolabi Epega and Philip John Neimark. *The Sacred IFA Oracle*, 2nd edn. Brooklyn, NY: Athelia Henrietta, 1999.

Regina Gemignani and Jacob Olupona. *African Immigrant Religions in America*. New York: New York University Press, 2007.

Benjamin Ray. *African Religions: Symbol, Ritual, and Community*, 2nd edn. Upper Saddle River, NJ: Prentice Hall, 2000.

Reference and research

Ibigbolade S. Aderibigbe and Toyin Falola, eds. *The Palgrave Handbook of African Traditional Religion*. London: Palgrave Macmillan, 2022.

Kwame Anthony Appiah and Henry Louis Gates, eds. *Encyclopedia of the African and African American Experience*. Philadelphia, PA: Running Press, 2003.

Elias Kifon Bongmba, ed. *The Wiley-Blackwell Companion to African Religions*. Oxford: Wiley-Blackwell, 2012.

Stephen D. Glazier, ed. *Encyclopedia of African and African American Religions*. New York: Routledge, 2001.

Ama Mazama and Molefi Kete Asante, eds. *Encyclopedia of African Religion*. Thousand Oaks, CA: Sage Publications, 2008.

Harold Scheub. *A Dictionary of African Mythology: The Mythmaker as Story Teller*. New York: Oxford University Press, 2000.

CHAPTER 6

Religions of Oceania
The power embedded in place

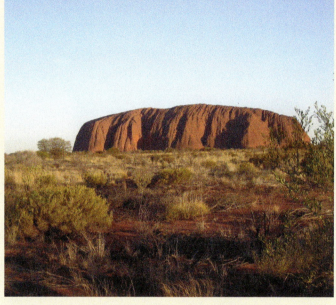

Uluru, or "Ayers Rock," in central Australia. This monolith is sacred ground for Indigenous Australians. Source: Reproduced by permission of Mary N. MacDonald.

DID YOU KNOW …

Singing is used throughout the religions of Oceania to influence the spirit world. Songs can reduce the pain of childbirth, encourage plants to grow large and healthy, and increase one's spiritual power, or *mana*. Some men and women have personal "song lines" that pertain just to them.

Understanding the Religions of the World: An Introduction, Second Edition.
Edited by Will Deming.
© 2025 John Wiley & Sons Ltd. Published 2025 by John Wiley & Sons Ltd.

OVERVIEW

The term **Oceania** refers to the world's largest ocean, the Pacific, and the landmasses it encompasses. Covering more than a third of the world's surface, the Pacific Ocean surrounds some 30,000 islands as well as the continent of Australia. In a recent census, the population of the region was estimated at about 45 million, which included both indigenous and settler peoples. The indigenous peoples, whose religions are the subject of this chapter, number somewhere between 12 and 18 million.

The four regions of Oceania

Scholars of religion generally divide Oceania into four regions: Australia and three groupings of the Pacific Islands—namely, Polynesia, Micronesia, and Melanesia (Figure 6.1). This threefold grouping of the islands goes back to the French explorer Jules Dumont d'Urville (1790–1842).

- The most easterly grouping is called **Polynesia**, a name which means "area of many islands." It extends over a triangular region that includes Hawai'i, Rapa Nui (also called Easter Island), and **Aotearoa** (also called New Zealand) at the corners of the triangle, as well as Samoa, Tonga, the Cook Islands, Tahiti and other islands of French Polynesia, and Niue. In addition, Polynesia includes Tuvalu, Wallis and Futuna, and Tikopia, which are just west of the triangle.

> **Talking about Religion**
>
> ### A Change of Name
>
> In earlier times, the Maori called the northern part of their homeland Aotearoa, meaning the Long White Cloud. Now Aotearoa has become their preferred name for what most westerners still call New Zealand. Likewise, the indigenous people of what westerners call Easter Island prefer the traditional name Rapa Nui.

- **Micronesia**, which means "area of small islands," is to the west and north of Polynesia. It is a 2000-mile-long archipelago, extending from Kiribati and the Gilbert Islands in the southeast, to the Marianas, the Carolines, and Palau in the west.

- South of Micronesia is **Melanesia**. It runs along the northeast coast of Australia, stretching from Papua New Guinea in the west to Fiji in the east, and includes the Solomon Islands, Vanuatu (New Hebrides), and New Caledonia. The name Melanesia means "area of black islands" and refers to the skin color of the people that d'Urville had encountered. At the time it seemed a useful term to distinguish this region from Micronesia and Polynesia. But d'Urville never saw the large populations of inland New Guinea, many of whom are relatively light-skinned.
- Finally, Oceania includes the continent of Australia, a nation whose indigenous population, known as Aboriginal peoples or **Aborigines**, makes up around 4 percent of the total population, or just over a million people.

Diversity and commonalities

The indigenous religions of Oceania are diverse, as one might expect from an area that is home to about one-fourth of all the world's languages. Each religious tradition has a distinct perspective on the world, its own stories and rituals, and its own social structures. Several other religious influences, including Hindu, Muslim, and Christian, have also been introduced into the region, making the situation more complex still. Nonetheless, there are many commonalities among Oceanian religions, deriving from both a widely held understanding of place and local community as sources of life-giving power, and the shared experiences of encountering foreign missionaries and colonialists.

All of the indigenous religions of Oceania may be understood as *orientation to the power embedded in place*. Access to this power, which is gained through proper behavior and ritual activities, maximizes the well-being of the community and the fertility of the land, and overcomes illness and misfortunes on personal, communal, and cosmic levels. In return for this power, the indigenous peoples are committed to "caring for place," meaning the fields, mountains, forests, and seaboards they call home (see the chapter-opening photo), as well as the plants, animals, and unseen beings who live there.

When western and Asian religions came to Oceania, the indigenous peoples did not simply abandon their ancestral traditions. Instead, they integrated the notions of god that they received from merchants and missionaries into their own practices and beliefs. For example, some of their concerns for the fertility of crops and game animals, which were once addressed through appeals to ancestors and land spirits,

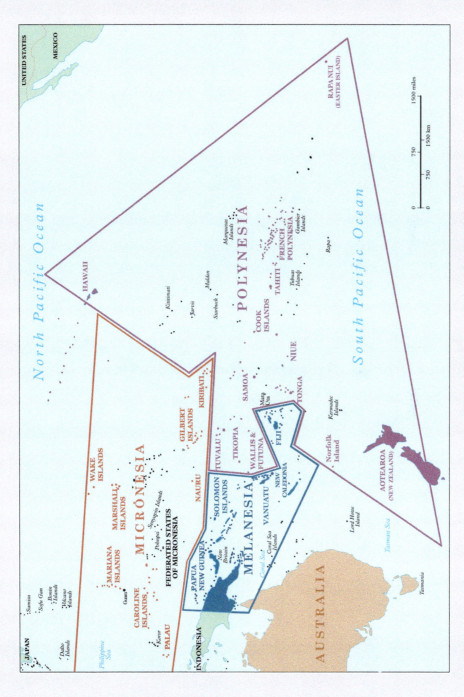

Figure 6.1 The many islands of Oceania are traditionally divided into Polynesia, Micronesia, Melanesia.

are today addressed to the Christian God. God and Jesus are also invoked to extend social and political boundaries. Candidates for parliament might appeal to potential voters outside their kin groups as "children" of the same God and "brothers and sisters" of Jesus. In fact, while about 90 percent of indigenous Oceanians in the islands identify themselves as Christian, it is not as though Christianity has replaced the indigenous gods and spirits. Quite to the contrary: the Christian Trinity (God, Jesus, the Holy Spirit) has joined their company. As a result, indigenous traditions have generally become more universal in outlook, drawing on both indigenous and imported wisdom to empower their lives in the modern world.

Because the central focus of Oceanian religions is the life-giving power of place, the claims to land and resources made by European colonialist have led to common practices of resistance across indigenous traditions. To some degree, members of Oceanian religions have even made common cause with members of other indigenous religions around the world as they fight for ecological concerns and their own political voice. The indigenous religions of Africa and the Americas are similarly embedded in the landscapes that are home to particular communities. They, too, have a concern for the fertility of their land and its inhabitants; and they, too, have experienced the oppression and exploitation of European and U.S. imperialism. Joining in solidarity with these other peoples, the practitioners of Oceanian religions have worked for legal enfranchisement, such as they received in the 2007 United Nations Declaration on the Rights of Indigenous Peoples.

In sum, the diversity of Oceanian religions is tempered by common beliefs and experiences. Consequently, we will sometimes speak of Oceanian religions generally, while at other times we will need to distinguish between the religions of Australia and those of the Pacific Islands (Polynesia, Micronesia, and Melanesia), and at still other times we will distinguish between the religions of the individual island groupings.

History

Timeline	
60,000–40,000 BCE	Peoples from Africa arrive in Australia and New Guinea via Asia and the Indo-Malayan archipelago.
30,000 BCE	Earliest known Australian Aboriginal rock art.
3000–1400 BCE	Polynesian and Micronesian cultures form; people settle in Aotearoa by the end of this period.
16th century CE	European first contacts.
1668 CE	Christian missionaries arrive in Micronesia.
1768–1771	James Cook reaches Australia and Aotearoa on HMS *Endeavour* and claims Australia for Britain.
1778–ca. 1930	The indigenous populations of Australia and Aotearoa decline sharply because of British colonization.
1915	The Australian and New Zealand Army Corps (ANZAC) undertake a mission to capture the Gallipoli Peninsula.
latter half of 20th century	The renewal of indigenous religious practices and the appearance of reconciliation efforts between indigenous and settler peoples.

Until the twentieth century, most Pacific Islanders did not have systems of writing. In the absence of written records, scholars of religion have turned to genetic research, historical-linguistic analysis of oral languages, archeological evidence, and traditional indigenous stories to reconstruct their past. Genetic research suggests that early human beings from Africa migrated east across Asia. From there they turned southeast and traveled by boats and land bridges from island to island through the Indo-Malayan archipelago, some reaching the continental shelf called Sahul (when Australia and New Guinea were joined). This occurred between 60,000 and 40,000 years ago. Linguistic analysis indicates that some of the settlers in New Guinea may have moved east to the Solomon Islands, and from there to the rest of what is now Melanesia.

Thousands of years later—perhaps 4000 years ago—the language profiles behind Polynesian and Micronesian cultures formed as Austronesian speaking groups from southeast Asia entered New Guinea and came into contact with the descendants of the people who had first settled there, who spoke Papuan. Interaction between these peoples can be traced though changes in genetics, culture, and language. Eventually, some of them left New Guinea and traveled east to populate the region we now refer to as Polynesia. Skilled navigators, they sailed as far as Tahiti and Hawai'i, and then swung back southwest to Aotearoa. The last cultural groups to form in Oceania were the Micronesians, whose earliest ancestors seem to have come from the Philippines. They are culturally and linguistically related to peoples from both Polynesia and coastal Melanesia.

A Closer Look

Easter Island's Talking Boards

Among the indigenous cultures in the Pacific, only the people of Rapa Nui (Easter Island) developed a system of writing. Known as Rongorongo, it was inscribed on wooden tablets, which became known as "talking boards" (Figure 6.2). Yet Rongorongo probably began only in the 1770s, following first European contact, and was discontinued around the middle of the nineteenth century. Attempts to decipher the boards have met with little success.

Figure 6.2 In the 1860s, Rongorongo, the hieroglyphic script of Rapa Nui (Easter Island), came to the attention of Eugene Eyraud, the first European missionary to work there. He noticed that houses contained wooden tablets with rows of geometric shapes and symbols of animals, birds, plants, and celestial objects. Today only a few of these tablets remain. Rongorongo was read by turning the board 180 degrees after each line, as the glyphs of each line are upside down with respect to the line before it. Source: Wikimedia Commons.

Regarding the religions of Oceanian, evidence comes from archeological finds such as rock carvings and paintings, and remnants of shrines and ceremonial grounds. Rock paintings dating back tens of thousands of years have been found in Aboriginal sites in Australia. Some of these portray community ceremonies, while others depict various animals, including carnivorous lizards, turtles, fish, possums, wallabies, and the now-extinct Tasmanian tiger. These may have been painted to establish connections between hunters and the spirits of the animals they intended to kill. Still other paintings portray the **Rainbow Snake**, a sacred being who is said to have shaped large parts of northern Australia during a period of creative activity known as **The Dreaming**. From these and other findings, scholars surmise that earlier inhabitants of Oceania maintained religious practices and beliefs that linked them to both the natural environment and their ancestors.

From the sixteenth century onward, we are able to supplement this early evidence with **first contact** reports of European traders and colonists. More recently our knowledge has been shaped by oral traditions collected by early explorers, missionaries, and anthropologists, as well as by the early written testimonies of Pacific Islanders educated in government and mission schools. Used with care, this information gives us some insight into the last few decades before the arrival of the Europeans. One rather striking piece of information we glean from these materials is that human sacrifice and the consumption of human flesh (necrophagia) were a part of some Oceanian religions. In Polynesian societies, enemies captured in battle were sacrificed to the gods for the sake of the community and the land. The practice seems to have been motivated by an understanding of the redistribution of life force, or *mana*. People nourished the gods and honored their chiefs with gifts that contained this precious life force, and in return the gods energized the people and the land.

A Closer Look

Captain Cook and the King of the Friendly Islands: A First Contact Report

THURSDAY, JUNE 26, 1777:

Having, therefore, some days of leisure before me, a party of us, accompanied by Poulaho [king of the Friendly Islands] set out, early next morning, in a boat, for Mooa, the village where he and the other great men usually reside. ...

As soon as we got ashore, the king desired Omai to tell me, that I need be under no apprehensions about the boat, or any thing in her, for not a single article would be touched by any one; and we afterward found this to be the case. We were immediately conducted to one of Poulaho's houses not far off, and near the public one, or *malaee*, in which we had

(continued)

> been, when we first visited Mooa. This, though pretty large, seemed to be his private habitation, and was situated within a plantation. The king took his seat at one end of the house, and the people, who came to visit him, sat down, as they arrived, in a semicircle at the other end. The first thing done, was to prepare a bowl of *kava* [a drink made from roots], and to order some yams to be baked for us.
>
> *The Journals of Captain James Cook on His Voyages of Discovery*, ed. J. C. Beaglehole, Cambridge, Published for the Hakluyt Society at the University Press, 1955–69, vol. 1, pp. 311–312.

Polynesian warfare and Australian funerary rituals, in turn, employed forms of cannibalism. During intertribal warfare, Polynesians seem to have used cannibalism to "completely destroy" the enemy, or perhaps ingest their warrior qualities. As a part of Aboriginal funerary practices in Australia, cannibalism was undertaken within kinship groups, specific parts of the deceased being given to specific kin. In these instances, it may have been thought that the *mana* of the deceased would pass to their relatives. Naturally, in evaluating the extent and significance of cannibalism, we need to be wary of exaggerations by early Europeans and distinguish between mythic accounts of cannibalism and its actual practice. Aboriginal stories of creation events, for example, often depict cannibals who prey on the community, but we do not know if this was an invention of the storyteller or an echo of an earlier reality. Even so, some cannibalism continued well after the Europeans arrived, as reported by eyewitnesses, and a few incidents are documented as late as the mid-twentieth century.

European first contacts, especially, must be used with caution in writing the history of Oceanian religions because they resulted in more than just reports and information. They also produced significant changes in indigenous cultures. To take just one example, the staple crop of the Papua New Guinea highlands is now the sweet potato, which comes from South America. It is possible, of course, that seeds from this plant could have reached Polynesia before human occupation, but more probably the sweet potato was introduced by traders about 350 years ago. Before that time, grass seed seems to have played an important part in the diet of the highlanders. At least this is one conclusion that can be drawn from the presence of mortars and pestles. At some point in the past, these mortars and pestles were added to a collection of egg-shaped stones that were used in the secret rituals of male cults; and today both the stones and the surviving mortars and pestles are associated with ancestral spirits. In all likelihood, however, this was not their original purpose, and their association with the egg-shaped stones came about after they had fallen out of use in food preparation. It is thus quite possible that their original use was for crushing grass seed prior to the European introduction of the sweet potato.

European imperialism and Christian missions

Starting in the 1500s, European explorers entered the Pacific in search of *Terra Australis Incognita*, a Latin phrase meaning "unknown south land." By the end of the seventeenth century, explorers from various countries had charted and claimed many of the Pacific Islands, and the Dutch had sighted and charted parts of Australia and Aotearoa. Between 1768 and 1771, Lieutenant (later Captain) James Cook, sailing on HMS *Endeavour*, charted the east coast of Australia and most of the coastlines of Aotearoa's North and South Islands, claiming Australia for the British empire. Subsequent to Cook's voyage, European and North American whaling and sealing ships entered the area.

By 1778 the British had established a penal colony at Botany Bay, near the modern city of Sydney, Australia. This was to hold convicts who, prior to the American Revolution, would have been sent to North America. On completing their terms of imprisonment, many convicts stayed on as settlers, as did retired British officers, who received land grants from the Crown. They were soon joined by other British settlers, who claimed land in Australia and Aotearoa for farming wheat and grazing sheep and cattle. The indigenous population of Australia at the beginning of this colonization effort has been estimated at about 350,000 (although some recent studies argue for a much higher figure, closer to 6 million). It and the native population of Aotearoa, the **Maori**, declined dramatically over the next 150 years due to several causes, including (1) the introduction of firearms and infectious diseases (measles, smallpox, tuberculosis, influenza, and whooping cough); (2) the forced resettlement of native people; and (3) the removal of children from their families in a misguided effort to preserve and civilize future generations of indigenous people. Today Australia and Aotearoa are distinctive among the nations and territories of Oceania in having a large settler population and only a small minority of indigenous people.

> ### Talking about Religion
>
> ## The Abduction of Children
>
> As a result of colonialism, the cultures and worldviews of indigenous peoples throughout the world have been devastated. These groups have been deprived of their homelands, their ways of livelihood, their sacred places, and even the custody of their children. It was only in 1992 that an Australian high court overturned the continent's legal status as *terra nullius*, or "empty land," that was given to it during the era of European settlement. Then, in 2008, there was cause for great celebration when the injustice of successive Australian governments was officially recognized, and an apology delivered in parliament by Prime Minister Kevin Rudd. In his remarks below, the prime minister refers, in particular, to the **Stolen Generations**—those children who were taken away from their families and placed in boarding schools or adopted into white families so they could be assimilated into the majority culture. The prime minister's apology was a significant ritual moment in the national process of reconciliation (Figure 6.3):
>
> > Today we honour the Indigenous peoples of this land, the oldest continuing cultures in human history. We reflect on their past mistreatment.

(continued)

We reflect in particular on the mistreatment of those who were Stolen Generations—this blemished chapter in our nation's history.

The time has now come for the nation to turn a new page in Australia's history by righting the wrongs of the past and so moving forward with confidence to the future. We apologize for the laws and policies of successive Parliaments and governments that have inflicted profound grief, suffering and loss on these our fellow Australians. We apologize especially for the removal of Aboriginal and Torres Strait Islander children from their families, their communities and their country.

For the pain, suffering and hurt of these Stolen Generations, their descendants and for their families left behind, we say sorry. To the mothers and the fathers, the brothers and the sisters, for the breaking up of families and communities, we say sorry. And for the indignity and degradation thus inflicted on a proud people and a proud culture, we say sorry.

House of Representatives Official Hansard, no. 1, 2008, Wednesday, 13 February 2008, p. 67.

Figure 6.3 The then Prime Minister of Australia, Kevin Rudd, embraces members of the "Stolen Generations" in 2008, after delivering an apology from the Australian government for its presumptuous and tragic mistreatment of Aboriginal peoples. Source: Reuters/Mark Baker.

Colonial interventions in the Pacific also paved the way for Christian missionary activity, the earliest missionaries being Spanish Jesuits. First active in the Philippines, they sailed east to the Mariana Islands in 1668, establishing the first Catholic churches there. About a century later, both Protestant and Catholic missionaries began making inroads in east Polynesia. Christian groups also settled in Aotearoa and eventually converted most of the native Maori population. In Hawai'i, missionaries from the

American Board of Commissioners for Foreign Missions gained the support of Queen Kaahumanu (1768–1832), establishing Congregational churches there. In 1797 the largely Congregational London Missionary Society sent its first missionaries to Tahiti. At first, the Tahitians were unresponsive to their message, but when their ruler, Pomare II, became a Christian in 1815, his constituents followed suit. The London Society's strategy was to establish churches and then move west. Thus, missionaries from Tahiti moved on, accompanied by Pacific Island evangelists, to the Cook Islands and Samoa, and from there to Tuvalu, the Loyalty Islands, Kiribati, and New Guinea.

During this period, English Methodists established churches in Tonga and Fiji, where, to this day, the majority of people are Methodist. Presbyterians, in turn, established churches in the New Hebrides, and Anglicans established them in the Solomon Islands, where Methodist and the South Seas Evangelicals also found a footing. Generally, Catholic missions followed Protestants into these islands, although in this westward missionary sweep across the Pacific, Catholics were the first to arrive in New Caledonia, where Marist missionaries ministered to French settlers as well as the indigenous people. In 1871 the London Missionary Society began its work in Papua New Guinea, where it was soon joined by Methodists, Anglicans, Lutherans, and Catholics.

As Christian missionaries began work in Fiji, however, Hindu and Muslim communities were also developing there. In the nineteenth century, Hindus and Muslims came to Fiji from India to work as indentured servants on British sugar plantations. At the end of their contracts, many stayed, becoming a significant component of Fiji's population. Likewise, the western part of New Guinea experienced an influx of Hindu and Muslim traders, some as early as the tenth century. Now part of Indonesia, this area's population is about half Muslim because of the country's policy of encouraging the emigration of people from Java.

The resilience of Oceanian religions

The manner in which Christian missionaries assessed and interacted with Oceanian religions varied from place to place and developed over time. The first missionaries characterized the localized, indigenous worldviews, in which people, trees, animals, and stones were said to share life and influence each other, as "infantile," "savage," and "primitive" misunderstandings of the world. Their approach was to condemn the beliefs and practices of the indigenous religions while working to replace them with Christianity. In the last century, however, most missionary efforts have concluded that it is more productive to accommodate the Christian message to indigenous worldviews.

As a result of this second approach, indigenous peoples of Oceania have often adopted aspects of Christianity, but on their own terms. Some understand the Christian God as a fuller revelation of an indigenous god or spirit. Others find parallels between their ancestral traditions and biblical narratives, and today it is common for students in the region's theological colleges to write theses on these parallels. Outwardly accepting Christianity and attending church, indigenous people continue to practice the "ways of the ancestors." Indeed, a history of Christianity in Oceania could well be written by tracing the way Christian elements have been integrated into the beliefs and practices of the various indigenous communities. By the beginning of the twenty-first century, most of the peoples of Oceania had become Christian; but the dialog and interaction between Christianity and indigenous traditions is far from over. It continues in daily household conversations, political oratory, and in Pacific theology.

> ### Sacred Traditions and Scripture
>
> ## Narratives of the Great Flood
>
> Since most peoples of Oceania today are Christian, it is common for them to see parallels between biblical stories and indigenous traditions. Here is an indigenous account of the great flood that serves as a Micronesian counterpart to the biblical flood narrative:
>
> The stars are the shining eyes of the gods. A man once went into the sky and stole one of the eyes. (The Pelew [Palau] Islanders' money is made from it.) The gods were angry at this and came to earth to punish the theft. They disguised themselves as ordinary men and went door-to-door begging for food and lodging. Only one old woman received them kindly. They told her to make a bamboo raft ready and, on the night of the next full moon, to lie down on it and sleep. This she did. A great storm came; the sea rose, flooded the islands, and destroyed everyone else. The woman, fast asleep, drifted until her hair caught on a tree on the top of Mount Armlimui. The gods came looking for her again, but they found her dead. So one of the women-folk from heaven entered the body and restored it to life. The gods begat five children by the old woman and then returned to heaven, as did the goddess who restored her to life. The present inhabitants of the islands are descendants of those five children.
>
> Theodor H. Gaster, *Myth, Legend, and Custom in the Old Testament* (New York: Harper & Row, 1969), pp. 112–13.

In Aotearoa, for example, the native Maori population received Christianity and developed their own indigenous churches. Before the arrival of Christian missionaries, the Maori had worshipped in places called *marae*, where they encountered the sacred power of the land. These were usually rectangular clearings with a meeting hall, a dining hall, and several other buildings. The architectural features of the *marae* were fashioned around a traditional Polynesian understanding of the cosmos. The Maori say that the world we live in (the "world of light") was created when the divine parents, the Sky Father Rangi and the Earth Mother Papa, were forced apart by their son to create a habitation for people. Accordingly, the floor of the ceremonial area (which is also called *marae*) corresponds to the Earth Mother; the sky above it corresponds to the Sky Father; and the meeting hall itself is the son who forced them apart. Today many Maori Christians, including Anglicans, Presbyterians, and Catholics, participate in ancestral rituals that take place in buildings called *Te marae*, which are the successors to the traditional meeting halls.

Another example of indigenous innovation is the so-called **cargo cults**. When Europeans first came to the Pacific, Oceania consisted of small-scale, subsistence economies augmented by trading networks that facilitated the exchange of indigenous foods and artifacts between peoples and islands. With the introduction of European goods, these trading networks flourished. Impressed by the abundance of material goods, formerly unknown in Oceania, indigenous peoples began to form religious movements around this exchange of goods. Combining ideas and rituals of wealth and reciprocity from both indigenous traditions and Christianity, the participants in these movements awaited the dawning of a utopian

Figure 6.4 Tanna Island in Vanuatu is home to one of the last remaining "cargo cults." Founded by John Frum after the islanders came into contact with the material wealth of American troops during World War II, it borrowed and adapted several Christian images. This painting, for example, depicts a black Mary weeping at the foot of a red cross on which her son, a black Jesus, has been crucified. Frum always used a red cross, which he may have seen on equipment brought by American medical units. Source: NNN.

world filled with material possessions and harmonious relationships. In New Guinea, where these movements blossomed, they acquired the name cargo cults—which is more informative of the views of western observers than of the theology and practices of the participants (Figure 6.4). While instances of these "cults" have waned since the 1950s, new religious movements that emphasize the power of the Christian Holy Spirit have appeared, satisfying indigenous desires for tradition-rooted ways of defining life in a modern, materialistic environment. Pentecostal and Evangelical churches, which promote miraculous gifts of the Spirit, have become especially popular in Australia.

Pluralism

Oceanian religions have shown their vitality and resilience not only in appropriating aspects of Christianity, but also in dealing with modern environmental and political realities. This can be seen especially in Australia and Aotearoa, where the indigenous peoples are only small minorities in their homelands. In the give-and-take of these pluralistic societies, indigenous people have taken the initiative to invite nonindigenous people to share in some of their religious festivals.

For hundreds, if not thousands, of years, the Aboriginal people of Australia celebrated periodic festivals associated with food crops. With their displacement from traditional lands, however, some of these festivals were interrupted. The **Gubbi Gubbi** people of southeastern Queensland in Australia were formerly hunters and gatherers, but now earn their living in a variety of occupations. Even so, they have revitalized the Bunya Dreaming Festival and sought to protect the ecosystem of their traditional territory along the Mary River from the Traveston Crossing Dam proposed by the Queensland government in 2006. They see both the ritual action (the festival) and the political action (their protest of the dam) as aspects of their religious commitment to "care for Country."

The **Bunya Dreaming Festival**, which brings Aboriginal groups together along Australia's central eastern coast, takes place when the bunya tree, an evergreen conifer, bears its fruit. A native plant that belongs to the genus *Araucaria*, the bunya dates back 180 million years to the Jurassic era and is sacred to the Aboriginal people. It bears nuts in a heavy cone, which can weigh more than 20 pounds. The individual nuts, which resemble chestnuts and are somewhat similar in taste, are a nutritious food that is eaten raw, roasted, boiled, or ground into a paste and mixed with other foods. A renewed form of the traditional celebration, the Bunya Dreaming Festival is an opportunity to share food, to hear traditional stories, to reflect on the relationship of people to the land, and to get to know people throughout the region. In this way the Bunya Dreaming Festival has become part of the reconciliation process between Aboriginal Australians and settler Australians.

The Gubbi Gubbi also have a special relationship to the Queensland lungfish, or Dala, which lives in the Mary River (Figure 6.5). They have adopted it as their identifying emblem, and are sometimes referred to as the Dala people. On account of this relationship, when the Traveston Crossing Dam was proposed in response to an extended period of drought, they felt an obligation to protect the lungfish from this project. Since there was also strong opposition to the dam from the larger community and from groups such as the Australian Conservation Foundation, the Gubbi Gubbi drew many white Australians into their efforts to care for Country. Two Gubbi Gubbi women, Dr. Eve Fesl and Beverly Hand, took leading roles in protesting the dam, making public statements such as the following, which invoke religious values:

> I know this river intimately. I know its tributaries, and its plants and animals. My mother told us stories about this area—oral history that has been passed down from generations. There is a history of more than 1000 years along this river and surrounding ranges, with burial sites, Bora rings

Religions of Oceania

Figure 6.5 The Queensland lungfish (Dala) of the Gubbi Gubbi people is one of only six extant lungfish species in the world. Recognized as a vulnerable species, the fish is potentially at risk with the construction of dams and weirs to regulate the waters of the Mary and Burnett rivers. Source: Wikimedia Commons.

[initiation precincts], and ceremonial sites in the area which would be inundated by the proposed dam.

> Beverly Hand, as quoted in Adele Coombs, ed., *Love, Mary* (Kandanga, Qld: Save the Mary River Coordinating Group, 2008), p. 37.

In 2009, the efforts of all who had cooperated in opposing the dam were brought to fruition when the Federal Environment Minister announced that the project would not go forward.

Religions of national identity

In Australia and Aotearoa, we find not only indigenous religions, and indigenous and western versions of Christianity, but also **civil religions**. These are systems of beliefs and practices related to national identity in which most members of a society participate. A good example of the practice of civil religion is **ANZAC Day**, during which the citizens of Australia and Aotearoa forge bonds with the land, with the national community, with their families, and with the people who have gone before them.

Because Australians and Aoteaoans fought side-by-side in World War I and World War II, they share April 25 as a day to honor their veterans and war dead. On that day in 1915, the Australian and New Zealand Army Corps, or ANZAC, set out to capture the Gallipoli Peninsula from the Turks to open a way to the Black Sea for the Allied navies. The final goal of the Allies was to capture Istanbul, the capital of the Ottoman empire. Landing on Gallipoli, ANZAC forces met fierce resistance. The campaign dragged on for eight months, until the Allied forces were evacuated, both sides suffering heavy casualties.

ANZAC Day is a most solemn occasion, for it commemorates not only the sacrifices of the original ANZAC, but also those of the men and women who fought in

World War II, the Korean War, and the Vietnam War, as well as in the wars in Iraq and Afghanistan. In recent years many citizens of Australian and Aotearoa have made pilgrimages to Gallipoli to pay their respects and hold ceremonies there. As scholars of religion have observed, there is a spiritual, transcendent element in these commemorations that comes to expression in the rather paradoxical behavior of its participants. On the morning of ANZAC Day, the heroic sacrifice of the ANZAC is remembered with formal street parades, somber outdoor services, and wreath-laying, while the afternoon is marked by alcoholic excess.

Contemporary Beliefs and Practices

The religions of Oceania enable adherents to orient themselves to the life-giving power that is embedded in *place*. Most indigenous peoples in Oceania still live in small-scale societies and depend on the natural bounty of the surroundings fields, rivers, forests, and seas for their livelihood. A few are hunters and gatherers, but the majority live as subsistence horticulturalists. They eat a diet of tubers and green vegetables, supplemented with game and fish, and pigs that they keep for ceremonial purposes. Even those who work for wages in towns or in large cities like Suva, Port Moresby, Sydney, and Auckland, consider it important to stay connected to the land. Thus, an office worker in the town of Goroka in Papua New Guinea might refer to his paycheck as his "garden," because it provides his food.

But the **power embedded in place** is more than just the fertility of the natural world, for Oceanians understand "place" as both geography *and community*. In other words, the life-giving power that is localized in a place is localized in all of its inhabitants as well. It not only suffuses the rocks and streams and plants and animals, but also the people, along with their tools and weapons and ritual objects, and especially the many unseen beings of a place. To orient oneself to the vital power or life embedded in place, therefore, is to maintain and cultivate fruitful interactions with a wide spectrum of objects and beings that are believed to inhabit one's particular social and geographical location in the world. Beyond this, one must also nurture relations with the inhabitants of other, adjacent locations. This is because one's place is always tied to a larger network of places, each inhabited by its own communities of plants, animals, people, objects, and spiritual beings. Among the Kewa of the New Guinea highlands, for example, the cosmos includes many settlements of human beings, a distant world of sky people, forests inhabited by various kinds of spirits, and settlements of ghosts reached by taking paths through the forests.

> **Did you know …**
>
> Currently, the biggest danger to the religions of Oceania is not secularism or missionaries from other religions. It is climate change, which threatens to submerge many of the smaller Pacific Islands.

The cosmic order

According to the peoples of Oceania, the order of our world is the work of spirit beings. These beings came from below the earth, from the sea, from the sky, or from over the horizon. Appearing in animal and human form, they moved across a region, forming mountains, rivers, animals, plants, rocks, and people, and implanting life-enhancing power in many places. In founding human communities, they imparted knowledge of hunting and warfare, healing, cooking, and building. They also established the social structures that define the relationships between groups and individuals. Certain places where they stopped on their journeys became sacred places where rituals are now carried out. After shaping an area and all that is in it, these beings then moved on to other territories or were transformed into trees, rocks, waterholes, or stars, leaving it to human beings to sustain what they had put in place.

While this general story is repeated across Oceania, there is no single, authoritative version of how things came into being. Instead, accounts of the spirits' ordering of the world vary from place to place, the people of one community describing the route the spirits took through their territory, the people in adjacent areas continuing the story sequence, or **song line**, of the spirits' passage through theirs. Some versions of the story are accessible to everyone in a community, while others are meant only for people of a certain age or status. There are even versions known only to men or only to women, and each person can have their own personal song line, inherited through one's mother or father. The Gaagudju people of Australia, for example, tell stories of a woman called Warramurrungundjui who came out of the sea with a womb full of children. She traveled through the land, giving birth to her children and instructing them in the languages that have been passed down through the generations. She also carried a digging stick and a dilly bag (a mesh bag made of plant fibers) holding yams, water lilies, and other plants. Warramurrungundjui planted foods and, using her digging stick, created waterholes. Other creator beings then appeared to help in her work of shaping the land. After Warramurrungundjui completed her tasks she turned herself into a rock, which can be seen to this day.

In the traditions of the Pacific Islands—Polynesia, Micronesia, and Melanesia—the stories typically feature sky gods and culture heroes. These beings distribute a sacred, efficacious power, known in Austronesian languages as *mana*. The sky gods, in some cases, endowed certain people with *mana*, thereby establishing hierarchical societies whose royal families can trace their lineage back to these gods through intermediary deities, such as the god of the forest or the god of warfare. On this basis, the indigenous people lay claim to the various resources of the region for themselves and their clans. **Culture heroes** are spirit beings somewhere between gods and humans, and in Melanesia they are often said to have traveled in pairs or groups. Their role was to introduce important institutions into human society, such as warfare, agriculture, and marriage, and to empower humans with important skills, such as sea navigation, weaving, building, and food preparation. If they are brothers, like Kilibob and Manup in the stories from Madang Province in New Guinea, they portray two contrasting ways of life and behavior, such as hunting and gardening. Pacific Islanders also tell stories that recount the creation of the world—as opposed to its ordering after the fact—during which the gods pull the world up from under the ocean.

> ### Sacred Traditions and Scripture
>
> ### The Culture Hero Tidalap
>
> On reaching manhood, Tidalap took a hero girl from a village nearby as his wife. In the beginning everything went well, but he was by nature suspicious and soon accused her of infidelity. Although she protested innocence, he not only refused to listen but beat her so unmercifully that the blood flowed from the wounds. His relatives, fearing her kinsmen might take vengeance on them for failing to prevent such cruelty, decided to launch their canoe and sail away. Tidalap, now alone, became terrified and also followed. But his brothers, in the interests of their own safety, killed him and dismembered the body. The trunk turned into the island of Mushu, which is low and flat, the head into the hilly island of Kairiru, the fingers into various coral reefs, and the legs into the Torricelli Mountains of the New Guinea mainland.
>
> Ian Hogbin, *The Island of Menstruating Men* (Scranton, PA: Chandler, 1970), pp. 30–31.

The Dreaming

In Australia, stories about the cosmic order emphasize ancestors and gods of natural forces as the primary actors, who are said to be part of something called The Dreaming. While the name The Dreaming might give the impression of a distant, dreamlike foundation for the world, nothing could be further from the truth. For the Aborigines, the events, the people, and the places of The Dreaming are so real that they continually sustain and energize the land in a timeless fashion. In the Warlpiri language, for example, the word that is rendered into English as The Dreaming means "to see and understand the Law."

Several versions of The Dreaming feature a being known as Rainbow Snake (Figure 6.6). This creative spirit, portrayed in some places as female and in others as male, is always associated with watercourses such as billabongs

Figure 6.6 The Rainbow Snake, here depicted on a wall mural, is both a benevolent protector and a punisher of law breakers. In northern Australia, where monsoons are prevalent, the Rainbow Snake often has a violent persona. In the central desert, where seasonal changes are less dramatic, she is depicted as treating the landscape with greater calm. Source: © Bill Bachman/Alamy.

(seasonal rivers), rivers, creeks, and lagoons. The Rainbow Snake is the protector of the land and its people, and the source of all its life, but she can also be a destructive force if not given the proper respect. One popular account describes the world long ago as flat and bare and cold. The Rainbow Snake slept under the ground with all the animal tribes in her womb, who were waiting to be born. When her time came, she pushed up, calling to the animals to come forth. She threw the ground up, making mountains and hills, and she spilled water over the land, making rivers and lakes. Then she made the sun, fire, and all the colors. In a more localized version, told by the Gagudju, the Rainbow Snake is known as Almudj, and lives under a waterfall in Kakadu. In their rendition of the story, Almudj forces passages through rocks, creating beneficial waterholes. Each year she appears in the sky as a rainbow and brings the wet season, causing all forms of life to multiply. The Gagudju also fear Almudj, however, because she punishes those who break the law by drowning them in floods.

Some variations of The Dreaming in northern Australia attribute the primal ordering of the world to a spirit-being known as the All-Mother, while in the southeast the events of The Dreaming are often located in the time before 1788 (when the British First Fleet arrived, with disastrous consequences for the native populations), and the principal actor is called the All-Father, who lives far off in the sky. Since about 1980, many Aboriginal peoples throughout Australia have attributed the ordering of the world to a common Mother Earth, who watches over the entire continent. In all three of these variations the tendency is toward a more universal understanding, envisioning a united Aboriginal community located in a single, common *place*, which is Australia.

Maintaining the cosmic balance

Once the order of the world has been established, it becomes the responsibility of human beings to maintain and care for it—a responsibility that is often called **the Law**. Humans need to sustain the sacred balance of their places by nurturing and repairing the relationships between the diverse beings that live there, and by ensuring the continual, abundant flow of power from a place to all the members of its community. Most often this is accomplished through everyday activities, such as gardening, fishing, and animal husbandry, which participate in the proper order of things through the rhythms expressed in nature.

> ### Talking about Religion
>
> #### Law and the Song Lines of Oceania
>
> No matter if they are fish, birds, men, women, animals, wind or rain.... All things in our country here have Law, they have ceremony and song, and they have people who are related to them.
>
> Mussolini Harvey, a Yanyuwa elder from central-northern Australia, quoted in M. Harvey, "The Dreaming," foreword to J. Bradley, *Yanyuwa Country: The Yanyuwa People of Booroloola Tell of Their Land* (Richmond, VA: Greenhouse, 1988), p. xi.

Fishing groups, for example, have rituals to ensure a good catch, while gardening is accompanied by songs and chants that encourage yams to swell and warn destructive insects to stay away. Gardeners sometimes use spells and Christian prayers to invite the sun and rain to visit the garden and to cast out plant disease. The prohibition of sexual intercourse during the growing season as well as a couple's ritual of sexual relations in a new garden are also ways for gardeners to manage the flow of power through their crops. Beyond this, there are rituals for weather, child raising, attracting members of the opposite sex, hunting, trade, and healing. Everyone practices some rituals in the course of their daily routine, and a variety of part-time healers, mediums, and shamans are also active in most regions. When plants, animals, or people fare poorly, it is an indication that the flow of power has been impeded. If there is a severe blight or illness, or an unexplained (unnatural) death, an investigation must take place to determine if an enemy or an angry spirit has inhibited the proper movement of life-enhancing power through the community.

Storytelling

Another important way that Oceanians maintain the order and balance in their communities is through storytelling. Stories are expressed in a variety of forms, including myth, legend, song, painting, dance, and ceremony. These not only pass important information from one generation to the next about the power that is localized in a place, but they also evoke a community's network of relationships in both intellectual and emotional ways. Stories of The Dreaming, for example, contain Aboriginal knowledge of sacred areas and rituals, and norms for behavior; and when a particular group honors a spiritual being by singing to it, the song welcomes that being into the reality of The Dreaming. Storytelling also solidifies the younger generation's connection to The Dreaming ancestors, which establishes a person's rights to hunt and gather in certain territories, as well as the responsibility to care for that land. For Oceanians, storytelling is not so much concerned with what happened in historical time, but with how a way of life was established, and how one can maximize the well-being of the land and community in one's particular place.

Reciprocity and redistribution

Given the importance of balance, relationship, and the proper flow of power, it is not surprising that the principles of reciprocity and redistribution play a significant role in Oceanian religions. Sometimes called **payback**, these principles are envisioned as the proper management of *mana*. Ritualized gift-giving and wealth redistribution are common practices throughout the region, as are offerings to gods and spirits. In addition, when a clan identifies closely with a particular animal or plant (its so-called *totem*), its members may abstain from eating that plant or animal, thereby making it available to other clans.

Mana, as we have noted, is the Austronesian term used by the indigenous peoples of Polynesia, Micronesia, and Melanesia for the power that is embedded in place. It is understood to be a quality or force that energizes people and things, giving them the ability to reach their goals. A strangely shaped stone, a person successful in trade, and a forest spirit are all understood as expressing the potency of *mana*. As some scholars have pointed out, many non-Austronesian languages in these areas treat *mana* not as a noun but as a stative verb. In other words, in these cases it may be more accurate to say that things *are mana*, rather than *possess mana*. Thus, a canoe that is *mana* takes a steady course. A spear that is *mana* reaches its target. And a chief who is *mana* exercises effective leadership.

Rituals, Rites, Practices

The Return of a Traditional Dance

The *hula* ritual is well known to those who have visited Hawai'i or have seen performances by Hawaiian dance troupes. Prior to the arrival of western missionaries, it was performed to honor the gods, pay tribute to chiefs, and celebrate nature and community. Believed to have been instituted by the goddess Laka, its chants and dance movements evoked the natural environment—valleys, forests, and rivers, as well as plants and flowers. When missionaries arrived in Hawai'i, starting in 1820, they were offended by what they perceived as the erotic element of the *hula*, and denounced as "heathen" its depiction of human love and the fruitfulness of nature. This led to a decline in the traditional performance of *hula*, and the development of a new form, known as *hula kui'i*, which combined traditional and new elements. Later, to appeal to an increasing tourist trade, the *hula* was presented as an entertainment with a focus on the beauty and charms of the dancers. But beginning in the 1960s, with support from the Hawaiian Cultural Renaissance, the study and practice of ancient *hula* has once again become popular, as have indigenous forestry and farming practices, and traditional outrigger canoeing and Polynesian voyaging.

There are also different types of *mana*, deriving from different sources. The Maori, for example, speak of *atua*, *tupuna*, and *whenua* types, among others. *Mana atua* comes from the particular god (*atua*) associated with an individual or group. *Mana tupuna*, which expresses itself as the power of a chiefly lineage, is part of a ruling family's inheritance from ancestors and the natural world. And *mana whenua* is derived from the land, being the power that the gods planted within Mother Earth so that she could produce abundance in the land. Thus, a person or tribe who controls a region is said to *be* the *mana whenua* of the area, and has the right to derive a living from that land. Because certain types of *mana* express themselves only in certain individuals and groups in a community, it is necessary that these individuals and groups make their *mana* available for the benefit of all through acts of reciprocity and redistribution. This is so important that the Anglican missionary and amateur anthropologist R.H. Codrington (1830–1922), who worked in eastern Melanesia, even characterized religion there as largely the process of acquiring *mana*.

Figure 6.7 In the highlands of New Guinea, periodic exchanges called pig-kills serve to cement alliances, remember the ancestors, and, in the contemporary period, express Christian faith. People gather, make speeches, dance, feast, and renew communal life. Source: © Danny Lehman/gettyimages.

Gods and spirits are known to increase a person's *mana* in return for songs, dances, and offerings, while humans engage in gift-giving and ritual redistribution of wealth between individuals and clans to keep *mana* flowing in various directions. In the highlands of New Guinea, ritual exchange can take the form of a large-scale slaughter of pigs, followed by transactions in pork and shells (Figure 6.7). In places with hereditary chiefs, harvest and first-fruit ceremonies function to redistribute the *mana* of the land in ways that validate the structures of society. On the Trobriand Islands, for example, yams are ceremonially eaten in succession by priest, chief, men, women, and children, while exchanges of yams take place between the hierarchies of individuals and lineages.

On the other hand, it also becomes necessary to preserve, protect, and restrict the flow of *mana*, both to keep it properly distributed and to prevent it from being depleted. In these cases, a restrictive force called *tapu* comes into play, usually translated into English as **taboo**. Objects, persons, and behaviors that manifest power not available to others are said to be set apart by taboo, making them potential sources of danger. For example, places where spirits dwell are usually taboo, including caves, swamps, rivers, mountains, and trees. These locations can be fraught with peril, and people who violate their sanctity are said to have encountered capricious and often harmful spirits, and even cruel monsters and ogres who shoot arrows into trespassers and ambush those who disturb their peace. When it is necessary to harvest nuts or to hunt in dangerous places such as these, Oceanians must perform protective rituals and purification rites. Likewise, before making a substantial change to their environment, such as felling a tree, they placate the local spirits with gifts and politely entreat them to move to another area.

Taboo may also require regularly avoiding certain relationships or objects, or staying away from certain events, such as birth or death. A husband, for instance, must be isolated from his wife during childbirth, or its taboo will destroy his *mana*. The consumption of food and drink can also be governed by taboo, and word-taboo and name-taboo are examples of this restrictive force in speech. Thus, many religious argots (insider terminology) have taboo, such as the special languages that can be employed only during the annual harvest of pandanus (screw pine) fruit in the Southern Highlands of Papua New Guinea.

Power in the human life cycle

As in many other religions, the adherents of Oceanian religions find it necessary to reaffirm, renew, or further develop their connections to ultimate reality as they move through important junctures in their own lives or in the life of their community. In these **rites of passage**, the concerns and priorities of the inhabitants of a place must be taken into account and properly addressed. As we have indicated above, these include not only the human inhabitants, but also deities (including the Christian Trinity); lesser spirits localized in caves, swamps, grasslands, and waterfalls; culture heroes; ancestors and ghosts; and plants, rivers, hills, and rocks. The extent to which all of these entities are understood as actual members of the community can be seen from the fact that local languages often refer to deities and spirit beings as people—sky people, forest people, cave people, cannibal people, and so on—who are akin to village people or settlement people, which are names that refer to human beings. While invisible under ordinary circumstances, these spirit people have an existence in the community parallel to that of human beings, and all of them have a stake in the distribution and flow of life-enhancing power.

In Australia, rites of passage can take place around a **focal area**, which is a particular spot in the land marked by a certain tree or stone, or a small depression in the ground. In the Pacific Islands, where power is imbedded in people and things as *mana*, the focal area is usually more elaborate and not so closely tied to the land. It can be a building or an enclosed platform, or the image of a deity. It can even be persons of great *mana*, such as ancestors, kings, or other influential people ("big men"). In such instances, ritual specialists may be needed to control the flow of *mana* by removing taboos.

To encounter spirit beings during rites of passage, participants prepare themselves by painting and decorating their bodies and by manipulating sacred objects that are normally kept secret. For example, a **bullroarer**, which is a low sounding whistle whipped around on the end of a string, may be employed so that those present can hear the voice of the ancestors and become privy to the invisible world around them. To encourage the spirit beings to take part, participants sing and dance, make offerings, and engage in the ceremonial redistribution of food and wealth. The spirits make themselves visible through masks and paintings, and communicate with humans through dreams, prophecy, and **trance**, in which the spirits take possession of the bodies of ritual specialists called **mediums** and speak or act through them.

Birth

One of the most important junctures in life is birth, not only because it begins life, but also because this is when the power of place is apportioned to a new member in the community. During childbirth, songs may be sung to encourage an easy delivery, and various food taboos may be observed by members of the family. This is also a time when it is vital that men keep their distance, lest contact with the birthing process deplete their share of power.

Adulthood

When boys and girls reach the age of adulthood, they often engage in ceremonies restricted to members of their gender. In the past, these were discouraged by colonialists and missionaries, but they nonetheless persisted and have undergone a revival in many communities. For both boys and girls, there are foods they should eat and foods they should avoid to develop the appropriate gender identity. Rituals for girls are usually linked to the beginning of menstruation and to marriage. The former involve isolating the menstruating girl in a hut or a separate settlement, while using some of her menstrual blood in ritual activities. She is then reintroduced into the community with a new, adult identity. Marriage rituals have several stages and require the exchange of valuables between the couples' families. Wives-to-be have a repertoire of rituals to ensure the well-being of their gardens, their future children, and the pigs entrusted to their care. After marriage, moreover, a wife in more traditional communities is expected to avoid her husband and members of his bloodline during menstruation. She will not even prepare food for her husband, for fear that the taboo of her menstrual blood will contaminate it and weaken him.

Boys, by contrast, are taken away from their parents and secluded under the direction of senior men for weeks or months. In some communities, induction into a male religious cult and one's first participation in warfare is what changes a boy into a man; in other areas, boys undergo an elaborate system of graded initiation. Typically, they are instructed in ritual behavior, shown secret objects such as bark paintings (Figure 6.8) or sacred masks, and taught songs and stories that convey tribal secrets. In some regions boys are introduced to sacred flutes or bullroarers, which, as adults, they will use to produce the voices of the spirits. They may also undergo scarification, tooth removal, tattooing, or incision of the **foreskin** or **urethra** to give them a particular status in their group. Like a girl's menstrual blood, the blood from these incisions often becomes part of the initiation rituals.

Death

Death is perhaps the most important of life's junctures in Oceania because it is the moment when an individual's spirit, understood as their share of power, is restored to the community for use by future generations. In Australia, it is believed that human life does not come from one's mother and father, but literally out of the earth, to which it must be returned. Oceanian funerals generally feature gift-giving and wealth redistribution, and a great deal of song, by which the participants attempt to *sing* the deceased back into the spirit world. Methods for disposing of the body include burial in the family house, exposure on platforms in the forest (Figure 6.9), burial at sea, and European-style interment in cemeteries or individual burial sites. After the funeral, additional rituals are performed to solidify the relationship between the living and the dead. Some involve sacrificing animals, such as marsupials and pigs, and sharing these and other foods with the dead. They can also include speeches, singing, and dancing. Rituals expressing a community's loss can last for months or years.

Funerals enable the transition from life in the human world to life in the domain of the spirits. The deceased are thought to continue as members of their communities, but now as important onlookers who oversee the community's ceremonies and social norms. They are envisioned as dwelling in birds, fish, and aspects of the natural world, or dwelling in settlements under the ground, in the sea, beyond the horizon, or on islands inaccessible to humans. In Polynesia they return to a homeland called Hawaiki. Both good and bad persons inhabit these places, and provisions are given to the dead during their funerary rites to ensure a successful passage there. Initially spirits of the dead hover around the human

Figure 6.8 Bark paintings are created on the inside of a strip of tree bark. Traditionally they served educational and ceremonial purposes, depicting clan emblems and ritual information. Here three spirits from The Dreaming are depicted: two trickster/culture hero spirits and a bird spirit. Today, artists produce them for collectors on the world market. Source: © Franck Metois/Alamy.

settlement to make sure that proper ceremonies are carried out on their behalf. If and when they are satisfied, they move on, returning from time to time when they deem it necessary, as when something is amiss in the human community and they feel they must bring it to light. If, on the other hand, they are not satisfied with the funerary rituals, there is a danger they will disrupt the community as troublesome ghosts, inhibiting the proper flow of power.

Over time, the deceased join the community of the long dead, which includes culture heroes. As with other spirit beings, they are regularly invited to ceremonial events to interact with the living community, and their exploits are celebrated in songs and legends. On such occasions, carved figures and masks may be produced for them to inhabit. These are either stored in special religious buildings or discarded

Figure 6.9 A drawing of a funeral platform, from a French first contact in New Guinea. The corpse is covered with leaves and exposed to the elements on a hammock made of branches. Source: Roger-Viollet/Topfoto.

after the ceremonies, when the ancestors leave. Finally, we should note that indigenous funeral and death rituals throughout Oceania have changed under the influence of Christianity and modernization. Regarding such changes in Micronesia, the Jesuit priest Francis Hezel observed:

> With the decline in the old spirit beliefs, or at least the reluctance to continue ritualizing these beliefs, the emphasis shifted to ensuring that family relationships were in good order. Funerals became occasions to repair damaged family bonds. Throughout Micronesia a funeral is a rare opportunity for straight talk and tears within the family, as individuals accept blame for problems they may have caused and apologize for their harsh words and actions.

> Francis X. Hezel, *The New Shape of Old Island Cultures: A Half Century of Social Change in Micronesia* (Honolulu: University of Hawai'i Press, 2001), p. 100.

CONCLUSION

The indigenous peoples of Oceania experience ultimate reality as the power imbedded in place. Bill Neidjie, a Gagudju elder and one of the last speakers of his native language, explained it this way: "Our story is in the land … it is written in those sacred places…. My children will look after those places. That's the Law" (Bill Neidjie, with Stephen Davis and Allan Fox, *Australia's Kakadu Man* [Darwin: Resource Managers, 1986], p. 65).

Understanding "place" in terms of both geography and community, indigenous Oceanians strive to cultivate fruitful interactions in the spiritual, natural, and human worlds through everyday activities, song, storytelling, and ritual. Although there was a period in which the indigenous understanding of the cosmos was disrupted and threatened by foreign intrusions, it has survived, and in recent years undergone a revitalization. Many indigenous ceremonies have been reinstituted, and cultural festivals have developed, drawing into their circle of influence even those Oceanians not indigenous to the region. For all the peoples of Oceania, moreover, actions that sustain life and call on localized, life-enhancing power have taken on a particular urgency in the light of climate change and globalization.

For review

1. What are some of the islands and island groups encompassed by Oceania?
2. What is "civil religion," and how is it practiced in Oceania? Is it practiced in western countries?
3. How is storytelling used as a religious act in Oceania?
4. Describe the difference between *mana* and *tapu* (taboo).
5. What do Aborigines mean by The Dreaming and the Law?

For discussion

1. If ocean levels continue to rise due to climate change, what might be the consequences for the religions of Oceania? What are their options?
2. Some anthropologists estimate that one-fourth of the world's discrete religions are practiced in Oceania. With this much diversity, how is it possible to speak of a single entity such as "Oceanian religions"? How is this different from speaking of Hindu or Chinese religion as single entities?

Key Terms

Aborigines	The indigenous people of Australia; also "Aboriginal peoples."
ANZAC Day	An expression of civil religion based on memories and shared experiences of the Australian and New Zealand Army Corps.
Aotearoa	Also known as New Zealand; the name the Maori prefer to call their island.
bullroarer	A device used in initiation ceremonies to make audible the voice of the ancestors.

Bunya Dreaming Festival	A festival of the Gubbi Gubbi that takes place when bunya trees bear their fruit, celebrated, in part, to build community with settler people.
cargo cults	What settler peoples called utopian religious movements in Oceania that formed around the exchange of material goods.
civil religions	Religions whose beliefs, practices, and membership are determined by cultural priorities and national identities.
culture heroes	Spirit beings responsible for introducing important traditions, institutions, and skills into one's culture.
first contacts	Western explorers' first experiences and reports of Oceania, which often distorted or changed the cultures and religions they depicted.
focal area	An area within a community that is marked as being particularly efficacious.
Gubbi Gubbi	The Aboriginal people of southeastern Queensland in Australia who have promoted the protection of their ecosystem through religious rituals.
hula	A traditional dance ritual in Hawai'i performed to celebrate nature and community and honor important beings.
mana	The sacred power distributed among Pacific Island people by their sky gods and culture heroes.
Maori	The indigenous people of Aotearoa.
medium	A religious specialist who conveys messages from the unseen world when possessed by a spirit.
Melanesia	"Area of black islands"; includes New Guinea, the Solomon Islands, Vanuatu (New Hebrides), New Caledonia, and Fiji.
Micronesia	"Area of small islands"; the archipelago defined by the Gilbert Islands in the southeast and the Mariana Islands in the northwest.
Oceania	The Pacific Ocean and the land masses of Australia and the Pacific islands, the latter comprising Polynesia, Micronesia, and Melanesia.
payback	A term for the religious principles of reciprocity and redistribution among Pacific Islanders.
Polynesia	"Area of many islands"; includes Hawai'i, Easter Island, Aotearoa, Samoa, Tonga, Tahiti, and others.
power embedded in place	A central element of Oceanian religions that defines "place" as both geography and community.
Rainbow Snake	The principal creative spirit of the Aboriginal landscape.
rites of passage	Rituals undertaken by individuals at important junctures in life to reaffirm their connection to their community and its gods and spirit beings.

song line	One part of a larger story that situates people and places with respect to the creative work of the spirits as they passed through the land.
Stolen Generations	Aboriginal children who were taken away from their parents so they could be assimilated to settler culture.
taboo	A restrictive force that prevents *mana* from being depleted or monopolized. English for *tapu*.
Terra Australis Incognita	"Unknown south land"; a Latin term Europeans used in the sixteenth century to describe the lands they were colonizing in Oceania.
terra nullis	"Empty land"; a Latin term Europeans used for Australia to justify their colonization of the continent.
The Dreaming	A creative period during which the Rainbow Snake and other spirit beings were active.
the Law	The responsibility in Oceanian religions to preserve the primal order and harmony that was established during The Dreaming.
trance	Spirit possession, especially by mediums, leading to communication from the spirit world.

Bibliography

A good first book
Tony Swain and Garry Trompf. *The Religions of Oceania*. London and New York: Routledge, 1995.

Further reading
Marie Alohalani Brown. *Ka Poʻe Akua: Hawaiian Reptilian Water Deities*. Honolulu: University of Hawaiʻi Press, 2022.

Daniel De Coppet and Andre Iteanu, eds. *Cosmos and Society in Oceania*. Oxford, UK, and Washington, DC: Berg Publishers, 1995.

Phyllis Herda, Michael Reilly and David Hilliard, eds. *Vision and Reality in Pacific Religion*. Canberra: Pandanus Books, 2005.

Jeanette Marie Mageo and Alan Howard, eds. *Spirits in Culture, History, and Mind*. New York and London: Routledge, 1996.

Albert C. Moore. *Arts in the Religions of the Pacific: Symbols of Life*. London and Washington, DC: Cassell, 1995.

Pamela J Stewart and Andrew Strathern. *Sacred Revenge in Oceania*. Cambridge: Cambridge University Press, 2018.

Reference and research
Brij V. La and Kate Fortune, eds. *The Pacific Islands: An Encyclopedia*. Honolulu: University of Hawaiʻi Press, 2000.

Linsey Jones, ed. *Encyclopedia of Religion*, 2nd edn, 15 vols. Chicago: Macmillan Reference USA, 2004.

CHAPTER 7
Indigenous Religions in the Americas
Cooperation between human and nonhuman people

Two Kogi *mamo*, or shamans, of northern Colombia. The seated man holds a *poporo*, a gourd containing lime powder made from seashells. As he chews coca leaves, he licks the powder from the stick he holds. The *mamo* who is standing wears a bag in which he keeps ritual tools. Source: Wikimedia Commons.

DID YOU KNOW …

The term "Indian," which has been used to refer to indigenous peoples throughout the Americas, is also used for the residents of India. Confused? So was Columbus when he landed in the Bahamas in 1492. Believing he had reached an island in the Indian Ocean, he assumed that the people he encountered were of South Asian descent. As a result, the Europeans who arrived after Columbus began identifying indigenous people throughout the western hemisphere as Indians. Not only was this a geographical mistake, but by using the single term Indian for everyone they encountered, Europeans badly misrepresented the cultural, religious, and linguistic diversity of the Americas. Characterizing all Indigenous Americans simply as Indians is a bit like thinking that all Asians are basically Japanese.

Understanding the Religions of the World: An Introduction, Second Edition.
Edited by Will Deming.
© 2025 John Wiley & Sons Ltd. Published 2025 by John Wiley & Sons Ltd.

OVERVIEW

The indigenous peoples of the Americas are the modern descendants of the first inhabitants of the western hemisphere. Their religions are found from the Pacific to the Atlantic Oceans, and as far north as Greenland and Canada, and as far south as the southernmost parts of Chile and Argentina. This is an area of some 16.4 million square miles, which is almost a third of the earth's total land mass. The practitioners of these religions belong to over 1700 cultural groups and speak as many as 1000 distinct languages and dialects. Given this enormous cultural and linguistic diversity spread over such an extensive geographical area, any comprehensive study of these religions would require several volumes, written with constant attention to difference, variation, and nuance. Since such an undertaking goes well beyond the scope of this chapter, the following account attempts a considerably more modest goal: that of introducing students to several elements shared by many of these religions.

One of the most fascinating of these shared elements is the belief that our universe is inhabited by multiple communities of "other-than-human persons"—a phrase coined by the late American anthropologist A. Irving Hallowell (1894–1974). These communities are comprised of animal persons (e.g., salmon, bear, and anaconda peoples), crop persons (e.g., corn and squash peoples), and weather persons (e.g., thunder and wind peoples). Each community has its own realm or living space. Some live in the sky or in the regions above the sky; others live below the ground or in deep underworlds; and still others live on the peripheries of human communities, in mountains, forests, jungles, lakes, deserts, and grasslands.

Like human persons, other-than-human persons exercise volition, or freedom of will, and have their own needs, desires, and traditions of doing things. Indigenous American religions teach that to achieve well-being and balance in life, and avoid illness and misfortune, humans must maintain relationships of respect with these other-than-human counterparts. Such relationships do not come automatically, however. They must be established by seeking contact with representatives of these nonhuman communities, and then nurtured by interacting with them on a regular basis. From the perspective of Indigenous Americans, there is often little or no difference between behaving religiously and behaving properly as a human being.

History

Timeline	
5050 BCE	Mummification begins among Chinchorro.
3500 BCE	Sechin Bajo spiritual center established.
3200–1800 BCE	Aspero and Caral spiritual centers active.
900 BCE	Chavin de Huantar established.
900–400 BCE	La Venta spiritual center active.
500 BCE–100 CE	El Mirador spiritual center at its height.
350 BCE	Kaminaljuyu spiritual center established.
100 BCE–400 CE	Hopewell spiritual center active.
100–700 CE	Moche and Nazca religions.
450 CE	Yaxchilan spiritual center established; Teotihuacan is at its height.
550–1200 CE	Effigy mounds built.
750 CE	Pueblos begin to appear.
900–1150 CE	Chichen Itza spiritual center active.
1050	Cahokia is built.
1250–1519	Aztec empire.
1200–1533	Inca empire.
1492	Christopher Columbus encounters Indigenous Americans; beginning of European invasion.
1531	Apparition of Mary to Juan Diego.
1536–1572	Inca rebellion.
1680	Pueblo revolt.
1763–1766	Pontiac War.
1781	Siege of La Paz.
1799	Longhouse religion begins.
1847–1915	Caste War of Yucatan.
1881	Shaker Church is founded.
1889–1890	Ghost Dance and Massacre at Wounded Knee.
1913	Native American Church chartered.
1960s	Renewal begins within Indigenous American religions; Liberation Theology spreads in Latin America.
1970s	Pentecostalism and the Catholic Charismatic Revival movement spread throughout Latin America; adherents of the New Age movement appropriate elements of Indigenous American religions.
1980s	Neo-Pentecostalism comes to Latin America.

(*continued*)

1994–2004	The United Nations celebrates the Decade of the World's Indigenous Peoples.
2004	The National Museum of the American Indian opens on the National Mall in Washington, DC.
2007	The United Nations adopts the Declaration on the Rights of Indigenous Peoples.

Our earliest evidence for religion in the Americas comes from isolated archeological finds dated to various time periods, from all over the western hemisphere. From these we gain no unified picture of religious life, only partial glimpses. Starting in the fourth millennium BCE, however, we can describe various spiritual centers that indigenous communities built. While not widely known, Indigenous Americans built tens of thousands of earthen mounds all over the western hemisphere. They built them in the Andes, from Ecuador to Argentina; in the Amazon regions of Brazil, Suriname, and Venezuela; in Cuba and the Dominican Republic; and in the United States and Canada. There are an estimated 800 of these mounds in Louisiana alone, and another 200 in southwestern Guatemala. Some are 6 feet high while others are a 100 feet or more. Some cover an area of 30 or 40 square yards, while others cover dozens of acres. Some have flat tops, some have rounded or ridged tops, some are conical, and some have straight sides like a pyramid. While many of these mounds were used for elevating farmlands or houses, especially the houses of the elite members of a community, and some functioned as middens (trash mounds containing broken pottery, shells, and bones), hundreds, if not thousands, of them had religious functions.

One such function was the proper burial of the dead to ensure their well-being in an afterlife. Some mounds housed burial chambers made of logs or stone in which a body was laid to rest with servants, animals, or finely crafted items made from expensive materials such as turquoise, obsidian, gold, and copper—all, presumably, for use in an afterlife. In other instances, religious leaders were buried with quartz crystals and ritual masks used to communicate with deities or animal spirits, as well as paraphernalia for preparing and ingesting hallucinogens used for journeys into the spirit world. Larger mounds were often built up in stages, as successive ceremonies and feasts for the dead took place on their summits. For example, charnel houses—structures containing corpses being prepared for burial and bones previously buried, dug up, and cleaned for a second burial—were sometimes built on top of new mounds. These structures were then ceremonially burned down and covered over with dirt, whereupon another charnel house was built on top of that, and so forth, increasing the size of the mound over time.

The religious nature of many mounds is also indicated by large plazas built near their bases to accommodate feasting, dancing, and perhaps witnessing rituals that took place on top of these mounds. Archeologists call these mounds and their adjacent plazas "ceremonial centers," because they were probably also used for political, military, and administrative ceremonies. But since our focus is religion, and because Indigenous Americans (then as now) did not clearly distinguish religion from other human activities, we shall refer to them as **spiritual centers**.

A Closer Look

Effigy Mounds

Indigenous Americans in the upper midwestern United States constructed earthworks in the shape of animals, including birds, bear, deer, panthers, turtles, and snakes. There are dozens of clear examples in Illinois, Iowa, Wisconsin, and Michigan, and some scholars estimate that their true number may be in the thousands. Most were built between 550 and 1200 CE, although who built them and why is unknown. The most famous of these effigy mounds is an outlier in central Ohio in the shape of an undulating snake (Figure 7.1). Known as the Serpent Mound, the snake is over a quarter of a mile long, 3 feet high, and 6–7 yards wide, and holds a round object in its mouth (an egg? the sun?).

Figure 7.1 An aerial photo of the Serpent Mound in Peebles, Ohio. The coiled tail of the serpent is on the far left, the serpent's mouth holding the round object is on the upper right. Source: © Mark Burnett/Alamy.

To gain an appreciation for the vast amounts of labor it took to build these spiritual centers, we need to know that prior to the arrival of Europeans in the fifteenth century, Indigenous Americans had no wheeled vehicles or iron tools. Plazas were leveled and stone was cut with hand tools made from wood, bone, stone, and soft metals such as copper, and the earth needed to construct the mounds was transported by the basketful. So why were these costly structures built, and how did they function?

The answer appears to be that they served not only local communities, but also surrounding populations, and even attracted groups living hundreds of miles away. People came to these centers to experience religion on a scale and of a quality that was otherwise unavailable to them: to worship at an artificial mountain or other human structure grander than any they had ever seen; to engage in ceremonies of dance and prayer and feasting on plazas that could accommodate thousands of others; and to be part of elaborate rituals directed by renowned specialists arrayed in awe-inspiring apparel. A few visitors also came for professional reasons: to acquire specialized knowledge, gain access to powerful spiritual beings through initiation into esoteric traditions, and obtain finely crafted religious objects made from costly materials. To use a comparison from the world of commerce, these spiritual centers were trading posts at the center of extensive political and cultural networks—but not trading posts that dealt in material goods. Rather, they specialized in hard-to-get *spiritual* goods and services.

This intriguing picture of early indigenous America leads to two important insights. First, it tells us that Indigenous Americans understood religion to be so vital to their existence that they devoted vast resources to it. Second, because they traveled great distances to these places, it tells us that they saw value in the spiritual practices of others. In the next section we will take a closer look at several of America's early spiritual centers, beginning in Canada and the United States and moving south into Meso- and South America (see Figure 7.7).

Canada and the United States

Hopewell

Along the Ohio and Scioti rivers in south central Ohio, a spiritual center that archeologists call Hopewell began to form around 100 BCE. It eventually covered more than 4 square miles and remained in use until about 400 CE. At its height, it consisted of over 30 conical mounds surrounded by plazas in the shape of rectangles, an octagon, and a circle. The octagonal plaza measured 50 acres and was enclosed by an earthen wall 5–6 feet high. Hopewell was not a city, however, for there is no evidence of extensive, long-term habitation. Rather, it seems to have been a pilgrimage destination that drew visitors from hundreds of miles away, for religious art found there is made of nonlocal materials such as mica, copper, obsidian, and shark teeth, imported from Canada, Florida's Gulf coast, and the Rocky Mountains. This art depicts people dressed as bears, panthers, and deer, and includes stone pipes for smoking tobacco and herbs. The pipes, some carved with animal images, may have belonged to religious professionals called shamans, as the animal images face the smoker when the pipes were used and may represent spirit beings with whom the shamans communicated.

Cahokia

East of the Mississippi River in Illinois, within sight of the modern city of St. Louis, a very different sort of spiritual center appeared rather suddenly around 1050 CE. Named Cahokia by archeologists, it was a planned city with a population of 10,000 and a metropolitan area of some 30,000. It attracted visitors from throughout what scholars call the Mississippian Culture Area, which extended north and west into

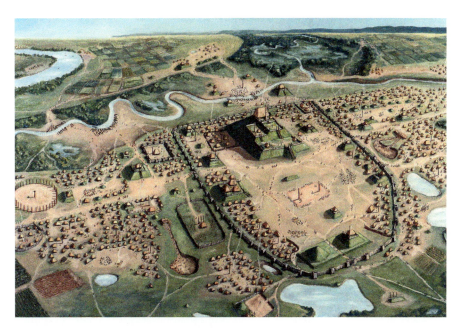

Figure 7.2 An artist's depiction of the Cahokia site in southwestern Illinois. The enormous Monks Mound stands at the center; the woodhenge is on the far left. Source: Cahokia Mounds State Historic Site; Artist: William R. Iseminger.

Canada and Minnesota, south into Texas and Florida, and east to the Atlantic Ocean. Cahokia contained over 100 mounds, many of which had buildings on top such as charnel houses, administrative centers, elite residences, and temples. At its center was an imposing flat-topped mound that rose 100 feet in height and covered a rectangular area of 14 acres (Figure 7.2). Now called Monks Mound because of its brief use by Trappist monks, this mound had buildings on four separate terraces and was surrounded by four large plazas. The southern plaza, which is the largest, encompassed 50 acres of artificially leveled ground. A half mile to the west of Monks Mound stands a wood henge, a solar observatory similar to the more famous Stonehenge in England. It consisted of 28 large posts arranged in a circle around a center post, and had a radius of over 400 feet. It was one of four such wood henges at the site, which were used to determine the precise date for religious ceremonies.

A half mile to the south of Monks Mound stands a mound known simply as Number 72, which contained over 260 bodies sacrificed in ritual fashion. Some were strangled, others beheaded, others shot with arrows or clubbed to death. Underneath the mound, as its foundation, are a decommissioned wood henge and two bodies: a male and female, positioned one on top of the other and laid on a covering of 20,000 imported shell beads strung together in the shape of a bird. Other indications of religious activity at Cahokia include: evidence of elite warrior cults dedicated to thunderbird spirits (giant eagles who create lightning, thunder, and rain); images of a fertility goddess with a collection of human bones and a winged, horned snake; art pieces in the shape of eyes and hands placed in burials; and the seeds of jimson weed, used as a hallucinogen.

Ancestral Pueblo kivas

Although most spiritual centers in the Americas featured tall mounds, some did not. An example of the latter type are the spiritual centers built by the Ancestral Pueblo culture at the nexus of what is now Utah, Colorado, Arizona, and New Mexico. Around 750 CE, this culture began building *pueblos* (towns) in the form of one-room, single-story row houses, using stone, wood, and adobe (brick made from mud and straw and dried in the sun). By around 900 CE, these towns began to take the form of ancient apartment buildings, called great houses, rising five to six stories high and containing hundreds of rooms. Next to these great houses we find ceremonial precincts consisting of plazas and *kivas*, which were underground ritual spaces, usually a large circular room, that connected humans with spirits who lived below the earth. Some kivas had brightly painted interior walls depicting rain, wind, and other forces of nature as anthropomorphic spirits. The largest of these kivas, called great kivas, were 60 or more feet in diameter and accommodated hundreds of worshippers.

The most impressive Ancestral Pueblo site is located in northwest New Mexico in Chaco Canyon. It had dozens of great houses built into the canyon walls, over 100 kivas, many of which were great kivas, and a solar observatory. Scholars estimate that building the great houses alone required more than 200,000 large trees to support the stone blocks and adobe bricks. The largest great house in the canyon, called Pueblo Bonito ("beautiful town"), could accommodate as many as 2000 people in its 600–800 rooms, and overlooked a plaza that had three great kivas as well as some 30 smaller ones (Figures 7.3 and 7.4). Based on the number of cooking hearths, burials, and trash middens found at Pueblo Bonito, scholars estimate that it never had more than about 70 permanent residents. These were probably the founders and overseers of the spiritual center, along with their families. The majority of rooms were evidently for the temporary use of religious pilgrims who came to Pueblo Bonito from an area of 25,000 square miles around the canyon, traveling on an elaborate road system that radiated out from the canyon.

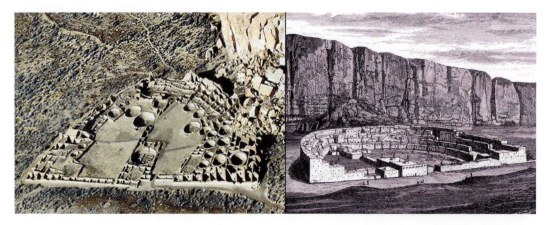

Figures 7.3 and 7.4 On the left (Figure 7.3) is an aerial view of the remains of Pueblo Bonito in Chaco Canyon, New Mexico, showing its large plazas and many underground *kivas* (the circular structures). On the right (Figure 7.4) is a reconstruction of what it might have looked like around 1000 CE. Source: Wikimedia Commons.

Some rooms in Pueblo Bonito stored ritual equipment such as flutes, trumpets, bells, incense burners, and prayer sticks, often made from expensive or exotic materials like copper, turquoise, macaw feathers, and marine shells. Mummies were also discovered at the site. These had been repeatedly moved and unwrapped after their initial placement, indicating a belief that the owners of these bodies had not fully departed and were expected to participate in the spiritual life of the community.

Mesoamerica

The term **Mesoamerica** refers to the indigenous cultural region that once extended from modern-day southern Mexico as far south as Costa Rica. It was a region populated by many peoples, including the Maya and the Aztecs, where large urban centers developed, royal families offered their blood to the sun god, and early writing systems and calendars were used in religion.

Much more clearly than in Canada or the United States, powerful groups in Mesoamerica combined religion with political control. Spiritual centers were located within the region's dominant city–states and were used to extend political influence over surrounding populations. Representatives from these populations visited the centers on a regular basis to worship the gods of the city–state and pay homage to its rulers, who assumed the roles of chief priests, divinely appointed kings, and even gods. The leaders of lesser city–states were allowed to govern their own communities as semi-independent entities and follow their own religious traditions if they fulfilled these diplomatic obligations and paid the necessary tribute. If they did not, they were replaced with someone who would.

The Olmec

The earliest example of this religio-political system is the Olmec culture, which built major cities in southern Mexico. The best preserved of these cities is La Venta, near the coast of the Gulf of Mexico, which flourished ca. 900–400 BCE. This was a spiritual and political center occupied by the Olmec royalty, while tradesmen, artisans, and other residents lived in a settlement 3 miles away. The city had a number of ceremonial platforms and mounds, under which archeologists have found massive caches of offerings, including tons of finished serpentine (greenish) mineral blocks. La Venta's largest mound was a stepped, flat-topped pyramid built of clay and located on an enclosed ritual platform.

The integration of religious and political forces in La Venta can be seen in three ways. First, the city had both public and restricted ceremonial precincts. The former were used by the common people and pilgrims; the latter, including the main pyramid, were reserved for royalty and visiting dignitaries. Second, the Olmecs honored their kings with monumental images of their heads, carved from nonlocal basalt boulders weighing between 6 and 45 tons each. The considerable resources needed to memorialize their kings in this way argues for a belief in divine rulers. And third, basalt thrones measuring 6 feet high, 12 feet long, and 5 feet wide have been found at

La Venta with depictions of were-jaguars (figures that are part human and part jaguar), as well as what many scholars have interpreted as references to the underworld and to human sacrifice.

The Maya

We know considerably more about the ancient Maya than we do about the Olmec, for several reasons. To begin with, they wrote down many of their religious traditions, and a few of their documents have managed to survive in one form or another. They also left a rich archeological record, including inscriptions and depictions of deities and religious ceremonies. In addition, they interacted with the first Europeans to arrive in America, who often recorded what they saw among the Maya. And finally, descendants of the ancient Maya are still with us today, practicing religious traditions that may, in some form, contain elements from ancient times.

The ancient Maya saw mountains, caves, springs, and other natural features in the landscape as places where they could communicate with gods and ancestors. In their cities, they even oriented important buildings with respect to some of these places, and they conducted pilgrimages there at various times of the year. The Maya worshipped a god known as the Feathered Serpent and saw a close connection between jaguars and the spirit world. Maya royal families made special blood offerings to the gods, and according to their origin stories, their kings were descended from the gods. Because they believed that people continued to be present in their bodies after death, the Maya mummified their dead, consulted them as advisors, and brought them to important religious festivals.

El Mirador What has been called the Maya empire was actually a system of independent city–states that prospered and declined in relation to one another through cooperation, alliances, and war. As with other centers of power in Mesoamerica, each of these city–states had its own spiritual center, although Maya spiritual centers were conceived and built on a much grander scale. An example from Guatemala is El Mirador, which flourished between the sixth century BCE and the first century CE. Its ceremonial mounds were flat-topped pyramids that supported various buildings. They were built of fill dirt and covered with a layer of cut stone, which was then smoothed out with limestone plaster and painted with colorful images of deities. The main pyramid was an astounding 235 feet tall. Many of El Mirador's pyramids had three buildings on top, perhaps indicating their use in the worship of three related gods.

Kaminaljuyu The city of Kaminaljuyu, also in Guatemala, is now located beneath the modern capital of Guatemala City. It flourished as a regional spiritual center around 350 BCE, and over the course of its history it saw the construction of almost 200 plazas, platform pyramids, and other mounds. These were used to worship a remarkable variety of divine beings, indicating a broad, multicultural approach to religion. Dozens of female figurines have been found there, as well as images of a maize (corn) god, a bird deity, kings dressed as jaguars, and spirit beings in the form of owls, bats, jaguars, and snakes. Kaminaljuyu's plazas were enclosed by stone walls depicting bloodletting and human sacrifice, a practice that is corroborated by the discovery of a burial urn containing more than 30 severed human heads.

Yaxchilan Located in Mexico just north of the Guatemala-Mexico border, the Maya city–state of Yaxchilan came to prominence around the middle of the fifth century CE. Like other Maya cities, its spiritual center had a number of pyramids and plazas. What makes Yaxchilan distinctive, however, is the discovery of four stone lintels (structural supports above doorways) on which queens are depicted performing bloodletting ceremonies known as **auto-sacrifice**. In one scene, a king holds a burning torch while a queen draws a barbed rope through a hole in her tongue (Figure 7.5), and in two other scenes, a queen offers her blood while an ancestor in the form of a serpent god rises up before her.

Chichen Itza The final Maya spiritual center we shall consider was located in Chichen Itza, a city–state in Mexico on the northern-most part of the Yucatan Peninsula. At its height, which was between 900 and 1150 CE, Chichen Itza had a temple to the Feathered Serpent, the patron god of

Figure 7.5 One of the lintels from the Maya city of Yaxchilan. On the left, King Itzamnaaj Baalm II (r. 681–742 CE) holds a burning torch over his queen, Lady Xoc, who draws a barbed cord through her tongue during a bloodletting ritual. Drops of her blood fall on pieces of paper, which are burned as an offering to the gods. Source: Wikimedia Commons.

warriors. Among its many other religious buildings were two temples to the Jaguar God, a platform for displaying severed heads, and another platform dedicated to the planet Venus, revered as a god. The city also boasted 13 ballcourts, some or all of which may have served religious functions. To the city's east, at a distance of about 2½ miles, there are a number of caves that contain offerings to the deities who could be contacted there; and within the city itself is a large sinkhole (*cenote*) into which pilgrims to Chichen Itza threw offerings made of gold, jade, animals, and pottery to the rain god. In 2024, a chamber containing the sacrificial remains of more than 60 children was discovered near the sinkhole. All were boys, and several were twins, including at least two sets of identical twins. The rituals in which these children were sacrificed were performed between 500 and 900 CE, and may have been part of ceremonies intended to replicate Maya origin stories.

Teotihuacan

To the north of the Maya, and 25 miles northeast of modern-day Mexico City, an ethnically diverse metropolis known as Teotihuacan began to take shape perhaps as early as the first century BCE. Referred to by the later Aztecs as the Place of the Gods, or as one scholar has recently argued, Place of the Sun, it may have had as many as 150,000 residents at its height around 450 CE. Its spiritual center was located along a grand avenue 50 feet wide and 2½ miles long. At the north end of the avenue stood the Temple of the Moon (Figure 7.6). It faced a large ceremonial plaza that was surrounded by 10 pyramid platforms. Toward the south end of the avenue, along the eastern side, stood the Temple of the Sun and the Temple of the Feathered Serpent. The former was well over 200 feet high and is considered one of the three largest pyramids in the world. Around these two temples and along either side of the avenue were almost 100 raised platforms for religious rituals and ceremonies.

> **Talking About Religion**
>
> ### A Comparison with Rome
>
> If we had no written records from the Roman Empire and no more archaeological data than we have for Teotihuacan, the course of Roman history between 100 BCE and 400 CE might look as uneventful as Teotihuacan's history looks now. ...
>
> George L. Cowgill, *Ancient Teotihuacan: Early Urbanization in Central Mexico* (New York: Cambridge University Press, 2015), p. 246.

In contrast to Teotihuacan's remarkable size and religious influence, which extended throughout Mesoamerica, is the enigma of its origin, function, and demise. It is still unknown who founded this city, how it was governed, if it had a writing system, or why its main religious structures were looted and burned in the sixth century. We do not even know what its citizens called it: the name Teotihuacan as well as the names of its three principal temples and its grand avenue (Avenue of the Dead) were all coined by the Aztecs centuries after the city had been abandoned.

Religious practices in the city were diverse, indicating that Teotihuacan's massive spiritual center drew visitors from many cultures and subcultures. The main deity seems to have been a goddess who controlled life and fertility. She lived beneath the earth, and the many caves and passages in and around the city were seen as locations where worshippers could bring offerings and communicate with her. Beneath the Temple of the Sun is an artificial cave that Aztec origin stories identified as a paradise ruled by the goddess before the first human emerged into the world. As in other spiritual centers in Mesoamerica, rulers in Teotihuacan practiced human sacrifice, but how often and to what extent is unclear. Along with eagles, jaguars, snakes, and wolves, more than 200 men dressed as Teotihuacan warriors were sacrificed near the

Figure 7.6 The Temple of the Moon at the north end of the Avenue of the Dead in Teotichaucan. It is fronted by a large plaza surrounded by pyramid platforms. At the center of the plaza stands a large ceremonial stage. Source: Wikimedia Commons.

Temple of the Feathered Serpent, and mass graves of commoners, perhaps captured in war, were found near the Temple of the Moon.

The Aztecs

The Mexica, now better known as the Aztecs, migrated into central Mexico as early as 1250 CE and founded their capital city, Tenochtitlan, on islands along the western coast of Lake Texcoco. In 1428, they joined with two nearby cities to form the Triple Alliance, and by the late 1470s Tenochtitlan had become the dominant power in the region. At its height it had a population around 200,000, making it the largest city in the world at that time.

Aztec temples were flat-topped pyramids crowned with one or two temples, before which stood sacrificial altars. The main temple in Tenochtitlan, envisioned as a mythical serpent mountain (Coatepec), stood within a walled precinct 25 acres in size. It was dedicated to the Aztecs' two patron deities, Huitzilopochtli, the Sun and warrior god, and Tlaloc, the god of life and fertility. Other temples in the city included a conical temple dedicated to the wind god, Ehecatl, who was a form of the Feathered Serpent. In addition, Tenochtitlan had numerous plazas and ceremonial platforms, some displaying rows of human skulls, some dedicated to Tzitzimime, who were patron goddesses of healers and midwives. These goddesses were often depicted as monstrous, skeletal figures holding bones and skulls, although bones and skulls were symbols of life in Aztec religion.

The Aztecs had two calendars, a solar calendar of 365 days and a ritual calendar that marked off 18 months of 20 days each. Religious specialists used these in combination to discern the possible fates that individuals could merit in their lifetimes, and to predict a person's lucky and unlucky days. During each of the 18 months of the ritual calendar, religious activities specific to that month took place, involving all sectors of society: kings, priests, nobles, artisans, and commoners; men, women, and children alike. The first days of each month were given over to the retelling and reenactment of origin stories and mythical themes, usually related to fertility. These set the tone for the activities that followed, which included oratory, processions, sacrifice, feasting, dance, and musical performances, the responsibility for which fell to various social groups, professional organizations, and religious societies.

To promote themselves as the rightful rulers of central Mexico and parts of Guatemala (the southern most reach of their empire), the Aztecs drew heavily on the traditions of earlier ruling cities in Mesoamerica. They claimed descent from the once powerful Toltecs, appropriating the Toltec god Tezcatlipoca (Smoking Mirror), and they excavated the ruins of Teotihuacan, removing symbols of royal authority for use in Tenochtitlan. Especially important was their continuation of the earlier traditions of blood sacrifice, by which they claimed to maintain the order of the cosmos.

According to one of their origin stories, the sun came into being at Teotihuacan when a god sacrificed himself by jumping into a blazing bonfire. It was then learned that the newly created sun needed offerings of blood to begin its movement across the sky, and so the other gods sacrificed themselves as well. But because it was necessary both to keep the sun moving and to repay the gods for their self-sacrifice, the Aztec royalty took it upon themselves to provide offerings throughout the year, making them the principal mediators between humans and gods.

While the gods, including the sun, demanded praise and gifts such drink offerings, quail, vegetables, grain, and precious objects, it was believed that their power ultimately depended on receiving human blood, which contained a vital spiritual force. For this reason, the Aztecs engaged in auto-sacrifice, or voluntary bloodletting. Their priests did this on a daily basis, sometimes inserting hollow reeds into their veins to increase the offering. More usually, however, they used sharp objects to pierce their ears, tongues, chests, arms, thighs, or genitals, which, over time, left scars over most of their bodies.

But auto-sacrifice by itself was insufficient, so human sacrifice was also needed. The victims were mostly adult male slaves and male prisoners of war, although on certain occasions the gods required children or young women. They were put to death variously—in fire pits, tied down and unarmed in contests with experienced fighters, as targets for arrows, and on altars that stood before the temples. The most elaborate of these sacrifices in terms of preparing the victim was the feast of Toxcatl, which took place during the fifth month of the ritual calendar. In the year leading up to this sacrifice, a young captive warrior was groomed to imitate the god Tezcatlipoca.

His skin was painted black and he was taught to play the flute, sing, and speak like an Aztec noble. Then, dressed in fine clothing and adorned with jewelry, he was led through the capital city in religious processions and greeted like a deity. He ate sumptuously, met with the king, and ritually married four women who represented goddesses. At the end of the year, he mounted the steps of Tezcatlipoca's temple where priests laid him on an altar, cut open his chest and ripped out his still beating heart as an offering. After this, he was decapitated and his skull put on a display rack near the foot of the temple. His corpse was flayed and his skin given to members of the nobility to eat.

To validate their claim as guardians of the world order, the Aztecs also performed the **New Fire Ceremony**, or Binding of Years, which took place every 52 years. The sun of the Aztec origin stories that came into being at Teotihuacan was not the first sun, but actually the fifth. The others had been destroyed when catastrophes had overtaken the previous four worlds: an attack of jaguars, hurricanes, fiery rain, and a flood. The present sun, along with the rest of the world, was destined to be destroyed through earthquakes. In each previous instance, moreover, destruction had taken place at the end of a 52-year cycle, counting from the beginning of each world.

The New Fire Ceremony was thus performed every 52 years in an attempt to ward off such an eventuality. People throughout the empire rid themselves of all vestiges of the previous 52 years as a way of preparing for the next cycle, should it come. They cleaned their yards and discarded clothes, mats, and cooking utensils. They also extinguished all fires, including those in temples and family hearths, and then, on the final day of the fifty-second year, waited in darkness. Toward dawn, if the Pleiades constellation crossed the sky's zenith, it was believed that the sun would return for another 52 years. The moment this took place, priests on a sacred mountain near Tenochtitlan lit a new fire in the chest cavity of a human sacrifice, and from this fire started a great bonfire that could be seen throughout much of the Valley of Mexico. Runners were then sent to the capital to relight all the fires, beginning with those in the temples and palaces.

Andean civilizations

The term **Andean** refers to the related cultures of indigenous people who inhabited, and still inhabit, the coastal deserts, valleys, and highlands of the Andes Mountains—from modern Ecuador and Peru to northern Chile and northwest Argentina, including parts of southwest Colombia and western Bolivia. The center of the Andean world was, however, Peru, where some of the largest cities and grandest spiritual centers in the Americas developed, and where the Inca empire was born.

People in the Andean world communicated with gods, spirits, and ancestors by using *huacas*, which were manufactured objects or features in the landscape that gave access to fertility, life, and other manifestations of sacred power. Natural *huacas* took the form of caves, mountain tops, sources of water, and boulders. Manufactured *huacas* included temples, shrines, entire spiritual centers, figurines, ceramic and clay objects, and mummies.

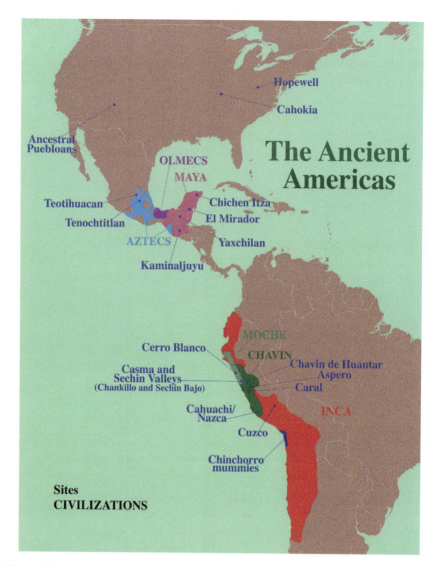

Figure 7.7 A map showing sites of ancient spiritual centers in the Americas, as well as major civilizations.

Early spiritual centers As early as 3500 BCE, spiritual centers began to appear in central Peru in the valleys and coastal areas associated with the Casma and Sechin rivers. Here we find stone reliefs and painted murals depicting warriors, severed heads, human sacrifice, mythical fish, and anthropomorphic beings in the shape of crocodiles and felines. At Chankillo on the coast, a walled, hill-top fortress looks out onto a nearby ridge where 13 upright monoliths were set in a row 325 yards long and used to track the movements of the sun. In the Casma Valley at Sechin Bajo, a raised ceremonial platform 6 feet high stands next to several circular, sunken plazas. The platform dates to ca. 3000 BCE, while the oldest plaza was built ca. 3500 BCE. In the Sechin Valley, there is a spiritual center that includes a pyramid 115 feet high, built between 1600 and 1400 BCE. It is surrounded by a stone wall with hundreds of low relief carvings and five plazas built of stone and adobe brick.

Ninety miles south of the Casma Valley, the Supe Valley was home to 18 urban centers, each of which had platform mounds. Aspero, near the coast, for example, had 17 mounds, the largest of which was approached by walking through a sunken plaza located at the center of a round, raised platform. Further inland, the city of Caral had six spiritual complexes at its center, each with its own pyramid mound and plaza. One of these plazas, moreover, has yielded a cache of over 30 flutes and 30 trumpets. Both Aspero and Caral were occupied from 3200 to 1800 BCE.

Chavin de Huantar One hundred and sixty miles north of Lima and 65 miles from the coast, a very different sort of spiritual center began to take shape as early as 900 BCE. Known as Chavin de Huantar, it was located at the confluence of two rivers, which was understood as the convergence of two powerful spiritual forces. The main structure at the site consisted of three temples in a U-formation, all facing a circular plaza 65 feet in diameter. Carvings of a deity with large eyes, claws, fangs, and snakes lunging from his waist and head adorned the outer walls of the temples, while a frieze depicting jaguars and men transforming into jaguars was carved into the stone wall surrounding the plaza. Some of these men hold pieces of the San Pedro cactus, which was used as a hallucinogen.

Unlike other temples, which were fairly simple structures perched atop earthen mounds, the temple complex at Chavin de Huantar took the form of a multistory labyrinth with interior passageways and chambers that were ventilated and lighted by shafts and mirrors. The passageways, which were sometimes quite narrow, contained brightly painted stone carvings of spiritual beings, some hiding in niches, others looming out from the walls. Some of the chambers, in turn, contained religious paraphernalia and offerings, indicating that they were used for private rituals. At the heart of the central temple was a room in which a 15-foot granite sculpture, part-human, part-feline, and part-serpent, rose out of a large shaft in the floor. Referred to by scholars as the Lanzon, this probably depicted the principal deity of the site, and may have functioned as an oracle.

In all, what made Chavin de Huantar distinct and innovative as a spiritual center was that it catered especially to an elite clientele. The innerworkings of its temple complex, which could only accommodate small groups, would have been reserved for visitors of status and wealth. Through disorientation, mystery, surprise, and the use of hallucinogens, these privileged few were guided into the spirit world, where they could consult the Lanzon oracle and acquire new forms of power under the direction of Chavin's distinguished order of priests. By undergoing these remarkable experiences at Chavin de Huantar, chief priests, rulers, and important administrators from surrounding areas legitimized their positions of authority in the towns and cities from which they came. To maintain this clientele, some of whom came from over 100 miles away, the authorities at Chavin continually offered new experiences. By around 200 BCE, however, the center was in serious decline.

The Moche The independent cities and villages of the Moche people dotted the northern coastal valleys of Peru from 100 to 700 CE. Within this region, which ran 350 miles from north to south, communities competed with their neighbors in both war and religion, building hundreds of pyramids, temples, and plazas. The largest of these, the Sanctuary of the Sun, belonged to the leading city, Cerro Blanco, located 4 miles from the coast in Moche Valley. While only about a third of the structure survives today, its original footprint was around 40 acres, and scholars estimate that it required over 140 million adobe bricks to build. It was probably used for royal, administrative, and military functions. Across from it, and built into the western slope of the mountain that gave the city its name, stood the smaller Sanctuary of the Moon. Much better preserved than the Sanctuary of the Sun, it was the city's spiritual center, consisting of a pyramid temple and multiple raised plazas, platforms, and terraces. One of these, named Platform II by archeologists, could accommodate more than 5000 worshippers at a time.

The nature of religion at Cerro Blanco, and more widely among the Moche, can be discerned from the imagery on Moche pottery and from the many painted stucco murals on the interior walls of the Sanctuary of the Moon. One of the most widely represented figures, probably the principal deity, has a spider's body and a human face. As this being often has fangs or holds a knife and a severed head, scholars refer to him as the Fanged Deity or the Decapitator God. There are also scenes from specific rituals, depicted multiple times in slightly different versions. In one of these scenes, known as the Presentation Theme (Figure 7.8), three large figures on an upper register (a heavenly realm?) have just presented a fourth figure with a goblet, while figures on a lower register (the earth?) collect blood from prisoners whose hands are tied.

Figure 7.8 A line drawing of one of the many depictions of the Presentation Theme from Cerro Blanco and other Moche sites. The figure in the upper register with the owl's head has offered a chalice to the main figure (left detail, the Fanged Deity?). Blood is collected from two bound figures in the lower register (right detail). Source: Moche Archive, Dumbarton Oaks, Trustees for Harvard University, Washington, D.C.

While scholars have offered various interpretations of these images, it is quite clear that human sacrifice and blood offerings were central to religion at Cerro Blanco and other Moche settlements. Regarding the Presentation Theme, some have proposed that the men being subjected to bloodletting are warriors who were captured in skirmishes between rival cities, while others have suggested that they are the losing participants in ritual competitions between royal families. There is, however, a consensus among scholars that the ceremonies depicted in these scenes were actually performed with rulers and religious leaders playing the parts of the four deities in the upper register. The main evidence for this is the discovery of elite burials in which the bodies of rulers and priests are dressed in the same attire as that worn by these deities. Burial in this manner may have celebrated a person's status as a ritual actor.

The Nazca During the same period in which Moche religion flourished in northern Peru, the Nazca people maintained several spiritual centers in southern Peru, 240 miles south of Lima. The largest of these was a pilgrimage site along the Nazca River called Cahuachi. It had some 40 mounds that were built over preexisting hills. One of these mounds is a series of terraces built into the side of a hill. It measures 450 feet across the front and overlooks several plazas of different heights and sizes. Other mounds, many of which had adobe structures on top, were built in groups and surrounded by empty space. Described as "islands" by one scholar, these probably belonged to individual communities that frequented the site.

Offerings found at Cahuachi include fine pottery, clay pan flutes, feathers, and corn, while the remains of around 200 camelids (such as alpaca and vicuña) attest to sacrifice and ritual feasting there. The bodies of 23 guinea pigs, each with its neck broken and (perhaps) its stomach slit open, suggest practices of divination. Among the images found on the pottery are musicians, spirit beings, masked people, birds, agricultural rituals, and both men and women chewing coca leaves. A structure of particular interest to archeologists is a room containing a number of upright posts made of wood from the huarrango tree. These vary in age and height, and were placed in small groups and rows. One is carved with the image of a human head with a flute. It is believed that this "Room of the Posts" was used to worship and communicate with ancestors, as the huarrango tree, which is native to this area, has traditionally been used as a symbol of ancestors and family heritage. Unlike most other structures at Cahuachi, the interior of this room was painted with images of pan flutes and faces with lines emanating from them like rays. In the middle of the room stands a low, square block of clay with a sunken area on top that is thought to have been an altar of some kind. Offerings found in the room include spondylus shells, pottery vessels filled with corn, huarrango pods, gourd rattles, and peppers.

A number of cemeteries have been found in the area surrounding Cahuachi, although no elite burials with costly grave goods have been discovered. This seems to indicate the absence of wealthy or politically powerful families who might have controlled the site. Several burials, however, contain what have been termed "trophy heads." These are severed heads of adult males, prepared in such a way that they retained a lifelike appearance: the skin and hair, including facial hair, were preserved; the brains, eyes, and tongues were removed; the eye sockets and mouths were filled with cotton; and the lips were held closed with splinters of huarrango wood. To facilitate carrying them around, for they were only later placed in graves, a short piece of rope was inserted into a hole drilled into the frontal bone. The current thinking among scholars is that these heads were valued as repositories of spiritual forces that promoted strength and fertility, and that they were acquired through either military encounters with foreign peoples or ritualized battles between Nazca communities.

The most mysterious aspect of the Cahuachi pilgrimage site is not at the site, however, but on the flat desert terrain of the Pampas, just east of it. This is the location of the famous Nazca **geoglyphs**, which are line drawings on the earth made by brushing away the thin layer of dark soil and gravel that covers the Pampas, exposing the white sand beneath it. These geoglyphs include depictions of plants, animals, birds, humans, and geometric shapes, as well as hundreds of straight lines. The choice of particular life forms—monkey, spider, condor (Figure 7.9), flower, orca, to name only a few—is no mystery, as they were part of Nazca culture, appearing again and again on Nazca pottery. What makes the geoglyphs extraordinary is their size. Many of them are so big it is impossible to see what they are unless one is flying overhead. The largest, which is a hummingbird, could fill two and a half football fields. The lizard, in turn, is over 600 feet long, and the monkey is almost 300 feet tall.

The geoglyphs do not seem to be placed in any pattern or order, and only a few are even next to one another. By contrast, the straight lines, some of which run almost perfectly straight for miles, cut through them indiscriminately, as if the geoglyphs were not there. So, why were these line drawings created? No one knows for sure—although they are definitely *not* landing areas for alien spacecraft, as one popular author in the 1960s claimed! Most likely, they served multiple purposes. The biomorphic figures were probably created over time by separate communities as expressions of group identity, and perhaps appealed to certain gods who saw them from above. Members of these communities would visit them as part of an annual pilgrimage to

Figure 7.9 The condor geoglyph, 1 of over 80 Nazca figures drawn on the Pampas desert terrain in southern Peru. It is approximately 135 yards long. Note the straight lines that run through the image. Source: Wikimedia Commons.

Cahuachi, when they visited their communities' mounds. Some of the areas defined by the geometric shapes, by contrast, may have been ceremonial plazas used for ritual dancing, while others may have been astronomically oriented for the observance of planet and star alignments. Finally, the straight lines may have functioned as directional indicators for different times of the year. They may also (as there are hundreds of them) have pointed toward shrines (*huacas*) in the distant mountains.

The Inca Sometime in the thirteenth century, the Inca settled in Cuzco Valley, 280 miles east of Lima, taking their place among several groups that were already there. Under their ninth king, Pachacuti, who was in power for more than 30 years (1438–1471), they began a period of rapid political expansion. They first conquered their neighbors in the Cuzco Valley, and then began subduing peoples to the north and south. By the first decades of the sixteenth century, they had created an empire that stretched 2500 miles along the Pacific coast. It included much of modern-day Peru, as well as parts of Colombia, Ecuador, Bolivia, Chile, and Argentina. At its height, it had a population estimated between 6 and 14 million people. The Inca called their empire Tawantinsuyu, Land of Four Jurisdictions, and established their capital city at their original settlement in Cuzco, where these jurisdictions came together.

Theirs was not an absolute monarchy, but a regime of coerced cooperation. Cities and towns brought into the empire were provided with protection from their neighbors, improved roads and irrigation systems, agricultural terraces for more productive farming, and monthly religious celebrations that included royal pageantry and feasting. In return, these communities gave much of their wealth to the Inca king and promised him their loyalty and military service. Refusal to join the empire brought swift reprisals, but even in these cases the sons of deposed and executed rulers were often taken to Cuzco for re-education and marriage into Inca royal families, after which they returned to their people to govern in place of their fathers. If a city was uncooperative, its ancestral idols were whipped, and if it continued to resist, its people were deported.

Scholars believe that the Inca devised this system of governance because, quite simply, there was no alternative. Given the limited population of the Inca, it would have been impossible for them to disenfranchise or enslave the entire empire and maintain any semblance of stability or prosperity. This is also why they accepted the religions and the gods of the people they ruled: they really had no choice. Andean peoples recognized tens of thousands of private, local, and regional *huacas* that formed the basis of their religious practices. Any attempt by the Inca to demand the worship of their own gods to the exclusion of these would have been disastrous. Instead, they made every effort to promote their patron god, Inti, the Sun God, while at the same time subordinating other gods and spirits to him.

The main Inca spiritual center, called the Golden Enclosure (Coricancha), was located in the heart of Cuzco. Its principal shrine was dedicated to Inti, and since maize was Inti's special gift to the Inca, a garden adjacent to the shrine contained a miniature cornfield with golden corn cobs. This was ritually tended by the Inca ruler, or **Sapa Inca**, who was Inti's son. Other gods enshrined in the Golden Enclosure included the Creator, the Moon Goddess, the Thunder God, and the Earth Mother. The Creator, called Viracocha, was said to be the father of Inti. According to one Inca origin story, Viracocha fashioned human beings out of clay and painted them different colors to divide them into ethnic groups. Inti then appointed the Inca royal family to rule these groups and bring order to the world. The Moon Goddess, who was Inti's wife, was the mother of the first Inca king and queen. She had oversight of the (lunar) ritual calendar, which determined the times of all state-sponsored religious festivals. The Inca Thunder God controlled the rain and water sources, on which the empire depended for farming and herding; and the Earth Mother had charge of the earth's fertility. She lived in the underworld, which was associated with the dead, and from time to time caused earthquakes.

As descendants of Inti and the Moon Goddess, Inca royal families claimed special access to the divine world through their ancestors. When a member of one of these families died, their body was mummified and used as a *huaca*. These mummies were housed by the thousands in the hills around Cuzco, in caves equipped with doors so they could be visited periodically. Food, drink, clothing, and gifts were brought to them, and they were consulted on important matters and asked to use their influence to ensure adequate rain and good harvests. In southern Peru, mummies were sometimes placed in specially built burial towers (*chullas*) rather than caves, and retrieved on auspicious occasions to participate in religious ceremonies. They were also taken to visit one another to maintain the relationships they had established during their lifetimes. This was done, in part, because their social standing in clan genealogies determined land ownership. It was even possible to improve a mummy's social standing through marriage to another mummy.

A Closer Look

Mummification

… the Inca royalty enjoyed unusually energetic careers after death. With the help of a coterie of assistants, kings and queens carried on as though their spirits had never left them. Royal mummies ate, drank, urinated, visited one another, sat at councils, and judged weighty questions.

Terence N. D'Altroy, *The Incas* (Oxford: Blackwell, 2002), p. 141.

Mummification was practiced by several Andean peoples long before the Inca. Among the Chinchorro, who occupied the dry coastal regions in northern Chile and southern Peru ca. 7000–1500 BCE, mummification has been documented as far back as the late sixth millennium BCE—that is, two millennia before the Egyptians began to mummify their pharaohs. Rather than embalming their dead, as in Egypt, they let the corpses dry out naturally or through the use of hot coals. Over time, they also developed several techniques of mummification. For the so-called black mummies, for example, they separated the head and limbs from the trunk of the body, and removed the skin as well as the organs, muscles, and brains. After these parts dried out, the skeleton was reassembled with rope and pieces of cane. The body cavity

(continued)

was then stuffed with wool, shells, and grass, and the entire body was covered with a paste made of ash. After this, the skin was replaced and the body was painted black (Figure 7.10).

Figure 7.10 A mummy from the Chinchorro culture. Note the use of string to hold the torso together, the wooden slats on the chest, and the stylized black clay mask. Source: Wikimedia Commons.

The mummies of the Sapa Incas were given special honors. Seated next to one another on a golden bench in Inti's shrine, they were attended to night and day. Each wore royal attire and jewelry, held a golden scepter, and spoke through a priest assigned to him. On occasion, a Sapa Inca's mummy might be transported to his palace so he could visit with mummies of other royal families or hold court with important dignitaries visiting Cuzco. At other times, the mummies would be escorted, as a group, from the Golden Enclosure to preside over major festivals or sacrifices. The family of each deceased Sapa Inca continued to live in his palace, performing the services of a *panaca*, a clan organization responsible for upholding a Sapa Inca's honor.

To promote loyalty to the empire, Inca law required all non-Inca to participate in religious ceremonies sponsored by the state. One of these, called *capacocha*, required municipalities to dedicate a boy and a girl to the state each year. They needed to be virgins with no physical defects. The boys were assigned to serve at court in Cuzco, while the girls were placed in various Houses of Chosen Women where they were taught to make alcoholic beverages, called *chicha*, and weave fine textiles for use in religious festivals. At critical moments in the life of the empire, as when a new Sapa Inca was installed or a drought threatened the year's harvest, a *capacocha* was undertaken. A number of these dedicated children were paired as husband and wife, dressed in royal attire and sent out from Cuzco to the most important *huacas* in the empire. Their journeys could take several months, for they traveled by foot along the straightest routes possible from Cuzco to the *huacas*, which led them over mountains, across rivers, and through valleys. When they arrived at their destinations, the children were given alcohol to drink and coca leaves chew, and then killed, usually by strangulation. The goal was to send these children to the gods as ambassadors for the common good of the empire. This is why they had to be perfect physical specimens, because the Inca wanted to send only the very best of their people.

The European invasion

In October of 1492, Christopher Columbus, an Italian adventurer sailing under the Spanish flag, landed in the Bahamas, believing that he had found a western maritime route to China and India. Over the next 50 years, religion in the Americas changed dramatically.

Columbus's encounter with Indigenous Americans ignited the imagination of European kings, queens, and religious leaders, as well as countless adventurers, colonists, and opportunists. Sailing as military forces and missionaries, European settlers came in waves, primarily from Spain, England, Portugal, France, the Netherlands, Sweden, and Russia. Indigenous peoples soon came to understand the European incursion for what it was—an open assault on their lands, cultures, and religions—but they were unable to repel the invading peoples. Following the Spanish destruction of the Aztec empire in 1519 and the Inca empire in 1533, over 100 unsuccessful indigenous uprisings took place, including an Inca rebellion (mid-1500s), a revolt by Pueblo peoples (1680), Pontiac's War (1763–1766), the Siege of La Paz (1781), the Battle of Tippecanoe (1811), the Great Sioux War (1876), and the Caste War of Yucatan (1847–1915). While European success in battle relied heavily on superior military technology and leveraging conflicts between indigenous groups, the Europeans' most powerful weapon was infectious disease. Unknowingly, they had brought with them numerous pathogens for which the indigenous peoples had no immunities: smallpox, measles, influenza, tuberculosis, cholera, and typhus, to name the most important. As a result, indigenous peoples died by the tens of millions, in many cases even before encountering Europeans, for these highly infectious diseases traveled quickly along indigenous trade routes and spread among those visiting spiritual centers. The death and illness they caused brought on further suffering and death through disruptions in trade, sharp declines in agricultural production, and increased fatalities in war.

Talking About Religion

A Train Wreck in the Caribbean

When looked at from a fairly long view, the meeting between the Spanish and the indigenous people of the Caribbean was an "encounter" of peoples the way a train wreck is an encounter.

> Samuel M. Wilson, ed., *The Indigenous People of the Caribbean*
> (Gainesville: University of Florida Press, 1997), p. 29.

It is estimated that of the 110 million people in the Americas at the time of Columbus's arrival, less than 15 percent survived the European invasion, and some areas were hit harder than others. In places where Europeans had enslaved the indigenous people, death from infectious disease was hastened by malnutrition, overwork, and squalid living conditions. Thus, in the first 100 years of colonization, the population of Mesoamerica fell from over 25 million to around 1 million; the Tupian people along the coast of Brazil, once estimated at about 1 million, were nearly wiped out; and indigenous peoples in the Caribbean were brought to near extinction on most of the islands. The few who survived did so by fleeing to the mainland or by cooperating and intermarrying with the Spanish.

The consequences of a population collapse of this magnitude are difficult to fathom. Consider the hardships and disruptions caused by the COVID-19 pandemic that began in 2020, which killed less than 2 percent of any single nation's population, and in most cases far less than 1 percent. Compared to that, an 85 percent death toll would be nothing short of a postapocalyptic dystopia—which was basically how Europeans, to their shock and horror, described what they saw when they came to the Americas in the mid-sixteenth century. Because neither the Europeans nor the indigenous peoples knew about microbes or bacteria, neither had the scientific means to explain what was happening. Both groups, consequently, turned to religious explanations.

European approaches

Europeans saw the Great Dying, as it became known in Latin America, as the Christian god's judgment on the indigenous peoples for practicing idolatry and demon worship, and for refusing to accept Christian salvation. To put an end to idolatry and demon worship, European monarchs working with church officials undertook what could be characterized as the systematic destruction of indigenous religions. In Mesoamerica, where writing systems had been used to record important traditions about gods, rulers, and rituals, the Spanish burned hundreds of religious libraries. They also publicly executed religious leaders in Aztec, Inca, and Maya cities, and dismantled the spiritual centers there. They stripped gold and silver furnishings from temples, defaced statues and monuments depicting spiritual beings, burned or confiscated ancestral mummies, looted sacred burial sites, and repurposed the stone blocks from raised platforms and pyramid temples to build churches, monasteries, and administrative buildings. Further north, *kivas* were closed down or demolished; and throughout the Americas, masks, drums, rattles, ceremonial pipes, priestly attire, and other religious paraphernalia were confiscated or destroyed.

By the eighteenth century, European colonists began to assert their independence from their homelands and form nations of their own, and in almost every case, this led to an immediate reduction of church oversight in state affairs. Yet this did little to slow the religious persecution of Indigenous Americans, for the presumption of European Christian superiority continued. Throughout the western hemisphere, indigenous children were taken from their parents and educated in European-style boarding schools, and whole communities were relocated from their native lands and sacred places and forced to live in Portuguese reduções, Spanish reduccíones, U.S. reservations, and Canadian Indian reserves. Even without the direct intervention of the church, laws prohibiting indigenous religious ceremonies became part of national and local legal codes. In the United States and Canada, for example, the Thirst Dance ("Sun Dance") of the Great Plains and the Potlatch of the Pacific Northwest were prohibited by law. In addition to offending Christian sensibilities, the first was banned due to its practices of "self-mutilation," which were judged to be incompatible with civilized societies. Potlatches, by contrast, were ceremonies in which goods were given away so as to reapportion authority, spiritual power, and wealth within a community. This practice, it was argued, was contrary to the morally beneficial nature of capitalism and the associated blessings of the Protestant work ethic, individualism, and the ownership of private property.

Sacred Traditions and Scripture

Indigenous Systems for Recording Ideas

Long before the arrival of the Spanish, systems of writing and recording ideas had developed among the Maya, Aztecs, and Inca. The Inca (as well as the Wari empire before them) made records by tying different styles of knots on cotton and wool strings. These were attached to a connecting string to create larger bodies of information called *khipu* (Figure 7.11). At one time there were libraries of these knotted strings throughout the Inca empire, each with a *khipu* maker—a librarian who could create and read these records. Over time, however, the process of recording information in this way fell into disuse. Although a number of examples still exist, and although a few people continued to use the *khipu* system as late as the nineteenth or early twentieth century, scholars have so far made little progress in determining their meaning.

By contrast, the Maya and Aztecs wrote using small pictures (somewhat like Egyptian hieroglyphs), which could be quite detailed. These pictures stood for ideas, sounds, and even short phrases (called logographs). Unfortunately, large libraries of Maya and Inca books were destroyed in the sixteenth century by Spanish authorities who believed they contained demonic teachings. Even so, examples of Maya and Aztec writing are preserved in inscriptions and in a few books that managed to survive.

(continued)

Figure 7.11 An example of a *khipu*, a series of knotted strings arranged along a common top string. *Khipu* were used to record many types of information, including inventory in storage facilities, census data, laws, religious ceremonies, and narratives. The knots vary in style, and the strings are made of cotton or wool, dyed with distinct colors, and twisted in particular ways. These details, together with the sequence in which they are tied to the top string, seem to have been important elements in storing the information they record. Source: Archives Center at the Smithsonian's National Museum of the American Indian (NMAI).

Given the wholesale destruction of the material aspects of indigenous religions, non-indigenous academics and intellectuals in the late nineteenth and early twentieth centuries feared the extinction of indigenous cultures in their lifetimes and advocated for what was called "salvage ethnology." In response, governments authorized the confiscation of indigenous religious objects so they could be preserved in museum collections for future generations. On the popular level, indigenous cultures were romanticized in history books, novels, and motion pictures as noble civilizations of the past, as if they had already died out.

Indigenous approaches

The European explanation for the illness and death that was ravaging indigenous communities simply did not make sense within indigenous worldviews. While gods and spirits punished people for neglecting to worship them properly, they did not, in the indigenous experience, punish anyone for worshipping other gods and spirits. From an indigenous perspective, monotheism, or the exclusive allegiance to one god, was wrong and dangerous, as it deprived other divine beings of their due. Some divine beings were more important than others, naturally, because they had more power or controlled vital resources such as water or fertility; but none could be ignored or excluded, unless their power had waned.

From the indigenous perspective, the great evils that Europeans had brought upon them were caused by sorcery. The Europeans, in other words, had used their influence and relationships in the spirit world to inflict harm. This was nothing new, for communities and city-states in conflict with one another had often relied on their spiritual leaders to inflict sickness and death on their enemies. When this happened, counter-sorcery and spiritual cures were needed. The problem with European sorcery was that the illnesses it inflicted were of a magnitude far greater than indigenous peoples had previously experienced, and traditional cures and counter-sorcery proved ineffective in warding them off. Some even feared that the Europeans, in gaining knowledge of machines and in producing material goods, had so misused the world's resources that they had upset the balance of creation. The way forward from the indigenous perspective was to gain access to more effective spiritual powers, either by establishing relations with the European god, or by learning new ways to access their own deities, which was the responsibility of indigenous prophets and messiahs.

Prophets and messiahs Prophets and messiahs were active in indigenous religions long before the arrival of the Europeans. When weather patterns changed and communities were threatened by drought or floods, prophets sought instructions from the spirit realm on the necessary course of action. Through the divine guidance they received in dreams and visions, prophets had implemented changes to important rituals and ceremonies, established new pilgrimage sites, reinterpreted the meaning of calendrical and astronomical calculations, and forged relations with new gods. In times of extreme crisis, prophets had taken on messianic roles, leading their communities to new settlements altogether. In these cases, indigenous origin stories, which often recounted how the present world had emerged from the destruction of a previous world, served as a model for what might lie ahead.

One response to the European invasion, therefore, was the appearance of hundreds of prophetic and messianic movements. Among the earliest was Taki Onqoy, the Dancing Sickness, which began in the latter half of the sixteenth century in southwestern Peru and spread into Bolivia. The *huacas*, or spirits of the land, began to take possession of Andean people, causing them to dance and shake. The leaders of the movement explained that this dance would drive out the Christian god and the Spanish invaders, and it was even reported that some of the Catholic saints had joined forces with the *huacas* in this effort. The people, in turn, were to divest themselves of all Christian and European influence and return to their traditional ways of life.

Similar movements featuring dance appeared independently in North America, the most well-known being the Ghost Dance. During a solar eclipse on January 1, 1889, a Northern Paiute prophet called Wovoka had a vision of the Christian God, who told him that native peoples would soon be separated from the Europeans and live in peace: the ancestors would lead them to abundant lands teaming with bison, and the death and illness brought by the Europeans would go away. To achieve this, indigenous peoples needed to promote harmony and work together, and perform a round dance for five consecutive nights at certain prescribed intervals. The round dance was a traditional ceremony in which dancers used a slow shuffle to move silently in a circle to the beat of a drum. It was explained as an imitation of the dead, or of the sun's movement across the sky, and was called the Circle Dance, the Dance to Christ, or the Ghost Dance, as it promised to draw the spirits of ancestors near. News of Wovoka's vision spread quickly from the Great Basin region, attracting leaders from indigenous communities in California and the Great Plains. When they returned home, these leaders taught versions of the dance and Wovoka's message to their own peoples. As the movement grew, the U.S. government grew wary of possible insurrections at large dance gatherings, leading U.S. soldiers in one instance to attempt to disarm a group of Lakota near Wounded Knee Creek in South Dakota. When chaos ensued, the soldiers responded by killing more than 150 of the Lakota, including some dancers and many women and children. Soon after the Wounded Knee Massacre, public performances of the dance ceased, although it continued to be practiced for a time in private sessions.

Indigenous engagement with Christian worship Indigenous Americans rejected many aspects of Christian theology as wrong or dangerous. These included the doctrine of original sin; salvation of the individual apart from one's family or community; belief in a single, absolute truth; and the idea that there was a worldwide community of saved people as opposed to the great majority, who were damned. Similarly, most indigenous communities condemned the buying and selling of natural resources to accumulate wealth. While not part of Christian theology proper, the commodification of goods was deeply ingrained in the Christian culture Europeans brought with them, while indigenous peoples found it reprehensible for two reasons. First, it inspired greed and individualism at the expense of the community; and second, it dishonored the spiritual beings who provided these resources and imbued them with their power. Corn, for example, was not an inanimate object in the indigenous worldview. Rather, it was a source for health and strength that flowed from the person of the Sun and the person of the Corn Goddess for the benefit of the human community. Like other resources supplied by the spirit world, it was wrong to hoard it or take more than one needed.

Conversion to Christianity was thus rarely an option for indigenous peoples. Nonetheless, they often approached Christianity with curiosity and interest, and saw nothing wrong with establishing the same sort of relations with God, Jesus, or one of the saints as they had with their own gods. Learning from the religions of others was a longstanding practice among Indigenous Americans, for they assumed that there was only one spirit world, which was common to all. For many Indigenous Americans, the most viable way forward was to gain power and knowledge from the gods who had enabled the Europeans to become so dominant.

> **Did you know …**
>
> One of the effects of the European conquest was to make indigenous religions more patriarchal. Not only did European Christians object to women taking leadership roles in religion, but they also tended to target women in their efforts to irradicate indigenous practices of magic, since they associated women with witchcraft. As a result, many of the leadership roles in religion that women had performed either vanished or were suppressed, and many of the ceremonies in which men and women had played complementary roles became androcentric.

Almost from the beginning of the European invasion, therefore, indigenous peoples appropriated divine beings from Christianity in an attempt to gain access to their power. Some gave the Christian god, Jesus, or Mary important roles in the spiritual realm, assimilating them to powerful deities like the sun and moon. Andean people, for example, identified the Virgin Mary with Pachamama, the goddess of earth and fertility. Others were baptized to gain access to the saints, localized the saints as *huacas* in the mountains, forests, and rivers around them, or assigned them traditional roles. In some areas St. Peter became the patron spirit of rain, or corn, or beans. Even Judas, who had betrayed Jesus, was sometimes elevated to the status of spirit-saint, being understood as a trickster who worked to undermine European religion.

In the southwestern United States and in Central and South America, the Catholic church actively encouraged indigenous populations to participate in Christian festivals and processions such as Holy Week, the feast of Corpus Christi, and All Saints' Day. This appealed to indigenous people as a substitute for the religious activities that had taken place at their spiritual centers, which now lay in ruins. All Saints' Day, which became known as the Day of the Dead (Día de los Muertos), was particularly popular because of the massive death toll in indigenous communities.

An important catalyst for engaging with Catholicism was the many appearances of Mary to indigenous people. The most significant of these apparitions was experienced by Juan Diego, a member of the Chichimec community in central Mexico. Coming to him four times in 1531 as a dark-skinned woman who addressed him in his native language, Mary soon became known as the Dark Virgin and Our Lady of Guadalupe, and was venerated widely as the spirit-saint who gave indigenous people special access to the Christian god.

Yet Indigenous Americans appropriated gods and participated in Christian worship on their own terms, not according to Christian theology. Thus, during Holy Week and the feast of Corpus Christi, Quechua peoples of the Peruvian Andes brought food to the church to be blessed by the priests before taking it to gravesites for a common meal with their ancestors. Puebloans followed Easter services with traditional dances dedicated to animal and plant peoples, spirits of healing, and weather deities; and indigenous groups farther north used Christmas as a time for giveaways—the practice of rewarding those who participated in rituals with gifts—which the Europeans had banned.

Indigenous churches   As an alternative to taking part in Christian worship, Indigenous Americans sometimes created their own churches. Examples from North America include the Good Message (or Longhouse Religion), the Native American Church (or Peyote Religion), and the Shaker Church, all of which continue to the present. The Shaker Church (which should not be confused with the millenarian Christian group known as the Shakers) was founded in Washington State by the Squaxin couple John and Mary Slocum. In 1881 John is said to have died and gone to Heaven, where he spoke with angels or Jesus. Upon returning to earth and reinhabiting his body, he announced that he had been commissioned to begin a church guided by a new medicine, which prohibited alcohol, smoking, and gambling, and employed certain shamanic rituals. Within a year John became seriously ill, but recovered through Mary's prayers, during which Mary was overcome by uncontrollable shaking. The couple chartered their church in 1892, based on a gospel that was communicated directly to members from God. Worship services took place on Sunday and included public testimony and confession of sin, the use of crucifixes, and healing sessions in which leaders used a shaking technique.

In Latin America (i.e., Central and South America), most indigenous churches developed out of Pentecostalism or the Catholic Charismatic Renewal movement. By the late 1970s, Pentecostal Christianity began to spread rapidly through indigenous communities in Argentina, Guatemala, El Salvador, Nicaragua, Brazil, and Chile. Its emphasis on the activity of the Holy Spirit in the life of individual Christians was equated by many indigenous Latin Americans to their own traditions of communicating with spirit peoples. Many joined Pentecostal churches, while others began their own brand of spirit-led churches. In response to the large-scale conversion of their members to Pentecostal churches, the Catholic church introduced its own version of Pentecostalism into Latin America. This was the Catholic Charismatic Renewal movement, which had begun in the United States in 1967. Finally, in the 1980s, neo-Pentecostalism came to Latin America, promising both spiritual powers and material riches. As a result of these influences, around 30 percent of the churches in Latin America are now Pentecostal or Charismatic, and many of these are indigenous organizations that combine Christian elements with indigenous music and dance, shamanism, and rituals of healing.

Renewal

Beginning in the 1960s, several factors coalesced to revitalize the practice of indigenous religions in the Americas. In the United States, a pan-Indian movement took shape, growing out of the interaction between different groups on reservations, and through powwows. The latter are occasions for indigenous groups to come together to showcase their respective traditions of dance, song, and dress. Having their origins in the late nineteenth century, powwows became an opportunity for indigenous people to pass their traditions along to successive generations, take pride in their cultural identity, and become aware of their common struggles and challenges. In South America, a similar role was played by the *dabucuri* ceremonies of the northwest Amazon and the *Toré* festivals of northeast Brazil.

> ### Talking About Religion
>
> ## Human Origins
>
> Because Indigenous Americans have their own traditions of creation, which include accounts of how human beings came into the world, they often object to academic accounts of human evolution or theories of human migration from Asia.

The 1960s also saw the passage of civil rights legislation in the United States and the proliferation of Marxist-leaning Liberation Theologies in Latin America, both of which raised awareness of the oppression of indigenous peoples and eventually led to some protections under the law. By the 1970s, indigenous religious practices had become popularized in non-indigenous circles, such as the New Age movement; Native-way schools and colleges began to appear; and undergraduate programs in Indigenous Studies were offered for the first time at major universities in North and Latin America. All of this emboldened a new generation of Indigenous Americans to reclaim their cultural history and reshape it for the future. More recently, the United Nations declared 1994–2004 the Decade of the World's Indigenous Peoples; in 2004 the Smithsonian Institute opened the National Museum of the American Indian on the National Mall in Washington, DC; and in 2007 the United Nations adopted the Declaration on the Rights of Indigenous Peoples. Because of these developments, the practice of indigenous religions in the Americas is currently growing, although with the rise of authoritarian politics in the United States and Latin America, it is perhaps premature to predict a secure future for these religions.

Contemporary Beliefs and Practices

Other-than-human persons

Fundamental to any understanding of indigenous religions in the Americas is the indigenous belief that humans are not the only people in the world. There are, in other words, nonhuman or "other-than-human" people with whom they must coexist and share resources. These include animals and plants, weather phenomena (such as thunder), and celestial bodies (such as the sun). Even mountains, rocks, lakes, clay, and pollen can be people, or be infused with the power of a nonhuman person. Among the Shoshone, for example (see Figure 7.12), the Grand Teton mountains are powerful people to whom one must show respect by not pointing at them or calling them by their true name. To distinguish between themselves and these other peoples, the Zuni refer to themselves as "cooked" people, as opposed to "raw" people; the Diné (Navajo) call themselves earth-surface people; and the Ava-Chiripa of Paraguay see themselves as "true people."

> ### Rituals, Rites, Practices
>
> ## Where Are the Photos?
>
> Unlike other chapters in this book, the Contemporary Beliefs and Practices section of this chapter has no photographs. While religious people in general do not appreciate outsiders treating their religion as a "spectator sport," Indigenous Americans rarely allow outsiders even to take pictures. This is because the effectiveness of their religious ceremonies and rituals depends on interacting with spirit people, with whom they have personal relationships of trust and cooperation; and personal relationships are by their very nature private matters. Indigenous Americans are also justifiably wary of outsiders, especially those of European descent, intruding into their affairs.

In the indigenous context, "people" are living beings who exercise individual volition. As individuals, they make decisions, desire certain things, and express preferences. This perspective is very different than a secular or scientific view of the world, in which animals act according to instinct, plants grow through photosynthesis, and matter is controlled by the laws of physics. From an indigenous perspective, the sun rises each morning and begins his journey across the sky because he has decided to do so. Like a human person, he has a daily routine. At times, however, he can shine too brightly and destroy the crops that humans depend on. When this happens, ritual experts are assigned the task of dissuading Father Sun from acting in this way. The Kogi of Colombia, for example, have a respected order of priests (the *mamo*) who train for up to 18 years so they can, among other things, dissuade Sun from shining too brightly and Rain from flooding their lands (see the chapter-opening photo). During the winter solstice, when the days are shortest, many indigenous communities perceive that Sun may lack the strength to continue his routine. As a remedy, they perform rituals designed to support and encourage the Sun in his travels. Similarly, during a solar eclipse, the Diné perceive that the Sun, whom they call Our Father, is undergoing a process of dying and renewal. Out of reverence, they neither eat nor drink anything, and they remain indoors praying and chanting. Throughout the Americas, indigenous peoples also perform rituals to change the path of a dangerous storm as it bears down on a community—rituals that communicate with Thunder, Lightning, Rain, and Wind. Members of the Iroquois False Face society, for example, perform exorcisms on tornados.

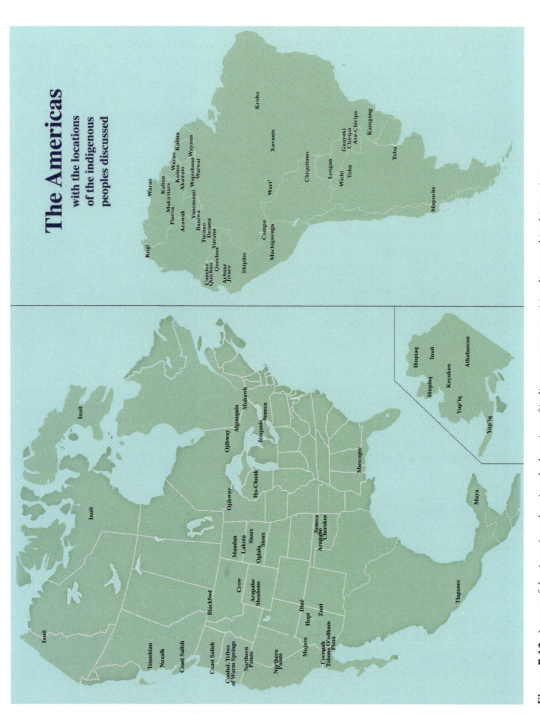

Figure 7.12 A map of the Americas showing the location of indigenous communities discussed in this section.

Animate versus inanimate

More than one anthropologist has noted that the community of Indigenous Americans they are studying does not consistently distinguish between animate beings and inanimate objects. For example, in communities that depend on fishing as a source of food, nets and traps are understood to be effective because they "have" or "are associated with" spirits who attract the fish. While we might understand this to mean that inanimate objects such as nets contain spirits, the indigenous view is quite different. Because they believe that spirits can choose to make themselves visible by wearing inanimate objects as a body or as skin, they see their nets and traps as living manifestations of the spirits, with attributes of personhood. Likewise, when spirits dwell in stones, as they sometimes do in the northwest Amazon, the stones themselves gain sensory perception and must be treated with care and respect. Among the Ojibway of the Great Lakes region, stones sometimes roll on their own and speak to people. By contrast, Maya of the Mexican highlands consider their physical houses to be alive, but not necessarily persons. They can become persons, however, through certain ceremonies, which make them members of the community.

Origin stories

A principal source of this distinctive view of the world is Indigenous American **origin stories**. Almost all indigenous communities have an origin story, and it is not uncommon for a community to have more than one. These stories explain how our present world came into being through the actions of deities and other-than-human peoples who lived long ago. Some describe how a god began or created the world. The Ho-Chunk of Wisconsin relate how Earthmaker wept out of loneliness, thereby creating the seas, while the Baniwa of the upper Rio Negro describe a Jaguar bone-deity who played his trumpet over a small stone ball, expanding it to create the world. Rarely, however, do Creators do more than just begin the process of creation. After performing the initial act or acts of creation, thereby setting the standard for what will follow, they leave the further details of creation to powerful beings who come later.

Other origin stories do not report the actions of a Creator or describe the beginning of the world. Instead, they simply assume the existence of the world and recount what happened in the "distant past" or "early times," when various powerful beings roamed freely. This is pictured as a chaotic and often violent period. It is full of trial and error, discovery and invention, terrible disasters, and narrow escapes, all of which move in the direction of our present world. There are few givens in this early period. Life forms are fluid, and aspects of the world change freely and abruptly. In many South American origin stories, various species of plants, fish, birds and animals come into existence, although some are too monstrous to survive. These are killed or die out, and improved life forms take their place. Alternatively, entire eras end in catastrophic earthquakes, fires, or floods, and new, more promising ones begin.

Among these early deities and other powerful beings, often referred to as supernaturals, there is a great deal of conflict and animosity. They are sometimes related to one another and harbor family jealousies—younger siblings murdering older siblings, spouses betraying spouses. Twins are featured in many of these stories, banding together for good or evil, going their separate ways, or killing one another.

In these primal times, supernaturals also experiment with creating the first humans, the ancestors of the present human race. Their initial attempts, however, come out badly: mud people, stick people, or humans who cannot move or speak. But in the end they succeed.

Some of the supernaturals in these origin stories are remembered for creating or procuring things that are beneficial to humans. Scholars call these beings **culture heroes**. They are given credit for bringing tobacco, or corn, or farming techniques into the world. They name beneficial plants, invent nets for fishing and bows for hunting, and teach humans how to weave and create pottery. They are especially remembered for stealing fire from other supernaturals and giving it to humans. Another class of supernaturals who contribute to the making of the world are the changers, or transformers. As their name suggests, they create by transforming one thing into another. Among the Campa of eastern Peru, for example, a transformer is given credit for having changed members of his family into insects and monkeys. Finally, there are supernaturals whom scholars call **tricksters**. These beings live by their wits—the Desana of Colombia and Brazil, for example, tell stories of a female turtle trickster who manages to outsmart monkeys, foxes, deer, and jaguars.

> ### Sacred Traditions and Scripture
>
> ## The Earth Diver
>
> In North American origin stories, a widely disseminated tradition recounts how land was created with the help of a figure known as the earth diver. The basic story begins with a watery world, sometimes the result of a flood. Various animals dive into the water, trying to retrieve mud from the bottom. After several attempts, one of the animals succeeds, and the mud that this earth diver manages to retrieve is used to make dry land. A Cherokee version of this story begins with the birds and animals living in the sky or on a rainbow. Since living conditions there are crowded, it is decided that the water beetle should descend to the waters below and search for dry land by skating in all directions on the surface of the water. When the beetle finds none, he heads in the only direction left, diving deep into the water and returning with a bit of mud from the bottom. He then continues to dive and retrieve mud, eventually creating enough dry land for the rest of the birds and animals.
>
> Other versions of the earth diver tradition involve a culture hero. The Mohawk version begins with a woman falling through a hole in the sky. A flock of ducks breaks her fall and sets her on the back of a turtle who is swimming in the waters below. The woman calls on various animals—a beaver, an otter, and a muskrat—to dive to the bottom and retrieve mud. The beaver and the otter fail, and die in the process. Only the muskrat is able to return with the mud, which the woman spreads around the edges of the turtle's shell. The woman then falls asleep, and when she awakes the mud has grown into dry land around the turtle, as far as the eye can see.

(continued)

> A woman is also the culture hero in an Iroquois version, although she is pregnant when she falls (or is let down) from the sky. After the muskrat helps her create the dry land, she gives birth to Corn Mother. In an Arapaho version, the culture hero is Flat Pipe. During the primordial flood, he finds himself alone and calls on all the birds and animals for help. After several ducks dive and fail to return with any mud, a turtle succeeds. Man Above then uses the power of Flat Pipe to expand this mud into the dry land. In a Crow version, Old Man Coyote is identified as the culture hero, while for the Ojibwe it is a being named Nanabozho. To save himself from the primordial flood, Nanabozho either climbs a tree, builds a raft, or clambers onto the back of a turtle who swims by. He then successively commissions a loon, an otter, a beaver, and a muskrat to dive for the mud. When the muskrat finally brings him a small clod, he spreads it out and breathes life into it to create a fertile earth.

It is not always easy to distinguish between culture heroes, transformers, and tricksters, which are, after all, academic terms. Those who qualify as tricksters, however, are usually the most colorful and entertaining, and one of their functions in origin stories is to teach listeners how *not* to act by producing disorder. They are known for doing what they want and getting their own way. As often as not, however, their cleverness leads them to inflict harm on themselves, which they simply laugh off. They have insatiable appetites for food, drink, and sex, and express these appetites in ways that are horrifying or disgusting, humiliating themselves in the process. They violate taboos, such as incest; they become fascinated with their own bodily functions and think up creative ways to use their own excrement; and they antagonize powerful beings to their own detriment. They are braggarts and liars, and above all, far too curious for their own good. Raven, for example, a trickster in origin stories from the Pacific Northwest, manages to open a box containing the sun, thereby burning himself black. Tricksters are usually animals (like Raven), although they appear in origin stories in human form. They can be male, female, or androgynous, or switch between genders. In North America, along with Raven, popular trickster figures include Coyote, Spider, and Blue Jay, while in Latin America, Opossum, Tree Frog, and Monkey are widespread.

One purpose for telling these origin stories is to give listeners insight into how humans relate to the nonhuman peoples with whom they share the earth. Audiences learn how the creative and destructive powers of former times have shaped the present hierarchy of beings, and consequently who should be thanked for this year's harvest of beans, or propitiated to cure an illness. But most importantly, audiences learn that they are heirs to a balanced and harmonious world that was achieved through the chaos and violence of earlier times, and that they must maintain this balance and harmony for the sake of all peoples, seen and unseen, lest chaos and violence return. In this way, origin stories provide the basis for indigenous peoples' norms and principles of life, which in most instances is indistinguishable from their religion. Thus, for the Yup'iq of Alaska, religion is simply the "way of being human," and for the Diné of the southwest United States, maintaining harmony and balance in one's life is to "walk in beauty." Similarly, the Xavante of west-central Brazil equate living morally with being beautiful.

Cooperation

Indigenous Americans engage with other-than-human peoples because it is necessary. Since every aspect of life depends on the actions of some person or group of persons, nothing can be taken for granted, nothing happens "naturally." Jivaro women of eastern Ecuador and northern Peru, for example, sing to Mother Earth while planting, so she will be persuaded to push the plants up from below. Similarly, without a science-based assumption of regularity in the natural world, Hopi farmers in northern Arizona plant a particular type of seed to obtain a certain crop, not because the seed is genetically disposed to produce that crop, but because this communicates to the deity of germination what plants they need. When humans want to harvest these plants, moreover, they must ask permission. This is the equivalent of asking the plants for their power, or "medicine," which for corn, squash, and other staples is their nutrition. Likewise, for herbs to have the potency to heal, for ice to support a traveler's weight, and for garden tools to dig the earth properly, humans must appeal to these people for their power.

> ### Talking About Religion
>
> ### "Medicine"
>
> The term "medicine" occurs in translations of many expressions used by indigenous North Americans: medicine man, medicine pipe, medicine lodge, medicine bundle. The intent is to convey the healing power of these entities, but not with reference to the use of medication. That would be a modern western perspective. In the indigenous North American context, "medicine" is the power or force that enables humans to thrive and prosper. It comes from spirit persons and can be used to control weather patterns and animal migrations; ensure plentiful harvests; and enable children to become responsible adults in their communities. And, yes, medicine in this sense is also used to cure illnesses, since illnesses are primarily understood to be spiritual problems with bodily symptoms.

Fortunately, most nonhuman people are generous and willing to help, for several reasons. First and foremost, spirit people have needs and desires just like human people, and so cooperation among all peoples becomes a basic rule of existence. A tree, for example, might desire tobacco smoke and cornmeal, things it can only get from humans. But it needs rain and sunlight, too, which only come from Thunder, the Winds, and Sun. But since tobacco and corn also require rain and sunlight, and since Thunder, the Winds, and Sun have their own particular needs, some of which are satisfied by humans, it is in everyone's best interest to work together for the good of all.

A second reason nonhuman peoples stand ready to help humans is that they, like humans, have their origins in the events of earlier times, as recounted in the origin stories. Consequently, they, like humans, are devoted to maintaining the harmony and balance of the present world to stave off a return to that evil, primal existence. A third reason, which is closely related to this, is the belief that during the chaos and violence of those former times, spirit peoples formed close bonds and even kinship ties with human beings. Origin stories commonly depict other-than-human peoples as having human form, sharing a language with humans, living in human communities, and joining forces with humans against powerful supernaturals. In these stories, clear distinctions between human and nonhuman people also tend to blur, as one species or group changes into another: humans become monkeys, fish, and features in the landscape, while rocks, rain, and orcas are transformed into humans. Given this history of closeness and cooperation between human and nonhuman peoples, it is only natural that they should continue to work together. Indeed, throughout North America, indigenous people give expression to this ongoing closeness by addressing spirit people with kinship titles such as "grandmother," "sister," and "brother"; and in the Great Plains, the expression "all my relations" refers to human and nonhuman people alike.

Lastly, it is a common belief among many Indigenous Americans that cooperation between peoples is facilitated by the influence of a Supreme Being. Male, female, and at times androgynous, the Supreme Being is understood as both the source of life and power in the universe, and the source of divine wisdom. Consequently, all creatures are indebted to the Supreme Being, whom they experience as the wind that circulates among them, the air that they breathe, or the rays of the Sun, which shine on all alike. In granting a portion of life, power, and wisdom to all, however, the Supreme Being obligates each person and each community of persons to work with others, lest these gifts be withdrawn.

Reciprocity   An important aspect of cooperation is **reciprocity**. If one receives, one should give in return, and likewise, if one gives one should receive. In the normal course of events, Indigenous Americans approach spirits and deities with offerings, sacrifices, thanksgiving, praise, and entertainment in exchange for the necessities of life—food, clothing, protection from the weather, procreation, and good health. The theological basis for this giving and receiving is often understood along the lines of a negotiated agreement between two parties for the benefit of both. In a number of rituals, however, humans make themselves weak and pitiful through fasting, physical exertion, lack of sleep, and self-inflicted pain in the hope of obligating the spirit world to take pity on them and grant their requests. As we will see, this technique is used in North America during vision quests and the Thirst Dance, while in northeastern and central Brazil it can take the form of scarification.

Ceremonies of thanksgiving

Regardless of how one engages in the system of reciprocity, it must be done with respect for the other party. Spirit people are not expected to cooperate if humans approach them in an undignified manner. They are, after all, people too. They live in villages where they maintain their own cultures and traditions, and often have relatives and acquaintances in other villages. According to the Koyukon of Alaska, for example, porcupine and bear are cousins, and squirrel, mink, and fox are sisters. In parts of southwestern Amazonia, spirits make beer, live as married couples, and dress up. In all these things, spirit persons take pride in what they do; and since, like humans, they have feelings and emotions, they expect other persons, human and nonhuman, to treat them with respect.

An important way Indigenous Americans show respect is by holding thanksgiving ceremonies that express their appreciation to the spirit world for providing the necessities of life. These typically occur annually, during harvest and hunting seasons, and involve the entire community. Since spirit people will be the honored guests on these occasions, the human participants, especially the religious leaders, undergo purification rituals to be in their presence. These rituals involve fasting, washing, and the use of emetics, which cause vomiting, and purgatives, which are strong laxatives. In addition, smoke created by burning certain leaves and grasses can be used to purify the participants, the ceremonial site, the ritual equipment (such as musical instruments and ritual attire), and any food or drink that is to be offered to the spirit guests. In many cases, taboos are also imposed. For example, during the Green Corn Ceremony, which is performed in the southeastern United States, participants are prohibited from using alcohol and drugs, engaging in sexual intercourse, and digging in the earth.

The act of thanking the spirits during these ceremonies is achieved through formal statements of thanksgiving by community leaders, as well as offerings and entertainment. Foremost among the offerings is tobacco, which spirits are thought to crave or even be addicted to. In North America, it is widely believed that only humans have access to tobacco, either because the deities did not think to save any for themselves when they first gave tobacco to humans, or, according to some Seneca traditions, because the daughter of the sky god ripped the tobacco plant from the heavens when she fell to earth, grasping it to break her fall. In South America, where spirits primarily crave tobacco smoke, humans are seen as the sole providers because only they have fire. For the same reason, cooked food is also an important offering there.

Rituals, Rites, Practices

Primordial Power

Origin stories always begin in earlier times, either when the world began or simply "long ago." Scholars who study South American stories call these earlier times the **primordium**. It is a period when great power was concentrated in the hands of a few supernaturals who wielded this power freely and chaotically. Then, over time, this power was distributed among deities, spirit people, and humans, and conventions of respect and reciprocity were put in place. This brought the world into balance and created our present existence.

With this understanding of the past, several indigenous traditions attempt to gain access to the primordium to make use of the concentrated, unbridled power that was then available. For example, the Kalina, who live in parts of Venezuela, Guyana, Suriname, and French Guiana, use songs that were taught during the primordium, because present-day spirit peoples find the power of these songs to be irresistible. Likewise, in other parts of South America, shamans are able to journey into the primordium with their souls. They do this to

(continued)

gain knowledge and power from the primordial Bird, or Monkey, or Jaguar, or an ancient proto-shaman. Thus, among the Yanomami, shamans journey to the primordial home of the Anaconda people to learn their powerful dances.

A very different approach is taken by the Diné, who use sandpaintings to make the power of the primordium accessible to members of their communities who need healing and blessing. At ceremonials called Holy Way, Evil Way, and Blessing Way, Diné religious artists use colored sand and pollens to create pictures of events from the distant past that commemorate an incident when a hero was aided by supernaturals called Holy People. As these events are recounted through chanting, the person in need of healing or blessing sits in the middle of the picture and becomes the hero, and in this way receives the same power that was given to the ancient hero. Likewise, during Diné and Apache puberty rites, girls are transformed into the culture hero Changing Woman or White Shell Woman, respectively, thereby enabling them to heal and bless others through the power of these supernaturals.

Finally, this desire to access the power of the primordium may explain the drinking festivals that are undertaken in several areas of South America. During these festivals, the women of a community force the men to drink large quantities of fermented beverages, particularly a type of beer made from manioc tubers. The men must drink until the supply of beer is exhausted, sometimes vomiting up what they have just consumed in order to accept more. In some communities, if a man refuses to drink, the beverage is poured on his head. One explanation that scholars have offered is that these drinking festivals replicate the primordial flood that is recounted in many origin stories. While this flood brings chaos and ultimately destroys the world, which is mirrored in the drunkenness (and sometimes violence) of the drinking festivals, it also brings renewal through the new world that follows. Thus, participation in these festivals may be an attempt to ward off a recurrence of the primordial flood by symbolically drinking it. In other words, by entering into both the mayhem and the power of the primordium, the men in these festivals are able to use their bodies in a manner that exceeds its capacity, so as to prevent the world from once again plunging into disorder and tumult.

To entertain spirit guests at thanksgiving ceremonies, groups of men and women sing, dance, and play drums and wind instruments for the spirits' enjoyment—activities that can last for days. Performers typically retell and reenact episodes from origin stories in which the spirit guests achieved great things, and their dances often honor the spirits through imitation. Dancers wear masks, animal skins, horns, feathers, and vegetation, and move in ways indicative of certain animals, birds, fish, and plants. When possible, they also imitate animals' noises, such as bird calls and the grunts of peccaries (large hog-like animals).

The plants and animals to which Indigenous Americans give thanks number in the thousands. Plants alone, for example, include innumerable berries, fruits, and nuts, as well as tubers and root vegetables (potatoes, yams, manioc), beans, tomatoes, squash, cactus, avocados, pumpkins, peppers, quinoa, and, above all, corn. Likewise, land animals include alpaca, vicuña, armadillo, porcupine, sheep, guinea pig, rabbit, peccaries, elk, fox, bear, beaver, deer, jaguar, and tapir—just to name the most well-known—and this does not take into account scores of birds and aquatic animals. Naturally, it would be impossible for a community to hold separate festivals to thank each plant, animal, fish, and bird on which it relies, and so some communities focus on the ones they consider to be the most important. The Confederated Tribes of Warm Springs, Oregon, for example, hold a Root Festival, a Huckleberry Feast, and a Wild Celery Feast. Other communities, in turn, offer gratitude to the Supreme Being, or the Creator, or Mother Earth for all plants and animals. Finally, as a third option, communities can express their appreciation to **spirit masters**. These are powerful beings who are understood to be the early ancestors of the plant and animal peoples. They oversee multiple plant or animal communities and grant respectful humans access to those under their protection. In some areas of North America, for example, the master of domesticated plants is known as the Daughter of Earth or the Corn Maiden, whereas the Maya offer thanks to the "owners of maize," who control all plants. In Brazil, plant and animal masters are often a spirit couple, whereas the Wichí of Argentina and Bolivia teach that the master of uncultivated fruits lives in the Orion constellation, tending miniature versions of these fruits.

Ceremonies of thanksgiving invariably end with an elaborate feast, enjoyed by human and spirit peoples alike, and a formal send-off, after which the spirits return to their homes and communities in the spirit world. Aside from offering gratitude to spirit peoples for their generosity during the year, these ceremonies foster solidarity in the human community. In the weeks and months that lead up to these events, various groups work side by side, preparing food, constructing arbors and cooking stations, practicing dances, and gathering supplies so that things can start on time and run smoothly. During the festivities, moreover, children learn the traditions of their communities through orations, singing, and storytelling. This not only benefits the community and ensures its continuity into the future, but it is also essential for the community's standing with the spirit world, for spirits will not cooperate with humans who do not practice cooperation among themselves.

Becoming fully human

In the religious traditions of indigenous America, the primary aspiration of an individual is to establish and maintain a personal relationship with one or more persons in the spirit world. Until this is accomplished, one cannot develop fully as a human being within their community. Since the human community is surrounded by innumerable spirits and spirit communities, this is the first step in a process of socialization, and, as stated earlier, humans are not able to survive without help from the spirit world. By entering into a relationship with a spirit person, one gains the necessary power and knowledge to benefit their community and becomes a person of consequence for others. Using this power or knowledge for personal gain, on the other hand, would render them less-than-human—an antisocial being who becomes a danger to others. The Maya teach that acting in this way leads to soul loss and death.

In most instances, the power and knowledge that comes from spirits equip humans with practical abilities for day-to-day living—the ability to hunt and fish, weave, and work with leather, as well as cook, build a shelter, and perform as a midwife. While non-indigenous people might see these as tasks that can be acquired on one's own through practice or training, Indigenous Americans would disagree. Because almost everything is associated with or under the power of a spirit, it is a very real concern that baskets, for example, may not function properly if the weavers do not know the spirits of the reeds they are using. Likewise, wooden beams may not be able to support a roof if one has no relationship with the spirits associated with trees.

Finally, if a person has no helping spirits, they become vulnerable to malevolent spirits and sorcerers. This is such a pressing concern that married couples among the Guayaki of Paraguay choose names that connect children with guardian spirits even before birth. Similarly, the Waiwai of Guyana and northern Brazil present a newborn's soul to the moon to receive a spirit name; and the elders in various communities in North America seek protective names for newborns from the spirit world through dreams. In sum, without close ties to spirit people, there can be no cooperation, reciprocity, or respect, and human communities will languish.

Relating to spirits

Spirit persons are often encountered first through dreams, which are both windows and doorways into the spirit world. If a spirit appears in a dream, it can be a sign that they are calling the dreamer into a relationship. When this happens, the soul of the dreamer may be taken on a journey through part of the spirit world to gain some special knowledge, such as the spirit's name, or a song or dance. Since these journeys establish a personal relationship with the spirit, the individual receiving the dream will reveal the name of the spirit or the details of the experience only in very special circumstances, and only for the benefit of the community. If the dreamer does otherwise, any knowledge or access to the spirit that was gained during the dream may be lost. One's dance or song may, however, be performed publicly at some later date as a way to thank and honor the spirit in the presence of the community. Songs are often quite simple, having only a few words or, occasionally, no words at all, the melody and rhythm being their defining elements.

A personal relation with a spirit is, like personal relations with friends and family members, something that has to be maintained or it will be lost. Maintaining these relationships consists of feeding the spirit, confiding in and praying to the spirit, and, as just indicated, performing a spirit's song or dance. It may also involve avoiding certain things—that is, abiding by taboos—as well as wearing objects or clothes or colors that are favored by one's spirit. It is especially important for a person to learn a spirit's desired foods and needs, for while a person may revere or even love a helping spirit, the underlying principle of this and other relations with the spirit world is reciprocity: when one gives, one should receive, and when one receives, one must give in return. Just as people engage with spirits out of necessity, spirits make themselves known to people because they need or desire certain things. If a person knows what these things are, they can put a spirit under obligation to help out in difficult times.

Puberty rituals

Many indigenous communities have rituals for introducing spirits to boys and girls when they reach puberty. With the aid of spirit people, these rituals transform adolescents into adults by equipping them with things that benefit the community, such as practical knowledge, physical strength, diligence, bravery, and fertility. Parents and other family members, community leaders, and mentors prepare these children and see them through the process, which typically includes fasting, periods of isolation and silence, sleep deprivation, and confinement in a special structure or area for several days or weeks. Candidates are also subject to food taboos and, in some cases, prohibited from touching their own bodies: if they have an itch, they must use a scratching stick or stone. Throughout South America, but especially in French Guiana and the Amazon, boys and girls undergo ceremonial whipping to test their endurance, stimulate growth, and induce fertility. In northeastern Brazil and the adjacent countries of Colombia, Venezuela, and Guyana, they may also undergo scarification, as when the Wapishana make deep cuts in a boy's back. The resulting wounds are treated with a mixture of honey and ashes from certain plants, which introduces powers into the candidate's body and leaves a pattern of raised scars. For this procedure to be successful, the Wapishana boys are required to remain silent while the scarification takes place.

During these puberty rituals, one or more spirit people will make themselves known, either in a dream or a waking vision, or in a ritual object that embodies the spirit. Boys may be shown masks and musical instruments that are never to be seen by females, and taught secret traditions by members of men's societies. Likewise, girls can encounter a female culture hero who reveals matters that are specific to women's lives. Girls' puberty rituals are particularly concerned with female procreative power, which manifests itself in menstrual fluids and is said to be especially strong when a girl has her first period. Until she learns to control her newly acquired power of fertility and regeneration, a girl may be vulnerable to malevolent forces and is a danger to all males. For this reason, mountain spirits appear as masked dancers during an Apache girl's puberty ritual to provide strength and protection. As the girl dances, secluded in a tipi, they dance outside in support. Among the Shipibo of Peru, the men of a village perform a similar function by staging a Big Drink. Consuming large quantities of manioc beer, they dance around the girl's initiation hut and cut each other on the head with small knives to ward off spirits that would harm her. Masked dancers of the Lengua in Gran Chaco, on the other hand, appear to the girl to teach her about the dangers brought on by her first period.

Men and women are thought to have mutually dependent but mutually exclusive powers and knowledge that come from the spirit world. In practice, this means that neither should interfere with the gender-specific activities of the other or handle the other's tools or ritual objects, as it would weaken them. The Guayaki, for example, do not allow women to touch men's bows, or men to touch women's baskets. In many traditions these precautions are especially important during women's menstrual periods. Because of this, men typically avoid looking at or being seen by a woman during her monthly period, and women, until they enter menopause, must seclude themselves from men when menstruating.

Vision quests

After puberty rituals, or in place of them in communities that do not have these rituals, men and women can have direct encounters with spirit peoples through **vision quests**. This is an umbrella term used by scholars for a variety of practices undertaken to acquire new powers and knowledge or gain the trust and help of a new spirit guide. Vision quests can last several days or weeks, and begin with ritual purification and instruction by an elder or religious expert. A person then fasts and goes into seclusion in areas where spirits are thought to have their homes. These can be mountains, lakes, waterfalls, and caves; ancient ruins, such as temples and pueblos; and sites with petroglyphs (ancient rock carvings and paintings).

Once a person arrives at the appropriate destination, they might construct a small shelter—a simple hut, a shallow ditch, or a tree house—and purify the vicinity by scattering fragrant leaves or twigs, or using a fumigant made from these. Tobacco leaves or smoke are then offered to attract spirits. Having made these preparations, the person remains there, prayerfully and humbly, exposed to the weather and without food or water or sleep until a spirit arrives. Spirits come in many forms: as an animal or bird, as a gust of wind, or as a clap of thunder. In rare cases, they do not come at all. If and when a spirit does appear, however, it imparts some of its power by revealing a special song or dance, or perhaps a ritual technique. The spirit may also take up residence in the person's body (in the form of a clear crystal) or instruct the person to collect specific stones and plants through which it makes itself accessible. When the person undertaking the quest returns home, they debrief with a mentor to gain a fuller understanding of what took place.

> ### A Closer Look
>
> ## Hallucinogens
>
> In North America, most indigenous religions rely on physical deprivation and exertion to bring on states of trance. These include food, drink, and sleep deprivation; isolation from others, as in puberty rites and vision quests; and light deprivation and exposure to extreme heat, as during the Spirit Lodge. They can also include exposure to extreme cold through immersion in the ocean, as practiced in the Pacific Northwest; continuous dancing, as in the Thirst Dance; and running, as used in vision quests among the Tohono O'odham and Hopi, and in girls' puberty rites among the Apache and Diné. Only a few North American groups—the Hopi, the Muscogee, the Tohono O'odham, and adherents of the Peyote Religion, for example—combine these practices with the ingestion of psychotropic substances such as peyote, datura, *psilocybe* mushrooms, "black drink," and the fermented juice of Saguaro Cactus fruit.
>
> In South America, by contrast, psychotropic substances are regularly used to induce trance. One of the most widely used is tobacco, especially the species known as *mapacho* (*nicotiana rustica*), as its leaves contain exceptionally high

(continued)

levels of the alkaloid nicotine. It is smoked in large, combustible tubes made from reeds or corn husks, or rolled into massive cigars. Among the Warao, these cigars can be as long as 3 feet, and are smoked by shamans in order to travel to the heavenly House of Tobacco Smoke, crossing a celestial bridge made of tobacco smoke. Tobacco is also taken as snuff or made into a syrup that is "drunk" through the nose. In all these cases, high doses of nicotine produce extreme nausea, followed by unconsciousness and states of dreaming or delirium.

In the upper Amazon Basin, the hallucinogen *ayahuasca* is also used. Boiled and fermented into a thick drink from a plant called *yagé* or "soul vine" (*banisteriopsis caapi*), it is typically mixed with other substances that prolong or heighten its effect. Among the Campa, *ayahuasca* and tobacco are considered the spirit-wives of shamans, whereas elsewhere in Amazonia, shamans take a combination of *ayahuasca*, tobacco, *vilca* (*anadenanthera*), and alcohol to transform themselves into jaguars.

The narcotic datura is favored by several groups, including the Canelos Quichua and Achuar Jivaro peoples of Ecuador. Among the Canelos Quicha, women use datura to gain the knowledge and power they need to incorporate their souls into the pottery they make. The men, in turn, take datura to journey into spirit worlds, including the primordium, which gives them the authority to establish their own households. Other psychotropic substances used in South America are derived from coca leaves, *psilocybe* mushrooms, morning glory seeds, the San Pedro cactus, secretions containing bufotenine from the skin of certain frogs, and the inner bark of trees from the *Piptadenia* and *Virola* genera, which is made into snuffs.

Vision quests in South America frequently require the participants to ingest hallucinogenic substances. For example, among the Jivaro and Quechua people of eastern Ecuador and northern Peru, young men undergo hallucinogenic experiences in small groups, using the narcotic datura. Then, over the next several days, they drink large quantities of tobacco syrup, causing them to have visions and extended dreams, which they discuss with one another each morning at dawn. In the indigenous context, however, hallucinogens are not understood as having a chemical effect on the brain, as they might be in other cultures. Rather, it is believed that the plants, leaves, and barks contained in these hallucinogens are associated with spirit people who grant humans the power to travel into the spirit world. Accordingly, if humans use them without the spirits' permission or the guidance of a spiritual mentor, they risk being transformed into ravenous jaguars or going insane.

Secret religious societies

To enhance their contact with spirit persons on an ongoing basis, men and women often join secret religious societies that focus on particular rituals or deities. These are usually gender-exclusive—either men's groups or women's groups—but there are exceptions. Because nonmembers cannot attend society meetings, most of what we know about these secret societies is gleaned from their performance of public rituals. The Iroquois Little People Society, for example, is dedicated to interacting with tiny spirit persons who are both playful and harmful. This society performs songs in the language of the Little People and enlists spirits of the dead in private, nocturnal healing rituals. The Bear Society of the Keresan Puebloans, on the other hand, specializes in bringing rain and curing illnesses caused by witchcraft, while the Bird Societies of central and eastern Brazil enable their members to enter the spirit realm of bird peoples to benefit their communities in other ways.

Societies of clowns are found throughout much of North America. Members of these groups add a component of morality to the rituals of others by showing up as "contraries" who mock tradition, dress inappropriately, and do things in a backward manner, including speaking. They dance out of step, portray human failings, mimic speakers during orations, and generally exhibit antisocial and self-contradictory behavior. Among the Lakota, for example, they perform an around-the-kettle dance, during which they remove pieces of meat from a boiling pot with their bare hands. The goal of clowns, much like that of tricksters in origin stories, is to provide examples of how *not* to act. They also disrupt order to introduce new order. While clowns may be farcical, they are not to be treated lightly, for they embody powerful spirit people. Among the Zuni, where clowns are specialists in relieving stomach pain, it is considered dangerous to touch them; and in many communities they impose discipline, cure disease, and promote agricultural fertility.

Rituals, Rites, Practices

Hearing the Spirits

In the South American lowlands (such as the Amazon Basin), indigenous communities play flutes, trumpets, and clarinets during religious ceremonies to hear the sounds of the spirit world. These musical instruments are understood as the bodies of supernaturals and spirit persons, or parts of their bodies—a bone, a leg, the trachea, the penis—and flutes are sometimes called "bones" and made of bone, as among the Wayana of French Guiana. When played separately, a wind instrument makes the sound of a particular spirit person, but when played together they can create the loud, disharmonious cacophony that characterized the chaos of primordial times, when dangerous deities and supernaturals used their powers freely.

In the lowlands of South America, there are hundreds of secret societies dedicated to the spirit power inherent in wind instruments, including indigenous flutes, trumpets, and clarinets. In northwest Amazonia, these instruments are said to derive from the body of an ancestral spirit—part culture hero, part transformer, and part monster—known as the Animal, the child of the Sun, or the Pleiades. The societies are exclusively male, since part of their mission is to keep these wind instruments safe from women. During Tucanoan and Arawakan harvest festivals, for example, men bring baskets of ripe palm fruit into the village to the sound of giant trumpets, which give voice to the spirits of vegetation and growth. While women and children are required to hear these sounds, they must remain indoors so as not to see anything. When the instruments are not in use, the men hide them in a special building or underwater in rivers and lakes. As part of their puberty rituals, the boys in these communities are introduced to the instruments and instructed in their proper use and connection to the spirit world.

The Thirst Dance and the Spirit Lodge

Two additional ways in which Indigenous Americans enhance and renew their relationships with spirit people are the **Spirit Lodge** and the **Thirst Dance**. The former ritual, which is popularly called the Sweat Lodge, is found in southern Canada, Alaska, parts of the continental United States, Mexico, and in Central America among the Maya. It requires a small, closed structure, used like a sauna, which, depending on where one is, can be a semi-subterranean room dug into the earth, a section of a longhouse, a small hut constructed of stone, wood, or adobe, or a domed tent made from bent saplings covered with blankets, tarps, hides, or bark. In the center of this structure is a fire pit into which hot stones are placed and sprinkled with water to create steam, although in some traditions only dry heat is used.

In the Great Plains and Eastern Woodlands traditions, a Spirit Lodge ritual begins when the leader enters through an east facing door, followed by no more than six to eight people who move in a clockwise (sunwise) direction to form a circle around the fire pit. Ritual objects, such as a drum, a pipe, or a shaker (rattle) are then handed to the leader from outside, after which a fire keeper passes in the heated rocks, called Grandfathers, from a nearby fire, known as Grandfather Sun. At this point, the doors of the lodge are shut by outside door keepers, and the leader pours a small amount of water over the Grandfathers, adding cedar leaves and tobacco to create smoke.

Over the next couple hours, or sometimes the better part of a day, the participants sit in sweltering heat and total darkness, praying and singing to Mother Earth, the Grandfathers, and other spirit people who have come to be present among them. At intervals the leader passes around a pipe, from which each participant takes four puffs, honoring the spirits in all four cardinal directions. The leader may also pass around a drum, known as Little Boy. When in possession of this drum, it is one's turn to say a prayer or confess wrongdoings. Depending on how long a Spirit Lodge lasts, the door keepers open the doors one or more times to let in cool air, and a drink of water is offered to cool down the participants before resuming the ceremony. At the end of the Spirit Lodge, the participants emerge warm and wet, as from a womb, being renewed people.

The Spirit Lodge has many functions. It is almost always seen as a means of purification, and therefore frequently conducted in advance of other rituals and ceremonies. At times it is used to call upon the spirits to cure a disease, while at other times the participants may experience a vision or a mild trance during which the spirits communicate with them. Finally, it is an important way to remove negativity and anger, bringing its participants into solidarity with one another before making an important decision or embarking on a major undertaking.

The Thirst Dance, by contrast, is practiced mostly among the indigenous peoples of the Great Plains, from Canada to Texas. While it is popularly known as the Sun Dance, indigenous people refer to it as the Thirst Dance, the Offering Lodge, the New Life Lodge, the Renewal Lodge, and the Prayer Lodge, as well as the Fringed Ankle Dance and Dry Standing Dance. The preparation for a Thirst Dance begins a full year before it takes place. Those who will dance, both men and women, seek out a mentor and then take a vow to benefit their community by suffering for family members, those in prison, those addicted to alcohol, and those overcome by grief. In addition, they will seek to strengthen the bond between their community and the spirit world, and more generally, bring the world back into balance. With the help of their mentor, they engage in a year-long regime of meditation, prayer, and exercise, abstaining from all alcohol and drugs. Their hope is that the pain they are preparing to endure will make the spirits pity them and grant their requests out of reciprocity for the sacrifice of their suffering.

Among the Blackfoot, a respected female member of the community, known as the Thirst Dance Woman or Sacred Woman, must assume the role of the primary sponsor for the Dance and organize community support. Her authority comes from being the keeper of a particular medicine bundle, which is a coterie of spirit people in the form of objects, living together in a leather packet. Her husband is obliged to undertake multiple Spirit Lodges, and she fasts during the time of the dancing.

The ceremonial site for the Dance is prepared in the week prior to the ceremony, which takes place in late spring or summer and lasts for four days. Volunteers seek out and "capture" an appropriate tree to use as a center pole, asking the tree and the birds that live in it for permission to cut it down. They then carry the tree back to the site and set it upright in the center of a circular dance area, around which they then build arbors, cooking stations, and separate sleeping quarters for male and female dancers. The night before the Dance, the dancers, their families, friends, and other members of the community hold a feast and then pray, dance, and play drums until dawn. On the first morning of the Dance, and each morning thereafter, the dancers undertake a Spirit Lodge. They also abstain from all food and water throughout the four days of the ceremony. During the heat of the day, they dance around the center pole, stopping from time to time to rest. As they do this, their supporters stand under the surrounding arbors and encourage them to continue on, while musicians sing and play drums.

The dancers may wear feathers, body paint, or small medicine bundles, and on one or more of the days, male dancers may run a skewer through the skin on their chests and attach the skewer to the center pole with a length of cord. Alternatively, they may use eagle talons instead of a skewer. During the day, they dance facing the center pole and lean backward, supported only by the cord. At sundown, they run and pull on the cords with their body weight to tear themselves free from the skewer or talons, after which their resulting wounds are treated by their mentors. Women dancers may also sacrifice their flesh by having a ritual leader raise the skin on their upper arms with a needle and cut a circle around the resulting cone with a razor blade. At the end of each day of dancing, the dancers retire to their assigned sleeping quarters and fall unconscious or into a deep sleep brought on by hunger, thirst, and exhaustion, at which time spirits appear to them in dreams and visions. On the afternoon of the fifth day, when the dancers have completed their vow and begun to recover, a feast is held to thank the spirits and reward everyone who took part.

Shamans

Religious leaders and specialists are those who have more knowledge and power from the spirit world than others in their communities. This enables them to act as a resource for their communities in several ways. They predict weather patterns and migrations of game animals; they select the appropriate plants for medicines; they oversee the proper performance of rituals; they pass on religious traditions to the next generation; and they diagnose and heal diseases. Scholars often refer to religious leaders using names such as diviners, prophets, herbalists, priests, chanters, elders, confessors, knowledge keepers, healers, medicine men and women, and shamans. Yet there is considerable variation in each of these categories, and they frequently overlap with one another. Not all priests do the same thing, nor are all healers alike; and some healers are herbalists, while some are shamans. Indigenous people actually have thousands of names in their own languages, and make thousands of distinctions between different types of religious leaders. In terms of their intimacy with spirit peoples, however, the most powerful religious leaders are often the **shamans**. They are distinguished by their ability to join forces with dozens of spirit persons and to travel outside their bodies for extended excursions into the spirit world. Shamans are found throughout South America and in many parts of North America, especially in the west and northwest regions, and as far north as the Arctic.

Talking About Religion

Indigenous Names for "Shaman"

The word "shaman" comes from Siberia, not the Americas. In the study of indigenous peoples, both in America and around the world, anthropologists use it as a general label for religious leaders who have special access to the spirit world. An older umbrella term, used specifically for North America, is "medicine man." While these designations are convenient (we use "shaman" in this chapter), they oversimplify the diversity among these leaders. To gain some perspective on how Indigenous Americans characterize shamans, here are some of their designations for these religious leaders:

"walks with pipe"	(Ojibwa, Oglala)
"man of tricks"	(Yup'iq)

(continued)

"blower"	(Tsimshian)
"where power sits"	(Northern Paiute)
"one with special helper spirits"	(Waiwai)
"man of songs"	(Piaroa)
"light head"	(Kraho)
"master of fire"	(Warao)
"clairvoyant"	(Kalina)
"jaguar"	(Campa)

The training of shamans

People become shamans in various ways. They can be called by a spirit in a dream or vision, or chosen by an older shaman, especially if they are known to dream excessively or display sensitivity to certain foods. They may also inherit the position, or purchase it; and quite often spirits inflict people with a severe illness to compel them to become shamans. Among the Maya of the Yucatan in Mexico, prospective shamans can be identified before birth through their movements in the womb; and in North America, "two-spirit people," who identify as neither male nor female, are thought to have special access to spirits and the spirit realms and, consequently, promising candidates for shamanism. Most shamans are men, but women are rarely barred from shamanism. Instead, because women's power is understood to be dangerous to men, and because shamans work with other shamans and religious leaders, women who become shamans often do so following menopause. Exceptions include female shamans in northern California; Yanomami women in Brazil and Venezuela, who become shamans but do not practice during their menstrual periods; and shamans among the Warao of Venezuela, who often work as married couples. The Mapuche of Chile have both female and transvestite shamans.

Regardless of how a person becomes a shaman, they must be accepted by spirit persons who are willing to enter into a relationship of respect and dependency. This is accomplished by undergoing a period of apprenticeship with the spirits, which can last anywhere from a year to more than 20 years. During this time, apprentices must remake themselves to be more like the spirits—seeing, hearing, speaking, and traveling like the spirits. For this reason, apprentices use emetics and avoid foods thought to make them heavy, so they can fly. In indigenous communities in northern parts of South America, apprentices eat insects to strengthen their voices or drink large quantities of water to make their voices beautiful to the spirits. They also rub their eyes with creams made from tobacco, ginger, and pepper to enable them to see things others cannot. The training of future shamans also includes learning to take complete control over their own souls, for this is vital to their survival. Their souls must be able to exit and reenter their bodies as needed, without being abducted by evil spirits or becoming lost in another world. If either of these things were to happen, the shaman's body would die, making it impossible for the soul to return.

Incredibly, most of an apprentice's preparation takes place in the spirit realm, with or without the help a human guide or mentor. After entering into a trance induced by fasting, sleep deprivation, or drugs, apprentices meet powerful spirit persons and learn new songs. In many parts of South America, shamans also see horrific ordeals during trance. As they look on, their skin is removed so they can learn the names of their bones; they are dismembered and reassembled in new ways; they are killed and brought back to life; and they endure inhuman levels of pain and protracted periods of fasting and isolation. Some scholars believe that these visions of torment are designed to increase an apprentice's endurance, both to acquire knowledge of ancient traditions and to be able to resist enemy spirits even in a weakened condition.

A Closer Look

The Universe

Indigenous Americans envision the universe as having multiple layers, regions, or worlds, where deities, supernaturals, spirit people, and the dead make their home. At minimum, there are four levels: the sky, where the Supreme Being, Sun, Moon, and Father Sky live; the atmosphere, inhabited by bird people; the surface of the earth, which is home to humans; and a region below the earth, where one finds Mother Earth, fertility spirits, various other spirit peoples, and the souls of the dead. The surface of the earth, moreover, contains mountains, bodies of water, forests, deserts, and the horizon, which provide habitat for the four winds, cloud people, aquatic spirit beings, etc. For example, the principal Zuni spirits (*Kokos*) live in a village at the bottom of a lake, whereas a similar class of spirits in the Hopi tradition (*Katsinas*) live on mountain peaks.

In South America, especially, the universe is believed to have many layers above and below the earth, usually envisioned as flat discs. Thus, the universe of both the Kogi and the Yucuna have 4 layers above and 4 below the earth, while that of the Baniwa has 12 above and 12 below. The Campa universe, by contrast, has an unlimited number of layers. The closest analogy in North America, by contrast, is found among the Diné, whose universe has 3 subterranean levels, from which the First Man and Woman emerged.

Typically, the lower layers of universes in South America are inhabited by unfriendly and malevolent beings. One of the Yanomami underworlds, for example, is home to cannibal spirits who devour the souls of babies; and the lowest level of the Machiguenga universe is ruled by an evil being and filled with corpses that float in the River of Death. Among the Baniwa, who associate several nether regions with friendly beings, one is filled with spirit people who are pure evil. As many South American origin stories relate, some of the layers of these universes are the bygone worlds of the supernaturals, now superseded by our present world. Although they belong to much earlier times, they are still accessible to shamans, and are sometimes experienced by others during certain ritual practices, such as stylized violence.

(continued)

> Travel between the layers of the universe is made possible by a world axis, often envisioned as an enormous mountain or tree whose base or roots are in the lowest level, and whose top is in the highest. Other images of the world axis include ladders, pillars, ropes, and poles. Since this axis can be used to communicate with helpful spirit people, religious structures and houses are often built with center poles said to have a comparable function. This is true for houses among the Canelos Quichua and Makiritare, ceremonial buildings among the Inuit and Kogi, and the Thirst Dance structures of the Great Plains. Moreover, an analogous feature, called a *sipapu*, can be found in Puebloan kivas. This is a hole dug into the floor of a kiva's underground chamber, which provides access to spirits who live below the earth.

Apprentices also begin the task of acquiring spirit helpers, for the more they acquire, the more powerful they become in service to their communities. During their initial ventures into the spirit world, they are introduced to powerful beings from origin stories by their mentors or by deceased shamans who accompany them as guides. These beings, who include culture heroes, giant jaguars, and ancient proto-shamans, become trusted helpers and present them with small stones and crystals that embody other spirits. The spirit helpers of Machiguenga shamans in southeast Peru, for instance, are said to raise spirit-pets in these stones. The apprentices are instructed to ingest these stones and crystals and retain them in their chests or stomachs as darts, thorns, or small bones for future use, regurgitating them when needed. Alternatively, they may keep the crystals in a rattle, or use the stones to empower their breath by putting them in their mouths.

Spirits are also obtained by using tobacco juice. Akawaio apprentices, for example, consume large amounts of tobacco juice to become unconscious and to attract spirits, with whom they then dance, sing, and form bonds. By assimilating spirits into their own bodies, apprentices form a symbiotic relationship with them. Their personalities and temperaments change, and they are compelled to feed these spirits with tobacco and sing to them on a regular basis. After one becomes a shaman, they will continue to acquire spirits during journeys into the spirit realm.

The healing role of shamans

Shamans are called to help when a member of the community is suffering from an unusual illness, or the community as a whole is in danger. From an indigenous perspective, such evils are not to be explained in terms of western science, but as the consequence of humans or spirits transgressing the principles of cooperation, reciprocity, and respect. It may be that members of the community have acted selfishly toward one another or have taken something belonging to a spirit master without seeking permission. They may have violated a taboo by trespassing on spirit lands in forests or on mountains, or failed to thank spirits properly for their help. Or it may be that a malicious spirit or a **dark shaman** has contravened these essential principles.

Dark shamans, also known as witches and sorcerers, are religious experts who use their powers to harm others. Their victims may be the residents of an enemy village, or persons with whom the dark shaman or his paying customer has a vendetta. Beyond this, dark shamans can align themselves with malicious spirits. Among the Warao, for example, dark shamans work for the spirits of the dead, feeding them with human life. But dark shamans do not always act intentionally. Some are thought to be born with a tendency to do wrong, or to have inherited a longing for human blood from an evil ancestor; others are said to cause harm because their negative feelings toward others make use of their powers without their consent. Moreover, it is sometimes the case that enemies and persons with whom one has a vendetta deserve punishment. For these reasons, dark shamans can be ambiguous figures, and the distinction between them and beneficial shamans is seldom without complication.

When shamans are needed to cure an illness, they must first diagnose its cause and devise a solution. They can do this themselves or use experts who specialize in diagnoses. The Diné, for example, rely on men and women known as hand tremblers to determine an illness's cause. When shamans make the diagnosis themselves, some call on spirits for help, while others use their enhanced vision to look through a patient's skin and examine their bones and organs. The Pima and Tohono O'odham shamans of Arizona blow tobacco smoke over a patient's body to illuminate the cause of sickness, while those of the Shoshone, their neighbors to the north, diagnose illnesses with their eyes closed.

Rituals, Rites, Practices

Categorizing Illnesses

In modern western medicine, illnesses are categorized with reference to physical causes: viruses, bacterial infections, cancers, etc. In Indigenous American religions, conditions are categorized according to spiritual causes. A particularly clear example of this approach is the ceremonial practices of the Diné. Unlike other indigenous communities in the Americas, the Diné only perform religious ceremonies when an individual needs help. These ceremonies, called chantaways, have many subtypes, which include Holy Way, Evil Way, Enemy Way, and Blessing Way procedures.

Holy Way chantaways are the largest subtype, comprising almost 60 distinct ceremonies. These include Wind Way, Bead Way, Eagle Way, Flint Way, Mountain Way, and Night Way, among others. Holy Way ceremonies alleviate suffering that is caused by offenses against spirits or Holy People. Evil Way ceremonies, in turn, are applied to conditions caused by malevolent ghosts of Diné ancestors. If, however, an illness has been caused by a non-Diné ghost, then Enemy Way ceremonies are applied to the patient. Finally, Blessing Way ceremonies are preventive medicine. They protect against evil spirit persons and provide blessings. They are also used to correct mistakes that are made during Holy Way and Evil Way ceremonies.

Serious or unusual illnesses are thought to have one of three causes: taboo violations, spirit darts, or soul loss. If the illness is due to violating a taboo, then the shaman must negotiate with the offended party in the spirit realm, and on the basis of this negotiation prescribe certain rituals of confession, contrition, and purification. **Spirit darts** are pathogens that have been shot into a person's body by a dark shaman or malicious spirit. If they remain in the person's body, they can be removed, but if the darts have gone through the body and passed out the other side, nothing can be done, and the patient will die. **Soul loss** typically happens when a person's soul ventures into the spirit world while sleeping or during a trance and becomes lost or is imprisoned there by an angry spirit or a dark shaman. When the person awakes, they experience disorientation, fever, and blackouts, all of which foreshadow their death. Among peoples in the Pacific Northwest, soul loss can also be caused by severe grief or trauma, and express itself initially as depression or fatigue.

If the cause of a person's illness is determined to be soul loss, the shaman must journey into the spirit world to find it or do battle with the forces that have taken it captive. These journeys can last several days and require the support of others, including family members, assistant shamans, and other ritual specialists such as singers, dancers, chanters, and musicians, who empower the shaman on his quest. In some cases, shamans enter the spirit world as a beam of light or a breeze, or by riding atop a spirit bird. In other cases, they use spirit alter-egos and travel into spirit realms as jaguars or vultures. They do this, moreover, in states of trance brought on by fasting, sleep deprivation, various drugs, or prolonged periods of dance accompanied by drums and chanting. The spirit reality they experience is both vivid and concrete, and filled with strange sights. They are confronted with perilous challenges, such as canyons they must cross on fragile bridges, or craggy mountains they must ascend. When they encounter spirit people, they address them in spirit language, speaking in low, gravelly tones or singing in falsetto, sometimes using whistles to amplify their words. Among the Coast Salish of the Pacific Northwest, the retrieval of a lost soul takes the form of an expedition party in which several shamans pack ritual weapons and effigies of helping spirits into a canoe and ritually travel across water and land to the realm of the dead. Along the way they gather plants and hunt, and exchange gifts and songs with the spirits they meet. Shamanic journeys to retrieve lost souls end when the soul is found or wrested from the control of its captors and returned to the body of the patient. In communities of the Amazon Basin, the presiding shaman then seals the soul within the body by blowing tobacco smoke on the patient's extremities.

If, on the other hand, the cause of a person's illness is found to be a spirit dart still lodged in their body, the shaman must determine the nature of the dart and find a cure. Using their enhanced sight, the shaman can see the true nature of the spirit dart—a spider, snake, insect, or other pathogen—and ascertain its song or design, which is the source of its power. The standard curing techniques employ sucking, blowing, and massage. These are performed, with variations, throughout the Americas, from the Arctic Circle to the Southern Cone of South America. To extract spirit darts by sucking or blowing, shamans rely on the power of the spirits they have internalized in their chests or stomachs. Prior to sucking, these are sometimes regurgitated into the shaman's mouth to catch the dart as it exits the patient's body.

> ### Rituals, Rites, Practices
>
> ## The Disposal of Pathogens
>
> When Shamans remove pathogens, such as a spirit dart, from their patients, they sometimes undertake a special procedure to dispose of its malevolent power. When a Yup'iq shaman extracts a spirit dart, he swallows it and disarms it with spirit helpers he keeps in his stomach. Both Shoshone shamans and those of the Chiquitano of Bolivia dispose of harmful spirits by burning them; and shamans in parts of Amazonian Brazil and Peru use special stones to absorb the illnesses.

At times it is necessary to relocate a spirit dart before sucking it out, which is done by massaging it into a different part of the body. The Kaingang shamans of southern Brazil use massage in this way, then bite the spirit dart to extract it with their teeth. Blowing on an affected area can also drive out or otherwise eliminate a spirit dart. Shamans often enhance this technique by blowing with tobacco smoke, or with a spirit stone in the mouth, as among the Waiwai. Shamans can also blow smoke into their cupped hands, along with tobacco-suffused saliva, and rub it into a patient's body as a balm. Among the Chiripa, shamans blow on a patient's head, as this is believed to have an opening where the soul exits and reenters the body during sleep; and in Shoshone communities, shamans focus the power of their breath by forming a hollow fist to blow through.

Ritual Tools

In their rituals, Indigenous Americans use a variety of objects to interact and communicate with spirit persons. What is distinctive about these **ritual tools** is that they embody the power of spirit persons, or the spirit persons themselves. In the latter case, they are handled with great care and fed to keep the spirits strong and cooperative. Some ritual tools are made by human beings, while others are said to have been given to humans by deities or culture heroes and passed down from generation to generation. Those made by humans require traditional materials and must follow traditional designs. These materials, which are thought to contain power from the spirit world, include quartz crystals, animal pelts, colored paints, feathers, corn husks, and wood from forests where spirits live, to mention just a few. The designs, in turn, are passed down through generations, and their application is often overseen by religious leaders. Among the Piaroa of the Orinoco Basin in Venezuela and Colombia, for example, shamans must supervise the making of musical instruments and masks.

Because each indigenous community has its own rituals and traditions for interacting with the spirit world, no ritual object is used universally or uniformly in the Americas. Many are limited to specific communities or geographical areas, and those with wider currency are used and understood differently in different places.

Prayer sticks, for example, are ritual tools used mostly by Puebloans, and thus largely confined to New Mexico, Arizona, and Texas. Made from branches of the red willow, they are carved with traditional designs, painted in different colors, and often decorated with feathers—all of which invests them with power. In petitioning the spirits for rain or crops, Puebloans breathe their prayers into them and place them in their fields.

Sacred bundles, also called medicine bundles and spirit bundles, are used much more widely. These are collections of objects such as hair, shells, small bones, pebbles, feathers, and leaves of certain plants (to name just a few), which are wrapped in cloth, basketwork, leaves, tree bark, or animal skin to keep them together. While their contents may seem rather random to an outsider, the objects in a bundle are selected by people on the basis of instructions received in dreams or visions, or are believed to have been assembled by a deity.

The process of creating a sacred bundle "tethers" certain spirit persons to the objects it contains. In this way, bundles localize and concentrate spiritual power. In return, the spirits are said to receive clothing and shelter through the bundling, and are fed, often with the smoke from herbs or tobacco. In addition, bundles are treated with great respect and are frequently subject to taboos regarding where they are kept and how they are handled. Some bundles must even be protected from loud noises. The power inherent in a bundle is actualized by songs and dances associated with each bundle. These honor the spirits tethered inside, describe their nature, recount the circumstances surrounding the bundle's creation, and explain its powers.

> **Did you know ...**
>
> When the horse of conquistador Hernán Cortés fell ill in 1525 and was left behind, a Guatemalan named Nojpeten-Tayasal cared for the animal until it died, and then made a spirit bundle from its bones. He used the bundle to communicate with Thunder and Rain, equating the sound of thunder with the horse's pounding hooves.

Bundles are not owned by anyone, but are given by spirits to individuals, secret societies, religious leaders, or entire communities for safe keeping. Among the Tlapanec in southern Mexico, for example, religious leaders are responsible for community bundles that contain a specific number of small sticks or pine needles, which they use to bring rain or protect the community from certain dangers; and in the Great Plains of North America and throughout Lowland South America, secret societies keep large bundles that contain musical instruments through which spirit persons speak during ceremonies. Bundles kept by individuals usually have only one or two songs or dances connected with them, and are rarely opened. Those kept by communities, on the other hand, can have multiple dances and dozens of songs, and are opened periodically during rituals that can last hours or days.

Bundles kept by communities and secret societies are passed down to the next generation, while those owned by religious leaders and individuals are variously entrusted to another person, exchanged, sold, or buried with its keeper. Among the Mandan of North Dakota, personal bundles are passed down through matrilineal inheritance. Whatever the process, when a bundle changes hands, the songs and dances associated with it must be passed along as well. Otherwise, the new keeper will not know how to care for the bundle or access its power.

Like bundles, ceremonial masks give physical presence to spirit persons, but in a much more interactive way. When a ritual participant wears a mask, the spirit embodied in the mask not only becomes present in the ritual, but, through the body of the wearer, can also speak, dance, give blessings, be entertained, and receive honor and thanks from community leaders. Among the Yup'iq of Alaska, for instance, when a community plans a feast to honor animal spirits for supplying its members with food during the hunting and fishing season, masks enable the spirits to enjoy the celebration through those who wear them. Similarly, during dances performed by the Piaroa of Colombia and Venezuela, animal masters are able to use the vocal cords of masked dancers to make the distinctive sounds that cause game animals to multiply; and the spirits who embody the Iroquoian Husk Face masks use the bare hands of those wearing the masks to handle hot coals.

Beyond this, masks work in the other direction as well, allowing their wearers to participate in aspects of the spirit world. In the Yup'iq feast just mentioned, mask wearers are often given visions and the ability to see into the spirit world. Throughout many communities in South America, moreover, masked dancers engage in ritual or stylized violence, whereby they can participate in events that took place among supernaturals during the primordium.

While tobacco pipes are used throughout the Americas, indigenous peoples in North America regard certain pipes as ritual tools, not simply a means for inhaling tobacco smoke. To begin with, these pipes are often said to be gifts from the spirit realm, not things made by humans. The pipe's bowl is usually stone, or in some cases clay; and the stem is wood, usually a hollowed-out reed. The bowl and stem are kept separate until needed in a ceremony. When they are put together, the pipe unifies powerful forces, creating a special ritual time. The bowl, which is considered female, can be black, connecting it with Mother Earth, or red, indicating the spiritual forces of life, procreation, and menstrual blood. The pipe's stem is considered male, seen variously as the path of life, the power of voice, or male reproductive power.

The purpose of smoking a ritual pipe is to offer tobacco to the spirit realm and to share the experience of smoking with them. Typically, after it has been assembled, a pipe is purified in the smoke of various herbs. Then, at the beginning of a ceremony, it is filled with tobacco and lit, and its stem is pointed in each of the four cardinal directions, held up to the sky, and touched to the ground. In this way, smoke is offered to all the gods, without exception. In a variation on this, the Lakota also point the pipe's stem to the spotted eagle, who carries their prayers to the Great Spirit Wakantanka. During the ceremony, the pipe is also passed in a circle among the ritual's human participants, always in the direction of the sun's path. Some communities have different pipes for different people (a women's pipe, a council meeting pipe), or for different ritual occasions, such as the Thirst Dance or the Spirit Lodge.

Offering the pipe to others builds trust. When shared with strangers or potential enemies, it establishes a bond of cooperation, and when shared with the spirit realm, it can curry the favor of spirit persons for help in bringing rain or healing a disease. Because the pipe promotes relationships of reciprocity, ceremonial smoking is often the occasion for recounting interactions that have taken place in the distant past between ancestors and spirit persons. Most pipes are not decorated, but when they are, the bowl may be carved with a figure facing the smoker to remind them of these stories and the values they convey. Such is the case among the Sioux nations of the upper Midwest and the Algonquin nations of Quebec and Ontario. Pipes may also be adorned with feathers or ribbons, the different colors of which are identified with the four cardinal directions, the sky, and the earth.

> ### Did you know …
>
> In North America, ceremonial pipes are used to smoke a variety of plants, not just tobacco. These include the dried berries, leaves, or the inner bark of dogwood, sumac, juniper, and kinnikinic (bearberry), each of which is understood as a spirit person with a distinct power. In all, as many as 100 plants are used in this way.

Finally, rattles of various kinds are used as ritual tools by many indigenous peoples. As percussion instruments, they often convey the sound, and hence the presence, of spirit persons during dance ceremonies. The rattle's hollow chamber is fashioned from gourds, turtle shells, bark, or animal hooves, and a wooden handle is usually attached. Seeds, pebbles, or small quartz crystals are then placed inside as a way of tethering spirit persons, much like the objects inside a bundle.

In the shamanic traditions of South America, moreover, rattles take on special significance. Considered the most powerful ritual tool of the shaman, they are the means by which shamans send spirits out into the world to do their bidding, and they serve as defensive weapons during travels in the spirit world. Among the Kalina, who live along rivers and coastal areas of northern South America, the stones in the shaman's rattle are believed to be tethered to the four winds. Known as "the fathers," these winds perform tasks for the shaman when he blows tobacco smoke into his rattle through the slits in its gourd. In northwestern Amazonia, shamans treat the rattle's handle and gourd, respectively, as a second body and soul, external to themselves; while shamans among the Warao enter the spirit world by traveling up the shaft of the rattle into the gourd, which becomes a microcosm of that world. On these journeys, the seeds and rocks in the gourd act as a shaman's ancestors and spirit helpers.

The soul and the afterlife

There is no uniform concept of a soul among Indigenous Americans, although the dominant belief is that a person has two or more. In North America, for example, most communities hold that a person has two souls, although the Mojave and the Lakota teach that a person has four (envisioned differently by each group); and in South America, the Bolivian Chiquitano believe that people have three souls, one associated with breath, one with blood, and one with a person's shadow. Other indigenous communities hold that particular body parts, especially the bones, contain souls. Thus, the Canelos Quichua locate a soul in the right shin bone, the Campa of the Peruvian Andes locate one in the heart, and the Nuxalk of the Pacific Northwest believe that a soul establishes itself in a bone at the back of the neck when one is born. The Waiwai, in turn, teach that each person has an eye-soul as well as a soul responsible for the rest of the body, linked especially with the breath and the heart; and both the Maya and the Yanomami in northern Brazil and southern Venezuela hold that one of a person's souls lives outside of their body, in the body of an animal. Not surprisingly, Indigenous Americans hold a variety of views as to what happens to these souls after death. Even so, there seems to be widespread agreement on at least two matters: that the soul associated with a person's physical vitality returns its power to a Supreme Being or Creator, or more generally, releases it back into the universe; and that a soul identified with one's personality and character goes to be with other souls in a realm of the dead.

It would be difficult, if not impossible, to catalog all the different teachings about the afterlife current among Indigenous Americans. Indeed, it is not unusual for a community or even an individual to hold multiple views. Thus, the realm of the dead can be a place very much like ours, except far away; or a world filled with animals for hunting; or one that somehow works opposite to our world, where night is day, summer is winter, and people speak backward. In the Americas it is widely held that the dead reside in a realm that is clearly separate from the world of the living, and in origin stories that feature culture heroes who are brothers or twins, it is often the first brother or twin to die who establishes this realm and governs over it. A different view, however, is found among the Inuit of Canada and among several communities in Alaska, including the Yupik and the Iñupiaq, who believe that certain qualities of people who have passed away can be reborn in the next generation.

Entry into the realm of the dead is sometimes understood as open to all, not just those who have lived an exemplary life of good deeds. In parts of Latin America, however, communities teach that the quality of a person's life, or status in the community, or manner of death determines whether one enters a favorable or unfavorable afterlife. In these cases, a soul may be confronted with a series of challenges or face a tribunal following death. The Canelos Quichua, for example, envision a judgment by tiny shamans. Depending on how a soul meets these challenges or responds to questions posed at the tribunal, it will receive punishments or rewards.

End-of-life practices

While departed family members often assume the role of ancestors and continue their involvement in the community, their initial transition to the afterlife can be fraught with peril. This is because souls of the dead often want to remain in the world of the living, but the longer they remain, the more they become a danger to their families and communities. Among the Shoshone they appear as whirlwinds or move around at night as skeletons, visible only in the moonlight, whereas the Waiwai believe that they become vengeful nocturnal animals. For this reason, end-of-life rituals seek to expedite a soul's departure to the realm of the dead. Some communities place food and clothing at the gravesite to provide a soul with the necessary supplies for its journey into the unseen world. Other communities hold farewell banquets for the deceased as a way to honor them and, at the same time, obligate them to leave. Among the Cocopah of Arizona, Baja California, and Mexico, this type of feast and send off is sponsored annually by the community for all those who died in the previous year. Lasting between four and six days, it includes orations honoring the deceased and a retelling of how the Creator built the first house of the dead. A different approach can be seen in the Stick Dance of the Alaskan Athabascan, during which the identity of a deceased man is temporarily transferred to the leaders of the ceremony. Dressed in the man's clothes, these leaders are honored at a feast with song and dance. Following this, they receive parting gifts, say their farewells to the man's family, and ritually take their leave. A similar result is achieved by members of the Hopi One Horn Society, who invite the bodiless souls of the dead to use their bodies, and then conduct them to the cemetery in a formal procession. Shamans in various parts of South America take the additional step of guiding souls into the spirit world, as among the Ava-Chiripa of Argentina and Brazil; and the Mapuche shamans of Chile do this to ensure that the deceased is not co-opted by a dark shaman for evil purposes.

A very different approach is taken by the Campa of eastern Peru, who believe that souls can remain in or around bodies after death. To protect the community from this danger, they either weigh the body down with rocks and sink it in a river, or place it on a raft and set it adrift. The Guayaki of Paraguay also do away with bodies for this reason, but by eating parts of them, as if the bodies were wild animals, or by exhuming them after burial to cremate them and crush their skulls. Indigenous communities on the upper Orinoco River and in north Amazonia cremate their dead, crush the bones, and consume the ashes of these bones in a fermented beverage.

After the dead leave our world, precautions are also taken to ensure that they do not reenter it, unless, perhaps, by invitation for a special ceremony. On all other occasions, the return of souls to this world is understood to violate the balance and harmony of existence, as the dead are not to consort freely with the living. For this reason, funerals in the Sierra Nevada de Santa Marta require priests to locate the entrance to the house of death, where the grave will be dug, and then secure its doors after the burial. Among the Yanomami, shamans put tobacco into the mouths of the deceased, both to provide their souls with food for the journey to the afterlife and to entice the spirits there to embrace them as their own.

Other communities engage in activities that make the former towns of the dead unfamiliar or uninviting. For example, the members of a Campa family whose child has died dress in unaccustomed ways for two months so that the child's soul will not recognize them; and among the Zuni, a town ceases to speak a dead person's name, and after four days of mourning, burn the deceased's personal items. Iroquois families distribute the personal property of the deceased to members of the community so ghosts have nothing to come back for, while the Kaingang of Brazil destroy all the property of the dead as a way of shipping it to them in the afterlife. The Toba of Argentina, in turn, take an additional precaution: the relatives of a deceased man not only destroy his belongings, but also seal up his house and burn it down.

The Wari' of western Brazil are perhaps the most thorough in destroying the property of a deceased male head of household—burning his house, possessions, clothes, crops, and even stored food supplies. Some scholars have proposed that this total erasure of a man's life serves another purpose as well, beyond preventing his return. In their view, it also promotes reciprocity and mutual dependence in the community by completely doing away with inheritance, which puts the family of the deceased under obligation to friends and relatives for their survival. In support of this view, these scholars point to the Wari' belief that the dead either return to the community as peccaries, or encourage large schools of fish to volunteer themselves as food, which enables the community to support the bereaved family.

CONCLUSION

The indigenous religions of the Americas are diverse, and yet share several elements that distinguish them, as a group, from other religions in the world. One of these elements is the conviction that the world is populated with other-than-human people with whom humans must establish and maintain relations of mutual benefit and respect if they want to thrive and live happy lives.

Some of the great diversity of these religions has been sketched in this chapter, but there is still much to be learned. In the last two decades, for example, LiDAR (Laser imaging, Detection, and Ranging) has been used to locate and produce 3-D images of hundreds of previously unknown ancient temples and effigy mounds in the rainforests of Brazil. More importantly, however, research into indigenous religions in the Americas is now advancing with the benefit of a new approach. Rather than letting their religions be studied primarily by outsiders—non-indigenous ethnographers, anthropologists, and linguists—Indigenous Americans are curating and presenting their own religious traditions in ways that they understand and value them. Protocols are now in place to guarantee that outsiders participate in this venture only when invited, and only as advisors and partners, ensuring that the people who practice these religions control the larger narrative of research. As indigenous communities continue to revitalize themselves from within, as they create venues for religious and cultural exchange with other communities, and as they engage in the larger scholarly discussion through the publication of journal articles and books, a more comprehensive and multi-dimensional understanding of indigenous religions in the Americas will certainly emerge.

For review

1. Describe two or three ancient spiritual centers—what did they look like and what went on there?
2. What are "other-than-human" persons?
3. Why is it important to show respect to plants and animals?
4. According to Indigenous Americans, how do hallucinogens work?
5. In what ways are young people introduced to the spirit world?
6. Who are shamans, and how are they trained?
7. Describe one or two of the healing techniques used by shamans.
8. What is the purpose of funeral rites?

For discussion

1. What perspectives do Indigenous Americans have on religious diversity and religious syncretism?
2. How do you envision the peaceful coexistence and interaction of Indigenous Americans with other Americans (including Brazilians, U.S. citizens, and Canadians, etc.) who hold modern western views?

Key Terms

Andean — The cultural area in western South America along the Andes Mountain range, including the ancient sites of Chavin de Huantar, the Moche, the Nazca, and the Inca.

auto-sacrifice — Self-administered, ritual bloodletting practiced by the ancient Maya and Aztec.

culture heroes — Spirit beings responsible for introducing important traditions, institutions, and skills into one's culture.

dark shaman — A shaman who uses power from the spirit realm to inflict harm on others.

geoglyph — Lines or images drawn on the earth, as at Nazca in southwestern Peru.

huacas — In Andean religions, either deities, or objects and places in the landscape that give access to their power.

kivas — Underground ritual chambers used by Pueblo peoples in the southwestern United States.

Maya — Indigenous people in Mexico and Central America.

Mesoamerica — The ancient cultural area extending from southern Mexico to Costa Rica. Home to the Maya and the Aztecs, among others.

New Fire Ceremony — An Aztec ceremony performed every 52 years to renew the world.

origin stories — Indigenous accounts of how the present world came to be.

primordium — The earliest period of the world in the origin stories of Indigenous Americans, when supernaturals were active, power was wielded freely, and chaos reigned.

pueblos — Towns in the southwest United States consisting of large complexes of rooms, much like apartment buildings.

reciprocity — An important religious principal in Indigenous American religions that promotes the proper flow of spiritual power between human and nonhuman peoples.

ritual tools — Ritual objects such as sacred bundles, masks, pipes, and rattles by which religious leaders gain access to the spirit world.

sacred bundles — Objects to which spirit persons are tethered, collected together in a pouch or bundle.

Sapa Inca — The Inca emperor.

shaman — A religious leader who has many spirit helpers and who can travel into the spirit world.

soul loss — A condition that can occur during dreams and which can lead to death.

spirit darts — Weapons used by dark shamans to inflict pain, illness, and death on their victims.

Spirit Lodge — A small gathering in an enclosed space heated with hot rocks, during which the participants commune with spirits and prepare for ceremonies and group decisions.

spirit master	A principal spirit who oversees an animal or plant species or multiple species.
spiritual centers	Religious sites in pre-European America with earthen mounds, *kivas*, pyramid temples, and plazas, where indigenous people met to worship and exchange spiritual goods and services.
Thirst Dance	A ritual undertaken for the benefit of a community, during which individuals dance for four days in a slow circle around a central pole without food or drink.
trickster	A clever, mischievous god or spirit who mediates between the human and spirit worlds, usually causing confusion or worse.
vision quest	A ritual undertaken to establish a lasting personal relationship with a spirit person.

Bibliography

A good first book

A. Irving Hallowell. *Contributions to Ojibwe Studies*. Lincoln: University of Nebraska Press, 2010.

Further reading

Joseph Epes Brown and Emily Cousins. *Teaching Spirits: Understanding Native American Religious Traditions*. Oxford: Oxford University Press, 2001.

Davíd Carrasco. *Religions of Mesoamerica*, 2nd edn. Long Grove, IL: Waveland, 2013.

Suzanne J. Crawford and Inés Talamantez. *Religion and Culture in Native America*. Lanham, MD: Rowman and Littlefield, 2021.

Suzanne J. Crawford and Inés Talamantez. *Native American Religious Traditions*. Upper Saddle River, NJ: Pearson Education, 2007.

Robin Wall Kimmer. Braiding Sweetgrass: Indigenous Wisdom, Scientific Knowledge and the Teaching of Plants. Minneapolis, MN: Milkweed Editions, 2015.

Jordan Paper. *Native North American Religious Traditions: Dancing for Life*. Westport, CT: Praeger, 2007.

William K. Powers. *Yuwipi: Vision and Experience in Oglala Ritual*. Lincoln, NE: University of Nebraska, 1984.

Robin M. Wright. *Mysteries of the Jaguar Shamans of the Northwest Amazon*. Lincoln, NE: University of Nebraska, 2013.

Reference and research

Suzanne J. Crawford and Dennis F. Kelley, eds. *American Indian Religious Traditions: An Encyclopedia*, 3 vols. Santa Barbara, CA: ABC-CLIO, 2005.

Arlene Hirschfelder and Paulette Molin, eds. *Encyclopedia of Native American Religions: An Introduction*. New York: Facts on File, 2000.

Deborah L. Nichols and Christopher A. Pool, eds. *The Oxford Handbook of Mesoamerican Archaeology*. Oxford: Oxford University, pp. 741–784, 2012.

Timothy R. Pauketat and Kenneth E. Sassaman, eds. *The Archaeology of Ancient North America*. Cambridge: Cambridge University, 2020.

Lawrence E. Sullivan. *Icanchu's Drum: An Orientation to Meaning in South American Religions*. New York: MacMillan Publishing, 1988.

CHAPTER 8

Judaism
Holy covenant, chosen people

A Jewish boy prepares to become a "son of the commandment," or *bar mitzvah*. Wearing a *yarmulke* (skullcap) and a *tallit* (prayer shawl), he holds a Torah scroll wrapped in a velvet mantel and adorned with a silver shield and reading pointer. In the background is the case, or ark, where the scroll is kept when not in use. Source: Reproduced by permission of Mark Lewinsohn.

DID YOU KNOW …

The Jewish understanding of God as a single, monotheistic deity is the basis for the monotheistic beliefs of both Christianity and Islam, and both these religions claim Judaism's founder, Abraham, as their spiritual father.

Understanding the Religions of the World: An Introduction, Second Edition.
Edited by Will Deming.
© 2025 John Wiley & Sons Ltd. Published 2025 by John Wiley & Sons Ltd.

OVERVIEW

There are about 15.7 million Jews worldwide. The majority lives in two countries, Israel (7.2 million) and the United States (5.7 million). The third-largest population is in France, with about 510,000 Jews, many of whom came from the once-large Jewish communities in Algeria, Morocco, and Tunisia. There are also around 390,000 Jews living in the West Bank, 375,000 in Canada, and 280,000 in the United Kingdom (see Figure 8.1).

Jews who live outside of Israel are said to be part of the **Diaspora**. In modern times, many of these Diaspora communities have lost members through intermarriage, secularization, and other forms of assimilation to non-Jewish cultures. This situation led Emil Fackenheim (1916–2003), a rabbi, philosopher, and Holocaust survivor, to formulate the now popular 614th commandment: "Thou shalt not give posthumous victories to Hitler." Since late antiquity, Jewish tradition had maintained that scripture contained 613 religious commandments, or **mitzvot**. According to Fackenheim, modern times necessitated the addition of one more commandment, which prohibited Jews from contributing to the eradication of Jewish life through a type of spiritual suicide. By forsaking their Jewish heritage, Fackenheim contended,

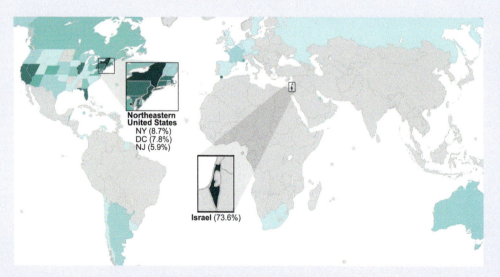

Figure 8.1 A map showing Jewish populations as a percentage of each area's population. While many Jews now live in Israel, even more live outside the homeland in the Diaspora, especially in large metropolitan areas in North America. Source: Wikimedia Commons.

Jews were effectively carrying on Hitler's genocidal program, the goal of which was to make the world *Judenrein* or "clean of Jews."

God and covenant

Judaism envisions ultimate reality as both the Creator of the world and the God of a particular people, the Jews. According to Jewish tradition, after God created the world, early humans rebelled against Him. In consequence, God entered into a covenant, or agreement, with a particular man named Abraham. The purpose of the covenant was to establish Abraham and his descendants as a people who would be faithful to God and play a distinctive role in human affairs.

The Jewish God is thus simultaneously a universal God and a national God—the God of all humanity and the God of the Jewish people, whom he chose to be "a light to the world." Just exactly what this entails, however, is a matter of discussion. Some Jews understand this task as one of modeling a godly lifestyle in the midst of non-Jewish cultures and nations. Other Jews see their very existence and survival as a statement of God's presence in the world; and still others believe that their faithfulness in keeping the commandments is the means by which God will initiate an age of renewal and salvation. None of these possibilities is necessarily exclusive of the others.

Jews and non-Jews

Jewish theology assumes a reciprocal and nonnegotiable link between the Jewish people and the Jewish religion. Not only has Judaism developed through the experiences of the Jews, but the Jews have had these experiences *because* of Judaism. They share its history even as it defines their destiny. From the beginning of the religion, Jews have been careful to distinguish themselves from all non-Jews, whom they speak of collectively as Gentiles (*goyim*, "nations"). While it is possible for non-Jews to become part of Judaism, it is not possible for the religion to pass from the Jews to another people, for Judaism is not transferable. In the absence of this specific ethnic group, there can be no Judaism.

Regarding the Gentiles, a strong tradition within Judaism holds that they, too, will share in God's blessings if they keep the laws that God gave to Adam, the first man. Known as the Seven Noahide Laws, because they were later also given to Noah, hero of the Great Flood, these commandments include the injunction to live under a rule of law and to observe prohibitions against idolatry, blasphemy, murder, theft, adultery, and the eating of parts torn from a living animal. Following World War II, Jewish theologians expanded this tradition, dedicating an Avenue of Righteous Gentiles in Yad Vashem, the Holocaust Museum in Jerusalem. Both sides of this avenue are lined with trees and plaques in honor of non-Jewish men and women, not because they kept the Noahide Laws, but because they risked their lives to save Jews during the Holocaust.

Sacred literature

At the heart of all forms of Judaism is a positive relationship to the sacred literature of the past. While various branches of the religion interpret sacred literature differently, giving greater or lesser credence to its status as inspired and authoritative, there is a common recognition that it constitutes the very foundation of Jewish existence and identity. Foremost among this literature is the Tanak, known by Christians as the Old Testament. This is an ancient collection of 24 writings, the most important of which are the first five: Genesis, Exodus, Leviticus, Numbers, and Deuteronomy. Jews refer to these to as the Torah (teaching, tradition)—a term that can also refer to *all* sacred traditions in Judaism (Figures 8.2 and 8.3).

After the Tanak, the most important religious literature in Judaism is the works of Jewish teachers known as rabbis (teachers). The first work of this rabbinic literature is a legal text called the Mishnah, edited in Palestine at the beginning of the third century CE. The Mishnah was later expanded and analyzed in a document called the Talmud, which synthesizes the teachings of the Tanak and Mishnah with centuries of rabbinic scholarship and interpretation. A Palestinian version of the Talmud appeared around 400 CE, and the more authoritative Babylonian version around 500 CE. Today, Jewish religious law, known as halakhah, has its basis in the Babylonian Talmud, although it has also developed in many ways since the finalization of the Talmud.

Orthodox, reform, and conservative Judaism

In the modern period—that is, since the European Enlightenment of the eighteenth century—several different religious communities emerged within Judaism, defined by the extent to which they affirm the Torah and Talmud as works inspired directly by God. Orthodox Jews hold that the contents of the Torah were revealed by God directly and literally to the prophet Moses, while Conservative and Reform Jews see them as more of a human response to the call of God. The Talmud is regarded as sacred and

Figures 8.2 and 8.3 On the left, columns of text in an open Torah scroll. Note that Hebrew reads from right to left. The detail on the right, from another Torah scroll, shows some of the letters decorated with "crowns," a convention used to mark the Torah's exceptional holiness. A reading pointer, or *yad* (literally "hand") is used so as not to touch the page. This practice is explained variously as a way to keep the scroll clean, or as a consequence of a Talmudic teaching that when one touches the Torah (except in the Temple in Jerusalem) it "makes the hands unclean." Source: Will Deming.

authoritative by Orthodox Jews, less so by Conservatives, and of more marginal importance by Reform Jews. Reform Judaism and some progressive groups within the Conservative movement have even modernized the *halakhah* to such an extent that it is almost unrecognizable to Orthodox and traditionalist Conservative Jews.

The designation "Orthodox" is actually an umbrella term referring to all Jews who oppose modern innovations in the religion. Reform and Conservative Jews, by contrast, are specific branches of the religion that parted ways with this premodern stance. Orthodoxy includes a wide spectrum, ranging from the **Ultra-Orthodox** to those who are nominally Orthodox. The latter group carries on some of the rituals of Judaism, and may attend prayers in Orthodox synagogues, but are otherwise secular in outlook. Between these extremes are groups who identify themselves as **Modern-Orthodox** and simply **Orthodox**.

The study of Judaism

The study of Judaism as a living religion is comparatively recent. It was only after the Enlightenment that Jewish scholars were able to attend universities in Europe and apply academic standards to their own tradition. Until then, the scholarly study of

Judaism was undertaken by Christians—mainly clergymen—who approached the Tanak as the Old Testament of the Christian Bible and regarded the rabbinic writings as a degraded form of Judaism whose value was primarily background material for understanding the life of Jesus. This narrow perspective assumed that Judaism had been entirely superseded by Christianity, and that the tradition that survived into the Christian era was not a true form of Judaism. The notion that Jews could even practice their religion after Jesus had come as the Messiah was incomprehensible to many Christians. The modern study of Judaism, by contrast, focuses on Judaism as a living religion.

> **Talking about Religion**
>
> ### A Jewish Perspective on Christianity and Islam
>
> Throughout the centuries, Jews living in Christian and Muslim lands have reflected on how these cultures viewed Judaism, and how they, in turn, should view these larger host cultures. One of the greatest Jewish thinkers of the Middle Ages, Moses Maimonides (1136–1204), gives this assessment in his magnum opus the *Mishneh Torah*:
>
> > As for Jesus of Nazareth and the Ishmaelite [Muhammad] who arose after him, they were only to prepare the way for the King-Messiah, and to rectify the whole world to serve God together. ... How is this? The whole world is already full of ideas about the Messiah, about the Torah, and about the commandments. These ideas have spread to far islands and among many heathen nations. They discuss these matters and the commandments of the Torah. Some say that these commandments were valid, but they have been abolished at this time, and were not meant to be practiced throughout the generations. Others say that there are hidden meanings in them and they are not to be taken literally, and the Messiah has already come and revealed their hidden meanings. When the true King-Messiah will arise, however, and will be successful and elevated, immediately they will all repent and know that their fathers inherited falsehood, and that their prophets and fathers led them astray.
>
> *Sefer Shoftim, Hilkhot Melakhim* 11:11–13, uncensored version

History

Timeline	
early 2nd millennium BCE	Traditional dating of God's covenant with Abraham and Sarah.
1500–1200 BCE	Traditional dating of the Exodus from Egypt and receipt of the Mosaic covenant.
1200–1000 BCE	Religious leadership under the Judges and the Ark of the Covenant.
10th century BCE	The rise of kingship and the appearance of prophets; the First Temple is built.
722 BCE	The fall of the northern kingdom (Israel) to Assyria; the "Ten Lost Tribes" are assimilated with other conquered peoples.
586–538 BCE	The fall of the southern kingdom (Judah) to Babylonia; the Babylonian Exile; the beginning of the Diaspora.
515 BCE	The Second Temple is completed.
late 4th century BCE	The beginning of Greek influence in the Mediterranean world.
167–165 BCE	The Maccabean Revolt and the rededication of the Temple.
63 BCE	The beginning of Roman rule in Palestine.
66–74 CE	The Jewish Revolt against Rome and the destruction of the Second Temple.
late 1st century CE	The synagogue becomes a primary institution of the religion; the rise of rabbinic Judaism and its tradition of *halakhah*.
early 3rd century CE	Creation of the Mishnah.
400–500 CE	Appearance of the Jerusalem and Babylonian Talmuds.
8th century CE	The Khazars convert to Judaism; Karaite Jews reject the authority of the Talmud.
1096 CE	The Crusades begin, followed by the killing of thousands of Jews by Christian crusaders.
end of 12th century	Moses Maimonides compiles the *Mishneh Torah*.

(continued)

end of 13th century	The *Zohar* appears and medieval Kabbalah develops.
1391	Many Spanish Jews are forcibly converted to Christianity.
1492–1499	Sephardi Jews are expelled from Spain and Portugal.
1565	Joseph Caro compiles the *Shulchan Arukh*.
17th and 18th centuries	Messianic movements appear in Europe and the Ottoman empire; Hasidism is born.
late 18th century	The beginning of the Jewish Enlightenment movement and Reform Judaism; France grants citizenship rights to Jews.
mid-19th century	Neo-Orthodoxy and Conservative Judaism are founded; anti-Jewish ideologies become widespread in Europe; Zionism begins.
late 19th century	The Dreyfus Affair takes place; Theodor Herzl convenes the First Zionist Congress in Basel, Switzerland.
1917	The British government issues the Balfour Declaration.
mid-20th century	The Nazi regime rises to power, followed by the Holocaust.
1948	The modern state of Israel is founded, followed by the War of Independence.

Beginnings

The beginning of Judaism is recorded only in the Tanak, in narratives passed down for theological, not historical purposes. Because of this, much of what took place before the end of the eighth century BCE cannot be verified using historical methods. What follows in this section is an account of what the Tanak says about this early period.

According to the Tanak, the Jewish people come into being when a man named Abram entered into a **covenant** with God. A covenant in this sense is an agreement between two parties, the parties here being Abram and God. Under the terms of this covenant, God promised to make Abram and his descendants into a great nation, giving them land and prosperity. In return, Abram pledged that he and his descendants would be loyal to God as His particular people, following all of God's commandments. God later renames Abram **Abraham**, meaning "father of many nations." **Israel**, one of the names given to Abraham's descendants, derives from Abraham's grandson. Originally named Jacob, he is reported to have encountered and wrestled with a mysterious man who renamed him "he who struggles with God," or Israel. The sons and grandsons of Jacob became the heads of tribes known collectively as the "Sons of Israel," or simply Israel.

The Exodus and the Mosaic covenant

Before Jacob's death, Israel had moved into northeastern Egypt, where, over time, the Egyptians enslaved them and attempted to control their numbers through infanticide. When this happened, God appointed Moses to be His **prophet** (spokesman). It fell to Moses to free the Israelites from bondage by bringing a series of disasters on the Egyptian people and leading the Israelites to the land that God had promised Abraham. As part of his preparation for this task, a new name for God was revealed to Moses: YHWH, meaning "I am" (or perhaps "I create"). The story of Moses' liberation of the Israelites from Egypt, known as the **Exodus**, became a model in Judaism for God's deliverance of His people in times of peril.

After their escape from Egypt, the Israelites entered into a second covenant with God. This consisted of hundreds of commandments that would become the law of the land for the new Israelite nation. Since it was given by God to Israel through the prophet Moses, it became known as the Mosaic covenant, and Moses is remembered as Israel's greatest prophet and lawgiver.

Sacred Traditions and Scripture

The Mosaic Covenant

The commandments given through Moses constituted an all-inclusive code of behavior for God's people. They regulated not only ritual matters, but also agricultural law, civil and criminal law, military service, and even the treatment of skin diseases. Here is an except, taken from Leviticus 19:1–19.

> The LORD spoke to Moses, saying: Speak to the whole Israelite community and say to them: You shall be holy, for I, the LORD your God, am holy. …
>
> When you reap the harvest of your land, you shall not reap all the way to the edges of your field, or gather the gleanings of your harvest. You shall not pick your vineyard bare, or gather the fallen fruit of your vineyard; you shall leave them for the poor and the stranger. …
>
> You shall not render an unfair decision; do not favor the poor or show deference to the rich. …
>
> You shall not let your cattle mate with a different kind; you shall not sow your field with two kinds of seed; you shall not put on cloth from a mixture of two kinds of materials.

Jewish Publication Society TANAKH Translation (JPSTT)

The Ark

Following Moses' death, the Israelite tribes invaded and settled the land promised to Abraham, known as the Holy Land or Promised Land. Before it was invaded by the Israelites it had been inhabited by Canaanites and Philistines, which is the origin of the land's additional designations as Canaan and Palestine. In his capacity as prophet, Moses is described as having directed not only the religious practices of his people, but also their military and civil affairs. This precedent of combining religion and government under a single leader was continued under his successor, Joshua, and then under a series of leaders known as Judges. Throughout the period of Moses, Joshua, and the Judges, Israel is pictured as worshipping God by means of a movable sanctuary, which consisted of an elaborate tent (tabernacle) that housed the **Ark of the Covenant**. This Ark was a wooden chest covered in gold and adorned with images of heavenly beings. It served as a point of communication between God's world and the human world, for God was believed to be present on the lid of the Ark. When tribes from Israel went to war against their neighbors, they took this chest with them as one might carry a king to the battlefield on a portable throne to oversee the fight.

Rituals, Rites, Practices

The Ark Returns from Battle

Many biblical scholars believe that when the Israelites returned from battle with the Ark, it was given a royal welcome. In one of the songs that may have been used on such occasions, the city gates are commanded to lift their heads and receive the Ark as God and King:

> O gates, lift up your heads!
> Up high, you everlasting doors,
> so the King of glory may come in.
> Who is the King of glory?—
> The Lord, mighty and valiant
> The Lord, valiant in battle!
>
> Psalm 24:7–8 JPSTT

Monarchy and the first temple

The system of governing through Judges was eventually replaced by a monarchy, uniting the tribes under a single king. Kingship was understood as a hereditary office, each new king ascending to the throne of his predecessor through a ceremony in which a priest anointed him with oil. Because of this practice, one of the king's titles was God's "anointed one," which in Hebrew is the word *messiah*. After the downfall of the monarchy, the word *messiah* took on other connotations signaling important developments in the religion.

Solomon, who was the third king, built a temple in the capital city of Jerusalem, envisioned as God's house. Israel's Ark was installed in the inner sanctuary of this building—a room known as the Holy of holies, or the most holy place on earth. The worship of God at the Jerusalem Temple was presided over by an order of priests, and consisted of chanting songs (psalms), attending annual pilgrimage festivals, and providing offerings and sacrifices that were stipulated in the Mosaic covenant.

The divided kingdom

After Solomon's reign, the nation was divided by civil war into a northern and a southern kingdom. The northern kingdom was inhabited by 10 of the 12 tribes and became known as Israel. The southern kingdom was inhabited by the remaining 2 tribes and became known as Judah, which is the origin of the names Judea, for the land, and Jews for the people. Each kingdom had its own religion, although the southern kingdom claimed to have the only legitimate place to worship God, as it retained the Temple and the Ark of the Covenant.

Beginning with the united monarchy and continuing into the period of the divided kingdoms, prophets appeared, their main purpose being to deliver messages from God to the kings. Much of what the prophets reported were warnings from God that the Jews were not living up to the stipulations of the Mosaic covenant. Sometimes their messages pertained to religious practices, but just as often they advised or criticized a king on his social and military agenda. One recurring issue was Israel and Judah's relation to the non-Jewish nations around them. Israel and Judah were relatively small kingdoms situated between empires: Egypt to the southwest, and Assyria, Babylonia, and Persia, successively, to the northeast. To survive, the Jewish kings often made treaties with these empires or formed alliances with other petty kingdoms in the area. According to the prophets, however, this was a violation of the covenant, since Abraham's descendants had pledged themselves to be His people, not the ally or satellite state of another nation. The prophets were especially critical of kings who adopted the religions of these nations, which almost always required the Israelites to worship statues and other images of foreign gods. This practice, called idolatry, was strictly prohibited by the Mosaic covenant, not only because the Israelites had been commanded to worship only God, but also because it confused the Creator with stone and wooden objects of his creation.

A Closer Look

Idolatry

The prophetic tradition vehemently denounced the worship of idols. Here, the eighth-century prophet Hosea associates idolatry with sexual sins and derides it as a violation of common sense:

> My people:
> it consults its stick,
> Its rod directs it!

(continued)

> A lecherous impulse has made them go wrong,
> And they have strayed from submission to their God.
> They sacrifice on the mountaintops
> And offer on the hills,
> Under oaks, poplars, and terebinths,
> Whose shade is pleasant.
> That is why their daughters fornicate
> And their daughters-in-law commit adultery!
>
> Hosea 4:12–13 JPSTT

Exile, diaspora, and a second temple

Eventually the northern and the southern kingdoms succumbed to empires invading from the northeast. In 722 BCE, Israel was conquered by the Assyrians, and effectively vanished from history. This has given rise to popular theories and speculations about the so-called Ten Lost Tribes of Israel. In 586 BCE, Judah fell to the Babylonians, who destroyed the Temple and exiled its leaders. In both instances, these military defeats were interpreted by the prophets as God's punishment for the Israelites' violation of the Mosaic covenant. Within less than 50 years, however, the Babylonians were themselves overthrown by the rising Persian empire, which allowed the exiles from Judah to return to their homeland as subjects of Persia. While many Jews saw this as a sign of God's forgiveness, not all chose to return to the Promised Land, which lay in ruins. Some remained in Persia while others migrated to Egypt. This begins the Diaspora—the "dispersion" or "spreading out" of Jews into foreign lands.

The destruction of Judah in 586 BCE and its aftermath marked a major turning point in Judaism: God's house (the Temple) had been destroyed, the people had been subjugated to foreign powers, and many now lived in Diaspora communities outside the homeland. Jewish prophets and theologians from this period began asking questions that went to the heart of the religion: In what way were the Jews still God's chosen people? What had happened to the promises of land, political autonomy, and prosperity given to Abraham? How could Jews worship God without the Temple? Was there still a covenantal agreement between God and the Jews? In turn, literature after the exile contained many new elements, including expectations of a future king, or messiah, speculation about the afterlife, and visions of God's plans for a reunification of the Jewish people in a utopian age.

By 515 BCE, Jews had resettled in Jerusalem and built a second, smaller temple to replace the first one. While this provided those in the homeland a place to worship, Jews living in the Diaspora had to create new religious practices if they wished to continue to be part of Judaism. One solution was to build additional temples. We know of three that operated sometime between the fifth and the first centuries BCE: two in Egypt and one in the old northern kingdom. But none of these had any lasting impact on the religion. Another solution, which eventually became central to Judaism, was to seek God through the Mosaic covenant, which was edited and set within a narrative history of God and Israel, beginning with the Creation and ending with the death of Moses. This new work was the Torah, which may have begun to take shape as early as the latter half of the sixth century. Both in the Diaspora and in the homeland, the study, interpretation, and translation of the Torah became the religious focus of many Jews.

> ### Sacred Tradition and Scripture
>
> ## Exile and Diaspora
>
> The Babylonian exile and the Diaspora produced many expressions of doubt and searching in Jewish theology. In this Psalm, the author asks how the worship of God can continue outside the homeland:
>
> > By the rivers of Babylon,
> > there we sat,
> > sat and wept,
> > as we thought of Zion.
> > There on the poplars
> > we hung up our lyres ...
> > How can we sing a song of the Lord
> > on alien soil?
>
> Psalm 137:1–4 JPSTT

The Jews under Greek and Roman rule

By the end of the fourth century BCE, the great empires of Persia and Egypt had fallen to the armies of Alexander the Great (356–323 BCE), a Macedonia king. His expansive empire, which eventually stretched from Greece to India, promoted Greek language and culture throughout its major cities, creating a Hellenized urban elite—"Hellas" being the name of ancient Greece. When Alexander died in 323 BCE, his empire was divided among his generals, who established the Seleucid dynasty in the former territories of Persia, and the Ptolemaic dynasty in Egypt. At the beginning of the second century BCE, the Land of Israel transitioned from Ptolemaic to Seleucid control, and in 175 BCE the Seleucid king, Antiochus Epiphanes IV, sought to impose Greek culture and religion on the Jews. In short order, Antiochus brought Jerusalem (which he renamed Antioch) under martial law, banned the teaching of Torah and other Jewish practices, looted the Temple treasury, and turned the Temple into a place for worshipping Greek gods.

While many in Jerusalem had initially supported Antiochus' vision of bringing their city into the world of Greek culture, Antiochus proceeded too rapidly with major changes, even replacing the Jewish high priest twice within four years with priests loyal to him. His impatience soon occasioned a religious uprising, led by a priestly family called the Maccabees. By 165 BCE, the Maccabees had gained control of Jerusalem and rededicated the Temple to God, observing the first celebration of Hanukah (Dedication). By 142 BCE, the Maccabees had gained control over most of Judea, establishing the Hasmonean dynasty, which lasted until 37 BCE. Thereafter, the Romans, who had expanded into this area, incorporated the Holy Land into its empire.

Sacred Traditions and Scripture

Scripture Interpretation in Egypt

Philo, a Jewish philosopher and theologian from Alexandria, Egypt (ca. 20 BCE–ca. 50 CE), produced extensive commentaries on the Torah in which he tried to reconcile Jewish traditions with Greek philosophy. In this passage from his *Allegorical Interpretation of Genesis,* Philo gives Genesis 3:8 a distinctively Stoic reading:

"And both Adam and his wife hid from the face of the Lord God in the midst of the trees of the garden."—Here Moses introduces a teaching demonstrating that the bad man is an exile. For if virtue is a city suited exclusively for the wise (*sophos*), then one who has no capacity for sharing in virtue has been driven away from that city.... If the wise, being God's friends, are visible to Him, it is evident that all bad men keep themselves hidden from God, as is to be expected of those who are haters and enemies of right reason (*logos*).

Allegorical Interpretation of Genesis 3.1

During the reign of the Hasmoneans, Judaism became a diverse religion, branching out in several directions. Worship, including animal sacrifice and pilgrimage festivals, continued at the Temple under the supervision of priests. But there were also competing schools of scripture interpretation, some in Egypt and some in Palestine, which practiced Judaism in ways that were not dependent on the Temple or its priests. One of these Palestinian schools was the Essenes, who most scholars associate with the Dead Sea Scrolls, a library of hundreds of religious texts discovered in caves near the Dead Sea in 1947. Another was the Pharisees, whose intense study of the law foreshadowed the later rabbinic tradition. In Egypt, several vibrant schools of scripture interpretation existed in Alexandria, the best-known scholar there being Philo of Alexandria, who sought to understand Jewish traditions in light of Greek philosophy. Several groups, including the Essenes, lived in anticipation of the coming of God's messiah. The most consequential messianic group from this period were the followers of Jesus, who eventually became known as Christians.

Post-destruction Judaism

Such diversity continued in Judaism until 74 CE, which marked the end of the Jewish Revolt against Rome. In 66 CE, leaders in Jerusalem revolted against their Roman masters. By 70 CE, the Romans gained control of Jerusalem and destroyed the Temple, and over the next four years they crushed the revolt entirely by laying siege to the mountain fortress of Masada by the Dead Sea. The period after the destruction of the Second Temple was crucial for Judaism. The biblical religion with its priestly establishment, its Temple, and its sacrifices gave way to a religion in which rabbis replaced priests, the home and local meeting places replaced the Temple, and prayer, ritual, and Torah study replaced sacrifice.

A Closer Look

Masada in the Modern Israeli Consciousness

Masada, an imposing fortress built by King Herod the Great (reigned 37–4 BCE) on a plateau by the Dead Sea (Figure 8.4), was the last stand of the revolutionaries in the Jewish Revolt. When it became clear that they could no longer defend the fortress against the Romans, the revolutionaries are reported to have

Figure 8.4 Masada, a fortress built on a plateau, as seen from the northeast. On the left side is the Snake Path (white line), which was the only approach to the top until the Romans built an earthen ramp (arrow, upper right) to breach the walls in 74 CE. Source: Wikimedia Commons.

(continued)

> committed suicide rather than submit themselves to their enemies. According to the Jewish historian Josephus (37–ca. 100 CE), some 960 men, women, and children set fire to the buildings and then killed themselves in groups, drawing straws to determine who would oversee the deaths of his fellow group members before ending his own life.
>
> Although this wartime tragedy at Masada is not in the *halakhic* (legal) category of a "commendable suicide," the heroism of the revolutionaries has captured the imagination of modern Israelis. Masada is now the site where members of the Armored Corps of the Israel Defense Forces swear allegiance with the words: "Masada will not fall again."

While the destruction of the Second Temple was traumatic for Judaism, the change in religious orientation enabled it to survive in the Diaspora. The Jews had gone through a similar trauma after 586 BCE, when the First Temple was destroyed and many Jews were sent into exile in Babylon. There they had begun to create a new type of sacred space for the expression of Judaism, called the house of assembly. Similarly, by the end of the first century CE, meeting places known as **synagogues** had appeared, and the religious activities of the home and synagogue fast became the real heart of Judaism. One advantage of this dramatic change was that Judaism became a "portable" religion. Even though Jews were still attached spiritually to the Holy Land, and expected the temple to be rebuilt, Judaism's new identity as a religion of home and synagogue ensured its practice anywhere that Jews chose to settle. As a result, Jews increasingly envisioned God as a universal deity, rather than a god localized in the Holy Land.

Post-destruction Jewish literature

Within a century and a half of the destruction of the Second Temple, Jewish leaders known as rabbis began to reformulate Judaism in ways that would essentially determine its future. They not only finalized the contents of the Tanak, Judaism's most authoritative scripture, but also published, in oral form, a large collection of civil and religious decisions called the Mishnah. Soon thereafter, commentaries on biblical texts also appeared. Known as *midrash*, these analyzed the precise wording of scripture in an attempt to establish its legal and ritual meaning, or *halakhah*. In addition, many nonlegal writings, collectively known as *aggadah*, were produced, providing moral guidance in the form of narratives and reflections on theology and ethics. Finally, sometime after 300 CE, rabbis in Palestine began to compile a commentary on the Mishnah, known as the Jerusalem Talmud. This work, together with the midrashic collections, was designed to be the principal vehicle both for adopting new concepts and practices into Judaism, and for denouncing heretical innovations.

> **Sacred Traditions and Scripture**
>
> ### The Mishnah
>
> The Mishnah's concise style can be seen from this discussion of activities that violated the Torah's prohibition of work on the Sabbath:
>
> He who builds, how much can he build before he is guilty [of violating the Sabbath]?
> —Whoever builds anything at all, or cuts any stone, or uses a hammer or adze, or drills any hole, is guilty … Rabbi Simeon ben Gamaliel said, "Even if he strikes a hammer on an anvil, since he is like one who is preparing for work.
> —He who attempts any ploughing or weeding or cutting dead leaves or pruning is guilty. He who gathers any amount of wood to sort it, or burns any amount to cook even the smallest egg; or who harvests plants for the purpose of caring for fields or feeding livestock—even just to feed a lamb one morsel.
> —He who writes out two letters of the alphabet, with either hand, whether the same letter or different letters, whether with the same ink or different inks, in any language, is guilty.
>
> *Mishnah Shabbat* 12:1–3

The Babylonian Talmud The intellectual center of Jewish life eventually moved away from the Holy Land to the Aramaic-speaking Jews of Babylonia. A new edition of the Talmud was edited there around 500 CE. Like the Palestinian version, the Babylonian Talmud was a collection of teachings around the Mishnah text, but much larger and more wide-ranging.

In the following centuries, Jews spread westward in the Roman empire, flourishing in Italy and northern Europe, and particularly in Spain after its conquest by Muslims in the early eighth century. In these areas and elsewhere in the Diaspora, rabbis continued to study the Tanak, the Mishnah, and midrashic collections. Yet, for the rabbis of this period, it was the Babylonian Talmud that offered the most appealing vision of Judaism, with the result that it eventually supplanted the Jerusalem Talmud as the highest expression of rabbinic ideology. This new role for the Babylonian Talmud was not without opposition, however. One powerful group that took issue with the Talmudic tradition altogether was the Karaite movement, founded in the eighth century in Babylonia. Rejecting the interpretive methods used in creating the Talmuds, the Karaites advocated a return to more literal understandings of the Tanak. Throughout the Middle Ages the Karaites challenged the Rabbanites (supporters of the Talmud), but eventually their competing view of Judaism was neutralized and contained. Today Karaites are only a small minority within Judaism, with little influence on the wider Jewish outlook.

Rituals, Rites, Practices

The Ruins of the Jewish Temple

After the Romans destroyed the Temple in 70 CE, only a small section of a retaining wall west of the actual Temple still stood above the rubble. Beginning in the late first century, Jews undertook pilgrimages to this Western Wall to mourn the destruction of God's house. Today pilgrims stand or sit before the Wall in prayer (Figure 8.5), touch the Wall as a way of drawing near to God, and leave written prayers between its massive stone blocks. A large plaza, divided into a men's and a women's section, has been built in front of the Wall to accommodate its many visitors.

Figure 8.5 Jews and others pray before the enormous stone blocks of the Western Wall in Jerusalem. Source: Reproduced by permission of H. Richard Rutherford, C.S.C.

Jews in Spanish and German lands

As Jews in the Diaspora spread to different lands, they found themselves divided between Christian and Muslim host cultures. Eventually a split occurred between Jews living in Muslim Spain, known as **Sephardim**, and those living in Christian central and eastern Europe, known as **Ashkenazim**. The Sephardim spoke a Judeo-Spanish dialect called Ladino, while the Ashkenazim spoke several varieties of Yiddish, which were Judeo-German dialects.

Some of the greatest achievements of the Sephardi Jews came during the time that Spain was ruled by the Muslim Umayyad dynasty. Under the Umayyads, these Jews were exposed to Greek philosophy through Arabic translations, and were stimulated theologically by interacting with Islamic scholars. By contrast, Ashkenazi Jews in central and eastern Europe had little intellectual contact with Christianity, generally shunned Greek philosophy, and concentrated their energies on developing and performing the ritual side of Judaism.

Codification of law

During the Middle Ages various attempts were made to codify part or all of the *halakhah* of the Talmud, the most important of these early codifications being that of the Spanish scholar Moses Maimonides (1136–1204). His achievement, the *Mishneh Torah*, systematically organized and explained most of the ritual and legal material found in rabbinic literature up to his time, including even laws affecting the Temple and the renewal of kingship, which were, it was thought, applicable only in the future messianic age. The few elements that Maimonides omitted were those he regarded as superstitious, because these were not supported by Aristotelian philosophy.

Maimonides' code was initially influential only among Sephardi Jews in Spain and Portugal. After the Christian reconquest of Spain, however, and the expulsion of Jews from Spain in 1492 and Portugal in 1499, Sephardi refugees spread the code of Maimonides into eastern parts of the Mediterranean world (Figure 8.6), where it became popular among the so-called Eastern Jews of those areas. Even so, it was largely rejected by the Ashkenazi Jews of central and northern Europe, who had different customs and a different approach to *halakhah*.

Although Maimonides' code never won universal acceptance, all later codes held this twelfth century *tour de force* in high regard. It took another 400 years before a *halakhic* code was acknowledged to be authoritative by all sectors of Jewry. This was the *Shulchan Arukh*, written in 1565 by Joseph Caro. Because Caro, like Maimonides, was a Sephardi Jew, additions were soon made to his work by Moses Isserles (1525–1572), incorporating Ashkenazi traditions from Germany and Poland.

In its combined Sephardi and Ashkenazi form, the *Shulchan Arukh* appeared at a time when printing was making books more available and affordable. Prior to this, books were in short supply, as they had to be painstakingly copied out by hand, which required Jews to rely on the libraries of their local synagogues or study centers. But the revised *Shulchan Arukh* was in print soon after its composition and distributed widely. When it was later combined with rabbinic commentary, it soon became the *halakhic* standard for practice in most Jewish communities. Thus, while differences between Ashkenazim and Sephardim still exist, there is also an impressive uniformity in the celebration of festivals, dietary laws, marriage and divorce, and liturgy.

Jews under Christian rule

In lands controlled by Muslims, Jews fared significantly better than in lands under Christian rule. In Muslim areas, Jews had a legal status as second-class citizens (*dhimmis*). In theory, at least, this meant they had some legal protections, and only occasionally faced mob violence and forced conversion. In Christian countries, by contrast, their very existence was fraught with danger. Called "Christ killers" and disciples of the

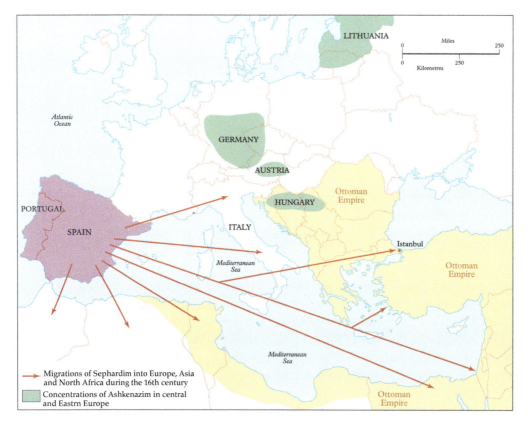

Figure 8.6 When Christian rulers expelled Jews from Spain and Portugal at the end of the fifteenth century, Sephardi teachings and customs spread into Italy, northwest Africa, and parts of the Mediterranean world controlled by the Ottoman empire.

Devil, they were often accused of desecrating Christian communion wafers and practicing ritual murder. In cities, Jews were regulated to separate areas, or ghettos, which were often gated, locked at night, and overcrowded. They faced vigilantes and legal persecution, and large populations were expelled from their Christian host countries.

Some Jews opted to live a double life, outwardly appearing to be Christian but secretly continuing Jewish practice. This was dangerous, however, for if their secret practices were discovered by church authorities, these so-called Conversos or Marranos (a reference to pigs) forfeited their possessions and faced torture and being burnt at the stake. Not surprisingly, the picture of Christianity found in medieval Jewish texts and Ashkenazi folk memory depicts a cruel and intolerant religion whose use of images and belief in a Son of God were idolatrous. Until the Enlightenment of the eighteenth century, when European Jews in western and central Europe began to emerge from the ghettos into European culture, very little changed.

Jewish mysticism

At the end of the thirteenth century, a strange book appeared in Spain, promoting **Kabbalah**, a form of Jewish mysticism. Known as the **Zohar**, or *Book of Splendor*, it originated in a devout enclave associated with Moses de Leon. While it drew on a long mystical tradition that can be traced back to the early centuries CE, it was nonetheless a new synthesis that profoundly affected the outlook of its readers.

The *Zohar* purported to be a second-century Palestinian collection of the teachings and sayings of Rabbi Simeon bar Yochai and his followers. According to a Talmudic legend, Rabbi Simeon and his son became students of the ancient Israelite prophet Elijah while hiding in a cave for 13 years. Kabbalah often named Elijah as a source of its teachings because, according to the Tanak, Elijah never died, but was taken alive into heaven by a fiery chariot with fiery horses. From there Elijah was said to return from time to time, bringing messages from God and secret teachings for mystics.

The true essence of Judaism, according to the *Zohar*, is accessible only through Jewish mystical traditions. While non-mystical scholars understood Torah as merely stories and laws, it was the secret teachings of Kabbalah that unveiled the truth of scripture. According to this truth, our world is an emanation of the unknowable God, the Unbounded One (*Ein Sof*). This God created the world by expressing Himself through 10 semi-divine emanations (*sefirot*) that now underlie all existence, particularly the reality of human beings (Figure 8.7).

The powers of evil, in turn, are a world of antimatter called the Other Side (*Sitra Achra*), which itself was a product of the divine emanation but subsequently became an independent force. The Other Side draws its power from the sinful actions of humans, which enables it to take control of the Unbounded One's female aspects, causing chaos and human misery. But human beings can resist evil through prayer and ritual. This enables the female aspects of God to reunite with the male aspects in a harmonious relationship, bringing about a messianic age in which the power of the Other Side will be broken and God's holiness will dominate. A major effect of the *Zohar* was to provide an alternative to the authority of the *halakhah*. It validated many folk ideas and customs,

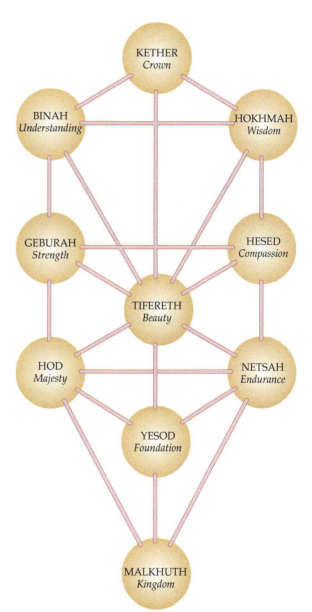

Figure 8.7 According to Kabbalistic traditions, although God is unbounded, he allowed his divine qualities to be divided into 10 emanations in order to create our world. As this tradition further developed, some mystics speculated that one or more of these emanations had shattered its bounds. This cosmic tragedy accounted for the chaos and evil in the world and called Jews to the divine task of *tikkun*, or repairing the world.

including a belief in reincarnation, understood as an atoning punishment for sexual sins committed in past lives.

Lurianic Kabbalah

In 1492, following English and French precedents, the Spanish monarchy expelled all Jews from Spain. Aside from disseminating an advanced form of Sephardi Judaism (as noted above), this expulsion was the catalyst for a new mystical movement called Lurianic Kabbalah. With its basis in the traditions of the *Zohar*, Lurianic Kabbalah made the sufferings of exile, both from Spain and from the Jewish homeland, the very heart of its teachings. It taught that in the beginning of time God was synonymous with all existence, but to make room for our world, God exiled himself during creation through an act of contraction (*tzimtzum*). With this new understanding creation, it became possible to view exile as an experience also shared by God, being the price God had paid to create human beings. Accordingly, the solution to exile and its hardships was the reparation of the world (*tikkun*) through good deeds that would return all things to perfection.

Messianic movements

In the seventeenth and early eighteenth centuries, under the influence of Lurianic Kabbalah two messianic movements spread quickly in Europe and the Ottoman empire, both of which ended by leaving Jewish communities in disarray. The Sabbatean movement demanded allegiance to the Turkish-born mystic and messianic pretender Sabbatai Zevi (1626–1676). After having won a large and enthusiastic following in many Jewish communities, including those in Christian Europe, Sabbatai traveled extensively in the eastern part of the Mediterranean world. But in 1666 he arrived at the Muslim-ruled city of Constantinople, where he was arrested and forced to convert to Islam under threat of death. His movement, which held much of the Jewish world in eager anticipation of a messianic era, came to a traumatic and humiliating end. Those who continued to believe in Sabbatai as the Messiah claimed, on Kabbalistic grounds, that breaking the law—even conversion to Islam—was a necessary part of messianic redemption. A small number even followed Sabbatai's lead, outwardly converting to Islam while secretly continuing the practice of Kabbalah.

A little more than a century later, the Frankist movement met a similar fate. Strongly influenced by Sabbateanism, its leader, Jacob Frank (1726–1791), advocated a higher form of Torah observance characterized by teachings and rituals that explicitly contradicted Jewish law. Having previously led underground cells in Poland from what remained of Sabbatai Zevi's movement, Frank was hailed as a messiah and divine incarnation. In the end, however, Frank and his followers converted to Catholicism to escape persecution from other Jews.

The Hasidic movement

In the wake of the Sabbatean and Frankist debacles, Hasidic spirituality offered a Jewish renewal movement that remained within rabbinic orthodoxy. Its founder was Israel ben Eliezer (1698–1760), a Ukrainian Kabbalist known as Master of the Good

Name, or **Baal Shem Tov**—usually abbreviated as the Besht. The title *baal shem* (master of the name) had originally designated a wonder worker whose mastery over YHWH, the name that God had revealed to Moses, gave him the power to cast spells, work miracles of healing, and engage in magical activities.

A Closer Look

God's Special Name

From ancient times, God's personal name was considered a powerful symbol, giving unparalleled access to God. In the period of the First and Second Temples, the high priest used the name on the Day of Atonement (Yom Kippur) to gain favor with God on behalf of the Jewish people. After the fall of the Second Temple, however, it became blasphemous for anyone to pronounce the divine name. In Jewish mystical traditions, however, it was manipulated in written form and used alongside magical terms and other names of God to bring about miracles and visions.

In modern Hebrew editions of the Torah, God's name is printed using conventions that alert the reader to substitute a traditional euphemism (Figure 8.8), such as *Ha Shem* (The Name) or *Adonai* (my Lord). The standard convention in English translations is to render the divine name as LORD (with small caps), to distinguish it from the actual Hebrew word for Lord.

Figure 8.8 The word in the middle of this text, underlined in gray, is the divine name of God (YHWH). Unlike the words around it, it has no vowels (the dots and lines, which are called "pointing"). This is one way to remind the reader not to pronounce the word out loud, but to replace it with a traditional substitute. Source: Will Deming.

Baal Shem Tov's approach to God valued prayer undertaken with ecstatic fervor over the intellectual study of Torah advocated by his rabbinic contemporaries. While he was known for having visions, many Jews were drawn to him on account of his charismatic personality and spiritual insights. At the core of his teaching was the practice of *devekut*, "cleaving to God," which could be performed in everyday activities that promoted personal holiness and the joy of human relationships. These simple actions gave people ready access to God, and at the same time hastened the reparation of the world (the Lurianic *tikkun*).

Although developing only after the Besht's death, the **Hasidic movement** spread throughout eastern and central Europe, forming many submovements. Each of these was headed by a great-souled leader (*tzaddik*) who had been touched by God's Holy Spirit. At first, opposition to Hasidism was extreme. Prominent rabbis leveled accusations that the movement was merely a variation of previous heresies, a charge they supported by pointing to ritual changes made by the movement, as well as its encouragement of singing, dancing, and drinking alcohol. But as it gained in popularity among the people, Hasidism eventually won the approval of even the Orthodox establishment.

The Jewish Enlightenment

At approximately the same time that Hasidism was transforming Jewish life in eastern Europe, the Enlightenment in western and central Europe heralded the beginning of modernity for Jews in those areas. Until this time, Jews had lived in physical and intellectual isolation, driven into ghettos by Christian persecution as well as by their own desire to preserve their religious identity. The Enlightenment, however, made the larger society more accepting of Jews. In France, for example, where Napoleonic rule had emerged as a product of the Enlightenment, far-reaching changes led to the acceptance of Jews as free citizens—a process known as Jewish emancipation.

Out of the general European Enlightenment, a Jewish Enlightenment (*Haskalah*), developed in the late eighteenth century. This was intended as a path by which Jews could participate in and enjoy the fruits of modern European culture. In Germany, the person most responsible for the promotion of the Jewish Enlightenment was Moses Mendelssohn (1729–1786), grandfather of the famous pianist and composer Felix Mendelssohn.

> ### Did you know …
>
> God's name "Jehovah" was created because the vowels for *Adonai* (my Lord) were sometimes placed with the consonants of YHWH, the divine name. This was done to remind readers not to say the divine name out loud, but "*Adonai*" instead. Some early readers and translators, however, took this to be a regular word, pronouncing it "Jehovah."

Mendelssohn was educated in the traditional manner of reading, memorizing, and interpreting Jewish texts, but he also learned European languages and literature, mostly through his own efforts. He won recognition from leading non-Jewish intellectuals for his philosophical writings in German; and he translated the Tanak into German for Yiddish speaking Jews who did not know the European alphabet by writing out the German in Hebrew letters. His goal was to encourage Jews to abandon Yiddish, which was despised by many Europeans as a coarse German dialect.

Emboldened by leaders like Mendelssohn, many Jews emerged from their isolation, became part of European society, and for the first time identified themselves with Christian civilization—albeit an *enlightened* Christian civilization. Emancipated Jews now spoke, dressed, and behaved like their Christian neighbors, and began to engage in craft work, agriculture, and other professions previously closed to Jews. They also undertook secular studies. Such developments were criticized by traditional Jews in eastern Europe, for whom Torah study was the sole focus of a Jewish education. In their eyes, secular studies were irrelevant at best, and at worst heretical, since they tempted young people into alien cultures and religions.

Even though Mendelssohn remained an Orthodox Jew throughout his life and won the support of several traditional rabbis, he was blamed after his death for the secularization of German Jewry. His efforts at Enlightenment had inadvertently led some Jews to abandon the religion of their upbringing and become almost entirely assimilated into European culture. In addition, the Jewish Enlightenment had the unintended consequence of promoting conversion to Christianity, especially among better educated and wealthier Jews. In fact, all of Mendelssohn's grandchildren became Christians. To stem the tide of secularization and conversion, Reform Judaism emerged—and thus Orthodox Jews also blamed Mendelssohn for the changes that this progressive version of Judaism brought to Germany, Austria, and France.

Reform Judaism

It was Reform Judaism that prevented many assimilated Jews from completely rejecting their religion. The early Reformers reshaped Judaism in aesthetic ways and created synagogues modeled on churches. This allowed Jews to embrace their newfound European identity and its Christian influences while still feeling at home in Judaism. Yet some Reformers insisted on going further. Leaders like Rabbi Samuel Holdheim (1806–1860) believed that synagogues should not only cater to Christian tastes in decoration, but also adopt the vernacular language of the country, abandoning the Hebrew liturgy. Under such pressures, changes in ritual and belief were inevitable, and so the Reformers both forestalled and aided the process of Jewish assimilation.

A Closer Look

The Spanish Synagogue

A striking example of the Jewish effort to enter into European society during the Jewish Enlightenment is the so-called Spanish Synagogue in Prague, Czech Republic (Figure 8.9). Its foundations were laid in 1868, one year after the Jews of that city received political emancipation. It departs from traditional synagogue architecture by incorporating Christian and Muslim features. The façade is neo-Moorish, drawing on the geometric decor of Muslim architecture in Spain, and its interior includes such Christian elements as pews, stained glass windows, and an organ.

Figure 8.9 The Spanish Synagogue in Prague. Source: Will Deming.

Orthodox Judaism

The Jewish Enlightenment and Reform Judaism encountered virulent resistance from Jews who became known as Orthodox. One of these was the German-Hungarian rabbi Moses Sofer (1762–1839), who taught that "anything new is forbidden by the Torah." Another opposing voice was Shneur Zalman (1745–1813), a Russian rabbi and first head of the Lubavitch branch of Hasidism. Even though the Russian government was extremely hostile to Jews, Zalman encouraged his followers to support the czar against Napoleon, because he judged Napoleon's agenda for Jewish emancipation as the greater threat to Jewish Orthodoxy. Other Orthodox leaders tried to reconcile themselves to modernity, while still condemning the Reform movement as a heresy. Known as the Neo-Orthodox movement, founded by Samson Raphael Hirsch (1808–1888), they argued that one could fully participate in European Enlightenment culture while remaining strictly Orthodox in belief and practice.

Conservative Judaism

Between the Reform and Orthodox positions there emerged a middle ground, called the Historical movement. This, in turn, gave birth to Conservative Judaism, begun in the mid-nineteenth century by European Jews who wanted Orthodoxy to reflect the realities of Jewish life in America. At the end of the century, when the radical platform of official American Reform Judaism blocked all attempts at compromise, Conservative Judaism expanded rapidly, becoming the most popular form of Judaism in North America, with branches throughout the United States and Canada. Although Conservative Judaism claimed to be the authentic continuation of premodern rabbinical Judaism, Orthodox rabbis condemned it outright. In the early twentieth century, Reconstructionist Judaism also appeared, founded by the liberal elements within Conservative Judaism. It adopted an even more dramatic program of changes, but its appeal was largely limited to intellectual circles.

Zionism

Although the nineteenth century saw many Jews embrace European society, the Enlightenment did not live up to its promise of full integration and acceptance. This was because anti-Jewish sentiments were deeply ingrained in Christian society, and because the discovery of genetics enabled non-Jews to reformulate their religious hatred into "scientifically proven" ideologies based on race. Unlike the older formulation, which allowed Jews to win acceptance through conversion, the new ideology, called **antisemitism**, claimed that even converts and their descendants were unacceptable because "Jewishness" was genetic. Even as the old Europe reshaped itself into modern nation–states, emancipated Jews, despite their considerable efforts, continued to be regarded as outsiders and aliens.

Partly because of their disappointment with the Enlightenment, and partly as a response to the rise of European nationalism, Jewish nationalism began to assert itself in the late nineteenth century, both at the grassroots level and among Jewish intellectuals. The man who brought coherence and unity to these yearnings for an independent Jewish nation was Theodor Herzl (1860–1904), a Hungarian Jew from Vienna. The movement he led eventually became known as **Zionism**, Zion being a biblical name for Jerusalem in the messianic age. As founder of an organization called Political Zionism, Herzl summoned various nationalist groups to the First Zionist Congress, held in Basel, Switzerland, in 1897. The participants included socialist, secularist, religious, and messianic Zionists.

> **Did you know ...**
>
> At one point in its deliberations, the First Zionist Congress considered Uganda as a place to establish the new Jewish nation.

As an assimilated journalist and playwright, Herzl had been drawn to nationalism because of his own experience of anti-Judaism as a student in Vienna. At first he proposed solving the problem of social ostracism by having all Jewish children baptized in the Cathedral of Vienna, but nothing came of this plan. His experience of anti-Judaism was renewed and heightened when he worked as a journalist in Paris covering the Dreyfus Affair. A Jewish captain in the French army named Alfred Dreyfus had been falsely accused of spying for Germany and sentenced to life imprisonment on flimsy evidence. Efforts to appeal the verdict ended in anti-Jewish protests and public rioting, making it quite clear that it was not Captain Dreyfus who had been found guilty, but Dreyfus the Jew. This whole experience, which took place in the heartland of the Enlightenment and Jewish emancipation, convinced Herzl that Jews would never be acceptable to a culture so permeated by anti-Jewish sentiment. Rather, Jews needed their own nation. As a secularist, he saw no reason to establish this new nation in the land of ancient Israel, even though it had been promised by God to Abraham in the Torah. It was only after traditional Jewish nationalists from eastern Europe weighed in that he agreed to settle on "the land of Israel." At first, Zionism was only a minority interest among Jews. The Ultra-Orthodox, though they prayed every day for God to return His people to Zion, would have nothing to do with a purely secular, nationalist movement. Reform Jews, on the other hand, were content to remain in their home countries despite the strong undercurrents of anti-Judaism they encountered in their daily lives.

The Holocaust and the modern state of Israel

During World War II, the racist policies of German fascism culminated in the Nazi-led genocide known as the **Holocaust**, ending any hope of full integration for European Jewry. Now known as the *Shoah*, a Hebrew word for "destruction," the Holocaust led many to question whether God had abandoned His people. The refrain of Jewish theologians and other intellectuals soon became, "Where was God at Auschwitz?" (Auschwitz being the largest of the death camps). How could a Jew make sense of the goodness of God after millions of unarmed Jewish civilians had been methodically murdered through starvation, exposure, hard labor, and poison gas in German facilities built specifically for that purpose?

The horrors of the Holocaust renewed and strengthened the original message of Zionism. Since Jews had been singled out because of their ethnic identity and race, neither social assimilation nor renunciation of their religion could keep them safe; they needed a nation of their own that they could defend. In the early decades of the

Figure 8.10 A 100-shekel coin from the 1980s, reflecting the hope of some Jews that the modern homeland would be rebuilt according to ancient Jewish patterns. The monetary denomination "shekel" is found in the Bible, and the menorah stamped on the back recalls the famous lamp stand used by the Maccabean liberators to rededicate the Temple. By contrast, the word "Israel" appears in Hebrew, Arabic, and English—a reminder of the diverse population of the emerging nation. Source: Will Deming.

twentieth century, Zionism had already made some inroads into the Jewish consciousness, and under the 1917 Balfour Declaration, the British government authorized the creation of a Jewish homeland in Palestine. But it was the unthinkable tragedy of the Holocaust that finally brought to fruition Herzl's vision of a return to Zion. In 1897, after the First Zionist Congress had met, Herzl wrote in his diary that people would laugh at his claim that he had founded the Jewish State. "Yet," he continued, "if not in five years, certainly in fifty years, everyone will know it." This proved to be prophetic, for the Holocaust changed everything. After the war, on November 29, 1947, the United Nations passed a resolution to establish the modern state of Israel.

For many Jews, the rebirth of a Jewish state was a miraculous event revealing that, despite the Holocaust, God was still active in the world (Figure 8.10). Likewise, subsequent events quickly reinforced this conviction. Against all odds, Israel fended off the attack of five Arab nations during the War of Independence in 1948; and in 1967 it annexed other areas of the Holy Land by defeating Egypt, Syria, and Jordan in the Six Day War. This unexpected and spectacular rebirth of the nation of Israel has since inspired a new messianic vision among both religious Zionists and Lubavitch Hasidic Jews. The former see the return to Zion as a precursor to the coming of the Messiah, whereas the latter were emboldened to announce that their leader, Menachem Mendel Schneerson (1902–1994), was the Messiah.

Contemporary Beliefs and Practices

The Jewish covenant with God is the centerpiece of Judaism. It grants Jews special access to God as his chosen people and establishes them as the custodians of his divine wisdom. The covenant also provides Jews with moral guidance, encouraging them to live a holy lifestyle and to embrace a divine destiny. The covenant's legal aspects, or *halakhah*, explain how God's commandments, or *mitzvot* (good deeds), should be implemented in everyday life, while the narrative sections, or *aggadah*, offers models for Jewish behavior based on Jewish figures of the past. Importance is especially given to holy men and women who lived when the prophets were actively communicating God's messages to His people.

In addition, both *halakhah* and *aggadah* enable Jews to extend their membership in God's community *into the past*, for all the individuals in scripture who are part of Israel's history of salvation continue to live on, almost as contemporaries, with the Jews of each age. Modern Jews join in solidarity with God's people throughout history in a manner that transcends their immediate historical or social context. Through the reenactment and celebration of past events, Jews take part in the experiences—the joys, the tragedies, the hopes—of these previous generations, beginning with Abraham.

The Jewish scripture

Most Christians are familiar with the Jewish scripture, since it is included in their Bibles (in a somewhat different arrangement) as the Old Testament. But because Jews consider this name derogatory, they speak of their scripture as the Tanak, which is an acronym—a word created from the first letters of words in a phrase. The phrase is *Torah, Neviim,* and *Ketuvim,* which is Hebrew for Teaching, Prophets, and Writings.

Jewish scripture is thus a library of ancient writings organized into three divisions. The first division, Torah, is also known as the Books of Moses or the Pentateuch (Five Books). It contains the account of Creation and God's covenant with Abraham, as well as the Exodus from Egypt, the giving of the commandments through Moses, and many other narratives of Israel's earliest interaction with God. The second division, the Prophets, contains writings by and about the many prophets who followed in the steps of Moses, including such figures as Joshua, the Judges, Elijah, Isaiah, Jeremiah, and Ezekiel. The last division of the Tanak, the Writings, encompasses several genres of literature, such as wisdom sayings (Proverbs), hymns and chants (Psalms), and revelatory visions (Daniel). By far the most important of the Tanak's three divisions is the Torah—described by mystics as "the root of the souls of Israel." It is not only considered the oldest division, but it also contains God's covenant with the Jewish people, including the commandments that guide Jewish life.

> **Sacred Traditions and Scripture**
>
> ### The Writings
>
> The division of the Tanak known as the Writings is a mix of several literary genres and theological perspectives. Below are examples that illustrate Israel's wisdom theology, liturgical songs, and revelatory visions.

(continued)

Proverbs 29:2–5

> When the righteous become great, the people rejoice,
> But when the wicked dominate, the people groan.
> A man who loves wisdom brings joy to his father,
> But he who keeps company with harlots will lose his wealth.
> By justice a king sustains the land,
> But a fraudulent man tears it down.
> A man who flatters his fellow
> Spreads a net for his feet.
>
> JPSTT

Psalm 40:1–3

> I put my hope in the LORD;
> he inclined toward me,
> and heeded my cry.
> He lifted me out of the miry pit,
> the slimy clay,
> and set my feet on a rock,
> steadied my legs.
> He put a new song into my mouth,
> a hymn to our God.
> May many see it and stand in awe,
> and trust in the Lord.
>
> JPSTT

Daniel 10:1–9

In the third year of King Cyrus of Persia, an oracle was revealed to Daniel … It was on the twenty-fourth day of the first month, when I was on the bank of the great river—the Tigris—that I looked and saw a man dressed in linen, his loins girt in fine gold. His body was like beryl, his face had the appearance of lightning, his eyes were like flaming torches, his arms and legs had the color of burnished bronze, and the sound of his speech was like the noise of a multitude. … I was drained of strength, my vigor was destroyed, and I could not summon up strength. I heard him speaking; and when I heard him speaking, overcome by a deep sleep, I lay prostrate on the ground.

JPSTT

The synagogue

Jewish communities gather for prayer and study of the Torah, sometimes on a daily basis, at meeting places variously called synagogues, schools (*shuls*), and temples. All synagogues (including *shuls* and temples) have a **Torah ark**, the successor to ancient Israel's Ark of the Covenant, which today is a cabinet containing one or more handwritten scrolls of the Torah (Figure 8.11). These scrolls are the holiest objects in the

Figure 8.11 An ark in the chapel of a Conservative synagogue. When closed, this ark resembles a large Torah scroll with a burning bush on its pages—an allusion to Moses' first encounter with God. The text on the bush quotes Exodus 3:2, "And the bush was not consumed," while the words above the ark state: "For out of Zion shall Torah go forth" (Isaiah 2:3). Source: Will Deming.

synagogue. They must be handwritten without mistake on parchment (leather) by professional scribes—a task that can take up to two years; and if a word or even a letter of a scroll becomes unreadable through use, the scroll must be repaired. Synagogues position the Torah ark against a wall facing the Temple Mount, where the ancient Ark once stood. When a congregation prays, it addresses God by turning toward the ark.

In Orthodox synagogues men and women sit in separate areas, the women's area being an upstairs gallery or a space on the main floor marked off with a curtain. As a rule, the more Orthodox the synagogue, the less visible the women will be. According to the late Rabbi Moses Feinstein (1895–1986), the curtain needs to be at least 5 feet high, although lower heights have been suggested by other Orthodox rabbis. In synagogues that identify themselves as Modern-Orthodox, the curtain is quite low, and in Conservative and Reform synagogues men and women sit together.

At the center or front of the synagogue is the *bimah*, a low platform where worship leaders stand to read from the Torah scroll and direct the congregation in prayer. It is raised above floor level for two practical reasons: first, so that people can hear the words spoken from it, and second, because *halakhah* teaches that if a Torah scroll is on the same level as the congregation, everyone needs remain standing out of respect for it. If, however, the scroll is elevated to a "domain" of its own, the congregation may be seated.

Scripture readings and prayer services

During the course of the year, the entire Torah is read aloud to the congregation, beginning with the creation story in Genesis and ending with the death of Moses at the end of Deuteronomy. The principal readings take place on Saturday morning, while smaller selections from the Torah are read on Monday and Thursday mornings (the old market days), and Saturday afternoons. There are also special readings on festival days and at the new moon. When the Torah is read in public, the reader uses chanting-rhythms and pitches suitable to the occasion, and these differ between Ashkenazi and Sephardi Jews.

Every male Jew is required to pray three times a day, preferably in a synagogue, although on weekdays many Jews pray at home. In the synagogue, the daily liturgy provides morning, afternoon, and evening prayer services. During morning and evening services, attendees recite the Jewish affirmation of faith, known as the *Shema*, and the standing prayer (*amidah*), while at afternoon services they recite the standing prayer alone. The weekday liturgy also includes hymns and traditional blessings of the type, "Blessed are You, O Lord our God, King of the universe." To read Torah and recite certain parts of the prayers a quorum (*minyan*) of 10 adult males must be present. Smaller synagogues may have members of the congregation lead the prayers, while larger synagogues often have a professional cantor with musical training.

> **Rituals, Rites, Practices**
>
> ### The Jewish Affirmation of Faith
>
> The *Shema*, an ancient affirmation of faith, consists of three passages from the Torah (Deuteronomy 6:4–9; 11:13–21; and Numbers 15:37–41). Here is the first:
>
> > Hear (*shema*), O Israel, the Lord is our God, the Lord alone. You shall love the Lord your God with all your heart and with all your soul and with all your might. Take to heart these instructions with which I charge you this day. Impress them upon your children. Recite them when you stay at home or when you are away, when you lie down and when you get up. Bind them as a sign on your hand and let them serve as a symbol on your forehead; inscribe them on the doorposts of your house and on your gates.
>
> > JPSTT

Appropriate dress

During prayer, men and boys cover their heads with a hat or a *yarmulke* (skullcap; also *kipah* or *kappel*). This is considered the proper way to present oneself before God in prayer, although many Orthodox men wear head coverings even when not praying. Married women in the Orthodox tradition are required to cover their hair in the synagogue, for their hair is considered part of a women's bodily beauty, and thus also part of her nakedness. Once a woman marries, she can expose her hair only to her husband, and never in a holy place. Orthodox women cover their hair with wigs or full headscarves, while Modern-Orthodox women wear hats. Women in Conservative Judaism sometimes wear a *yarmulke* during prayer services, either a traditional cloth *yarmulke* or a jeweled one.

At morning prayer men also put on a *tallit*, or prayer shawl, and *tefillin*, which are scripture boxes. A **tallit** is a white, rectangular cloth worn over the shoulders, and sometimes over the head. Its distinctive feature is that it has a tassel at each of its corners consisting of eight thin strings, or **tzitzit**, as commanded in the Torah. These are knotted and woven together in a particular pattern. In the past, *tzitzit* included one purple string, but since the biblical technique of dyeing this thread was lost over time, most Jews wear only white strings. The purpose of wearing the tassels is to keep one's focus on God's commandments. Orthodox Jews have extended this practice outside of morning prayer, wearing a small, fringed undergarment, also called a *tzitzit*, throughout the day.

A Closer Look

Tassels

The biblical instructions for putting tassels at the corner of one's garment (Figure 8.12) make up the third passage of the *Shema* (Numbers 15:37–39):

The Lord said to Moses as follows: speak to the Israelite people and instruct them to make for themselves fringes on the corners of their garments throughout the ages; let them attach a cord of blue to the fringe at each corner. That shall be your fringe; look at it and recall all the commandments of the Lord and observe them.

JPSTT

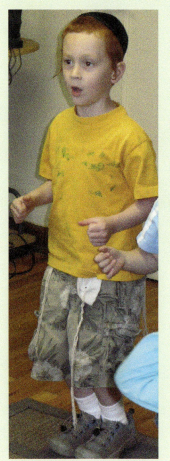

Figure 8.12 A boy participates in games at a Jewish summer camp, his *tzitzit* hanging down almost to his shoes. Source: Will Deming.

Figure 8.13 A man prays the morning prayer wearing a *tallit* (prayer shawl) and *tefillin* (black scripture boxes). Source: Ira Berger/Alamy.

Tefillin consist of two black leather boxes that contain four short passages from the Torah, handwritten on parchment. These boxes are attached by black leather straps to one's forehead above the hairline, and to the left forearm (Figure 8.13). This is done to fulfil the biblical commandment and first passage from the *Shema*, that one should "bind" God's instructions "as a sign on your hand and let them serve as a symbol on your forehead."

Women are excused from wearing a *tallit* and *tefillin* because of a rabbinic ruling that exempts women from all "positive commandments dependent on time." This means that women, who bear and nurture children, are not to neglect these important maternal obligations to engage in rituals that must be performed at specific times. Even so, some holy women in the past are rumored to have put on *tefillin*; and some modern women, mainly in the Conservative movement, put on *tefillin* and (more commonly) a *tallit*.

The religious calendar

Jews measure time according to a very full calendar of religious activities. This gives them access to God through regular interaction with His people, both those now living and those who served God faithfully in the past. During the observance of Sabbaths (see below), new moons, and yearly religious festivals, Jews are able to enter into events in the life of God's people, take part in important miracles of the past, and fulfil commandments that are required only on these occasions.

The Hebrew calendar is based on a lunar year, whose months are approximately 29½ days long. The first day of each month is the new moon, which is a minor festival day. The major festivals also fall on specific days of the lunar months, and since some of these are associated with seasons and harvests, which follow a solar year, the lunar calendar must be adjusted by adding an extra month (called Second Adar) seven times every 19 years to keep the lunar months aligned with the seasons.

The Sabbath

The Jewish week is defined by the **Sabbath** (*Shabbat*), a Hebrew word meaning "He (God) rested," referring to God's resting after the Creation. The Sabbath is the seventh day of the week, which in Judaism begins on Friday evening just before sunset and ends with the appearance of three medium-sized stars on Saturday evening. Since God rested from His labors following the six days of Creation, the Torah commands Jews to rest from their labors on the Sabbath as a way to imitate the divine action. For Orthodox Jews, this has meant that the Sabbath is structured around restrictions on actions that exercise control over nature. For example, the Orthodox do not switch electrical appliances on or off, drive motor vehicles, or operate any kind of machinery on the Sabbath. Many non-Orthodox Jews, by contrast, keep the Sabbath in a more general way. They drive to synagogue, use appliances, and exercise other forms of control over nature, while still regarding the Sabbath as a day of rest.

In addition to connecting Sabbath observance with God's resting after Creation, the Torah also links it to God's redemption of the Israelites from Egyptian slavery during the Exodus. For this reason, Sabbath observance celebrates the freedom of the Jewish people through expressions of joy and thanksgiving, special food and drink, sexual relations, and general "Sabbath delight." In Orthodox homes, the Sabbath day begins with the women of the household lighting two candles, and the father "making *kiddush*," which are blessings over wine. A second *kiddush* is made the following afternoon at lunchtime over wine or other alcohol, and at the conclusion of the Sabbath there is a ceremony called *havdalah*, involving prayers over wine and spices and the lighting of two candles intertwined with one another, which end the Sabbath by marking the division between sacred and secular time.

> **A Closer Look**
>
> ### The Role of Wine in Jewish Ritual
>
> Wine is common in Jewish rituals, for as the Tanak states, wine "cheers the hearts of men" (Psalms 104:15 JPSTT). Because of the joyful and intoxicating effects that wine has on the human spirit, both the Sabbath and Jewish festivals are sanctified over wine. Likewise, two cups of wine are used in the wedding ritual, one at circumcisions, and four during the Passover meal.

The New Year

Although the biblical names of the months are simply "first month," "second month," etc., the annual calendar currently in use among Jews was borrowed from the ancient Babylonians during the exile of 586–538 BCE. For this reason, the New Year festival (Rosh Hashanah) falls on the new moon days at the start of the biblical *seventh* month. These are regarded as days of judgment for Israel and for the whole world. During this time God sits as a heavenly judge, assessing human activity for the past year. The ram's horn (*shofar*) is blown in the synagogue to awaken people to repentance, and the prayer service is longer than usual, with an emphasis on sin and repentance. It is customary for people to go to a river to "throw their sins" into the flowing water. Even so, the New Year festival is not a sad occasion, because God is merciful and accepts human repentance, and so it is celebrated as a festive day with special foods, which give a foretaste of a sweet new year.

The Day of Atonement

The high point of repentance comes 10 days into the new year on the Day of Atonement, or **Yom Kippur**. This "day" lasts 25 hours, during which there is no eating or drinking, no sexual relations, no washing or anointing oneself with cosmetic oils, and no wearing of leather shoes. This is the rabbinic interpretation of the biblical command to "afflict one's soul" on this day. The message of Yom Kippur is that God will forgive sins if one is truly penitent, and if reconciliation with an offended party takes place first.

All adult Jews must observe Yom Kippur, adults being defined as males above the age of 13 and females above the age of 12. Children are encouraged to fast for part of the day, depending on their age and understanding of the significance of Yom Kippur. On the day before Yom Kippur many Orthodox Jews perform a ceremony of atonement (*kapparot*), by swinging a chicken over their heads, which is then slaughtered as a substitute for the person. Modern-Orthodox Jews prefer to use money as the sacrificial victim in this ritual, which is given to charity.

> **Did you know …**
>
> When making a new copy of the Torah, if a scribe happens to misspell the divine name, the area of the leather on which the mistake was made must be cut out and replaced with a patch.

The festival of Tabernacles

Five days after Yom Kippur is the festival of Booths (*Sukkot*), also called Tabernacles. This festival comes at the end of the harvest year and affirms that God is the Lord of Nature. One of its rituals celebrates God's gift of the four species of produce, represented by a citrus fruit, a palm branch, a willow, and a myrtle. Participants hold these items together and shake them while walking around the synagogue and chanting *hosanna!* (deliver us!) in response to the recitation of Psalms 113–118, which are known as praise Psalms (*Hallel*).

The affirmation of God as Lord of Nature is also the basis for another ritual during Tabernacles. This requires Jews to live for seven days in a temporary structure—the tabernacle or booth (*sukkah*)—the roof of which must be made of loosely woven branches, exposing its interior to the sky. In the Torah this activity is explained as a way to join with the ancient Israelites after the Exodus, when they lived 40 years in the wilderness under God's protection. In the contemporary context, the ritual also carries the message that God, rather than the walls or roof of one's house, guarantees security and protection. The seventh day of Tabernacles, known as the Great Hosanna, ends the period of repentance and divine judgment which began with the New Year festival. According to Jewish folklore, if a person does not see their shadow on the night of the Great Hosanna, God may have decided that this person will not live out the coming year.

On the eighth day of Tabernacles the yearly reading of the Torah is concluded and begun again in a ceremony known as the Rejoicing of the Torah (*Simchat Torah*). Two individuals, known as the bridegrooms of Torah and Genesis, respectively, are appointed in each synagogue to make blessings over the concluding and beginning of the Torah. It is a great honor to be chosen for one of these roles. During this time all of a synagogue's Torah scrolls are taken out of the ark and people dance with them, sometimes for hours, celebrating God's gift of revelation through the Torah.

Celebrating the dedication of the Temple

Two months after the end of Tabernacles, usually falling around Christmas time, Jews celebrate Hanukah. This festival is based on the story of the Maccabean revolt, which took place in the second century BCE after the Seleucid rulers of Palestine seized the Jewish Temple and used it as a sanctuary for their own gods. The Maccabees, who led the uprising, soon recaptured Jerusalem and rededicated the Temple to the worship of God.

It is this dedication (*hanukah*) that is celebrated at the festival. Rabbinic traditions convey the story of how, when the Temple was recaptured, the priests found only one container of oil still sanctified with the high priest's seal. When this was used to fill the seven lamps of the Temple lamp stand (*menorah*), it miraculously burned for eight days. To celebrate and take part in this miracle, contemporary Jews light small lamps or candles on a nine-branched candle stand over an eight-day period, lighting one branch on the first night, two on the second, and so forth, the middle branch (the ninth) being used to light the others. By focusing on the incidental story of the jar of oil, rather than the Maccabean military victory, the emphasis is placed on divine intervention. It is customary to eat foods cooked in oil on Hanukah, to give children gifts of special festival money (*Hanukah gelt*), and to gamble with this money using a four-sided top (*dreidel*), on which are printed the Hebrew letters of the acronym for "there was a great miracle there."

Casting lots

Two-and-a-half months after Hanukah comes the festival of Purim, a one-day carnival that reenacts and celebrates events from the biblical Book of Esther. In this story, the Jews of Persia are saved from a plot to destroy them devised by a wicked official in the king's court named Haman. Being not only wicked but arrogant, Haman casts lots (*purim*) to decide what day is best for their annihilation. A striking aspect of Esther is that God is never mentioned directly. Rather, the heroes of the narrative are the beautiful and resourceful Esther, who becomes queen of Persia, and her cousin Mordecai, who suggests that God may be working behind the scenes.

As a way of aligning themselves with this hidden God during Purim, Jews put on fanciful costumes to act out the message that things are not always what they seem. Rabbis even allow men to dress as women and vice versa—which is normally prohibited—and suggest that people should get drunk to the point where they can no longer tell the difference between "blessed is Mordecai" and "cursed is Haman." In the synagogue liturgy, the entire Book of Esther is read aloud from its own handwritten scroll, and whenever the name of the villain Haman is pronounced, the participants boo and make other disruptive noises to fulfil the biblical saying that "the name of the wicked rots" (Proverbs 10:7 JPSTT). Finally, giving gifts of food to at least one friend, and charity to at least two persons in need is prescribed on Purim.

Passover

Next in the Jewish calendar is the festival of **Passover** (or *Pesach*), which commemorates God's redemption of the Israelites from Egyptian slavery. This usually falls four weeks after Purim. During this festival, Jews do not eat regular bread made with yeast or other rising agents, but unleavened, crisp bread known as ***matzah***. This was the bread of slaves and the bread that was baked quickly when the Israelites hurried out of Egypt. In preparation for Passover, all leavening products are removed from the home, and the kitchen is thoroughly cleansed in a process known as kashering, which usually involves washing or immersing items in boiling water, or heating cooking vessels to a red heat.

On the first night of Passover a family gathers for the ***Seder***, a meal of various ritual foods, including *matzah*, bitter herbs (usually horseradish or lettuce), and a dipping paste made of nuts, wine, and spices. Eating these, a family relives the harsh life of the Israelite slaves. Then, to celebrate their liberation from slavery, family members drink four cups of wine or grape juice. During the course of the meal, stories of the Israelites in Egypt, the Ten Plagues brought by God on Pharaoh, and the Israelite Exodus through the desert are read and sung from a special text called the *haggadah* (not to be confused with *aggadah*). As opposed to the Torah tradition, the *haggadah* focuses almost entirely on God's activity during the Exodus. The great prophet and liberator Moses merits only one passing reference.

Pentecost

Seven weeks, or 49 days after Passover, the festival known as Pentecost ("fifty") or Weeks (*Shavuot*) celebrates the giving of the Ten Commandments to Moses at Mount Sinai. Many Jews stay awake the night of Pentecost, studying the Torah in preparation to receive it once again. On Pentecost day, synagogues are decorated with flowers and greenery, following the rabbinic account that Mount Sinai burst into flowers with the revelation of the Torah, and the Ten Commandments are read aloud from the book of Exodus. It is customary to eat milk and cheese dishes on Pentecost in imitation of the first Israelites to receive the Torah, who are said to have kept all the dietary laws it contained. Since it was quite complicated to eat meat products under these laws, the Israelites ate only dairy at the beginning.

Dietary laws

Many regulations govern the preparation and consumption of food in Judaism, conveying the Jewish belief that eating, which is among the most basic of human acts, can strengthen or weaken one's relationship to God. For this reason, the rabbinic tradition regards the dining table as an altar, and the rituals associated with eating as a quasi-sacrificial offering. Different ritual practices are mandated before and after meals depending on what major food groups are eaten. For example, before eating bread, diners must ritually wash their hands; and when a bread-based meal is over, a long grace is recited or sung.

An extensive *halakhic* analysis designates certain foods as edible and others as inedible, the word for edible being **kosher**. For example, fish are kosher only if they have both fins and scales. While most common species of fish meet these criteria, shrimp, scallops, oysters, and calamari can never be eaten, and catfish and swordfish are in dispute among rabbis because their scales are so different from those of other fish. Kosher foods must also be prepared in certain ways. For example, an animal such as a cow or sheep must be killed by cutting through its windpipe in a single, smooth motion. Then its carcass is examined for serious defects in its vital organs, which would render it inedible. For the hindquarters to be kosher, certain sinews and fats must be removed, a practice call porging. Otherwise, the hindquarters must be cut away completely and not sold on the kosher market.

Dietary laws make it particularly clear that Jews cannot eat blood, because it is thought to contain an animal's life. The blood of every animal, including birds, is consequently drained after it is killed, and the animal is cut into pieces that are washed and salted with a coarse salt ("kosher salt") to draw out additional blood. Finally, the meat is drained and washed a second time to remove any remaining loose blood. The alternative to this method is to sprinkle the meat with salt and grill it on an open flame.

Apart from the many restrictions that Jewish dietary laws place on the types of food that are kosher, and on its preparation, there are special limitations on cooking and eating meat and milk products. This comes from the thrice-repeated biblical commandment, "You shall not boil a kid in its mother's milk," which was interpreted by rabbis to be a prohibition against cooking meat with dairy products, eating such a dish, or "deriving any benefit" from it. There is also *halakhah* that prohibits eating milk products and meat together in one meal, even if they were cooked separately. Instead, Jews must observe a waiting period between meat and milk dishes, ranging from one to six hours. Even different plates and utensils are sometimes used for milk products and meat. Orthodox Jews keep this division so strictly that they have separate sinks for washing up, and sometimes separate dishwashing machines.

It is especially in the area of diet that the various types of Judaism distinguish themselves. Conservative Jews and many Modern-Orthodox Jews, for instance, keep some but not all the dietary laws, while Reform Jews regard all dietary laws as belonging to the past and not relevant to the spiritual condition of modern Jews. Ultra-Orthodox Jews, in turn, insist on food that is produced under the supervision of an eminent rabbi, and often demand that meat be extra, or "smooth," kosher (*glatt*), which designates meat from animals that are free of even tiny lesions on the lungs.

Jewish family life

Since most Jewish practices take place in the context of family, the expectation for young people is that they find a Jewish life partner, get married, and start a family of their own. A person who remains single is considered incomplete, while having children fulfills God's commandment to "be fertile and increase." It is in the family that one develops his or her identity as a Jew and as a member of the people of Israel. Not surprisingly, the Jewish home is a sanctified place, a "little temple." In imitation of the ancient Temple, now destroyed, the *halakhah* requires that a small section of one wall in the home remain unplastered. This is still practiced in Ultra-Orthodox homes, although Jews who live in countries west of Jerusalem may simply have a plaque on the wall facing Jerusalem. This is imprinted with a stylized picture of Jerusalem and the Hebrew word for East (*mizrach*). When praying at home, they face in that direction.

The wedding ceremony

A traditional Jewish wedding ceremony is, with some variation, followed in all sections of Jewry. Before the public ceremony begins, the groom visits a room where the bride is seated in order to see her face before covering it with a veil. The purpose of this ritual is to ensure that the bride is indeed the woman he wishes to marry. It is a reenactment of what the biblical figure Jacob *should* have done—a precautionary

Figure 8.14 A *mikveh*, or ritual bath. When more water is needed, rain water is channeled through the hole that is now covered by the small wooden panel with the round handle. Source: Will Deming.

measure to avoid his mistake of marrying the wrong woman. It is also customary for Orthodox couples to bathe before the wedding in a small ritual pool called a *mikveh* (Figure 8.14).

A Closer Look

The Ritual Bath

The *mikveh* is a pool of water, often tap water, connected to a source of spring water, rainwater, or melted snow. In this way it gains the required *halakhic* status of "natural" or "living" water. Some Jews bathe in a *mikveh* just before the Day of Atonement, others bathe every Friday in preparation for the Sabbath, and Hasidic Jews bathe every morning before prayers. Among Orthodox Jews it is also used by the bride and groom before a wedding, by a married woman after her period of menstruation, for the initial cleansing of kitchen utensils that are acquired from non-Jews, and for purifying converts to Judaism.

The wedding ceremony requires a canopy (*chupah*), under which the groom stands and into which the bride is led. The canopy is the groom's "house," and so at the beginning of the wedding, the groom is the first to enter the canopy, which may be set up in the synagogue, a hall, or the open air. The latter is especially common among Ashkenazi Orthodox communities, who regard marriages inside a synagogue as too much like Christian weddings. A canopy under the heavens is also thought to engender fertility on the model of Abraham, who received God's promise that his descendants would be "as numerous as the stars in heaven." Once under the canopy, the groom faces toward Jerusalem and his bride enters, attended by members of her family or her bridesmaids. It is customary for the bride to walk around the groom, often seven times, formally establishing her arrival in his domain.

The ceremony proper begins with a blessing over a cup of wine, from which the groom and bride take a sip. The groom then gives his bride a ring in front of two witnesses who must verify that the ring belongs to the groom and that it has an "unambiguous value." For this reason, a plain band of gold or other precious metal is used, without a stone, as the true value of a precious stone is difficult to determine in such circumstances.

> **Sacred Tradition and Scripture**
>
> ### Jacob Marries the Wrong Woman
>
> Now Laban had two daughters; the name of the older one was Leah, and the name of the younger was Rachel … Jacob loved Rachel…. And Laban gathered all the people of the place and made a feast. When evening came, he took his daughter Leah and brought her to him; and he cohabited with her…. When morning came, there was Leah! So he said to Laban, "What is this you have done to me? I was in service for Rachel! Why did you deceive me?" Laban said, "It is not the practice in our place to marry off the younger before the older."
>
> Genesis 29:16–26 JPSTT

After the ring is given, it is customary to read the wedding certificate (*ketubah*) out loud. In traditional ceremonies it is read in its original Aramaic, sometimes with a translation. Following the reading, the couple takes a second cup of wine, over which seven marriage benedictions are recited. The ceremony usually ends with the groom stomping on a glass that has been wrapped in cloth or paper, an act that is greeted by cries of "good luck!" (*mazel tov*). This custom of breaking a glass arises from an account in the Talmud of a rabbi who smashed some valuable glasses at a wedding to remind those present that, despite their joy, they should never forget the destruction of the Jerusalem Temple. At some weddings the groom recites verses from Psalm 137 just before breaking the glass: "If I forget you, O Jerusalem, let my right hand wither … if I do not keep Jerusalem in memory even in my happiest hour" (JPSTT). Various folk beliefs have also grown up around the glass-breaking ritual. It is said that it symbolizes the breaking of the hymen of a virgin bride, or that if the groom fails to break the glass on his first attempt, the bride will dominate him in their life together.

Circumcision

The desire of traditional Jewish newlyweds is to have children. Although the *halakhah* states that a couple should try to have a daughter as well a son, there is generally a greater desire for sons. This reflects the androcentric nature of Judaism whereby the male's role in performing the commandments is much greater than the female's role, and in his morning prayers he acknowledges God's blessing of not making him a woman.

Rituals, Rites, Practices

Entering a Jewish Home

At the entrance to a Jewish home, one often finds a small case affixed to the doorframe containing a rolled-up parchment (Figure 8.15). The parchment is called a *mezuzah* (doorpost), and on it is a handwritten text of the first two

Figure 8.15 A jeweled and gilded *mezuzah* reading "Shalom" (peace, well-being), with a hinged door and latch, so that the parchment it contains can be checked periodically. Source: Will Deming.

(continued)

> paragraphs of the *Shema*. The homes of strict Orthodox Jews have a *mezuzah* on interior doors as well, apart from the toilet or bathroom, and they kiss the *mezuzah* at the front door when they enter and leave their homes. It is important to check the condition of the parchment every few years to ensure that the writing is still intact, and if not, it must be replaced.

If a boy is born, his parents bring him into the covenant with God through circumcision. This practice, which involves cutting away the foreskin of the boy's penis, should occur on his eighth day of life. It is performed by a trained circumciser (*mohel*), who examines the child a couple of days before the operation to determine that the child is healthy. Apart from the father, the mother, and the circumciser, certain other individuals are assigned roles in the ceremony. The boy is brought from his mother into the place of circumcision by his godparents, a married couple known among Ashkenazi Jews as *kvaters*. It is customary to choose a couple who themselves do not yet have children, since acting as godparents is thought to promote conception. In the ceremony, the godmother takes the boy from his mother as the congregation proclaims, "Blessed be he who comes." She then hands him to the godfather, who brings him to the circumciser.

The person who holds the child on his lap during the operation is the **sandek**. This is usually a grandfather or the local rabbi. To act as a *sandek* is considered a great *mitzvah* (good deed), equivalent to offering up an incense sacrifice to God. If the *sandek* is worthy, it is expected that the prophet Elijah will attend the circumcision. According to Kabbalists, serving as a *sandek* atones for having "sinned with one's thighs" in an illicit sexual relationship. In addition to his role in the ceremony, the *sandek* becomes someone to whom the boy can later turn for help or advice, a kind of patron or honorary uncle. It is not customary for a woman to act as the *sandek* when an able man is present. When the child is placed on the *sandek*'s lap, the circumciser says a benediction and cuts away the foreskin as the father says another benediction. Those in attendance respond with the words, "Just as he enters the covenant, so may he enter the worlds of Torah, the wedding canopy, and good deeds."

Growing up

In many Orthodox families a male child does not have his hair cut until he is three years old. The most popular occasion for this haircut is a minor festival that falls between Passover and Pentecost, at which guests are given the opportunity to cut off a lock of hair. The sideburns, however, are always left untouched in fulfillment of the biblical command, "You shall not round off the side-growth on your head, or destroy the side-growth of your beard." In many Orthodox communities, after the boy's haircut, he begins to learn Hebrew and wear the tasseled undergarment (*tzitzit*).

Adulthood for Jewish children begins at puberty, traditionally 13 for a boy and 12 for a girl. At these ages they become responsible for keeping all of God's commandments. After their initiation into adulthood, a boy is known as a **bar mitzvah**, or "son

Figure 8.16 A girl reads from the Torah at her *bat mitzvah*, using a gilded, silver reading pointer. Source: Reproduced by permission of Paul W. Rizzo Photography.

of the commandment," and a girl as a **bat mitzvah**, or "daughter of the commandment." The initiation ceremony for boys, which is also called *bar mitzvah*, requires a boy to make a blessing over a section of the Torah during a synagogue service (see the chapter-opening photo). Usually, he also reads the Torah passage for that week, and possibly a section from the Prophets. To prepare for this, a boy must begin practicing his Torah passage weeks or months beforehand learning to read it correctly and with the proper tonal pitches. The *bat mitzvah*, for girls, is largely modeled after the *bar mitzvah* (Figure 8.16), although in Ultra-Orthodox communities there is no public ceremony.

The afterlife

The bodily resurrection of the dead, mentioned in the biblical book of Daniel, is regarded in early rabbinic literature as an essential part of Jewish faith. It is envisioned as a reunion of body and soul that takes place in the messianic age. In the synagogue liturgy, belief in resurrection is part of the standing prayer (*amidah*), which is included in every service:

> You are mighty for eternity, O Lord, bringing the dead back to life. You are great to save…. You revive the dead with great mercy … and keep faith with those that sleep in the dust…. Blessed are You who revives the dead.

As an alternative to resurrection, many Jews believe in a disembodied afterlife, called "the world to come." In this scenario, the souls of the righteous exist in the heavenly Garden of Eden, while the souls of the wicked are punished in a place called *Gehinnom*. Belief in the disembodied afterlife plays a greater role among modern Jews than the idea of the resurrection, and Reform Judaism rejects resurrection altogether as antiquated and contrary to modern science. A third possibility is reincarnation, which has its roots in Kabbalah and is endorsed by Hasidic and many Sephardi Jews. It is not popular among other Jews, however, with the exception of those who are influenced by New Age teachings, who accept both reincarnation and the teachings of Kabbalah as truths that open the way for a dialog with Buddhism and Hinduism.

A Closer Look

Idolatry and the Visual Arts

The creation of visual arts in Judaism has been limited due to the biblical injunction against the carving of images for use as idols, which the rabbinic tradition applies to *all* graphic and three-dimensional art forms. Consequently there is no strong tradition of drawing, painting, or sculpture in Jewish cultural history. An important exception to this rule has been the creation of objects for ritual use, often in precious or semiprecious metals. These include spice boxes, candlesticks, reading pointers (*yad*; see Figure 8.17), and synagogue furnishings. Also included is a category of ornaments used to decorate the Torah scroll. These consist of cloth coverings, (known as mantels), breastplates, and a crown or two pomegranates (finials) to cover the staves at the top of a scroll.

Figure 8.17 A fanciful *yad* on its ornate carrying case. Source: Will Deming.

Burial

Most Jews bury their dead, which is in line with the biblical view that a human being "comes from the dust and returns to the dust." Kabbalists and others believe that this is a necessary preparation for the resurrection of the dead. Reform Jews, by contrast, practice cremation, but this is highly criticized in Orthodox circles, and many rabbis will neither officiate at a cremation nor allow any mourning rituals for someone who has been cremated.

According to Orthodox Jews, a dead body, before burial, should never be left alone. This not only honors the dead, but also prevents evil spirits from attaching themselves to the deceased. While some Orthodox communities still rely on semiprofessional watchers who recite psalms over the body until the funeral, others are content with the secure conditions of a morgue; non-Orthodox Jews do not follow any of these practices. Before burial, the body is washed and dressed in a white shroud (*kittle*) by members of a voluntary burial society known as the Holy Fellowship. A man's prayer shawl (*tallit*) is buried with him, but its fringes (*tzitzit*) are cut off because the man can no longer keep the commandments. This is also the reason that men tuck in their *tzitzit* when they visit a cemetery, so as not to mock the dead.

CONCLUSION

Jews see themselves as a holy people guided by their covenant with God. This covenant is known to them through Torah, and its good works (*mitzvot*) extend into all areas of life. Since Judaism puts such great emphasis on the ritual side of life, preferring concrete practices over abstract theologies, American Jews have more in common culturally and ideologically with other Americans than with, say, Italian Jews. But when it comes to ritual and personal lifestyle, they share many things: prayers, dietary laws, and Sabbath rituals; attitudes toward life and death; values associated with family and children; an appreciation for Torah study; a common religious calendar; hopes of messianic redemption and a return to Zion; and a sense of destiny as God's Chosen People. Given the many persecutions and expulsions that mark Jewish history, moreover, many believe that it is precisely this ritual structure of Jewish life that has preserved Jewish identity. As the modern Zionist thinker Ahad Ha-Am said: "More than the Jews have kept the Sabbath, the Sabbath has kept the Jews."

For review

1. In what ways can Judaism be seen as the religion of a particular ethnic group?
2. How did the destruction of the Jewish Temple, both in 586 BCE and in 70 CE, change the course of Judaism?
3. What are the meanings of "Torah" in Judaism?
4. What is the relation between Torah, Tanak, and Talmud?
5. Give an instance of how Jews interact with God by participating in the events of sacred scripture with great figures of Israel's past.
6. Provide some examples of how the three principal branches of Judaism, Orthodox, Reform, and Conservative, differ in belief and practice?
7. List several ways in which Jews use the Torah in synagogue services.
8. What are some ways in which purity and impurity are defined in Judaism?
9. List some of the rules for preparing food to be kosher.
10. How do Jews envision an afterlife?

For discussion

1. How are politics and religion related in Judaism? Is it possible for Jews to observe a separation of "church and state"?
2. What is the Jewish notion of salvation?

Key Terms

Abraham	A man whose covenant with God marks the beginning of the Jewish people, who are Abraham's descendants.
aggadah	Nonlegal Jewish traditions (see *halakhah*); to be distinguished from *haggadah*, which is a text used at Passover.

antisemitism	A form of anti-Judaism based on the spurious belief that Jewish identity can be determined by a person's DNA.
Ark of the Covenant	A wooden chest covered in gold and adorned with images of heavenly beings; used for communication with God.
Ashkenazim	Jews who trace their roots to Christian host communities in eastern Europe.
Baal Shem Tov	The title given to the founder of the Hasidic movement, meaning "Master of the Good Name."
bar and *bat mitzvah*	"Son/Daughter of the Commandment"; the Jewish rite of initiation into adulthood for boys and girls, respectively; also the titles of those initiated.
bimah	A raised platform in a synagogue from which the Torah is read and the worship service is directed.
Conservative Judaism	A branch of Judaism that understands the Torah as an authoritative expression of ancient Israel's response to God's call, and the Talmud as an important but not definitive guide to matters regulating Jewish religious life (see Orthodox and Reform Judaism).
covenant	A binding agreement made between God and an individual or group of people.
Diaspora	A term for Jews living outside the land that God promised to Abraham.
Exodus	The departure of the Israelites from Egypt under the leadership of Moses.
halakhah	Jewish religious law and legal traditions.
Hasidic movement	A popular movement in Judaism that emphasizes personal piety and joy in human relations, making God accessible through the practice of "cleaving to God."
Holocaust	"Burnt offering"; a term for the murder of millions of Jewish civilians by the Nazis during World War II (see *Shoah*).
Israel	"Struggles with God"; the name given to Jacob, the grandson of Abraham, which later became the name for the the ancient and modern Jewish nation.
Kabbalah	The Jewish mystical tradition.
kosher	A designation for food that is edible according to *halakhah*.
matzah	A crisp, unleavened bread eaten during Passover.
messiah	Hebrew for "anointed one"; usually a king, but also a priest or a kingly person in the service of God; most Jews hold that a messiah will appear in the future.
mikveh	A small pool for ritual bathing.
Mishnah	The earliest work of rabbinic literature, a legal compendium from the early third century CE.
mitzvot	Both "commandments" and "good deeds"; plural of *mitzvah*; actions prescribed by God in the Torah.

Modern-Orthodox	A version of Orthodox Judaism that favors some accommodations to modern life.
Moses	The Israelite prophet who led the Exodus and to whom God revealed the commandments of the Torah.
Orthodox Judaism	A branch of Judaism that regards the Torah as divinely revealed truth, and the Talmud as sacred and authoritative (see Conservative and Reform Judaism).
Passover	The annual commemoration of God's redemption of the Israelites from Egyptian slavery.
prophet	A spokesperson for God, inspired by God's Spirit.
rabbi	The teacher, pastor, and leader of a Jewish community; usually a scholar of Torah and rabbinic literature.
Reform Judaism	A branch of Judaism that understands the Torah as an authoritative but not definitive guide to religion, and the Talmud as having only marginal importance (see Orthodox and Conservative Judaism).
Sabbath	The day of the week on which work is prohibited, beginning Friday evening and concluding Saturday evening.
sandek	A grandfather or rabbi who holds a male baby on his lap during circumcision.
Seder	The Passover meal.
Sephardim	Jews who trace their roots to Spain.
Shema	A statement of faith from the Torah, recited as part of morning and evening prayers.
Shoah	"Destruction"; a name for the Holocaust currently preferred by many Jews.
Shulchan Arukh	The definitive compendium of the Jewish *halakhic* code, published in 1565 and expanded to its final form in the following decades.
synagogue	A building where Jews meet for worship, containing a *bimah* and a handwritten, leather Torah scroll.
tallit	A prayer shawl with tassels at its corners, made according to *halakhic* specifications.
Talmud	A compendium of rabbinic teachings compiled in the fifth and sixth centuries CE; it exists in a Jerusalem and a Babylonian version, the latter being considered authoritative.
Tanak	A designation for the Jewish scriptures; an acronym created from the Hebrew words for Torah, Prophets, and Writings.
tefillin	Small black leather boxes containing passages from the Torah that are strapped to the arm and forehead during morning prayer.
Torah	"Teaching, tradition"; the first five books of the Tanak.
Torah ark	An ornate cabinet that holds one or more Torah scrolls, usually placed at the front of the sanctuary in a synagogue.

tzitzit	The tassels on the four corners of a *tallit* (prayer shawl); also a fringed undergarment.
Ultra-Orthodox	A version of Orthodox Judaism that favors a strict application of biblical and Talmudic teachings.
Yom Kippur	The Day of Atonement, which comes on the tenth day of the new year.
Zionism	A nineteenth- and twentieth-century nationalistic movement that lobbied for a politically autonomous Jewish homeland.
Zohar	The *Book of Splendor*, an important work of medieval Jewish mysticism.

Bibliography

A good first book
Oliver Leaman. *Judaism: An Introduction*. London: I.B. Tauris, 2011.

Further reading
Martin Goodman. *A History of Judaism*. Princeton and Oxford: Princeton University Press, 2018.
Eliezer Segal. *Introducing Judaism*. New York: Routledge, 2009.
Jack Wertheimer. *The New American Judaism: How Jews Practice Their Religion Today*. Princeton, NJ: Princeton University Press, 2018.

Reference and research
Encyclopaedia Judaica, Rev. edn. Jerusalem: Keter, 2006.
Simone Gigliotti and Berel Lang, eds. *The Holocaust: A Reader*. Maiden, MA: Blackwell, 2005.
Steven T. Katz, ed. *The Cambridge Companion to Antisemitism*. Cambridge: Cambridge University Press, 2022.
Byron L. Sherwin. *Kabbalah: An Introduction to Jewish Mysticism*. Lanham, MD: Rowman and Littlefield, 2006.
Michael Tilly and Burton L. Visotzky, eds. *Judaism*, 3 vols. Stuttgart: W. Kohlhammer, 2021.
Adele Berlin and Marc Zvi Brettler, eds. *The Jewish Study Bible*. New York: Oxford University Press, 2004.
Milton Viorst. *Zionism: The Birth and Transformation of an Ideal*. New York: St. Martin's Press, 2016.

CHAPTER 9

Christianity
Salvation through Jesus Christ

A Gothic altarpiece at Washington National Cathedral in Washington, DC, showing various events in the life of Jesus, whom it calls "the Way the Truth and the Life" (quoting the Gospel of John). Source: Will Deming.

DID YOU KNOW …

The eucharist is a ritual in which Christians eat a stylized meal of bread and wine. Most Christians believe that Christ's risen body and blood are physically present in the bread and wine once they have been consecrated. These Christians typically drink all the wine and store any remaining bread in a safe place so as not to dishonor Christ's body.

Understanding the Religions of the World: An Introduction, Second Edition.
Edited by Will Deming.
© 2025 John Wiley & Sons Ltd. Published 2025 by John Wiley & Sons Ltd.

OVERVIEW

Christianity is the world's largest religion, encompassing almost one-third of the world's population, or around 2.6 billion people. Its adherents worship the God of the Jewish and Christian scriptures and call themselves **Christians**, meaning followers of Christ. They believe that God is accessible to all human beings through the death and resurrection of **Jesus of Nazareth**, a first-century Jewish teacher and healer who lived in what is now northern Israel. Although Jesus was put to death as a criminal by Roman and Jewish authorities, Christians believe that he rose from the dead after three days and is the savior of the world. They consider him both the **Christ** (anointed king) who was promised in the Hebrew Bible, and God's very own son.

Motivated by their belief in Jesus as the savior of all humankind, Christians have spread their religion throughout the world. Today about 28 percent of all Christians live in Africa, and about 23 percent live in Latin America. Europe accounts for another 21 percent, Asia for about 16 percent, and Northern America for about 10 percent (Figure 9.1).

In Latin America and Africa, where the religion continues to expand, Christians constitute 88 percent and 51 percent of the total populations, respectively. In Europe and Northern America, by contrast, the percentage of people who identify as Christian has been declining. In the United States, for example, surveys show that Christian affiliation decreased 15 percent between 2007 and 2021. Globally, however, the percentage of people who are Christian is expected to remain constant for the next several decades.

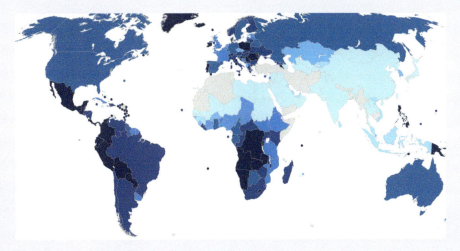

Figure 9.1 A map indicating the Christian population of different countries as a percentage of each country's total population. Source: Wikimedia Commons.

Varieties of Christianity

Christians belong to a worldwide community, or **church**, which is a single fellowship of believers. But since Christians are also divided into various **denominations**, they disagree on who belongs in this worldwide church. Some of their differences derive from regional and cultural variations, but the three main divisions of Christianity differ over basic questions of who leads the church and how Christians relate to God through these leaders.

> **Talking about Religion**
>
> ### The Many Meanings of "Church"
>
> Christians use the term "church" to refer to many things, including the fellowship of all Christians throughout the world, a localized gathering or association, and even the building used for worship. In addition, most localized churches (also called congregations), are part of regional, national, or international denominations, which can also be called churches. For example, the Idlewild Presbyterian Church in midtown Memphis, Tennessee, is part of the Presbyterian Church (USA). There are literally hundreds of denominations. Denominations popular in the United States include the Roman Catholic Church, the Southern Baptist Convention, the Assemblies of God, the United Methodist Church, the Orthodox Church in America, the Lutheran Church–Missouri Synod, and the Church of God in Christ.

The largest division is the **Roman Catholic** Church, accounting for more than half of all Christians, or 1.31 billion people. This church, also known simply as the Catholic Church, is governed by celibate men called **bishops**, who oversee other celibate men called **priests**. Women and married men are excluded from these positions of authority. The most important bishop is the bishop of Rome, who has supreme authority over the church. Known as the **pope**, he is seen as Christ's chief representative and spokesman on earth. In consultation with other bishops and the laity, the pope determines God's will based on scripture and longstanding Catholic traditions. Other authority figures in Catholicism include the saints, who are deceased men and women now communing with God in heaven.

Eastern Orthodox Christians constitute around 11 percent of Christianity, or 290 million people. Like Roman Catholics, they maintain that God draws close to human beings through the mediation of church officials and saints. They do not, however, require celibacy of their priests, nor do they acknowledge the pope as the supreme authority. Instead, the Orthodox Church is led by celibate male bishops who preside over several national and regional churches, most of whom recognize the head of the church in Constantinople (Istanbul) as the "first among equals." Several other churches are connected to the Orthodox tradition through historical associations, but are no longer in communion with it. These include Eastern-Rite Catholics, who accept the authority of the pope, and the churches of Oriental Orthodox Christianity, who understand the humanity and divinity of Christ in a different way.

The third major division of Christianity is **Protestantism**. Numbering around 950 million people, it represents about 36 percent of all Christians. Following the teachings of Martin Luther and other sixteenth-century reformers, Protestants hold that Christians can establish communion with God without the aid of bishops, priests, or saints. For them the Bible is the supreme religious authority. But since Protestants have never agreed on a common interpretation of the Bible, they have divided themselves into hundreds of separate denominations with differing beliefs and practices.

Aside from Catholic, Orthodox, and Protestant Christians, there are also about 90 million Anglican Christians who belong to a tradition begun by the Church of England. While some Anglicans consider themselves Protestants, others see themselves as having more in common with Catholics, and still others claim to be following a middle way between the two. Another 35 million Christians hold beliefs that place them somewhere on the margins of the Christian tradition. These include Mormons, Unitarians, Jehovah's Witnesses, Seventh-day Adventists, and Christian Scientists.

The type of Christianity found in a particular area varies widely (Figure 9.2). Some nations, such as Poland, are mostly Catholic, while others, such as Greece, are mostly Orthodox. In North America, where more varieties of Christianity are practiced than anywhere else, Protestants outnumber Catholics two to one, while most countries in Latin America are overwhelmingly Catholic.

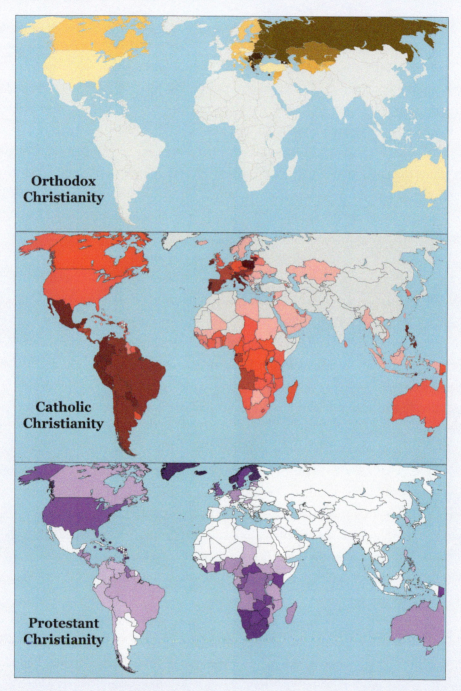

Figure 9.2 Maps showing the locations and relative population densities of the three largest divisions within Christianity. Source: Wikimedia Commons.

History

Timeline	
end of 1st century BCE	The birth of Jesus of Nazareth.
ca. 29–31 CE	Jesus' ministry and crucifixion.
ca. 45–65 CE	The apostle Paul's missionary activities.
2nd–4th century CE	The appearance of Gnosticism, early creeds, and widespread martyrdom.
3rd–4th centuries CE	The appearance of monasticism.
313 CE	The emperor Constantine legalizes Christianity in the Roman empire.
325 CE	Constantine convenes the Council of Nicaea.
330 CE	Constantinople is founded as the center for Christianity in the east.
590–604 CE	The papacy of Gregory the Great.
8th century	The iconoclastic controversy.
early 10th century	Cluny reforms begin.
11th century	Gregorian reforms begin.
1054	The Great Schism.
11th–13th centuries	The Crusades, the Scholastic movement, and the appearance of mendicant orders of monks and nuns.
14th–15th centuries	The papal schism leads to Avignon popes.
15th–16th centuries	European colonization and missions begin.
16th century	The Protestant Reformation; the establishment of the Church of England (Anglican church); the Catholic Reformation.
16th–17th centuries	Religious wars ravage Europe.
18th century	Christianity enters the modern period; appearance of liberalism and Evangelicalism.
1869–1870	The First Vatican Council.
early 20th century	The appearance of the Pentecostal movement and fundamentalism.
mid-20th century	The ecumenical movement promotes cooperation among different denominations.
1960s	The Second Vatican Council; the appearance of Liberation Theology.
end of 20th century	The expansion of Christianity in the Global South.

The Christian religion appeared shortly before the close of an important era in Judaism. This era began in 586 BCE with the Babylonian destruction of the first Jewish temple and it ended in 70 CE with the Roman destruction of the second Jewish temple. During these six-and-a-half centuries, several new types of Judaism appeared both inside and outside of the Jewish homeland, developing new ways of envisioning God and salvation. Christianity was one of these new types of Judaism, but soon broke ties with the mother religion over assertions about its founder, Jesus of Nazareth, and its belief in a universal mission.

Jesus of Nazareth

Christianity began in the Roman province of Palestine—roughly the land of modern Israel—around 31 CE. Shortly before then, an apocalyptic prophet called John appeared in central Palestine near the Jordan River and announced that God was about to interact with the world in a new way. The "kingdom of God" was coming and people needed to prepare for God's reign by repenting of their sins and undergoing a ritual cleansing, an immersion in water called **baptism**. One of the people who came to John was Jesus of Nazareth. After his baptism, Jesus returned to his home in northern Palestine, where he began his own prophetic ministry.

A Closer Look

Miracles and Parables

The gospels, which contain our earliest reports of Jesus' ministry, present Jesus as performing miracles and teaching in **parables** (comparisons of various kinds). Some of the miracles he performed were exorcisms, by which he removed unclean spirits from people. Below is an exorcism and a parable from the Gospel of Mark.

An exorcism:

> Just then there was in their synagogue a man with an unclean spirit, and he cried out, "What have you to do with us, Jesus of Nazareth? Have you come to destroy us? I know who you are, the Holy One of God." But Jesus rebuked him, saying, "Be silent, and come out of him!" And the unclean spirit, convulsing him and crying with a loud voice, came out of him.
>
> Mark 1:23–26: New Revised Standard Version (NRSV)

(continued)

> A parable:
>
> He also said, "The kingdom of God is as if someone would scatter seed on the ground, and would sleep and rise night and day, and the seed would sprout and grow, he does not know how. The earth produces of itself, first the stalk, then the head, then the full grain in the head. But when the grain is ripe, at once he goes in with his sickle, because the harvest has come."
>
> Mark 4:26–29 NRSV

For the next two or three years Jesus traveled through the villages and cities of Palestine, teaching in parables and performing miracles, miraculous healings, and exorcisms. His ministry ended when he was arrested in Jerusalem on charges of violating Jewish law and encouraging sedition against the Roman empire. Shortly thereafter, he was put to death by **crucifixion**, a humiliating process of torture and execution that was reserved for Rome's worst criminals. Persons were tied or nailed to a giant wooden cross and left to die of exhaustion and asphyxiation as they struggled to hold themselves upright to breathe.

While Jesus' followers disbanded after his death, they soon regrouped, claiming that his crucifixion had established a new relationship between God and humanity. For them, Jesus had shown himself to be God's Christ by voluntarily dying to save the world. Furthermore, his followers claimed that Jesus was both divine and God's own son. Although he had died, his heavenly father had raised him from the dead. Jesus now lived in a glorious, imperishable body and commanded a position of authority in the cosmos second only to God the Father. He would return soon to punish evil doers and to reward his followers with eternal life in the presence of God. In the meantime, God had given Jesus' followers the **Holy Spirit**, to guide and encourage them, and to supply them with spiritual gifts such as the ability to heal, speak in unknown languages, and prophesy.

Talking about Religion

Jesus the Christ

The title Christ is from the Greek word for "anointed one" (*christos*). It refers to a ceremony in ancient Judaism in which priests and kings were anointed with oil at their installation. Thereafter they would be known as God's anointed one, the Hebrew for which is *messiah*. After the Davidic monarchy fell in the sixth century BCE, Jewish prophets began to speak of a future king who would

(continued)

> bring salvation to God's people, envisioned as either a military or spiritual leader. In early Christianity, this expected messiah was identified with another figure spoken of by these prophets, namely God's servant who would suffer to redeem Israel. Thus, after his crucifixion, Jesus became the *suffering* messiah, and Christians claimed that Jesus' death was God's way of bringing salvation to the whole world.

Christianity to the end of the first century

By about 50 CE, Christians had spread as far west as Rome. Their practice of worship included fellowship with one another, prayer, baptism, and the **eucharist**. In fellowship they sought to imitate the love Jesus had shown for them by suffering on the cross; in prayer they communicated with God through Jesus' divine authority; and in baptism and the eucharist they participated in Jesus' crucifixion and resurrection. In the eucharist, Christians ate Jesus' body and drank his blood in a stylized meal, and in baptism they died to their former lives and were raised to a new life in the imperishable body of Christ, which they identified as the church.

The foremost leaders of the early church were the apostles (emissaries) Jesus had chosen during his ministry, Simon Peter being chief among them. The title apostle was soon applied to others as well, including the very active and influential Paul of Tarsus. Paul was an observant Jew and scholar of the Torah who had persecuted Christians until the resurrected Christ appeared to him in a vision. Thereafter, Paul traveled through northern Mediterranean cities proclaiming Jesus as savior, converting non-Jews to Christianity, and founding churches. Eventually he traveled to Rome in the hope of taking his message of good news, or **gospel**, as far as Spain.

Sometime between the late 40s and mid-60s CE, Paul wrote letters to several of his churches to encourage new converts and clarify his message. In this same period, other Christians passed on accounts of Jesus' deeds and teachings, which were later collected and used in narratives of Jesus' ministry called gospels. Over the next several centuries, four of these gospels, Paul's letters, and several other early Christian writings, were codified as scripture and used alongside the Jewish scripture. To distinguish these two bodies of scripture, Christians referred to the latter as the Old Testament and the former as the New Testament, thereby naming the two main parts of the Bible.

Early divisions

In the second century, an influential Christian leader named Marcion taught that the creator God of the Old Testament was a completely different God than the God of the New Testament. Other Christians, known as Gnostics, held similar views. They proposed that Jesus was a purely spiritual being who had never really taken on a human body, and that he had given his disciples secret knowledge (*gnosis*) that enabled them to escape the defilement of the physical, created world.

Sacred Traditions and Scripture

The *Revelation of Adam*

In the *Revelation of Adam*, a Gnostic text found in Nag Hammadi, Egypt (Figure 9.3), the first man explains that he and his wife Eve were originally superior to the creator god, having the glory of the *true* god. This changed, however, when the creator god made them follow his moral commandments (the Mosaic law). They were reduced to slaves, and their knowledge of the true god was taken from them.

Figure 9.3 A map showing the location of Nag Hammadi, a town in modern Egypt where a small library of formerly unknown Gnostic writings was found in 1945.

The revelation that Adam taught his son Seth in the seven hundredth year, saying, "Listen to my utterances, my son Seth! After god had made me of earth, along with Eve your mother, I used to go about with her in glory.... And we resembled the great eternal angels. For we were superior to the god who had made us and to the powers that are with him. ...

"Next, god ... angrily gave us a command. Next ... the glory that was in our hearts—your mother Eve's and mine—left us. ...

"After those days, eternal acquaintance with the god of truth became distant from your mother Eve and me. From that time on, we learned about mortal affairs, like human beings.

(continued)

> "Next, we became acquainted with the god that made us. ... And we served him in fear and servility. And after this, we became dark in our hearts."
>
> Bentley Layton, trans., *The Gnostic Scriptures*, (New York: Doubleday, 1987), pp. 55–56.

Many Christian leaders regarded these teachings as falsehoods that threatened Christian salvation. They responded by circulating short summaries of theology they considered to be true, called **creeds**, which they recited especially at baptisms (see Figure 9.4). Among the oldest of these summaries is the Apostles' Creed, which is still recited in churches today. Central to the position of these Christians was the claim that proper authority in the church belonged to the reigning bishops. These were Christian leaders who had been consecrated by earlier bishops who could trace their authority back to the first apostles. In the absence of Jesus, this succession of bishops was to oversee the church's theology and its other leaders.

Figure 9.4 Beginning in the second or third century, Christians used the drawing of a fish to express their beliefs. The Greek word for fish is ICHTHUS, which was used as an acronym for the short creed: "Jesus Christ, Son of God and Savior." Source: Will Deming.

Sacred Traditions and Scripture

The Apostles' Creed

I believe in God, the Father almighty,
Creator of heaven and earth,
and in Jesus Christ, his only Son,
our Lord,
who was conceived by the Holy Spirit,
born of the Virgin Mary,
suffered under Pontius Pilate,
was crucified, died and was buried;
he descended into hell;
on the third day he rose again from the dead;
he ascended into heaven,
and is seated at the right hand

(continued)

> of God the Father almighty;
> from there he will come to judge
> the living and the dead.
> I believe in the Holy Spirit,
> the holy catholic Church,
> the communion of saints,
> the forgiveness of sins,
> the resurrection of the body,
> and life everlasting. Amen.
>
> From the *Roman Missal*, https://www.usccb.org/prayers/apostles-creed, accessed 04.01.23

Martyrs and saints

From the first century to the early fourth, the Roman empire occasionally persecuted Christians for failing to honor the Roman gods. The problem was that Christians, like Jews, were monotheists who could only worship their own god. While Romans usually tolerated Judaism, because it was an ancient tradition, they insisted that the members of the new Christian religion offer sacrifices to their gods out of loyalty to the empire. When Christians refused, Roman officials sometimes condemned them to death in public spectacles. On these occasions, their fellow Christians regarded them as martyrs who "witnessed" (Greek, *martureo*) their faith in Christ by reenacting his sacrificial death with their own lives. Soon, Christians began venerating the graves of martyrs and praying to them for help, for by dying in this way martyrs had become saints, which gave them the ability to intercede with God on behalf of others. Over time, Christians who displayed exceptional dedication to Christ in ways other than martyrdom were also venerated as saints.

A Closer Look

Roman Persecution of Christians

Below are excerpts from a letter written in the early second century by the Roman governor of Bithynia (present-day northern Turkey), Pliny the Younger, to the Emperor Trajan (r. 98–117). In it Pliny asks what sort of measures, if any, he should take against Christians in his jurisdiction.

Pliny to the Emperor Trajan:

> Having never been present at a trial of the Christians, I am unacquainted with the method and limits to be observed either in examining or punishing them. Whether any difference is to be made on account of age, or

(continued)

> no distinction allowed between the youngest and the oldest; whether a pardon can be granted upon repentance, or if a man has once been a Christian it avails him nothing to recant; whether the mere profession of Christianity, albeit without crimes, or only the crimes associated therewith are punishable—in all these points I am greatly doubtful. …
>
> A placard was put up, without any signature, accusing a large number of persons by name. Those who denied they were, or had ever been, Christians, who repeated after me an invocation to the gods and offered adoration to your image with wine and frankincense … and who finally cursed Christ … these I thought it proper to discharge. …
>
> I judged it necessary to extract the real truth, with the assistance of torture, from two female slaves who were styled "deaconesses." But I could discover nothing more than depraved and excessive superstition.
>
> Pliny the Younger, *Letters*, book 10, letter 96

Christianity as the imperial religion

In 313 CE, the Roman Emperor Constantine legalized Christianity, thereby ending the persecution of Christians. He and succeeding emperors functioned as protectors and benefactors of the church, financing it with government funds, appointing clergy, and enforcing orthodoxy (correct belief). In 325, Constantine invited all the bishops of the church to an official meeting, or council, at Nicaea (near Constantinople) to resolve a theological dispute about the divinity of Jesus. Some Christians led by a priest named Arius insisted that Jesus had been *created* by God out of nothing, like the angels and the rest of the universe. While Jesus was worthy to be called divine or even God, he was not God himself. Other Christians declared that Arius was spreading dangerous lies. They argued that unless Jesus was both fully human *and* fully God, he would not have been able to overcome sin and death in a way that established communion between human beings and God. The creed that was finally approved at Nicaea condemned Arius' views and defined Jesus as "the Son of God, begotten of the Father as an 'only begotten'—that is, from the substance (or essence) of the Father, God from God, Light from Light, true God from true God, begotten, not made, being of one substance (or essence) with the Father." Later expanded by the Council of Constantinople in 381, a version of this Nicene Creed is now recited every Sunday in Catholic, Anglican, and some Protestant churches, and daily during the Orthodox eucharist.

By the end of the fourth century, Christianity was the Roman empire's official religion, which brought a new splendor to the church. Church buildings were richly decorated with images of Christ and the saints, imperial pomp and ceremony was incorporated into the worship service, and many Christians even saw the emperors as leaders of an earthly kingdom of God, or Christendom. Under royal sponsorship, magnificent churches were erected at sacred locations (see Figure 9.5), including Jesus' birthplace in Bethlehem, his empty tomb (Holy Sepulcher) in Jerusalem, and Simon Peter's grave in Rome (see Figure 9.5).

Figure 9.5 Dedicated in Constantinople in 360 CE, Hagia Sophia (Holy Wisdom) became the seat of authority for the patriarch of Constantinople. The building that presently occupies the site was built between 532 and 537 CE at the direction of the Byzantine Emperor Justinian, after the original structure, as well as an earlier replacement, had been destroyed in riots. Source: David R. Bains.

Together with churches that were located near the tombs of other saints, these churches became a catalyst for pilgrimage and the veneration of sacred relics. By forsaking their day-to-day activities and traveling to these places, Christians were able to detach themselves from the world and contemplate the work of salvation accomplished by Christ and witnessed by his saints.

Leaving the world behind

In the third and early fourth century, even before the legalization of Christianity, a growing number of Christians had objected to the ease and comfort of their lives in human society. Many became monks and nuns, seeking to imitate Christ more fully by denouncing attachments to this world. Some lived alone as hermits, while others formed small communities for mutual support. They took vows of poverty, chastity, and obedience to spiritual mentors, and they pursued regimens of prayer and fasting and practiced charity, especially for weary travelers and the poor. The holiness of these monks and nuns, which manifested itself in their piety, their ordered lifestyle, and their spiritual insight, caused other Christians to seek them out for miracles and intercession with God, sometimes making financial contributions to their work. It was through the practices of these monks and nuns that a Christian tradition of mysticism arose, which used constant prayer and acts of self-denial to achieve an experience of union with God. Drawing on metaphors found in scripture, especially in the Song of Songs, some spoke of God as a divine lover, using erotic language to describe their longing for God or union with him.

> ### A Closer Look
>
> ### Mystical Union with God
>
> In this passage from *On Divine Names*, attributed to Dionysius the Areopagite (late fifth to early sixth centuries), the author contrasts the physical worship of God with the experience of a union between the soul and the Godhead.
>
> We ought to know, according to the correct account, that we use sounds, and syllables, and phrases, and descriptions, and words, for our physical senses. But when our soul is moved by intellectual energies to the things it contemplates, the perceptions that come to us by aid of sensible objects are superfluous. The soul, having become godlike through a union beyond knowledge, throws itself against the rays of the unapproachable light by sightless efforts.
>
> *On Divine Names* 4.11

The development of Eastern and Western Christianity

From the fourth century onward, several factors contributed to a gradual separation of churches in the western part of the Roman empire from those in the east. Politically, the Roman empire had been divided into western and eastern administrative districts; and intellectually, Latin, the language of Roman law, became the medium for theological innovation in the west, whereas Greek, the language of philosophy and literature, underlay the work of eastern theologians. In 330 CE, moreover, Constantine founded the city of Constantinople near the town of Byzantium on the Bosporus Strait and moved the imperial capital there. This young metropolis, the beginning of what would become the Byzantine empire, was seen by many as New Rome and quickly became the Roman empire's leading city. This, in turn, gave the eastern church access to intellectual and material resources that earlier were only available in Rome. All these factors contributed to a growing isolation—politically, intellectually, and culturally—between the eastern and western halves of the empire (Figure 9.6). One important consequence of this isolation for Christianity was that western theologians came to understand the nature of humanity and God somewhat differently than their eastern counterparts.

In the fifth century, the north African Christian Augustine of Hippo (354–430), who was to become one of the west's most influential theologian, articulated the doctrine of original sin for western Christianity. He reasoned that because the first humans, Adam and Eve, had sinned, all humans thereafter (who were their descendants) were sinners from the moment of conception. Eastern Christians, by contrast, had earlier developed the doctrine of ancestral sin, from which they concluded that humanity's separation from God was not nearly as severe as Augustine would claim.

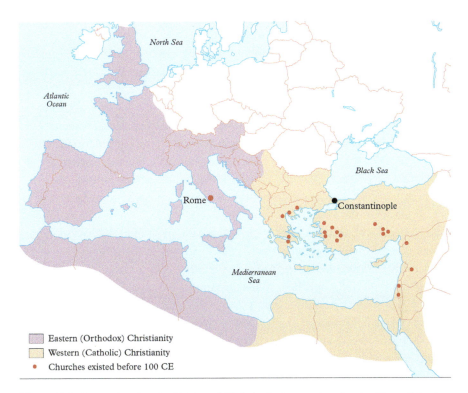

Figure 9.6 A map showing the division of Christianity into west and east, with capitals at Rome and Constantinople. The red dots mark cities where churches were known to have existed before 100 CE.

They held that, although Adam and Eve's sin had caused the world to fall away from God, it had not created a sinful human nature or an inherited guilt. Thus, instead of exploring the consequences of original sin, as was done in the west, eastern theologians took a different path, which allowed them to understand the goal of Christian living as *theosis*—the divination of human beings. In the words of the eastern theologian Athanasius of Alexandria (ca. 293–373 CE), God, in his Son, "assumed humanity that we might become God."

Overshadowed by Constantinople's rise to prominence, the now neglected city of Rome declined during the fourth century, and in 410 was sacked by an army of Visigoths from the north. But as the city's imperial power faded over the next few centuries, the status of the western church increased, for people in the west turned more and more to the church as the source of order in society. Led by the bishop of Rome, who became known as the pope (Latin, "father"), western Christianity adopted the name Catholic (universal) church. Eastern Christianity, in turn, took the name Orthodox (correct doctrine) church, and was governed jointly by the bishops of Jerusalem, Antioch, Alexandria, and Constantinople, each of whom bore the title **patriarch** (Greek for "male head of household"). Over the next several centuries, the office of pope, or papacy, not only came to dominate the political affairs of the Roman west, but began to claim universal religious authority.

The Eucharist

Between the fourth and the seventh centuries, especially in the west, Christians increasingly approached God through the image of ritual sacrifice. From its beginning, Christianity had explained the crucifixion as a sacrifice, and now, as western Christianity moved north into Germanic lands, a sacrificial explanation for the eucharist became central to the understanding of this new audience. This resulted in the multiplication of sacrificial "altars" for eucharistic celebrations in local churches and monasteries. Priests began to receive payment for offering the eucharist to benefit certain causes, especially the welfare of the dead; and lay patrons and rulers endowed monastic communities that celebrated the eucharist in a daily cycle of prayers known as the divine office.

Concurrent with these changes, Pope Gregory the Great (590–604) set in motion several reforms that shaped other aspects of Christianity in the west. Having been a monk before he became pope, Gregory supported the growth of monasticism throughout western Europe. He extolled the virtues of the monk Benedict of Nursia (ca. 480–547) and promoted Benedict's *Rule* as the standard guide for monastic life. He also extended the reach of the Roman church by sending missionaries to England. This westward push culminated in 800 CE when Pope Leo III crowned the Frankish king Charlemagne emperor of the Roman west.

The use of images in worship

As early as the fourth century, Christians began to create pictures of Jesus, his mother **Mary**, and other saints. Known also as **icons**, these soon became an important way for Christians to experience Christ and the saints as present in their worship. In the east, some Christian leaders saw this new practice as a violation of the Old Testament prohibition against making idols. By the seventh century, Islam had come into being, and its almost complete ban on images, combined with its rapid expansion into Christian lands, may have strengthened this view. In 726, the eastern emperor Leo III ordered the removal and destruction of all icons. But this iconoclasm (image smashing) drew strong opposition, especially in monastic communities. In the west, Pope Gregory III (731–741) mustered political support against the emperor's decree, and eastern theologians such as John of Damascus (ca. 675–749) argued for a connection between the legitimacy of icons and the doctrine of Christ's incarnation: to forbid the making of an image of Christ was to deny that he had become part of our physical world. The dispute was resolved in 843 in favor of using icons, but the controversy it generated further alienated Rome from Constantinople.

> **Did you know …**
>
> For the first two centuries of the church, Christians did not use statues or icons in worship. Because many detractors of the new religion equated idols with gods, they accused Christians of being atheists.

Reform of the monasteries

In the spiritual economy of medieval Christianity, priests and monks began to function as ritual and prayer specialists. As such, they were supported by wealthy patrons for the purpose of securing God's grace for these patrons, their families, and their associates. By the tenth century, however, the gifts given to monasteries often made the monks subject to the control of these wealthy donors, compromising their devotion to the monastic life. A key reform began in 910 with the founding of a new monastery in Cluny, France. Unlike other monastic organizations, it was independent of the surrounding rulers. The only authority above it was the pope—at the time a distant figure with little direct influence in France. Soon, several other monasteries in western Europe were founded by the leaders in Cluny, forming one of the largest networks, or orders, of monastics. Because of their independence from local rulers, the Cluniac monasteries were able to set very high standards for discipline, purity, and prayer.

Papal supremacy

In the eleventh century, the pattern of reform that had begun at Cluny extended to all clergy in the western church. This so-called Gregorian reform, initiated by Pope Gregory VII (1073–1085), also enforced celibacy on all priests, heightening the distinction between clergy and laity. In addition, Gregory enhanced papal authority by becoming the first pope to visit churches north of the Alps and by asserting the papacy's supremacy over civil rulers. While this new power over the temporal realm was often challenged, the arguments for papal supremacy increased steadily until popes in the early fourteenth century could claim supreme authority not only over the church, but also over all aspects of Christian civilization east and west—and indeed over the whole world.

Two Churches: A Parting of the Ways

Eventually, the assertions of papal authority and the other differences that had developed strained the relationship between eastern and western Christianity to the breaking point. A key theological issue was whether the Holy Spirit proceeded "from the Father," which was preferred in the east, or "from the Father *and the Son*," which was the western position. Beginning in the ninth century, this and other disputes resulted in the occasional excommunication, or breaking of communion, between the pope and the east; but these were always resolved and communion restored. In 1054, however, Pope Leo IX sent a legate (official envoy) to Constantinople. Among other things, this legate demanded that the phrase "and the Son" be added to the Nicene Creed. When the patriarch of Constantinople refused, the leader of the legate excommunicated him in the name of the western church, and the patriarch, in turn, excommunicated the members of the legate. While this did not seem exceptional at the time, later events intervened, making this particular break between the churches permanent. In retrospect, historians have seen this as the **Great Schism** (splitting away).

The Crusades

Despite controversies and disagreements between east and west, in 1095, Pope Urban II responded to a request from the Byzantine emperor Alexios I Komnenos to help win back territory in Asia Minor (modern-day Turkey) that Muslim Seljuk Turks had recently conquered. The pope called for a crusade—essentially an armed pilgrimage through Asia Minor to Christ's tomb in Jerusalem, which had also fallen into Muslim hands (Figure 9.7). In asking knights to redeem the honor of Christ's holy tomb by waging war on Muslims, Urban II succeeded in combining the Christian practices of pilgrimage and self-denial with the medieval knight's ideals of honor, duty to one's lord, and assisting the weak.

This and subsequent Crusades (into the thirteenth century) affected the theology of western Christianity. With the Crusades' focus on Jerusalem and the Holy Land—where God, in the person of Jesus, had walked on earth with his disciples, suffered, and died—Catholicism directed its attention more than ever to Christ's existence as a human being. The Crusades also caused the west to re-envision Christianity as a religion that opposed "the other." Initially this "other" was the Muslim Turks, but soon it expanded to include Jews, Christian heretics, and even eastern Christians. There had long been a teaching in Christianity that identified the Jews as "Christ killers" because of the role that first-century Jewish leaders had played in Jesus' execution. Partly on this account, some soldiers in the first Crusade turned their fury against Jews in

Figure 9.7 A fourteenth-century Bible depicts the Crusaders being led into battle by Christ himself. Astride a white horse, Christ holds out the Gospel. In his mouth he brandishes a sword, which is both a cross and the word of God. Detail from the Queen Mary Apocalypse, 14th century, MS Royal 19 B XV f. 37. Source: British Library, London.

German cities such as Mainz while on their way to the Holy Land. The violence that ensued was so horrendous it is sometimes called the *first* Jewish Holocaust. In the coming centuries, Jews would be expelled from much of western Europe, forcing many to migrate east into Muslim lands. In Christian regions where they were permitted to remain, they were increasingly made to live in separate districts (ghettos) in each city, lest they contaminate the purity of Christian society.

The rise of academic theology

The time of the Crusades also witnessed a major theological movement in the west that attempted to create a comprehensive system of knowledge—a fully integrated understanding of the world that took into account all learning and explained all phenomena. To this end, monks and priests freely combined the wisdom of Christian writings with the philosophy and science of classical texts, especially the recently rediscovered works of Aristotle. Since this movement grew out of the schools, including the emerging universities, rather than the monastery or parish, it was called scholastic theology, or **Scholasticism**. The movement's most celebrated figure, Thomas Aquinas (1224/25–1274), insisted that the spiritual and material realms were not so much opposed to one another as they were complementary: the supernatural brought the natural to completion.

One outcome of Scholasticism was a precise analysis of cause and effect in Christian belief and ritual. On the one hand, this provided bishops with the means to identify and pursue heretics. On the other, it developed the church's theology of the **sacraments,** which were its principal tools for drawing close to God. From the religion's earliest days, most Christians had simply affirmed that they received the body and blood of Christ in the bread and wine of the eucharist. With one or two notable exceptions, theologians had never tried to define what this actually meant. In scholastic theology, however, the inner workings of the eucharist became the focus of vigorous debate. Some took the position that the bread and wine were only figuratively Christ's body and blood; others condemned this view as heresy and insisted on a more literal interpretation. The issue was finally settled in 1215 at the Fourth Lateran Council, where it was declared that the bread and wine did, in fact, become the actual body and blood of the resurrected Christ. Its metamorphosis was attributed to a process called transubstantiation, during which the "essential substance" of the bread and wine was completely transformed into Christ's body and blood, while their "outward accidents" of taste, smell, and appearance remained intact.

> **Did you know …**
>
> The words school, scholarship, and scholasticism all come from a Greek word for "leisure time." In the economies of ancient Greece and medieval Europe, the time commitment required for academic study was incompatible with earning a living and providing for a family.

Like the eucharist, the other sacraments underwent scrutiny as well. Although earlier theologians had counted as many as 20 or more sacraments, scholastic analysis now determined that there were exactly 7 sacraments, no more and no less. Around 1152, the scholastic theologian Peter Lombard identified them as baptism, eucharist, confirmation, penance (now called reconciliation), extreme unction (now called anointing of the sick), ordination, and marriage. His list of 7 would later be adopted as the official position of the Catholic church.

Changes in monastic life

Scholasticism remained largely foreign to the thought of the eastern church. Officially it was held that Orthodox theology and worship were complete and unchanged since the iconoclasm controversy—and to a remarkable degree this was so. Eastern theologians practiced a strict fidelity to the earliest church theologians, or Greek Fathers, and assigned the work of ongoing theological reflection to the relatively isolated monasteries rather than urban schools and universities. As a consequence, the most significant area where some change did occur was the monastic practice of solitary contemplation. A new technique, known as *hesychia*, guided one's contemplation of God by the continual repetition of the simple prayer, "Lord Jesus Christ, Son of God, have mercy on me, a sinner." As the practice developed over time, monks claimed that they could see the energy of God as "uncreated light," or entered into the same communion with God that Adam and Eve had enjoyed before the fall. Some even claimed to have achieved the highest possible communion with God, which made them divine.

Orders of begging monks and nuns

As western Europe became more urban, monks and nuns were persuaded that their devotions did not require seclusion in a monastery but could also be pursued in the city, where their lifestyle of prayer and poverty could be combined with preaching, teaching, and caring for the poor. New religious orders appeared, supporting themselves through donations rather than physical labor or endowments. The most significant of these mendicant (begging) orders were the Franciscans, or Order of the Little Brothers, which emphasized poverty and service to others, and the Dominicans, or Order of Preachers, whose goal was to encourage a truer faith among the uneducated populace by preaching and teaching.

The founder of the Franciscans, Francis of Assisi (1181/82–1226), had been influenced especially by a new school of thought that stressed the human aspects of Christ. Unlike earlier efforts to understand Christ's humanity, which had served to lessen his divine nature, this was a way to explore Christ's decision, *as God*, to embrace human vulnerability, suffering, and death. In art, images of Jesus increasingly depicted him not as a triumphant king, but as a child nursing at his mother's breast or a as sacrificial victim in agony on the cross. Inspired by a similar understanding of Christ, Francis created a dramatization of Jesus' lowly, human birth and introduced it into Christmas celebrations. Francis also became the first Christian known to have received *stigmata*, or mysterious wounds on his hands, feet, and side, paralleling the five wounds of the crucified Christ. This fixation on Christ's suffering, which so affected Francis and other Christians of his day, reached its apex between 1347 and 1351, when a pandemic known as the Black Death traumatized western Europe by killing a third of its population, taking as much as two-thirds in some areas.

The pope's departure from Rome

In 1309, political events forced Pope Clement V to move his residence to Avignon, in southern France. But because the pope's authority depended solely on his status as the bishop of Rome, opposition to his departure increased over time. The incongruity of his and his successors' absence from Rome was especially felt by the pilgrims to St Peter's tomb there. In 1377, Pope Gregory XI, the seventh of these Avignon popes, moved back to Rome. But when he died in the following year, two rival popes were elected, one in Rome and one in Avignon.

As the years dragged on, many came to the twofold conclusion that only a council of bishops could resolve the situation, and that supreme authority in the church should belong to such a council rather than the pope. In 1409, a council met at Pisa, but succeeded only in electing a third pope. In 1417, the Council of Constance finally healed the schism by electing a new pope after deposing or receiving a resignation from each of the three competing popes.

Slavic orthodoxy

In 1453, Muslim armies from the Ottoman empire conquered Constantinople. This had the effect of elevating Slavic churches, especially in Russia, to a more prominent leadership role in eastern Christianity. Orthodox missions to Slavic peoples had begun in the ninth century, and Vladimir the Great and his Russian subjects were converted in 988 by missionaries who employed a different approach than their western counterparts. While Roman Catholic missionaries insisted that the church's scriptures and formal worship remain in Latin, the Orthodox freely translated them into Slavonic languages. They also allowed the churches of individual nations—Russia, Bulgaria, and Serbia—to operate independently of the patriarch in Constantinople. As a result, after Constantinople fell to the Ottomans, autonomous Orthodox churches continued to thrive in Slavic lands. The Russian head of state claimed the role of emperor, taking the title czar (from Caesar), and labeled Russia the Third Rome. The Russian church, in turn, came to think of itself as the protector of all Orthodox believers who lived under Muslim control.

Reformers and the birth of Protestant Christianity

On October 31, 1517, Martin Luther (1483–1546), a Roman Catholic priest and professor at the University of Wittenberg in Germany, initiated what he expected would be a lively academic discussion by posting 95 theses (academic propositions) on the door of the city's main church (Figure 9.8). Similar discussions had been initiated by earlier theologians seeking to reform the church. These had included the Englishman John Wycliffe (d. 1384), whose work was condemned by the church after his death; the Czech Jan Hus (d. 1415), who had been burned at the stake; and the Dutch humanist and contemporary of Luther, Desiderius Erasmus (1496–1536), who remained in good standing with the church. In particular, Luther objected to the increased availability of indulgences. These were certificates that freed a Christian from performing the works of penance that priests assigned them after they received

Figure 9.8 Martin Luther's legendary nailing of the 95 Theses to the door of a Wittenberg church is celebrated by Protestants as a heroic act of religious liberation. Painting by Petru Botezatu, now displayed in the Andrew Gerow Hodges Chapel, Samford University, Birmingham, Alabama. Source: Reproduced by permission of David R. Bains.

the sacrament of confession. While Luther initially expected other scholars, and eventually the pope, to accept his point of view, within a few years he had alienated himself from Rome and created a major theological crisis in the west. In 1521, Pope Leo X excommunicated Luther, precipitating the Protestant Reformation, during which churches in many areas of western Europe broke from Rome.

Reconciliation to God

In addition to being a priest, Luther belonged to the Augustinian Hermits, a religious order with loyalties to St Augustine, and as Luther's thought developed, Augustine's understanding of original sin became central to his theology. Luther's main disagreement with Rome, as he saw it, was over the matter of justification—that is, being reconciled to a holy and just God by becoming a righteous person. Convinced that humans were thoroughly and permanently corrupted by original sin, Luther argued that they were incapable of pleasing God even in their best thoughts and actions. Christians were and would remain sinners their entire lives. Their reconciliation to God, therefore, could not be the result of their own accomplishments; rather Christians were "reckoned" sinless by God because of Christ. The Christian's sole task was to believe—and even this required God's help. As Luther phrased it, justification came "by grace through faith"—that is, by God's grace, received through Christian faith, which was also a gift from God.

Catholic theologians, on the other hand, insisted that reconciliation to God meant entering into a sinless condition of holiness. Against Luther, they saw this as a real condition, not something simply reckoned to people. Furthermore, they argued that justification depended not only on God's grace, but also on human cooperation and effort, which included demonstrating one's love for God through prayer, fasting, pilgrimage, and giving to the poor. For Luther, this was precisely the sort of "works theology" that St Paul and St Augustine had condemned, as it created only an *illusion* of justification, not true justification.

Scripture alone as the source of authority

Luther eventually became convinced that he must reject both the authority of the pope and the tradition of the Roman church in favor of his own interpretation of the Bible. *Sola scriptura*, or "scripture alone," became his guiding principle. He rejected the doctrine of purgatory, prayers for the dead, and the veneration of saints because he found no evidence for them in the Bible. Likewise, after forsaking his vows of celibacy, he married; he reduced the number of sacraments to two—baptism and eucharist; and he abandoned the notion that Catholic priests could mediate between people and God, claiming instead that *all* believers had the status of priests.

Following the principle of scripture alone, Luther renounced the idea that celebrating the eucharist was a sacrifice offered by the church. He also rejected the theory of transubstantiation in favor of another explanation of Christ's presence in the bread and wine of the eucharist. With regard to the scripture itself, because Luther found the doctrine of justification by faith most clearly expressed in St Paul, he evaluated the other books of the Bible largely on the basis of this author. Consequently, he denounced the New Testament Letter of James as theologically superficial, and he excluded seven books and portions of two others from the Old Testament, both on theological grounds and because they were missing from Jewish Bibles.

> #### Did you know ...
>
> When Luther translated the Bible into German, he reduced the size of the Catholic Bible by making the contents of his Old Testament identical with that of the Jewish scriptures. This became the standard for all later Protestant translations.

The splintering of Protestant Churches

To Luther's dismay, his appeal to the sole authority of scripture soon led other Christian leaders to demand changes far beyond what he proposed. He had been relatively cautious in his reforms, leaving many church practices untouched; but other reformers read the Bible in ways that called for a thorough reassessment of Roman Catholicism. Initially active in Switzerland, these Christians became known as the Reformed and Anabaptist wings of Protestantism. The Reformed churches later spread to the Netherlands and other parts of Europe, and triumphed in Scotland as Presbyterians. Ulrich Zwingli, a former Catholic priest and almost exact contemporary of Luther, led the movement in Zurich. He died in 1531 at the age of 47 in a battle with neighboring Catholic cities. Soon thereafter, a much younger contemporary of Luther, John Calvin (1509–1564), became active in Reformed churches in Geneva. Shaped to a greater degree than Luther by the humanism of the Italian Renaissance, both Zwingli and Calvin held that finite, earthly things could not contain God's grace or Christ himself, which were infinite. On that basis they rejected the use of both statues and icons, as well as the affirmation that Christ was physically present in the eucharist. Zwingli maintained that Christ was only figuratively present in the bread and wine, while Calvin affirmed a real presence, but in spiritual terms that satisfied neither Catholics nor most Lutherans.

Reformed Protestants also found in the Bible specific guidelines for worship and church life. Calvin, for example, rejected singing hymns of human composition, insisting that only the inspired songs of the Bible, chiefly the Psalms, could be sung in public worship. At the heart of Calvin's theology was an emphasis on God's complete sovereignty over his creation. This led him to teach that human salvation and damnation were both predestined by God; and while he agreed with Luther that Christians were saved by grace and not by works, he put more emphasis on the need to grow in holiness through the performance of religious duties.

In contrast to both Lutherans and Reformed Christians, the Anabaptists agitated for even more far-reaching changes. Agreeing with Luther's initial insight that faith was necessary for Christians to be reconciled to God, they maintained that only those who could profess their faith—that is, adults—could be baptized. It was on this account that they were called Anabaptists (re-baptizers), for they insisted that anyone who had been baptized as an infant must also be baptized as an adult. In addition, the Anabaptists rejected all alliances between church and state, which had been the norm since the fourth century. They reasoned that defending one's nation was incompatible with Christ's teaching of nonresistance.

Reform in England

While the Protestant Reformation was transforming Christianity on the European continent, Christians across the channel in England went their own way. Unlike Lutherans, Reformed Christians, and Anabaptists, English Christians did not initially separate from Rome over demands for religious reform. Instead, at the urging of King Henry VIII, parliament declared in 1534 that the Church of England was free of the pope's authority on *legal* grounds, contending that a bishop's jurisdiction did not extend beyond the empire in which he lived. Henry had taken this step when European politics prevented the pope (*Rome's* bishop) from granting him an annulment for his marriage to Catherine of Aragon, who had not provided England a male heir to his throne.

But once the Church of England, or Anglican church, was independent of the papacy, Protestants in England vied with former Roman Catholics for control. By the end of the sixteenth century, a moderate Protestantism prevailed, yet this moderation was not enough for some and too much for others. Reformed groups called Puritans appeared, their name deriving from their desire to further purify the English church of its Roman traditions. Some of these left for North America, where they founded a New England.

From the Reformation to the Enlightenment

The sixteenth century produced much more than the Protestant and Anglican Reformations: it also produced reforms within the Roman Catholic church; foreign missions to non-European lands; and decades of religious wars.

Catholic reform

Beginning in 1545, Catholic bishops met at the Council of Trent to respond to Protestantism. They charted a course to eliminate corruption in the church and to strengthen and standardize the religion by reaffirming Catholic doctrine and promoting education. A number of new religious orders emerged from this "Catholic Reformation," chief among them being the Society of Jesus, or Jesuits. Founded by Ignatius Loyola (1491–1556), the Jesuits vowed fidelity to the pope and the traditional teachings of Catholicism. They also sought to develop the faith of individual Christians by emphasizing the mission of the church as well as the individual's personal religious experiences and commitment to Christ.

> ### A Closer Look
>
> #### Commitment to Tradition
>
> As a proponent of the Catholic Reformation, Ignatius Loyola wrote a work entitled *Spiritual Exercises* in which he provided rules to help Roman Catholics embrace their faith and resist Protestant ideas. He believed so deeply in the correctness of the Catholic church and its traditions that he even advised in Rule 13, "To be right in everything, we should always hold that the white which we see is black, if the Church so decides it."

Foreign missions

In the fifteenth and sixteenth centuries, the Spanish and Portuguese established colonies in Africa, the Americas, Asia, and the Pacific Islands (Oceania). Their military forces were accompanied by Catholic priests and missionaries, who initiated a new phase in the expansion of Catholicism. Anglican and Protestant nations soon followed suit, sending their colonists and missionaries across the globe as well. Most Europeans, however, considered the peoples of Africa, Oceania, and the Americas little more than savages, presenting Christian missionaries with a daunting challenge. They needed to adapt Christianity to these "primitive cultures" without compromising its basic doctrines and rituals. The Jesuit missionaries, because they emphasized an individual's experience of Christ rather than outward rituals, were often the most successful in reshaping Christianity so that it would appeal to non-European cultures.

Religious wars, piety, and reason

In the second half of the sixteenth century, it became evident that the divisions within western Christianity came at a high price. Every group assumed that their version of Christianity was the only authentic form, and all but the Anabaptists believed that it was the state's function to suppress all other forms. Accordingly, from 1562 to 1651 religious wars ravaged Europe, resulting in a tremendous loss of life. Above all, this carnage persuaded many Protestants that Christian unity was impossible on the basis of scripture alone. While there was overwhelming agreement on the authority of the Bible, there was simply too much disagreement on how to interpret it. This began a search for additional sources of truth and authority, as well as new possibilities to build human community independent of religious affiliation.

Some Protestants proposed that a personal religious experience with God was the truth that would bring people together. Known as Pietists and Evangelicals, they resolved to bring everyone to Christ through the experience of a personal conversion by confronting Christians and non-Christians alike with the true depth of their sinfulness. In shifting the emphasis from theological education to personal experience, they sought to create a society in which doctrinal disputes would be pushed aside as citizens filled their days with the gospel message, Christian resolve, and pious lifestyles. The Pietist/Evangelical movement encouraged a new breed of lay preachers whose energetic and sometimes fiery sermons touched people in their souls and led to thousands of tearful and emotion-filled conversions (Figure 9.9). But their success, ironically, only added to religious divisions in society, for many of these lay preachers went on to found their own congregations, resulting in a proliferation of smaller movements and even some new denominations, such as the Methodist and the Baptist churches.

Other Protestant groups proposed that human reason could bring Christians together. Drawing inspiration from the European Enlightenment of the seventeenth and eighteenth centuries, they based their hopes on the human ability to establish a common, universal truth by observing the natural world and drawing logical conclusions. Indeed, a sea-change began in the west—a completely new understanding of

Figure 9.9 John Wesley, one of the founders of Methodism, worked tirelessly for spiritual revival within the church. In England he traveled by horse from town to town, often preaching two or three sermons a day. Source: © Print Collector/Alamy.

human knowledge that placed the natural sciences and critical thinking alongside the Bible and church traditions as sources of ultimate truth. As this approach to truth spread, people became convinced that science and reason, combined with a flexible and general belief in God, was the recipe for peaceful coexistence. New political theories arose from this approach as well, assigning basic human rights to all citizens regardless of religion, and claiming that governments were human creations, not divine institutions. In line with this, fully autonomous churches, created without governmental support or interference, appeared for the first time in North America.

Human reason did not always accord with church traditions, however, which led theologians to reassess long-held Christian doctrines through a more human-centered lens. Treatises on correct doctrine and on receiving grace through sacramental rites gave way to writings on moral transformation; and practically all theologians applied themselves to the problem of reconciling God's wrath with his divine love. Unitarians, in particular, were affected by this turn toward reason, rejecting the doctrine of the **Trinity** as irrational. Rather than claim that a single God consisted of three persons—Father, Son, and Holy Spirit—they endorsed the belief that Jesus was not God, but God's adopted son. Unitarians also rejected the doctrine of original sin by insisting that human ethical reasoning, which came from God, led to the conclusion that a good God would not condemn people for something done by their ancestors.

> ### A Closer Look
>
> ### Non-Trinitarian Christians
>
> While all Christians speak of God, Jesus Christ, and the Holy Spirit, not all accept the doctrine of the Trinity, which envisions a single God existing as these three persons. Latter-day Saints, who are popularly known as Mormons, regard the Heavenly Father and Jesus as two separate individuals, while Jehovah's Witnesses consider the Son of God to be a created spiritual being also distinct from God. Some Pentecostals, in turn, hold a Oneness Theology that affirms the unity but not the Trinity of God, while Unitarians reason that if "God is one," then Jesus is not God.

Recent challenges and developments

In the late eighteenth and early nineteenth centuries, modern scholarship and science also began to challenge what some Christians understood to be the very foundation of their religion. Geology demonstrated that the Earth and the human race were much older than the biblical chronologies suggested. Evolutionary biology challenged the six-day account of creation in the book of Genesis, and the academic study of scripture argued that many books in the Bible were not written by the individuals traditionally assigned to them, but by multiple authors and at a later date.

Liberal and conservative Christianity

This new approach to biblical interpretation nurtured a modernist, or liberal Christianity, which insisted that all claims of truth and authority must be evaluated on the basis of critical thinking and scientific fact. This led many to the conclusion that some portions of the Bible were not God's word but the ethics and beliefs of human authors. Instead of continuing Christianity in its traditional forms, they called for adapting it to the demands of contemporary society.

Others, however, defended biblical truth and authority. The Bible, they maintained, was God's book, and Christians needed to lead their lives according to the "plain sense of scripture." By the early twentieth century, these Christians had become known as conservatives and **fundamentalists,** the latter term indicating their commitment to what they defined as the fundamental, and therefore nonnegotiable, truths of Christianity. In particular, fundamentalists defended the inerrancy of the Bible, which usually (but not always) meant that they held the Bible to be completely true with respect what it said about God and morality, as well as history and science.

The initial Catholic response to the challenge of modern science and critical thinking was also conservative. At the First Vatican Council (1869–1870), the bishops reaffirmed their belief in the inerrancy of the Bible and the truth of the Catholic tradition. Further, they declared that the ultimate measure of truth in matters of faith and morality did not depend on scientific discovery, but on pronouncements of the pope when he spoke from his seat of authority (*ex cathedra*) as the successor to St Peter.

> **Did you know …**
>
> Although the pope has the ability to speak infallibly on matters of Christian doctrine, this authority has been explicitly invoked only twice, both times to affirm long-held beliefs about the Virgin Mary.

Christians with gifts of the spirit

In 1906, a small group of Protestants at a church in Los Angeles began worshipping God in a new way. They claimed they were following the example of the first apostles, who had received supernatural gifts from the Holy Spirit during the festival of Pentecost. These gifts included speaking in tongues (human and angelic languages), miraculous healings, and prophecy. Soon **Pentecostalism**, as it was called, spread throughout the world. Together with the somewhat earlier Holiness movement, Pentecostals taught that Christians needed to be baptized in the Holy Spirit. Unlike baptism with water, this was a miraculous event that came directly from God in answer to fervent prayer. Until the appearance of these movements, most Protestants had taught that the age of miracles had ceased once the New Testament had been written. But reasoning that "Jesus Christ is the same yesterday and today and forever," Pentecostal and Holiness followers insisted that the Spirit was again working in people to perform miracles, just as it had in the apostolic age. Many even took this to be a sign that the "last days" had arrived, when Christ would return in judgment.

> **A Closer Look**
>
> ### Speaking in Tongues
>
> According to the New Testament Book of Acts, the church came into being when the Holy Spirit descended on the Apostles in Jerusalem on the day of Pentecost, enabling them to communicate the gospel to people from all corners of the Roman empire.
>
>> When the day of Pentecost had come, they were all together in one place. And suddenly from heaven there came a sound like the rush of a violent wind, and it filled the entire house where they were sitting. Divided tongues, as of fire, appeared among them, and a tongue rested on each of them. All of them were filled with the Holy Spirit and began to speak in other languages, as the Spirit gave them ability.
>>
>> Acts 2:1–4 NRSV

Beginning in the 1960s, a second wave of Pentecostalism appeared. Frequently called the Charismatic movement (from Greek *charisma*, "gift"), it held that all Christians, regardless of their denomination, could participate in the spiritual gifts of tongues, healing, and prophecy. Today, Charismatic Christians are found in Catholicism and many mainstream Protestant denominations. Along with Pentecostal Christians, they constitute one of the religion's fastest growing constituencies.

Cooperation among the churches

An impulse toward Christian unity known as **ecumenism** became prominent in the mid-twentieth century. Following World War II, an organization called the World Council of Churches held its first meeting, bringing Orthodox and Protestant churches together to discuss their differences and agree on common projects. Even before this, similar organizations had appeared on a local scale, and some regional denominations had merged into single churches. Such was the case in 1947 when Reformed, Methodist, and Anglican churches in India united to form the Church of South India.

Although Roman Catholics did not initially participate in the ecumenical movement, things changed in 1958. In that year, the newly elected Pope John XXIII surprised Catholics everywhere by calling a council to grapple with issues that confronted Catholicism in the modern world. Perhaps no single event since the European Enlightenment had a greater impact on Christian belief and practice than this **Second Vatican Council** (1962–1965). Prior to this, Roman Catholicism had mounted a dogged defense of traditional beliefs and practices. Catholics isolated themselves from modern society by marrying only other Catholics and by creating their own network of schools, from elementary to graduate education. But Vatican II, as this council became known, brought Catholicism into a dialog with modernity. It encouraged critical, academic study of the Bible, and signaled that it was no longer possible or desirable for Catholics to speak of certain areas of the world as Christendom—the domain of Christ—thereby renouncing the church's longstanding claim to religious authority over the world. The Catholic church began to support religious freedom as a fundamental human right, and it gave qualified recognition to other forms of Christianity and even non-Christian religions. Accordingly, it admonished Catholics to see themselves as pilgrims on this earth, humbly witnessing the truth of Christianity amidst other religions and ideologies.

Changes in Catholic worship

Some of the council's most notable reforms were in the area of worship. Vatican II permitted the eucharist to be celebrated in the everyday languages of the people, rather than in Latin only, which had been the practice since the fourth century. It also encouraged priests to face their congregations when consecrating the eucharist. Previously, they had consecrated the bread and wine with their backs to the people, standing between them and God as intercessors. Now the altar was moved from the front wall of the sanctuary to a more central location so the priest could stand behind it and look toward those who had come to receive the eucharist. This encouraged the laity to think of the eucharist as a ritual in which they also participated, rather than as a sacrifice performed by the priest on their behalf. They were soon offered the wine as well as the bread, whereas for several centuries before Vatican II only the priest had been allowed to drink the wine.

While the council's reforms led to more participation in worship by those who attended, it did not lead to larger congregations, which is what the bishops had hoped. Instead, in the decades following the council, the Catholic church experienced a major decline in attendance, especially in western Europe and the United States. In response, two recent popes, John Paul II (1978–2005) and Benedict XVI (2005–2013), committed themselves to a more cautious application of the council's teachings. Yet their successor, Pope Francis (2013–present), has decided in favor of a more progressive approach. A Jesuit from Argentina, he has frequently called for priests to minimize the distance between themselves and their congregations, saying that they should be "shepherds with the smell of sheep." In 2021, he began a four-year, worldwide "synodal process" to encourage Catholics at all levels to meet together to hear what the "Holy Spirit is saying to the Church." He has asked that Catholics work toward a more consultative church by being open to advancing the place of women in church governance and by listening to "those at the margins," including LGBTQ+ individuals.

Christianity South of the equator

Pope Francis is the first pope to be chosen from outside of Europe and the Mediterranean world, and his appointment of bishops from countries south of the equator to the Church's college of cardinals (the body that elects new popes) reflects the shift in Christianity's center of gravity. At the beginning of the twentieth century, only 18 percent of all Christians lived outside of Europe and North America. By 2024 it was over 68 percent, most of whom lived in Latin America, Africa, and south Asia—areas that scholars refer to collectively as the **Global South**. This demographic shift is transforming Christianity in terms of both morality and worship. In parts of Africa, for example, not only is it lawful for Christian men to have multiple wives, but indigenous practices, such as ritual dance, can dominate worship services to the point that these services become unrecognizable to Christians from Europe and North America.

In addition, Christians in the Global South are *socially* and *doctrinally* more conservative than their European and North American counterparts. They typically interpret the Bible in a literal, fundamentalist way, and they reject most tenets of the feminist movement, especially the call for the ordination of women. Yet *politically* they are more progressive and left-leaning than Christians north of the equator. Pointing to the west's history of colonialism, slavery, and economic exploitation, southern theologians criticize many of the church's norms as supporting the mistreatment of peoples in the south. Latin American theologians, in particular, have pioneered what is known as liberation theology, which defines the central goal of Christianity as helping improve the lives of those who suffer economic and political oppression.

Pentecostal and Charismatic practices of healing and speaking in tongues have flourished in the Global South, as have various indigenous traditions of prophecy, healing, and spirit possession. As these churches grow, and as they increasingly supply church leadership—as in the case of Pope Francis—it seems inevitable that their perspectives will become a major factor in Christianity's future development.

Divisions over sexuality and gender

For most of its history, Christians allowed only men to be ordained as priests and pastors. But beginning in the nineteenth century, Protestant groups that emphasized the ongoing work of the Holy Spirit began ordaining women. Christians committed to traditional theologies and gender roles objected to this practice, but other Protestant denominations followed suit, leading to new divisions between progressives and traditionalists.

More recently, debates over non-heterosexual lifestyles have added to the controversy. This is perhaps most clearly seen among Anglicans. In 2008, bishops from Nigeria, Kenya, Uganda, and Rwanda united with conservatives from the United States and elsewhere to form the Global Anglican Future Conference (GAFCON). In part, this was to protest the consecration of a gay man as bishop in the United States. Fourteen years later, many GAFCON bishops refused to attend the gathering of Anglican bishops at the Lambeth Conference in Canterbury, England, because the Episcopal Church in the United States was ordaining LGBTQ+ clergy and celebrating same-sex marriages. Then, early in 2023, the Church of England authorized the blessing of unions, but not marriages, for same-sex couples, complicating matters still further.

Contemporary Beliefs and Practices

The focus of Christianity is the God of the Bible, envisioned as a divine Trinity of three distinct yet unified persons: God the Father, God the Son, and God the Holy Spirit. This God created the world and everything in it, and now longs for a loving relationship with all human beings. But humans are unable to conform themselves to God's will. They are estranged from God and need his help. This help, called grace, is supplied by God through his divine Son, Jesus Christ, who became human, was put to death by crucifixion, and rose from the dead to bring humanity back into communion with God.

Christians attribute humanity's estrangement from God to sin, which is both an evil force in the world (sometimes personified as Satan) and the evil actions of people who come under sin's power. Sin first appeared when Adam and Eve, the first humans, disobeyed God's commandment not to eat fruit from the "tree of the knowledge of good and evil." While Christians understand Adam and Eve variously as history, myth, or symbol, their conclusion is the same. The disobedience of the first humans introduced sin and mortality into the human condition, and since that time people have continued to sin and die. If they are not reconciled to God before death, they will be permanently separated from God.

A Closer Look

The Trinity

Christians depict the mystery of the Trinity in many ways. One of the most common is the trefoil, a design formed by three intersecting arches. Triangles are also popular. The three circles in the triangle in Figure 9.10 contain: an all-seeing eye as the Father; the Greek letters *chi* and *rho* from *Christos*, the Son; and a dove as the Holy Spirit.

Figure 9.10 A depiction of the Trinity at St. Rose of Lima Roman Catholic Church in Hastings, Michigan. Source: Reproduced by permission of David R. Bains.

Christians believe that Jesus is able to reconcile people to God because he willingly surrendered his divine status and being on their behalf. Coming into the world as a helpless infant born to an unwed peasant woman, Jesus lived a lowly human life without sin. As an adult, he taught people God's ways and healed their illnesses through God's power. Then, condemned unjustly as a criminal and a heretic, and undergoing a horrific death by crucifixion, he gave his perfect life in payment for the sins of the world. Because his self-sacrifice on behalf of unworthy sinners was voluntary and perfect, God raised Jesus from the dead, destroying death not only for Jesus but for all people who commit themselves completely to God through Jesus. In this way, Jesus became the savior of the world and the indispensable mediator between God and humanity. When he returns at the end of time to judge the world, Christians will be raised from the dead as he was, and enter into eternal communion with God.

> **Talking about Religion**
>
> ## Satan
>
> Christians identify the serpent in Genesis with a figure they call Satan or the Devil. According to one interpretation, Satan was originally a heavenly being created by God, but rebelled against his maker and was cast down from heaven to earth. He and his own company of angels now have the power to tempt humans and work evil among them until the end of time, when God judges the world. While some Christians understand Satan to be a real figure, others see him as only a personification of evil human tendencies.

Christians use several images to clarify the manner in which Jesus brings about their justification. Perhaps the most pervasive is the image of sacrifice. Thus, Christians speak of Jesus as the Passover lamb, equating his crucifixion to the Israelites' slaughter of lambs during the Exodus, the blood of which protected them from evil. Closely related to the idea of ritual sacrifice is the claim that Jesus' death paid the price for human sin, thereby satisfying the demands of God's law. Both of these images envision Christ's death as a substitutionary sacrifice, meaning that Jesus died *in the place of* human beings, who would otherwise have suffered eternally for their sin.

Another way Christians explain their salvation is to see Jesus as conqueror. Here the emphasis is on Christ overcoming the power of sin and death, an image that is favored particularly by the Orthodox tradition. In Orthodox churches, the hymn "Christ is risen from the dead, trampling down death by death" resounds throughout Easter, the annual celebration of Christ's resurrection. A final popular image of salvation holds that Jesus' voluntary death established the model for Christian living. Here the cross is seen as the highest expression of God's love for humanity, calling Christians to return this love by conforming their hearts and their actions to God's will.

Whichever image or images of salvation Christians use, they almost universally agree that to be saved people must "believe in Christ." This means that people must give Christ their complete trust and allegiance, to the extent that Christ becomes their Lord and they become Christ's servants, willing to bear his cross themselves. When this happens, a person enters into communion with God, becomes holy in God' eyes, and receives the promise of eternal life. In what follows, we will investigate Christian beliefs and practices under three broad headings: *entering* into communion with God; *sustaining and deepening* this communion; and *extending* this communion to non-Christians for their salvation.

Entering into communion with God

No one is born a Christian. Even if one is born into a Christian family, they must be born anew as a Christian, an event that is linked to baptism.

Baptism

In **baptism**, an individual is immersed or otherwise symbolically washed with water in the name of the Father, the Son, and the Holy Spirit—that is, the Trinity. This ritual is believed to cleanse the person from their sin, or, alternatively, bury the person with Christ in preparation for their rebirth. In the latter explanation, baptism becomes an act by which the individual participates in Christ's crucifixion, which brings an end to their former, non-Christian self. Then, rising from this death, which in immersion baptism is identified with rising up out of the baptismal pool, the individual is reborn as a new, forgiven person and follower of Christ. Christians describe the result of rebirth in several ways. First, it brings one into God's family as a child of God and brother or sister of Christ. Second, it enables Christians to approach God *through* Christ, which is why Christians often end prayers with expressions like, "we ask this in Christ's name." And third, it incorporates a person into the risen body of Christ, which is the church. As a member of this body, the Christian is guided by the Holy Spirit, which flows through Christ's body like a human spirit flows through a human body. In Christian living, the Spirit urges and motivates people to do things that please God.

> **Talking about Religion**
>
> ### Living in a State of Grace
>
> Gaining access to God's Holy Spirit is sometimes called sanctification. Being sanctified, Christians enter into a state of grace where they are protected from the powers of evil. A few churches teach that truly sanctified Christians stop sinning altogether. Most Christians, however, regard this sort of unqualified description of sanctification as a goal to be pursued, not a state to be achieved in the here and now.

The rite of baptism can be accompanied by other practices that reinforce its transformation of the individual. In Eastern Orthodoxy and increasingly in Roman Catholicism, infants are re-born in baptism just as they were first born—in the nude. These and other Christian groups clothe the newly baptized in white to signal their purity. Frequently a cross is traced on the person's forehead with water from the baptism or with sacred oil, marking them as forever belonging to Christ; and throughout their lives, many Christians trace the cross on their chests in commemoration of their second birth.

Declaring one's faith

Baptism is preceded by a renunciation of sin and a declaration of belief in Jesus Christ. When infants are baptized, these pronouncements are made on their behalf by parents or sponsors. Some Protestant churches refuse to baptize infants on grounds that only the person being baptized can profess their faith. Churches that practice this "believer's baptism" include Baptists, Mennonites, and most Independents and Pentecostals. But even among these churches there is considerable variation as to what one should profess. Some have candidates for baptism make a public statement of their personal decision to accept Christ as Lord their lives, while others expect candidates to testify about having had an experience of God's presence.

Confirmation and first eucharist

For Protestant groups that practice infant baptism, **confirmation** is the occasion for young Christians to give the solemn profession of faith that they, as infants, could not make for themselves. They typically prepare for confirmation by studying their denomination's tradition and deciding whether they truly desire to embrace this religion as their own. If they go on to make a profession of faith, a pastor or bishop will lay their hands on them and pray for the Holy Spirit to confirm their decision. Among Catholic and Orthodox Christians, confirmation is a sacrament in which a priest places the seal of the Holy Spirit on confirmands by anointing them with a fragrant oil known as chrism. In Orthodoxy, this sacrament is called chrismation and takes place immediately after baptism, even for infants. Chrismation conforms a person to the image of Christ—*christos* being the Greek word for "anointed one"—thereby opening the door to *theosis*, a Christian's deification.

Like confirmation, receiving one's first eucharist can also be part of Christian initiation. For most Christians, joining others for the first time in the eucharist finalizes their membership in the church. The practice of first eucharist varies considerably, however, as Orthodox Christians serve communion to adults, young people, and newly baptized infants, whereas Catholics admit Christians to the eucharist only after the age of discretion (usually eight), and only after they have made their first confession. Protestant practices vary by denomination.

Baptism in the spirit

Holiness, Pentecostal, and Charismatic Christians believe that most other Christians have never received the full measure of the Holy Spirit. By contrast, their doctrine of baptism in the Holy Spirit envisions the possibility of God's Spirit descending and imparting gifts to modern Christians as it did with Christians at the founding of the church (Figure 9.11). Usually occurring at some point after water baptism, baptism in the Spirit is a supernatural event that enables Christians to speak in tongues, prophesy, and heal the sick.

Sustaining and deepening one's communion with God

Once individuals have become Christians, they seek to sustain and deepen their newly won communion with God. The principal ways of doing this are public worship, individual or small group Bible study and prayer, and practices and lifestyles known as pastoral rites.

Christianity 427

Figure 9.11 In a church in Tanzania, a man receives the "laying on of hands" by a Pentecostal minister in preparation for being baptized in the Holy Spirit. Source: © Jake Lyell/Alamy.

Worshipping in public

In public worship Christians conform their thoughts, voices, and bodies to God's will, presenting themselves to the world, each other, and God as a people unified in salvation through Christ. Some churches offer mid-week prayer meetings where individuals can give public testimony of God working in their lives. Others engage in public worship on a daily basis. Most Catholic churches, for example, offer a daily morning eucharist. Perhaps the most extensive form of public worship is the cycle of daily services practiced by monastic orders devoted to prayer, such as the Benedictines. Known as the divine office, liturgy of the hours, or daily office, these services include singing and chanting psalms, meditative readings from scripture, and brief prayers. There can be as many as eight gatherings per day, the most common being morning prayer (lauds and matins) and evening prayer (vespers).

Typically, however, Christians worship publicly on what they call the Lord's day, which is generally understood to be Sunday. This is the day of the week Christ rose from the dead. Because Christians also associate the Lord's day with the Jewish Sabbath, some abstain from all forms of work on this day in accordance with Old Testament teachings. Catholic Christians understand the Lord's day as beginning on Saturday evening, following the Jewish practice of beginning each day at sundown rather than at dawn. This allows them to celebrate the Lord's day eucharist on Saturday evening. A relatively small number of Christians, including Seventh-day Adventists, insist that the proper day is the actual Jewish Sabbath, which the Old Testament defines as the period between sunset on Friday and sunset on Saturday.

Worship leaders and the order of worship Public worship is typically led by clergy, who are responsible for presiding at the sacraments, crafting the sermon, and leading the main prayers. In most churches, the structure and content of worship on the

Lord's day are provided by texts called liturgies. The principal liturgies include the *Roman Missal* used by Catholics, *The Liturgy of St. John Chrysostom* used by Orthodox Christians, and the *Book of Common Prayer* used by Anglicans and a few others. Liturgies are important ways to maintain continuity with a church's past, and to unify Christians around the world in the same worship. Most Protestants, by contrast, regard the use of liturgies as an impediment to worship, believing that authentic worship requires each group of Christians to be guided freely by the Bible and the Holy Spirit.

Worship services can last an hour or several hours, and involve many components. All worship services offer praise to God for his greatness and for his gift of redemption in Christ. Sometimes this praise is expressed in recited words or dance (as in many churches in Africa), but it is more commonly expressed through musical instruments and song. Frequently, fellowship is also a component of public worship, and in many traditions worshippers greet one another with a hug, a handshake, or a kiss, saying, "The peace of Christ be with you." Other traditions prefer less formal interactions, such as warm greetings or a reception with coffee or tea after the service.

Additional elements of public worship include communal prayer, financial contributions, and proclamation of God's word. When praying communally, Christians assume a posture that honors God's superiority. For Eastern Christians this posture is standing, punctuated by bowing; Catholics and Protestants prefer kneeling, sitting with one's head bowed, or standing with arms outstretched toward heaven. On special occasions, Catholic and Orthodox churches even prescribe lying on one's stomach in full prostration.

As a way of acknowledging their dependence on God, Christians make monetary contributions to the work of the church. They see this as an act of returning to God a part of the wealth with which he has blessed them. Some Pentecostals teach that when Christians give generously to God, they can expect to receive blessings in return, including financial success. Most often, contributions are collected unobtrusively, but a few traditions require their members to present them with great ceremony before church leaders. Many Christians contribute 10 percent of their annual income to the church, based on the Old Testament practice of tithing. Others object to tithing as a form of legalism, which is following Old Testament laws so closely that worshipping God becomes a matter of keeping rules.

All churches today set aside time during public worship for proclaiming the Christian message through sermons and readings from the Bible. For some traditions this takes as little as 15 minutes, for others, an hour or more. Christians who use liturgies read two or three biblical passages from a predetermined list of passages known as a lectionary. Orthodox Christians follow a list that repeats every year, while Catholics and others follow a three-year cycle so that those attending worship are exposed to more of the Bible. Most Protestants attend nonlectionary churches in which the ministers choose Bible passages that serve as the starting point of their sermons.

Books used for reading scripture to the congregation include the Bible, a ceremonial book containing only the four Gospels, or a selection of passages printed in the liturgy. In Catholic and Orthodox churches this book is handled with great respect, sometimes being carried into the sanctuary by a procession and then honored with incense, which purifies the worship area. Protestants, on the other hand, frequently bring their own Bibles, often with passages highlighted or underlined from regular study. They do this so they can confirm the message of the sermon for themselves and highlight additional passages cited in the sermon.

The eucharist   One of the most important components of public worship is the eucharist, which many Christians see as the primary reason to meet. With the exception of the Quakers and the Salvation Army, all denominations celebrate this ritual; and in Catholic and Orthodox churches, most Anglican churches, and some Protestant churches, the eucharist is celebrated at least weekly.

The eucharist goes by several names, which reflect the different ways it is thought to bring Christians close to God. The word eucharist itself, which is in general use among Christians, comes from the Greek word for thanksgiving and reflects a focus on praising and thanking God for his gifts of creation and redemption. Orthodox Christians also use the name Divine Liturgy, which suggests two things. Because it is *divine*, it is a way for Christians on earth to participate with the saints in heaven in their worship of God. And because *liturgy* in this context means "work of the people," the eucharist becomes a meritorious work offered to God by the community. Among Protestants the eucharist is known as the Lord's supper, the Lord's table, and communion, which all emphasize the unifying aspect of gathering for a meal. Catholics most often refer to the eucharist as the **mass**, a term that derives from the formal Latin dismissal of the congregation at the end of the service. Because Catholics, like Orthodox Christians, view the eucharist as a sacrifice, Catholics frequently call it the sacrifice of the mass.

The eucharist's place of importance in public worship derives from a consensus among Christians that it is the religion's single most profound experience of communion with God. It is a ritual by which Christians seek to be emptied of their own concerns and take on the self-sacrificing mind of Christ. Formal confession of one's sins to a priest before receiving the eucharist is sometimes required by Orthodox and Catholic churches. In addition, Catholic, Orthodox, Lutheran, and some Methodist and Anglican churches believe that the bread and wine truly become the body and blood of the risen Christ. In eating the eucharist they receive Christ's divine body and blood into their own bodies as a spiritual food that perfects their communion with God. Accordingly, in all these denominations the consecrated bread and wine are treated with special reverence. In Catholic and Orthodox churches, a priest oversees the rite, and care is taken that no crumbs from the bread fall on the floor. Catholic churches commonly use individual wafers of unleavened bread that produce few if any crumbs when broken, and Orthodox priests dip the bread into the wine with a spoon and then place it carefully into the mouths of the communicants. After the eucharist, any remaining wine is consumed, and Catholic, Orthodox, and some Anglican and Lutheran churches retain any remaining bread so that it can be taken to the sick or served to those who desire the eucharist at times other than the eucharistic service. Catholic and Orthodox Christians keep the bread in locked cases called **tabernacles** (Figure 9.12), named after the Old Testament structure that served as God's house on earth. Tabernacles are often given places of prominence in church sanctuaries, or

Figure 9.12 Catholic and Orthodox Christians keep eucharistic bread, once it has been consecrated and become the body of Christ, in ornate cases called tabernacles. This particular example is in the shape of a church. The writing on the front (IC XC NIKA) is a Greek abbreviation for "Jesus Christ conquers." Source: Will Deming.

placed in special chapels and illuminated with candles or lights to honor the physical presence of Christ. Worshippers can visit a tabernacle outside of regular worship services to pray and express their adoration to God the Son.

Protestants also see the eucharist as an intimate experience of communion with God, but they hold very different views on how it works. They frequently pass the eucharist to one another as an affirmation of the Reformation teaching that all believers belong to a holy priesthood. Lutherans as well as some Methodists and Anglicans believe that Christ is physically present in the bread and wine, but reject (along with the Orthodox) the Catholic doctrine of transubstantiation. Other Protestants hold that Christ's presence is only spiritual or symbolic. Finally, out of a concern for recovering alcoholics, many Protestants use grape juice rather than wine, a practice that originated with Thomas Welch in the Methodist tradition and eventually led to the production and sale of Welch's Grape Juice.

> **Did you know ...**
>
> Kellogg's Corn Flakes were created in the 1890s by two Seventh-day Adventists, Dr. John Kellogg and his younger brother Will Kellogg, as a way to diversify the vegetarian diet recommended by their church.

Church buildings Church buildings often provide an important context for public worship. Some Christians see their buildings as temples or houses of God, others see them as only meeting-houses or gathering places, and many regard them as some combination of both ideals. As a rule, Catholic and Orthodox churches tend toward the temple ideal, whereas Protestant churches, particularly the more Evangelical or Pentecostal ones, tend toward the meeting-house ideal. As a temple, the building is a special place where God is present and can be experienced in a unique way. Several things enhance this experience, including the presence of holy objects and the way in which the architecture of the building separates it from the outside world. Holy objects include icons, devotional statues of Jesus and the saints, relics, the altar on which the eucharist is offered, and most especially, the consecrated bread and wine. The specific means by which a building's architecture defines it as sacred space varies from culture to culture, but often includes limited or focused light, acoustic resonance, imposing height, and rich decoration with costly materials. As a meeting-house, by contrast, a church building is a practical, utilitarian structure, sometimes taking the form of an auditorium that directs the worshippers' attention to musicians or a speaker's podium.

But whether temple or meeting-house, most churches have a pulpit or ambo from which the word is proclaimed, a baptismal font or pool, and a table or altar where the eucharist is celebrated. In Protestant churches the pulpit is usually quite prominent, while the eucharistic table may be brought out only as needed. In Catholic and Orthodox churches, the altar is the focal point of the church; and Orthodox churches often do not even have a stationary pulpit. The Orthodox altar, moreover, stands behind an iconostasis, or icon screen, which separates and often hides the altar from the congregation (Figure 9.13). Only priests and their male assistants can go behind the iconostasis, a practice that marks it off as holy space. Similar taboos are observed in some Catholic churches and, more rarely, in Protestant churches. Since music is an important component of worship for many traditions, a prominent spot may also be given to a pipe organ, an area for singers (called a choir), a stage where a band leads songs, or a screen onto which the words of songs are projected.

The Christmas season Most Christians gather to observe a number of annual holy days and seasons of worship. The celebration of Jesus' birth, or **Christmas** (Christmass) is the best-known Christian worship season, although it ranks after Easter in theological importance. Western Christians typically prepare for Christmas by observing the season of **Advent**, which begins four Sundays before Christmas. Eastern Christians, however, observe the Nativity Fast, which begins on November 15 and lasts 40 days. Since both practices encourage Christians to reflect on Christ's first advent (coming), and on his final advent in judgment at the end of time, it can be a time of hopeful expectation or sorrow and repentance.

Christmas proper begins on December 25 and lasts 12 days, during which there is a focus on the mystery of God becoming human. The initial worship service often begins the evening before Christmas (Christmas Eve) or at midnight, in imitation of the gospel story of angels announcing Jesus' birth to shepherds at night. A public reading of Jesus' birth narrative from the gospel is sometimes acted out by children in a Christmas pageant. The story of a lowly woman giving birth to the Son of God in a stable, this narrative often gives the service a quiet, tender quality, while the announcement that God has become human to save the world makes it a festival of great joy.

The Christmas season concludes on January 6 with the observance of the Epiphany, when the infant Jesus was first presented to the world. In the west, this is associated most closely with the Gospel of Matthew's account of wise men from the east coming

Figure 9.13 In accordance with the Orthodox tradition, this Ukrainian church has an iconostasis (screen of icons) between the congregation and the eucharistic table. (The table in front of the screen is for displaying icons related to the particular events remembered in the worship service.) Source: Will Deming.

to worship the baby Jesus. Their gifts of gold, frankincense, and myrrh provide one of the religious rationales for giving gifts at Christmas. Orthodox Christians call Epiphany the Theophany, and associate it with Jesus' baptism, when God proclaimed that Jesus was his beloved son.

> ### Sacred Traditions and Scripture
>
> #### Wise Men Visit the Baby Jesus
>
> Matthew's is the only gospel to record that wise men from the east (perhaps Persian astrologers) visited the newborn Jesus. In later Christian tradition, the wise men are identified as three kings (Figure 9.14). Luke's gospel, which is the only other gospel to record Jesus' birth, describes shepherds coming to Jesus.

(continued)

Figure 9.14 A child plays the part of one of the wise men, bearing a gift for Jesus in a nativity play. Source: Will Deming.

> In the time of King Herod, after Jesus was born in Bethlehem of Judea, wise men from the East came to Jerusalem, asking, "Where is the child who has been born king of the Jews? For we observed his star at its rising, and have come to pay him homage." . . . When they saw that the star had stopped, they were overwhelmed with joy. On entering the house, they saw the child with Mary his mother; and they knelt down and paid him homage. Then, opening their treasure chests, they offered him gifts of gold, frankincense, and myrrh.
>
> Matthew 2:1–11 NRSV

The Easter season   The most important annual festival is **Easter**, which celebrates Jesus' bodily resurrection from the dead. The date of Easter in western churches can be any Sunday between March 22 and April 25 because, like the Jewish Passover with which it is associated, it follows a combined lunar-solar calendar. The Orthodox, who call Easter by the Greek name Pascha, follow a different calendar, often observing Easter later than Catholics and Protestants. In all three traditions Easter is preceded by a season called **Lent**, during which most Christians undertake special acts of prayer, abstinence, and service in order to distance themselves from the distractions of the world and focus their lives on God. In many cultures this somber period is preceded by a celebration of excess known as Carnival or Mardi Gras ("Fat Tuesday"). While not officially part of Christianity, Carnival serves to moderate Lenten observances by first celebrating the things from which Christians must abstain.

In western Christianity, Lent begins on Ash Wednesday and lasts for 40 days. Sundays are not included in counting these days as they are celebrations of the resurrection, on which fasting is inappropriate. On Ash Wednesday, worshippers are marked with ashes on the forehead or scalp to remind them of their mortality—from which Christ's death and resurrection has redeemed them. As they mark them in this way, ministers traditionally recite God's words to Adam after the fall: "You are dust and to dust you shall return." Orthodox Christians count the 40 days of Lent differently and thus begin the season on a Monday. They commonly abstain from meat, fish, eggs, and dairy products during Lent, while Catholics observe Ash Wednesday and Good Friday (the last Friday in Lent) as solemn fasts, and the other Fridays in Lent as days of abstinence from meat. The Fridays of Lent are a time for Catholics to trace Jesus' path to Easter through a devotion called the **Stations of the Cross**. This involves meditating on 14 events that led to Jesus' death and burial by viewing images of these events. Lent is also a customary time to prepare for baptism, especially in Roman Catholicism. Adults are received into the church on the evening before Easter (Easter Vigil), after having completed a course on the Catholic faith during Lent.

Rituals, Rites, Practices

The Stations of the Cross

A set of 14 images are often used to mark the Stations of the Cross in a church. Figure 9.15 depicts station 12, Jesus dies on the cross surrounded by his female followers and a Roman guard; and Figure 9.16 depicts station 13, Jesus' body is taken down from the cross.

(continued)

Figure 9.15 Station of the Cross 12. Source: Will Deming.

Figure 9.16 Station of the Cross 13. Source: David R. Bains.

The last week in Lent, called Holy Week, observes the events that took place in the week prior to Jesus' death. It begins with the celebration of Jesus' triumphal entry into Jerusalem on Palm Sunday. In Catholic and many Protestant churches, it is customary on this day to read the biblical account of Jesus' death and burial, taking worshippers from the triumphant entry to his death in the same service. Holy Thursday, also known as Maundy Thursday, commemorates the Last Supper, when Jesus met with his disciples to institute the eucharist and, according to Catholic interpretation, the office of priesthood. Good Friday commemorates Jesus' crucifixion. Its liturgical observance differs sharply from the rest of the year. Churches are usually stripped of ornamentation, such as brass candlesticks and altar cloths, and the eucharist is not celebrated.

The celebration of Easter begins before dawn on Easter Sunday and continues for 50 days. It has become more and more common for Roman Catholic, Eastern Orthodox, and some Anglican and Protestant churches to begin their celebration on Saturday night. For those who attend, this is the chief service of the year. The Easter candle is lit from a new fire, just as the light of Christ was restored through his resurrection; the story of salvation is recounted through many readings from the Old Testament; baptisms take place; and the first eucharist of Easter is celebrated. In the Orthodox tradition, the congregation assembles in a darkened church before midnight and then leaves the building to process around it. When they return to the front, the resurrection is proclaimed. The congregation then reenters the church and a triumphant celebration of the eucharist commences. On the fortieth day of Easter, Jesus' return to heaven is observed, and 10 days later the Easter season concludes with an observance called Pentecost, which celebrates the descent of the Holy Spirit on the apostles as they were gathered in Jerusalem.

Saints' days and other festivals Apart from the Christmas and Easter cycles, the passage of the year is regarded by most Christians as ordinary time. This term refers to time that is "ordered" by lectionary readings that lead congregants through one of the gospels over the course of a year. During ordinary time there are some additional special days. A few of these, such as All Saints' Day (Figure 9.17), Trinity Sunday, and the Feast of the Body and Blood of Christ, commemorate theological doctrines. Many more, however, commemorate events in the lives of Jesus and Mary, while the vast majority commemorate the lives of saints, although after Vatican II, the number of saints' days observed by Catholics was greatly reduced to increase their focus on the events and teachings recorded in the Bible. Protestants ignore most special days, although Mother's Day and Father's Day were created by American Protestants to honor parents, and festivals that celebrate the local community and its founders can function like special days.

Private devotions

Christians pursue their communion with God not only in public worship, but also in individual and group devotions. While these vary, prayer and the study of scripture are common to almost all denominations.

Figure 9.17 As in many eastern European countries, these Polish Catholics observe All Saints' Day by visiting the graves of deceased relatives and adorning the cemetery with flowers and candles. Source: Reproduced by by permission of John Thaxter.

Scripture study The goal of scripture study is not to master the content of the Bible, but to encounter God and discern his will. Many Christians, especially Evangelicals, set aside a regular time each week or each day to read and study the Bible by themselves; and many take part in group Bible studies, which offer encouragement and fellowship. A popular way to study scripture meditatively is *lectio divina* (divine reading), which has four stages. First, Christians read over a passage of scripture slowly and expectantly, listening for ways the passage might speak directly to them. Second, they meditate on the entire passage or on key words that stand out. Third, they engage in prayer, inwardly or out loud. And finally, they move to contemplation, described as resting in the presence of God.

Scripture study invariably involves interpretation, and Christian denominations differ on the extent to which their members can interpret scripture without the guidance of church officials. Evangelical Christians encourage individual interpretation, since they place religious authority in scripture itself, rather than in a church hierarchy. Catholic and Orthodox Christians, on the other hand, give much more weight to the official pronouncements of the church. While individuals are encouraged to read the Bible for devotional purposes, the authority to determine the Bible's theological meaning rests with the clergy. Another option is offered by Protestants such as Lutherans and Presbyterians, who use what are called confessions. These are statements of the denomination's core beliefs, intended as guides for biblical interpretation. Confessions carry authority, not because persons in authority wrote them, but because they are believed to reflect biblical truth.

Finally, the way in which a particular church interprets the Bible also depends on its understanding of the divine inspiration of scripture. Fundamentalist Christians usually insist that the Bible is entirely without error. For example, when the Bible says that Joshua caused the sun to stand still in the sky, it must be accepted as historically and scientifically true. Other conservative Christians, however, hold a more limited notion of biblical inerrancy by taking into account the scientific limitations of its ancient authors and the Bible's literary genres: one should not credit the biblical authors with an understanding of quantum physics, nor should one interpret poetry in the same way that one interprets law or narrative. Liberal Christians, in turn, argue that the Bible is not God's actual words but only a human record of God's words as they were handed down over time. They hold that many things contained in the Bible, such as historical statements or teachings concerning the roles of women, should not be accepted as inspired or authoritative. Finally, Pentecostals favor an *experiential* interpretation of the Bible, which understands God's inspiration as ongoing. In their view, biblical passages can have multiple meanings, and these become known with certainty only when a Christian experiences God's spirit as their guide to interpretation.

Not surprisingly, differing views on biblical inspiration have influenced how the Bible has been translated into modern languages, leading some churches to prefer one translation over another. In English-speaking countries, for example, conservative Protestants often insist on the King James Version, first published in 1611. They consider only this translation to be scripture, not the New American Bible, which is used by many Catholics, or the New Revised Standard Version, which is preferred by more liberal Protestants. Study Bibles have also become quite popular since the 1970s, reinforcing a particular view of inspiration through introductory materials and commentary. Recently, these have begun catering to specialized audiences such as teenagers, feminists, and environmentalists.

Sacred Traditions and Scripture

Bible Translations

Modern translations of the Bible have increasingly sought to soften or eliminate altogether the male-centered language of the Bible. "Brothers" is often rendered "brothers and sisters," and "Father and Son" can be couched as "Parent and Child." The challenge of this undertaking can be seen from the following passage, taken from the *New Testament and Psalms: An Inclusive Version* (Oxford, 1995):

> Jesus said, "Now the Human One has been glorified, and in that one God has been glorified. If God has been glorified in the Human One, God will also glorify that very one in Godself and will glorify that one at once …
> Having spoken these words, Jesus looked up to heaven and said, "Father-Mother, the hour has come; glorify your Child so that the Child may glorify you.

Gospel of John 13:31–32; 17:1

Prayer   Like Bible study, prayer is an important component of private devotion. Whether one prays as an individual or in a small group, private prayer becomes a conversation with God in which one both speaks and listens to God. Some Christians detect God speaking to them through an insight, a change in their inner disposition, or a scripture reading, while others claim to hear God in audible words and see visions sent by God.

Broadly speaking, there are prayers of adoration, confession, supplication, and thanksgiving. Adoration praises God for his greatness, while confession acknowledges human sinfulness and seeks God's forgiveness. Supplication makes requests of God, and thanksgiving offers gratitude for blessings already received. Some Pentecostal and Charismatic Christians reject the idea that Christians must ask God for blessings. As proponents of the so-called Word of Faith theology, they teach that the Bible has already promised blessings to Christians, and to receive them Christians need only confess their faith in these promises and believe that God is already fulfilling them. Charismatics, moreover, pray to God "in tongues," which they understand as a special prayer language that God gives them through his Spirit.

Intercession of the saints   Catholic and Orthodox Christians not only pray to God, but also to the saints. Saints, as we have seen, are Christians from past times who led such exemplary and holy lives that they now have a special standing with God in heaven. When Christians pray to a saint, they are asking the saint to use their special standing to intercede for them. The saint, in turn, prays to God on their behalf. This intercessory relationship with the saints is clearly seen in the last lines of the "Hail Mary," a common prayer to St Mary, Jesus' mother:

> Holy Mary,
> Mother of God,
> pray for us sinners, now
> and at the hour of our death.

Praying to saints is appealing to many, because people often find saints more approachable than God or Christ. Having once lived on earth as sinners, saints are believed to have special empathy for certain human concerns. There are literally thousands of saints associated with thousands of causes, professions, and other activities. For example, St Jude, one of the 12 apostles, is the patron saint of lost causes. Devotion to him includes a set of prayers to be prayed for nine days, called a novena. St Joseph, the husband of Mary, is the patron saint of fathers and fatherhood, and St Ambrose (ca. 337–397) looks after animal husbandry and beekeeping. When new causes arise, saints are assigned to them as well. For instance, Isidore of Seville (560–636), who compiled a well-organized dictionary-like work, has become the patron saint of the internet.

> **Talking about Religion**
>
> ## The Many Meanings of "Saint"
>
> The New Testament uses the term saint (Greek, "holy one") to refer to all Christians, and modern Christians sometimes use the term in this way. More usually, however, the term refers to a Christian who has passed away and now has special access to God. In earlier centuries there was no formal process for canonizing saints. They were simply identified by popular acclaim and recognized by the local bishop. This procedure is still the practice in Orthodox churches. In Roman Catholicism, by contrast, to be declared a saint, a person must be recognized by the church hierarchy in Rome as having lived a model life and demonstrated their power as an intercessor before God by having performed at least two miracles. If the person was martyred, only one miracle is required. The miracles for recently canonized saints are often unexplained medical cures that resulted from a saint's intercession on behalf of the sick. Protestants do not seek intercession through saints, nor do they formally recognize new ones, although they may refer to figures like the apostle Paul or Francis of Assisi as saints. Many Protestants also celebrate the memory of exemplary figures such as John Calvin, John Wesley, and Martin Luther King, Jr.

Mary is by far the most important saint because of her role in giving birth to the Son of God. Catholics commonly refer to her as the Blessed Virgin Mary, and Orthodox Christians call her the Bearer of God (*Theotokos*). Roman Catholics maintain that Mary entered into the world without original sin, a doctrine called the Immaculate Conception; and both Catholics and Orthodox teach that she left this life by being taken, body and soul, directly into heavenly glory. Catholics call this the Assumption of Mary. Among Catholics a common devotion to Mary is the rosary. It consists of repeating the Hail Mary, the Lord's Prayer, and a few other prayers while meditating on certain saving events, or "mysteries," in the lives of Mary and Jesus. Because this devotion requires dozens of repetitions, a string of beads, also called a rosary, is used to keep count.

Mary can be approached as the patron of any good work, and is associated with innumerable causes, such as cooking, aviation, fishing, silk manufacture, motherhood, virginity, and tile making. She is also linked to many locations—dioceses, hospitals, cities, and countries. As the Immaculate Conception she is the patron saint of the United States, and as Our Lady of Guadalupe she is the Queen of Mexico, Patroness of Latin America, and Empress of the Americas. Her association with these regions is indicative of another important role of saints. Because of their close relation to God, saints can localize access to God in a particular place. To emphasize this point, Pope John Paul II (1978–2005) canonized 476 saints from different places around the world and recognized (beatified) another 1,315 men and women who might be canonized as saints by a future pope.

A Closer Look

Holy Objects

Almost all Christians believe that God "became flesh" (Latin, *carnis*) in Jesus' physical being. Based on this incarnational principle, Christians often maintain that certain physical objects can bring one close to God. The most common of these are icons, statues, and relics.

Orthodox churches use two-dimensional depictions of Christ and the saints, called icons, which worshippers bow before and kiss, and clergy honor with incense during the liturgy (Figure 9.18). Catholics use both icons and statues, often with a stand for votive candles in front of them so that worshippers can honor the saint by lighting a candle. Both Catholic and Orthodox churches display relics, which are meaningful remnants from the life of a saint, such as bones, ashes, or devotional objects.

Figure 9.18 This icon of Saint Andrew, one of Jesus' original disciples, is illuminated by a hanging votive lamp and stands behind a brass altar containing sand, in which worshippers put tall candles. Source: Will Deming.

Pastoral rites

A Christian's communion with God frequently needs to be repaired or redefined in order to sustain it. For most Christians this requires clergy to perform sacraments, and all traditions rely upon clergy or other ministers to provide personal counsel and spiritual direction throughout an individual's life. These are called pastoral rites, and they include reconciliation, pastoral care and healing, death rites, and vocations.

Reconciliation When Christians sin, their communion with God is strained, impeded, or altogether broken. This requires Christians to be reconciled to God by repenting of their sin and seeking God's forgiveness. Protestants and Anglicans believe that individuals can do this on their own without clergy, although they often say communal prayers of confession in public services. Catholics and Orthodox Christians, on the other hand, teach that forgiveness for some sins occurs in the sacrament of reconciliation, which must be performed by a priest. In reconciliation, also known as confession or **penance**, a penitent verbally confesses their sins to a priest. The priest then imposes a penance, and grants absolution from the sins. *A* penance (as opposed to penance) is an act by which a Christian expresses remorse for sin, seeks to destroy their selfish will, and works for the welfare of others. Confessors impose a penance suited to an individual's spiritual state and the gravity and nature of their sin. It can include prayer, self-denial, or works of mercy. Orthodox Christians who receive the eucharist infrequently (a few times a year) must confess their sins prior to receiving it. Among Catholics it is only very serious sins (mortal sins) that must be confessed to a priest before receiving the eucharist, because these destroy the individual's love for God. Lesser sins, known as venial sins, merely wound an individual's love for God. They do not require the intervention of a priest, but regular confession to a priest is encouraged nonetheless.

Pastoral care and healing the sick In some cultures, it is common for clergy to make regular visits to the homes of their church members. While unannounced pastoral calls are becoming increasingly rare, clergy or other church leaders still visit the sick and those experiencing major life-transitions, such as the birth of a child, divorce, or a death in the family. In eastern Christianity an annual visit by the priest to bless a family's house and its Christmas decorations remains an important rite, and in large parishes decorations must remain in place for weeks for the priest to make his rounds. In the United States and other western societies, it is more common for clergy to offer pastoral care at their church offices, where they provide advice and counseling by appointment. This is especially true for prenuptial counseling, although this can also take place at retreats or seminars attended by groups of couples.

When Christians become ill, Catholic and Orthodox priests perform the sacrament of anointing the sick. Formerly known as extreme unction and reserved for those on their death beds, this sacrament is now also performed at weekly or monthly healing services in local churches. The anointing with oil and the laying on of hands in these healing services seek to address the physical aspects of illness in a way that prayer alone cannot. When Pentecostal and Charismatic ministers practice healing, recovery is attributed to the faith of the sick person and the work of the Holy Spirit.

Death rites The final days of life present Christians with their last opportunities to affirm their communion with God or repair it if it has been broken. If they are successful, they enter into eternal communion with God, called heaven; if not, only eternal separation from God, or hell, awaits them. For this reason, clergy and other church leaders visit Christians on their deathbeds, and sometimes conservative pastors challenge the dying to repent of any remaining sins that might separate them from God. The last rites as performed by Catholics and Orthodox Christians include anointing the sick with oil, performing the sacrament of reconciliation, and serving the eucharist.

In anticipation of a bodily resurrection from death, most Christians bury their dead, although cremation is becoming increasingly acceptable. Because Catholics envision a transitional state of punishment between earthly life and eternal communion with God, called Purgatory, their funerals include prayers that the dead will be relieved of these punishments. This can be done at a wake, where people view the body, or later at the gravesite. Between the wake and the burial, Catholics ordinarily celebrate a mass, sometimes called a requiem mass, in which they pray for the dead to receive final repose in heaven.

Hearing God's call Christians sometimes speak of having a calling or **vocation**, meaning that they believe God intends for them to take up a particular line of work. For lay Christians, vocations can be specifically Christian pursuits, such as evangelism or serving on an important church committee, or they can be any professional career that is undertaken *as a Christian*, especially if it helps others or contributes to a just society. For those who wish to enter into one of the spiritual vocations of the church—for example, the priesthood or the monastic life—a formal process of personal reflection called discernment must take place to establish that one has, indeed, been called by God to this work (Figure 9.19). Candidates for the priesthood also undergo ordination by a bishop, a ritual that can include solemn vows, lying prostrate on the floor, and receiving certain tools of ministry, such as a chalice to celebrate the eucharist or a Bible. Candidates for the Catholic priesthood must be unmarried at the time of their ordination and remain unmarried throughout their lives. By contrast, Orthodox and Anglican priests as well as Protestant clergy are usually expected to be married, although Orthodox priests may not enter into marriage *after* ordination, and only unmarried priests may be promoted to the office of bishop.

The monastic life In Catholic and Orthodox churches, one may also receive a call to become a monk or nun, which is a nonordained calling, meaning that these Christians remain laypersons. Monks and nuns are distinguished from priests by taking the title brother or sister instead of father. Some live independently in society, and a few become isolated hermits, but the majority join religious orders and live in community with other monks or nuns. Priests can also join orders and live in community with monks. Some of these orders, like the Trappists, several Benedictine orders, and most Eastern Orthodox orders, devote themselves to a life of contemplative prayer, teaching, and spiritual exercises. Others, such as the Society of Jesus (Jesuits) and the Missionaries of Charity founded by Mother Teresa of Calcutta, pursue active ministries that benefit the sick and poor. Some orders are also found in Anglicanism, and a few in

Figure 9.19 Since the 1950s, women clergy have become increasingly common in mainline Protestant denominations. In 2024, however, there was a backlash against women clergy in the Southern Baptist Convention, the world's largest Baptist organization. Here, two female Presbyterian ministers preside over the eucharist celebration. Source: Will Deming.

Protestantism. Ecumenical orders, such as the Taizé Community in France, now draw members from all major Christian groups. Overall, however, the number of men and women who join Christian orders has declined since the 1960s.

Marriage Almost all churches acknowledge marriage as a vocation, and for Catholic and Orthodox Christians it is defined as one of the seven sacraments. In most cases the marriage ceremony must be performed in a Christian setting and be presided over or witnessed by a priest. In Orthodox ceremonies, the priest or members of the wedding party put crowns on the couple, an act that identifies the bride and groom as martyrs who pledge to sacrifice the self for the benefit of the spouse. Most Christian marriages follow a conservative interpretation of the Bible in which the husband's calling is to be a leader in the church and the head of his family, while the wife is called to submit to her husband's decisions, work inside the home, and raise children. Liberal Christians often argue for equality within marriage, criticizing the biblical model of female submission as coming from a time when all societies were male-centered. But as Christianity continues to expand in the Global South, where societies can be quite androcentric, the biblical model of wives submitting to their husbands will most likely remain the norm among Christians for the foreseeable future. While several Protestant and Anglican denominations now perform same-sex marriages, and some European Catholic bishops permit blessing same-sex relationships, this practice is strongly opposed by more conservative Christians in all denominations.

> ### A Closer Look
>
> ## The Role of Women in Christian Marriage
>
> Because the Bible contains several views on the role of Christian women, the proper relationship between husbands and wives continues to be a point of controversy. Here are two contrasting statements on gender relations from the New Testament:
>
> > There is no longer Jew or Greek, there is no longer slave or free, there is no longer male and female; for all of you are one in Christ Jesus.
> >
> > Galatians 3:28 NRSV
>
> > Wives, be subject to your husbands as you are to the Lord. For the husband is the head of the wife just as Christ is the head of the church … Just as the church is subject to Christ, so also wives ought to be, in everything, to their husbands.
> >
> > Ephesians 5:22–23 NRSV

Extending communion with God to others

One of the most common Christian prayers, the Lord's Prayer, addresses God with the petition, "Your kingdom come, your will be done, on earth as in heaven." Similarly, the Gospel of Matthew culminates with Jesus' so-called Great Commission to "make disciples of all nations, baptizing them in the name of the Father, and of the Son, and of the Holy Spirit." Both of these important statements reflect the Christian desire to bring the whole world into communion with God. Accordingly, Christians attempt to extend God's salvation through Christ to the world by sharing their religion with others and by correcting what they, as Christians, regard as sins and injustices in their societies.

Evangelism

For many Christians there is a great urgency to evangelize—that is, to spread the gospel (Greek, *euangelium*). Believing that those who die outside of communion with God will forever suffer in hell, they strive to give everyone a chance to hear the gospel message at least once. Not surprisingly, some Christians feel called to **evangelism** as a vocation, and a few become professional evangelists, supported by the prayers and financial contributions of their churches.

Throughout much of the modern period, Christians in the western world engaged in foreign missions, sending missionaries from Europe and North America to Latin America, Africa, Asia, and Oceania. These missionaries were, on the whole, remarkably successful, with the result that Christianity is now practiced in all parts of the world. Today, western missionaries still travel to these regions, but many of the Christians in recently evangelized nations, such as South Korea and Nigeria, now travel to the west to evangelize. As a consequence, the phrase foreign mission has been replaced by global mission.

In their home countries, Christians witness their faith through their behavior in everyday activities, share their beliefs with friends and acquaintances, and invite non-Christians to attend church services. At church, their preacher might end the Sunday sermon with an altar call, which is an invitation for non-Christians in the audience to come to the front of the church and publicly accept Jesus as their savior. Other Christians share the gospel by supporting preachers and evangelists who go door-to-door in a neighborhood, preach on the radio, TV, or internet, and hold revival meetings. In recent American history the best-known evangelist and revivalist was Billy Graham (1918–2018), whose preaching drew such large crowds that his organization had to rent out sports stadiums to accommodate them.

Social reform and social justice The purpose of sharing the gospel is not confined to bringing individuals into communion with God. Many Christians seek to advance the reign of God by reshaping society according to Christian principles. Among some Christians this means working for social justice, which includes such things as advocacy for the poor and oppressed, promotion of religious freedom, and protection of the environment. For many liberal Christians, furthering social justice has even replaced the goal of converting others to Christianity. This is because liberal theologians often teach a theology of universalism, which advances the notion that all religions lead to the same all-merciful and all-loving God who grants salvation to everyone.

Conservative Christians, on the other hand, may strive to establish God's kingdom on earth by denouncing abortion and homosexuality as sins, and objecting to public schools teaching evolutionary theories that undermine belief in the Bible's story of creation. Leaders of many conservative denominations also take the position that a nation's prosperity is determined by the righteousness of its society. If a nation keeps God's laws, it will thrive; if not, God will punish it with natural disasters, political instability, and financial woes. Envisioning the United States as a Christian nation, these denominations prominently display the American flag in their sanctuaries and hold patriotic celebrations on the Fourth of July. The extent to which this connection between Christian righteousness and national prosperity is current in the United States is indicated by the presidential inaugurations of Dwight Eisenhower (1953, 1957) and Ronald Reagan (1981, 1985). Both men took the oath of office with a hand on a traditional King James Bible, opened to 2 Chronicles 7:14: "If my people, which are called by my name, shall humble themselves, and pray, and seek my face, and turn from their wicked ways; then will I hear from heaven, and will forgive their sin, and will heal their land."

Theologies of withdrawal and isolation

Not all Christians consider evangelism a priority, however. In churches where people become members of the congregation as infants, there is sometimes much more emphasis on Christian formation (instilling Christian values) than on conversion. Other churches fear the corrupting influence of the larger society and seek to create a separate, Christian society. In America, the best-known isolationist Christians are the Amish, who see modern, secular society as detrimental to their communion with God. Living in their own communities, they operate their own schools, dress in ways that express their understanding of modesty, and ban or curtail the use of conveniences such as cars, electricity, and telephones, which increase the pace of life in distracting ways.

In rare cases, isolationist groups view the world around them not simply as a bad influence, but as evil, and sometimes interpret this to be a sign that the end of the world is at hand. Following certain interpretations of biblical books such as Daniel and Revelation, which scholars classify as apocalyptic literature, they close themselves off from the larger society to remain pure in anticipation of Christ's second coming. Over time, when their expectations of Christ's return have been disappointed, they either moderate their views or become even more radical, even taking up arms against those on the outside. An example of the first type is the Seventh-day Adventists, who broke away from the earlier Millerite movement, which had predicted that Christ would come again on October 22, 1844. Two prominent examples of the second type are the Peoples Temple (1954–1978) and the Branch Davidians (1955–1993). Both movements became involved in standoffs with agencies of the U.S. government that ended in violence and death.

CONCLUSION

Christianity offers communion with ultimate reality, which most Christians understand to be a single God who exists in the three persons of the Trinity: God the Father, God the Son, and God the Holy Spirit. This communion is made possible through God the Son, who became incarnate as the man Jesus. Through Jesus' teaching, crucifixion, and resurrection, humans can become free from sin and death. Christians experience this communion with God as members of a church, which most Christians join by being baptized, repenting of their sins, and making a profession of belief, although not always in that order. The Christian life then becomes a matter of remaining in this communion and offering it to non-Christians around the world. After death, Christians expect to enjoy eternal communion with God in a manner more intimate and loving than is possible here on earth.

For review

1. Name two Christian sacraments and explain how they orient people to Christ and God.
2. Who are the "persons" of the Trinity? How do Christians relate to each of them?
3. Why is Jesus' crucifixion the basis of communion with God?
4. What are some of the meanings of the word "church"?
5. What are some of the many images of Jesus Christ used by Christians?
6. How do the interiors of Roman Catholic, Eastern Orthodox, and Protestant churches differ in appearance?
7. Who are the saints, and what role do they play?
8. Name some of the Christian vocations.
9. What are some of the ways that Christians extend communion with God to others?

For discussion

1. Given that most Christians believe in God, Jesus Christ, and the Holy Spirit, as well as saints, angels, and Satan, how is Christianity still a monotheistic religion?
2. What is the relation between the Christian religion and Judaism, both historically and theologically?

Key Terms

Advent	The period of expectation before Christmas, lasting four weeks.
baptism	The Christian initiation rite, seen as a purification and rebirth through water.
bishop	The highest-ranking leader in many forms of Christianity.
Christ	The Greek translation of the Hebrew word *messiah* (anointed one); a king sent from God.
Christian	A follower of the messiah (Greek, *christos*).

Christmas	The annual celebration of Jesus' birth.
church	Local, regional, national, and international communities of Christians; also a building where Christians meet.
confirmation	A rite that follows baptism, more fully incorporating a Christian into the church.
creeds	Summaries of important Christian beliefs.
crucifixion	Death by being hung on a giant wooden cross; the manner of Jesus' death.
denomination	One of several divisions or church traditions within Christianity.
Easter	The annual celebration of Christ's bodily resurrection from the dead.
Eastern Orthodoxy	One of three major types of Christianity, having its origins in the eastern part of the Roman empire (see Roman Catholicism and Protestantism).
ecumenism	A unifying movement that began in the twentieth century whereby different denominations and churches join in common causes.
eucharist	A stylized meal of bread and wine through which Christians experience the body and blood of the crucified and risen Christ.
evangelism	The promotion of the Christian message (gospel) among non-Christians in an effort to convert them.
fundamentalist	A Christian committed to the authority of the Bible above all other truths.
Global South	Christian populations living in areas south of the equator; now the largest contingent in Christianity.
gospel	"Good news"; the Christian message of salvation; also the name of the first four books of the New Testament.
Great Schism	The separation of the Roman Catholic and Eastern Orthodox churches in 1054 CE.
Holy Spirit	One of three persons of the Christian godhead, or Trinity.
icon	A two-dimensional image of Jesus or the saints.
Jesus of Nazareth	Founder of Christianity; held by Christians to be God's son and messiah.
Lent	The 40-day period of solemn reflection and abstinence that precedes Easter.
Mary	The mother of Jesus and the principal saint in Catholic and Orthodox Christianity.
mass	The Catholic name for the eucharist.
messiah	The Hebrew term for "anointed one," translated into Greek as "Christ"; the title given to Jesus of Nazareth, the founder of Christianity.
parables	Various kinds of comparisons used by Jesus in his teaching.
patriarch	A principal leader in the Orthodox church.
penance	A ritual of confession; an act of contrition necessitated by sin.

Pentecostalism	A movement within Christianity in which Christians receive miraculous gifts from the Holy Spirit, including the ability to speak in spiritual languages.
pope	The bishop of Rome and leader of the Roman Catholic church.
priest	A type of ordained church leader found in many forms of Christianity.
Protestant Reformation	A sixteenth-century reform movement in Europe which gave birth to Protestant Christianity.
Protestantism	One of three major types of Christianity, having its origins in the Reformation (see Eastern Orthodoxy and Roman Catholicism).
Roman Catholicism	One of three major types of Christianity, having its origins in the western part of the Roman empire; headed by the bishop of Rome (the pope). (See Eastern Orthodoxy and Protestantism.)
sacrament	A ritual which imparts a special grace from God. Some churches recognize seven sacraments, others recognize only baptism and the eucharist.
Scholasticism	A form of scholarship begun in Catholicism in the twelfth century that sought to create a unified understanding of the world.
Second Vatican Council	A council of Roman Catholic bishops convened in the 1960s to address the challenges of modernity and pluralism.
Stations of the Cross	Fourteen images that depict the last hours of Jesus' life, including his crucifixion and burial.
tabernacle	A locked case where Catholic and Orthodox Christians store uneaten bread from the eucharist.
theosis	The process by which Orthodox Christians achieve divinity.
Trinity	The three persons of the Godhead: God, Christ, and the Holy Spirit.
vocation	A particular line of work or holy lifestyle to which Christians feel called by God.

Bibliography

A good first book

Linda Woodhead. *Christianity: A Very Short Introduction*. New York: Oxford University Press, 2004.

Further reading

Mary Farrell Bednarowski, ed. *Twentieth-Century Global Christianity. A People's History of Christianity*. Minneapolis, MN: Fortress Press, 2008.

Patrick Collinson. *The Reformation: A History*. New York: Modern Library, 2004.

Philip Jenkins. *The New Faces of Christianity: Believing the Bible in the Global South*. New York: Oxford University Press, 2006.

James M O'Toole. *The Faithful: A History of Catholics in America*. Cambridge, MA: Belknap Press of Harvard University, 2008.

Melanie C. Ross. *Evangelical Worship: An American Mosaic*. New York: Oxford University Press, 2021.

A Edward Siecienski. *Orthodox Christianity: A Very Short Introduction*. New York: Oxford University Press, 2019.

Keith Ward. *Christianity: A Short Introduction*. Oxford: Oneworld, 2000.

Reference and research

James Joseph Buckley, Frederick Christian Bauerschmidt and Trent Pomplun, eds. *The Blackwell Companion to Catholicism*. Oxford: Blackwell, 2007.

Diarmaid MacCulloch. *Christianity: The First Three Thousand Years*. New York: Viking, 2010.

Jaroslav Pelikan. *The Christian Tradition: A History of the Development of Doctrine*, 5 vols. Chicago: University of Chicago Press, 1971–1989.

Lamin O. Sanneh and Michael McClymond, eds. *The Wiley-Blackwell Companion to World Christianity*. Oxford: Wiley-Blackwell, 2016.

Geoffrey Wainwright and Karen B. Westerfield Tucker, eds. *The Oxford History of Christian Worship*. New York: Oxford University Press, 2006.

Gina A. Zurlo. *Global Christianity: A Guide to the World's Largest Religion from Afghanistan to Zimbabwe*. Grand Rapids, MI: Zondervan Academic, 2022.

CHAPTER 10

Islam
The oneness of God

Muslims on pilgrimage surround the Kabah ("Cube") in Mecca, unified in their submission to the one true God.
Source: Photo by Fadi El Binni.

DID YOU KNOW …

Muslims have their own traditions about figures found in Jewish and Christian writings, such as Noah, Abraham, Moses, Mary, and Jesus (see Figure 10.3). The Quran, Islam's holy book, even refers to Jesus as the messiah, although without the implication that Jesus was the savior of humanity or the Son of God.

Understanding the Religions of the World: An Introduction, Second Edition.
Edited by Will Deming.
© 2025 John Wiley & Sons Ltd. Published 2025 by John Wiley & Sons Ltd.

OVERVIEW

Islam appeared in the seventh century CE, making it the youngest of the major religions. With nearly 25 percent of the world's population, however, it is also the second-largest religion (Figure 10.1). Most Muslims live in the eastern hemisphere in a broad geographical corridor that stretches from Morocco to Indonesia. Within this corridor Islam encompasses hundreds of cultures, languages, and ethnic groups.

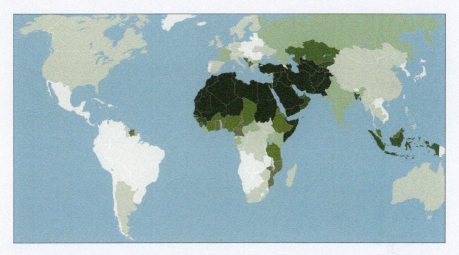

Figure 10.1 A map indicating the Muslim population of different countries as a percentage of each country's total population. Source: Wikimedia Commons.

Because Islam originated on the Arabian Peninsula, which is still home to its most sacred building, and because its main scripture, the Quran, is written in Arabic, Americans typically think of Muslims as Arabs, and Islam as a religion of the Middle East. Yet both these notions are incorrect. The nation with the largest Muslim population is Indonesia—where almost 13 percent of all Muslims live (243 million). After Indonesia comes Pakistan (233 million), India (200 million), and Bangladesh (151 million). These are followed by Nigeria (97 million), Egypt (90 million), Iran (83 million) and Turkey (80 million). Of these eight countries only three are in the Middle East (Egypt, Iran, and Turkey) and only one of these is Arab (Egypt). By comparison, the countries that Americans most often associate with Islam are relatively small: Saudi Arabia (32 million), Afghanistan (38 million), and Iraq (37 million) (see Figure 10.2).

Figure 10.2 Of the eight countries with the largest Muslim populations, only three are in the Middle East (in purple), and only one of these is Arab. Since Pakistan and Bangladesh were part of India until the 1947 Partition, almost a third of the world's Muslims can be said to live in Indonesia and the former territories of India (in green).

A Closer Look

The Islamic Diaspora in the West

Aside from Muslim populations in Asian, Middle Eastern, and African countries, there are significant populations of Muslims in western Europe and the Americas. These populations have been on the rise, moreover, due to the displacement of people by wars in Afghanistan, Iraq, Syria, and Yemen, as well as conversion. Many Muslims in England and France are immigrants from their former colonial territories, while many of those in Germany are Turks who arrived after World War II as guest workers.

In the Americas, Muslim communities in Suriname and Guyana are a result of indentured labor brought from India and Indonesia during colonial times, while Muslim communities in Argentina came to the New World with Spanish and Portuguese explorers and conquerors. In the United States, early Muslim populations developed much like other immigrant communities, settling, for example, in Dearborn, Michigan. Later groups sometimes came from the ranks of physicians, engineers, and other professionals

(*continued*)

> who immigrated to the United States from Pakistan and Arab countries, beginning in the 1960s. Others are part of the Nation of Islam, a form of Islam indigenous to American soil. This "Lost-Found Nation of Islam in the Wilderness of North America" began in the 1930s in impoverished Black communities in Detroit and Chicago, and catered exclusively to African Americans. Gaining national prominence under the name Black Muslims during the Civil Rights Movement, it split into two groups in the 1970s. The larger group affiliated itself with Sunni Muslims worldwide.

Despite Islam's wide geographical and cultural dispersion, it has remained a remarkably unified religion. One important source of this unity is the Muslim vision of *tawhid*, or oneness. In Islam God is understood to be a single god whose oneness resonates throughout his creation. He has given a *single* message to humanity through the *one* messenger, **Prophet Muhammad**, instructing humanity to join together in a *single* community, regardless of racial, national, social, or ethnic differences. Muslims also agree on a single version of their sacred scripture, the **Quran**. Unlike Catholic, Orthodox, and Protestant branches of Christianity, each of which has its own version of the Bible, containing a different number of books and translated in different ways, Muslims recognize only one text of the Quran in Arabic, which they recite and often memorize, regardless of their ability to understand Arabic. Beyond this, Islam requires five common practices that unify Muslims worldwide in a life of service to God and each other.

Yet Islam's common scripture and practices have not made it a monolithic religion. Its leaders never developed a strict orthodoxy, and within certain boundaries Islam encourages a diversity of views. Muslims promote a flexible system of legal rulings on lesser points of law, and there are two distinct branches of the religion, **Sunni** and **Shia** Islam. While this division is sometimes a source of conflict, Sunnis and Shias nonetheless worship together in Mecca and unite in common Islamic causes.

History

Timeline	
ca. 570 CE	The birth of Muhammad ibn Abd Allah.
610 CE	The Night of Power: Muhammad receives his first revelation in a cave near Mecca.
613 CE	Muhammad begins his public career as Prophet of God by reciting the Quranic message in Mecca.
619 CE	The death of Muhammad's uncle Abu Talib and Muhammad's wife Khadijah.
621 CE	Muhammad's Night Journey to Jerusalem and ascent to God.
622	The Muslim emigration from Mecca to Yathrib (Medina), marking year 1 of the Muslim calendar (AH 1).
627	The Battle of the Trench.
630	Mecca yields to Muhammad's armies; the beginning of Islamic rule in Mecca.
632	Muhammad dies in Medina; leadership of the religion goes to his close friend, Abu Bakr.
632–661	The "rightly guided period" of the first four caliphs (the Rashidun). The Arabian Peninsula is unified, Islamic rule extends into the Levant and Iraq through allegiances and battle.
644	The Quran is standardized with the creation of the Uthmanic Codex.
656–661	A civil war (*fitnah*) breaks out between those who supported Ali's right to leadership and those of Uthman's clan who supported Muawiyah, the eventual founder of the Umayyads.
661–750	The Umayyad dynasty, which moved the center of Islam from the Hijaz to Damascus.
750–1258	The Abbasid dynasty, which moved the center of Islam from Damascus to Baghdad.
9th–10th centuries	Formation of Islamic legal schools; Sufi groups take Islam into sub-Saharan Africa and northern India. Umayyads form a dynasty in Spain, and Shia Muslims spread into central Asia.
ca. 900	Rise of the Fatimids, the first Shia dynasty.
11th–13th centuries	Muslim and Christian armies fight in the Crusades.

(continued)

12th–13th centuries	The golden age of Islamic culture in Spain.
14th century	Rise of Naqshbandi Sufism; Sufi groups take Islam into southern India and Indonesia.
1453	The Ottomans, a Sunni dynasty, capture Constantinople, ending Byzantine rule.
early 16th century	The Safavids establish a Shia dynasty in Persia; Mughal rulers establish a Sunni dynasty in India; Suleyman the Magnificent becomes sultan of the Ottoman empire.
1722	Fall of the Safavid dynasty.
1730s	Beginning of the Wahhabi reform movement.
1757	Battle of Plassey, foreshadowing the end of Mughal rule in India.
1798	Napoleon invades Egypt, initiating the era of European colonialism in the Middle East.
19th century	Appearance of various Mahdist movements.
World War I–World War II	Period of intensive European colonization of the Middle East.
1919	The end of World War I; the Treaty of Sèvres dismembers the Ottoman empire.
1924	The Ottoman caliphate is abolished.
20th century	Autonomous nation states form in Muslim lands; Sayyid Abu al-Ala Mawdudi (1903–1979) and Sayyid Qutb (1906–1966) are active as reformers.
1932	The Kingdom of Saudi Arabia is founded.
1938	Oil is discovered in Saudi Arabia.
1940s–1960s	Pan-Arab and pan-Islamic movements appear.
1960s	Militant forms of Islam appear.
1979	The Ayatollah Khomeini comes to power in the Iranian Revolution.
late 20th–early 21st century	The U.S. invasion of Afghanistan and involvement in two Gulf wars.
2011	The Arab Spring: popular uprisings topple dictatorships in Tunisia, Egypt, and Libya.
2014–present	Religious and political unrest in Egypt, Syria, Iraq, and Afghanistan; the rise and fall of ISIS; Tunisia adopts a democratic form of government.

Islam began in a remote pocket of the seventh-century world—the western shore of the Arabian Peninsula, known as the Hijaz. At this time, two longstanding empires ruled over the territories that would become the heartland of Islam. The first was the Sassanian empire, a Persian dynasty in what is now Iraq and Iran. The second was the Byzantine empire, the successor to the eastern half of the old Roman empire. These two powers competed for control of the major trade routes that connected them with the Indian Ocean. The area of the Hijaz was of little interest to the rulers of these empires. It was mainly populated by Arab tribes, many of whom lived nomadic or semi-nomadic lifestyles, moving with flocks and herds from one oasis to another.

The Arab people before Muhammad

The Arab tribes on the Arabian Peninsula had no central government or codified law, and the Arabic they spoke consisted of numerous tribal dialects. There was no standard written form, although there did exist a widely cultivated genre of oral poetry. While some Jews and Christians also lived in the region, the religious life of the peninsula was dominated by polytheism and the worship of idols. Later, Muslims would identify these religious practices as belonging to a period of *jahiliyyah*, or spiritual ignorance in Arab history. The Arab tribes, who were often in conflict with one another, nonetheless joined in worship at several common shrines. Among the most important of these was a building named for its distinctive shape, the **Kabah**, or Cube. Standing about 45 feet high and made of granite from the nearby hills, the Kabah was located in the oasis town of Mecca. In the last month of every lunar year, tribal peoples from all over Arabia would come to Mecca to participate in a pilgrimage festival. This brought significant wealth to the people of the town, which they invested in an overland trading route from southern Arabia to Syria. Islamic sources suggest that Meccan society was becoming increasingly mercantile by the sixth century CE, showing the signs of social dislocation and economic disparity that such change often brings.

The life of the Prophet

Muhammad ibn Abd Allah, the prophet and founder of Islam, was born in or around 570 CE. Muhammad's father died before he was born, and his mother died when he was still a small child. Without parents or siblings, he was raised by his grandfather and his uncles. As a young man, Muhammad worked for a widow named Khadijah, representing her interests in the Yemen–Syria trade. The two grew fond of each other, and Khadijah, who was reportedly 15 years his senior, proposed marriage. Muhammad accepted and the two lived a modestly prosperous life. They had a number of children, although only three daughters survived to adulthood.

Islamic tradition holds that Muhammad avoided the polytheistic practices of his fellow Meccans, describing him as a *hanif*—a monotheist in the tradition of the Jewish patriarch Abraham. In Muslim accounts, Abraham expelled his concubine Hagar and their son Ishmael from his household. After wandering for days, Hagar found a well in the middle of the desert. Abraham, regretting his treatment of Hagar and Ishmael, eventually went looking for them. When he found them still alive, he settled by the well and built the Kabah to commemorate God's mercy on his family. The religious community that grew from this settlement is thought to be the ancestors of the *hanifs* in Mecca.

While little is known about Muhammad's early years, several miraculous incidents are said to have foreshadowed his religious destiny. On one occasion, during a business trip to Syria with his uncles, Muhammad encountered a Christian monk who interpreted a birthmark on his back as a sign that he would become "the great prophet of his people." These and other prophetic episodes in Muhammad's life connected him with traditions of prophecy that traced back to Moses, Abraham, and Adam.

Muhammad's call to prophecy and his years in Mecca

Muhammad's prophetic career began when he was about 40. During a religious retreat in a mountain cave outside of Mecca, he was visited by a being who took hold of him and gave the order, "Recite!" When the bewildered Muhammad replied that he could not, the being commanded twice more, "Recite!," and revealed to him his first prophetic pronouncement:

> Recite in the name of your Lord, who created!
> Who created man from an embryo.
> Recite! And your Lord is most generous,
> Who taught by the pen,
> Taught men what they know not.
> (Quran 96.1–5)

After doing as he was commanded, Muhammad ran from the cave. Halfway down the mountain, however, he was stopped by the same being, who bore down on him from across the horizon. Identifying himself as Gabriel, the archangel found in Jewish and Christian traditions, this being announced that Muhammad was the Messenger of God. When Muhammad arrived home, he was quite shaken and had to be reassured by Khadijah that he was not insane. Khadijah later took him to see her Christian cousin, who substantiated the divine nature of Muhammad's experience and foretold his success as a prophet. After the **Night of Power**, as this initial encounter with Gabriel became known, revelations came to Muhammad for the remainder of his life.

At first, Muhammad shared these revelations only with close friends and family members. Aside from Khadijah, this included his younger cousin Ali (who would marry one of Muhammad's daughters) and Abu Bakr (whose daughter was later betrothed to Muhammad). Both these men would lead the Islamic community after Muhammad's death. In 613, Muhammad was commanded by God to proclaim His message before a broader audience. Muhammad first turned to his clan, where he succeeded in converting his powerful uncle Hamzah and securing the protection—but not the conversion—of his uncle Abu Talib, the clan's leader. Yet most members of Muhammad's clan, who represented Mecca's elite citizenry, rejected Muhammad's message. They feared that his condemnation of tribal allegiances, his message of charity for the poor, and his call to end polytheistic worship at the Kabah would undermine their privileged way of life.

Muhammad also attracted a small number of followers from other groups in Mecca, some of whom, as a consequence, were persecuted by his clan. Muhammad's own person and possessions were initially protected by the benefaction of Abu Talib. But Abu Talib's death in 619 opened the way for reprisals from his clan. To compound his adversity, Khadijah also died that year. Isolated and threatened with poverty and physical harm, Muhammad fled to the nearby settlement of Ta'if, only to be rejected and driven off.

This year of Muhammad's greatest despair was followed by a divine encounter that not only reaffirmed his religious convictions, but also led to a closer relationship with Christians and Jews in the area. On what became known as the **Night Journey**, Muhammad mounted a winged horse named Buraq and was guided by the angel Gabriel to Jerusalem, to the site where the Jewish temple once stood. Once there, Muhammad ascended through seven heavens and came to within "two bow lengths" of God himself. When he returned to earth he carried with him the instructions for what would become Islam's unique form of prayer, and for nearly five years after the Night Journey, Muhammad and his followers prayed toward Jerusalem, in solidarity with Jews and Christians.

Muhammad's years in Medina

In 622, the fortunes of Muhammad and his followers improved greatly. This is the year of their *hijra*, or emigration from Mecca to Yathrib, a date-farming oasis community about 250 miles north of Mecca. The clans of Yathrib had been locked in a power struggle and needed a prestigious figure from the outside to arbitrate for them. They chose Muhammad because his following in Mecca had grown to perhaps 40 families, and he had been able to stand up to the Meccan authorities, who were at odds with the leadership of Yathrib.

The Muslim defection from Mecca was executed piecemeal and secretly, Muhammad's followers stealing away by night toward their new home. Within a few years, Muhammad had become the political and religious head of Yathrib, which he reorganized as an Islamic society. This first independent community of Muslims referred to themselves as an *ummah*—a community organized on the religious principle of *tawhid* rather than clan or ethnic ties. In Islamic history, this was seen as a watershed event: Muslims began to identify themselves collectively as the *ummah*, even across borders and ethnic identities; Yathrib was renamed Medina, which was short for City of the Prophet (*Medinat al-Nabi*); and the Islamic lunar calendar was created, designating the year of the *hijra* as year 1 of a new era.

> ### A Closer Look
>
> ## The Muslim Lunar Calendar
>
> Muslims use the Hijra calendar to keep track of the years, beginning with AH 1 (after *hijra*), or simply H 1 (*hijra*), which is the western (Gregorian) year 622 CE. Because the Hijra calendar is a lunar calendar having 6 months with 29 days and 6 with 30, for a total of 354 days, Muslim years are shorter than western years by about 10 days. As a result, the seasons are not aligned with the months: over a 32½-year cycle, summer, fall, winter, and spring are experienced in each of the months.

During the Medinan years, Muhammad established many of Islam's legal and social precedents. The month-long fast of **Ramadan** was instituted, commemorating God's initial revelation to Muhammad; the direction that Muslims faced during daily prayer was changed from Jerusalem to Mecca; and it was from Medina that Muhammad led a pilgrimage to Mecca near the end of his life, thereby defining the sequence of activities during **Hajj**, Islam's annual pilgrimage. Yet the move to Medina was not without difficulties. Muhammad's followers fled to the city leaving most of their possessions behind in Mecca. In 624, this situation encouraged a group of Muslims to attack a Meccan caravan returning from Syria, leading to formal armed conflict between the Meccans and the Muslims.

In the first year of combat, the Muslims won an important battle at a site called Badr. Since they were reportedly ill-equipped and outnumbered, the Battle of Badr was hailed as a confirmation of God's support for Muhammad. The following year, however, Muslims were routed at the Battle of Uhud, leaving Muhammad severely injured and his uncle Hamzah dead. Then, in 627, the Meccans and their allies attacked Medina itself. The attack failed, however, because the Medinans had fortified their city with a defensive trench, making it impossible for the Meccans to enter with their cavalry. The Meccan forces laid siege to the city until their supplies ran out, and then returned home demoralized. Often referred to as the Battle of the Trench (although no real combat took place), this incident was a major turning point.

Until this time, Muhammad had also struggled with political and religious resistance within the Medinan community. Insincere converts to Islam ("the hypocrites") and the city's three Jewish clans had become quite critical of Muhammad and his teachings. Matters got so bad that Muhammad exiled two of the Jewish clans, and when the third was accused of treason during the Battle of the Trench, all its men were executed.

In 628, Muhammad was inspired by a dream to lead his followers to Mecca on a pilgrimage. Although the Meccans barred the city's entrance, and no pilgrimage took place, the Muslims returned home with a 10-year truce promising them access to the city the following year. In 630, after an alleged violation of the truce by the Meccans, Muhammad marched on Mecca with his forces, only to have the Meccan elders surrender the city without a fight. In the wake of this Muslim triumph, the inhabitants of Mecca adopted Islam, and the Kabah was emptied of its idols and dedicated to the worship of the one true God. But Muhammad did not resettle in Mecca. Rather, he returned to Medina, where he died two years later.

The first four successors to Muhammad

During the last years of his life, Muhammad used his spiritual authority and charismatic presence to unite many groups under the banner of Islam. Most of the polytheistic Arabs of the peninsula had adopted Islam and pledged their loyalty to the leaders of Medina, and Muhammad had urged all members of the now substantial Muslim community to view one another as "brothers." Shortly after his death, however, some of this unity threatened to unravel. Muslims who were native to Medina seemed content to return to self-governance, while some of those who had emigrated to Medina with Muhammad rejoined their clans in Mecca.

Caliph Abu Bakr

Sensing the danger of a political schism, Muhammad's closest followers resolved to find a successor to Muhammad who would be acceptable to most Muslims. In a hasty meeting arranged even before Muhammad was buried, they agreed upon Muhammad's close friend and father-in-law, Abu Bakr. Muhammad's cousin and son-in-law, **Ali** ibn abi Talib, who was not at the meeting, seems to have been displeased with the choice of Abu Bakr. According to some reports, he felt that the leadership of the community should have fallen to him, and so he distanced himself from the new leader for several months. Although Ali eventually reconciled with Abu Bakr, the tradition of his claim to leadership would later become the basis for Shia Islam.

Most Muslims believed that Muhammad had not given any explicit instructions as to how the Islamic community should be governed after his death. Instead, he had urged the *ummah* to imitate his way of life, or *sunnah*, to respect one another as brothers, and to adhere to the revelations God had given him. These revelations, which were known collectively as the Quran, made it clear, moreover, that Muhammad was the last of God's inspired messengers, the "Seal of the Prophets." As a result, Abu Bakr came to power as a pious and wise person who had been a trusted companion of the late Prophet, not as an inspired religious leader guided by continuing revelations from God.

Assuming the title "commander of the believers," and later **caliph**, or "successor" to Muhammad, Abu Bakr began his rule in 632. Before his death two years later, he had undertaken a military campaign against Arab tribes who rejected his caliphate, and he nominated another early companion and father-in-law of Muhammad, Umar ibn al-Khattab, as the second caliph. Abu Bakr's military campaigns, known as the Wars of Apostasy, also ventured north and east, provoking border clashes with peoples in what are now the nations of Iraq and Syria.

Figure 10.3 Muslims see the New Testament figure John the Baptist (Yahya) as a prophet who renewed the message of Islam within Judaism. This shrine in the prayer hall of a mosque in Damascus, Syria, is said to contain John's severed head. Source: Reproduced by permission of Jerry Fish.

Caliph Umar

Succeeding caliph Abu Bakr, caliph Umar ruled from 634 to 644, during which time he extended Islamic rule over the Byzantine territories of present-day Syria and Egypt, and the Sassanian territories of present-day Iraq and Iran. Even though the land controlled by Muslims grew tremendously under his caliphate, it would take several centuries for the populations in those regions to become Muslim. This was because Umar and the caliphs who followed him governed the lands they conquered from within military garrisons. The conquered peoples—Christians, Jews, and Zoroastrians—were allowed to continue practicing their religions, provided they paid a per capita tax to Islamic rulers for protection and other services. In this way they became a separate class within Muslim society, known as *dhimmis*, or protected persons.

> ### Talking about Religion
>
> ## People of the Book
>
> Religious tolerance toward certain groups of non-Muslims has been a part of Islam from its early days. The Quran refers to Muslims, Jews, Christians, and a few other groups as **People of the Book**, thus distinguishing them as people who had received a sacred book of revelation through one of God's earlier prophets.
>
> According to Islamic tradition, God sent a prophet to every people in the world. Some 25 of these prophets are mentioned by name in the Quran, and it is commonly held that their total number is over 100,000. Their task was to reveal God's truth and warn people about his judgment. In a few instances, they delivered sacred books to humanity. This was the case with the prophet Moses (Musa), who delivered the Torah (*al-Tawrah*), as well as David (Daud), who delivered the Jewish Psalms (*al-Zabur*).
>
> The biblical patriarch Abraham (Ibrahim), who preceded both Moses and David, was also a prophet, but is understood as a monotheist and a Muslim, rather than a Jew. From the Muslim Abraham came two groups of monotheists, the Jews and the Arabs. God also sent the prophet Jesus (Isa) to the Jews to deliver the Gospel (*al-Injil*). Over time, however, the Torah, the Psalms and the Gospel all became distorted and unreliable, necessitating the appearance of God's last prophet, Muhammad, who delivered the Quran.

Caliph Uthman

Before his death, Umar instructed six of Muhammad's remaining inner circle to elect the third caliph. They chose Muhammad's early companion and son-in-law, Uthman ibn Affan. While Uthman continued Islamic military advances into North Africa, his greater contribution was his initiative to preserve Muhammad's most precious legacy—the Quran.

During Muhammad's prophetic ministry, his revelations often came suddenly and unexpectedly, and his followers memorized them or wrote them down on what was at hand. From what was written down, "pages" began to circulate, which were eventually grouped into collections that were commissioned and owned by families close to the Prophet. Islamic tradition reports that after Muhammad's death, these collections were combined with oral traditions, and the entire corpus of Muhammad's revelations was copied onto "sheets," which were safeguarded by the caliph Umar and his daughter Hafsah, one of Muhammad's widows. By 644, disagreements on the correct recitation of Muhammad's revelations prompted Caliph Uthman to prepare an official version of the Quran. Using Hafsah's copy as a guide, a committee of former companions to the Prophet collated and edited the surviving sources, both written and oral, and produced what has become known as the **Uthmanic Codex**. Uthman then made four copies of this codex and sent them to the major centers of Islamic authority in his continually expanding empire. Despite his enormous contribution to the preservation of the Quran, Uthman's legacy was later sullied by charges of favoritism. In 656, he was assassinated in his Medinan home by dissidents from Egyptian and Iraqi territories.

Caliph Ali

Immediately following Uthman's murder, an impromptu election designated Ali as the fourth caliph. Although Ali had waited 24 years to assume this office—which he had initially claimed at the time of the Prophet's death—his caliphate lasted only four years and ended with his assassination. The trouble began with Ali's refusal or inability to bring Uthman's assassins to justice. This escalated into a civil war in which Ali faced rebels from Iraq and then Syria. After putting down the first rebellion, Ali relocated his headquarters to an area within Iraq to better position himself against the Syrians, effectively removing the seat of Islamic governance from Medina forever. As the fighting escalated, Ali's own camp split, and a substantial number of his supporters formed the Kharijites, or secessionists, who opposed both Ali and his enemies. When the war ended with a discredited arbitration between Ali and his Syrian opponents, the Kharijites accused Ali of grave moral error and assassinated him in 661.

The first Muslim dynasties

With Ali's death, the period known as the Rashidun, or rightly guided caliphate, came to a close. Despite the turbulence of those early years, Muslims look back on this time as a golden era in which the *ummah* was led by Muhammad's wisest and most righteous companions, chosen by a consensus of the community's leading men. Thereafter, the caliphate passed from father to son within family dynasties, obscuring the earlier ideal of the caliph's accountability to the larger Muslim community.

The Umayyad dynasty (661–750)

The fifth caliph, and the first of the dynastic caliphs, was Muawiyah, who had been Ali's chief opponent in the civil war. Cousin to the murdered Caliph Uthman, and governor of Syria by appointment of Caliph Umar, Muawiyah assumed the caliphate by default after Ali's death. Since Muawiyah belonged to the Umayyad clan of Muhammad's tribe, this was the inception of the **Umayyad dynasty**, which lasted almost a century.

During their reign, the Umayyads were remarkably successful as conquerors, spreading Islam further across north Africa and up into Spain (Figure 10.4).

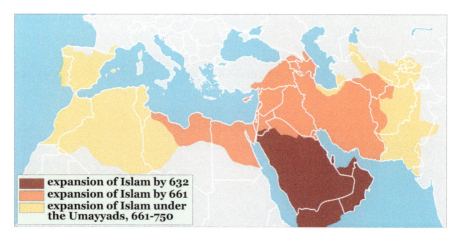

Figure 10.4 By the time of the Prophet's death in 632, Islam was embraced by much of Arabia. By the death of Caliph Ali in 661, it had begun its expansion into northern Africa, Persia, and areas along the Black and Caspian seas. Under the Umayyad dynasty, Islam spread further east into Asia, and further west along the north African coast and up into western Europe via Spain and Portugal. Historians still debate whether the Franken king Charles Martel's defeat of Muslim forces near the cities of Tours and Poitier was the decisive battle that prevented Islam's further expansion into western Europe.
Source: Wikimedia Commons.

Their clan, however, had been one of the Meccan groups most opposed to Muhammad before the conversion of Mecca, and so their claim to authority over the Muslim community was not universally accepted. Further opposition arose from their authoritarian style of governing, the questionable moral conduct of many of their caliphs, and charges that the Umayyads favored Arab Muslims over non-Arab Muslims.

In 750, the Umayyad dynasty fell victim to a widespread rebellion led by followers of the murdered Ali. They had rallied around Ali's two sons, Hassan and Husayn, and formed the Party (*shiaht*) of Ali, which soon evolved into Shia Islam. The last Umayyad caliph and the royal family were all killed, save Abd al Rahman, who escaped and eventually made his way to southern Spain. There he founded a new dynasty in the former Umayyad emirate of al-Andalus. Lasting until 1016, it governed large populations of Christians, Jews, and Muslims, and fostered a multicultural environment that produced such grand figures as the mystic Ibn al-Arabi, the Jewish philosopher Maimonides (who wrote his major work in Arabic), and the Muslim philosopher Averroes (Ibn Rushd), whose writings influenced the Roman Catholic theologian Thomas Aquinas.

The Abbasid dynasty (750–1258)

The rebellion that ended the Umayyad dynasty is known as the Abbasid Revolution because it brought to power another important Meccan clan—the Abbasids, who were descended from Muhammad's uncle Abbas. Initially, the Abbasids sought to shore up their political and religious authority by appealing to the Muslim community's

Shia constituency, the principal group that had brought them to power. But radical elements within Shiism insisted that the authority to rule belonged to the descendants of Ali, not those of Abbas, and so the Abbasids abandoned their former allies and appealed to a broader spectrum of Islamic society for support.

Whereas the Umayyad dynasty had done much to expand the borders of the Islamic empire, the Abbasids worked to consolidate the empire from within, building the foundations of what has been called classical Islamic civilization. During the Abbasid era, political power moved to the city of Baghdad, making it the new center of Muslim rule. In Baghdad's environment of ethnic pluralism and relative peace, a distinctively Islamic artistic and literary culture emerged, as did the classical schools of Islamic theology and legal science.

Legal scholars and mysticism   By the ninth century, Islamic legal scholars had compiled six important collections of *hadith*, which were witnessed reports of what Muhammad had done or said on particular occasions. These were used to reconstruct Muhammad's habitual practices—his *sunnah*—which served as a model for all Muslims. By comparing Muhammad's words and deeds to God's words, which Muhammad had delivered and which were recorded in the Quran, legal experts determined ("discovered") God's will for humanity, which they disseminated in codes of conduct named *Sharia*. By the tenth century, four distinct schools of "Sunni" law (from *sunnah*) had developed, offering somewhat different versions of Sharia, due to differing approaches to interpretation. These legal schools were led by a new class of religious authorities called the *ulama* (legal experts).

Another development of this period was the growth of Islamic mysticism, or *Sufism*. The term Sufism likely derives from the word "wool" (*suf*), referring to the coarse hair-shirts worn by certain holy men in the eighth and ninth centuries. Gaining renown for their pious and ascetic lifestyles, a number of Sufi masters founded separate brotherhoods to perpetuate their own particular teachings and techniques.

The end of the caliphate

Although the rise of both legal scholars and Sufi masters posed a challenge to the authority of the Abbasid caliphs, a more formidable challenge came from powerful tribal leaders, known as emirs, who held sway over certain areas within the Abbasid empire. Early caliphs were able to deal with these emirs indirectly by assigning their concerns to a chief minister known as a vizier, but over time the emirs grew too strong for this system. As a result, Baghdad fell to an army of Buyids in 945, a Shia group from Persia. This was followed a century later by an invasion of Seljuk forces of Turkish origin. While these dynasties left the Abbasid caliph in place, the caliphate became subservient to Buyid emirs and Seljuk sultans and retained only symbolic authority for most Muslims. Then in 1258, Baghdad fell to Mongol invaders from central Asia, bringing an end to the caliphate system of governance.

A Closer Look

Islam and the Arts

Islam has never allowed three-dimensional sculpture, which Muslims associate with idolatry, and depictions of persons are rare in the tradition, because they are thought to impinge on God's role as creator. A notable exception are the miniatures found in some illuminated manuscripts, mostly Persian and Indian, that recount the great deeds of the Prophet, Muslim saints, kings, and heroes. Another exception is certain expressions of Sufi and Shia religious art. But even in these exceptions, when depicting the Prophet artists often leave out the details of Muhammad's face, and on pages of the Quran or Hadith, one rarely encounters any form of representational art.

On the other hand, Muslim artists have made extensive use of calligraphy, especially in works of art that reproduce verses from the Quran or the 99 Most Beautiful Names of God. Geometric (Figure 10.5) and floral designs have also

Figure 10.5 An example of Islamic art that combines geometric design with calligraphy (in the center). The stylized letters of the calligraphy form the phrase, "In the name of God, the Most Gracious, the Most Merciful." Source: Reproduced by permission of Jerry Fish.

(*continued*)

> been an important outlet for artistic and religious expression, as have fanciful patterns known as arabesque, which combine geometric shapes with the natural curves of the plant world. The more complex and intricate of these designs and patterns are attempts to depict God's divine oneness (*tawhid*).

Shia developments and the Fatimid dynasty

Shia groups continued to be active under Abbasid rule despite persecution from the government. By the end of the eighth century, they had developed their own school of legal scholarship, and by the early tenth century Shia Islam offered a viable alternative to Sunni Islam in the areas of theology, law, and political theory. But even when they received political support from the Buyid dynasty later in the tenth century, most Shias were content to stay out of politics. Instead, they identified themselves as the persecuted yet righteous remnant within Islam who looked to God rather than political regimes to bring justice to the world. A striking exception to this tradition of quietism was the rise of a Shia group known as the Ismailis (Seveners). Having organized an extensive clandestine network, they came to power around 900 in Syria, Arabia, Egypt, and parts of north Africa, which they united under the Fatimid dynasty. In Cairo, their capital, they established one of the great centers of Islamic learning, Al-Azhar University; and until their demise in 1171, Fatimid leaders posed a formidable challenge to the Sunni caliphate in Baghdad.

Jerusalem and the Crusades

Since the time of the Prophet, Muslims had regarded Jerusalem as a sacred city. Called simply "the Holy," Jerusalem was the site of Muhammad's ascension to the seventh heaven, and it was to Jerusalem that early Muslims turned in prayer. In 638, six years after the Prophet's death, a Muslim force took the city without resistance from its residents. By the end of that century, Muslims had built two important religious structures there: the al-Aqsa (Far) Mosque (Figure 10.6), and the **Dome of the Rock**. The latter was a shrine built over an area of bedrock that was not only thought to be the site of the first and second Jewish temples, but also where Abraham attempted to sacrifice his son Ishmael, and the very point from which Muhammad ascended from earth into the presence of God.

Early in the eleventh century, a group of Muslims from Egypt traveled to Jerusalem and burned down the Church of the Holy Sepulcher, which Christians had built in the fourth century to mark the place Jesus was crucified and buried. Christians in western Europe responded by initiating the first Crusade to win back the city. In 1099, they occupied Jerusalem and preceded to convert the Dome of the Rock into a church, and the al-Aqsa Mosque into the headquarters of an elite military association called the Knights Templar. In 1187, the city was retaken by Muslims under the famous military commander Saladin, changed hands again in 1229 and 1244, and then came under the jurisdiction of the Mamluk Muslim dynasty in 1250. From these

Figure 10.6 The al-Aqsa Mosque (upper right) stands near the southwest corner of the temple mount in Jerusalem, near the Western Wall (foreground), an important pilgrimage site for Jews. Source: Reproduced by permission of H. Richard Rutherford, C.S.C.

military encounters with the Crusaders, Muslims began to envision western medieval Europe as a cultural backwater, inhabited by a barbaric people they called Franks.

Sufi missions into sub-Saharan Africa and India

While the early Muslim dynasties vied with each other and with Christian Crusaders for control of the Islamic heartlands, Sufi missionaries were taking Islam into India and sub-Saharan Africa. By the tenth century, Sufi groups had followed trade routes down the east and west coasts of Africa, where they converted local rulers and helped establish small Islamic kingdoms; and by the eleventh century, they had crossed the Himalayas into northern India. In both sub-Saharan Africa and northern India, they planted an eclectic form of Islam, combining their mystical traditions with local practices. In India, for example, they adopted a variation of the Hindu caste system, based on ethnic ancestry rather than social class. Later, in the fourteenth century, Sufi missionaries traveled from Arabia and southern Indian to Indonesia, where they combined Islam with aspects of Hinduism, Buddhism, and local folk traditions.

The last of the great Islamic dynasties

In the centuries immediately before and after the fall of the Abbasid dynasty, political control of the Islamic world became fragmented under a number of smaller dynasties. The Mongols, who had sacked Baghdad, controlled Iran and parts of Iraq for only about a century before their royal line died out and their empire was divided among several Turkic dynasties. In Spain, the Umayyad dynasty was broken into a number of local kingdoms, and by 1492 the Spanish Reconquest had succeeded in removing the last Muslim rulers from the Iberian Peninsula. In northern India, the Delhi Sultanate—which itself was a succession of five dynasties between 1206 and 1526—was divided up and ruled by a series of Turkic and Afghan dynasties. And the region stretching from Syria to northern Africa was ruled successively by the Fatimids, the Ayyubids, and the Mamluks.

Starting in the early fourteenth century, however, Muslims began to reunite under three major empires. These were the so-called "gunpowder dynasties" because their rapid expansion relied, in part, on their deft use of this newly adopted military technology. The first to appear was a Turkic people known as the Uthmaniyyah, or "Ottomans." Spreading out from their base of power in eastern Europe and Turkey, the Ottomans expanded into Syria, Palestine, the Arabian Peninsula, and North Africa. Within two centuries they brought an end to the Byzantine empire by capturing Constantinople, and established their rule over much of the region, including Islam's three holiest sites, Mecca, Medina, and Jerusalem.

The second great empire was the Safavids, a Shia dynasty with origins in a Sufi brotherhood. Beginning in 1501, they swept through and conquered all of Iran, and at times controlled parts of Iraq and central Asia. Establishing **Imami** (or Twelver) Shiism as their state religion, they presented a constant political and religious challenge to the Ottomans. This prolonged conflict between Sunni Ottomans and Shia Safavids contributed greatly to the present-day tensions between Sunnis and Shias. The last major dynasty to take shape was the Mughal kingdom in India, also founded around the beginning of the sixteenth century. Led by a Turkic clan claiming descent from earlier Mongol rulers, it expanded the former Delhi Sultanate to include much of the Indian subcontinent.

Political and religious changes under the last great dynasties

At their height, the Ottoman, Safavid, and Mughal dynasties governed much of the eastern hemisphere, but unlike the Umayyad and the early Abbasid dynasties, which were ruled by caliphs, these dynasties were ruled by sultans, shahs, and rajas. These were military, not religious leaders, and their responsibility to their Muslim populations consisted in upholding Islamic laws and defending the religion. They were not required to display personal religious piety, and in some cases they were only nominally Muslim. Eventually a two-court legal system arose in which a religious court oversaw ritual law, marriage, inheritance, and religious endowments, while a separate nonreligious court under the authority of the dynastic rulers dealt with civil and criminal offenses. Faced with this reality, Muslim political theorists began to argue that legitimate Islamic government required only that a ruler be properly installed and govern in a way that did not violate Islamic law.

With this shift away from earlier Muslim statecraft, the Ottoman and Mughal dynasties made significant concessions to Christian, Jewish, and Hindu populations living under their rule. The Mughal ruler Akbar the Great (1542–1605) relaxed Sharia laws to accommodate Hindu practices, while the Ottomans organized Christians,

Jews, and Muslims alike into self-governing communities called *millets*, each of which reported directly to the sultan. This tendency toward religious tolerance also benefited prominent Sufi orders, whose brotherhoods grew into communities that encompassed whole towns or regions. As in former times, Sufism was highly eclectic, introducing novel ideas and practices into Islam, especially in Africa, India, and Indonesia. In northeast India, for example, Sufis venerated Hindu sages, leading to the Sufi-Hindu synthesis called Sikhism.

The decline of Islamic political power

Even though the beginning of the sixteenth century saw Islam's greatest extension of imperial rule and cultural influence, the seeds of its political decline had been germinating since the beginning of the fourteenth century. This was when Islamic preeminence in science and scholarship began to pass to western Europeans, who were awakening to the discoveries of the Italian Renaissance. Advancements in navigation led European countries to explore and colonize distant lands, including the Americas, and the resources and knowledge they gained brought wealth and advances in military technology. The Renaissance, which lasted into the seventeenth century, was succeeded by the European Enlightenment of the seventeenth and eighteenth centuries. During this period, Europeans saw the beginnings of critical thinking and scientific methods of research. Yet as European nations became stronger and consolidated their power, Muslim rulers and intellectuals took little notice. None of the Muslim dynasties engaged in colonization, and European inventions such as the printing press and more effective weaponry were regarded by Muslims as novelties and curiosities. While Muslims sometimes imported these inventions, they showed no interest in manufacturing them, and very few books were translated from European languages for Muslim audiences.

The Safavid dynasty, which had been weakened by sustained warfare with the Ottomans, as well as intermittent challenges from the Mughals, Russians, and Afghans, was overrun by an Afghan army in 1722, leaving its territories exposed to Russian and British influence. In India, Britain's East India Company was able to undermine Mughal control in several provinces, and by the Battle of Plassey in 1757, Muslim rule of the subcontinent had effectively run its course. A century later, India became subject to the British crown, and Queen Victoria was proclaimed Empress of India.

A Closer Look

Islam and Science

In the first 600 years of Islam, Muslims made significant contributions to mathematics and the natural sciences. Science was, and still is, regarded as an extension of religion, a way of understanding God's nature and plan for humanity. Since the Quran encourages human beings to see signs of God's creative power

(continued)

in the physical world, Muslims have seldom felt that religious faith was incompatible with scientific inquiry. Early Muslim thinkers explored the scientific and philosophical writings of the civilizations they encountered, especially those of the Greeks, Persians, and Indians. Upon conquering Iraq, Muslims found there an advanced understanding of medicine, largely based on Greek and Persian sources. This they developed further, producing precise understandings of human anatomy and bodily functions. The Arabic numeral system was developed from Indian origins by Muslims and Arab Christians, and proved vastly superior to Roman numerals in supporting complex mathematics. Sometimes new contributions to science were inspired by religious concerns. The need to determine the direction of Mecca for prayer (the *qiblah*) led to advances in astronomy, geography, and geometry. Likewise, the Quran's complex rules of inheritance inspired al-Khwarizmi (d. ca. 850) to develop algebra (*al-jabr*), and a version of al-Khwarizmi's name became the mathematical term "algorithm."

Under the Abbasid caliphate, Baghdad attracted the finest minds of the era to its House of Wisdom, a state-supported institute for all branches of knowledge. One of its many contributions to society was the development of the hospital, beginning in the tenth century. This innovation spread throughout its Muslim provinces, and in 1284, the Mansuri hospital was founded in Cairo, accommodating some 800 patients in separate wards for different maladies—a principle of quarantining that is still in use today.

The Ottoman empire had seen its zenith under Suleyman the Magnificent (1520–1566). In 1683 it laid siege to Vienna, hoping to expand into western Europe, but was rebuffed and forced to sign a peace treaty for the first time as the defeated party. As the Ottomans continued to suffer defeat over the next two centuries, they set about modernizing their society in an attempt to keep pace with European progress. In the nineteenth century, they granted equal rights to all citizens, adopted western models of bureaucracy, created a ministry of justice to replace the *ulama*, and modernized their military.

Despite these measures, the Ottoman empire was weakened by wars with Russia and by domestic struggles between traditionalists and westernizers—the latter styling themselves Young Ottomans, and later Young Turks. European newspapers began to characterize this once great empire as the "sick man of Europe," and in the closing years of the nineteenth century the Ottoman sultan, in a desperate attempt to secure the support of Muslims in other parts of the world, revived the caliphate and appointed himself to the office. But the end came just decades later. Sealing their fate by joining Germany against the European allies in World War I, the Ottomans declared a worldwide *jihad* (military campaign) against Britain and France. Yet this call to arms went largely unheeded, and at the Treaty of Sèvres the allies dismembered the Ottoman empire into European-dominated mandates and zones of influence, bringing the empire to a close. Two years later, the newly founded Republic of Turkey—an avowedly secular state—claimed the heartland of the former empire, and in 1924, it abolished the caliphate (Figure 10.7).

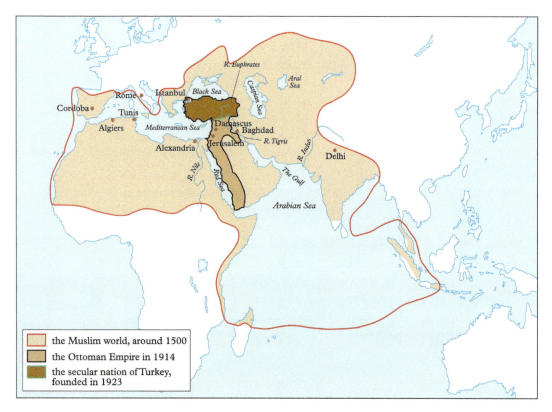

Figure 10.7 Between the beginning of the sixteenth century and the early 1920s, the three Muslim empires (Ottoman, Safavid, and Mughal) declined and vanished in the face of foreign imperialism. Turkey, a secular state, became heir to the Ottoman legacy.

Islamic reform in the twentieth century

The dramatic reversal of Islam's political fortunes became the source of much soul-searching among Muslims, prompting its political and religious leaders to call for a thoroughgoing reform of the religion in light of the modern world. This was not Islam's first attempt to reform from within, for reform movements had appeared in Muslim lands long before European encroachment. In the fourteenth century, Ibn Taymiyyah tried to restrict the Sufi practice of venerating past teachers as quasi-divine beings, and criticized the legal schools for incorporating non-Muslim elements into Sharia. In that same century, a Sufi reform movement called the Naqshbandi brotherhood appeared in central Asia, banning Sufi traditions of dancing and music, and later the practice of Sikhism. Finally, beginning in the 1740s, a reformer named Muhammad ibn Abd al-Wahhab from the Arabian Peninsula advocated a strict, puritanical return to Islam's earliest years, which was embraced by the powerful Saud tribe.

All of these earlier reformers had styled themselves **Salafis**, thereby promoting their reforms as a return to the practices of Islam's "pious forebears" (*salaf*). Likewise, the reformers of the twentieth century also advocated Salafism, but with a different meaning. Their goal was not to return to an earlier period of the religion, but to reformulate the practices of that earlier period to address the challenges of modernity—the world of science and technology that had emerged from the Enlightenment and become the foundation of modern western societies. Among these reformers there developed a wide consensus that the Quran and the Hadith alone were the basis for any legitimate reformulation of the religion. The earlier scholarship of the legal schools was to be only a resource, not an authoritative tradition. There was also wide agreement that the modernization of Islam did not mean its westernization. To the contrary, the reformers argued that the Quran and the Hadith far surpassed the resources of western scholarship. In addition, two of the most influential voices of this period, Sayyid Abu al-Ala Mawdudi (1903–1979) and Sayyid Qutb (1906–1966), argued that western imperialism over Islamic lands had subjected Islamic peoples to a new age of spiritual ignorance (*jahiliyyah*), from which they must escape through a modern-day emigration (*hijra*).

According to Mawdudi and Qutb, Islam had no need of western civilization because Islam was a complete way of life in itself, older than and superior to the west. It had supported pluralism, democracy, and human rights long before they became popular among westerners, and it had done so in an Islamic way that did not depend on secularism, nationalism, or capitalism, which were manifestly un-Islamic. By the 1960s, this stance had evolved into the contention that all western advances were really Islamic in origin, and that, rightly understood, Islam was and is truly modern. Islamic intellectuals held that democracy and parliamentary debate had their origins in the Muslim concepts of consultation (*shura*) and consensus (*ijma*), while modern scholarship itself had antecedents in Islamic legal scholarship. Western scholarship, by contrast, was based on materialism and a deep ignorance of spiritual matters. The philosophical and theological basis for this Muslim intellectual stance was God's *tahwid*, which Qutb promoted as the fundamental principle of Islam. Because God is one, and because his world reflects this oneness, there can be no contradiction between revelation and modern discoveries, and all good things in the world have their roots in God's religion, Islam. On this basis some reformers even called for the Islamization of knowledge, whereby Muslims could challenge western mathematics with Islamic mathematics, and western science with Islamic science, just as they challenged western religion with Islam.

A Closer Look

Mawdudi's Vision of Islamic Revival

Islamic Revival is neither striking compromises with un-Islam, nor preparing new blends of Islam and un-Islam, but it is cleansing Islam of all the un-Godly elements and presenting it and making it flourish more or less in its original pure form. Considered from this viewpoint, a *mujaddid* (a figure of religious renewal) is a most uncompromising person with regard to un-Islam, and one least tolerant as to the presence of even a tinge of un-Islam in the Islamic system.

Abul a'la Maududi, *A Short History of the Revivalist Movement in Islam*, 7th ed. (Lahore: Islamic Publications, 1992), pp. 35–36.

Nation building

Aside from the important challenges posed by western science and culture, the most pressing issue for the reformers was to reconcile Islamic tradition with the realities of Muslims living in modern nation–states. Until the end of World War I, most Muslims in the world thought of themselves as members of a larger Islamic empire. But the dismemberment of the Ottoman empire left Muslims with political identities determined by the various colonial powers and victors of the war. Then, within decades, the allied forces and colonial powers began to withdraw from Muslim lands, leaving behind numerous independent nation–states and the daunting task of forming governments suited to both the values of Islam and the demands of a modern world. Some Muslims argued that the modern nation–state was simply incompatible with Islam. God, through his Prophet, had called all peoples into a universal Muslim polity, the *ummah*. No particular people, ethnic group, or culture should claim the sort of autonomy and independence that was required to form a modern nation. Others accepted the reality of national divisions among Muslims but came to a general consensus that neither communism, socialism, nor democracy, as practiced by other countries, was acceptable. Communism promoted atheism, and both communism and socialism called on individuals to make sacrifices for the good of the political system, rather than surrender themselves entirely to God. Democracy, on the other hand, divided the *ummah* into competing political parties, and its principle of "rule by the people" ran counter to Islam. God made laws, not the people, and justice came from the proper application of Sharia. As an alternative, they urged Muslims to draw on their religious traditions to create Islamic forms of socialism or democracy. Mawdudi, for example, envisioned a "democratic caliphate," or "theo-democracy," in which all citizens served as God's vice-regents on earth. Similarly, Qutb proposed a "shuracracy," in which the Islamic principle of consultation (*shura*) would guarantee a democracy without party divisions or dissent.

In actual practice, however, the process of modern nation building among Muslims took many paths, as the following six examples illustrate.

- The Republic of Turkey was founded in 1923 with a secular government that sought to privatize Islam by mandating a secular education for its citizens and prohibiting religious expression in the public sphere (Figure 10.8).
- The Republic of Indonesia was founded in 1945 as a "guided democracy" based on five essential principles (*pancasila*). The first of these principles mandated a common monotheism for the entire nation by which all citizens needed to profess either Islam, Hinduism, Buddhism, Catholicism, or Protestant Christianity.
- The Islamic Republic of Pakistan came into existence between 1947 and 1956, after the British colonial authority designated certain provinces in northern India as an Islamic homeland. Meaning "Land of the Pure," Pakistan was founded specifically to be an Islamic nation.
- Libya became an independent kingdom in 1951, but in 1969 a military dictatorship came to power under General Muammar Gaddafi, who founded the Socialist

Figure 10.8 In the new, secular nation of Turkey, Mustafa Kemal Ataturk, Turkey's first president, introduced European writing to replace the Arabic alphabet. Source: Wikimedia Commons.

People's Libyan Arab *Jamahiriya* ("mass community"). This regime ruled using an idiosyncratic mix of Islamic socialism and Arab and African nationalism. Gaddafi was overthrown in a popular revolution in 2011, and since then Libya's political system has been in turmoil due to regional factionalism, a civil war (2014), military interventions by ISIS, Egypt, the UAE, and Turkey, and catastrophic flooding (2023).
- The Kingdom of Saudi Arabia was established in 1932 when the Arab tribal chieftain ibn Saud joined with Wahhabi leaders and conquered most of the Arabian Peninsula. Ibn Saud created an absolute monarchy guided by the very conservative Wahhabi theology.
- The Islamic Republic of Iran came into being in 1979 through a popular revolution that overthrew a monarchy supported by the United States. While it has an elected president, a constitution, and regular parliamentary elections, a Council of Guardians has the authority to veto any candidate's bid for office on religious grounds. It is distinct from other Muslim nations in that it promotes Shia Islam as the state religion.

International Muslim organizations

Despite being divided by national allegiances, Muslims retained an understanding of themselves as members of a *global* religious community. This prompted several Muslim leaders to create international organizations that would unite Muslims across national borders. In 1945, the Arab League (also League of Arab States) was founded in Cairo, Egypt. Its mission was to unify the Arab world under the banner of Arab nationalism or Arab socialism. It argued that Arab peoples were the core of Islam, and that Islam had been compromised by its spread into non-Arab lands. A short-lived experiment in Arab nationalism was the joining of Egypt and Syria between 1958 and 1961, forming the United Arab Republic. The League lost credibility in 1967, however, when Arab countries led by Egypt suffered a humiliating defeat to Israel in the Six Day War.

Another pan-Arab movement, with more lasting consequences, was established a few years earlier in Damascus, Syria. Called the Arab Baath (renewal) Socialist Party, it was cofounded by an Arab Muslim and an Arab Orthodox Christian. It adopted the slogan, "Islam is the soul, Arabism is the body," and by 1950 the Baath Party was active in Syria, Jordan, Lebanon, and Iraq. A prominent figure in the party was Saddam Hussein, former dictator of Iraq.

In 1962, to counter the influence of the Egyptian-based Arab League, Saudi Arabia established the Muslim World League in Mecca. Seeking to unite Muslims on the basis of their Islamic, rather than Arab, identity, it funded international conferences on Sharia and networked with other Islamic nations and organizations on issues affecting the global *ummah*. In 1969, it was instrumental in forming the Organization of the Islamic Conference (OIC), a Muslim counterpart to the United Nations, with 57 member states.

Transnational Muslim organizations

Another path to uniting Muslims of different nationalities came from the **Muslim Brotherhood** movement, which began in Egypt in 1928. Denouncing national identities and promoting Islam as an all-sufficient way of life, it worked outside the Egyptian government on the neighborhood level. It built schools and organized community centers, and eventually formed a network of hundreds of branches, each with its own mosque, school, and community outreach program. Beginning in the 1930s, the Brotherhood also spread to other countries, including Syria, Iraq, and Saudi Arabia in the Middle East, and Libya, Somalia, and Sudan in Africa. In these countries, it remained independent of governmental oversight, becoming one of Islam's most powerful transnational NGOs, or non-governmental organizations.

An early spokesman for the Brotherhood was the reformer Sayyid Qutb, who was known for his critique of American culture as soulless, racist, and sexually permissive. Qutb divided the world sharply into two categories, Islamic societies and anti-Islamic societies, the latter including not only the west but also Muslims whom Qutb considered tainted by western influences. Based on the principles that God alone was sovereign and that Islam claimed authority over all areas of human life, Qutb concluded that opposition to all anti-Islamic societies, even to the point of armed resistance, was mandatory for individual Muslims as well as Muslim nations. Influenced by this and similar ideologies, localized resistance movements appeared in the 1960s and early 1970s, known variously in the west as *jihadists*, Islamists, or Muslim fundamentalists. But it was not until the late 1970s that Islamic resistant movements crossed boarders to become transnational.

Following a 1978 coup in Afghanistan that brought a communist dictator to power, religious warriors called *mujahidin* attacked the new regime in defense of Islam. When Russia intervened on the side of the dictator, Muslims from Pakistan and several Arab nations joined the *mujahidin*, and by 1992 this transnational force had driven out the Soviets and toppled the dictatorship. Two years later, Muslim religious students organized themselves into another militant group to restore civil and religious order to the country. Called the Taliban (Students), they have continued to promote their strict interpretation of Sharia in Afghanistan, and have crossed into the neighboring countries of Pakistan and India. In addition, they have been supportive of another transnational form of militant Islam, the al-Qaeda (the Base) organization, founded by the late Osama bin Laden. This group was responsible for the attack on the Pentagon and the destruction of New York's World Trade Center on September 11, 2001. It currently remains active through secret militant cells throughout the Middle East, Afghanistan, and Pakistan. In 2011, bin Laden was killed by U.S. Navy SEALs in Abbottabad, Pakistan, and in 2022 his successor, Ayman al-Zawahiri, was killed by a CIA drone strike in Kabul, Afghanistan.

The Arab Spring and ISIS

Near the end of 2010, popular demonstrations began in Tunisia and quickly spread to other Arab nations. Citizens took to the streets in large numbers to voice their anger against the economic, social, and religious conditions in their countries. Soon, popular revolutions broke out in Tunisia, Yemen, Egypt, and Libya, overthrowing the dictators who ruled these countries and replacing them with various forms of constitutional democracies. A popular uprising and civil war also broke out in Syria, but was unsuccessful in overthrowing the government. Since the countries involved were Arab, and since the ousting of dictators occurred in the spring of 2011, these events became known as the Arab Spring, with "spring" carrying overtones of "renewal."

With new governments in place in Tunisia, Yemen, Egypt, and Libya, Salafi forms of Islam, which had been persecuted under the former regimes, became more active, both in society and politics. In Egypt, a member of the Muslim Brotherhood was elected president, but early into his term many Egyptians criticized his government for promoting a Salafi agenda that impinged on their freedoms and threatened the future of Egypt's infant democracy. In 2013, the president was deposed in a military coup and negotiations began between the Muslim Brotherhood and the military concerning what role, if any, the Brotherhood sould play in Egyptian politics. Not long thereafter, membership in the Brotherhood was declared to be illegal, and since 2014 a popularly elected president, Abdel Fattah el-Sisi, has been in office.

In 2014, another Salafi-inspired organization, called ISIS, drew international attention when it captured the Iraqi city of Mosul and began the genocide of Iraqi Yazidis. Identifying itself as the Islamic State and global caliphate, by late 2014 it had taken military control of an area that included about 40 percent of Iraq and a third of Syria. By early 2019, however, it had lost all of this territory to a U.S.-led international military coalition, and was driven underground. At present, differences over Islamic law and struggles over democracy, militancy, and engagement with the global community continue to shape societies in North Africa and the Middle East.

> **Did you know …**
>
> The name Pakistan, which means Land of the Pure, is an acronym created from the former Indian provinces of *P*unjab, *A*fghania, *K*ashmir, *S*ind, and Baluch*istan*.

Contemporary Beliefs and Practices

One approach to understanding contemporary Islam is through three related concepts: *tawhid*, *islam*, and *jihad*. *Tawhid*, which is the most abstract of the three, refers to God's oneness. This is God's hallmark characteristic, leading not only to the Muslim affirmation of a single god (monotheism), but also to the belief that God's unity is reflected throughout his creation, and especially in his plan for human society. Human beings, however, constantly stray from God's plan, dividing and organizing the world in ways that contradict his oneness. They give inordinate value to money, individual freedom, and sexual pleasure, and split human society into competing nationalities, ethnic groups, and social classes. These actions create inappropriate associations (*shirk*) in human society, and distance human beings from God's truth.

Islam, which means "submission," is the solution to this human rebellion. It is the term from which the religion gets its name, and refers to human submission to God's will under the guidance of the Prophet Muhammad. Those who submit to God are Muslims literally, the "submitting ones." Yet submission to God is no easy task since human beings are prone to follow their own ways. A third concept, therefore, becomes important, namely, *jihad*, which means "struggle." Although this term can refer to a military campaign or armed struggle, its range of meaning is much broader, such that it encompasses *all* human effort to conform to the divine plan. If we construe *jihad* in this wider sense, we can summarize our brief consideration of these terms in the following way: people who submit (*islam*) themselves to God must undergo a struggle (*jihad*) to bring themselves into harmony with God's oneness (*tawhid*).

Sharia: The Islamic way of life

Human beings conform to the divine plan in concrete ways through Sharia. Literally, "the straight path," Sharia defines the Muslim way of life. It is a guide to living that orders society and individuals according to revelation. Especially concerned with family and ritual law, Sharia divides human actions into five categories:

- Obligatory
- Recommended
- Permitted
- Reprehensible
- Prohibited

The first category, *obligatory*, covers actions that must be performed, such as daily prayer. God rewards people for doing these actions and punishes them for leaving them undone. *Recommended* actions are those that God rewards for doing but does not punish for omitting. Considered highly desirable but not absolutely necessary, they include such things as weekly fasting and reading the Quran during the Islamic month of Ramadan. *Permissible* actions are neutral undertakings that merit neither reward nor punishment. They include incidental choices such as whether one attends this or that school, or drives this or that make of car. *Reprehensible* actions, by contrast, are actions said to be hated by God. While one is rewarded for avoiding them, they are not, however, forbidden. Sometimes described as "immoral but not illegal," the classic example of a reprehensible action is divorce. Finally, *prohibited*, or forbidden, actions are those that God punishes for committing and rewards for avoiding. Eating pork, for example, is forbidden. In some Muslim societies, religious scholars and judges—called *ulama* and *faqihs*, respectively—assign penalties for violating the injunctions of Sharia, but most rewards and punishments are anticipated in the afterlife.

As a divinely prescribed way of life, Sharia is understood to preexist all human law. As something that already exists, moreover, it cannot be created, but must be "discovered" through study. Those responsible for its discovery are the *ulama*, who are expected to put forth the utmost scholarly exertion (*ijtihad*, a term related to *jihad*) in determining God's will on a particular issue. *Ulama* are also called upon to give sermons at mosques, lead daily prayer, and teach in religious schools; and it is under the guidance of the *ulama* that human beings become God's representatives or "vice-regents" on earth. As an often-quoted passage from the Quran declares to Muslims, "You are the best community sent forth to mankind; you enjoin right conduct and forbid what is wrong; and you believe in God" (Quran 3.110).

The four sources of law

To discover Sharia, the *ulama* rely on four sources ("roots") of law: the Quran, the Hadith, consensus (*ijma*), and analogy (*qiyas*). Muslims consider the Quran to be the very words of God, spoken to Muhammad by the angel Gabriel. Muhammad is not its author. Rather, it is an uncreated book, reflecting a heavenly original that remains with God. But this does not mean that *ulama* necessarily employ literalist readings to interpret the Quran. On the contrary, the legal sciences (*fiqh*) are a sophisticated area of study, determining, for example, whether a revelation that Muhammad received later in life might clarify or abrogate an earlier one.

Whereas the Quran contains the very words of *God*, the Hadith are records of the words and deeds of *Muhammad*. These are considered a source of law because Muhammad is believed to have been protected by God from sin and error, making him the perfect model of what a Muslim should be. For this reason, the person and life story of the Prophet are revered among all Muslims, who typically follow the mention of his name with the expression, "May God bless him and grant him peace," or "Peace be upon him."

As with the Quran, interpretation of the Hadith is a highly sophisticated task, taking into account the reports of Muhammad's words and actions and their context in his life (the actual *hadith*), as well as the chain of witnesses who are responsible for having transmitted a given report, which is the **isnad** that accompanies each report. It is common for scholars to categorize individual reports as "weak," "good," "sound," or "certain" according to their estimation of the witnesses' reliability. The third source of Sharia is the principle of consensus, which refers to the agreement of legal experts and is based on Muhammad's assertion that "my community will never agree in an error." Analogy, finally, is the legal science of reasoning from the known to the unknown. For example, one of the legal arguments against buying and selling insurance in Muslim societies is that it resembles gambling, which is forbidden in the Quran.

Five obligatory activities

According to a widely accepted Hadith, Muhammad proclaimed that "Islam is built upon five fundamentals." This is understood to refer to five actions that are obligatory for all Muslims, known as the **Five Pillars**. They are:

- Public testimony,
- Daily prayer,
- Charity for the needy,
- Fasting during the month of Ramadan, and
- Pilgrimage to Mecca.

Public testimony   The first pillar of Islam is called the **Shahadah**, which is a public statement that affirms the oneness of God and the authority of Muhammad. It is expressed in Arabic in the set formula, *la ilaha illa allah, Muhammad rasulu-llah*, which can be rendered into English as, "There is no god but God, and Muhammad is the Messenger of God." Reciting the Shahadah before two witnesses is widely understood to be the procedure by which members of other religions convert to Islam, and all Muslims who utter the Shahadah must be considered Muslims in good standing from a legal point of view, regardless of their actions or other qualities.

Daily prayer The second pillar of Islam is daily prayer (*salat*). While there are many types of prayer in Islam, daily prayer is a practice required of all believers five times a day at set times. These are: dawn, just after midday, in the afternoon, just after sunset, and at night. In most Muslim societies, these times are announced by a public call to prayer, sometimes from a public address system, sometimes interrupting radio and television programs. The call to prayer has several elements, most of which are said more than once. They include the statement that God is most great (*Allahu akbar*), the Shahadah, an encouragement to come to prayer, and an encouragement to come to salvation. The call to morning prayer adds the admonition, "prayer is better than sleep."

Daily prayer must be undertaken in a ritually clean place by Muslims in a state of purity. Since impurities come from many things encountered in daily life, such as feces and urine, blood, semen, and dog saliva, Muslims engage in ritualized acts of washing before prayer. After focusing their mind and heart, which establishes the proper intention to pray, a Muslim applies water to the face, rinsing the mouth and nostrils, and to the hands, forearms, head, and feet. If water is not available, the same washing movements can be enacted without water. The prayer itself consists of performing two or more cycles of set movements and phrases, called *rakahs*. The movements include raising the hands beside the head, bowing, kneeling, half-crouching, and touching one's forehead to the ground in prostration before God. The phrases include "God is most great," passages from the Quran, and the closing benediction, "Peace be upon you and the mercy of God," directed at fellow Muslims as well as God's prophets and angels. When praying, Muslims must face in the direction of the shortest path between themselves and the Kabah in Mecca. This ensures that Muslims participate in *tawhid*, God's oneness, by turning toward a single geographical point at the heart of the Islamic world.

Daily prayer can be done alone, with one's family, or in a large gathering. Muslims frequently pray communally in prayer halls called **mosques** (Arabic, *masjid*), where prayer is conducted by a leader called an **Imam**. This ensures that those gathered pray and perform the *rakahs* in unison. The direction of Mecca in a mosque is indicated by a niche or alcove in a wall, or by lines on the floor. Noon on Friday has become the preferred time for Muslims, especially men, to gather for prayer at the mosque, and most mosques offer an extended period of worship at that time, including a sermon on religious, moral, or political topics, readings from the Quran, and informal prayers (*dua*). At the mosque, women pray separately from the men, either behind them, blocked from view by a partition, or in another room, since it is considered unseemly and distracting for men to see women performing the *rakahs*.

Charity for the needy Charitable giving, in various forms, is one of the highest moral acts in Islam. Almsgiving, however—charitable giving specifically for the needy—is Islam's third pillar, and thus a mandatory act of generosity. Called by its Arabic name *zakat*, it is usually given at the end of the Islamic month of Ramadan. Those considered deserving of *zakat* are not required to pay it, while anyone not in need of *zakat* must pay it.

The theological principle behind *zakat* is threefold. First, since Muslims are those who practice submission to God, they give *zakat* as a way of surrendering even their wealth to God's purposes. Second, as those who participate in God's oneness by belonging to the unified Islamic community, Muslims must look out for the welfare of other Muslims, and not just as fellow citizens, but as brothers and sisters. And third, since God is the creator and provider of everything, Muslims give *zakat* in recognition that the wealth they retain is not their private property, but a trust from God. In fact, the word *zakat* means purification, and giving to the needy is seen as the means by which Muslims purify God's bounty for their own use while purifying themselves from the sins of greed and selfishness. Today, the standard amount for *zakat* is set at 2.5 percent of one's total wealth, excluding real estate and inventories.

Fasting during the month of Ramadan Muslims fast on many occasions. Some fast for six days in Shawwal, the tenth month of the Islamic calendar; others fast monthly to fulfill a vow or atone for a sin; and Shia Muslims fast during their observance of Ashura, a yearly memorial dedicated to the death of Muhammad's second grandson, Husayn. As with prayer and charitable giving, however, one practice of fasting has been designated as one of the Five Pillars. This is the practice of fasting during daylight hours for the entire month of Ramadan, the ninth month of the Islamic year. Every day during this month, from dawn to sunset, Muslims must refrain from food and drink, as well as from other physical satisfactions such as smoking and sexual intercourse. Many Muslims also perform extra acts of piety, such as contributing to charitable causes, reading through the entire Quran, and attending additional prayer services at the mosque. The last 10 days of the month are considered particularly important, because the night of Muhammad's first revelation, the Night of Power, is said to have occurred on one of the odd-numbered nights in this period. Pious Muslims often increase their fervor during these final days by practicing a type of spiritual retreat or by offering additional prayers and supplications.

All Muslims over the age of puberty are expected to fast during Ramadan, although exemptions are made for persons whose health might be threatened or for whom it would pose a particular hardship. These include the sick, the elderly, those traveling substantial distances, and women who are pregnant or breastfeeding. Menstruating women are forbidden to fast, as they are ritually unclean. If one is unable to fast because of travel or a temporary condition, they must make up all missed days of fasting later in the year. For Muslims whose condition is permanent (such as old age), a charitable payment should be made in place of fasting.

The fast of Ramadan is said to discipline the appetites and purify the soul, strengthen community, reinforce one's dependence on God, and increase solidarity with the poor. It is also thought to be good for one's health. When Muslims break the fast at the end of each day, they often take a light snack of water and dates, after the example of Muhammad. This is followed by evening prayer and a full meal, characterized by festivity and community spirit. At the end of Ramadan, Muslims celebrate **Eid al-Fitr**, the Feast of Breaking Fast, one of two major festivals in the Islamic calendar (the other being the Eid al-Adha, discussed below). Participants exchange gifts, renew friendships, dress up and wear new outfits, and give to the poor. The celebration, which lasts for three days, begins with an obligatory congregational prayer on the first morning of the new month, and on that day it is forbidden for anyone to fast.

Pilgrimage to Mecca The last of the Five Pillars is the Hajj, a pilgrimage to the Saudi Arabian city of Mecca and its environs. While Muslims can visit Mecca at any time of year, the Hajj must be performed during the first and second weeks of the Month of Hajj, which is the twelfth month of the Islamic lunar year. Pilgrimage to Mecca at any other time constitutes only a lesser Hajj (*umrah*), which, though meritorious, does not satisfy one's obligation to God. Every Muslim who has sufficient health and financial resources is required to undertake the Hajj once in their lifetime. Having sufficient wealth means being free of debt and able to pay for the trip without borrowing money. Muslims must satisfy all financial obligations before leaving, including support for dependents and payment of *zakat*, and do so without jeopardizing their ability to fulfill those obligations in the future. Because many Muslims are unable to meet these financial conditions, some *ulama* have ruled that the Hajj can be performed by proxy. Even so, only a small percentage of the Muslim world is able to participate in this pillar: some 2–3 million pilgrims perform Hajj each year, out of a worldwide population of around 2 billion.

Mecca and the area that immediately surrounds it are called the *haram*. It is a sacred place into which only Muslims may enter. When they arrive, pilgrims often proclaim, "Here I am, O God, here I am. You have no associate. Here I am." Upon entering the *haram*, pilgrims adopt a status called *ihram*, a state of special purity that they must maintain throughout the five days of the Hajj rituals. *Ihram* requires that Muslims refrain from sexual intercourse, killing animals, uprooting plants, manifesting anger or violence, and cutting one's hair or nails. Men are required to wear two seamless pieces of white cloth, one around the waist, and one across the chest so that it covers one or both shoulders. In this way they participate in the oneness of the Islamic community by eliminating all signs of national, ethnic, and economic status that clothing might otherwise reveal. Women typically wear white or light-colored, modest clothing, including a scarf for covering the head, although they are prohibited by tradition from covering their faces during the Hajj.

The rituals of the Hajj are said to have been first performed by Abraham after he and his son Ishmael restored the Kabah, which had been built originally by Adam and destroyed during the great flood of Noah's day. The current sequence of rituals that pilgrims follow was established by the Prophet Muhammad during his Farewell Pilgrimage in 631. The rituals allow pilgrims to imitate the faithful actions of Abraham, Ishmael, and Abraham's wife Hagar, and they must be completed in sequence for a pilgrimage to be a valid Hajj.

Pilgrims begin the Hajj by circumambulating (walking around) the Kabah seven times counterclockwise, each sevenfold circuit constituting a *tawaf*. This is performed in imitation of Abraham, as well as God's angels, who continually circumambulate God's throne in heaven (see the chapter-opening photo). At the beginning or end of each *tawaf*, pilgrims kiss, touch, or point to the Black Stone, which is a meteorite set into the southeast corner of the Kabah. This stone is said to absorb people's sins, which is also the reason given for its black color.

Then pilgrims perform two prayer *rakahs* at the place Abraham is remembered to have stood as he supervised the rebuilding of the Kabah. This is followed by "hurrying"—running or walking rapidly—seven times between two nearby hills in imitation of Hagar's desperate running back and forth in the Meccan wilderness in search of water for her child Ishmael. The path they hurry along is now partly enclosed in an air-conditioned, multilevel extension to the Masjid al-Haram, the Grand Mosque that surrounds the Kabah. Near one hill is the spring Zam-Zam, which God is said to have revealed to Hagar in response to her prayers ("zam-zam" being the noise the spring made to catch Hagar's attention). Pilgrims drink water from this spring (which is saline and something of an acquired taste) and take bottles of it home.

On the second day of Hajj, pilgrims begin a three-day circuit outside of Mecca. First, they travel about four miles by bus to Mina, a sprawling city of tents (Figure 10.9), where they spend the night in prayer and contemplation, preparing for the important tasks ahead. On the following day, they arrive at the valley of Arafat, where they observe a vigil of prayer and remembrance from noon until sundown. It is on this plain, which is about seven miles from Mecca, that Adam and Eve were said to have lived after their expulsion from Paradise. It is also here that Muhammad gave his last sermon, standing atop a hill called the Mount of Forgiveness, and that the final judgment is expected to take place. During their vigil, pilgrims reflect on their sins, repent, and submit themselves to God's great mercy. It is something of a dry run for the Judgment Day. Some climb the Mount of Forgiveness, believing it to be the place on earth closest to God, from which he best hears prayers. The vigil at Arafat is generally considered the most important part of the Hajj.

Figure 10.9 The city of Mina, on the way to the valley of Arafat, houses millions of pilgrims in tents during the season of the Hajj. Source: Photo by Arisdp.

A Closer Look

The Final Judgment

Islam teaches that all morally responsible beings in the created world will be held accountable to God for their actions. These include *jinn* and human beings. *Jinn* (singular: *jinni*, from which westerners get the word "genie") are spirits whom God created from smokeless fire. Angels, by contrast, were created by God from light. The Quran mentions several angels by name, including Jibril, Israfil, and Mikail, whose counterparts in the Jewish and Christian traditions are Gabriel, Raphael, and Michael. With the exception of Iblis, or Satan, all angels are good, and as they have no free will, they will not face judgment. They serve God by guarding the entrances to hell, watching over the affairs of human beings, and circumambulating God's heavenly throne while singing his praises. Iblis is different, however, not only because he is referred to as both an angel and a *jinni*, but also because he is reported to have rebelled against God by refusing to bow before Adam at God's command.

The Islamic understanding of an end-time judgment is complex and receives considerable attention in the Quran. Unlike the natural order, which always submits to God's will, humans have a choice. God created them specifically to be tested, having given them a divinely inspired motivation to choose good and avoid evil, sometimes called an inner light. But Iblis, aided by a class of *jinn* called satans, works as a counterforce to this inner light. While he cannot compel people to sin, he is able to tempt them through their own pride and forgetfulness. Iblis is thought to whisper temptations into their ears, and is sometimes associated with human appetites. In the popular imagination, it is widely believed that everyone is paired with both an angel and a satan, each of which constantly gives a person advice.

On the Last Day, the precise date of which is known only to God, all humans will be resurrected from the grave and brought to judgment. A great host of witnesses will then attest to each person's good and evil actions. These witnesses include the earth, the skin, hands, and feet of one's own body, and God and his angels, who possess books in which they have recorded human deeds. Believers and unbelievers alike will proclaim the truth of God and his prophets; all conflict and difference of opinion will be resolved; and people will stand defenseless in the immediate presence of the just and merciful God. Based on the choices they made during their lives, people will be judged as both individuals and as groups. Their evil deeds, which are light and insubstantial, will be weighed on a scale against their good deeds, which are heavy. Those whose evil deeds are heavier will be sent down to the hellfire, along with Satan, his satans, and the other bad *jinn*. There they will be guarded by the angel Malik

(continued)

> and his 19 angelic helpers, whose task is to oversee their punishment. Those who lived in submission to God will be sent up to paradise, envisioned as a garden of delights. As they go to their respective places, believers and unbelievers will address and call to one another, affirming the truth of God's earlier warnings and promises.

After sundown, Muslims travel to an area between Arafat and Mina, where they collect 49 pebbles. On the following day, they return to Mina to stone the Devil (Iblis), casting their pebbles at pillars called Jamarat (Figure 10.10). These pillars commemorate the three times the Devil is said to have tempted Abraham to rebel against God by telling him not to sacrifice his son Ishmael, which God had commanded Abraham to do. By throwing their pebbles at the pillars, Muslims imitate Abraham's resistance to temptation and faithfulness to God.

After stoning the Devil, the pilgrims return to Mecca and pay butchers to slaughter sheep, goats, cows, and camels, and package up the meat to be sent to the poor. This activity commemorates God's last-minute substitution of a ram for Ishmael so that Abraham did not have to sacrifice his son after all. Contact with the animals' blood

Figure 10.10 During the Hajj, pilgrims participate in Abraham's defiance of Satan by throwing pebbles at one of three large pillars, or walls (Jamarat). Source: Fadi El Binni of Al Jazeera English.

and other fluids also breaks the state of purity (*ihram*) and thus signals the conclusion of the Hajj. Male pilgrims have their hair cut or heads shaved while females have a lock of hair cut off; and preparations are made for the **Eid al-Adha**, or Festival of Sacrifice. This is the most important religious celebration of the Muslim calendar, and Muslim families around the world join in. They slaughter their own animals, using a third of the meat for the family feast, giving a third to neighbors and friends, and donating a third to charity. All Muslims who are able should eat meat that has been ritually butchered on this day.

Following the Eid al-Adha, which takes place on the tenth day of the month of Hajj, pilgrims perform one or more sevenfold circuits (*tawafs*) around the Kabah and return to Mina to stone the Devil again. On the twelfth or thirteenth day of the month, they return to Mecca for a farewell circuit around the Kabah before heading home, although many travel to Medina first, where Muhammad is interred. Those who have undertaken the Hajj may add "hajji" to their names, either as a prefix or a suffix, and it is said that they return home with the purity of a newborn baby.

Sharia beyond the Five Pillars

In addition to defining the Five Pillars, Sharia sets standards for many other areas of Muslim life. These include food and food preparation, family relations, and end-of-life practices.

Food and food preparation   Sharia categorizes all foods as either permitted (*halal*), prohibited (*haram*), or questionable (*mashbuh*). Prohibited meats include pork, meat from animals already dead before slaughtering (carrion), and beasts and birds of prey. The meat of other animals is permitted provided that it is slaughtered properly. This usually means facing the animal toward Mecca and cutting its jugular vein and windpipe with a quick motion while an onlooker says, "In the name of God," or "God is most great." Its blood must then be completely drained, as blood is a source of impurity.

All alcohol is also prohibited by analogy with the Quran's ban on wine. Other drugs and intoxicants, however, such as tobacco, hashish, opium, and *qat* (a caffeine-like stimulant), are sometimes put in the permitted or questionable category, rather than the prohibited category. In accordance with the Muslim understanding of God's oneness and its pervasiveness throughout creation, it is widely believed that permitted foods are beneficial to one's health, whereas prohibited foods are unhealthy.

Family relations   Another area carefully regulated by Sharia is family law. Sharia places great emphasis on being kind and deferential to parents; and legal experts point out that in several Quranic passages the injunction to respect one's parents follows immediately on the command to worship God, suggesting an important connection between the two. According to one passage, even if the parents are unbelievers, a son or daughter has a duty to speak and act kindly toward them, while being careful not to follow them into unbelief. Sharia also emphasizes the importance of maintaining good relations with one's extended family. One accomplishes this by visiting them often and helping them generously and willingly to the extent one is able. In most Islamic communities, a person's identity and social life are largely defined by their nuclear and extended family, and the first claimants to one's charity are family members, then close neighbors, and then the wider community.

> ### Did you know …
>
> In the nation of Iraq, there are three distinct Muslim populations: Arab Shias, Arab Sunnis, and Kurdish Sunnis. In neighboring Iran, most of the population is Persian Shia. But none of these groups is friendly with the others, either because of the Sunni–Shia divide, or because of ethnic differences—or both.

In Muslim-majority countries, dating and courtship can be quite limited, and many families in these countries still practice arranged marriage, often between first cousins. Even if a marriage is not arranged, parental consent is expected for both men and women, and required if it is the woman's first marriage. The principle of parental consent assumes that parents, who have a long experience with marriage and its challenges and know the personality and needs of their children, are best suited to identify appropriate marriage partners. All marriages also require the consent of the individuals who are to be married.

From the perspective of Sharia, Islamic marriage is a binding contract between the groom and the bride, the latter's interests traditionally upheld by her father or legal guardian. The marriage contract (*kitab*) states that the partners accept their responsibilities in marriage, and often specifies financial obligations, such as the amount of the bridal gift (*mahr*). This is a payment that all Muslim men must make to their brides, although its precise value is negotiable. Neither it nor any other wealth the bride possesses can be taken from her or used by her husband without her consent. The marriage contract may also specify a wife's living arrangements and a stipulated payment to be made to the wife should she be divorced or widowed. In addition, it can include financial stipulations to provide for a wife's education or future career, and, according to some views, stipulations that provide the wife with extended powers of divorce or restrict the husband's options for polygamy. Widows are encouraged to remarry, and the Prophet is said to have promoted remarriage by example, as all but one of his wives had been a widow or a divorcee.

Death, burial, and inheritance Regarding death and burial, Sharia prescribes that dying persons be faced toward Mecca and the first half of the Shahadah recited for their benefit. Corpses must be washed and wrapped in a burial shroud made from the same seamless, white cloth that men wear during the Hajj. Men are wrapped in three pieces of this cloth, women in five. A special prayer (*salat*) is then performed, the body is laid in the grave on its side with the head toward Mecca, and just before closing the grave the Shahadah is pronounced in the corpse's ear. The principal exception to these conventions is for religious martyrs. Since they have died "in the way of God," they are already considered holy and can be buried in the clothes they have on, without the washing or the white shroud.

Because private property is considered a trust from God, and because all Muslims are responsible for establishing a just society, a deceased person's estate must be divided among as many heirs as possible, and only a third of the estate may be directed away from these heirs to establish a charitable bequest (*waqf*) to support a mosque, fund education, or help the needy. Other trust funds or investments are not allowed.

Variety within Sharia

Sharia can vary from one Islamic community to another, for there is no single legal authority that is universally recognized by Muslims. Instead, Sharia is discovered in a living, dynamic process of legal discussion that takes place on both local and international levels, and everything in between. On the international level, there are five schools of Islamic law, each with its own legacy of scholars, particular emphases, and centers of study; and it is not considered proper to mix them. The most widely accepted school is the Hanafi, favored by perhaps one-third of the Muslim world. It has a reputation for being relatively liberal in the areas of individual freedoms and women's rights in marriage. By contrast, the Hanbali school, which is officially recognized only in Saudi Arabia and Qatar, is socially conservative but innovative in commercial and international law. While it prohibits western-style entertainment and limits the public activities of women, the Hanbali tradition has allowed U.S. industry and military forces onto the Saudi peninsula. The Hanafi and Hanbali, along with the Maliki and Shafii traditions, are all Sunni legal traditions. Shia Muslims have their own tradition called the Jafari school, which teaches, for example, that *salat*, the obligatory daily prayers of Islam, may be satisfied with *three* prayers in the course of a day, rather than the five that Sunnis require.

Talking about Religion

Religion or Culture?

It is often difficult to distinguish a tradition's religious symbols from its cultural symbols. For instance, is dressing up for church an essential part of Christian worship, or is it necessary only in certain cultures? In the latter case, one could argue that it is not Christian, per se, but just an aspect of the surrounding culture. Likewise, because Islamic life is regulated by the transcultural norms of Sharia law and, at the same time, is at home in a great variety of cultures, questions frequently arise among Muslims as to whether a given practice or image is actually Muslim or not.

One example is the image of the crescent, or crescent and star (Figure 10.11), which many take to be a symbol for Islam, much like the cross for Christianity. But while it appears atop mosques, on the flags of some Muslim countries, and

(*continued*)

Figure 10.11 The origins of the crescent and star, widely used as a symbol for Islam, are unknown.

elsewhere in Muslim contexts, the origins of this symbol are unclear, and it was formerly used by the Ottomans as an insignia for their empire rather than as a religious symbol.

A second example is circumcision. In most of the Islamic world, Muslim boys are circumcised between the ages of 7 days and 15 years, depending on local practice. An Arabic saying equates the importance of circumcision with that of marriage, and circumcisions are often planned for religious occasions, such as the birth month of the Prophet or in celebration of a boy's first full recitation of the Quran. Nevertheless, in some cultures Muslim boys are not circumcised. A final example concerns whether or not Muslim women must wear a veil. Most legal scholars today hold that Islam does not require women to veil their faces, explaining the practice as a carryover from earlier cultural norms. Yet some conservative groups do not permit women to be out in public or with men who are not close relations unless they are veiled; and many Salafi groups require women in these situations to wear *burqas*, a type of clothing that covers the entire body and masks the face with a cloth mesh (see Figure 10.12). They argue that *burqas* are necessary to preserve a woman's modesty and protect her from the exploitative fashions of the west. By contrast, Turkey, Egypt, Algeria, and Tunisia ban the wearing of *burqas* in some public settings.

(*continued*)

Figure 10.12 Astride a motorcycle, holding her twin girls, a woman in Turkey wears a veil, head scarf, and partial *burqa*. Source: H. Richard Rutherford, C.S.C.

On a national level, Muslim countries have taken different paths in adapting Sharia to the standards of modern legal codes. Pakistan, for instance, has three court systems: one for civil and criminal law, one for religious law, and one for tribal law. In Malaysia and Indonesia, Sharia is often informed by local customs and the residual practices of European colonial rule, while religious education, the collection of *zakat*, and the promotion of the Hajj are all under the direction of government bureaus.

Finally, on the local level, Sharia is shaped by a community's legal advisors, called *muftis*, who issue nonbinding rulings called *fatwas*. These are usually in response to questions on topics not yet covered by Sharia, or where Sharia is ambiguous: How can one pray on an airplane? Is it permissible to practice polygamy in modern societies? Can women participate in this or that current fashion trend? *Fatwas*, which are both practical and necessary, appear in newspaper columns, on radio talk shows, and on internet websites.

A Closer Look

A *Fatwa* on Friday Prayer

Question:
What is the smallest number of persons necessary for the Friday prayer and the giving of the sermon?

(*continued*)

> *Answer:*
> There is much difference of opinion in this matter among the scholars, but the most correct saying is that the minimum is three: The Imam and two others with him. So if there are three free, resident men in a village who are obligated to pray, they should establish the Friday [noon] prayer and not pray Zuhr [the usual noon prayer], because the evidences for the lawfulness of the Friday prayer and its obligation include them and any greater number.
>
> Cited from the online *fatwa* guide, http://FatwaIslam.com (accessed 11.22.2024)

Uses of the Quran beyond Sharia

In addition to being the first of the four sources of Sharia, the Quran functions in Islam in a number of nonlegal contexts. As the very speech of God, the Quran allows Muslims to hear God speak whenever the Quran is read aloud—or, more accurately, to hear God speak *in Arabic*. Because God's actual words came to Muhammad in Arabic, a translation of the Quran into any other language distorts God's words to a greater or lesser extent. Unlike in Christianity, where translations of the Bible are taken to be authoritative, only the *Arabic* Quran is considered scripture in Islam, and translations are used solely as aids for study. In consequence, the vast majority of Muslims understand little or nothing when the Quran is read out loud, since less than a fourth of the world's Muslims speak Arabic.

But the benefit gained by hearing the words of God need not involve understanding them, for most Muslims value readings from the Quran not for *what* it says, but for *how* it says it. Muslims often assert that Arabic has three modes of expression: prose, poetry, and Quranic style, which God used because of its unmatched ability to fulfill human needs and transform human hearts, whether or not one understands its meaning. For those who do understand Arabic, however, the Quran's cadences, word-plays, and overall structure add even more to their experience of God. They commonly attest that its style and organization reveal divine, nonlinear patterns in which sounds, phrases, and rhythms refract and cross-reference each other, making God's oneness, or *tawhid*, audible. The practical and moral message of the Quran, in turn, is said to coincide precisely with the natural sciences, while its narrations of otherwise unknowable realities attest to its origin in divine revelation.

For all these reasons, Muslims hold that the Quran is inimitable—something quite beyond the possibility of human imitation. The Quran itself even challenges its listeners to produce a chapter or even a few verses like it. Traditionally Muslims have identified the Quran as the Prophet's primary or sole miracle, and in the Science of Inimitability, a scholarly field developed to study the Quran's shifting patterns of rhetoric and style, scholars have compiled lists of the work's miraculous aspects. That an unschooled man with no ability for poetic composition could suddenly produce a work of such extraordinary quality late in life is held to be strong evidence for Muhammad's special status as the final Prophet of God.

A Closer Look

Popular Notions of the Quran's Inimitability

Popular traditions often circulate among Muslims that the miraculous nature of the Quran has been proven by scientists and computer experts. The following statement by an Egyptian pharmacist is a good example of this notion:

> As for the language of the Quran, scholars who speak Arabic have tried to write just one statement similar to this book in beauty. They could not. One computer scientist did a computer analysis of the Quran. He found that the number of chapters, the numbers of statements, and the number of times each letter is used are all multiples of nineteen (which is the number of angels in the Hellfire). Then he tried to see if he could write a book about any subject, using multiple numbers of any figure. No one could do it. The beauty of the Quran is pure, supreme.

From Mary Pat Fisher, *Living Religions*, 4th ed. (Upper Saddle River, NJ: Prentice Hall, 1991), p. 367.

The recitation of the Quran

Scholars most often derive the word Quran from an Arabic word for public reading or recitation, which is its principal use in the Islamic world. Memorization of the Quran is widely practiced, and specialists in this craft (Memorizers) perform at religious events and participate in competitions. Skillful recitation of the Quran from memory can elevate one to celebrity status in the Muslim world. Those who memorize the Quran attest to experiencing its formidable "kaleidoscopic composition," as verses and phrases repeat throughout the text, exposing different valences of meaning and aesthetic beauty. Reciting the text from memory demands constant vigilance against jumping from one familiar passage, theme, or word to another. In consequence, Memorizers must practice continually to keep the Quran fixed in their minds, often reciting the Quran from beginning to end once a week. Typically, however, a public recitation by *reading* the Quran is preferred over recitation from memory, because reading guards against the sorts of errors that enter into one's memory. In fact, the Quran itself promotes reading the Quran.

When one reads, they should face in the direction of Mecca and preface the reading with the words, "In the name of God the Compassionate, the Merciful," a phrase that precedes 113 of the Quran's 114 sections in all printed editions. It is generally held that one must be in a state of purity to formally recite or even touch the written text of the Quran, although this is sometimes disputed. The text used is the standard Arabic edition known as the Uthmanic Codex, and proper recitation follows an advanced science of reading that identifies even minor differences in vocalization. In its original form, the Uthmanic Quran was a consonantal text, with no written vowels. It was intended as a memory aid for those who already knew much of the Quran by heart, not as a guide to pronunciation. These limitations allowed for the development of different "voweling" of passages by early reciters. Today there are seven principal vowelings, or readings, of the Quran, although the publication of a royal Egyptian edition in 1924 has popularized one of these above the others. All these readings, however, agree on certain guidelines for pronunciation, making the sound of the Quran distinct from all other Arabic speech and song.

While recitations of the Quran occur throughout the year, they are especially popular during the celebration of the Prophet's Night Journey, and on his birthday, which falls on the twelfth day of the third lunar month. It is also popular to read the entire Quran aloud during the month of Ramadan as part of one's additional nighttime prayers. To facilitate this practice, printed editions of the Quran are often divided into 30 equal sections, one for each day of Ramadan. Other systems divide the text into 7 equal parts for recitation over the course of a week. During Ramadan and the season of Hajj, some Muslims take on the challenge of reading the entire Quran out loud in a single night.

Recitation and blessing

Holding a public celebration when a child has read the Quran out loud for the first time is quite common, and usually occurs before they have reached the age of five. While few of these children understand the words of the Quran as a language, the simple hearing of God's words is thought to convey a blessing on them, known as *baraqah*. For this reason, the Quran is also recited at other important transitions in life, such as birth, weddings, business agreements, and funerals. In some parts of the Muslim world, reading the Quran aloud is used to effect cures and exorcisms, or endow amulets (charms) with its *baraqah*. The Quran's blessing also can be received through physical contact with the written word. For example, verses from the Quran might be written on a piece of paper and then washed off by dipping the paper in water. When one drinks the water, they absorb the words' power.

The three orientations of Islam

Muslims typically identify themselves as believers according to three principal orientations: Sunni, Shia, and Sufi. All Muslims are either Sunni or Shia, and since Sunnis and Shias disagree on important aspects of belief and practice, these two orientations are exclusive of one another. While they may live harmoniously side-by-side, they normally do not worship together, except on the Hajj, and Shia Muslims have their own cycle of annual observances. Sufism, by contrast, is an orientation undertaken by many Sunni Muslims, and so we may think of it as a subset within the Sunni orientation. Most Sufis follow the beliefs and practices of Sunni Islam, but add to them or interpret them in ways that are distinctively Sufi.

While this is a convenient way to distinguish these orientations from one another, it is important to recognize that Muslims understand them as choices and variants within a unified tradition. From a Muslim perspective, the degree of diversity they engender within Islam is more readily seen as a gift from God than as a problem to be solved. As a famous saying attributed to the Prophet states, "Differences in my community (*ummah*) are a mercy from God."

Sunni Islam

Sunnis make up most of the Islamic world—somewhere between 85 and 90 percent. The starting point of their distinctive orientation is the belief that all divinely inspired teaching ended with the death of Muhammad. Through his recitation of God's words, and through his own words and actions, Muhammad became the Seal of the Prophets in the sense that God's revelation to humanity is now complete, without any possibility (or need) of adding to it. The highest religious authority for Sunnis is thus embodied in the Quran and the Hadith, the latter recording the "tradition (*sunnah*) of the Prophet" (*sunnat al-Nabi*), the expression from which Sunnis take their name.

Because no one can claim to have a new revelation, or even an infallible understanding of the Quran or the Hadith—since infallibility requires divine inspiration—religious leadership among Sunnis belongs to the *ulama*, the theologian-scholars who study these texts. Moreover, while some *ulama* are regarded as more insightful or learned than others, there is no standard system for training or licensing them, nor any universally recognized hierarchy among them. The degree of religious authority a scholar enjoys is mostly determined by the size his following and his reputation for religious integrity and knowledge.

A Closer Look

The Future Leader of the Muslim World

While Shia Muslims usually adhere to specific doctrines about the coming of the "Rightly Guided One," or **Mahdi**, Sunnis tend to share a set of unofficial, popular beliefs regarding this messianic figure. It is widely held by Sunnis that the Mahdi will come from the Prophet's family and bear the name of Muhammad's father, Abd Allah ibn Abd al-Muttalib. He will appear in a time of extreme moral confusion, perform miracles, and spread wealth, justice, and the religion of Islam throughout the world. Eventually he will be challenged to do battle with the false messiah Dajjal, "the Deceiver," during which time both Jesus and God will come to the Mahdi's aid. Then, with Jesus and the Mahdi's victory over evil, the Last Judgment will begin.

The decentralized nature of religious leadership in the Sunni community has three important consequences. First, Sunni Islam can accommodate many forms of government, since their *ulama* have sufficient flexibility to work within a range of political systems. In practice, because Sunnis also make a fairly clear distinction between religious and political authority, their *ulama* usually give local and national governments jurisdiction in most areas of law, reserving for themselves only ritual law and those aspects of family law covered by Sharia. The second consequence of a decentralized religious leadership is that Sunni Islam has no official theology or uniform code of Sharia. Certain elements of Sunni belief vary greatly from region to region and, as noted above, Sunnis have four distinct legal traditions, each of which is held to be valid. The third and final consequence is that Sunni beliefs and practices have become a common denominator among Muslims. Since Sunnis claim no special access to God through a continuing tradition of prophecy, there is very little in their orientation to God that is exclusive to them. In fact, most of what we have already covered in this section could serve as a description of Sunni Islam by itself.

> **Talking about Religion**
>
> ## The Different Meanings of Imam
>
> The Arabic term Imam means "one who leads," and it has a number of uses in Islam. Sunni Muslims sometimes use it as a synonym for caliph, referring to the leader of the Muslim community worldwide. They also use it as the title for a very learned religious scholar. In its most popular usage, however, Sunnis call anyone who leads a group of Muslims in prayer an Imam, and as such it can double as the title for those in charge at a mosque. Shias, on the other hand, use Imam quite differently. For them it refers to the divinely guided leaders who succeeded Muhammad after his death, and thus is a technical term reserved for Ali and his designated descendants.

Shia Islam

Shias comprise 10–15 percent of the Islamic world and mostly live in Iran, Iraq, and neighboring countries (Figure 10.13). The fundamental premise of Shia orientation is that divine guidance *did not* end with Muhammad. For Shias, the authority of the Quran and the Hadith are not a sufficient substitute for Muhammad's leadership, for individual Hadith can vary in their reliability and the Quran can be interpreted in a number of ways. Instead, Shias believe that divine inspiration passed from Muhammad to his cousin and son-in-law Ali (the fourth caliph), and then to several of Ali's descendants in successive generations. Today most Shias identify themselves as Imamis or "Twelvers" (*Ithna Ashari*). They hold that Ali and 11 of his descendants became Imams, a title Shias use to designate persons who wield infallible knowledge and authority. At present, the Twelvers await the return of Imam Muhammad, the twelfth and final Imam, who is believed to have been hidden away by God in the late ninth century. Named after the Prophet, Imam Muhammad is expected to return near the end of time as the Mahdi, to establish his authority over the entire Muslim community. He will also avenge wrongs that were committed against all the other Imams, all of whom are believed to have died as martyrs. Until that time, the Mahdi's gift of inspiration is mediated to the Shia community through the insights of its senior *ulama*.

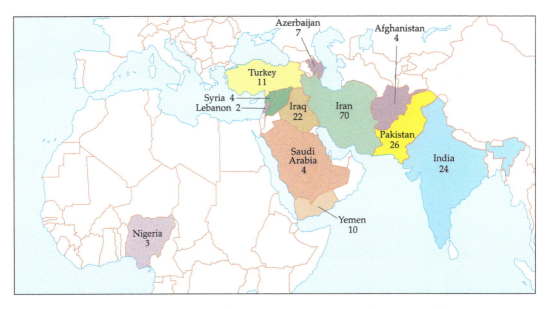

Figure 10.13 A map showing the location of major Shia populations (in millions).

A Closer Look

Non-Twelver Shia Sects

Twelver Shiism, which recognizes a succession of 12 divinely inspired Imams after the death of Muhammad, constitutes over 85 percent of all Shias. Of the non-Twelver Shia groups, the Zayidis, or "Fivers," parted company with other Shias after the death of the fourth Imam, electing to follow Zayd rather than Muhammad al-Baqir. Today Zayidis are found mostly in Yemen and are considered close to Sunnis in belief and practice. The Ismailis, in turn, who are also known as "Seveners," recognize a succession of seven Imams. They split off from the larger group when Ismail, the oldest son of Imam Jafar, the sixth Imam, died before his father. When Jafar appointed a younger son, Musa, as the seventh Imam, those loyal to Ismail rejected Musa in favor of Ismail's son Ahmad (Figure 10.14). Ismailis are found in Iran, Syria, east Africa, Pakistan, and India, and are the origin of two smaller groups: the Druze and the Nizaris. The Druze are distinctive in believing in reincarnation, while the Nizaris are the only Shias to recognize a living ("manifest") Imam. Known as the Aga Khan, his primary residence is the French city of Gouvieux, north of Paris.

The Alawis (also called Nusayris) are found mostly in Syria. They are usually called Shias, and apparently derive from a group that broke away from the Twelver line after the tenth Imam. Their rather secretive beliefs and practices appear to meld Ismaili Shiism with Persian, Gnostic, and Christian elements, and they gather in private homes rather than mosques for worship.

(continued)

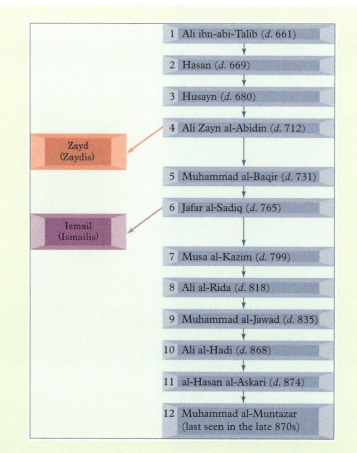

Figure 10.14 A chart showing the rightful succession of Imams (inspired leaders) according to various Shia groups.

Today, Alawis constitute perhaps 7 percent of the Syrian population, but they maintain control of the government. Finally, in northeast Turkey there is a group named the Alevis, who are sometimes identified as Shia. More likely, however, they are rooted in indigenous Anatolian culture mixed with Sufism. Among their distinctive practices is worshipping in assembly halls called *cemevi*, rather than mosques.

During the Mahdi's state of hiding, called the Greater Occultation, Shias are expected to seek out and follow a particular member of the *ulama*, who serves as a "model for imitation." Like their Sunni counterparts, Shia *ulama* study the Quran and the Hadith, although within the context of the Jafari school of law. In addition, their Hadith include biographical reports not only of the Prophet, but also of their Imams, to whom they attribute extraordinary knowledge and wisdom, and even miraculous powers. The *ulama* themselves are also expected to select a "model for imitation" from among their colleagues, and the most respected *ulama* in the Shia community are honored as Ayatollahs, meaning "signs of God," and Grand Ayatollahs.

The Shia assumption that believers should follow the example of a *living* religious scholar has meant that each new generation relies on a fresh set of scholars and their interpretations of Sharia. For this reason, Shia *ulama* are often less constrained by legal precedents than their Sunni counterparts.

Because Shias believe that divine guidance was passed down through the Prophet's bloodline via his daughter Fatimah and her husband, Ali, they practice a deep and personal devotion to all the members of this line. Collectively known the "Prophet's family" and "people of the house [of the Prophet]," Muhammad's descendants through Fatimah and Ali are addressed with the honorific titles Sayyid and Sharif, and supported financially by the Shia community. Since it is considered inappropriate to their dignity for them to receive *zakat* (alms), they receive part of an annual Shia offering known as *khums*. This is defined as 20 percent of a person's net profits for the year, which must be given to members of the Prophet's family, local religious leaders, and the poor. In origin, *khums* was the Prophet's share of goods and captives taken in battles and caravan raids.

Shia devotion to Fatimah, Ali, and their descendants is referred to as "befriending" the Prophet's family, and takes several forms. One is the regular public denunciation of the first three caliphs for usurping the rightful place of Ali as successor to the Prophet. A second involves pilgrimages and visitations to the tombs of the Imams and their family members. Upon death (and sometimes prior to death), Sayyids and Sharifs are honored as saints, and special shrines are built to house their tombs. Each shrine has a distinctive prayer that visitors say, and shrines housing the tombs of Imams are surrounded by cemeteries so that devotees can be buried near them. The Iraqi cities of Najaf and Karbala have elaborate shrines for Ali and Husayn, respectively, while a massive and architecturally stunning tomb complex in Mashhad ("Martyr's Tomb"), Iran, houses the body of the eighth Imam (Figure 10.15). For many Shias, pilgrimage to Mashhad is considered second only to the Hajj as a source of spiritual merit and honor. In addition to these and other major shrines, Iran and Iraq are dotted with the burial sites of lesser-known Sayyids and Sharifs, which attract both Shia and Sunni pilgrims.

A third type of devotion to members of the Prophet's house takes the form of weekly and annual religious observances. Ghadir Khumm, for example, which follows shortly after the Hajj, celebrates the day on which Shias believe the Prophet Muhammad appointed Ali to be his successor. Mawlid al-Husayn is the birthday celebration of the third Imam, held in Cairo; and for the birthday of Imam Muhammad, the twelfth, hidden Imam, it is customary for Shias to write him letters and send them off by placing them in a river. At solemn meetings throughout the year, Shias also narrate the events that led to the death of Imam Husayn, the third Imam and Ali's second son. Fighting for God's cause, abandoned by those who should have been his loyal supporters, in desperate need of water, and facing a vastly superior army, Husayn and his family were hacked to death and beheaded on the plains outside of Karbala by false Muslims under the command of the third caliph's son. He was then left unburied in the desert. For this reason, Husayn is honored by Shias as the **Prince of Martyrs**, and his death is seen both as an inspiration for resistance to all injustice and as a redemptive act undertaken on behalf of the Islamic community. Recitations of his

Figure 10.15 The entrance to the tomb complex in Mashhad, Iran, which contains the body of Imam Ridha, the eighth Shia Imam. The complex also contains several seminaries, a large mosque for staff and students, a museum, a library, and mosques for visitors.
Source: Photo by Iahsan.

story are held in special halls, courts, and tents called *husayniyahs* and *imambarahs*. These can last from two to eight hours, and scenes from Husayn's story are sometimes illustrated with large drawings. Tending to be highly emotional, they inspire prolonged wailing and even self-flagellation by participants and onlookers alike.

One of the most important and distinctive religious observances for Shias is Ashura, which memorializes the day of Husayn's gruesome martyrdom. Ashura begins on the first day of the lunar year and culminates on the tenth (*ashura*). During these 10 days, processions of mourners pass through Shia towns and cities, beating their chests and lacerating themselves with chains, knives, and swords. This is to express their grief for Husayn's unjust death, and a deep remorse for having abandoned him (a sin they take upon themselves) in his hour of need. Some carry branches of the date-palm tree, because Husayn's corpse was said to have been retrieved for burial on a stretcher made of such branches. Since the eighteenth century, Shias have also performed passion plays during Ashura, recounting and acting out the horror of Husayn's last days. Known as "consolation" (*taziya*), these are quite stark presentations using stylized props and minimal stage design—a bowl of water for the Euphrates River, a palm branch for an oasis. The heroes are dressed in green, the color of the Prophet, and sing their parts; the villains wear red and deliver their lines in shrieks and fits of anger (Figure 10.16). In the final scene, either a coffin or Husayn's severed head is carried to the court of the third caliph's son, where actors playing the roles of Jews, Christians, and Sunnis bow in sadness, humiliation, and disgrace. The Karbala massacre, and the injustices against the family of the Prophet both before

Figure 10.16 During a performance of the *tazyia* passion play in Tehran, actors playing the false Muslims under the command of Muawiyah celebrate their victory over the fallen Imam Ali. Source: Photo by Ninara.

and after this event, are foundational to the spiritual and emotional lives of devout Shias, making martyrdom, ritual mourning, and resistance to injustice central to the Shia self-understanding.

Sufism

Sufism is an orientation based on esoteric and mystical interpretations of Islam. Its practitioners, known as Sufis, are found throughout the Islamic world. Like Shias, Sufis believe that humans have access to divine revelation apart from the Quran and Hadith. Yet unlike Shias, most Sufis envision this access in a way that is acceptable to many Sunnis. Their point of departure is the teachings of the Quran and the Hadith on the Prophet's ascent to God. Known as the *Miraj*, Muhammad's ascent is said to have taken place in 621, just before he began his public ministry. After being taken to Jerusalem on the winged horse Buraq, Muhammad ascended through seven levels of heaven, greeting angels and prophets, and visiting hell and paradise. He was then ushered into God's presence by the angel Gabriel, where, alone with God, the Prophet received special teachings. In this tradition, Muhammad is said to have encountered the very person of God in a direct, unmediated experience. Since Muhammad did this as a human being, with no special powers of his own, and since he is the perfect model of a Muslim for all believers, Sufis hold that it is both possible and meritorious for Muslims to replicate the Prophet's encounter with God.

A key term for understanding Sufism is *tariqah*, which translates "way" or "path," and has at least three important meanings in Sufi thought. *Tariqah* can designate the spiritual path to God; or refer to a Sufi order; or refer to the teachings and practices of a particular Sufi master.

The Sufi path to God Sufis envision the path to God (*tariqah*) as a series of stations and states through which one progresses, both psychologically and spiritually. Since their model is Muhammad, the perfect human being, they attempt to internalize his *sunnah* as well as emulate it outwardly through ritual, thereby making his *sunnah* their own. Stations (*maqamat*) are attitudes such as sincere intention, gratitude, repentance, and hope, which one achieves through their own self-effort. States (*ahwal*), on the other hand, are significant breakthroughs on the path to God, which come as gifts from God. They expand and contract one's soul, bringing on experiences of profound joy, sadness, love, nearness, longing, and intoxication. Sufis often speak of their progress toward God as "polishing the heart." In this metaphor, the heart is a mirror in which one sees the very reflection of God. The more polished the mirror, the clearer its image of God becomes. The final goal of the Sufi path is to encounter God in such a way that one experiences God's *tahwid* through both annihilation of the self (*fana*) and continuance in God (*baqa*). When someone reaches this pinnacle of knowing God, they become a *wali*, or friend of God, with the religious status of a saint. Many *walis* are thought to have special power (*baraqah*) by which they can perform cures and healings.

The Sufi path to God has been controversial from the first and continues to be so because of the Sufi claim to achieving an essential unity with God. Their poetic descriptions of this mystical experience are also criticized since they sometimes resort to metaphors of intoxication, infatuation, and forbidden love, which many Muslims find offensive. Most often, however, controversies are centered on Sufi practices that take them beyond the Islamic mainstream, and sometimes this criticism comes from other Sufis. For these reasons, Sufism is currently banned in Saudi Arabia and censored by many reformist groups.

Sufi orders Sufis are organized into regional and transnational fraternities called *orders*, which is our second meaning for *tariqah*. Sufi orders are led by spiritual masters called *shaykhs* (or *pirs* or *murshids*), who derive their authority from an unbroken line of former masters that leads back to the *tariqah*'s founder. The founder, in turn, has his own teaching lineage, linking him to the Prophet, either through Ali or through one of the Prophet's other companions. By virtue of a *tariqah*'s lineage, modern *shaykhs* are believed to have access to Muhammad's *baraqah*—his divinely given power to bless and heal.

When a spiritual master dies (and sometimes while he is still alive), he can become a saint (*wali, marabout*) by popular acclamation. If this happens, the local members of his order create a shrine to house his body. Some shrines are elaborate buildings with domed roofs, while others are simple frame structures made of wood and draped with a cloth to cover the saint's grave. Their purpose is to make the Prophet's *baraqah*, which continues to reside in the saint's corpse, available to pilgrims. Visitors come throughout the year to ask for the saint's intercession before God, fulfill a vow for prayers that were answered, or make physical contact with the saint's *baraqah* by touching or kissing the cloth over his tomb, after which they may wipe their hands down their faces while saying, "Give us something from God, Sayyid." These visits are seen as especially powerful for persons related to the saint, and some shrines are considered particularly effective for women's needs, while others cater primarily to men's needs.

> **Did you know ...**
>
> Under current Swiss law, Muslims can build mosques in Switzerland, but not minarets, which are the slender towers that usually accompany them. This is because the Swiss find minarets too assertive or menacing.

An order's most important shrines are endowed with a religious trust (*waqf*) and hold annual observances. On a saint's birthday, for example, visitors circumambulate his tomb seven times and make a donation or offer a sacrifice. This is also a popular occasion for parents to have their sons circumcised. Some observances mark the death date of a saint, which is celebrated as his "wedding" to God. Annual observances have a festive atmosphere, with food, entertainment, and special pavilions for religious observances.

Like the Shia veneration of Sayyids, the Sufi veneration of saints is regarded by many Muslims as violating the Islamic principle that one should worship and pray only to God. Nevertheless, from the Asia Pacific to the Atlantic coast of Africa, millions of Muslims visit the graves of these holy persons for spiritual insight and blessing.

The devotional path of a Sufi master To practice Sufism, one becomes the disciple of a master, for it is considered dangerous to pursue the mystical path to God without an experienced guide. While masters are almost always male, there are a few recognized female masters (*shaykhah*). New members take an oath of allegiance to their master, typically sealed with a ritual handclasp that transfers *baraqah* from the master to the disciple. Ideally, through their devotion to the Prophet's *sunnah*, masters have reached a state of perfection like Muhammad's, possessing the highest levels of the Prophetic virtues, without, of course, attaining to the rank of Prophet. In this state of perfection, they mirror the qualities and virtues of the Prophet, and guide their disciples through a particular "path of devotional practices," which is our final meaning of *tariqah*.

One master's *tariqah* (in this sense) differs from another's with regard to style of dress as well as religious practices called **dhikr**. *Dhikr* are techniques of "remembrance and invocation" whose primary feature is repetition. The goal of performing *dhikr* is to bring the remembrance of God into everything that one does, exchanging all worldly distractions for a heightened awareness of God. Through *dhikr* a person is said to internalize Muhammad's experience of God, thereby losing all awareness of anything but God. The most common *dhikr* involve repetition of the name "Allah" (Arabic for God) or phrases taken from the Quran, such as "There is no God but God," and "God is the Eternal One." These verbal repetitions are often accompanied by repetitive movements such as swaying, regulating the breath, bowing, or "jerking" the head forward. It is also popular for Sufis to chant the 99 Most Beautiful Names of God, which derive from statements in the Quran and are believed to eliminate impediments to one's spiritual ascent. These names include such titles as "Protector," "Witness," "Most Kind and Just," "Defender," and "Light," and typically the one chanting them keeps count on a rosary of 33 beads.

Other forms of *dhikr* use singing and dancing, as well as the repetitive shapes in calligraphy that are produced when one copies out verses (*ayah*, literally "signs") from the Quran. An order of Turkish Sufis, the Mevlevi, has become famous in the west as Whirling Dervishes for its *dhikr* of highly choreographed dance in which disciples surround their master, rotating and orbiting in a circle like planets around the sun (Figure 10.17). *Dhikr* can be performed in a group, in unison with others, or by oneself. For many Sufi orders, Thursday night is a common time for congregational performances of *dhikr*, which also function more or less as entertainment.

Figure 10.17 The distinctive *dhikr* of the Mevlevi Sufi order has earned them the name Whirling Dervishes. Here several disciples dance while a master (*shaykh*) looks on. Source:Wikimedia Commons.

In the Quran—which reflects on its own repetitive style as a form of *dhikr*—the practice of *dhikr* is commanded, and in one instance the Quran asserts that *dhikr* is greater than daily prayer. But instead of classifying it as one of the mandatory acts of Sharia, legal scholars assign *dhikr* to the category of supererogatory acts, which are described in a widely known "sacred Hadith"—that is, one uttered by God himself:

> My servant does not draw near to Me through anything more beloved to Me than the rites I have ordained for him. *Then My servant continues to draw near to Me through supererogatory works*, until I am the sight by which he sees, the hearing by which he hears, the hand with which he grasps, and the foot with which he walks.

CONCLUSION

The religion of Islam proclaims that God is one, and that his oneness should guide all human action and serve as a pattern for human society. Access to God's final message to humanity comes through the Prophet Muhammad, whose recitation of God's words are recorded in the Quran, and whose life was an act of perfect submission to God. Through the Quran and Muhammad's example, Muslims around the world share a common set of practices and values, as well as the conviction that submission to God can bring all of humanity together as a unified community of believers and put an end to differences caused by race, nationality, culture, or ethnic identity.

For review

1. Where do most Muslims live in the world? Which countries have the largest Muslim populations?
2. What are the four sources of Sharia (Islamic law)?
3. What are the Five Pillars?
4. Describe the practice of daily prayer (*salat*).
5. Name at least three ways that Muslims use the Quran to orient themselves to God.
6. How do Muslims see themselves in relation to Judaism and Christianity?
7. What is the connection between the concepts *tawhid* and *islam*?
8. List some of the uses for the term *jihad*.
9. How do *fatwahs* function?
10. List several differences between Sunni, Shia, and Sufi orientations in Islam.
11. What are some of the meanings of the Sufi term *tariqah*?

For discussion

1. Given the Islamic vision of the ideal human community, how much room for dialogue is there between the Muslim world and the west?
2. Is the status of women in Islam better or worse than their status in Chinese religion, Hinduism, or Christianity? How do their prospects for the future compare?

Key Terms

Ali	Ali ibn-abi-Talib, the Prophet's cousin and son-in-law; the fourth caliph of Islam; considered by Shias to be the first inspired Imam.
baraqah	A blessing; especially a divine blessing or gift of power passed along in the family bloodline of the Prophet or bestowed by a Sufi *shaykh* or saint.
caliph	"Successor"; leaders that guided the Islamic community after Muhammad's death.
dhikr	A Sufi devotional practice designed to heighten one's awareness of God.

dhimmi	Formerly, a non-Muslim living in Muslim-controlled lands and paying a head tax for Muslim protection.
Dome of the Rock	A shrine built in the late seventh century commemorating Muhammad's ascent to God; located in Jerusalem on the Temple Mount.
Eid	One of two major festivals in the Islamic calendar, one following the annual time of the Hajj (Eid al-Adha), one following the Ramadan fast (Eid al-Fitr).
fatwa	A nonbinding legal ruling on a matter not sufficiently covered by Sharia.
Five Pillars	Five defining actions that are obligatory for all Muslims: profession of faith, daily prayer, almsgiving, the Ramadan fast, and the pilgrimage to Mecca.
hadith	Witnessed reports of what Muhammad said and did during his life.
Hajj	One of the Five Pillars of Islam; the pilgrimage to Mecca that Muslims make during the eighth month of the Islamic year.
hijra	The emigration of Muslims from Mecca to Medina in 622 CE.
Imam	Among Sunnis, the person who directs prayers at the mosque; in Shia Islam, one of several inspired leaders descended from Muhammad, beginning with Ali.
Imami	The largest sect of Shia Islam; also known as the Twelvers.
Islam	Literally "submission"; submission to God, which is the principal characteristic of the religion.
isnad	The chain of witnesses that accompanies each *hadith*.
jahiliyyah	A period of spiritual ignorance in Arab history; also used by reformist Muslims to describe the state of spiritual ignorance among fellow Muslims.
jihad	Literally "struggle"; used to describe the human effort needed to conform to God's will; sometimes refers to armed struggle against Islam's enemies.
Kabah	Literally "Cube"; the holiest shrine in the Muslim world, located in Mecca; Muslims must turn toward the Kabah during daily prayer.
Mahdi	The "rightly guided one"; a future leader of the Islamic community expected to appear before the final judgment.
Miraj	Muhammad's ascent to God during his Night Journey.
mosque	A prayer hall (Arabic: *masjid*).
Muslim Brotherhood	A grassroots Salafi movement with political aspirations, found in Egypt and elsewhere in the Middle East.
Night Journey	Muhammad's spiritual journey from Mecca to Jerusalem on a winged horse named Buraq.
Night of Power	The night of Muhammad's first revelation from God.

People of the Book	A Muslim designation for Muslims and other monotheists who have a sacred scripture (Jews, Christians, Zoroastrians).
Prince of Martyrs	A title given to Husayn, the second son of Ali and a focus of Shia theology and identity.
Prophet Muhammad	God's last messenger to humankind, who delivered God's message without error (the Quran) and lived a perfect life.
Quran	The most authoritative scripture in Islam, being the very words of God delivered in Arabic to humankind by Muhammad.
Ramadan	The ninth month of the Islamic year, during which Muslims fast during daylight hours.
Salafis	Reformers who look back to the first generations of Muslims as their guide for reform.
Shahadah	Profession of one's faith through the formula: "There is no god but God, and Muhammad is the Messenger of God"; the first of the Five Pillars.
Sharia	The Islamic way of life, often called Islamic law; established by legal scholars, it pertains largely to marriage, inheritance, and religious duties.
shaykh	A Sufi spiritual master; also known as a *pir* or *murshid*.
Shia	One of two principal types of Islam, comprising 10–15 percent of the Muslim world; it sees Ali and his descendants as having a divine authority comparable to Muhammad's (see Sunni).
Sufism	Sunni Islam's mystical tradition.
sunnah	"Tradition"; especially the tradition of the Prophet's life as recorded in the Hadith; origin of the name Sunni.
Sunni	One of two principal types of Islam, followed by 85–90 percent of all Muslims (see Shia).
tariqah	In Sufism: a spiritual path to God; a Sufi order; the teachings and practices of a particular Sufi master.
tawhid	"Oneness"; the principal attribute of the Muslim God, which suffuses his creation and establishes a pattern for human actions and society.
ulama	Muslim legal scholars who "discover" Sharia through their study of the Quran and the Hadith.
Umayyad dynasty	The first Islamic dynasty, established after the death of the fourth caliph.
ummah	The Muslim community, established by Muhammad in 622 CE and characterized by God's oneness (*tawhid*).
Uthmanic Codex	The Arabic text of the Quran as established by the caliph Uthman (d. 656) and now accepted by Muslims as definitive.
zakat	Obligatory charitable giving to the poor. One of the Five Pillars.

Bibliography

A good first book

Andrew Rippin and Teresa Bernheimer. *Muslims: Their Religious Beliefs and Practices*, 5th edn. New York: Routledge, 2018.

Further reading

Shahab Ahmed. *What is Islam? The Importance of Being Islamic*. Princeton, NJ: Princeton University Press, 2017.

Zahra M.S. Ayubi. *Gendered Morality: Classic Islamic Ethics of the Self, Family, and Society*. New York: Columbia University Press, 2019.

John L. Esposito, Tamara Sonn, and John O. Voll. *Islam and Democracy After the Arab Spring*. New York and Oxford: Oxford University Press, 2015.

Anna M. Gade. *The Qur'an: An Introduction*. Oxford: Oneworld, 2010.

Zareena Grewal. *Islam is a Foreign Country: American Muslims and the Global Crisis of Authority*. New York: New York University Press, 2013.

Juliane Hammer and Omid Safi, eds. *The Cambridge Companion to American Islam*. Cambridge: Cambridge University Press, 2013.

Amir Hussain. *Muslims and the Making of America*. Waco, TX: Baylor University Press, 2017.

Reference and research

Jane D. McAuliffe, ed. *The Cambridge Companion to the Qur'ān*. Cambridge: Cambridge University Press, 2006.

Knut S. Vikør. *Between God and the Sultan: A History of Islamic Law*. New York: Oxford University Press, 2005.

CHAPTER 11
Change in Religions and New Religions
The ongoing search for the divine

Two practitioners of Wicca perform a Handfasting ceremony, which unites them as husband and wife. Source: Reproduced by permission of Kam Abbott.

DID YOU KNOW …

New religious movements are constantly forming in all parts of the world, although few survive more than a generation. Some die out because their members lose interest. Others are abandoned when their leaders become involved in scandal; and a few movements have brought on their own demise through martyrdom or mass suicides.

Understanding the Religions of the World: An Introduction, Second Edition.
Edited by Will Deming.
© 2025 John Wiley & Sons Ltd. Published 2025 by John Wiley & Sons Ltd.

OVERVIEW

Even though many people see their own religion as unchanging and timeless, religions change constantly. Religious leaders feel the need to react to challenges, both internal and external, and each new generation wants its religion to be relevant for them. In truth, religions are *rarely* static. It is their nature to develop over time, and they do so in many ways, as the history sections in the previous chapters have demonstrated.

Sometimes change is the result of simple human nature. Human beings are inquisitive creatures who exchange ideas with one another, incorporate new experiences into their understanding of the world, and develop new expectations for the future. As far back as we have historical records, theologians have advanced new claims about the nature of the world, the gods, or ultimate reality. At times these claims come down to us in the form of reflective monologs and spiritual diaries in which religious leaders relate life-changing experiences, particular moments of insight, or bare their souls to make the case for religious change. Two such spiritual diaries are St Augustine's *Confessions*, and Mahatma Gandhi's *The Story of My Experiments with Truth*. At other times, calls for change can take the form of dialogs in which two or more characters work out an argument for religious innovation based on reasoned considerations of their tradition. We see this, for example, in the *Upanishads*. Some dialogs even feature a divine teacher whose arguments are beyond human criticism. The gospels, for example, depict Jesus teaching his disciples, and in the *Bhagavad-Gita* the god Krishna instructs King Arjuna on the topic of religious duty.

A Closer Look

Mary Baker Eddy Discovers Christian Science

Mary Baker Eddy (1821–1910) founded of the Church of Christ, Scientist, or Christian Science in 1879. Here is an excerpt from her autobiography, *Retrospection and Introspection*, describing her spiritual discovery:

> It was in Massachusetts, in February, 1866 ... that I discovered the Science of divine metaphysical healing which I afterwards named Christian Science. The discovery came to pass in this way. During twenty years prior to my discovery I had been trying to trace all physical effects to a mental cause; and in the latter part of 1866 I gained the scientific certainty that all causation was Mind, and every effect a mental phenomenon.

(continued)

> My immediate recovery from the effects of an injury caused by an accident, an injury that neither medicine nor surgery could reach, was the falling apple that led me to the discovery how to be well myself, and how to make others so. …
>
> I then withdrew from society for about three years,—to ponder my mission, to search the Scriptures, to find the Science of Mind that should take the things of God and show them to the creature, and reveal the great curative Principle,—Deity.
>
> Mary Baker G. Eddy, *Retrospection and Introspection*
(Boston: W. G. Nixon, 1891), pp. 24–25.

Religious change also can have its roots in the larger, external forces of history and culture. When Buddhism came to China from India around the first century CE, it underwent several significant developments as the Chinese interpreted it on their own terms. Making Buddhism relevant to their own religious and cultural expectations, images of the Buddha took new forms (Figures 11.1 and 11.2) and entirely new schools of Buddhism appeared.

Figures 11.1 and 11.2 Americans often encounter a fat, laughing Buddha in Chinese restaurants. This is because somewhere around the tenth century CE, the Chinese identified the future Buddha Maitreya with a jolly, rotund sage from their folk traditions. Known as Pu-tai (Budai) or Milo, he is much beloved by children, to whom he gives little presents. By contrast, Figure 11.1 is a serene, contemplative Maitreya in the Indian style from the second century CE. Source: Wikimedia Commons. Figure 11.2 is a laughing Milo from contemporary Chinese Buddhism. Source: Will Deming.

Intellectual developments, such as the European Enlightenment, and social developments, such as the feminist movement, have brought about changes as well, sometimes as small adjustments to a religion, sometimes as wholesale transformations. The same is true of the missionary activities that came with European colonialism in Asia, Africa, the Americas, and the Pacific Islands (Oceania). One result was conversions to Christianity, but another was the appearance of hundreds of new religious movements that borrowed selectively from the missionary religions.

The introduction of religious freedom into an area is yet another powerful catalyst for change, as can be seen in post-World War II Japan, with the popularity of hundreds of new charismatic sects. Finally, political developments and military encounters can bring about important innovations. Judaism, in particular, can trace major religious watersheds to such events: the Babylonian Exile, the Maccabean Revolt, the Jewish Revolt against Rome, the expulsion of Jews from Spain and Portugal, the Holocaust, and the establishment of the modern state of Israel.

A Closer Look

Western Forms of Eastern Religions

The diffusion of religious traditions outside their homelands continues to create new patterns of religious change in our century. For example, one sees an increasing number of western spiritual masters in eastern traditions. Swami Paramahansa Yogananda (1893–1952), founder of the Self-Realization Fellowship and author of the spiritual classic *Autobiography of a Yogi* (1946), passed his spiritual mantle to a *western*-born successor; and Willigis Jäger, a former Benedictine monk and highly successful Catholic meditation teacher in Germany, founded his own Zen Buddhist lineage in 2009 after joining and then leaving the Sanbô-Kyôdan Zen school. In an extension of this trend, Dharmachari Subhuti (aka Alex Kennedy), a leading member of the British organization Friends of the Western Buddhist Order, argued for creating a "real Western Buddhism" in his book *Buddhism for Today* (1983). Likewise, Guru Maharaj Ji, a popular Hindu guru in the 1970s, currently presents his Divine Light Mission using a "de-hinduized" terminology. Known as both Prem Rawat and Maharaji, he wears a western business suit and tie.

Traditional Patterns of Change

These particular catalysts for innovation, which can operate independently or in combination with one another, result in what can be categorized as "traditional" patterns of change, which include reactive and progressive reform movements, as well as schisms and syncretism.

Reactive and progressive reform movements

Some catalysts for change have the potential to arouse an internal dynamic in a religion, felt either as an urgency to return to a tradition's roots, or as a desire to update a religion to contemporary sensibilities. The first, which can be called a **reactive reform movement**, seeks a purer, more original version of the religion. This is typical of fundamentalist Christianity and Salafi Islam. The second is classified as a **progressive reform movement**, clear examples of which include Reform Judaism and the Second Vatican Council.

Schisms

When factions within a religious group result in new divisions of the tradition, this pattern of change is known as a **schism.** Like many religions, Christianity experienced schisms even in its beginning years: between apostolic leaders in the first century, and with Gnostic groups in the second. During the second millennium of its existence, moreover, Christianity underwent two major schisms. The first occurred in the eleventh century, when the western and eastern churches parted company, creating Roman Catholicism and Eastern Orthodoxy. The second came in the sixteenth century as a result of the Protestant Reformation, which divided the western church into dozens, and then hundreds, of new Christian denominations.

A Closer Look

An Early Christian Schism

Evidence for Christian schisms appears already in the New Testament. In the letter of 3 John, an author who identifies himself as the Elder writes to another leader named Gaius concerning a third leader, Diostrephes:

> I wrote to the church, but Diostrephes, who likes to put himself first, does not acknowledge our authority. So if I come, I will call attention to what he is doing in spreading false charges against us. And not content with those charges, he refuses to welcome the brothers, and even prevents those who want to do so, and expels them from the church.
>
> 3 John 9–10 NRSV

Schisms can lead not only to new schools or denominations within a religion, but also to entirely new religions. A good example of this development is Bahai, which began in nineteenth-century Persia (today's Iran) as a movement within Shia Islam. After 1848, however, the movement broke away and began creating its own rules, ceremonies, and ritual calendar. Today, no one (and certainly no Muslim) would call Bahai a branch of Islam. While one can discern elements of Islamic origins, Bahai has become a distinct religion in its own right.

An intriguing comparison, with a very different outcome, is the path taken by the Church of Jesus Christ of Latter-day Saints, popularly known as Mormonism. Established in 1830 under the leadership of Joseph Smith, Jr. (1805–1844), who had grown up Christian, this movement claimed a divinely appointed priesthood and an inspired scripture that augmented the Bible. Called the *Book of Mormon*, this scripture was held to be an ancient document recounting how early Hebrews had migrated to America, and how Christ had come to America after his resurrection. Smith himself undertook a new translation of the Bible to restore its true meaning, received revelations, and engaged in highly creative theological speculation, especially near the end of his short but active life.

Sacred Traditions and Scriptures

The New Doctrines of Mormonism

In the last few years of his life, Joseph Smith produced some of his most creative theological formulations. Here is his explanation of the origin of God, published in the year of his death:

> What sort of a being was God in the beginning? Open your ears and hear ye all ends of the earth; for I am going to prove it to you by the Bible, and I am going to tell you the designs of God to the human race, and why he interferes with the affairs of man.
>
> First, God himself, who sits enthroned in yonder heavens, is a man like unto one of yourselves, that is the great secret … if you were to see him to-day, you would see him in all the person, image and very form as a man; for Adam was created in the very fashion and image of God. …
>
> You have to learn how to be Gods yourselves; to be kings and priests to God, the same as all Gods have done; by going from a small degree to another, from grace to grace, from exaltation to exaltation, until you are able to sit in the glory as doth those who sit enthroned in everlasting power. … God himself finds himself in the midst of spirits and glory, because he was greater, and because he saw proper to institute laws, whereby the rest could have a privilege to advance like himself.

From the "King Follett" discourse, April 7, 1844 in *Times and Seasons* (Nauvoo, IL: August 15, 1844), pp. 612–617.

Because of its striking and provocative innovations, one might have predicted that Mormonism would have broken from Christianity and become a new religion altogether. But the attractiveness of the movement originally had nothing to do with its potential to leave mainstream Christianity—to the contrary, its members viewed it as a return to the religion's original, pristine form. Then as now, Mormons insisted that they are Christians, and while they parted ways with much of traditional Christian theology and developed their own distinctive beliefs and practices, they have managed to remain within the larger orbit of Christianity (Figure 11.3).

Figure 11.3 Along with their innovations in Christian belief and doctrine, the Latter-day Saints have created a distinctive architecture for their leading churches, which they call temples. On the highest spire of the temple stands a golden statue of Moroni holding a trumpet. This is the angel who directed Joseph Smith to the *Book of Mormon*, which is said to have been written on golden tablets in the Reformed Egyptian language. Source: Will Deming.

Syncretism

A final pattern of traditional change is **syncretism**, which is the fusion of elements from different religions. This has the opposite effect of reform movements, which seek to rid a tradition of outside influences that have accumulated over time. Both Chinese and Japanese religions are good examples of syncretism, the former fusing elements of Confucianism, Daoism, and Buddhism, the latter combining elements of Shinto and Buddhism. In our present, globalized world we are actually witnessing a broadening and acceleration of religious syncretism. It is no longer difficult for missionaries of all religions to travel the globe; and increasing numbers of people now migrate across continents and cultures, enabling interaction between religions on many levels. A few religions even share sacred places, such as sanctuaries, rivers, and mountains.

Syncretism is sometimes unintentional—a natural mixing or interpenetration of religious traditions. In other cases, elements from the outside are forced on a religious tradition. African-based religions, such as Vodun and Santería, for example, are the product of the enslavement and forced migration of west African peoples to the Caribbean and Brazil, where African traditions were mixed with elements from other religions, including Catholicism, Spiritism, and Indigenous American traditions. In still other cases, syncretism is voluntary and intentional—what scholars call conscious syncretism. A well-known instance of conscious syncretism is the Vietnamese Caodai religion, which is now active in the west. While retaining many beliefs and practices from its place of origin, it has also appropriated elements from western traditions, such as the clerical titles "pope" and "cardinal" from Roman Catholicism. Although many religious groups are wary of syncretism, the adherents of Caodai proudly advertise what they call their "synthetic approach." From their perspective, the process of mixing the achievements of different religions gives Caodai a claim to being the culmination and completion of everything that came before.

A Closer Look

Syncretism in African Christianity

The twentieth century witnessed a phenomenal development of Christianity in sub-Saharan Africa. All categories of Christianity—from Catholics to Pentecostals, from Adventists to Copts—established successful missions there. As this was going on, several missionary agencies became convinced that Christianity should not simply be imported into Africa, but adapted to local customs and cultures. As a consequence, many African churches began using indigenous forms of liturgical art and incorporating drums and dancing into their worship. An unexpected consequence was the appearance of African Initiated Churches (AICs), which diverge, sometimes

(continued)

quite substantially, from traditional forms of Christianity. While some AICs are primarily concerned with having their own African leadership and lines of authority, others are based on revelations received by African prophets and messiahs.

An instructive example of this phenomenon is the AIC called the Church of Jesus Christ on Earth by His Special Envoy Simon Kimbangu, which has converted about 10 percent of the Congolese population and expanded into neighboring countries. Many of its members give superhuman status to its founder, Simon Kimbangu (1887–1951), and celebrate Christmas on May 25, purportedly the real date of Jesus' birth, but also the actual birthday of Simon Kimbangu's second son.

The Brotherhood of the Cross and Star is another such AIC. In the following poem, one of its theologians envisions the Nigerian birthplace of its founder as a new Israel:

> The daughter of Zion is born again,
> The flesh couldn't prove the mystery.
> The Redeemer, the Saviour of our time—
> Go to Biakpan and see the manger ...
> Go down to the New Nazareth,
> See the Garden of Eden,
> The land Promised to our Fathers,
> The new Nazareth is now our own.
>
> Friday M. Mbon, *Brotherhood of the Cross and Star* (Berlin: Peter Lang, 1992), p. 145.

These types of universal, supersessionist claims are increasing as the process of globalization advances. Newly emerging groups see themselves as predestined to bring all religions to fruition in themselves, forging a grand message of spiritual unity. An example of one of these supra-religions from the Japanese context is Mahikari. Now divided into two groups, the World Divine Light Organization and the True Light Supra-Religious Organization, it incorporates elements not only from Japanese religion and Christianity, but also from alternative and esoteric western traditions. Its practices of spiritual purification, with the potential for concrete, physical blessings such as healing, have attracted converts from as far away as western Europe and Africa. Mahikari's followers justify its claims to universalism through the citation of Bible passages and through symbolic interpretations of a meeting that took place in 1973 between Mahikari's founder and Pope Paul VI. They also maintain that the founders of major religious traditions, such as Moses, the Buddha, Jesus, and Muhammad, were trained in Japan before preaching in their own religions. Jesus, in fact, is said to have escaped his crucifixion and returned to Japan, where he died after reaching a very old age.

> **Rituals, Rites, Practices**
>
> ### The True Light Supra-Religion
>
> The Art of True Light is generally practiced between two people, with one receiving True Light and the other transmitting it. True Light is transmitted from the palm of the hand, which is held at a certain distance from the body.
>
> Through the practice of giving and receiving True Light, it is possible to experience the existence and the power of God. One can also become aware of the great influence that the unseen spiritual world has on the physical world.
>
> From the official website of Sukyo Mahikari, Europe and Africa, https://www.sukyomahikarieurope.org/en/practice (accessed 03.29.23.)

New Patterns of Change

When religions innovate according to traditional patterns of change and new movements or religions appear, it is relatively easy to determine the religion from which they came—Buddhism, Islam, Hinduism, etc.—because they still bear family resemblances to their source religions. Thus, Zen and Pure Land emerged from earlier schools of Mahayana Buddhism, and Bahai emerged from Shia Islam. Likewise, groups as disparate and idiosyncratic as the Mormons, Unitarians, Jehovah's Witnesses, and Christian Scientists all clearly have Christian roots.

In the last two centuries, however, new patterns of change have arisen that cannot be classified among the traditional ones, for the groups they engender have no clear connection to earlier religious traditions—that is, they have no discernable source religion. The first stirrings of these new patterns can be seen in the creation of the Theosophical Society in New York in 1875. Founded by the Russian-born Helena Blavatsky (1831–1891) and the American Henry Steel Olcott (1832–1907), the Society emphasized esoteric and non-Christian sources of wisdom and advanced the notion that all spiritual knowledge originates in the East (Figures 11.4 and 11.5). As early as 1879, its two founders moved to India, where the Society contributed to a renewal movement within Hinduism at a time when British colonial interests dominated the country. Olcott eventually converted to Buddhism and played a significant role in the Buddhist revival in Sri Lanka.

Having established branches in India and across the western world, the Theosophical Society popularized and encouraged the spread of alternative religious traditions, engendering early prototypes of **seekers**. These are people who disavow membership in established religions to explore beliefs and practices that are different from, and often in opposition to, the mainline religions of their own cultures. In the west, interest of this sort in eastern and unconventional religions received additional impetus during the World Parliament of Religions, held in Chicago in 1893. This gathering invited religious teachers from all over the world to present their traditions, creating a kind of marketplace of religions. While traces of a Theosophical

Figure 11.4 While the Theosophical Society no longer commands the attention it once did, it maintains a presence in cities in America and areas that were formerly under British colonial rule. Source: Reproduced by permission of Jean-François Mayer.

Figure 11.5 The eclectic symbol of the Theosophical Society combines (from the center): an Egyptian ankh; a kabalistic, six-pointed star; a Gnostic serpent biting its tail; a South Asian swastika; and a Hindu "OM." The Society's motto is "There is no religion higher than truth."

legacy can still be found in a number of contemporary groups and movements, including New Age spirituality, the Society has declined in popularity as newer, competing organizations have proliferated. Yet, precisely for this reason—the proliferation of new seeker networks—the Society's contribution to new patterns of change has been quite significant.

A Closer Look

New Age: Cosmic and Individual Transformation

New Age thinking emerged in the 1970s and became increasingly popular with the publication of Marilyn Ferguson's 1980 bestseller, *The Aquarian Conspiracy*. New Age is not an organization, but a spiritual outlook emphasizing eclecticism. It teaches that humans now stand on the threshold of a remarkable planetary alignment that will usher in a new era. In this context, people should evolve with the times, following their own instincts about what is good for them. Some adherents have imagined the coming of the New Age in terms of colliding worlds and apocalyptic events. Most, however, put the emphasis on a new evolutionary phase in the human race, characterized by a shift in spiritual consciousness and the dawn of universal peace, cooperation, harmony, and respect for nature.

Because the events of the 1970s and 1980s did not result in a harmonious new era, the early 1990s saw the decline of New Age terminology. Some participants started to speak of a Next Age, putting the emphasis on a heightened personal transformation rather than a collective transformation. Whatever happened on the planetary level, a person could still enter their own New Age, thereby achieving increased physical vigor, a higher standard of living, and a personal sense of peace. Yet the excitement surrounding a Maya long-count calendar that was interpreted as ending on December 21, 2012, reignited theories of world renewal on or around that date. New Age ideas and literature are now widely disseminated, and even books that claim no direct affiliation with New Age, such as James Redfield's *Celestine Prophecy* (1993), have popularized forms of New Age religiosity.

The divine feminine

New Age themes are embraced especially by religious groups that promote the divine feminine. In an article entitled "The Revolution of the Divine Mother," Andrew Harvey gives this account of an impending spiritual metamorphosis:

> Unless we come to know what the sacred feminine really is—its subtlety and flexibility, but also its extraordinarily ruthless, radical power of dissolving all structures and dogmas ... we will be taken in by patriarchal projections of it. The Divine Mother, the fullness of the revolution that she is preparing, will be lost to us. ...

(continued)

> What is required is a massive and quite unprecedented spiritual transformation. There is no precedent for what we are being asked to do. Only the leap into a new consciousness can engender the vision, the moral passion, the joy and energy necessary to effect change on the scale and with the self-sacrifice that is essential to save the planet in the time we have left.
>
> Andrew Harvey, "The Revolution of the Divine Mother," *New Connexion*, vol. 20.1 (2011), p. 1.
>
> ## A New Age interpretation of the last supper
>
> With his disciples 2000 years ago, the Christ enacted a dramatic symbolic episode which pointed to his future work in the age of Aquarius. Before the Last Supper he instructed the disciples to go into the city, where they would meet a man carrying a pitcher of water [Latin, *aqua*]. They were to follow him to an upper room and there prepare a communion meal. The taking together of bread and wine symbolized the Principle of Sharing, the keynote of the coming age, and the implementation of right human relations on a worldwide scale.
>
> As we move into this new age of Aquarius, our activities are more and more governed and conditioned by the energy of Synthesis. The present turmoils and upheavals are partly due to the "conflict" between the old, separative and individualistic energies, which are gradually withdrawing, and the new synthesizing energies, which are now making their impact felt. The current situation of extreme polarization in the world is largely caused by the crumbling of the old order.
>
> Wayne S. Peterson, *Extraordinary Times, Extraordinary Beings* (Henderson, NV: Emergence Press, 2001), pp. 76–77.

An environment for seekers

To account for the new patterns of change, scholars of religion now refer to an entity they call the cultic milieu. To avoid the negative connotations associated with "cultic," however, we will use the term **seekers' milieu** instead. This milieu (or environment, or community) is a vast subculture, independent of any single religion and open to alternative ideas on a variety of topics. Its principal traits can be seen in numerous publications. Take, for example, the German magazine *Visionen* (Visions), which bears the subtitle "Spirituality, Consciousness, Well-Being." This magazine promotes yoga, schools of positive thinking, Sufism, evolutionary spirituality, Celtic astrology, and feminist values. It has articles on Hinduism and Daoism, and interviews with Catholic priests and Buddhist monks. Its advertisers offer a variety of spiritual seminars, a congress for spiritual healing, and membership in a spiritual political party. Although the magazine is modern, it endorses age-old practices such as herbal cures and shows a fascination for premodern cultures. And while it is published in Germany, it could just as well have come from a metropolis in America or Asia.

To someone who is rooted in a single religious tradition, this sort of presentation may look chaotic and haphazard. But bringing these topics together in the same publication makes perfect sense for seekers, who are searching for meaning and personal development beyond the confines of conventional religions. Naturally, readers of these publications do not synthesize or embrace *all* these paths and techniques. Typically, they experiment, successively or simultaneously, with only a few. Even so, they give some credence to most or all of them as legitimate and viable components of human spirituality, which they envision as coherent and unified, despite its diversity.

The seekers' milieu itself is held together precisely by its deviance from the dominant cultural orthodoxies, including mainstream Christianity. Rejecting the truth claims of all established religions, seen as fossilized corruptions of their original manifestations, and offering exciting alternatives, seekers are drawn together by a bond of rebellion and mutual respect. Their interactions with one another foster an environment in which seekership is accepted and admired, and in which divergent views inherently take on plausibility. For those who value individualism, religious freedom, globalism, and religious pluralism, the seekers' milieu is especially appealing.

Another attraction of the seekers' milieu is that it provides access to spirituality through a consumer-oriented, marketplace model. In contrast to membership in an established religious organization, such as a church or a mosque, participation in the seekers' environment is open, fluid, and changing. There is no institutional authority, no preference for established forms of a tradition over mixed forms, no conversion, no heresy. One's involvement is strictly voluntary and noncommittal, accommodating all individual quests and choices. Everyone has the freedom to fashion their own approach to religion.

While the news media regularly report that the number of "nones," a name given to those who choose "none of the above" on surveys of religious affiliation, has been steadily growing in the United States, Europe, Latin America, and Australia, these surveys are not necessarily evidence for a declining interest in religion. More often than not those surveyed are simply registering their lack of commitment to an established religious tradition. If, instead, they had been asked if they considered themselves to be spiritual, many would have classified themselves as seekers.

Rituals, Rites, Practices

Witches

The religious movement called **Wicca** is part of a larger category of, for the most part, loosely organized movements collectively known as Neo-Paganism. These include Celtic, Norse, and Egyptian branches, among others, which, consonant with today's environmental concerns, typically promote a reverence for nature. Most Wicca groups freely admit that they are deliberate modernizations of ancient traditions, devising their doctrines and practices on the basis of both scholarly and fictional literature. Here is an explanation of how Wiccans use ancient traditions, given by the religious scholar Carol P. Christ:

(continued)

> The sources for the symbol of the Goddess in contemporary spirituality are traditions of Goddess worship and modern women's experience. The ancient Mediterranean, pre-Christian European, native American, Mesoamerican, Hindu, African, and other traditions are rich sources for Goddess symbolism. But these traditions are filtered through modern women's experiences. ... Ancient traditions are tapped selectively and eclectically, but they are not considered authoritative for modern consciousness.
>
> Carol P. Christ, "Why Women Need the Goddess," in *Womanspirit Rising: A Feminist Reader in Religion*, ed. Carol P. Christ and Judith Plaskow (San Francisco: Harper & Row, 1979), p. 276.

The word Wicca comes from the Old English word for witchcraft. Its founding narrative is the claim that medieval witches were the continuation of the "Old Religion," a tradition purportedly going back to prehistoric times. Focused on fertility worship and a horned god, this Old Religion was suppressed by Christianity, which associated it with the devil. But, the narrative continues, small, family-based circles managed to maintain the ancient practices until modern times. Based on scholarship that is now over a century old, such as Margaret Murray's 1921 study, *The Witch Cult in Western Europe*, some Wiccans claim that their religion is a survival of the world's first religion.

The principal figure who stands at the beginning of the current Wicca movement is the Englishman Gerald Gardner (1884–1964). Gardner had no academic training, but reported encountering a group, or coven, of witches. Explaining later that a priestess had initiated him, he wrote several books, including *Witchcraft Today* (1954). In his view, Wicca centered on magic, the Goddess, and her male counterpart. Rituals were practiced in a circle, and participants frequently observed ritual nudity, often called "working skyclad." Through his books, Gardner's understanding of Wicca spread, and people began to come to him to be initiated. In the 1960s, Wicca came to the United States, where it was given an enthusiastic welcome and has since flourished.

Wicca has never been a unified movement, in the United States or elsewhere. There are federations, independent and semi-independent local groups, solitary practitioners, informal gatherings, and seasonal festivals. As a consequence, there are many interpretations of what Wicca is and how it should be practiced. Gardnerian Wicca has become just one expression among many, and some Wiccans "take up the craft" based on reading books, without any contact with an existing coven. Indeed, many Wiccans today do not claim direct lineage from ancient practices.

Since the 1970s, Wicca has increasingly blended with feminist spirituality due to their mutual promotion of the Goddess. *The Spiral Dance* (1978), by an author known simply as Starhawk, has played an important role in that development. Positing that Wicca and Goddess worship are a return to older patterns of life that spoke to "female needs and experience," Starhawk argues

(continued)

Figure 11.6 The pentacle, circle, and three moons are common images in Wicca. The pentacle, or five-pointed star, evokes the five elements (earth, air, fire, water, and spirit) as well as the cardinal directions plus the center. The circle is used to inscribe sacred space. The full moon flanked by the crescent moons indicate the phases of the moon, which control the ritual calendar and evoke the life stages of womanhood: maiden, mother, and crone. Source: Wikimedia Commons.

that "wise women" had formerly practiced a woman-centered, nature-centered spirituality, but were oppressed and persecuted by patriarchal religions.

Despite the movement's diversity, some practices and beliefs have a fairly wide currency. It is common for Wiccans to gather during one of eight annual Sabbats, some groups distinguishing between the four principal Sabbats (Halloween, the first signs of spring, May Day, the fall grain harvest) and the four lesser ones (the solstices and equinoxes). These are seen as particularly powerful times for casting spells, and on these occasions Wiccans often perform rituals within a sacred circle that is created using various purification rites. At the center of the circle there may be an altar equipped with ritual tools such as a knife, a wand, incense, candles, a chalice, or a pentacle, which is an amulet inscribed with a five-pointed star (Figure 11.6). These are used to "raise power" in the group. If the Goddess is the focus of worship, she is typically identified as the Triple Goddess—Virgin, Mother, and Crone. Wiccans are also known to practice Wiccaning, which is the naming of infants, and Handfasting, which is the Wiccan marriage ritual (see the chapter-opening photo).

Two Wiccan rituals

A self-blessing

In a self-blessing ritual, described by the Hungarian witch Zsuzsanna E. Budapest, an altar is prepared with two candles and a chalice containing a mixture of water and wine, and salt is strewn before the altar. After lighting the candles, the celebrant

(continued)

dips her fingers into the liquid and touches her forehead, nose, lips, breasts, genitals, and feet while reciting blessings. As Budapest explains:

> In self-blessing, you affirm the divine you. Self-blessing is very important for women, because too many of us have internalized our own oppression. It is important for us to change the influences working in our deep minds. Religion controls the inner space; inner space controls outer space. If a woman internalizes her oppression and thinks she is inferior, or unclean when she menstruates, she internalizes a policeman.... The easiest and most efficient way for small numbers to oppress large numbers of people is to sell them a religion.... Self-blessing rituals are a way of exorcizing the patriarchal policemen, cleansing the deep mind and filling it with positive images of the strength and beauty of women.
>
> Zsuzsanna E. Budapest, "Self-Blessing Ritual," in Womanspirit Rising: A Feminist Reader in Religion, ed. Carol P. Christ and Judith Plaskow (San Francisco: Harper & Row, 1979), pp. 269–272.

A celebration of menstruation and birth

Hallie Mountainwing and Barby My Own created a summer solstice ritual to celebrate menstruation and birth. The women simulated a birth canal and birthed each other into their circle. They raised power by placing their hands on each other's bellies and chanting together. Finally, they marked each other's faces with rich, dark menstrual blood saying, "This is the blood that promises renewal. This is the blood that promises sustenance. This is the blood that promises life."

Carol P. Christ, "Why Women Need the Goddess," in Womanspirit Rising: A Feminist Reader in Religion, ed. Carol P. Christ and Judith Plaskow (San Francisco: Harper & Row, 1979), p. 282, citing from Barby My Own, "Ursa Maior: Menstrual Moon Celebration," in Anne Kent Rush, ed., Moon, Moon (Berkeley and New York: Moon Books and Random House, 1976), pp. 374–387.

Observing the seekers' milieu at a fair, one might be struck by the vast array of offerings: tarot readings, health food, channeling, and alternative therapies; participation in utopian societies; initiation into esoteric forms of universal wisdom from Tibet or ancient Egypt; and interaction with the living founder of a sect or a spiritual guide. And yet, out of this seeming cacophony of elements borrowed from a potpourri of traditions, seekers are able to identify commonalities and affinities. Some seekers use theories of astrology to give their quests a coherent framework. Others combine spirituality with ecological concerns, producing eco-feminist spirituality, Neo-Pagan environmental activism, and theologies ostensibly based on indigenous principles of ecology. In still other cases, a popular divine figure can be enlisted as the organizing principle for one's spiritual activities. In this way, adherents of both New Age and Neo-Paganism have found it useful to identify Guanyin, the patron saint of compassion and childbirth in east Asian Buddhism, as an expression of their Great Goddess.

From Seekers to New Religions

When several people in the seekers' milieu develop common interests, distinctive groups can emerge, boasting new identities and the initial trappings of organizational structures. Such groups, while charting their own course, usually continue to interact with other seekers to a greater or lesser degree. If, however, seekers choose a course that increasingly distinguishes them from the larger culture of seekers, they eventually become what scholars call a **new religious movement**, or **NRM**. Many of these will be ephemeral, lasting only a few years or decades. But even if a movement disbands, its legacy may continue to live on in the seekers' milieu, which constantly absorbs and recycles older ideas. Movements that survive beyond a generation or two, however, might even set themselves apart further, becoming fledgling new religions.

An example of a group that developed in this way is Heaven's Gate, a religion that became instantly famous and simultaneously died out in 1997 when its 39 members committed mass suicide (Figure 11.7). More than 20 years prior to this, the two founders of Heaven's Gate had been active as freelance teachers in the seekers'

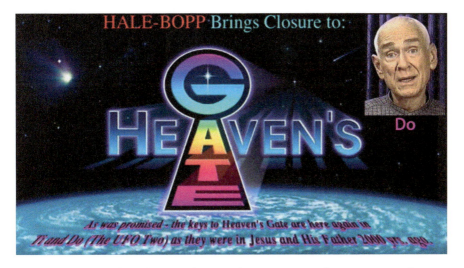

Figure 11.7 A page from the Heaven's Gate website announcing the opportunity to leave this world during the appearance of the Hale–Bopp comet in 1997. A picture of Do, one of the movement's two "witnesses," is superimposed in the upper right. Source: Reproduced by permission of the Telah Foundation.

community, but had failed to attract any dedicated followers or form a new movement. Heaven's Gate might never have seen the light of day had not its founders been invited in 1975 to address a group of seekers who gathered regularly to discuss esoteric interpretations of the Book of Revelation. Three weeks later, 24 of the 50 or so members of this group packed up everything to follow their new teachers, their earlier participation in the seekers' milieu having prepared them to accept their teachers' unconventional, far-flung ideas. Forming an NRM, they initially called themselves HIM (Human Individual Metamorphosis). Over the next nine years, their movement embraced a mixture of Christian, alternative, and heterodox beliefs, further differentiating and isolating them from other seekers. At the end of this process the nucleus of a new religion, Heaven's Gate, came into being, before its tragic demise.

The birth of new religions

Whether religions change according to traditional patterns or NRMs emerge from the seekers' milieu, is it impossible to predict if or when a new religion will arise. This is because change in religion is rarely linear, and younger movements, especially if they have a living founder, can change quickly and erratically. While numerous scenarios can move a group in the direction of becoming a new religion, the realization of one or more of these scenarios only serves as an indication of what *might* ensue.

The diverse and fluid nature of the seekers' milieu can, from time to time, even direct NRMs back to mainstream religious organizations. In 1968, for example, a new religious movement called the Holy Order of MANS was founded in San Francisco. It was a monastic organization based on several New Age beliefs. Prior to this, it had existed as a lay movement known as the Science of Man Church. By 1972, the Holy Order had branches in more than 40 states. But when its founder died in 1974, some of its members were drawn back into the seekers' milieu with its many exciting alternatives; and by 1988 a number of these had joined a noncanonical jurisdiction of the Eastern Orthodox Church that called itself Christ the Savior Brotherhood. Finally, when the Holy Order disbanded completely in the early 1990s, most of its former members had settled into mainstream branches of the Orthodox Church.

A second example involves a Buddhist lay group that appeared in Taiwan in 1989. Calling itself the Modern Chan Society, it was founded by an unconventional teacher who had risen to the rank of master in Yiguan-Dao, a movement that seeks to unify the elements of Chinese religions into a "single thread." At its inception, the Modern Chan Society claimed to be "a radical critique" of contemporary Taiwanese Buddhism, which it condemned as clinging to archaic rules that were inappropriate for modern people. Among other things, the Society challenged the authority of traditional Buddhist monastics, insisting on complete equality between monastics and laypersons. Shortly before his death in 2003, however, the founder encouraged his followers to reaffiliate with one of the traditional Buddhist schools, and then dissolved the movement. In this instance, what could have become a new religion was led back to conventional forms of Buddhism by its own founder.

> ### A Closer Look
>
> ## How Many NRMs? How Many Adherents?
>
> It is often difficult to determine the size of a particular NRM, and almost impossible to determine the current number of such movements. To begin with, the definition of a "member" is not the same in all movements. In movements that establish communes, membership may mean full-time, life-long dedication. Other movements, however, may require very little practical commitment, except for an occasional meeting. When the Indian guru Paramahamsa Nithyananda (b. 1978) claims to be "working and sharing with over twenty million people worldwide," or the Ukrainian Embassy of the Blessed Kingdom of God for All Nations claims 700 branches in 35 countries, it is not at all clear what these numbers represent. Movements such as the Spiritualist Churches, on the other hand, have small, dedicated core groups that are regularly joined by visitors, while meditational groups typically experience high levels of attrition. Thus, from the more than 6 million people reported to have been initiated into Transcendental Meditation, only a small percentage is still involved. The Jehovah's Witnesses, by contrast, keep very precise membership data, employing clear definitions of who is "in" and who is "out." In 2023, its leadership reported a peak of 8,816,562 active Witnesses in 118,177 congregations, broken down by country—but this is a rare exception.
>
> Finally, when we turn to estimating the total number of religious *movements*, it once again depends on definitions. What, precisely, constitutes an NRM, given that they can be such amorphous entities? Moreover, it is a quickly changing scene with few sources of reliable data. No one knows with certainty, for example, just how many guru movements there are in India.

An additional level of complexity is added when studying the development of movements that stem from established religions of other cultures. Since globalization has enabled NRMs to cross cultural barriers with surprising ease, this phenomenon has become increasingly common, especially with NRMs coming to the United States from India and Japan. With regard to India, in the 1890s the Hindu teacher Swami Vivekananda (1863–1902) began promoting his Ramakrishna Mission in the United States. Since that time, many other neo-Hindu movements have come from India, usually centered on a spiritual teacher, or guru, to whom followers often attribute superhuman qualities. But while these NRMs differ in many ways from conventional schools of Hinduism, they are not necessarily on their way to becoming new religions, for Hinduism has always accommodated innovative gurus. Some of these North American gurus, moreover, are popular in India as well—so much so that even mainstream Indian politicians curry their support.

Regarding Japanese imports, an instructive example is the Buddhist group Soka Gakkai, which was founded in 1930 as a lay movement within Nichiren Shoshu. After World War II, it began to spread outside of Japan, and in 1975 it became the global organization Soka Gakkai International (SGI). At present, SGI claims about 12 million adherents, three-quarters of whom live in Japan, and some 350,000 in North America.

SGI remains an NRM within Buddhism, however, even though certain events of the 1990s might have brought about its transformation to a new religion. In 1991, the mother religion, Nichiren Shoshu, decommissioned SGI as a legitimate Buddhist lay movement, and in 1992, it excommunicated SGI's president. Then, in 1997, it excluded all SGI followers from temple membership. But SGI, like Nichiren Shoshu, continues to identify itself as part of the larger Nichiren tradition, and both claim to represent true Buddhism.

Challenges for NRMs and New Religions

For NRMs that emerge from the seekers' milieu, the milieu itself can create formidable challenges. On the one hand, this milieu bolsters new movements, enabling them to communicate with a host of potential followers, quickly disseminating new techniques and products through seminars, books, websites, fairs, and individual consultations with therapists and clairvoyants. And once a master or teacher is on a seekers' speaking tour, there are audiences eager to listen. On the other hand, it is the tendency of seekers to look for new experiences, experiment with them, and then move on. Thus, the very nature of the seekers' milieu makes it difficult for leaders to retain followers or convince people to commit themselves fully.

An excellent example is the story of Luc Jouret (1947–1994), a popular speaker for a small group that used various names and came to be known by news outlets as the Order of the Solar Temple. When Jouret began to attract audiences of several hundred in France, Switzerland, and Quebec in the early 1980s, the group prepared itself for an influx of new members and made plans to expand. But Jouret's highly successful lectures and seminars brought only a modest number of new adherents. Those eager to listen were not so willing to commit themselves—which turned out for the best, since 74 of the Order's members (sadly including a number of children) lost their lives in three events in the 1990s that combined ritual suicide and murder.

In contrast to Jouret, some spiritual teachers show little interest in gaining long-term commitments from followers, simply accepting the fact that seekers move from one teacher to another. Those who belong to loose networks of western-born enlightened teachers, collectively known as the **Satsang** movement, sometimes do not even maintain a core group of followers. This satisfies their customers' conflicting demands of finding spiritual guidance *and* maintaining independence from any one teacher. And for those seekers who think that even this level of commitment is too much, a few groups associated with Satsang networks have, in the past, offered meetings without a master.

A Closer Look

UFOs

Just after Christmas 2002, the biotechnology company Clonaid held a press conference in Florida to announce that it had cloned a human being—a baby girl, appropriately named Eve. The timing was good. Between Christmas and New Year's, the news tends to be slow. Soon there were stories in newspapers around the world, along with voices condemning the venture. But Clonaid never produced any proof of a successful cloning, either in that purported case or subsequent ones. Clonaid's 2002 press conference was more than just a publicity stunt, however, and Clonaid is not a typical sort of business. It was created by members of the Raelian movement, a religious group claiming contact with extraterrestrials (ETs), and for whom cloning is a central doctrine of faith.

Inspired by flying saucer sightings, which began in 1947, individuals across western Europe and North America soon reported making contact with extraterrestrial beings. Some of the contactees told their stories in books while others created groups of UFO believers. The Raelians are an outgrowth of these activities. In some scenarios, contactees and their followers propose that ancient stories from the Bible and other religious texts are evidence for earlier ET contacts, written by people who were not yet able to understand them scientifically: life on Earth was not caused by divine creation, but the intervention of ETs. According to Raelian teachings, humans were created by a group of extraterrestrial scientists called the Elohim, a biblical term that, the ETs explained, should not be translated as "God," but as "those who came from the sky (Figure 11.8)."

The Raelian movement's founder was born Claude Vorilhon in France in 1946. While working as a sports journalist and singer, he experienced several encounters with ETs, the first in central France on December 13, 1973. Following this, he took the name Raël and wrote several books. Within a few years a religious organization was born.

While they profess no belief in a deity, Raelians practice rituals designed to achieve individual salvation, and they promote a doctrine of global salvation. In their view, the bombing of Hiroshima at the end of World War II marked the start of an era of doom. This is the Age of Apocalypse, and Raël was sent as the last of its prophets. The ETs that Raël encountered are expected to land officially on Earth in 2035 to save humanity from destruction. One of the tasks of the movement is to build an embassy to welcome them (Figure 11.8).

To become a member of the Raelian movement, a person must renounce their previous religion and undergo the transmission ceremony. This is a ritual in which a Raelian guide—the equivalent of a member of their clergy—places

(continued)

Figure 11.8 Members of the Raelian movement plan to build a diplomatic embassy to receive extraterrestrials and their space craft. Here they solicit support for their project in a public venue in Lyon, France. The tall figure in the background in the yellow costume and the person to his right in the silver costume are members of the movement dressed as ETs. Source: Serge Mouraret / Alamy Stock Photo.

their wet hands on the forehead and neck of an initiate, thereby transmitting the "cellular code" of each individual to the ETs. This allows the ETs to recreate the individual after their death, if they deem that person to be worthy. Initiates are also advised to leave instructions that a small piece of their forehead bone be removed after their death for safekeeping by the movement, as a record of their DNA. The movement currently claims to have more than 50,000 members, but this seems to match the number of Raelian initiations, not active members. Nevertheless, there are now thousands of people around the globe who identify themselves as Raelians.

The internet and cultural identity

Another challenge to the stability of NRMs and new religions is the popularity of the internet. Websites, blogs, and search engines create an openness to information that can threaten a group's unity and solidarity. Once misgivings have been posted on the internet, it is impossible for a group's leaders to ignore dissident voices or keep divisive issues purely internal. This can even cause mayhem in established groups. When one of the masters of the International Society for Krishna Consciousness (ISKCON) broke with the movement in 1998, it was possible to follow the developing firestorm online. Only a few years earlier, it would have taken weeks or months for even secondhand reports of the dispute to filter out beyond the inner circle (see Figure 11.9).

NRMs and new religions can also encounter limits to their potential growth due to what sociologists call **cultural capital**. The more a religious group diverges from the norms of the society from which it draws its members, the more its members must give up their "investment" in those norms—their education, their socialization, their outlook on life. An Episcopalian Christian, for example, will sacrifice more cultural capital by joining Soka Gakkai International than by converting to Roman Catholicism. Even when cultural divergence is seen as one of the attractions of joining an alternative group, a group's novelty can become a burden over time. It is not uncommon for former members of religious communes to admit that they simply grew weary of this social experiment in living together and sharing things in common. One way a group can reduce a convert's loss of cultural capital is to make concessions to the larger culture. Certain Japanese communities in Mexico, for instance, have rescheduled their ceremonies for the dead (*obon*) from the traditional Japanese date in the summer to a date in early November, where it coincides with local Day of the Dead observances.

Figure 11.9 Sculptures of devotees at the International Society for Krishna Consciousness center in Mayapur, Bengal. Source: Reproduced by permission of Jean-François Mayer.

The second generation

Even if the first generation of members maintains its interest in a NRM or new religion, a second generation also needs to be won over if the group is to survive. If a group takes an open-minded attitude toward alternative lifestyles, its live-and-let-live ethic can hinder parents from transmitting religious beliefs to their children. Out of respect for their children's individual choices, and to avoid forced indoctrination, these parents may make participation in the group voluntary. In other cases, where groups have the expectation that children will become full members, parents can make the mistake of assuming that their children will simply follow in their footsteps, forgetting that *they* had broken with the religious traditions of *their* parents. Especially in communes, teenagers not only focus their teenage rebellion against their parents, but also against the group itself.

Even groups that emphasize the importance of family and family values are not immune to these challenges. This can be seen from the recent history of the Family Federation for World Peace and Unification, founded by the late Rev. Sun Myung Moon. Formerly known as the Unification Church and popularly called the Moonies, this group promotes arranged marriages between members and sees a special role for children in its plan of salvation. Through the birth of children, Moon's followers establish Blessed Families, thereby fulfilling the mission given to Adam and Eve to "go forth and multiply." But some children reject the Federation's expectations for them, while others are born with disabilities, and so matters have become complicated. Sexual misconduct among young people, for example, has required the creation of a forgiveness ritual called the amnesty ceremony; and for children with special needs, it was necessary to develop a teaching that identified them as victims of cosmic justice. As one couple recounted:

> … we know why we have a handicapped son. The main cause is definitely spiritual. Of course, it is not his fault. Sometime, somewhere, somehow, somebody has to pay indemnity for the past or current mistakes. It is simply our time to take up the role and pay the indemnity so that our future generations will not have to suffer as much as we did or do now.
>
> https://www.tparents.org/Library/Unification/Talks/Ichijo/Ichijo-070102.htm (accessed 29 March 2023).

The death of a founder

The presence of a living master is often what holds a movement together, especially if they provide the movement with unique access to the divine world. India's "hugging guru" Mata Amritanandamayi, for example, travels the world to spread her message of love and worldly renunciation, and to hug her followers, frequently hundreds at a time. Through this hug, her followers, who affectionately call her Amma (Mother), are said to experience a divine warmth and sense of well-being. To survive much beyond her death, Amma's movement likely will need a fundamental change in direction, the emergence of an equally charismatic successor, or the development among its members of a strong organizational commitment.

But even a seemingly obvious prediction such as this may be premature, given that the once charismatic Bhagwan Shree Rajneesh (1931–1990) offers something of a counterexample. In the wake of fraud and scandal on Rancho Rajneesh, his central Oregon commune, Bhagwan was deported from the United States in 1985. Returning to India, he died in 1990, taking the name Osho a year before his death. Yet his movement has not disappeared. To the contrary, a network of Osho groups has continued after his death, establishing an international meditation resort in Pune, India.

A Closer Look

Amma: The Hugging Guru

It was 1988, in a rented hall in a European city. Some 100 people were expecting the arrival of the Indian sage, Mata Amritanandamayi, known by her audiences as Amma. She was not yet famous as a spiritual master in the west, but her name had begun to circulate among seekers. Amma arrived accompanied by a

(continued)

saffron-robed Hindu monk and mounted a stage where Indian musicians were waiting. "In this dark age," she proclaimed, "in order to reach inner concentration, devotional songs (*bhajan*) are better than meditation." The music started and Amma, surrounded by five Indian monks and four western women, began singing, eyes closed.

After the songs, Amma and her entourage led a guided meditation for 15 minutes. Then something quite unusual happened: Amma welcomed all those who came to her, methodically hugging everyone. She held each visitor on her lap like a mother with a young child, caressed the person's back with one hand and pressed her head against theirs. For many people, this embrace turned into an emotional and spiritual moment. Several reported that they had wept; and many soon became followers.

Mata Amritanandamayi was born Sudhamani Idamannel in 1953 in a village in Kerala (southern India). She came from a pious, lower-caste family of fishermen. Leaving school after four years, her status was that of a servant. She was treated poorly and despised by many of her fellow villagers, many of whom considered her to be simpleminded. As she grew older, however, she began to experience ecstatic states. Some said this was a result of her many religious devotions, others assumed she was suffering from a mental illness. At the age of 22, she reported experiencing a state of identification with the god Krishna, and later with the Mother Goddess. Around the age of 25, she garnered some acceptance as a spiritual master, and this led to the founding of a small commune (*ashram*) and the Mata Amritanandamayi Mission.

Today Amma draws enormous crowds, both in India and in the west. Following her spiritual presentations, thousands wait for hours to experience her mystical embrace. Her small birth village has turned into a pilgrimage site with a busy spiritual center and modern buildings with accommodations for her followers. Her present organization, created in 1981, was granted consultative status with the United Nations' Economic and Social Council in 2005, and her followers currently support several humanitarian ventures, including schools and hospitals.

Amma's devotees do not consider her just a spiritual master, but an *avatar*, an incarnation of the Goddess. When someone in her audience once asked how she became a holy woman, she gave the following reflection, speaking of herself in the third person:

> As far as Amma is concerned, She never became anything. She has always been fully aware of the unreality of the world and always knew that She is that Reality that underlies the world. Amma always wanted to know and imbibe the essential principles of life and She always wondered why people suffer in the world.

(continued)

> Even from Her early childhood, Amma knew that God alone is Truth. ... Thereafter, She performed severe spiritual practices, and once She started this, Her own parents and relatives couldn't understand the exalted spiritual state of Amma. So, out of ignorance, they began scolding Her and opposed Her spiritual practices. During that time, when even Her family members were against Amma and Her spiritual practices, the animals and birds took care of Her. They brought food for Amma, and they even used to dance briefly when Amma sang, or sometimes they tried to wake Her up when She was in a deep trance. Thereafter, Amma received an inner call, a revelation, that Her purpose in life was to uplift ailing humanity. From then onwards, Amma started this spiritual mission, spreading this message of Truth, Love, and Compassion throughout the world, by receiving one and all.
>
> *Amritanandam*, 3rd Quarter, 1995.
>
> Like many other religious masters, Amma has not been immune from accusations and controversies. Some of her longtime disciples have left her, including some who had been quite close, and there is now an active and growing online network of former members.

Sometimes founders attempt to ensure the stability of their movements after their death by conferring leadership on close relatives or establishing a corporate bureaucracy. Following the death of Sun Myung Moon (1920–2012), Hak Ja Han, known as Mother of Peace, succeeded her husband as the movement's leader. But being the founder's widow was not sufficient for preserving unity. One of Moon's sons had already split off a few years before his father's death to form his own group, and two other sons established a third group after his death, denouncing their mother as a heretic.

A different set of circumstances surrounded the founder of ISKCON, Swami Prabhupada (1896–1977). Family succession was not an option for him since he had never married. After his death, senior staff attempted to divide the organization into several geographical jurisdictions under the spiritual leadership of the Swami's closest disciples. But a number of these disciples failed to live up to expectations and eventually left the movement, sometimes under allegations of scandal. ISKCON was then reorganized a second time, allowing its members to choose spiritual masters from any of the geographical jurisdictions, and all masters were given a status clearly subordinate to that of the late founder. Considering that ISKCON is rooted in traditional Hinduism and had sufficient resources for dealing with such a crisis, it is easy to imagine how a similar challenge could be the undoing of a smaller, less traditional group.

CONCLUSION

Throughout history, religions have changed and new religious movements have come and gone. On rare occasions a new religion appears, and on even rarer occasions it establishes itself and prospers for decades or centuries, or millennia. Due to current trends toward freedom of religious choice and globalization, more changes than ever before are occurring in religions. A new environment for religious change has also come into being—the seekers' milieu. But there is still no recipe that guarantees the success of a particular group.

Currently, scholars are paying particular attention to new forms of religion and NRMs in Korea and China, for there is reason to believe that some of these could grow well beyond their respective countries and diaspora communities. The longing of human beings for religious answers spawns an almost inexhaustible religious creativity, and we cannot rule out the possibility that from among the movements now active, a major new religion will emerge, destined to redefine the economic, political, and ideological map of our world.

For review

1. Name some of the causes of change in religions.
2. In what way is it possible to think of Islamic or Christian fundamentalism as a "reform movement"?
3. What are some of the different types of syncretism?
4. How has the appearance of a modern seekers' milieu changed the way in which new religions form?
5. What are some of the characteristics of New Age?

For discussion

1. When do innovations in a religious tradition crystalize into a new religion, altogether separate from the original tradition?
2. Why do some religions intentionally and openly adopt the elements of other religious traditions? Does this undermine their credibility as valid religions?

Key Terms

cultural capital	A person's stake or "investment" in their culture; often a deterrent to joining a religion from another culture.
New Age	A spirituality that looks forward to the dawning of a new era in human moral development and spirituality.
new religious movement (NRM)	A group formed for the purpose of sharing novel religious beliefs and practices. Occasionally these groups develop into new religions.
progressive reform movement	An attempt to modernize or update one's religion.

reactive reform movement	An attempt to return to a purer, earlier form of one's religion.
Satsang	A loose network of enlightened teachers that demands no commitment to any one teacher.
schism	A split within a religion that results in new divisions.
seekers	Persons looking for religious experiences apart from membership in mainstream, established religions.
seekers' milieu	The subculture of seekers that offers opportunities to experiment with elements of many unconventional religions.
syncretism	The fusion of elements from different religions.
traditional patterns of change	Reactive and progressive movements; schism and syncretism.
Wicca	A modern spiritual movement that uses elements associated with pre-Christian traditions from Europe.

Bibliography

A good first book
Joseph Laycock. *New Religious Movements: The Basics*. New York: Routledge, 2022.

Further reading
Peter B. Clark. *New Religions in Global Perspective*. London and New York: Routledge, 2006.

Lorne L. Dawson, ed. *Cults and New Religious Movements: A Reader*. Malden, MA: Blackwell Publishing, 2003.

Olav Hammer and Mikael Rothstein, eds. *The Cambridge Companion to New Religious Movements*. New York: Cambridge University Press, 2012.

James R. Lewis and Inga Tøllefsen, eds. *The Oxford Handbook of New Religious Movements*, 2nd edn, 2 vols. New York: Oxford University Press, 2016.

Elijah Siegler. *New Religious Movements*. Upper Saddle River, NJ: Pearson-Prentice Hall, 2007.

Reference and research
W. Michael Ashcraft. *A Historical Introduction to the Study of New Religious Movements*. New York: Routledge, 2019.

David G. Bromley and J. Gordon Melton, eds. *Cults, Religion and Violence*. New York: Cambridge University Press, 2002.

Eugene V. Gallagher and W. Michael Ashcraft, eds. *Introduction to New and Alternative Religions in America*, 5 vols. Westport, CT: Greenwood Press, 2006.

Benjamin E. Zeller. *Prophets and Protons: New Religious Movements and Science in Late Twentieth-Century America*. New York: New York University Press, 2010.

CHAPTER 12
The Study of Religions

Those who know one, know none.
Source: Post of Moldova / Public domain.

Introduction

At American universities the study of religions is often an integral part of undergraduate education, taking its place alongside psychology, English, communication studies, biology, and other academic disciplines. But this is a fairly recent phenomenon, going back only to the 1960s. In the century or so before that, studying a religion other than one's own was hardly possible outside of graduate programs at elite universities; and before that, no one involved in higher education even considered the study of religions to be a legitimate academic pursuit. Most saw it as unnecessary or a waste of time, and many argued passionately against it. So how did we get from then to now? What changed?

This chapter provides an explanation of how the study of religions became an academic discipline and why it is currently part of the curriculum. It will consider the impact of European colonialism and the Enlightenment; the role of the church; and the various attempts by other emerging disciplines to discredit or debunk religion. This is a story of false starts, brilliant mistakes, and many misconceptions about religion. It also entails institutional power and colorful and remarkable academics. Ultimately, it is the story of the triumph of liberal education over dogmatism, prejudice, and fear.

Early Universities

Universities offered a form of instruction in religion from the very beginning. Over 1500 years ago, Buddhists in northeast India developed what may have been the first universities in the world. Their goal was to provide monks and nuns with the knowledge and skills that would help them understand and practice sophisticated Buddhist teachings. The most famous of these universities was Nalanda Mahavirhara, founded in the fifth century CE. At its height, it had thousands of residential students and a library of over 9 million manuscripts.

Universities in Muslim and Christian lands followed a similar pattern. Al-Azhar University in Cairo, arguably the oldest university still in operation, was founded around 970 CE to promote the study of the Quran and Islamic law (Sharia). A little more than a century later, Europeans started founding universities that advanced the Christian religion. They began in cities such as Oxford, Paris, Salamanca, and Cambridge, and eventually this model in the North American colonies. New College (now Harvard University), the College of William and Mary, King William's School (now St. John's College), and the Collegiate School (now Yale University) were chartered between 1636 and 1701, and all had faculties to train Christian clergy.

These early universities were not, however, entirely focused on religion. They also offered advanced instruction in such things as grammar, logic, mathematics, and rhetoric, and many universities in Muslim and Christian lands prepared students for careers in law and medicine. Even so, religion was central to their mission, resulting in a close, centuries-long connection between religion and higher education.

And yet—and this is the important point for us—the study of religions never developed as an academic discipline at any of these universities. Why? Because students were being educated in theology, which is a different matter altogether.

The difference between theology and the study of religions continues to cause confusion even today, so it is worth our time to clearly distinguish the two. **Theology** is an academic discipline designed to explain, develop, and justify the beliefs and practices of *one's own* religion (e.g., Roman Catholicism), sometimes as a defense against what are perceived as divergent forms of that religion (e.g., Eastern Orthodoxy), or against other religions altogether (e.g., Islam). The **study of religions**, by contrast, is also an academic discipline, but one that investigates one or more religions for no other reason than to gain insight into the nature of religion and religious people. It is a disinterested approach that attempts to examine all religions equally, without prejudice or favoritism toward any. It does not promote a particular religion.

> ### The Gardener and the Botanist
>
> Those who study theology and those who study religions are like gardeners and botanists, respectively. Gardeners care for plants they like. They do not bother with plants they dislike, and they will uproot them if these encroach on their gardens. Botanists, by contrast, attempt to gain an appreciation for all plants. They cannot ignore or destroy the ones they dislike. So also, theologians can favor one religion over others, and even denounce other religions, while students of religions must seek to gain an unbiased appreciation of one or more religions through the lens of scholarship. While they may practice a particular religion in their private lives, this should not prejudice their work.
>
> "… it belongs to a religion to claim to be the true religion."
>
> <div align="right">Schubert M. Ogden, <i>Is There Only One True Religion, Or Are There Many?</i>
(University Park, TX: Southern Methodist University, 1992), p. 13.</div>

With this distinction firmly in place, it becomes obvious that as long as universities approached religion solely from the perspective of theology, there was no room for the study of religion to develop. Universities would have to change. As we will see shortly, this began to happen only around 1500 and took several centuries to run its course. But something else had to take place as well: scholars needed to determine *what* religion was, and *how* to study it.

The What and How of Studying Religion

"Religion," as an intelligible category of research, did not exist in the west from the early Middle Ages until the eighteenth century. Earlier, during Greek and Roman times, religious toleration was widely practiced. While various groups—trade guilds, associations, cities, and even nations—knew that other groups worshipped gods different from their own, they generally respected the religion of others, and assumed that others would respect theirs. The important thing was that everyone reverenced the gods. What got Christians in trouble with the Roman authorities was not their demand for religious freedom, but their intolerance and criticism of other people's religions, especially emperor worship. But after the Roman empire adopted Christianity as its state religion in the late fourth century, intellectuals began to question the notion of "religion" as a unified category, preferring instead to divide religions into two opposing and irreconcilable categories: true religion and false religion. True religion was Christianity, and false religion was everything else—paganism, idolatry, polytheism, heresy, apostasy, magic, and demon worship. These were not only false, but they were also dangerous, since they violated the precepts of the true religion and put one's salvation at risk.

In this intellectual and spiritual atmosphere, the idea that anyone would want to study false religions, except perhaps to condemn them more thoroughly, seemed absurd; and even more absurd was the suggestion that someone should undertake the study of Christianity and these other religions without prejudice against the latter. Until Christianity's monopoly on true religion in Europe and North America showed signs of weakening, "religion" could not be reenvisioned as a unified category that encompassed all religions equally. And without this understanding of *what* religion was, there could only be theology, not the study of religions.

As it turned out, however, determining *what* religion was depended, in part, on *how* one studied religion. While this might strike us as a problem with an obvious solution, the solution was anything but obvious to those scholars who first attempted to study religion. After Christianity's monopoly started to wane in the mid-1700s, it would take another two full centuries before scholars gained any methodological clarity on this issue. As we will see in the coming pages, they applied various theories of knowledge to religion, as well as political and economic theory, linguistics, anthropology, sociology, and psychology before arriving at an approach specific to religion.

The Late Medieval Period Through the Enlightenment

The intellectual climate in Europe began to change, albeit slowly, as the Middle Ages (roughly 500–1500) gave way to the Renaissance (ca. 1300–1600), followed by the Enlightenment (ca. 1600–1800). During medieval times, scholars sought knowledge about the world through the study of a limited body of ancient traditions, guided by the Bible and church doctrine. But as interaction with other cultures increased through trade and through the exploration and colonization of lands in Africa, Asia, Oceania, and the Americas, Europeans saw their knowledge base increase exponentially. By the beginning of the Enlightenment, they were also developing methods by which they could make completely new discoveries on the basis of what they already knew. These methods included reason, critical thinking, evidence-based research, and controlled experimentation. It is worth noting that the last half of the Renaissance (which means "rebirth") is sometimes referred to as the Scientific Revolution, while another name for the Enlightenment is the Age of Reason.

The new information, methods, and discoveries of this period would eventually support the study of religions. But not at first. The rising demand for scientific explanations of the world, rather than explanations based on church tradition, called into question such things as miracles and divine revelation. Yet, instead of making room for the academic study of religions alongside theology, theologians and church officials initially blocked all movement in that direction and renewed their commitment to Christianity as the one true religion. In this intellectual environment, critical considerations of the Bible or church teachings could lead to serious consequences, such as losing one's teaching position or excommunication from the church.

In sharp contrast to the actions taken by the church, many Enlightenment thinkers insisted that science and reason had exposed traditional religion, especially Christianity, as a lie. The philosopher Immanuel Kant (1724–1804), for example, proclaimed that the only valid religion was "religion within the limits of reason alone." Some embraced **empiricism**, a theory of knowledge that first appeared in the seventeenth century in the writings of Francis Bacon and René Descartes. It demanded that nothing be accepted as true without observable, scientific proof. As a consequence, Deism became popular. This religion held that God existed but was only active at the time of the Creation. After creating the world and setting the laws of physics and morality in place, God essentially retired, leaving the oversight of the world in human hands. Others went further, insisting on a **materialist empiricism**. This approach to knowledge not only demanded scientific proof for ideas, but also denied the existence of anything that was not physical matter—things like gods and spirits. Materialist empiricists lobbied for the abolition of all religions and promoted atheism as the correct course for the future. As one might imagine, both Deism and atheism impeded the study of religions.

The research university

At first, Enlightenment thinkers discussed their ideas outside of the university setting, in coffeehouses and "salons," which were private gatherings in the homes of wealthy patrons. Those who participated in these discussions included educated people from all walks of life, both male and female. Universities, by contrast, initially resisted new ideas. At the beginning of the nineteenth century, however, higher education took an innovative turn. After Napoleon Bonaparte's humiliating defeat of Prussia and brief occupation of Berlin in 1806, Prussian leaders set about to rebuild and modernize their educational system. In 1810, they founded the University of Berlin as a public research university, dedicated to ongoing academic inquiry, unfettered by outside forces like the church or government. As other universities in Prussia followed suit, these German universities soon became the envy of the world and were replicated elsewhere in Europe and abroad. The first American research university, Johns Hopkins, was established in 1876 in Baltimore, Maryland; and a year later, the empire of Japan founded the University of Tokyo.

> ### The First Research University
>
> Berlin's new research university changed the rules of the game for aspiring scholars. Ludwig Feuerbach, whose critique of Christianity, *The Essence of Christianity* (1841), would influence Marx, Freud, and Darwin, described the new academic environment at the University of Berlin in this way:
>
> There is no question here of drinking, dueling, and pleasant communal outings; in no other university can you find such a passion for work, such an interest for things that are not petty student intrigues, such an inclination for the sciences, such calm and such silence. Compared to this temple of work, the other universities appear like public houses.
>
> Quoted from David McLellan, *Karl Marx, A Biography*. 4th ed.
(Basingstroke: Palgrave Macmillan, 1981), p. 15.

The reconceived university became the soil in which many new disciplines, including the study of religions, grew. But the study of religions, as we just saw, initially had to overcome resistance on two fronts: from theologians and church officials who felt threatened by scientific methods of research, and from Enlightenment thinkers promoting either Deism or atheism. It should not surprise us, therefore, that one of the first investigations into the nature of religion during this time came from a graduate of the University of Berlin who took employment outside of the university as a journalist and approached religion from a strict materialist empiricist perspective—namely, Karl Marx.

Born during the Industrial Revolution, Karl Marx (1818–1883) spent much of his life advocating for the working class as both a journalist and social activist. The economic opportunities made possible through industrial manufacturing enabled entrepreneurs to become quite wealthy by producing goods efficiently and at quantity, but only by taking advantage of their workers. Hours were long, work was strenuous and often dangerous, and salaries were meager. The families of workers lived in overcrowded factory towns, and child labor was rampant. Marx approached these social ills using a combination of political and economic theory, guided by a philosophical method known as dialectic. This method had been developed by G.W.F. Hegel (1770–1831), who had taught at the University of Berlin until shortly before Marx arrived as a student. According to Hegel, history was the stage of a back-and-forth interplay, or dialectic, between opposing ideas. Progress came about when two contrary ideas were resolved ("sublated") into a third, which overcame their contradictions. But while Hegel had confined the dialectic process to the world of ideas, Marx, who was a materialist, applied it to the struggle for survival between social and economic classes.

For Marx, what needed to be sublated in mid-nineteenth-century Germany was the contradiction between the rich, who owned the factories, or "means of production," and the impoverished factory workers, who did the actual work. As his research unfolded, he came to believe that religion (which he understood in terms of

Christianity) was both a symptom and a cause of the workers' misery. It was a symptom inasmuch as workers turned to religion as an outlet, expressing their suffering through prayer, confession, and penance. It was a cause, on the other hand, because the Christian values of hard work and submission, and the promise of a heavenly reward were used by industrialists to keep workers at their jobs and prevent them from organizing protests. In the introduction to his *Contribution to the Critique of Hegel's Philosophy of Right*, published in 1844, Marx framed the matter this way:

> Religious suffering is at the same time an expression of real suffering and a protest against real suffering. Religion is the sigh of the oppressed creature, the sentiment of a heartless world, and the soul of soulless conditions. It is the opium of the people. The abolition of religion as the illusory happiness of men, is a demand for their real happiness.
>
> Quoted from John Raines, ed., *Marx on Religion* (Philadelphia, PA: Temple University Press, 2002), p. 171.

In Marx's view, religion did not lead to a better life for the worker, but only benefited wealthy entrepreneurs. It was a drug whose effect was to convince the poor to be obedient and work hard in the false expectation of a better life in Heaven.

Marx's negative assessment of religion provides us with our first example of a methodology known as **reductionism**. This approach first "reduces" the object of inquiry to what it ostensibly *really* is, so it can be studied properly. To give a positive example outside the field of religion, the once common belief that all foreigners are intellectually and culturally inferior needs to be studied by reducing it to what it really is, namely, a form of xenophobia or racism, not a serious proposition based on evidence. One could even say that reductionism is an early form of what we now call "deconstructionism."

Marx, however, employed reductionism to argue that, *in reality*, religion was a malignant outgrowth of capitalism that oppressed the working class and enriched the wealthy. Later, in the nineteenth and early twentieth centuries, others would use reductionism to argue that religion was *really* a mental illness or a social construct. Until a majority of scholars became convinced that religion was actually a thing in itself, and not something else in disguise, there was no motivation to establish an academic discipline to study religions, just as there is no place at today's universities for a department of Foreign Inferiority. Fortunately, two developments in Europe and North America prevented both empiricism and reductionism from becoming the dominant approaches to religion, although it took some time. One was Romanticism, the other was European colonialism.

Romanticism and colonialism

As a counterbalance to the Enlightenment's emphasis on empiricism, Romanticism was an intellectual movement that valued and celebrated the mysterious, the irrational, and the emotional phenomena of human existence. Appearing late in the eighteenth century and receiving wide approval in the first half of the nineteenth, it encouraged scholars to reconsider those aspects of religion that earlier Enlightenment thinkers had discarded as irrational and unscientific.

> The heart has its reasons of which reason knows nothing: we know this in countless ways.
>
> Blaise Pascal, *Pensées*, no. 423.

European colonialism, which began in the late fifteenth century, encouraged a nonempiricist, nonreductionist approach to religion in at least two ways. First, colonizers needed a working understanding of the peoples they governed, which gave them an incentive to go beyond treating indigenous religions as irrational nonsense. For practical reasons they had to address religion on its own terms. Likewise, missionaries, who were religious themselves, and therefore had no interest in either empiricism or reductionism, were eager to study the worldview of indigenous religions. Their goal was to discover commonalities between these religions and Christianity for purposes of conversion.

Second, those who went to the colonies, whether as administrators, explorers, settlers, or missionaries, sent descriptions of foreign religions back home in letters and reports, and shipped never-before-seen texts and objects to collectors and museums. This not only provided a wealth of new information, which, as we saw earlier, had been an important catalyst for the Enlightenment itself, but for most scholars, it was also their first engagement with a living religion other than Christianity. Many Europeans knew something about ancient religions from their study of the Bible and classical texts, and most had acquired anecdotal impressions of Judaism and Islam through the teachings of church leaders. But now they were receiving an ever-increasing flow of eyewitness accounts from their contemporaries in colonies all over the world. This wealth of detail from multiple living religions not only made the study of religion less theoretical, but also complicated the reduction of religion to something else.

Yet colonialism also supported the European assumption of Christian superiority. Christian theologians had long taught that Christianity was demonstrably superior to all other religions. The colonization of indigenous peoples in the Americas, Africa, and Oceania now seemed to create a mountain of new evidence supporting this prejudice. As Europeans encountered group after group of what they described as "primitive" people, they became convinced that indigenous religions were not only inferior to Christianity, but had actually kept these people from evolving beyond mere savages. Christianity, by comparison, had blessed Europeans with the highest level of civilization in human history. Among theologians, this became an argument that God favored Europeans over other people and was now commissioning them to civilize the rest of the world to European standards through conversion to Christianity. Among scholars of religions, on the other hand, it became the basis for believing that indigenous religious practices were similar to or identical with those of prehistoric people. They viewed them as the living practices of the earliest humans, frozen in time. As a result, these scholars were encouraged to speculate about the origin of religion and promote the notion that indigenous religions belonged at the low end of any evolutionary development of religions.

Max Müller

The influence of all these factors—empiricism, reductionism, Romanticism, colonial discoveries, and assumptions about indigenous religions—can be seen in the work of Max Müller (1823–1900), whom many consider the founder of the study of religions. Müller earned a doctorate in philology (language study) at Leipzig University, where he mastered Greek and Latin and became proficient in Arabic, Persian, Sanskrit, and several modern European languages. Deciding to continue his study of Sanskrit, he moved first to Berlin, then to Paris, and finally to England, in pursuit of teachers and texts. In England, he was given access to the East India Company's trove of Sanskrit texts at Oxford University. He eventually became that university's first professor of comparative philology.

> The Science of Religion may be the last of the sciences which man is destined to elaborate; but when it is elaborated, it will change the aspect of the world, and give a new life to Christianity itself.
>
> Max Müller, *Chips from a German Workshop*, vol. 1: *Essays on the Science of Religion* (New York: Charles Schribner, 1869), p. xix.

Müller's interest in religion came from his study of India's earliest religious texts, which were written in the earliest known forms of Sanskrit. Starting from a novel theory of language development that assumed early humans had the thinking capacity of children, Müller proposed that religion had begun as a misunderstanding—a "disease"—of language. While Müller's linguistic explanation of the origin and nature of religion died shortly after he did, he nonetheless made a number of contributions to the study of religions. To begin with, he translated several religious texts from Sanskrit into English, giving scholars who had no knowledge of Sanskrit access to this literature. Along these lines, he edited the series *Sacred Books of the East* (Oxford, 1879–1910), in which experts in Sanskrit and other languages provided English translations of texts from Hinduism, Buddhism, Jainism, Zoroastrianism, Daoism, and Confucianism—50 volumes in all! Müller also drew attention to the importance of mythology for the study of religions and inspired others, mostly through their criticism of his theories, to develop better ways of interpreting mythology. Finally, Müller left an important legacy to the study of religions in his dictum, "He who knows one, knows none," which Goethe had once said of languages. What Müller meant was that comparison was absolutely necessary in the study of religion. Scholars simply cannot understand what religion is, or even what *a* religion is, if they know or practice only one—no more than people who eat only plums can grasp the broader category "fruit."

Grand Theories of Religion

Müller's theory of religions was a "grand theory" inasmuch as it attempted to explain all religions as well as religion itself. This became the norm in Müller's day, and like Müller, many of his contemporaries also sought the origin of religion based on speculation about early human beings. Also like Müller (and Marx before him), many reduced religion to something other than religion (although nothing quite so bizarre as a "disease of language"). Finally, just as Müller's grand theory attempted to analyze religion using comparative linguists, the theories of his contemporaries employed methodologies designed to study something other than religion—anthropology, sociology, and psychology. Methodologies specific to religion would come about only later.

E.B. Tylor

Born in London, E.B. Tylor (1823–1917) traveled to Central America in his early twenties, hoping that the warmer climate would help him recover from a case of tuberculosis. While visiting Cuba, he joined an archeological expedition to Mexico City, where he took notes on Mexican culture and archeological finds. These notes became the basis of his first book, which was part travelogue and part contribution to the emerging field of anthropology. Back in England, he continued his studies by reading the reports that were streaming into universities and learned societies from the European colonies. Piecing together bits of information from all over the world, Tylor argued for a unified history of human development. He proposed that ancient humans were intellectually no different than modern ones. They, too, sought to understand their world through logical thought. What made them "primitive" is that they lacked the knowledge that humans have today. In comparison to modern people, they were like inexperienced children rather than knowledgeable adults. Tylor assigned them to the "savage" age of human intellectual evolution, which was followed by the "barbaric" age, and ultimately the "civilized" age.

In his ground-breaking work, *Primitive Culture* (2 vols., 1871), Tylor argued that religion had its origins in two experiences common to all primitive people. First, noticing the change that took place when a person fell asleep, went into a trance, or died, primitive people reasoned that an animating spirit had left the person's body. Second, when they encountered visions of people and other beings in their dreams, they concluded that these were similar spirits. Early humans, according to Tylor, then used this knowledge of spirits to explain other things, such as movement and life in the world around them. They reasoned that these spirits, like those in human beings, lived in plants, animals, lakes, the sun, the moon, and so on. When they attempted to interact with these spirits, a crude form of religion was born, which Tylor called **animism**, from the Latin word *anima*, "life, soul, spirit." Religion thus began with a misunderstanding about the natural world, made by human beings with the knowledge base of children. As Tylor described it, this was the work of "primitive philosophers."

Over time, Tylor explained, the descendants of these philosophers added many new ideas to animism: rebirth through transmigration, spirit possession, the presence of spirits in inanimate objects (fetishes), and the worship of animals. Then, as human society grew more complex through the division of labor and the establishment of authority figures (clan leaders, kings), religions kept pace by assigning various duties to certain spirits and elevating some above others. In this manner, animism evolved into an early form of polytheism. Following this, a "structured polytheism" arose, characterized by a formal hierarchy of gods, as we find, for example, in ancient Greece. Finally, monotheism emerged, reaching its highest form in Christianity. Yet Tylor was no friend of Christianity, and so like many of his contemporaries, he predicted that Christianity would soon give way to a still higher system of thought, governed completely by logical reasoning.

One of the challenges Tylor faced in arranging animism, polytheism, structured polytheism, and monotheism on an evolutionary timeline was the presence of elements from the earlier forms of religion in later, more evolved forms. Why, for example, did some polytheists still worship animals? In other words, if religion evolved through distinct stages, as Tylor believed, why was there any carryover from one stage to the next? Tylor's solution was simple: as religions evolved, some older beliefs and practices were retained by sheer force of habit. Rather than being a problem for his evolutionary theory of religion, these "survivals," he suggested, were useful to scholars as a way of determining what an earlier form of the religion might have looked like. They could be easily identified, moreover, since they seemed out of place in the more evolved religion.

In 1896, after serving for more than a decade as a Reader (principal lecturer) in anthropology at Oxford, Tylor became the university's first professor of anthropology. Later he became a fellow of the Royal Society and received an honorary doctorate in Civil Laws from Oxford; and in 1912 he was knighted by the king of England, becoming Sir Edward Burnett Tylor. Today he is considered the founder of the discipline of Anthropology, and his *Primitive Culture* is seen as the beginning of the subdiscipline Cultural Anthropology. Without in any way diminishing these achievements and accolades, we must note that Tylor's understanding of the origin and development of religion derives almost entirely from his imagination. Having no knowledge of what early human beings actually thought, he simply constructed what he judged to be a credible story based on his best guess. His reliance on the theory of evolution also requires comment.

Twelve years before Tyler's *Primitive Culture*, Charles Darwin (1809–1882) published his landmark study, *On the Origin of Species*, arguing for biological evolution. The book was well received, and within a few years scholars began appropriating Darwin's theory for areas of study outside the field of biology. Economics, political science, sociology, and the analysis of religion (as seen in Tylor) each employed its own version of evolutionary theory. The problem with this broader application was that Darwin had presented evidence only for *biological* evolution, and had identified the mechanism behind it as "natural selection." In these other disciplines, however, there was no such mechanism to justify a natural or inevitable process that mirrored biological evolution. By the early 1900s, the whole venture of what became known as "social Darwinism" was under heavy criticism; and by the 1940s it had been thoroughly discredited. Tylor's purportedly scientific organization of religious materials in an evolutionary sequence thus proved to be arbitrary. At the turn of the century, however, it seemed reasonable enough, and Tylor may have adopted it for practical reasons as well. Like other scholars of the time, Tylor was confronted with a great mass of previously unknown information coming in from the colonies. The randomness of the material, moreover—a report on a ritual from Ghana, a note on a goddess from Peru, a mysterious artifact from Australia—necessitated some organizing principle. To be able to sort his evidence chronologically along an evolutionary timeline certainly simplified the challenge he faced. To do this, however, he had to solve another problem. Since much of his information related to religions that were still current in his day, how could he establish a timeline that relegated some beliefs and practices to the ancient past or prehistoric times? This is where his theory of survivals proved its worth. When he came across a belief or practice that struck his European sensibilities as crude and illogical, he explained it as a survival from an earlier period that, through force of habit, had managed to last into the present day.

Early Departments of Religion

Initially, scholars working with materials from the colonies did not give much thought to creating a separate discipline for the study of religions. The French scholar Eugène Burnouf (1801–1852), for example, studied texts and inscriptions from India. While he made significant contributions to the European understanding of Buddhism, Hinduism, and Zoroastrianism, his focus remained the Sanskrit language in which these texts and inscriptions were written.

In 1877–1878, however, the Netherlands established chairs for the History of Religions and the Philosophy of Religion in each of its four universities (Amsterdam, Groningen, Leiden, and Utrecht). Eight years later, Religious Sciences were added as a fifth section to the École Pratique des Hautes Études in Paris. The first Department of Comparative Religion was established at the University of Chicago in 1892, and in 1903 a chair in the study of religions was created at the Imperial University in Tokyo. By this time, the discipline had at its disposal several professional journals, reference works, and endowed lectureships. Scholars of religion also began to gather nationally and internationally. Of particular importance was the World's Parliament of Religion of 1893, held in Chicago in conjunction with the Columbian Exposition (the World's Fair). While this was more of an interfaith event than an academic congress, for the first time, Hindu and Buddhist spokespersons were able to address an American and European audience as equals.

James Frazer

Tylor's younger contemporary, the Cambridge scholar James Frazer (1854–1941), contributed to the study of religions by examining the practice of magic and by exploring the relation between myth and ritual. He also managed to organize a body of material several times larger than Tylor's two volume *Primitive Culture*. The third edition of Frazer's most famous work, *The Golden Bough* (1906–1915), filled 12 large volumes, while its smaller cousin, *Totemism and Exogamy* (1910), encompassed 4 volumes, each containing 400–600 pages.

Frazer's organizing principle for the *Golden Bough* employed both an evolutionary framework and a puzzling story about a priest, from which he derived several organizational headings. Ancient sources reported that this priest, who was also a king, lived in a grove of trees by Lake Nemi, south of Rome. This "King of Nemi," who served the goddess Diana, obtained his position by killing the previous priest in single combat. Frazer mistakenly thought that the aspiring priest first needed to pluck a bright yellow branch (the "golden bough") from a tree in the grove, although this was actually part of an unrelated tale. Proposing to explain this odd story, Frazer proceeded to use it as a cipher for understanding the origins and development of religion. He assembled a vast quantity of ethnological material from all over the world and sorted it into categories that mirrored elements in the account of the priest. He then devoted one or two volumes to each of these categories: magic and sacred kingship (2 vols.); taboos (1 vol.); dying and rising gods (3 vols.); scapegoats (1 vol.), etc. In his analysis of these categories—and dozens of subcategories within them—he compared disparate pieces of information across cultures and time periods for the purpose of identifying parallel practices and beliefs. For example, his treatment of rainmaking brings together magical charms from Armenia, practices of ritual bleeding among the Diyari of South Australia, songs to Indra from the *Rig-Veda*, and Aristophanes' description of Zeus in the ancient Greek play *The Clouds*. Quite controversially, he sometimes also made reference to elements from Christianity, inferring, for instance, that Jesus' death and resurrection resembled traditions of fertility gods who died and rose again with the change of seasons.

With these sorts of wide-ranging comparisons, over the course of thousands of pages, Frazer concluded that religion was an unfortunate blind alley or dead-end street in humanity's attempt to understand the world. His grand theory began with the practice of magic. Primitive peoples, Frazer argued, were problem solvers. In searching for patterns that would help them understand and control the natural world, they created systems of magic that operated, or so they thought, according to two principles: contagion and similarity. The principle of **contagion** dictates that one can gain influence over persons by manipulating things with which they have been in contact. Thus, a person's baby teeth, umbilical cord, hair clippings, or footprint can be crushed, burnt, or stabbed with a knife, respectively, to harm that person. The principle of **similarity**, in turn, dictates that similar things exercise sway over one another: like influences like. By imitating the movements of a game animal, a hunter can draw these animals to him; by pressing a red rock against a wound, a tribal healer can stop a wound from bleeding; and by carrying a wooden baby around with her, a woman can cure her infertility.

For Frazer, this sort of magical thinking was an early form of applied science. Primitive peoples were not misguided in looking for laws of nature; they had simply identified false laws. But when magic was found to be unpredictable and unreliable, early humans took the fateful step of speculating that life was controlled by a supernatural power that belonged to beings called gods. To curry the favor of these gods, they worshipped them, and magic slowly gave way to religion. But, Frazer continued, since science can now teach us the correct laws of nature, we no longer need either magic or religion.

> We shall perhaps be disposed to conclude that the movement of the higher thought, so far as we can trace it, has on the whole been from magic through religion to science.
>
> James Frazer, *The New Golden Bough: A New Abridgement of the Classic Work by Sir James George Frazer*, ed. Theodor H. Gaster (N.P.: Criterion, 1959), p. 738.

As mentioned earlier, Frazer is remembered especially for his analysis of magic and the attention he gave to mythology and ritual. In addition, his approachable writing style made vast quantities of religious materials from all over the world available to a wide audience. Like Tylor, Frazer received multiple accolades and honors for his work in religion. But also like Tylor, his grand theory was grounded in imagination and intelligent guesses. His work soon came under criticism for drawing too many parallels between unrelated phenomena. Although he assembled his information with great care, even writing letters to missionaries about specific topics, he was often unaware of its full context within a religion. He was, ultimately, an "armchair anthropologist" who never visited the cultures and the peoples he wrote about.

Émile Durkheim

A graduate of the prestigious École Normale Supérieure in Paris, Émile Durkheim (1858–1917) began his career as a philosophy teacher in secondary education. Soon, however, his attention shifted to the developing field of sociology. Contrary to the conventional wisdom, Durkheim became convinced that societies were not simply collections of individuals, but more like living organisms. When people interacted within a group, a social dynamic was created and things came into being that were particular to this social dynamic. In 1897 he gained recognition for his approach through the publication of *Suicide: A Study in Sociology*. Prior to this, suicide had been treated as the personal decision of an individual. By showing that suicide was more prevalent in some societies than others, however, Durkheim was able to identify it as a *social construct*.

A decade or so after writing *Suicide*, Durkheim turned his attention to the study of religion. In his *Elementary Forms of the Religious Life* (1912), he attempted to show that religion, too, was a social construct, and that its origin and function could be explained entirely through sociological analysis. Defining religion as "a unified system of beliefs and practices relative to sacred things," Durkheim posited that religious people always divided the world into what was "sacred" and what was "profane." These categories did not define good and evil, but rather what was special and what was ordinary. Sacred things were special. They belonged to the entire society, not individuals, and consequently demanded the utmost reverence and respect from all members of society. They could be approached or handled only by certain persons (e.g., priests) and only at certain times (e.g., festivals). At all other times they were "set apart and forbidden." Profane things, by contrast, belonged to the everyday, routine lives of individuals. They had far less significance for the larger society and required no special treatment.

As a test case for his ideas, Durkheim wanted to examine an uncomplicated religion in an uncomplicated society. The religion needed to be free of theology or mythological thought and show little historical development, and it must belong to a society with minimal organizational structure. In this way, he argued, he could most easily and convincingly reduce the religion to its "elementary forms," or building blocks, which would prove to be the basis for all religions. He ultimately decided on the religion of an Aboriginal people, the Arrernte of Australia. This was a form of totemism, which, in his view, was the simplest of all religions. Moreover, it had recently received thorough treatments in anthropological publications.

As Durkheim presented it, the various clans of the Arrernte wandered in small groups for much of the year, but on certain occasions each clan came together for the Intichiuma ceremony. During this ceremony, clan members experienced a "collective effervescence," an extraordinary experience that Durkheim identified as an encounter with the sacred. Since this experience belonged to the clan, not the individual, it was embodied in a "totem"—an animal or plant that symbolizes the clan itself. The totem became the clan's most sacred object and was worshipped as the source of the clan's strength and being.

Based on this depiction, Durkheim proposed that the totem functioned as a symbol for both the sacred and the clan, and, further, that when the clan assembled to worship and participate in the power of the sacred, they were actually worshipping and participating in the power of the clan. Religion, in other words, could be reduced to a social construct whose function was to sanctify and protect society by worshipping it as sacred.

Because Durkheim had identified totemism as the simplest form of religion, he also saw the Arrernte's Intichiuma ceremony as indicative of the origin of religion. This implied that religion had begun without gods or divine beings, for humans had originally worshipped society in the form of an impersonal sacred power. But since the sacred was identical with society, it mirrored society's structure and evolved in concert with it. Thus, according to Durkheim, gods appeared in religion as clans became more fully integrated into the larger society of the tribe. When this happened, the sacred took on the features of the tribal leader and was worshipped as a high god, or Supreme Being. Polytheism, in turn, came about when tribal councils, composed of clan leaders, developed, and individual clan totems were elevated to the status of minor deities in service to the high god. Finally, if a tribal society evolved into a monarchy, the sacred was envisioned as a king, and monotheism appeared.

Durkheim contributed to the study of religions mainly by drawing attention to the social dimension of religion: how religions affected societies and how societies affected religions. Because he had reduced religion to a social construct, however, and identified the sacred with society, his proposal concerning the nature and origin of religion received harsh criticism almost immediately. Some questioned the accuracy of his information on the Arrernte, others questioned his use of the data, and still others his assumption that religion was *only* a social phenomenon and *only* pertained to groups, not individuals. In the end, however, the most damning criticism was that his argument involved a certain circularity, for his initial assumptions about the sacred and its connection to society anticipated the gist of his conclusions.

Sigmund Freud and Carl Jung

The last two grand theories we will examine in this section were the creations of the psychiatrists Sigmund Freud and Carl Jung. Freud (1856–1939) was born in what is now the eastern Czech Republic, then a part of the Austrian Empire. Receiving his doctorate in medicine from the University of Vienna, he established a practice in Vienna as a neurologist, treating patients with psychological and emotional disorders. Early in his career, he used hypnosis to examine his patients, but eventually settled on a combination of free association and dream analysis in a process he called psychoanalysis.

Freud became convinced that mental illnesses are caused by the unintentional release of thoughts that his patients repressed in the unconscious part of their minds. While Freud did not invent or discover the notion of the unconscious, he explored it in ways that would change forever how western science understood mental processes and the human personality. In 1900, he published the *Interpretation of Dreams*, in which he argued that sleep allows repressed ideas to escape a person's unconscious and express themselves in strange and illogical scenarios of wish fulfillment that we call dreams. He determined that one of the principal wishes that males repress is sexual desire. All boys, Freud claimed, develop a sexual attraction to their mothers, resulting in a wish to kill their fathers and become their mothers' sexual partners. Since they also fear their fathers, however, they repress this wish in the unconscious part of their minds, and eventually identify with their fathers. Freud called this process the "Oedipus complex," after an ancient Greek drama in which a son unknowingly kills his father and marries his mother.

In 1907, Freud proposed that there were unmistakable similarities between religious rituals and the obsessive-compulsive disorders he observed in his patients. Both involved repeating certain activities out of a feeling of necessity, and in both, people gave careful attention to the details of what they were doing. In addition, both rituals and obsessive-compulsive behavior were distinct from everyday activities, and most religious people, like obsessive-compulsive people, were unable to articulate precisely what they were doing or why they were doing it. From these observations, Freud concluded that religion was a collective mental illness—a "universal obsessional neurosis"—that could be cured through psychoanalysis!

During the last 25 years of his life, Freud tried to explain how religion, this universal obsessional neurosis, had come into being. In *Totem and Taboo* (1913), he speculated that early human beings had lived in hordes in which a father dominated his sons and kept all the women for his own sexual pleasure. The sons, consequently, hated the father. Desiring to have his wives as their sexual partners, they killed him, took his wives, and ate his flesh as a way of acquiring his power. Later, however, they were overcome with unbearable remorse for what they had done. Resolving that this should never happen again, they established taboos (prohibitions) against murder and incest, and they enshrined the memory of their father in a totem, which became an object of religious worship. Finally, they repressed their guilt in a "collective unconscious" that all humans after them inherited. As humans evolved from primitive to civilized peoples, this repressed guilt matured into increasingly sophisticated forms of religion. Freud even suggested that the Christian eucharist—the ritual consumption of the body of God's Son—was an outgrowth of this process.

Fourteen years later, Freud published a second work on religion entitled, *The Future of an Illusion*. In this essay, he suggests that early humans were frightened by the dangers of the natural world and longed for the security of their childhood under the protection of the father whom they had killed to acquire his wives. As a wish fulfillment, their collective unconscious projected into the heavens the image of a god who was a protective, albeit stern, father figure.

> No, our science is no illusion. But an illusion it would be to suppose that what science cannot give us we can get elsewhere.
>
> Sigmund Freud, *The Future of an Illusion*, trans. James Starchey (New York: W. W. Norton, 1961), p. 56.

In a final essay on religion, *Moses and Monotheism* (1939), Freud attempted to uncover the origins of Jewish and Christian monotheism. This, like the other essays, described the repression of ideas in a collective unconscious, and their eventual reappearance in the form of religion. Since Freud relied on a creative retelling of Egyptian and Jewish history, and constructed a theory that was at odds with *Totem and Taboo*, we need not summarize its contents. Suffice it to say that, in all these instances, Freud sought to expose religion as a mental illness that could be cured through psychoanalysis.

Carl Jung (1875–1961) was a Swiss psychologist who collaborated with Freud between 1907 and 1913. After a falling out, Jung continued to practice a form of psychoanalysis that he called "analytical psychology." Like Freud, he understood religion as a psychological phenomenon, but unlike Freud, he saw religion in a positive light. For Jung, it was not a mental illness, but a source of mental health and wholeness.

Following Freud, Jung believed that everyone shared in a collective unconscious. But Jung's research led him to the conclusion that, instead of harboring memories of traumatic events from the dawn of humanity, this collective unconscious contained ideas, symbols, and mythological motifs that facilitated the healthy integration of one's personal psyche into the ethos of the collective unconscious. This integration, which he termed "individuation," was achieved by utilizing the contents of the collective unconscious to undertake a spiritual journey in search of "the Self"—Jung's term for a unique and whole person with meaning and purpose in life.

In past times, Jung explained, religious leaders had tapped into the collective unconscious, which they understood as the spiritual world, to retrieve religious tools that Jung labeled **archetypes**. Among the archetypes were images of the Virgin, the Mother, and the Wise Old Man; symbolic representations of good and evil, and male and female; and myths of the creator, the hero, and the trickster. Religious leaders then imparted these archetypes to their followers in the form of religious songs, rituals, stories, and art, so that their followers could achieve individuation, which they understood as experiencing the sacred. In the present day, Jung insisted, analytical psychology was able to facilitate this important spiritual journey through dream interpretation and psychoanalysis. But instead of doing away with religion, as Freud urged, Jung valorized religion as a resource for mental health, writing extensively on the mythologies and symbols of Hinduism, Buddhism, Christianity, Daoism, Gnosticism, and alchemy, and visiting India to learn from Hindu philosophers and examine religious art.

Despite their differences, both Freud and Jung made important contributions to the study of religions. Freud did so more broadly through his research into the nature of the unconscious. This presented western scholars with a vast and unexplored world of nonlogical symbolic thought, which has borne fruit not only in the study of religions, but also in psychology, anthropology, archeology, art history, literature, and many other disciplines. His work specifically on religion, by contrast, was largely a product of his dislike for Judaism and Christianity, and his reduction of religion to a universal mental illness gained little recognition from his peers. Jung, on the other hand, helped scholars of religion appreciate of the importance of religious symbols and mythology in an individual's quest for the sacred. Even though he also reduced religion to an aspect of psychology, Jung argued for the importance of religious traditions in the healthy development of the human psyche. Indeed, some critics have claimed that his valorization of religion went too far, leading him away from psychology and into theology and mysticism.

New Approaches in Sociology and Anthropology

By the late 1800s, the full implications of Romanticism and colonialism were being brought to bear on the study of religions. As Romanticism gained respectability in scholarly circles, the emotional, aesthetic, and spiritual aspects of religion became important topics of investigation, casting doubt on purely empirical approaches and making materialistic explanations of religion obsolete. Colonialism, in turn, brought western scholars face-to-face with an entire world of previously unknown religions. This expanded their knowledge and experience of living religions far beyond the boundaries of Christianity and made the distinction between the true and false religions increasingly difficult to maintain. Christian theologians became more open to the truth claims of other religions; reductionism yielded to more fruitful approaches; and an appreciation for "religion" as a unified category began to develop.

Max Weber

Émile Durkheim and Max Weber ("Váy-ber," 1864–1920) are often seen as the founders of the discipline of Sociology. Like Marx, Weber was a graduate of the University of Berlin (which by Weber's time had been renamed Friedrich Wilhelm University). Although Weber began his career teaching economics and publishing essays on the intersection of economics and politics, he soon became interested in the effect that religions had on economic systems. He did not, however, envision his subject as the intersection of religion with economics, but as the intersection of particular religions with particular economic systems. As a result, he differed from those who studied religion before him in a number of ways. He paid little attention to reductionism and theories on the origin and evolution of religion, and he saw no special value in studying the religions of "primitive" peoples.

Weber's first major foray into religion came in the form of two articles published in 1904 and 1905 under the collective title *The Protestant Ethic and the Spirit of Capitalism*. He set for himself the task of determining why early forms of capitalism had developed in Protestant countries but not Catholic ones. Looking into the theologies of Martin Luther and John Calvin, the principal leaders of the Protestant Reformation, Weber argued that Luther had broadened the notion of religious vocation to include the everyday occupations of all Christians. In Catholicism, both before and after Luther, a religious vocation, or "calling," was something that only religious leaders—priests, monks, and nuns—undertook, not laypersons. Luther's teachings had the effect of giving everyone the sense that their work, no matter how humble, contributed to the glory of God.

Luther's younger contemporary John Calvin added to Luther's theology by reasoning that if Christians wanted to dedicate their work to God in this way, they needed to lead well-ordered, exemplary lives. But Calvin also taught the doctrine of predestination, which held that God had already determined which people would receive salvation and which would be damned. As a consequence, Calvinist Christians began to look for signs that they were among the saved, and one of these signs became a person's success in their chosen occupation, for success indicated that a person had God's favor.

Success also produced wealth, and under the influence of these new teachings, many Protestant Christians became quite wealthy. To avoid the sins of greed and luxury, they saved what they earned, rather than spending it on themselves, and invested it in their livelihoods to achieve even more success and more assurance of God's favor. Weber described this behavior as "inner-worldly asceticism" because these entrepreneurs lived and worked in society, rather than apart from the world in monasteries and convents, but denied themselves the fruits of their labors by living frugal and industrious lives. Of course, the wealth that they saved and reinvested was the capital that gave rise to capitalism. While this became the economic engine in Protestant countries, noncapitalistic economies continued to prevail in Catholic countries.

> **Polymaths**
>
> Many of the pioneers in the study of religions were polymaths—intellectual giants who had mastered several areas of learning. One example is William Robertson Smith (1846–1894), who, at age 25, was a Fellow of the Royal Society of Edinburgh and held a chair in Hebrew at Aberdeen Free Church College in Scotland. In 1881, Smith lost his position at Aberdeen for comparing ancient Judaism to other Semitic religions and for suggesting that the Bible was not inerrant. Shortly thereafter, he was offered a position at Harvard University, not in Hebrew, however, but in *mathematics*. He eventually served as University Librarian and professor of Arabic at Cambridge, where he became a fellow of Christ College; and at 46 he was appointed chief editor for the 9th edition of the *Encyclopaedia Britannica*.
>
> Another example is Max Weber, who has been described with these words:
>
>> His mind was encyclopedic and absorbent, steeped in learning that embraced not only law and economics but also history, philosophy, art, literature, and music.... At age thirteen, his idea of a Christmas gift to his parents was a pair of essays: one on medieval German history, another on the later Roman empire.
>
> Daniel L. Pals, Ten Theories of Religion, 4th ed. (New York: Oxford University Press, 2022) pp. 144–145.

Weber's *Protestant Ethic and the Spirit of Capitalism* was well received by those in his field, and on the basis of its success he planned a series of books that would explore the influence of specific religions on economic systems. He entitled the series, *The Economic Ethic of the World Religions*, and managed to complete three volumes before his death: *The Religion of China: Confucianism and Taoism* (1915), *The Religion of India: The Sociology of Hinduism and Buddhism* (1916), and *Ancient Judaism* (1917–1919). In these books, as well as his *Economy and Society*, published posthumously in 1922, Weber made several important contributions to the study of religions.

Perhaps his most important contribution was in the area of comparative methodology. Under the name **ideal types**, Weber defined different categories of religious leaders, ideas, and change that could be applied to several religions for the purpose of comparison. Weber's ideal-typical method will be familiar to students of economics and the natural sciences. Economists, for example, construct economic models. These models are "ideal" in the sense that they make assumptions that may not always hold true in the "real" world. When applied to particular economies, however, they become a standard by which one can measure both how economies differ from one another, and how they are similar.

Weber defined three ideal types of religious leaders that could be applied to most, if not all, religions: the magician, the prophet, and the priest. These were larger-than-life roles that individuals took on, much like our notions of "hero" or "superstar." They differed from religion to religion, and from era to era, but were nonetheless sufficiently defined and stable to allow for meaningful, instructive comparisons. In this way, Weber distinguished between prophets in eastern religions and those in western religions. He called eastern prophets "exemplary prophets," since they led by example. They were the sages and gurus who encouraged individuals to attain inner peace in the midst of a chaotic world. They viewed sacred reality as an impersonal power, such as the Dao or the law of karma. Western prophets, on the other hand, were "ethical prophets." They delivered definitive pronouncements on right and wrong from a personal god who rewarded moral conduct and punished disobedience.

Weber also defined three ideal types of religious authority: charismatic, traditional, and legal-rational. Charismatic was an authority that rested on one's personal attributes, such as unusual insight into human nature and the ability to inspire confidence. It was the type of authority exercised by Weber's magician, prophet, and, to some extent, priest. Traditional authority, on the other hand, resided in an "office" or "profession" that was rooted in tradition, not in a person. It was the principal authority wielded by Weber's priest. Finally, legal-rational authority was the authority that belonged to bureaucrats and officials in rule-based institutions, such as governments and large religious organizations. It could be questioned only with respect to legal codes and rational arguments.

Among the other ideal types that Weber identified were theological doctrines, such as salvation and theodicy (the explanation of evil), and developments within religions and society, such as secularization (which Weber called "cultural disenchantment") and "routinization." The latter refers to the change in religious authority that takes place when a charismatic leader, such as a magician or prophet, dies. Weber explained that when this happens, charismatic authority, which was individual, intermittent, and extraordinary, is replaced by traditional or legal-rational authority, which is more constant and routine. Lastly, Weber regarded magic, polytheism, and monotheism as ideal types. In his view, they were not stages in an evolutionary process, as others had argued, but variations in religion that could appear again and again in a particular religion's history.

E.E. Evans-Pritchard and Clifford Geertz

By the 1930s, the field of anthropology had advanced considerably since its founding by Tylor and Frazer. It was no longer acceptable to collect reports from around the world and use them selectively to distill generalizations about religion. The emphasis now fell on careful fieldwork among a specific people for the purpose of contextualizing a particular religion within a particular culture. One of the earliest anthropologists to approach religion in this way was E.E. Evans-Pritchard (1902–1973). Having studied history at Oxford, and having received his PhD from the London School of Economics with a dissertation on the social organization of the Azande people of South Sudan, he published his first major study of religion under the title *Witchcraft, Oracles, and Magic Among the Azande* (1937). Based on two years of fieldwork among the Azande, during which Evans-Pritchard learned the

Zande language and took detailed notes on every aspect of Azande rituals, the book offered an analysis of Azande beliefs and practices from *their* point of view. In other words, with *Witchcraft, Oracles, and Magic*, Evans-Pritchard deliberately broke from the Eurocentric tradition of explaining, evaluating, and judging the religions of others from the outside, through comparisons with western standards of science and rational thought. Instead, he sought to present an empathetic, insider's understanding of Azande religion by underscoring the coherence of their distinctive world view and logic.

Evans-Pritchard continued his ethnographic work among the Nuer, also of South Sudan, publishing *Nuer Religion* in 1956. In the same detailed manner as his earlier study, he presented the religion of the Nuer as a fully coherent system, governed by its own internal logic. Finally, in his *Theories of Primitive Religion* (1965), Evans-Pritchard provided an incisive critique of several earlier attempts to study religion, especially those of Tylor, Frazer, and Durkheim. He rejected reductionism, evolutionary schemes, and the notion of survivals, demonstrating that magic, religion, and science are not antithetical and do not sequentially replace one another, but can coexist and complement one another as elements of the same cultural tradition.

Clifford Geertz (1926–2006) was trained in the American tradition of anthropology at Harvard and conducted fieldwork in Indonesia and Morocco, focusing on the cultural dimension of religion. In his view, religion was one element, albeit an important one, in the larger systems of meaning that we call cultures. Cultures, in turn, were human constructs, not objective universal truth accepted by everyone. Nonetheless, a particular culture *served as reality* for the people who belonged to it by providing order, meaning, and purpose in life. Religion's role in all of this, according to Geertz, was to connect or naturalize each people to its own culturally defined reality through rituals and symbols.

In his *Religion of Java* (1960), Geertz examined the tensions and interactions between Muslim, Hindu, and Javanese popular traditions in the pluralistic context of Javanese culture; and in his *Islam Observed* (1968), he compared the forms of Islam practiced in Indonesia with those practiced in Morocco. In neither of these books, as we might expect, did he study religion in isolation. Instead, he situated religion within the various political, social, and moral contingencies of Indonesian and Moroccan culture, and explored the changing role of rituals and symbols over time.

The methodologies pioneered by Weber, Evans-Pritchard, and Geertz highlighted the social and cultural dimensions of religion and demonstrated the importance of religion for the disciplines of sociology and anthropology. This guaranteed a place at the university for the study of religions, and, just as importantly, provided a viable alternative to reductionism. Indeed, by showing how fruitful it was to treat religion as a real thing, and not something else in disguise, all three scholars significantly raised the bar for theories that sought to "expose" religion as a tool of capitalism or dismiss it as an antiquated, unscientific way of thinking.

While this represented a significant step forward for the study of religions, it came at a price, for Weber, Evans-Pritchard, and Geertz treated religion as an aspect of a larger process, namely, economic, social, and cultural change. In consequence, "religion" did not emerge from their works as its own category of study. All three, moreover, dealt only with individual religions, one at a time or, in Geertz's case, through comparison with another religion. None of them attempted to develop a grand theory of religion; and only Geertz made the effort to actually define religion. As a result, not only did these scholars not contribute to the creation of a separate discipline for the study of religions, but they also, in large part, provided a powerful argument against it. After all, if religion could be adequately studied in the social sciences, was there any need for a department of religion? The combined work of the next three scholars, who are the last in our survey, would provide an affirmative answer to that question: yes, there was a need. By focusing on the *experience* of religion, their efforts identified an aspect of religion that called for its own branch of scholarly inquiry.

The Experience of Religion

William James

Born in New York City, William James (1842–1910) received an MD from Harvard University, but never practiced medicine. He returned to Harvard some years later to teach physiology and anatomy, and then philosophy and psychology. Even though he had never taken a course in philosophy or psychology, he established an international reputation in psychology with the publication of his two-volume, 1200-page *Principles of Psychology* (1890), and he is remembered as one of the founders of the American philosophical tradition called Pragmatism.

With regard to religion, our interest in James centers on his lecture "The Will to Believe," published in 1896, and on a series of lectures he published in 1902 under the name *The Varieties of Religious Experience*. In "The Will to Believe," James presented several arguments based in Pragmatism for the position that some beliefs are justified even when there is no evidence to support those beliefs. This is so, for example, when an unsupported belief may lead to an important truth that we would otherwise not know, or when it brings important benefits to one's life or the lives of others. While the right to believe something without sufficient proof may not strike us as the sort of issue that needs philosophical justification, it was a crucial matter in the intellectual circles of James's day. Advances in science and the popularity of empiricism and atheism in the latter half of the nineteenth century made it difficult for professors at prominent universities to hold religious beliefs while maintaining legitimacy as scholars. For many in higher education, scholarship and faith were incompatible, and theologians in particular were put on the defensive. We can get a sense of how serious this prejudice against religion was by noting that James introduced his lecture as "a defense of our right to adopt a believing attitude in religious matters," and later spoke of the option to believe as "lawful." Although James received criticism from other philosophers, both at the time of the lecture and later, he emboldened many theologians and other academics to reengage in the study of religion without the fear of losing their scholarly reputations.

Shortly after the publication of "The Will to Believe," James was invited to give the 1901–1902 Gifford Lectures at the University of Edinburgh in Scotland. These had been established in 1887 for the purpose of promoting "natural theology," which was defined as a system of thought that could justify belief in God on the basis of reason and science. The resulting 20 lectures were published in 1902 as *The Varieties of Religious Experience.*

James approached his subject by examining the religious emotions and impulses experienced by individuals, for unlike theological claims, these were facts that could be recorded, verified, and examined. He freely admitted that these experiences were not rational, and that they often moved people to act in ways that seemed eccentric and even pathological. But this alone, he continued, does not give us the right to judge whether they are good or not, for history has shown that such experiences and behaviors sometimes lead to astounding discoveries, feats of heroism, or the creation of great works of art and literature. In addition, even if we took the position of a medical materialist and concluded that all religious feelings and actions originated in chemical changes in the brain, we would still be in no position to judge their worth. This is because medical materialism finds the origin of *all* experiences and behaviors in biological and chemical change, including extraordinary experiences of love and acts of kindness. It is, James insisted, the benefits of religious experience, not its origins, that determine its worth and goodness.

James, as we just noted, was concerned with the religious feelings, actions, and experiences *of individuals*, not groups. Accordingly, he defined religion as what solitary individuals experienced and did in the presence of what they considered to be divine. Anything having to do with organized religion—churches, doctrines, rituals, etc.—were, in his view, secondary aspects of religion, which he called "over belief." Since these secondary aspects differed from place to place and from religion to religion, they offered no reliable insight into religion. But the religious experiences of individuals, he insisted, were constant.

In their purest and most exalted manifestation, which James called mysticism, religious experiences have four distinguishing marks. First, they are ineffable: they cannot be described, or taught, or explained to anyone else, but only grasped through direct encounter. Second, they give access to truth not otherwise available: they are revelatory, luminous, and full of significance. Third, they are transitory, lasting for only a short while. And fourth, they overwhelm the individual and leave their mark on the individual's psyche. James held that religious experiences of this sort came into an individual's conscious thoughts by way of their "subconscious" (similar to Freud's unconscious). It was for this reason that the individual perceived them as coming from "outside." Yet James did not thereby reduce religion to a purely psychological phenomenon. Staying within the guidelines of the Gifford Lectures, he suggested two options. *Either* these experiences put a person in touch with their Better Self, which was housed in a person's subconscious, *or* they were communications from a spiritual realm, being only *mediated* by one's subconscious. In other words, speaking with the authority of a scholar guided entirely by philosophical reasoning and the latest discoveries in psychology, James fulfilled his obligation to the Gifford Lectures by arguing that God might exist after all.

Rudolf Otto

Unlike the other figures we have discussed, Rudolf Otto (1869–1937) came to the study of religions as a Christian theologian. Having done his graduate work in both theology and philosophy, Otto taught these subjects at several German universities and spent the last 12 years of his career as a professor of systematic theology at the University of Marburg. He was initially attracted to Christian apologetics, or seeking philosophical arguments for the superiority of Christianity over other religions. While Otto admired the accomplishments of James's *Varieties of Religious Experience* (which had relied mostly on Christian examples of religious experience), he rejected the author's strictly academic approach. By bringing the insights of theology to bear on the analysis of religious experience, Otto wanted to show that a religious orientation to the world offered what the nineteenth-century philosopher Jakob Fries had described as a "feeling of truth."

Otto's perspective on his work broadened considerably during his travels in 1911–1912, which took him from the Canary Islands through Morocco, Egypt, China, Japan, and the United States. In 1917. he published his most influential book, *The Holy*, which bore the subtitle, *Concerning the Irrational in the Concept of the Divine and Its Relation to the Rational*. Here he proposed that an experience of the divine ("the Holy") was not only indescribable, as James had argued, but revealed the divine as "wholly other." Whereas James had compared religious experience to psychological states of pathology, Otto insisted that religious experience was without counterpart, analogy, or parallel anywhere in human experience. It was *sui generis*, "in a class by itself." As a shorthand for what one experienced, Otto employed the term *numinous*. This was a mysterious presence of the divine which, while it lacked logical and moral dimensions, had an "overplus of meaning" that elicited powerful feelings and emotions. It was at once overwhelmingly fascinating, drawing a person toward it, and overwhelmingly terrifying, reducing that same person to a helpless condition of submissiveness in its presence. Like James, Otto held that such experiences were the basis of all religions.

From his claim that experiencing the Holy was an encounter with something wholly other, Otto drew three conclusions. First, the radical uniqueness of the Holy meant that it had to be apprehended and appreciated entirely on its own terms. It was not reducible to anything else, nor was it accessible using the methods of sociology or psychology, or any other existing discipline. It needed a separate discipline of its own. Second, the Holy's *sui generis* nature elicited a distinctively *religious* experience, the basic structure of which would be the same everywhere. Third, since the overplus of meaning that came from an encounter with the Holy could not be adequately conveyed to others, but had to be experienced directly, only those who had undergone this experience were qualified to talk about it. Otto even invited readers who had never experienced the divine to stop reading his book! This was a bold reversal of the earlier sentiment that theologians and others with religious beliefs should be excluded from participating in the study of religions because their personal beliefs would prejudice their scholarly views. Now, according to Otto, it was *only* those who had religious experiences who were qualified to participate. Soon, *The Holy* was translated into multiple languages, and together with James's *Varieties*, it helped legitimize the study of religions by scholars who refused to embrace reductionistic theories or abandon their belief in god.

> The reader is invited to direct his mind to a moment of deeply felt religious experience.... Whoever cannot do this, whoever knows no such moments in his experience, is requested to read no farther ....
>
> Rudolf Otto, *The Idea of the Holy*, 2d ed. (Oxford: Oxford University Press, 1950), p. 8.

Otto's work was an early example of a phenomenological approach to religion. More generally, **phenomenology** is a method of understanding something by observing how that something "presents itself" *to someone*. For example, a phenomenologist might suggest that a falling star manifests good luck if it presents itself to someone in that way. Of course, we could argue that the notion of a falling star manifesting good luck is simply the product of an individual's imagination. The problem with this explanation comes about, however, when falling stars appear to multiple people in multiple cultures as manifestations of good luck. If this is a substantial number of people in a substantial number of cultures over thousands of years, a phenomenologist would conclude that it cannot be explained as a coincidence, but is due to some sort of "intentionality" in the human consciousness. As applied to religion, phenomenology insists that repeated manifestations of the Holy in certain objects or events must be understood entirely from the believer's point of view. According to most phenomenologists, it is not necessary to have had the experience of a believer to practice phenomenology, as Otto contended, but it does require that one recognize the reality or "fact" of the believer's experience, without reducing it to something else.

Mircea Eliade

In the decades following the publication of Otto's *The Holy*, many scholars pursued the study of religions through phenomenology. The most widely read and influential of these was the Romanian scholar Mircea Eliade (Mér-cha El-ee-á-day, 1907–1986). Born in Bucharest, Eliade was a child prodigy who read voraciously and became proficient in a number of languages. By age 14 he was a published author. He did graduate work in Romania, Italy, and India, where he lived five years studying Sanskrit, Indian philosophy, rural religious life, and yogic traditions. After receiving his PhD from the University of Calcutta in 1933 with a dissertation on yogic practices, he returned to Romania where he lectured on metaphysics and worked as a journalist and author. Following World War II, he moved to Paris and taught at the École Pratique des Hautes Études. During this time, he published many of his most significant works: *Patterns in Comparative Religion* (1949); *The Myth of the Eternal Return* (1949); *Shamanism: Archaic Techniques of Ecstasy* (1951); *Yoga: Immortality and Freedom* (1954); and *The Sacred and the Profane* (1957). In 1957, he accepted a professorship at the University of Chicago, where he taught and wrote until his death in

1986. While at Chicago, he founded the journal *History of Religions*, wrote a three-volume *History of Religious Ideas* (1978–1985), and edited the 16-volume *Encyclopedia of Religion* (1987).

Eliade held that religion was best understood by examining traditional peasant cultures, because religious world views in the modern west have become fragmented through the influence of secularism. By contrast, the people in traditional cultures, whom Eliade labeled "archaic," maintain a unified understanding of reality, which has two modes of existence: the sacred and the profane (à la Durkheim). The sacred mode is characterized by what is meaningful, powerful, and real; it is the perfectly ordered world of divine beings. The profane mode is the opposite: it is ordinary, random, and lacking in both power and meaning. Because archaic people yearn to immerse their lives in what is real and meaningful, they desire to live entirely in the sacred mode. This is impossible, however, for their origin stories, or myths, tell them that the sacred mode of living, which was available to all creatures at the time of creation, now belongs only to divine beings. Nonetheless, they can participate in the sacred from time to time through hierophanies and symbols.

Hierophanies are "manifestations of the sacred," which, according to Eliade, archaic people still experience because humans are inherently religious, or "*homo religiosis.*" Through these manifestations, the sacred confronts the human conscious as absolute reality—something wholly different from anything in the profane world—and symbols are created, facilitating future contact with the sacred. For example, if the sacred manifests itself to someone through an animal, or through an event or object connected to an animal, future interactions with that animal, such as showing the animal respect by not eating it, or asking permission to hunt it, become symbolic actions that establish contact with the sacred. If the sacred is manifested in a tree, moreover, that tree can become an especially powerful symbol, because trees, like mountains, ladders, and pillars, conform to a widely documented *pattern* of symbols that mediate between the profane and the sacred. A shaman, for example, might travel up a tree to acquire knowledge from the spirit world. Alternatively, a god might use a tree to descend into the human world. Eliade called this particular symbolic pattern the *axis mundi*, or world axis, because the tree, by defining an access point to what is ultimately real, becomes a center around which people in the random, unreal world of profane existence organize their lives.

> Works of art, like "religious data," have a mode of being that is peculiar to themselves; they exist on their own plane of reference, in their particular universe. The fact that this universe is not the physical universe of immediate experience does not imply their non-reality.
>
> Mircea Eliade, "History of Religions and a New Humanism," *History of Religions* 1 (1961): 5.

In his *Patterns in Comparative Religion*, Eliade presented several patterns of symbols from around the world and across time. Aside from trees, he examined the symbolic function of the sun, the moon, sky gods, Mother Earth, and bodies of water. He showed that each of these patterns not only has a common meaning in different cultures—the sun as the source of truth, the moon as a goddess of fertility, etc.—but in certain cultures they also had multiple meanings. Bodies of water, for instance, give access to the underworld, are a source of fertility, and provide a means of purification. Important symbols like these, in other words, offered access to the sacred in various ways. They were "multivalent." In addition, in his books on Shamanism and Yoga, Eliade demonstrated that symbols were not isolated entities, but integral parts of larger systems of meaning. By paying attention to their complementary and overlapping functions, one could arrive at a more comprehensive understanding of certain practices and beliefs.

Finally, in his *Myth of the Eternal Return*, Eliade considered the religious meaning of time. He argued that archaic people made a distinction between sacred time and profane time. Sacred time is only available at the moment of creation. It is only then that the world is new and pristine, the gods are present, and everything is brimming with clarity and meaning. Yet this moment is now past, and time has moved on. The gods are now distant, order is gone, and meaning slips away. Life is governed by profane time, and archaic people suffer from an emptiness, which they experience as nostalgia for a paradise now lost. Worse still, they develop a "terror of history," for as profane time marches forward, sacred time becomes increasingly remote and inaccessible.

The problem with profane time is that it is linear and unidirectional. It proceeds relentlessly into the future, day after day, year after year, without any end or goal or meaning. To protect themselves from this existential void, archaic people employ a cyclical understanding of time, which begins anew every month, or year, or sequence of years. Unlike linear time, cyclical time enables them to experience the sacred through recurring *hierophanies* of creation, including new moons and the arrival of spring. The principal *hierophany* of creation among archaic people, however, is beginning of the New Year. Often coinciding with the winter solstice, when the sun god begins to recover his strength and provide more hours of daylight, New Year celebrations destroy linear time through a cosmic reset. By erasing all past time, understood as the previous year, these celebrations give people renewed access to the sacred time of the beginning.

Throughout his almost 30 years of teaching and writing in the University of Chicago's History of Religions program, Eliade became an important advocate for the study of religions. Aside from his contributions to the analysis of religious symbolism, he promoted the notion that religion must be studied on its own terms rather than from the perspective of another discipline such as anthropology or sociology. His argument was that religion had a unique and irreducible element—the sacred—which demanded a separate tradition of scholarship with its own methods of research.

The Expansion of the University and Creation of Departments of Religion

The last portion of our narrative has to do not with scholarly theories, but with demographic, cultural, and institutional changes that took place following World War II, especially in the United States, but also in Europe. To begin with, higher education evolved. After the war, as populations in North America and Europe increased due to the post-war "baby boom," educational systems expanded. By the 1960s, when the first baby boomers were applying to college, the United States began a transition from elite to mass higher education. Universities and colleges received an unprecedented amount of support from the U.S. government, which had previously displayed comparatively little interest in higher education. In Europe, where universities already received ample public support, new universities were founded.

While higher education was expanding in this way, several factors came into play that made the study of religions attractive to college students. With the end of the war, a political standoff known as the Cold War began between the west and communist countries, and religion became an ideological weapon in this standoff. Western governments talked more openly about the importance of religious freedom, and in 1954, the U.S. congress added the phrase "under God" to the Pledge of Allegiance to teach elementary school children the difference between the "free world" and "godless Communism."

Even though most Americans in the 1950s identified religious freedom with the right to practice their "Judeo-Christian" traditions, this would change as information about non-Christian religions came to them in various ways. First, members of the military who had served in Japan during the war came back with personal accounts of East Asian religious traditions; and this scenario was repeated when soldiers returned home from the later Korean and Vietnam wars. Indeed, in some cases, they returned with spouses who practiced these traditions. Second, European colonial rule in Asia and Africa began to unravel after 1945, and by 1970, most European colonies had declared their independence and established sovereign governments. This meant that previously colonized people were able to travel abroad, and some emigrated to the west bringing their religions with them. As a result, religious diversity slowly increased in the United States, as well as in the United Kingdom, France, Australia, and Canada.

Naming the Discipline

Just as people associate the study of medicine with the practice of medicine, many people mistakenly associate the study of religion with the practice of religion, and this makes it difficult to find an apt name for the discipline. "Religious science," for example, by analogy with "political science," is considered inappropriate because science suggests analysis, and people who equate "religious" with "being religious" reject the notion that someone's personal faith can (or should) be analyzed. In turn, "religiology," by analogy with "biology," sounds more like a cult than an academic discipline; and describing someone as a "religionist," by analogy with "physicist," also suggests advocacy for religion. Even the seemingly innocuous "religious studies" can lead to confusion, depending on whether it is understood as a personal or a scholarly endeavor.

Third, the counterculture movements of the late 1950s and 1960s found inspiration in eastern religious practices. The so-called Beat Generation, or "beatniks," who included the literary figures Allen Ginsberg and Jack Kerouac and the expressionist painter Jackson Pollock, were outspoken critics of materialism in American society. Along with promoting sexual liberation and experimentation with psychedelic drugs, this group of progressives were drawn to the non-theistic teachings of Buddhism and Daoism. Their successors were the "hippies," a younger generation mostly in their teens and early twenties. Promoting nonconformity and opposition to authority, they rejected the value systems of their parents, including organized religion. While the media focused primarily on their propensity for "sex, drugs, and rock 'n' roll," and often depicted them as "godless," they explored various forms of spirituality, including Transcendental Meditation, yoga, and the devotional practices of neo-Hindu groups such as the "Hare Krishna" movement (ISKCON). Many also experimented with Neo-Paganism (especially Wicca) and the Occult, and joined religious communes.

In 1963, in response to a rising demand for religious education, the U.S. Supreme Court issued a two-fold decision. On the one hand, it ruled that if schools, including universities, received funding from the federal government, they could not engage in the "teaching *of* religion." On the other hand, it allowed these schools to "teach *about* religion." By making this distinction between theology and the study of religions, the Court gave universities (most of which received federal grants) a green light to establish departments of religious studies, and many did. Something similar also took place on an international level. At the 1960 conference of the International Association for the History of Religions held in Marburg, Germany, the German-born Israeli scholar of religions R.J. Zwi Werblowsky circulated a statement insisting that scholars of religions are not in the business of promoting or condemning religions; rather, they should examine religions as "a creation, feature and aspect of human culture." While he noted that endorsing a particular religion "may have its legitimate place in other, completely independent disciplines such as ... theology," he insisted that it had no place in the study of religions.

In practical terms, the demand for people who could teach religions under these new guidelines increased, leaving universities to scramble for qualified instructors. One impromptu solution was to hire religious leaders from surrounding communities, leading to courses taught by local preachers, rabbis, imams, and Hindu and Buddhist leaders. In other instances, universities that already had theologians and Bible instructors on their faculties encouraged them to shift their focus to the study of religions. Some did this out of personal interest, while many more acquiesced to teach survey courses in "world religions" to meet institutional needs. Parallel changes occurred on the level of professional associations. In 1964, for example, the National Association of Bible Instructors (founded in 1909) transitioned to become the American Academy of Religion. But these attempts to retool after the fact inevitably obscured the distinction between theology and the study of religions, a problem that continues to beset the work of the American Academy of Religion even today.

A more promising source of qualified teachers was the growing number of graduate programs in the study of religion. Preeminent among these in the English-speaking world were the University of Chicago's History of Religions program, associated especially with the Romanian scholar Mircea Eliade; the Religious Studies programs at the newly founded (1964) Lancaster University and at the University of California–Santa Barbara, both associated with the Scottish scholar Ninian Smart; and Harvard University's Religion program, associated above all with the Canadian scholar Wilfred Cantwell Smith. Those who received their PhDs from these and similar graduate programs were ultimately responsible for founding the first undergraduate departments of religious studies. Thus, in one way or another, by around 1970, one-third of U.S. universities had courses in non-Christian religions, and a separate department for the study of religions became a feature on many campuses.

Postscript: Further Defining the Field

At today's universities, students are often able to study religion in ways that go well beyond survey courses in world religions. Many universities offer courses in the sociology of religion, the philosophy of religion, religion and anthropology, religion and politics, religion and psychology, religion and literature, religion in art, religion in the media, and religion in cyberspace. There are also courses that approach religion through postcolonial and feminist critiques, queer theory, and Black and Latino studies. In addition, specialization in a particular religious tradition is possible in some departments of religion. It is not uncommon to find advanced courses in Judaism, Islam, Hinduism, Buddhism, and Native American religions, and undergraduates may even have the opportunity to begin language study in Hebrew, Arabic, Sanskrit, Hindi, Chinese, Japanese, and Indigenous American languages.

Finally, since the 1990s, a very different approach has emerged, although it is confined mostly to graduate programs. Known as the **Cognitive Science of Religion**, or CSR, it seeks to explain religion based on mental processes alone. Thus, it rejects the idea that religion should be examined as something *sui generis*, giving new life to reductionistic approaches. As an interdisciplinary field, however, CSR goes beyond the earlier medical materialism, drawing on discoveries in sociobiology, neurophysiology, and evolutionary psychology, and branching out into such areas as the cognitive ecology of religion, neurotheology, and cognitive anthropology. In 2006, the International Association for the Cognitive and Evolutionary Sciences of Religion was established as a resource and umbrella organization.

> In the end religion and science probably cannot be reconciled, if only because we do not really desire any such closure.
>
> James Gilbert, *Redeeming Culture: American Religion in an Age of Science* (Chicago: University of Chicago Press, 1997), p. 323.

Currently, many proponents of CSR seek to advance the notion that religion is an evolutionary byproduct of the brain's neurological development. Working from a theory called the Modularity of the Mind, they argue that neural complexes in different areas of the brain evolved to oversee separate and distinct cognitive functions, one of these functions being religious thought and motivation. Experimentation in CSR has, for example, sought to correlate religious experiences during meditation to events in the brain. Furthermore, because the cognitive mechanisms by which CSR tries to explain religion are not held to be species-specific, research is done not only on humans, but also on other advanced mammals, especially primates. For instance, the practice of bowing among certain nonhuman primates to indicate submission has been studied in relation to religious acts of reverence. Whether the grand venture of CSR will succeed in reducing all of religion to the electrochemical signals of certain neurons, or suffer the fate of the reductionist theories of the eighteenth and early nineteenth centuries, remains to be seen.

For review

1. How was the study of religion influenced by the Enlightenment?
2. Give some examples of a reductionistic approach to religion. Why were scholars attracted to this methodology?
3. What is Romanticism, and why was it so important to the study of religions?
4. Why was the use of evolutionary theory to study religion considered racist?
5. Give some reasons why the study of religions became so popular among college students, beginning in the 1960s.

For discussion

1. Which of the many ideas about religions presented in this chapter do you think are the best? Which are the worst? Why?
2. What responsibilities do scholars have to the religious people they study and write about? How can we reconcile these responsibilities with academic freedom?

Key Terms

animism	The belief that anything in the world—plants, mountains, arrows—can have a soul. A term used by E.B. Tylor to explain the origins of religion.
archetypes	According to Carl Jung, these were the ideas, symbols, and myths in the human collective unconscious.
Cognitive Science of Religion	The current attempt to explain religion entirely on the basis of mental processes.
contagion	One of two principles by which James Frazer explained how magic was thought to work (see similarity). Contagious magic assumes that people can be influenced by manipulating things with which they have been in contact.
empiricism	A theory of knowledge that requires scientific proof for anything to be considered true.
hierophany	The term used by Mircea Eliade for a manifestation of the sacred.
ideal types	Idealized or generalized models of important elements found in many or all religions. Used by Max Weber to compare religions to one another.
materialist empiricism	A theory of knowledge that not only demands scientific proof for establishing truth, but also denies the reality of anything that is not physical matter (i.e., anything spiritual or divine).
numinous	Rudolf Otto's term for describing the experience of the Holy as overwhelming, terrifying, mysterious, and irresistible all at once.

phenomenology	An approach to religion that attempts to explain religion on its own terms, as it "presents itself" to the human psyche. Associated especially with the work of Rudolf Otto and Mircea Eliade.
reductionism	A method for studying religion that first defines it as really being something other than religion.
similarity	One of two principles by which James Frazer explained how magic was thought to work (see "contagion"). Magic based on similarity assumes that similar things exercise sway over one another.
study of religions	An academic discipline that investigates one or more religions for no other reason than to understand the nature of religion and religious people; as opposed to theology.
sui generis	"In a class of its own." An expression used by phenomenologists of religion to describe the unique nature of religion.
theology	An academic discipline that explains, develops, and justifies one's own religion; as opposed to the study of religions.

Bibliography

A good first book

Eric J. Sharpe. *Comparative Religion: A History*, 2nd edn. LaSalle, IL: Open Court, 1986.

Further reading

David Chidester. *Empire of Religion: Imperialism & Comparative Religion*. Chicago: University of Chicago Press, 2014.

Daniel L. Pals. *Ten Theories of Religion*, 4th edn. New York: Oxford University Press, 2022.

Daniel L. Pals. *Introducing Religion: Readings from the Classic Theorists*. New York: Oxford University Press, 2009.

Stephen H. Webb. The Supreme Court and the Pedagogy of Religious Studies: Constitutional Parameters for the Teaching of Religion in Public Schools. *Journal of the American Academy of Religion* 70(1): 135–157, 2002.

Reference and research

Gregory D. Alles, ed. *Religious Studies: A Global View*. London: Routledge, 2008.

Lindsay Jones, ed. *Encyclopedia of Religion*, 2nd edn, 15 vols. New York: Macmillan, 2005.

Robert Alan Segal and Nickolas P. Roubekas, eds. *The Wiley-Blackwell Companion to the Study of Religion*, 2nd edn. Hoboken, NJ: Wiley-Blackwell, 2021.

GLOSSARY OF KEY TERMS

Abhidharma	"Higher Dharma"; teachings that synthesize and elaborate the Buddha's teachings.
Abhidharma-pitaka	The third and last division of early Buddhist scripture (see *Tri-pitaka*), which contains the "higher Dharma" teachings.
Aborigines	The indigenous people of Australia; also "Aboriginal peoples."
Abraham	A man whose covenant with God marks the beginning of the Jewish people, who are Abraham's descendants.
acupuncture	The practice of inserting slender needles into various points along the body's meridians to improve a person's flow of *qi*.
Advent	The period of expectation before Christmas, lasting four weeks.
African Initiated Churches (AICs)	Churches that are independent of European church authorities and combine African traditions with Christianity.
aggadah	Nonlegal Jewish traditions (see *halakhah*); to be distinguished from *haggadah*, which is a text used at Passover.
Agni	The Hindu fire god.
ahimsa	The Hindu and Buddhist principle of not destroying life.
Ali	Ali ibn-abi-Talib, the Prophet's cousin and son-in-law; the fourth caliph of Islam; considered by Shias to be the first inspired Imam.
Amaterasu-Omikami	The Japanese sun goddess, identified with Mahavairocana, the Great Sun Buddha; considered the ancestor of the imperial family.
Amida Buddha	The Japanese form of Amitabha Buddha. A Buddha who used his enormous store of merit to create a Pure Land for those in need of salvation.
Amitabha Buddha	See Amida Buddha.
an-atman	A Buddhist term meaning devoid of any stable core or self.
Analects	The teachings of Confucius as recorded by his disciples.
Ancestors	The spirits of exemplary human beings who have passed into the unseen world; central to African religions.
Andean	The cultural area in western South America along the Andes Mountain range, including the ancient sites of Chavin de Hauntar, the Moche, the Nazca, and the Inca.
androgynous	A being who is both male and female, a quality sometimes attributed to Supreme Beings.
animism	The belief that anything in the world—plants, mountains, arrows—can have a soul. A term used by E.B. Tylor to explain the origins of religion.

Understanding the Religions of the World: An Introduction, Second Edition.
Edited by Will Deming.
© 2025 John Wiley & Sons Ltd. Published 2025 by John Wiley & Sons Ltd.

Glossary of Key Terms

antisemitism	A form of anti-Judaism based on the spurious belief that Jewish identity can be determined by a person's DNA.
ANZAC Day	An expression of civil religion based on memories and shared experiences of the Australian and New Zealand Army Corps.
Aotearoa	Also known as New Zealand; the name the Maori prefer to call their island.
arati	A Hindu blessing received from a ritual flame.
archetypes	According to Carl Jung, these were the ideas, symbols, and myths in the human collective unconscious.
arhat	"One worthy of honor"; a monastic who attains enlightenment through the teachings of the Buddha.
Arjuna	The righteous king to whom Krishna reveals his divinity in the *Bhagavad Gita*.
Ark of the Covenant	A wooden chest covered in gold and adorned with images of heavenly beings; used for communication with God.
Aryans	The authors of the *Collections*; literally "Noble People."
Asen	A metal sculpture used by the Fon (Republic of Benin) as an altar and to remind people of their dependence on the Ancestors.
Ashkenazim	Jews who trace their roots to Christian host communities in eastern Europe.
atman	The imperishable soul in Hinduism (whose existence Buddhist teachings deny).
auto-sacrifice	Self-administered, ritual bloodletting practiced by the ancient Maya and Aztec.
Avalokiteshvara	The *bodhisattva* of compassion; see Guanyin.
avatar	One of 10 forms that Vishnu assumes in this world.
Baal Shem Tov	The title given to the founder of the Jewish Hasidic movement, meaning "Master of the Good Name."
baptism	The Christian initiation rite, seen as a purification and rebirth through water.
bar and *bat mitzvah*	"Son/Daughter of the Commandment"; the Jewish rite of initiation into adulthood for boys and girls, respectively; also the titles of those initiated.
baraqah	In Islam, a blessing; especially a divine blessing or gift of power passed along in the family bloodline of the Prophet or bestowed by a Sufi *shaykh* or saint.
bardo	A journey the soul experiences after death in Tibetan Buddhism.
Bhagavad Gita	"Song of the Lord"; a Hindu poem from the *Mahabharata* proclaiming the greatness of Krishna.
bhakti	"Devotion"; acts of devotion to images of deities.
bimah	A raised platform in a synagogue from which the Torah is read and the worship service is directed.
bishop	The highest-ranking leader in many forms of Christianity.
bodhisattva	A "being dedicated to awakening"; a compassionate, enlightened being who postpones buddhahood to work for the salvation of others.
body of bliss	The buddha body that enables buddhas to create their own lands of bliss and teach *bodhisattvas* who are on their way to buddhahood.
body of transformation	The buddha body that enables *bodhisattvas* and new buddhas to come into the karmic world.
brahman	Ultimate reality in Hinduism.

Brahmin	A Hindu priest; the highest class in traditional Hindu society.
Buddha	The Enlightened one, the Awakened one; the founder of Buddhism. An enlightened being who brings Buddhist salvation to a world.
buddha bodies	Three realms or states that *bodhisattvas* can attain after death: the body of transformation, and the body of bliss, and the Dharma body.
bullroarer	A device used in initiation ceremonies in Oceania to make audible the voice of the ancestors.
Bunya Dreaming Festival	An Australian festival of the Gubbi Gubbi that takes place when bunya trees bear their fruit, celebrated, in part, to build community with settler people.
butsudan	Traditionally, a large piece of furniture that serves as a Buddhist altar in China and Japan for memorializing a family's ancestors.
caliph	"Successor"; leaders that guided the Islamic community after Muhammad's death.
cargo cults	What settler peoples called utopian religious movements in Oceania that formed around the exchange of material goods.
chakras	In Hindu schools of yoga, disks along the spine and in the head where divine power resides.
Chan	"Meditation"; a Chinese school that emphasized meditation as a way to see the buddha nature in oneself.
Christ	The Greek translation of the Hebrew word *messiah* (anointed one); a king sent from God.
Christian	A follower of the messiah (Greek, *christos*).
Christmas	The annual celebration of Jesus' birth.
church	Local, regional, national, and international communities of Christians; also a building where Christians meet.
civil religions	Religions whose beliefs, practices, and membership are determined by cultural priorities and national identities.
class-and-life-stage *dharma*	One of three sources of *dharma*; duties determined by one's birth and stage in life.
Cognitive Science of Religion	The current attempt to explain religion entirely on the basis of mental processes.
collective unconscious	A repository of unconscious thoughts repressed over time by the human race and accessible to all humans. A universal counterpart to the individual's unconscious. It was used by both Freud and Jung in their explanations of religion.
Commoners	The third-ranking class in traditional Hindu society.
confirmation	A rite that follows baptism, more fully incorporating a Christian into the church.
Confucius	Founder of Confucianism (551–479 BCE).
Conservative Judaism	A branch of Judaism that understands the Torah as an authoritative expression of ancient Israel's response to God's call, and the Talmud as an important but not definitive guide to matters regulating Jewish religious life (see Orthodox and Reform Judaism).
contagion	One of two principles by which James Frazer explained how magic was thought to work (see similarity). Contagious magic assumes that people can be influenced by manipulating things with which they have been in contact.
covenant	In Judaism and Christianity, a binding agreement made between God and an individual or group of people.

creeds	Summaries of important Christian beliefs.
crucifixion	Death by being hung on a giant wooden cross; the manner of Jesus' death.
cultural capital	A person's stake or "investment" in their culture; often a deterrent to joining a religion from another culture.
culture heroes	Spirit beings responsible for introducing important traditions, institutions, and skills into one's culture.
cupping	The Chinese practice of applying small, heated glass jars to parts of the body to manipulate the flow of *qi*.
daimyo	Samurai lords, originally in service to the emperor. Beginning in the twelfth century they established military dictatorships throughout Japan.
dalit	The current name used in India for "outcaste."
dana	The Buddhist practice of giving to gain merit (good karma).
danka	The members of an extended family registered at a Japanese temple during the Tokugawa shogunate.
Dao	The Chinese universal Way, understood as a cosmic force that influences everyone and everything.
Daode Jing	An early writing of Daoism.
Daoism	A philosophical and religious tradition that sees the Dao (Way) as the reality behind our world.
dark shaman	A shaman who uses power from the spirit realm to inflict harm on others.
darshan	A visual exchange between a *murti* and a Hindu worshiper.
denomination	One of several divisions or church traditions within Christianity.
Devi	One of the three great deities of Hinduism.
dharma	Hindu religious duty; religion.
Dharma	The message of the Buddha, the truth of the universe.
Dharma body	In Theravada, the teachings of the Buddha; in Mahayana, the highest of the buddha bodies, being the essence of the Buddha's *nirvana*.
dharmas	In *Abhidharma* teachings, the individual "facts" or "truths" of existence in this world.
dhikr	A Sufi devotional practice designed to heighten one's awareness of God.
dhimmi	Formerly, a non-Muslim living in Muslim-controlled lands and paying a head tax for Muslim protection.
Diaspora	A term for Jews living outside the land that God promised to Abraham.
Dome of the Rock	A shrine built in the late seventh century commemorating Muhammad's ascent to God; located in Jerusalem on the Temple Mount.
dukkha	The dissatisfaction and suffering that Buddhism teaches is inherent in all life.
Easter	The annual celebration of Christ's bodily resurrection from the dead.
Eastern Orthodoxy	One of three major types of Christianity, having its origins in the eastern part of the Roman empire (see Roman Catholicism and Protestantism).
ecumenism	A unifying movement that began in the twentieth century whereby different denominations and churches join in common causes.

Eid	One of two major festivals in the Islamic calendar, one following the annual time of the Hajj (Eid al-Adha), one following the Ramadan fast (Eid al-Fitr).
Eight Trigrams	The eight possible combinations of three *yin* lines and three *yang* lines, used for divination in the Chinese *Classic of Change*.
empiricism	A theory of knowledge that requires scientific proof for anything to be considered true.
eucharist	A stylized meal of bread and wine through which Christians experience the blood and body of the crucified and risen Christ.
evangelism	The promotion of the Christian message (gospel) to non-Christians in an effort to convert them.
Exodus	The departure of the Israelites from Egypt under the leadership of Moses.
fatwa	A nonbinding legal ruling on a matter pertaining to Islam not sufficiently covered by Sharia.
fengshui	The Chinese art of arranging things and space to achieve the optimal flow of *qi*.
filial piety	The most important virtue in Confucianism, the obligation of a child to a parent.
first contacts	Western explorers' first experiences and reports of Oceania, which often distorted or changed the cultures and religions they depicted.
Five Classics	An early body of Chinese scripture that included five traditional writings: the *Classics of Documents*, *Change*, and *Poetry*, the *Record of Ritual*, and the *Spring and Autumn Annals*.
Five Flavors	The Chinese flavors associated with the Five Phases: sour, bitter, sweet, acrid, salty.
Five Phases	The five basic Chinese modes of *qi* under the influence of *yin* and *yang*: water, metal, fire, wood, earth.
Five Pillars	Five defining actions that are obligatory for all Muslims: profession of faith, daily prayer, almsgiving, the Ramadan fast, and the pilgrimage to Mecca.
Five Relationships	Five human relationships that Confucius held to be essential for all human interaction.
focal area	In Oceania, an area within a community that is marked as being particularly efficacious.
Four Noble Truths	A summary of the Buddha's teaching that comprises four foundational truths about the world.
Four Sights	An old man, a sick man, a corpse, and an impoverished holy man; the four things Siddhartha Gautama (later the Buddha) saw that began his search for truth.
fuda	Prayer slips or talismans available for purchase at Japanese temples and shrines.
fundamentalist	A Christian committed to the authority of the Bible above all other truths.
Gelede festival	The harvest festival for the Great Mother in Yoruba.
general *dharma*	Religious duties incumbent upon all Hindus.
genze riyaku	Practical benefits given by gods to human beings to enhance their lives in this world. Central to Japan's lived religion.
geoglyph	Lines or images drawn on the earth, as at Nazca in southwestern Peru.

Global South	Christian populations living in areas south of the equator; now the largest contingent in Christianity.
Gods of Good Fortune	The gods of longevity, prosperity, and progeny; found in most Chinese temples.
gospel	"Good news"; the Christian message of salvation; also the name of the first four books of the New Testament.
Great Schism	The separation of the Roman Catholic and Eastern Orthodox churches in 1054 CE.
Great Ultimate	In Chinese religion, the universal ebb, flow, and balance of *yin* and *yang*.
Guandi	A Chinese god of great spiritual power (*ling*) and a patron of many professions, including law enforcement.
Guanyin	A female form of the *bodhisattva* of compassion, Avalokiteshvara, popular in China.
Guanyin Pusa	"Hearer of Cries," a popular female *bodhisattva* popular in China, concerned especially with women and children.
Gubbi Gubbi	The Aboriginal people of southeastern Queensland in Australia who have promoted the protection of their ecosystem through religious rituals.
Gye Nyame	"Except God!"; a phrase used by the Asante of Ghana to honor the Supreme Being, expressing the notion that some things are unknowable or undoable except by God.
hadith	Witnessed reports of what Muhammad said and did during his life.
haiden	A worship hall at a Shinto shrine where gods come to hear prayers and be honored by ceremonies.
Hajj	One of the Five Pillars of Islam; the pilgrimage to Mecca that Muslims make during the eighth month of the Islamic year.
halakhah	Jewish religious law and legal traditions.
Han	The predominate ethnic group of China, which practices Chinese religion; also, a dynasty that reigned from 206 BCE to 220 CE.
Han synthesis	A synthesis of Confucianism, Daoism, and *yin–yang* theory under the Han dynasty.
Hasidic movement	A popular movement in Judaism that emphasizes personal piety and joy in human relations, making God accessible through the practice of "cleaving to God."
hierophany	The term used by Mircea Eliade for a manifestation of the sacred.
hijra	The emigration of Muslims from Mecca to Medina in 622 CE.
Hinayana	"Lesser Vehicle"; a demeaning name used in the *Lotus Sutra* to describe the Buddhism of the Pali Canon.
Holocaust	"Burnt offering"; a term for the murder of millions of Jewish civilians by the Nazis during World War II (see *Shoah*).
Holy Spirit	One of three persons of the Christian godhead, or Trinity.
honden	The structure in which a Japanese god's *shintai* is kept; the focal point of a shrine.
huacas	In Andean religions, either deities, or objects and places in the landscape that give access to their power.
hula	A traditional dance ritual in Hawai'i performed to celebrate nature and community and to honor important beings.
hun souls	In Chinese religion, the rational, or *yang*, aspect of human consciousness; one of two types of human souls found in each person.

icon	A two-dimensional image of Jesus or the saints.
ideal types	Idealized or generalized models of important elements found in many or all religions. Used by Max Weber to compare religions to one another.
ihai	A Japanese memorial tablet on which the posthumous name of a deceased person is inscribed.
image hall	The structure at a Buddhist temple in which the image of a Buddha or *bodhisattva* is displayed; the focal point of a temple.
Imam	Among Sunnis, the person who directs prayers at the mosque; in Shia Islam, one of several inspired leaders descended from Muhammad, beginning with Ali.
Imami	The largest sect of Shia Islam; also known as the Twelvers.
immanent	"Close by"; used to describe gods that dwell near human communities and are active in human affairs.
Indra	The king of the Hindu gods in the *Collections*.
ishta-deva	The Hindu deity chosen as the focus of one's religious devotion.
internal logic	A system of meaning unique to a particular religion that determines how one orients oneself and others to what is supreme or ultimate.
Islam	Literally "submission"; submission to God, which is the principal characteristic of the religion.
isnad	In Islam, the chain of witnesses that accompanies each *hadith*.
Israel	"Struggles with God"; the name given to Jacob, the grandson of Abraham, which later became the name for the ancient and modern Jewish nation.
Jade Emperor	The highest deity in the Chinese celestial bureaucracy.
jahiliyyah	A period of spiritual ignorance in Arab history; also used by reformist Muslims to describe the state of spiritual ignorance among fellow Muslims.
jati	"Birth"; the Hindu word translated into English as "caste."
Jesus of Nazareth	Founder of Christianity; held by Christians to be God's son and messiah.
jihad	Literally "struggle"; used in to describe the human effort needed to conform to God's will; sometimes refers to armed struggle against Islam's enemies.
Jizo	A popular Japanese *bodhisattva* known for protecting travelers and children.
jnana	Hindu divine knowledge.
Jnana-Yoga	A spiritual discipline in Hinduism for attaining divine knowledge (*jnana*).
junzi	"Gentleman," the word chosen by Confucius to designate the superior person.
Kabah	Literally "Cube"; the holiest shrine in the Muslim world, located in Mecca; Muslims must turn toward the Kabah during daily prayer.
Kabbalah	The Jewish mystical tradition.
kami	A Shinto god or divine force.
kamidana	Literally a "god shelf"; a home altar used in Japan to worship family and household gods.
karma	The good and bad consequences of one's actions.
Kitchen God	A minor Chinese deity who reports to the Jade Emperor after observing a family's interaction in the kitchen for a year.

kivas	Underground ritual chambers used by Pueblo peoples in the southwestern United States.
kofun	Large earthen memorials constructed in Japan for rulers between 300–550 CE.
kosher	A Jewish designation for food that is edible according to *halakhah*.
Krishna	A popular *avatar* of the Hindu god Vishnu.
lama	An accomplished spiritual leader in Tibetan Buddhism.
Lent	In Christianity, the 40-day period of solemn reflection and abstinence that precedes Easter.
li	The etiquette or protocol in Chinese religion that governs each human relation.
liminal	In rites of passage, the experience of being in between what one was and what one will be.
ling	In Chinese religion, the state of being spiritually powerful.
lingam-yoni	A popular *murti* of the Hindu god Shiva.
Lord Lao	The deified sage Laozi, the putative author of Daoism's *Daode Jing*.
Mahabharata	The longest of India's two epic poems; composed ca. 300 BCE–300 CE
Mahayana	"Great Vehicle"; one of the three branches of contemporary Buddhism.
Mahdi	The "rightly guided one"; a future leader of the Islamic community expected to appear before the final judgment.
Maitreya	The Buddha that is to come into the world when people have forgotten Gautama Buddha's Dharma.
mana	A sacred power distributed among Pacific Island people by their sky gods and culture heroes.
mandala	A diagram used in Buddhism as a spiritual and psychological map to salvation.
Mandate of Heaven	The belief in early China that a ruler's right to govern required Heaven's approval.
mantras	Sacred formulas chanted at rituals in Hinduism and Buddhism.
Maori	The indigenous people of Aotearoa.
Mary	The mother of Jesus and the principal saint in Catholic and Orthodox Christianity.
mass	The Catholic name for the eucharist.
materialist empiricism	A theory of knowledge that not only demands scientific proof for establishing truth, but also denies the reality of anything that is not physical matter (i.e., anything spiritual or divine).
matsuri	A Japanese festival in which a god is carried through a town or neighborhood in a portable shrine to bless the people of the area.
matzah	A crisp, unleavened bread eaten during the Jewish Passover.
Maya	Indigenous people in Mexico and Central America.
medium	A religious specialist who conveys messages from the unseen world when possessed by a spirit.
Meiji period	The reign of Emperor Mutsuhito (1868–1912), which brought the imperial family back to power and made important changes to religion in Japan.
Melanesia	"Area of black islands"; includes New Guinea, the Solomon Islands, Vanuatu (New Hebrides), New Caledonia, and Fiji.
Mencius	An important early interpreter of Confucian principles.

meridians	In Chinese religion and medicine, channels by which *qi* moves through the human body.
Mesoamerica	The ancient cultural area extending from southern Mexico to Costa Rica. Home to the Maya and the Aztecs, among others.
messiah	Hebrew for "anointed one"; usually a king, but also a priest or a kingly person in the service of God; most Jews hold that a messiah will appear in the future. Translated into Greek as "Christ," the title given to Jesus of Nazareth, the founder of Christianity.
Micronesia	"Area of small islands"; the archipelago defined by the Gilbert Islands in the southeast and the Mariana Islands in the northwest.
mikoshi	A portable shrine used in Japanese festivals called *matsuri*.
mikveh	A small pool for ritual bathing used in Judaism.
Miraj	Muhammad's ascent to God during his Night Journey.
Mishnah	The earliest work of rabbinic literature, a compendium of Jewish legal teachings from the early third century CE.
mitzvot	Both "commandments" and "good deeds"; plural of *mitzvah*; actions prescribed by God in the Jewish Torah.
mizuko kuyo	A Japanese funeral service for fetuses who die in childbirth or through abortion.
Modern-Orthodox	A version of Orthodox Judaism that favors some accommodations to modern life.
moksha	In Hinduism, release from the karmic world.
monism	The Hindu vision of ultimate reality as a single impersonal principle that pervades everything.
Moses	The Israelite prophet who led the Exodus and to whom God revealed the commandments of the Torah.
mosque	A Muslim prayer hall (Arabic: *masjid*).
moxibustion	The Chinese practice of heating various parts of the body with smoldering mugwort to manipulate a person's flow of *qi*.
murti	A consecrated image used by Hindu gods to interact with worshippers.
Muslim Brotherhood	A grassroots Salafi movement with political aspirations, found in Egypt and elsewhere in the Middle East.
New Age	A spirituality that looks forward to the dawning of a new era in human moral development and spirituality.
New Fire Ceremony	An Aztec ceremony performed every 52 years to renew the world.
new religious movement (NRM)	A group formed for the purpose of sharing novel religious beliefs and practices. Occasionally these groups develop into new religions.
Nichiren	The thirteenth-century founder of Nichiren Buddhism, which stresses the importance of the *Lotus Sutra* above all else.
Night Journey	Muhammad's spiritual journey from Mecca to Jerusalem on a winged horse named Buraq.
Night of Power	The night of Muhammad's first revelation from God.
nirvana	The Buddhist goal of extinguishing this life; liberation from *samsara*.
Noble Eightfold Path	Eight actions and attitudes in Buddhism that one must practice to attain release from *samsara*.
Nobles	The second-ranking class in traditional Hindu society.
Nok sculptures	Terra cotta figurines from central Nigeria depicting humans and animals; perhaps used to communicate with the spirit world, forces of nature, and culture heroes.

numinous	Rudolf Otto's term for describing the experience of the Holy as overwhelming, terrifying, mysterious, and irresistible all at once.
obon	A three-day Japanese Buddhist festival in August that welcomes and entertains the souls of the dead.
Oceania	The land masses of Australia and the Pacific islands, the latter comprising Polynesia, Micronesia, and Melanesia.
omamori	Traditionally, small pouches available for purchase at Japanese temples and shrines that contain a request for a *genze riyaku*.
origin stories	Indigenous accounts of how the present world came to be.
Orthodox Judaism	A branch of Judaism that regards the Torah as divinely revealed truth, and the Talmud as sacred and authoritative (see Conservative and Reform Judaism).
Oshun	A powerful goddess among the Yoruban.
outcaste	An older term for *dalit*; impure persons excluded from traditional Hindu society.
Pali Canon	The early threefold Buddhist scripture written in Pali, consisting of the *Sutra-*, *Vinaya-*, and *Abhidharma-pitakas*; see *Tri-pitaka*.
parables	Various kinds of comparisons used by Jesus in his teaching.
Passover	The annual commemoration of God's redemption of the Israelites from Egyptian slavery.
patriarch	A principal leader in the Orthodox church.
payback	A term for the religious principles of reciprocity and redistribution among Pacific Islanders.
penance	A Christian ritual of confession; also an act of contrition necessitated by sin.
Pentecostalism	A movement within Christianity in which Christians receive miraculous gifts from the Holy Spirit, including the ability to speak in spiritual languages.
People of the Book	A Muslim designation for Muslims and other monotheists who have a sacred scripture (Jews, Christians, Zoroastrians).
phenomenology	An approach to religion that attempts to explain religion on its own terms, as it "presents itself" to the human psyche. Associated especially with the work of Rudolf Otto and Mircea Eliade.
po souls	In Chinese religion, the source of bodily strength and movement, characterized by *yin*; one of two types of human souls found in each person.
Polynesia	"Area of many islands"; includes Hawai'i, Easter Island, Aotearoa, Samoa, Tonga, Tahiti, and others.
pope	The bishop of Rome and leader of the Roman Catholic church.
power embedded in place	A central element of Oceanian religions that defines "place" as both geography and community.
prasad	In Hinduism, a gift received from a *murti*.
priest	In Christianity, a type of ordained church leader found in many forms of Christianity.
primordium	The earliest period of the world in the origin stories of Indigenous Americans, when supernaturals were active, power was wielded freely, and chaos reigned.
Prince of Martyrs	In Isalm, a title given to Husayn, the second son of Ali and a focus of Shia theology and identity.

progressive reform movement	An attempt to modernize or update one's religion.
prophet	A spokesperson for the divine world; in Judaism and Christianity, inspired by God's Spirit.
Prophet Muhammad	In Islam, God's last messenger to humankind, who delivered God's message without error (the Quran) and lived a perfect life.
Protestant Reformation	A sixteenth-century reform movement in Europe which gave birth to Protestant Christianity.
Protestantism	One of three major types of Christianity, having its origins in the Reformation (see Eastern Orthodoxy and Roman Catholicism).
pueblos	Towns in southwestern United States consisting of large complexes of rooms, much like apartment buildings.
puja	In Hinduism, worship in which such things as fruit and flowers are offered to a *murti*. In Buddhism, the veneration of images.
Puranas	A literature that first appeared in Hinduism ca. 350 CE; used as devotional texts for worshipping Hinduism's three great deities.
Pure Land	A paradise created by Amitabha Buddha for the salvation of his devotees.
Pure Land Buddhism	A school of Buddhism that teaches that one can be reborn into Amitabha's Western Paradise (Pure Land) by practicing devotion to him.
qi	The most basic "stuff" of the universe in Chinese religion.
Quran	The most authoritative scripture in Islam, being the very words of God delivered in Arabic to humankind by Muhammad.
rabbi	The teacher, pastor, and leader of a Jewish community; usually a scholar of Torah and rabbinic literature.
Rainbow Snake	The principal creative spirit of the Aboriginal landscape.
Rama	A popular *avatar* of the Hindu god Vishnu; the hero of the *Ramayana*.
Ramadan	The ninth month of the Islamic year, during which Muslims fast during daylight hours.
Ramayana	One of India's two epic poems; composed ca. 200 BCE–200 CE.
reactive reform movement	An attempt to return to a purer, earlier form of one's religion.
reciprocity	An important religious principal in Indigenous American religions that promotes the proper flow of spiritual power between human and nonhuman peoples.
reductionism	A method for studying religion that first defines it as really being something other than religion.
Reform Judaism	A branch of Judaism that understands the Torah as an authoritative but not definitive guide to religion, and the Talmud as having only marginal importance (see Orthodox and Conservative Judaism).
reincorporation	The third and final part of a rite of passage, when someone emerges from the seclusion (liminal) stage with a new identity and is integrated back into society.
religion	The human activity of orientation to what is supreme or ultimate.
religions	Symbolic systems by which people orient themselves to a particular vision of what is supreme or ultimate.
ren	The Chinese virtue of humaneness or "human heartedness."
Rig-Veda	The earliest and most authoritative part of the Hindu Veda.

rites of passage	Rituals undertaken by individuals at important junctures in life to reaffirm their connection to their community and its gods and spirit beings.
ritual tools	Ritual objects such as sacred bundles, masks, pipes, and rattles by which religious leaders gain access to the spirit world.
Roman Catholicism	One of three major types of Christianity, having its origins in the western part of the Roman empire; headed by the bishop of Rome (the pope). (See Eastern Orthodoxy and Protestantism.)
Sabbath	The day of the week on which Judaism prohibits work, beginning Friday evening and concluding Saturday evening.
sacrament	A Christian ritual which imparts a special grace from God. Some churches recognize seven sacraments, others recognize only baptism and the eucharist.
sacred bundles	In indigenous American religions, objects to which spirit-persons are tethered, collected together in a pouch or bundle.
Salafis	Reformers who look back to the first generations of Muslims as their guide for reform.
samsara	"Flowing around." In Hinduism and Buddhism, the beginningless, meaningless cycle of birth, death, and rebirth controlled by karma.
samskaras	Hindu rituals performed at different stages of a person's life.
sandek	In Judaism, a grandfather or rabbi who holds a male baby on his lap during circumcision.
Sangha	The Buddhist community, composed of men and women, monastics and laypersons.
Sapa Inca	The Inca emperor.
Satsang	A loose network of enlightened teachers that demands no commitment to any one teacher.
schism	A split within a religion that results in new divisions.
Scholasticism	A form of scholarship begun in Catholicism in the twelfth century that sought to create a unified understanding of the world.
seclusion	The first stage in a rite of passage, when initiates are separated from their previous roles in society.
Second Vatican Council	A council of Roman Catholic bishops convened in the 1960s to address the challenges of modernity and pluralism.
Seder	The Jewish Passover meal.
seekers	Persons looking for religious experiences apart from membership in mainstream, established religions.
seekers' milieu	The subculture of seekers that offers opportunities to experiment with elements of many unconventional religions.
Sephardim	Jews who trace their roots to Spain.
Servants	The lowest-ranking class in traditional Hindu society.
Shahadah	The Muslim profession of one's faith through the formula: "There is no god but God, and Muhammad is the Messenger of God"; the first of the Five Pillars.
Shaivas	Devotees of the Hindu god Shiva.
Shaktas	Devotees of the Hindu goddess Devi.
shakti	The creative power of the universe; an aspect of the Hindu goddess Devi.
shaman	A religious leader who has many spirit helpers and who can travel into the spirit world.

Sharia	The Islamic way of life, often called Islamic law; established by legal scholars, it pertains largely to marriage, inheritance, and religious duties.
shaykh	In Islam, a Sufi spiritual master; also known as a *pir* or *murshid*.
Shema	A Jewish statement of faith from the Torah, recited as part of morning and evening prayers.
Shia	One of two principal types of Islam, comprising 10–15 percent of the Muslim world; it sees Ali and his descendants as having a divine authority comparable to Muhammad's.
shide	Slips of white paper folded in a zigzag pattern, indicating the presence of Japanese deities.
shimenawa	In Japan, a festoon, or length of rope, marking off sacred space.
shintai	An aspect of nature or a manufactured object that embodies a Japanese god. Often a sword or mirror.
Shinto	Literally, "the way of the gods." The current name for religious traditions associated with Japanese shrines.
Shiva	One of three great deities in Hinduism.
Shoah	"Destruction"; a name for the Holocaust currently preferred by many Jews.
shogun	A military dictator who commands *daimyo*. The shogunate form of government first appeared in Japan during the Kamakura period (1185–1333).
Shulchan Arukh	The definitive compendium of the Jewish *halakhic* code, published in 1565 and expanded to its final form in the following decades.
Siddhartha Gautama	The name of the man who became the Buddha; the founder of Buddhism.
sila	The Buddhist practice of keeping ethical precepts.
similarity	One of two principles by which James Frazer explained how magic was thought to work (see "contagion"). Magic based on similarity assumes that that similar things exercise sway over one another.
song line	In the religions of Oceania, one part of a larger story that situates people and places with respect to the creative work of the spirits as they passed through the land.
soul loss	In indigenous American religions, a condition that can occur during dreams and which can lead to death.
spirit darts	Weapons used by dark shamans to inflict pain, illness, and death on their victims.
Spirit Lodge	In indigenous religions in the Americas, a small gathering in an enclosed space heated with hot rocks, during which the participants commune with spirits and prepare for ceremonies and group decisions.
spirit master	In indigenous religions in the Americas, a principal spirit who oversees an animal or plant species or multiple species.
spirit money	Currency sent to the spirit world in Chinese religion to help the deceased garner favors or bribe minor gods.
spirit tablet	In Chinese religion, the final resting place of *hun* souls; placed on a family altar or in the clan's ancestral shrine.
spiritual centers	Religious sites in pre-European America with earthen mounds, *kivas*, pyramid temples, and plazas, where indigenous people met to worship and exchange spiritual goods and services.

Stations of the Cross	Fourteen images that depict the last hours of Jesus' life, including his crucifixion and burial.
Stolen Generations	Aboriginal children who were taken away from their parents so they could be assimilated to settler culture.
study of religions	An academic discipline that investigates one or more religions for no other reason than to understand the nature of religion and religious people; as opposed to theology.
stupa	In Buddhism, a building or model of a building (especially on altars) containing a relic or precious object.
Sufism	Sunni Islam's mystical tradition.
sui generis	"In a class of its own." An expression used by phenomenologists of religion to describe the unique nature of religion.
sunnah	In Islam, "tradition"; especially the tradition of the Prophet's life as recorded in the Hadith; origin of the name Sunni.
Sunni	One of two principal types of Islam, followed by 85–90 percent of all Muslims.
sunyata	"Emptiness"; an understanding of nirvana developed by Mahayana Buddhism.
Supreme Being	The creator and source of all life in most African communities.
the supreme or ultimate	The focal point of religion and religions; that which is the most important, real, and true in someone's life.
sutra	A Buddhist sacred writing chanted at temple rituals. Popularly understood as containing magical incantations.
Sutra-pitaka	"Basket of Discourses"; a collection of the Buddha's teachings, being the first division of the early Buddhist scriptures (see *Tri-pitaka* and Pali Canon).
symbol	The means by which people orient themselves to what is supreme or ultimate; depending on the religion, a symbol can be practically anything.
synagogue	A building where Jews meet for worship, containing a *bimah* and a handwritten, leather Torah scroll.
syncretism	The fusion of elements from different religions.
tabernacle	A locked case where Catholic and Orthodox Christians store uneaten bread from the eucharist.
taboo	In the religions of Oceania, the restrictive force that prevents *mana* from being depleted or monopolized. English for *tapu*.
taiji quan	Exercises of patterned breathing and fluid movement of the body that bring one into harmony with cosmic patterns; widely practiced in China.
tallit	A Jewish prayer shawl with tassels at its corners, made according to *halakhic* specifications.
Talmud	In Judaism, a compendium of rabbinic teachings compiled in the fifth and sixth centuries CE; it exists in a Jerusalem and a Babylonian version, the latter being considered authoritative.
tamagushi	Fresh branches of sakaki tied with *shide* and used in Shinto rituals as a purifying wand and as an offering to a god.
Tanak	A designation for the Jewish scriptures; an acronym created from the Hebrew words for Torah, Prophets, and Writings.
Tantras	Practices of asceticism and meditation in Hinduism and Buddhism; texts that contain information about these practices.

Tara	A female divinity in Tibetan Buddhism.
tariqah	In Sufism: a spiritual path to God; a Sufi order; the teachings and practices of a particular Sufi master.
tawhid	"Oneness"; the principal attribute of the Muslim God, which suffuses his creation and establishes a pattern for human actions and society.
tefillin	Small black leather boxes containing passages from the Torah that are strapped to the arm and forehead during morning prayer in Judaism.
Terra Australis Incognita	"Unknown south land"; a Latin term Europeans used in the sixteenth century to describe the lands they were colonizing in Oceania.
terra nullis	"Empty land"; a Latin term Europeans used for Australia to justify their colonization of the continent.
The Dreaming	The creative period during which the Australian Rainbow Snake was active.
the Law	The responsibility in Oceanian religions to preserve the primal order and harmony that was established during The Dreaming.
theism	Ultimate reality envisioned as a god or gods.
theology	An academic discipline that explains, develops, and justifies one's own religion; as opposed to the study of religions.
theosis	The process by which Orthodox Christians achieve divinity.
Theravada	"Teaching of the Elders"; one of the three branches of contemporary Buddhism.
the supreme or ultimate	The focal point of a religion; what is the most important, real, and true in someone's life.
Thirst Dance	In indigenous religions in the Americas, a ritual undertaken for the benefit of a community and world renewal, during which individuals dance for four days in a slow circle around a central pole without food or drink.
Three Jewels	Also known as the Three Refuges of Buddhism: the Buddha, the Dharma, and the Sangha.
Three Teachings	Confucianism, Daoism, Buddhism, each of which contributes to Chinese religion.
Torah	"Teaching, tradition"; the first five books of the Tanak.
Torah ark	In contemporary Judaism, an ornate cabinet that holds one or more Torah scrolls, usually placed at the front of the sanctuary in a synagogue.
torii	The gateway that marks the entrance to a Japanese shrine, consisting of two upright posts joined by one or two horizontal beams.
totem	The identifying emblem of a particular indigenous people, often a species of plant, animal, or bird.
traditional patterns of change	Reactive and progressive movements; schism and syncretism.
trance	Spirit possession, especially by mediums, leading to communication from the spirit world.
transcendent	"Far off" or "far above"; used to describe the Supreme Being's remoteness from humans.
transition	The second part of a rite of passage, when initiates leave their former identity behind in preparation for receiving a new identity.

Tri-pitaka	"Three Baskets"; the early threefold Buddhist scripture, consisting of the *Sutra-*, *Vinaya-*, and *Abhidharma-pitakas* (see Pali Canon).
trickster	A clever, mischievous god or spirit who mediates between the human and spirit worlds, usually causing confusion or worse.
Trinity	The three persons of the Christian Godhead: God, Christ, and the Holy Spirit.
Tudi Gong	"Lord of the Earth," a popular minor Chinese god who watches over villages and neighborhoods.
tzitzit	The tassels on the four corners of a *tallit* (Jewish prayer shawl); also a fringed undergarment.
ulama	Muslim legal scholars who "discover" Sharia through their study of the Quran and the Hadith.
Ultra-Orthodox	A version of Orthodox Judaism that favors a strict application of biblical and Talmudic teachings.
Umayyad dynasty	The first Islamic dynasty, established after the death of the fourth caliph.
ummah	The Muslim community, established by Muhammad in 622 CE and characterized by God's oneness (*tawhid*).
Untouchable	An older Hindu term for *dalit*.
Upanishads	Late texts of the Hindu Veda that contain ideas about karma, rebirth, and renunciation.
Uthmanic Codex	The Arabic text of the Quran as established by the caliph Uthman (d. 656) and now accepted by Muslims as definitive.
Vaishnavas	Devotees of the Hindu god Vishnu.
Vajrayana	"Thunderbolt/Diamond Vehicle"; one of the three branches of contemporary Buddhism; sometimes treated as a form of Mahayana.
Veda	The most authoritative collection of Hindu scripture, comprising the *Collections*, the *Brahmanas*, the *Aranyakas*, and the *Upanishads*.
Vedanta	Literally, "end of the Veda." A name for the *Upanishads*, the last scriptures to be added to the Vedic canon.
Vinaya-pitaka	"Basket of Discipline"; the Buddhist teachings on monastic discipline, being the second division of the early Buddhist scriptures (see *Tri-pitaka*).
Vishnu	One of the three great deities of Hinduism.
vision quest	A ritual undertaken in indigenous American religions to establish a lasting personal relationship with a spirit person.
vital force	In African religions, the life-giving power of the universe, distributed according to a hierarchy of beings and returned to the Supreme Being after death.
vocation	A particular line of work or holy lifestyle to which Christians feel called by God.
Wicca	A modern spiritual movement that uses elements associated with pre-Christian traditions from Europe.
wu wei	The Daoist principle of not taking any action contrary to the Dao; "doing without ado."
yakudoshi	In Japan's lived religion, "calamitous years." The years in a person's life considered particularly dangerous and requiring the protective services of a Buddhist or Shinto priest.

Glossary of Key Terms

yang	In Chinese religion, one of the two states of *qi*, characterized by bright, active, male attributes; the opposite of *yin*.
yangsheng	Chinese regimes of exercise and diet that nurture life.
yantra	A two-dimensional geometrical design used as an image of the Hindu goddess Devi.
yin	In Chinese religion, one of the two states of *qi*, characterized by dark, passive, female attributes; the opposite of *yang*.
yoga	A Hindu spiritual discipline using breath control and body posturing.
Yom Kippur	The Jewish Day of Atonement, which comes on the tenth day of the new year.
zakat	Obligatory charitable giving to the poor. One of the Five Pillars of Islam.
Zen	The Japanese form of Chan Buddhism.
Zhuangzi	An early writing of Daoism.
Zionism	A nineteenth- and twentieth-century nationalistic movement that lobbied for a Jewish homeland.
Zohar	The *Book of Splendor*, an important work of medieval Jewish mysticism.

Index

Abbasid dynasty 466–7, 469–71, 473
Abhidharma 70, 74
Abhidharma-pitaka 72, 74, 104
Aborigines 242, 258
abortion 101, 199, 446
Abraham 3
   in Islam 452, 459, 464, 469, 485–6, 488
   in Judaism 334, 337, 339, 344–8, 364, 366, 379
Abu Bakr, Caliph 459, 462–3
Abu Talib 460
Accounts of Ancient Things (Kojiki) 171, 179
acupuncture 5, 136, 139
Adam 339, 350, 399, 404–5, 410, 422, 434, 459, 485–7, 515, 536
adulthood 34, 228–9, 264, 314, 373, 381
Advent 431
Adventist 393, 427, 430, 447, 519
African Initiated Church (AIC) 209, 519, 520
African religions
   contemporary beliefs and practices 210–36
   history 206–10
   western study of 209
afterlife 16, 29, 64, 105, 120, 121, 150, 183, 192–3, 207, 274, 330–2, 348, 382–3, 481

Age of Declining Dharma 173
aggadah 352, 366, 376
Agni 16, 18, 35
ahimsa 20, 71
Ahmadiyyah Islam 209
Ainu 170, 181
Akbar the Great 471
al-Ala Mawdudi, Sayyid Abu 457, 475–6
al-Aqsa Mosque 469, 470
al-Arabi, Ibn 466
al-Khwarizmi 473
al-Qaeda 479
Alawis 499–500
alchemy 138–9, 147, 559
Alevis 500
Alexander the Great 21, 349
Ali, Caliph, Imam 498, 501, 503
Alinesitoue, prophetess 235
Allah 483, 506
All-Father 459
All-Mother 459
All Saints' Day 300, 436–7
altar 13, 98, 99, 104, 105, 111, 115, 142, 151, 156, 162, 177, 182, 190, 192, 195, 200, 201, 219, 238, 283, 285, 289, 367, 420, 431, 436, 441, 446, 527
Amaterasu-Omikami 171, 179
Amida Buddha 85–6, 174–5
amidah 369, 382
Amish 447

Amitabha Buddha 78, 82–5, 99, 105
Amitofo 83
Amma 536–8
Amritanandamayi, Mata 536–7
amulet 156, 177, 186, 188, 191, 220, 496, 527
Anabaptists 414, 416
Analects 123–4, 132
an-atman 65, 66, 70, 90, 108
ancestors 35, 37, 119, 120, 122, 127, 129, 135, 142, 148–52, 154–6, 184, 193, 197, 200, 208, 212, 217–20, 222, 224, 227, 229, 231, 233, 235, 236, 242, 245, 247, 252, 258, 260–3, 266, 280, 281, 285, 289, 292, 299, 301, 306, 312, 324, 329, 333
Andean civilizations 285, 292, 298, 300
Andrew, St 441
androgyny 42, 213, 307, 309
Anglican church 210, 251, 253, 261, 393, 402, 415, 416, 420, 422, 428–30, 436, 442–4
animism 551–2
Anthology of Ten Thousand Leaves (Manyoshu) 171, 179
Antiochus Epiphanes IV 349

Understanding the Religions of the World: An Introduction, Second Edition.
Edited by Will Deming.
© 2025 John Wiley & Sons Ltd. Published 2025 by John Wiley & Sons Ltd.

antisemitism 363
ANZAC Day 255–6
Aotearoa (New Zealand) 241, 245, 249, 250, 252, 254–6
apostles 398, 419, 436, 439, 440
Apostles' Creed 400–1
Aquinas, Thomas 409, 466
Arab Baath Socialist Party 478
Arab League 478
Arab Spring 479
arati 39, 51, 53
archaic 478–9
archetypes 559
arhat 74, 75, 77, 79, 80, 99, 101
Arjuna 23, 25, 40, 41, 56, 513
Ark of the Covenant 346–7
Arrernte 556–7
Aryan 11, 13–17, 20, 29
  (*see also* Nobles)
Asase 216
asceticism 20, 42, 44–6, 65, 77, 80, 99, 178, 460, 467, 560
  (*see also* renunciation)
Asen 219
Ashikaga 175–6
Ashkenazim 354–5, 356
Ashoka 21–2, 71–2, 82
Ashura 484, 502
Ataturk, Mustafa Kemal 477
atheism 130, 156, 406, 546, 547
atman 17–20, 24, 33, 35, 44, 53, 55, 65
Augustine 404, 412, 413, 513
authority, charismatic, traditional, and legal-rational 562
auto-sacrifice 281, 284
automatic writing 178
Avalokiteshvara 86–7, 101, 155
avatar 9, 25, 26, 40–2, 50, 52, 172, 537
Avenue of the Dead 282–3, 288
Averroes 466
Avignon popes 411
axis mundi 568

Ayatollah 500
Ayers Rock 240
Aztecs 279, 282–5, 293, 296–7

Baal Shem Tov (Besht) 359–60
Baghdad 467, 469, 470, 473
Bahai 517, 521
Balfour Declaration 365
banyan tree 11, 19
baptism 6, 396, 398, 400, 410, 413, 424–6, 431, 432, 434, 436
  in the Holy Spirit 419, 426, 427
baraqah 496, 504–5
bardo 105
bar mitzvah 337, 382
bat mitzvah 382
bazi (the Eight Characters) 140
Benedict XVI, Pope 421
Benin 213, 219, 224
Bhagavad Gita (*Song of the Lord*) 23–5, 26, 40–2, 513
Bhagwan Shree Rajneesh 536
bhakti 27, 37–9, 47–9, 55, 81
Bible 22, 40, 251–2, 342, 356, 365, 366, 370, 382, 393, 398, 413–14, 416–18, 421, 422, 426, 428, 429, 438, 443, 455, 494, 517, 520, 533, 545, 546, 549, 561, 571
biblical interpretation 251–2, 346, 352, 371, 375, 377, 381, 383, 391, 413–14, 416–18, 420, 426, 428, 437–8, 444–5, 447, 448, 464, 517, 520, 533, 561, 564
bimah 368
bin Laden, Osama 479
birth 140, 227, 234, 263, 264, 313, 321, 459, 528, 536
bishop 117, 132, 392, 393, 400, 405, 411, 415, 421, 422, 443
BJP (Indian People's Party) 31–2

black headed priests 154–5
Blavatsky, Helena 521
Bo tree 65, 82
Bodhidharma 84
bodhisattva 76–8, 80, 83, 86, 98, 101, 103, 108, 155, 170, 171, 176, 177, 185–6, 188, 189, 193, 194
body of bliss 80, 101, 105
body of transformation 79, 110
Bön 86
Book of the Dead 105
Brahma 17, 40, 44, 50, 66
brahman 5, 17–20, 33, 36, 37, 42, 47, 53, 54
Brahmanas 17
Brahmins 11, 16–17, 20–21, 32, 34, 36, 40, 50
Brotherhood of the Cross and Star 520
buddha bodies 78–9
Buddha, the 25, 61, 64–9, 72–3, 74, 86, 89, 94, 98–100, 102–4, 169, 187, 514, 520
Buddhaghosa 76, 77
buddhas 76–80, 82, 85, 87, 101, 155, 165, 172, 184
Buddhism
  history 63–91
  contemporary beliefs and practices 91–108
  modern study of 87–8
bullroarer 263, 264
Bunya Dreaming Festival 254
burial 120, 121, 135, 150–1, 167–8, 232, 265, 274, 277, 288, 289, 292, 331, 383–4, 443, 490–1, 501
burqa 492–3
butsudan 98, 177, 182, 192
Byzantine empire 403, 404, 408, 458, 463, 471

Cahokia 276–8
Cahuachi 288–9

calamitous years 190–1
calendar, religious 65, 101, 139, 284, 292, 372, 460–1, 523, 527
caliph 463–5, 467, 480
calligraphy 86, 116, 468
Calvin, John 414, 440, 560
Candomblé 224, 226
Caodai 519
capacocha 293
capitalism 179, 296, 475, 548, 560–1, 563
cargo cults 253
Caro, Joseph 355
caste 20–1, 31, 470 (*see also* class)
Catholic Charismatic Renewal 301
Catholic Reformation 415
Catholicism 117, 132, 224, 226, 251, 301, 392–3, 413–15, 418, 420–1, 428–31, 434, 436, 440, 442–3, 476, 519, 560
Celestial Masters 119, 127
cenote 282
ceremonies of thanksgiving 190, 219, 309–12, 429, 439
Cerro Blanco 288, 289
chakras 47–8
Chamunda 46
Chan 82, 84–5 (*see also* Zen)
Changing Woman 311
chantaways 324
chanting 15, 16, 27, 34, 35, 38, 42, 47, 49, 51, 55, 71, 81, 86, 98–9, 103–5, 188, 192, 324–5, 347, 366, 369, 506
charismatic movements 177, 178, 182, 187, 301, 420, 422, 426, 439, 442, 536
Chavin de Huantar 287
Chiang Kai-Shek 130
Chichen Itza 282
children 31, 35, 78, 94, 101, 142–3, 148–50, 155, 186, 194–5, 218, 230, 249–50, 282, 293, 380, 381, 535–6
Chinchorro 292, 293
Chinese almanac 140
Chinese religion
 history 119–33
 contempory beliefs and practices 133–59
Chinese zodiac animals 139, 140
chrismation 426
Christ 390, 391, 397–8, 406, 409, 410, 413, 414, 416, 419, 424–5, 428–30, 436, 445, 447
Christian Science 393, 421, 513–14
Christianity
 history 395–422
 contemporary beliefs and practices 422–47
Christmas 177, 301
Chronicle of Japan (*Nihonshoki*) 171
church 392–3
Church of England *see* Anglican church
Church of Jesus Christ of Latter-day Saints (Mormons) 393, 418, 517–18, 521
Church of Jesus Christ on Earth 520
circumcision 228–9, 373, 380–81, 492
civil religion 255
class and life stage *dharma* 33–6
class, Hinduism 20–21
Clement V, Pope 411
Clonaid 533
Cluniac monasteries 407
Code of Manu 20
Codrington, R.H. 261
Cognitive Science of Religion (CSR) 572–3
Collections, the (Hinduism) 16, 20
collective unconscious 558–9
colonialism 28–9, 87, 88, 181, 210, 235, 416, 472, 476, 549–50, 559, 570
Columbus, Christopher 271, 294, 295
Commoners 20, 30, 34
communism 476
confirmation 410, 426
Confucianism 62, 116, 118, 127, 129, 130, 132–3, 168, 169, 176
Confucius 122–4, 131, 147, 148, 156
Conservative Judaism 341, 363, 370, 377
Constantine 402, 404
contagion, the principle of 554
Conversos 356
Cook Islands 241, 251
Cook, Captain James 247–8, 249
cooperation 303, 308–9, 312, 313, 323, 329
Copts 519
Corn Maiden 312
cosmology 16, 17, 44, 55, 70, 75–80, 122, 133–41, 147, 152–3, 156, 184, 210–12, 220, 322–3
covenant 339, 344–5, 347, 365–6, 381
cow 6, 36, 51, 96
creed 400–401
cremation 16, 35–6, 45
crucifixion 397, 398, 406, 423, 425, 436
Crusades 408–9, 469–70
cultural capital 535
Cultural Revolution 131, 132
culture hero 208, 257–8, 306, 311, 314, 326, 330
cupping 136–7

Cuzco 291–92, 293
cyclical time 26, 40, 569

d'Urville, Jules Dumond 241–2
Dahomey 213
daimyo 173, 175–6, 178
Dalai Lama 87, 90
dalit 31
dana 68, 95–7, 102, 104
danka 177, 179
Dao 84, 124–6, 133–4, 138–9, 147, 152, 562
Daode Jing 124–5, 127
Daoism 62, 116, 118, 124–6, 127, 133, 168, 169, 176, 519
dark shaman 324–5, 331
darshan 38
Darwin, Charles 89, 209, 547, 552–3
Day of Atonement (Yom Kippur) 359, 373, 374, 378
Day of the Dead 300, 535
Dead Sea Scrolls 350
death 17, 18, 21, 26, 29, 34–5, 42, 69, 78, 80, 99, 104–5, 120, 150–1, 152, 155, 170, 171, 182, 184, 191–2, 193, 218, 219, 228, 231–2, 248, 260, 264–6, 280, 294, 298, 322, 325, 331, 384, 398, 410, 422, 423, 443, 484, 490–1, 496, 502, 536–8
Decapitator God 288
deism 546, 547
Delhi Sultanate 28, 471
Democratic Republic of the Congo 209, 217, 236, 520
denomination 3, 209, 292–3, 416, 420, 422, 426, 429, 436, 437, 444, 446, 516, 517
devekut 360
Devi 9, 14, 25, 26, 37–9, 45–8, 51
devotional Hinduism 26–7, 38–9, 40, 45–7, 49
dharma 11, 20–5, 30, 32–6, 37

Dharma 66, 69–72, 74, 77–9, 83, 86, 88, 91, 92, 97–9, 101–6, 108, 155, 188
Dharma body 79
Dharma Cloud 80
Dharma eye 74
dharmas 70, 74, 75
dhikr 505–7
dhimmi 464
diaspora 224, 338, 348, 349, 352, 353, 454–5
Diego, Juan 300
diet 2, 5, 34, 37, 71, 81, 94, 96, 129, 137–8, 141–3, 145, 146, 227, 248, 355, 376–7, 430
Dionysius the Areopagite 404
Dipankara Buddha 77
disease of language 550, 551
dividing the body 197
divination 47, 104, 119–22, 129, 140–1, 143, 154, 167, 168, 207, 220, 224, 226, 233–5, 263, 264, 288, 314, 315, 321, 372, 373, 375–7, 397, 429, 484, 489, 524
divination slips 196, 197
Divine Light Mission 515
Divine Liturgy 429
divorce 230, 481, 490
Diwali 52–3
Dizang Pusa 155
Dogen 175
Dome of the Rock 469
domestic worship 20, 36–8, 50, 96, 98, 115, 117, 129, 177, 190, 196, 197, 221, 235, 351, 352, 369, 372, 375, 377, 380–1, 486, 499
Double Five 144–5
dragon boat races 145
dragon dance 143–4
Dreaming, The 247, 254, 258–9, 260, 265
dreidel 375

Dreyfus Affair 364
Druze 499
Duke of Zhou 122
dukkha 65, 66, 68, 70, 80, 90, 91, 96
dumplings 142–3
Durga 46, 51–2
Durkheim, Émile 555–7, 560, 563, 568
Dussehra 51–2

earth diver 305–6
Earth Goddess 100
Earthly Branches 114, 139
East India Company 28–9, 472, 550
Easter 301, 424, 431, 434–6
Easter Island (Rapa Nui), 241, 246
Eastern Orthodoxy 393, 404–7, 408, 410, 411, 425, 428, 431, 442, 443, 530, 536, 544
ecumenism 420
Eddy, Mary Baker 513–14
Edo (Tokyo) 176, 178, 179
education 97, 107, 122–4, 129, 130, 146, 148, 149, 209, 210, 216, 265, 291, 361, 415, 416, 420, 476, 490, 493, 535, 543, 546, 564, 570, 571
effigy mounds 275
Egungun festival 224
Egypt 292, 296, 345, 347–50, 365, 366, 372, 375, 376, 399, 453–4, 463, 465, 469, 477–9, 492, 496, 518, 522, 525, 528, 558, 566
Eid al-Adha 484, 489
Eid al-Fitr 484
Eisai 175
Eisenhower, Dwight 446
Elementary Forms of the Religious Life 555–6

Eliade, Mircea 567–9, 572
Elijah 357, 366, 381
El Mirador 280
ema 188–9
empiricism 546, 548–50, 564
    materialist empiricism 546
Empress of Heaven 158–9
Enlightenment, the 340, 341, 363, 364, 416, 420, 475, 515, 543, 545–7, 548, 549
Eshu 216, 217
Essenes 350
Esther 375
Ethiopia 208, 209, 229, 233
eucharist 390, 398, 402, 406, 409, 410, 413, 414, 420, 421, 426, 427, 429–30, 431, 432, 436, 444
European invasion 293–4, 298, 300
Evangelicals 251, 253, 416, 430, 437
evangelism 251, 443, 445–6, 447
Evans-Pritchard, E.E. 562–3
Eve 350, 404, 405, 410, 422, 486, 536
evolution 89, 209, 302, 418, 446, 523, 550–2, 553, 554, 560, 562, 563, 572
excommunication 407, 412, 546
exercise 89, 137, 152, 319
exile 348–9, 352, 358, 373, 515
Exodus 345, 366, 372, 374, 376, 424
exorcism 129, 154, 190, 303, 396, 397, 496
extraterrestrials 533, 534

Fackenheim, Emil 338
faith 85, 89, 174, 369, 372, 401, 410, 413–15, 418, 425, 426, 439, 442, 446, 473, 488, 564, 570
Falun Gong 132

Family Federation for World Peace and Unification 535
family life 50, 98, 99, 115, 124, 129, 133, 134, 141–2, 143, 145, 146, 149–51, 183, 184, 190, 193, 222, 230, 231, 266, 314, 375–6, 377–82, 444, 489–90, 535–6
Fanged Deity 288, 289
faqihs 481
fast of Ramadan 461, 481, 482, 484–5, 496
fasting 54, 220, 309, 314, 322, 325, 403, 413, 434, 481, 482, 484
Fatimid dynasty 469, 471
fatwa 493–4
Feast of the Hungry Ghosts 145
feast of Toxcatl 285
Feathered Serpent 280–3
Feinstein, Rabbi Moses 368
fengshui 114, 135–6, 149
Ferguson, Marilyn 523
fertility 143, 150, 167, 216, 221, 234, 242, 244, 277, 283–5, 290, 298, 300, 314, 317, 322, 379, 526, 554, 569
Fesl, Dr Eve 251
festival of Booths 374
festival of Purim 375
festivals, holy days 101–3
fields of merit 97
Fiji 242, 251
filial piety 124, 150, 152
final Judgment 157, 330, 419, 431, 464, 486–8, 497
first contacts xi, 248
Five Classics 120, 127
Five Flavors 137
Five Ms 48
Five Phases 122, 134, 135, 137, 140, 144
Five Pillars 482, 484, 485, 488
Five Relationships 148–50

focal area 263
food *see* diet
Four Noble Truths 66–8, 70, 90, 92
Four Sights 64
four sources of law 481–2
Francis of Assisi 410, 440
Francis, Pope 117, 421, 422
Frank, Jacob 358
Frankist movement 358
Frazer, James 209, 554–5, 562
Freud, Sigmund 547, 558–9, 565
Friendly Islands 247–8
Frum, John 253
fuda 197–8
fundamentalism 418, 421, 437, 479, 516
funeral rites *see* death
future, assessing the *see* divination

Gaddafi, General Muammar 476
Gandhi, Mohandas 30–1, 513
Ganesha 9, 14, 44–5, 50–2
Ganesh Chaturthi 50–1
Ganges River 6, 20, 44, 46, 49, 53, 81
Gardner, Gerald 526
Garuda 40
Gautama, Siddhartha 61, 64, 77–9, 81, 83, 84, 99, 118, 155
Gayatri *mantra* 34–5
Geertz, Clifford 562–4
Gelede festival 223
general *dharma* 36–7
Gentiles 39–40
genze riyaku 183, 186–9, 197, 198
geoglyphs 290
Ghana 212, 213, 216, 220, 227, 233, 234, 553
ghetto 356, 360, 409
Ghosh, Aurobindo 30

Ghost Dance 299
ghosts 35, 74, 91–3, 103, 142, 143, 145, 151, 152, 155, 156, 212, 231, 256, 263, 265, 324, 332
Gifford Lectures 565
Global South 421, 422, 444, 446
Gnostics 398–400, 516, 522, 559
goddess 6, 9, 13, 16, 22, 26, 36, 39, 40, 44–8, 51–3, 87, 100, 167, 171, 172, 179, 180, 213, 216–18, 222, 223, 227, 233, 252, 261, 277, 282, 291, 299, 300, 526–9, 537, 553, 554, 569
godparents 381
Gods of Good Fortune 155–6, 190
Gohonzon 86
Golden Bough, The 554–5
Golden Enclosure 291, 293
gomagi 198–99
Good Friday 434, 436
gospel 301, 390, 396, 398, 408, 416, 419, 428, 431, 432, 436, 438, 445, 446, 464, 513
Graham, Billy 446
grand theories of religion 551, 554, 555, 557, 564
Grave Sweeping Day 515
graves 121, 133, 135, 149, 151, 192, 193, 197, 283, 289, 301, 331, 401, 402, 437, 487, 490, 505
Great Dying, the 295
Great Mother 213, 223
Great Schism 407
Great Ultimate 134, 141
Gregorian reform 407
Gregory I, Pope (the Great) 406
Gregory III, Pope 406
Gregory VII, Pope 407
Gregory XI, Pope 411

groundbreaking ceremony 31–2, 195
Guandi 157
Guanyin, Pusa 155
Gubbi Gubbi 254–5
guia 226
guru 36, 39, 48, 53–5, 515, 531, 536, 562
Gye Nyame 212

Hachiman 164, 171
hadaka matsuri 191
Hadith 467, 468, 475, 481–2, 497, 498, 500, 503, 507
haggadah 376
haiden 185
Hajj 461, 485–9, 490, 493, 496, 501
halakhah 340, 341, 352, 355, 357, 366, 368, 377, 380
halal 489
Hallowell, A. Irving 272
hallucinogen 97, 272, 277, 287, 315–16, 322, 325
Han 115–18, 133
Han dynasty 127–8
Han synthesis 127–8
Hanafi school 491
Hand, Beverly 254–5
hand tremblers 324
hanif 458–9
Hanukah 350, 374–5
haram 485, 486, 489
harvest festivals 146, 187, 190, 219, 222, 223, 262, 308, 310, 318, 372, 374, 527
Hasidic movement 358–9, 360, 362, 365, 378, 383
Hasmonean dynasty 350 (*see also* Maccabees)
havdalah 372
Hawaii 132, 261
healers 48, 98, 136, 138, 172, 178, 190, 194, 196, 198,

209, 210, 221–5, 228, 231–5, 257, 260, 283, 299, 301, 307, 308, 310, 311, 317, 320, 323, 329, 359, 391, 397, 419, 420, 422, 423, 426, 442, 489, 504, 513, 520, 524, 555
Heart Sutra 188
Heavenly Stems 114, 139
Heaven's Gate 528–30
Hegel, G.W.F. 547–8
Heian-Kyo (Kyoto) 171, 173, 174
Heian period 171–3
Henry VIII, King of England 414
Herzl, Theodor 363–5
hesychia 410
hexagrams 140–41
Hezel, Francis 266
hierophany 568–9
high god 119–20, 556, 557
Higher Dharma movement 70
Hijaz 458
hijra 460, 461, 475
Hinayana 75, 76
Hindu Renaissance 29–31
Hinduism
 contemporary beliefs and practices 32–55
 history 12–32
Hirohito, Emperor 182
Hirsch, Samson Raphael 363
Hitler, Adolf 14, 338, 339
Hokkaido 167, 170, 181, 182
Holdheim, Rabbi Samuel 361
Holi 50
Holocaust 338, 364–5, 409, 515
Holy Land 346, 350, 352, 353, 365, 408, 409
Holy Order of MANS 530
Holy People 311, 324
Holy Spirit 244, 263, 301, 360, 397, 400, 401, 407, 417–19, 421–3, 425–8, 436, 442, 445

Holy, the 469–7, 568–9
Holy Week 300, 436
honden 185, 188
Hong Kong 132, 144, 147, 157
Hopewell 276
Hosea 347–8
huaca 285, 291, 292, 298–300
Huitzilopochtli 283
hula 261
hun souls 150, 151
Hundred Schools period 124
Hungry Ghosts, Feast of the 145
Husayn, Imam 466, 484, 501, 502
Hymn to Jizo of the River Beach of Sai 193

Iblis 487, 488
icon 406, 414, 431, 432, 441
iconoclasm 406, 410
iconostasis 431, 432
ideal type 561–2
idolatry 295, 339, 347, 383, 468, 545
Idowu, E. Bolaji 210
Ife 208
Ignatius of Loyola 415
ihai 192, 193
image hall 99, 184
Imam 483, 494, 499–503, 571
Imami Shiism 471, 499, 500
immanent 213, 215
immortals 139, 152
Inari 186, 187
Inca 285, 290–93, 295, 296
Indian 271
Indigenous religions in the Americas
  contemporary beliefs and practices 302–32
  history 273–302
  western study of 333
Indo-European 15
Indonesia 10, 28, 82, 88, 181, 251, 453, 454, 470, 472, 476, 493, 563

Indra 16, 22, 53, 104, 554
Indus Valley 13–15
Industrial Revolution 179, 547
infertility 230, 234, 236, 555
inheritance 332, 471, 473, 491
intercession of the saints 403, 439–41
internal logic x, xi, 5–7, 33, 97, 134, 559, 563
International Society for Krishna Consciousness (ISKCON) 53, 534, 535
internet 439, 493, 534
Inti 291, 292
investiture with the sacred thread 34, 35
Iran 453, 454, 458, 463, 471, 477, 490, 498, 499, 501, 502, 517
Iraq 256, 453, 454, 458, 462, 463, 465, 470, 471, 473, 478, 480, 490, 498, 501
Ishmael 342, 459, 469, 485, 486, 488
Ishta-deva 38
Ishvara 55
ISIS 457, 477, 479, 480
Islam 480
  contemporary beliefs and practices 480–507
  history 456–80
Islamists 479
Ismailis 469, 499
isnad 482
Isserles, Moses 355
Izanagi 179

Jade Emperor 142, 156, 158, 162
Jafari school 491, 500
Jäger, Willigis 515
jahiliyyah 456, 475
Jainism 14, 550
Jamarat 488
James, William 564–5, 566, 567
Janmastami 50

Japan's lived religion
  contemporary beliefs and practices 183–99
  history 166–83
jati 20
Jehovah 360
Jehovah's Witnesses 393, 418, 521, 531
Jerusalem 340, 341, 346–54, 363, 374, 379, 397, 402, 405, 408, 419, 433, 436, 460, 461, 469–71, 503
Jesuits 250, 415, 443
Jesus of Nazareth 6, 117, 176, 177, 244, 253, 299–301, 342, 350, 390, 391, 396–8, 400, 402, 406, 408, 410, 415, 417–19, 422–5, 430–34, 436, 438–41, 443, 445, 446, 448, 450, 452, 464, 469, 497, 513, 517, 520, 554
Jewish emancipation 360, 362, 364
Jewish Enlightenment 360–61, 362
Jewish Revolt, the 351–2, 515
Ji, Guru Maharaj 515
Jiao 147
Jigong 148, 151
jihad 473, 479–81
jinn 487–8
jitong 159
Jizo 101, 186, 193, 194
jnana 24, 53–5
Jnana-Yoga 54–5
John Paul II, Pope 421
John the Baptist 396, 463
John XXIII, Pope 420
Joshua 346, 366, 438
Jouret, Luc 532
Judah 347, 348
Judaism
  contemporary beliefs and practices 365–84

history 343–65
modern study of 341–2
Judges 346, 366
Jung, Carl 557–9
junzi 122, 123, 152

Kabah 452, 458–60, 462, 482, 485, 486, 489
Kabbalah 356–8, 383
kaimyo 192
Kali 46
Kalki 40
Kamakura period 173–5, 179
kami 164, 170–2, 175–7, 180, 187
kamidana 177, 182
kami-kaze 164
Kaminaljuyu 280
Kamo no Chomei 174
Kanetomo Yoshida 176
Kannon 101, 177, 186, 189
Karaite movement 353
karma 18–25, 32–7, 44, 48, 53, 55, 60, 65, 68, 70, 74, 77, 80, 88, 94–8, 105, 129, 172, 183, 197, 562
karmic orientation 96–105
Kenya 209, 210, 213, 215, 219, 227, 230–2, 422
Khadijah 458–60
Kharijites 465
khipu 296–7
khums 501
kiddush 372
Kimbangu, Simon 520
Kinai 169
king 16, 21–3, 28, 40, 52, 53, 61, 64, 71, 82, 104, 105, 119, 120, 122, 123, 145, 155, 215, 218, 233, 247–8, 263, 279, 281, 282, 284, 285, 291, 292, 342, 346–9, 367, 369, 375, 391, 406, 410, 414, 432, 438
King of Hell 156

kingdom of God 396, 397, 402, 445, 446, 466, 468, 513, 517, 543, 552, 554, 557
Kinjikitile 235
Kiribati 241, 251
Kitchen God 141, 142, 156, 162
kiva 278, 295, 323
Knights Templar 469
koan 84, 175
kofun 167–8
kosher 276–7
kowtow 142
Krishna 23–6, 40–2, 49, 50, 52, 53, 513, 531, 534, 535, 537, 571
Kukai 171, 189
Kundalini Yoga 47, 54, 55
kyoha shinto 181, 182, 187

Ladino 354
Lady in the Moon 146
Lakshmi 40, 41, 51, 52
lama 75, 84, 101, 103, 104, 106, 132
Land of Bliss Sutras 78, 83
Lantern Festival 143
Laozi 118, 127
Latter-day Saints (Mormons) 393, 418, 517–18, 521
La Venta 279–80
Law, the 258–60, 267
leather 21, 33, 373
lectio divina 437
lectionary 428, 436
Lent 434, 436
Leo III, Pope 406
Leo IX, Pope 407
Leo X, Pope 412
li 147
Li Bai 146
liberation theology 302, 421
Libya 399, 476–9
liminal 226
ling 152, 155, 157
lingam 42–3, 44, 49

lingam-yoni 42–3
lion dance 143–4
liturgy 42, 147, 355, 361, 369, 375, 382, 427–9, 441
lived religion 165
Lombard, Peter 410
Lord Lao 127
Lotus Sutra 75–7, 78, 86, 99, 172, 175, 188
Loyalty Islands 251
Lubavitch 362, 365
Lunar New Year 141–3
Lurianic Kabbalah 358, 360
Luther, Martin 393, 411–14, 440, 560
lwa 224, 225

Maccabees 350, 374
Madhyamaka 74, 75
madrasa 210
magic 47, 81, 103, 116, 235, 236, 300, 359, 426, 545, 554, 555, 561–3
Mahabharata 22, 23, 25, 37, 40
maha-pari-nirvana 69, 77, 78, 99, 102, 187
Maha-shiva-ratri 49–50
Mahavairocana 172
Mahayana 61, 74–8, 80, 81, 84, 90, 94, 101–3, 107, 155, 521
Mahdi 497, 498, 500
Mahdism 209
Mahikari 520–21
Maimonides, Moses 342, 355, 466
Maitreya 77, 514
Malaysia 10, 115, 132, 181, 493
Mamluk dynasty 469, 471
mamo 271, 303
mana 240, 247, 248, 257, 260–63
mandala 86, 106, 108, 171
Mandate of Heaven 120–23, 127, 128
Manjusri 73, 101, 502, 503

mantra 34, 35, 38, 40, 51, 53–5, 57, 81, 93, 98, 99, 103–5, 111, 171, 188, 196
Mao Zedong 131, 156
Maori 246, 248–50, 258–9
Mara 65, 100, 101
Marcion 398
Marranos *see* Conversos
marriage 21, 23, 34, 35, 37, 50, 53, 62, 140, 228–31, 257, 264, 291, 355, 379, 410, 415, 422, 444–5, 471, 490–2, 527, 535
martyr 401, 440, 490, 498, 501, 512
Marxism ix, 130, 302
Marx, Karl 547, 548, 551, 560
Mary 117, 177, 300, 301, 400, 406, 419, 433, 436, 439, 440, 452
Masada 351–2
Mashhad 501, 502
masjid 31, 483, 486
Masjid al-Haram 486
mask 204, 219–21, 223, 224, 263–5, 274, 288, 295, 311, 314, 326, 328, 334, 492
mass 421, 429, 431, 443
matsuri 183, 188, 191
matzah 375
Mawdudi, Sayyid Abu al-Ala 475, 476
Maya 279–82, 295, 296, 305, 312, 318, 321, 330, 523
maya 44
Mazu 159–60
Mbiti, John S. 210, 219
Mecca 6, 452, 455, 458–62, 466, 471, 473, 478, 482, 483, 485, 486, 488–90, 495
medicine 133, 136, 137, 146, 155, 162, 169, 210, 214, 234, 235, 301, 308, 319, 320, 324, 327, 473, 514
Medina 460–2, 465, 471, 489, 509

meditation 5, 24, 38, 44, 45, 53–55, 65, 67, 68, 79, 84, 89, 90, 98, 99, 107, 108, 129, 138, 139, 171, 175, 185, 319, 515, 531, 536, 537, 571, 573
medium 154, 159, 178, 224, 226, 233, 235, 260, 264
Meiji period ix, 179–81, 187
Melanesia 241–5, 257, 260, 261
memorialization 190, 192
Mencius 123, 124
Mendelssohn, Felix 360–61
Mendelssohn, Moses 360
menorah 365, 375
menstruation 33, 175, 258, 264, 314, 321, 328, 378, 484, 528
meridians 136, 137
merit 33, 37, 38, 68, 78, 80, 92, 95–9, 103–5, 284, 429, 501
Mesoamerica 279, 280, 282, 284, 294, 295, 526
messiah 298, 342, 346, 348, 350, 358, 397, 398, 452, 497, 520
Mevlevi 506
Mexico 281–5, 300, 305, 318, 321, 331, 440, 535, 551
mezuzah 380–81
michi 175
Micronesia 241–5, 252, 257, 266
Mid-autumn festival 146
Middle Way 65
miko 188
mikoshi 188–9
mikveh 378
Mina 486, 488, 489
mindfulness 91, 175
miracles 41, 99, 102, 125, 172, 189, 253, 359, 365, 372, 375, 396, 397, 403, 419, 440, 459, 494, 495, 497, 500, 546
Miraj 503
Mishnah 340, 352, 353
Mishneh Torah 342, 356

mitzvah (pl. *mitzvot*) 337, 338, 366, 381, 382
miyamairi 194
mizuko kuyo 193, 194, 199
Moche 287–9
Modern Chan Society 530
Modern-Orthodox Judaism 340, 368, 370, 373, 377
moksha 18, 20, 22, 25, 32, 53–55
monism 20, 29, 32, 57
monks and nuns 63, 64, 68, 70–74, 76, 77, 80, 81, 84–86, 89, 90, 93–97, 99, 101–7, 118, 128, 129, 131, 138, 145, 151, 155, 170, 171, 173, 175, 178, 403, 406, 407, 409, 410, 443, 459, 515, 524, 530, 537, 543, 560
Monks Mound 277
monotheism 29, 38, 209, 210, 298, 337, 401, 458, 474, 480, 552, 557, 558, 562
moon blocks 154
moon poems 146
Moon, Rev. Sun Myung 535, 538
Moonies 535
Moroni 518
Mosaic Covenant 345, 347, 348, 365, 366, 381, 385, 399
Moses 345, 346, 349, 350, 359, 366, 368–70, 376
mosque 2, 31, 32, 132, 463, 469, 470, 478, 481, 483, 484, 486, 491, 498–500, 502, 505, 523, 525, 536–8, 559, 568
mother 36, 39, 42, 44, 46, 95, 99, 104, 129, 145, 147, 148, 158, 159, 213, 216, 222, 223, 227–9, 253, 259, 261, 291, 307, 308, 312, 318, 322, 328, 399, 406, 410, 433, 436, 438, 439, 523
Mother Earth 253, 261, 291, 308, 312, 318, 322, 328

mound building 167, 274–7, 279, 281, 287–9
Mount Hiei 172, 173, 176
moxa (mugwort) 136, 137, 144
moxibustion 136
Mozi 124
Muawiyah, Caliph 465, 503
Mughal dynasty 28, 471, 472, 474
mujahidin 479
Muhammad *see* Prophet Muhammad
Mulian 145
Müller, Max 550, 551
mummification 279, 280, 285, 292, 293, 295, 296
Murray, Margaret 526
murti 9, 32, 36–38, 42, 47, 48
Muslim Brotherhood 478, 479
Muslim World League 478
mutually destructive and engendering cycles 134, 136
mysticism 209, 356, 403, 467, 559, 565
mythology 25–27, 29, 37, 41, 44, 46, 49, 77, 130, 140, 169, 171, 172, 181, 214–15, 217, 233, 248, 252, 260, 283, 284, 286, 422, 550, 554–6, 558, 559, 567–9

Nagarjuna 74–5
Nakayama Miki 178
naked festivals 190–91
Nalanda 81, 543
names and naming 34, 148, 192–4, 214, 227, 228, 235, 263, 303, 306, 313, 332, 344, 345, 359, 374, 425, 459, 468, 482, 489, 495, 506, 527
Nandin 45
Naqshbandi brotherhood 28, 474
Nara 166, 170–71
National Learning 178–80

nature 34, 42, 44, 119, 120, 122, 125, 133, 146, 154, 185, 186, 208, 209, 215, 218, 259, 261, 278, 372, 374, 523, 525, 527, 555
Nazca 289, 290
nembutsu 85–6, 99, 174
Neo-Confucianism 129, 177
Neo-Paganism 525, 529, 571
neo-Pentecostalism 301
Netherlands 294, 414, 553
New Age, Next Age 302, 523–4, 529, 530
New Caledonia 242, 251
New Fire Ceremony 285
New Guinea 181, 245, 251, 253, 257, 258, 262, 266
New Hebrides 242, 251
new religions 517, 529–34
New Testament 398, 413, 419, 438, 440, 445, 463, 516
New Year 62, 102, 141, 143, 144, 156, 183, 193, 197, 373, 502, 569
New Zealand (Aotearoa) 241, 245, 255
Nicene Creed 402, 407
Nichiren 86, 99, 175, 532
Nigeria 208–10, 213, 214, 216, 224, 233, 422, 446, 453, 454, 520
Night Journey 460, 496
Night of Power 459
nikayas 70, 71, 77
nirvana 5, 60, 66–69, 72, 74–81, 83, 84, 92, 93, 99, 100, 102, 105, 107, 128, 155, 170, 174, 187
Nithyananda, Paramahamsa 531
Nizaris 499
Noahide Laws 339–40
Noble Eightfold Path 67, 68, 72, 77, 94
Nobles 20, 23, 29, 34, 40, 50

Nok sculptures 208
nones 525
novices 90, 94, 95, 107
numinous 566
nuns *see* monks and nuns
nusa 194, 195

obon 193, 197, 535
Oceania 5, 115, 133, 167, 241–4, 247, 249, 251–3
Oceanian religions
 contemporary beliefs and practices 256–66
 history 245–56
Oedipus complex 557
offerings (*see also* sacrifice) 16, 22, 23, 26, 27, 34, 36, 38, 39, 43, 49, 53, 60, 92, 98, 99, 102, 103, 120, 145, 147, 151–6, 171, 184, 185, 188, 192, 193, 195, 199, 217–19, 222–3, 225, 227, 232, 233, 235, 279–85, 287–9, 291, 310, 312, 315, 328, 329, 347, 348, 376, 381, 401, 402, 413
Ogun 218, 223, 260, 262, 263, 428, 429, 431, 433, 439, 484, 501, 505
Olcott, Henry Steel 88, 521
Old Testament 340, 342, 366, 398, 406, 413, 427–9, 436
Olmec 279–80
Om 35, 55
omairi 192
omamori 197–8
Omituo Fo 115, 155
opening of the curtain 187
Order of the Solar Temple 532
Organization of the Islamic Conference (OIC)
origin stories 280, 282, 284, 285, 291, 298, 305–7, 308, 310, 311, 317, 322, 323, 330, 568

original sin 404, 405, 412, 413, 417, 440
orishas 224
Orthodox Judaism 340, 341, 358, 360, 362–3, 368–70, 372, 373, 377–9, 381
Osho 536
Oshun 216
Other Side 357
other-than-human persons 302–3
Otieno, Silvano Melea 230–31
Otto, Rudolf 566–7
Ottoman dynasty 255, 355, 356, 358, 411, 471–4, 476, 492
Our Lady of Guadalupe 300, 440
outcaste 21

Pachamama 300
Pakistan 10, 31, 453–5, 476, 479, 480, 493, 499
Palestine 340, 346, 350, 352, 365, 374, 396, 397, 471
Pali 72, 87, 128
Pali Canon 72, 74–77, 79, 82, 94
Papua New Guinea 181, 242, 245, 248, 251, 256, 263
parable 76, 78, 396–7
Partition, the 31, 454
Parvati 44, 50–52
Passover 373, 375, 376, 381, 424, 434
pastoral rites 426, 442
Patanjali 53–4
Path of Purification 63, 76, 77
patriarch 403, 405, 407, 411, 459, 464
Paul of Tarsus 398, 413, 440
Paul VI, Pope 520
payback 260
penance 127, 410, 411, 442, 548
pentacle 527
Pentecost 376, 381, 419
Pentecostalism 253, 301, 418–20, 422, 426–8, 430, 438, 439, 442, 519

People of the Book 464
Persia 10, 11, 15, 347–9, 367, 375, 432, 454, 458, 466–8, 473, 490, 499, 517, 550
Pharisees 350
phenomenology 567
Philo of Alexandria 350
Pietists 416
pig-kill 262
pilgrimage 5, 22, 26, 36, 37, 45, 71, 96, 98, 132, 159, 172, 173, 177, 178, 187, 189, 190, 256, 276, 280, 288, 290, 298, 347, 354, 403, 408, 413, 452, 461, 470, 485–9, 482, 501, 537
pipe 220, 225, 226, 229, 276, 295, 307, 308, 318
Platform Sutra of the Sixth Patriarch 84
Pliny the Younger 401–2
polymaths 561
Polynesia 241–4, 247, 248, 250, 252, 257, 260, 261, 265
polytheism 209, 454, 458, 552, 556, 562
pope 117, 143, 176, 392, 405, 415, 419, 519
po souls 150, 151
Potlatch 296
poto mitan 225
power embedded in place 242, 244, 256, 260
powwow 302
Prabhupada, Swami 538
prajna-paramita 74, 76
prasad 38, 49, 50
Pratimoksha 94, 96, 103
prayer wheels 98, 103
pregnancy 177, 186, 223, 227, 234, 484
Presentation Theme 288, 289
priests, priestesses 11, 16, 17, 27, 34, 36–38, 42, 49, 87, 116, 118, 127, 130, 131, 145, 147, 150, 151, 153–5, 170, 172, 175, 179, 181, 182, 184–6, 188, 190–5, 197, 199, 210, 214, 216, 224, 226, 233, 262, 266, 279, 284, 285, 287, 288, 293, 295, 301, 303, 320, 331, 346, 347, 349–51, 359, 374, 375, 397, 402, 406, 407, 409, 411–14, 416, 420–22, 426, 429–31, 436, 442–4, 517, 524, 526, 554, 556, 560–62
primitive xi, 251, 416, 549, 551, 552, 554, 555, 558, 560, 563
primordium 310, 311, 316, 328
Prince of Martyrs 501
Princess Miaoshan 155
profane 556, 567–9
progressive reform movement 516
prophet 209, 235, 298, 299, 320, 340, 342, 346–8, 357, 365, 366, 376, 382, 396–8, 463, 464, 483, 487, 520, 533, 561, 562
Prophet Muhammad 455, 458–60, 462, 465, 466, 468, 469, 476, 480, 482, 485, 490, 492, 494, 496–8, 500–5
Protestant Ethic and the Spirit of Capitalism, The 560, 561
Protestant Reformation 395, 412, 415, 430, 516, 560
Protestantism 117, 132, 393, 411–15, 420, 444, 455, 476
psychoanalysis 557–9
puberty rites 228, 314, 315, 318, 331, 381, 484
Pudu 145
pueblo 278, 315
Pueblo Bonito 278, 279
puja 22, 46, 49, 52, 53, 96, 98–101

Puranas (*Ancient Tales*) 26, 27, 32
Pure Land Buddhism 82–86, 93, 98, 99, 115, 174, 175, 193
Purim 375

Qatar 491
qi 134–7, 138, 141, 142, 149, 150
qiblah 473
qigong 138
Qu Yuan 145
Quran 452, 453, 455, 459, 462, 464, 465, 467, 468, 472, 473, 475, 481–4, 487, 489, 492, 494–8, 500, 503, 506, 507, 543
Quran, inimitability of 494, 495
Qutb, Sayyid 475, 476, 478

rabbinic Judaism 340, 342, 350–53, 355, 358, 360, 361, 363, 368, 371, 373–7, 379, 382–4, 571
Raël 533
Raelians 533–4
Rainbow Snake 247, 258, 259
Rajneesh, Bhagwan Shree 536
rakah 483, 486
Ram-Lila 40
Rama 22, 23, 25, 31, 32, 40, 49, 52, 56
Ramadan 461, 481, 483, 484, 496
Ramakrishna Mission 531
Ramayana 22, 25, 40, 49, 52
Rapa Nui 241, 246
Rashidun 465
rattles 289, 295, 318, 325
Reagan, Ronald 446
real presence 413, 414, 430
rebirth *see* reincarnation
reciprocity 253, 260–61, 309, 310, 319, 329, 332
reclining Buddha 69, 99, 100

reconciliation 273, 410, 412–13, 442, 443
Reconstructionist Judaism 363
Record of Ritual 120, 121
red headed priests 154
Redfield, James 523
redistribution 247, 260–61, 262, 263, 265
reductionism 548–50, 559, 560, 563, 567, 572, 573
Reform Judaism 340, 341, 361–2, 363, 364, 368, 377, 383, 384
reform movements 29, 30, 131, 406, 407, 415, 420, 421, 474–6, 478, 504, 516, 519 (*see also* Protestant Reformation)
Reformed churches 414, 415, 420
reincarnation 14, 18, 21, 26, 33, 34, 54, 69, 76, 83, 84, 91, 93, 94, 104, 105, 115, 128, 133, 165, 174, 358, 383, 499, 552
reincorporation 226, 227, 229
religion
  definition 4–6, 544–5
  importance of 2
religious experience x, 17, 24, 33, 39, 42, 44, 48, 52, 79, 80, 85, 90, 105, 213, 214, 287, 309, 313, 316, 318, 322, 325, 328, 366, 403, 404, 406, 415, 416, 426, 429–31, 438, 494, 504, 506, 513, 521, 526, 533, 536, 537, 556, 564–5, 566–9, 573
religious orders 28, 90, 287, 303, 347, 407, 410, 412, 415, 427, 443, 444, 472, 479, 504–6, 515, 530, 532
religious specialists 97, 103, 119, 133, 136, 208, 232–3, 235, 236, 263, 264, 276, 284, 317, 320, 325, 407, 495, 584

ren 147
Renaissance 13, 29, 261, 414, 472, 545, 546
renunciation 13, 18–20, 22–5, 32, 36, 46, 48, 54, 55, 364, 425, 536 (*see also* asceticism)
research university 546–7
Revelation of Adam 399–400
Ricci, Matteo 130
Rig-Veda 15, 16, 29, 35
Rinzai Zen 175
rites of passage 221, 226, 227, 229, 232, 263, 265
ritual tools and paraphernalia 5, 171, 179, 220, 271, 295, 326–30, 409, 443, 527, 559
Roman Catholicism 3, 6, 117, 130, 132, 176, 224, 226, 250, 251, 253, 297, 300, 301, 358, 401, 402, 405, 408, 410–43 (*passim*), 455, 466, 467, 515, 516, 519, 524, 535, 544
Roman empire 282, 349–50, 351, 353, 354, 391, 396, 397, 402, 404, 405, 419, 458, 545, 561
Romanticism 548, 550, 559
Rongorongo 246
Room of the Posts 288–9
rosary 99, 440, 506
routinization 562
Rudd, Kevin 249–50

Sabbat 527
Sabbatai Zevi 258
Sabbath 353, 357, 358, 372, 427
sacrament 409, 410, 412, 413, 426, 427, 442–4
sacred bundle 327–8
sacred, the 556–7, 559, 562, 567–9

sacrifice 5, 16, 20, 40, 46, 48, 52, 71, 119, 120, 129, 217–19, 222, 223, 225, 227, 231–5, 247, 277, 280–82, 284–7, 289, 293, 309, 319, 347, 348, 350, 351, 401, 406, 413, 421, 423, 424, 429, 444, 469, 476, 488, 489, 505, 524 (*see also* offering)
Saddam Hussein 478
Safavid dynasty 471, 472, 474
Saicho 171, 172
saint 27, 28, 148, 151, 224, 298–300, 392–3, 401–3, 406, 413, 418, 431, 439–41, 449, 468, 501, 504, 505, 517, 518, 529
saints' days 436–7
Sakyadhita 90
Saladin 469
salafis 474, 479, 480, 492, 516
salat 483, 490, 491
salvage ethnology 297
salvation 18–19, 25, 32, 37, 40, 46, 47, 53, 55, 56, 72, 75, 76, 78–80, 83, 93, 99, 101, 104, 106, 109, 174, 295, 299, 366, 390, 396, 398, 400, 403, 414, 424, 436, 445, 446, 483, 533, 536, 545, 560, 562
samadhi 54, 55
Samoa 241, 251
samsara 14, 18, 25, 44, 55, 65, 66, 69, 75, 76, 79–81, 91, 105, 170
samskaras 34–5
samu 175
samurai 173
sanctification 425
Sanctuary of the Sun 288
sandek 381
Sangha 68, 69, 71, 72, 74, 88, 98
Sanskrit 14, 15, 26, 35, 48, 74–77, 81, 87, 128, 550, 553, 567, 572

Santería ix, 224–6, 519
Sapa Inca 291, 293
Sarasvati 29, 52
Sassanian empire 458, 463
Satan 422, 424, 487, 488
Satsang 53, 532
Saudi Arabia 453, 477, 478, 485, 491, 504
savage 251, 416, 549, 551
Sayyid 501, 505
schism 407, 411, 462, 516–17
Schneerson, Menachem Mendel 365
Scholasticism 409–10
Seal of the Prophets 462, 497
seclusion 226–9 (*passim*), 232, 315, 410
Second Temple, the 348–9, 351, 352, 359, 396
Second Vatican Council 6, 418, 420, 421, 436, 516
secret religious societies 314, 316–18, 327, 328
Seder 375
seekers, seekers' milieu 521, 523–9, 530, 532, 536
sefirot 357
self-blessing 527–8
self-cultivation 116, 124, 129, 133, 147, 152
Self-Realization Fellowship 515
Senegal 227, 235
Sephardim 354–6, 358, 369, 383
Serpent Mound 275
Servants 20, 30
seven, five, three ceremony 194–5
sexagenary cycles 139
Shabbatean movement 258
Shahadah 482, 483, 490
Shaivas 42, 44–47, 55
Shaker Church 301
Shaktas 46, 47, 55
shakti 42–44, 46–48
Shakya 46, 101

shaman 36, 87, 154, 167, 177, 207, 260, 271, 276, 301, 311, 316, 320–26, 329–31, 567–9
Shang Di 120
Shang dynasty 120, 121
Sharia 447, 467, 471, 478, 479, 481–93, 498, 501, 507, 543
Sharif 501
shaykh 504–6
Shema 369–71, 381
Shia Islam 455, 462, 466–9, 471, 477, 484, 490, 491, 496–503, 505, 517, 521
shichigosan 194
shide 185, 187, 188, 193–5
Shijia Fo 155
shimenawa 185, 187, 193
shinbutsu-bunri 179
Shingon 171, 172, 189
Shinran 85, 174
shinshukyo 182
shintai 185, 188, 197
Shinto ix, 62, 164, 165, 176, 181, 182, 184–7, 190, 193–5, 200, 515, 519
Shiva 13, 14, 25–27, 38, 39, 42–5, 46, 48, 50, 51, 53, 55
Shoah 364
shogun 88, 173, 175, 177–9, 181
shrine-temple 172, 174
shrines 28, 36–38, 62, 88, 98, 99, 105, 157, 165, 170, 172, 174, 176–80, 182–6, 189, 190, 194–200, 213, 214, 216, 219, 220, 224, 231, 233, 247, 285, 291, 293, 458, 463, 469, 501, 505
shukyo 181–2
Shulchan Arukh 355
siddha 80
Siddhartha Gautama *see* Gautama, Siddhartha
siddhi 47, 48
Sikhism 10, 28, 472, 747

sila 68, 94, 96, 98
Silk Road 128
sipapu 323
Six Day War 365, 478
six realms of rebirth 91, 92
Skanda 14, 44, 45
skill in means 75, 76, 78, 81
slavery 30, 208, 224, 372, 375, 421
Smith, Joseph 517, 518
social Darwinism 553
social justice 446
Sofer, Rabbi Moses 362
Soga clan 168
Soka Gakkai International (SGI) 532, 535
sola scriptura 413
Solomon 346, 347
Solomon Islands 245, 251, 424
Somin-sai 190
Song dynasty 129, 158
song line 240, 257, 259
sorcerer 157, 221, 231, 235, 298, 313, 324–6
Soto Zen 175, 186
soul 16–18, 33, 35, 40, 41, 53, 65, 66, 70, 105, 134, 150–52, 155, 192, 193, 199, 225, 233, 236, 311–13, 316, 321, 322, 325, 326, 329–32, 369, 373, 382, 383, 404, 440, 484, 502, 551
soul loss 312, 321, 325
South Africa 209
Spain 176, 250, 294–6, 298, 353–6, 358, 362, 398, 416, 454, 465, 466, 471, 515
Spanish Reconquest 471
Spanish Synagogue 362
spirit dart 323, 325, 326
spirit government 114, 152–9
Spirit Lodge 315, 318–19, 329
spirit master 312, 323, 328
spirit money 145, 150, 151, 154, 156

spirit tablet 105, 151, 192
Spiritism 224, 226, 519
spirits, non-human (African religions) 215–17
spiritual centers 274–95 (*passim*)
Spiritualist Churches 531
Spring and Autumn Annals 120, 121
Sri Lanka 10, 21, 22, 61, 63, 72, 76, 82, 87–90, 99, 521
Starhawk 526
Stations of the Cross 434–5
stigmata 410
stillbirth 152, 155
Stolen Generations 249–50
stoning the Devil 488
storytelling 5, 260, 312
study of religions 540–73
stupa 28, 88, 98, 100
subconscious 565
Subhuti, Dharmachari 515
Sudan 209, 213, 215, 217, 233, 399, 478, 562
Sufism 28, 209, 467, 468, 470–72, 474, 496, 500, 503–7, 524
sui generis 566, 572
Suleyman the Magnificent 473
Sun Myung Moon 535, 538
Sun Simiao 137
sunnah 462, 467, 497, 504, 505
Sunni Islam 455, 467, 469, 471, 490, 491, 496–8, 500–3
sunya, sunyata 75, 79, 81, 107, 108
supernaturals 306, 309, 311, 317, 322
Supreme Being 205, 210, 212–15, 216–20, 224, 226, 227, 231–3, 235, 237, 309, 312, 322, 330, 556
supreme reality *see* ultimate reality
Supreme Soul 40, 53

survivals 209, 552, 553, 563
sutra 74, 81, 107, 168, 170, 171, 175, 177, 188, 190, 192, 193
Sutra-pitaka 69, 70
swastika 14, 522
Switzerland 363, 414, 505, 532
symbol x, 5–7, 558, 559, 563, 568, 569
synagogue 2, 341, 352, 355, 362, 367–72, 373–6, 379, 382, 383
syncretism 515, 519–21

tabernacle 346, 429, 430
Tabernacles, feast of 374
taboo 233, 262–4, 307, 310, 313, 314, 323, 325, 327, 431, 554, 558
Tahiti 241, 246, 251
taiji quan 137–8
Taiwan 89, 115, 130–32, 138, 148–50, 153, 156, 159, 161, 530
taking refuge 72–4, 98, 99, 101
Taki Onqoy 298
Taliban 479
talisman 116, 197
talking boards 246
tallit 337, 370, 371, 384
Talmud 340, 352, 353, 355, 357, 379
tamagushi 194, 195
Tanak 340, 342, 344, 345, 352, 353, 357, 361, 366, 373
Tang dynasty 126, 128, 146
Tantra 38, 48, 81
Tanzania 209, 215, 233, 235, 427
Tara 101, 108
tariqah 504–7
tawaf 485, 489
tawhid 455, 460, 469, 480, 483, 494
Taymiyyah, Ibn 474
tefillin 370, 371

temple 2, 22, 27, 28, 30–32, 36–39, 42, 48, 49, 60, 62, 72, 88, 94, 96–101, 103, 105, 127, 128, 130-2, 140, 145, 147, 153–4, 155–9, 165, 169, 170, 172–5, 177–80, 182–7, 189–93, 196–9, 208, 214, 216, 220, 233, 277, 282–5, 287, 288, 295, 315, 333, 335, 341, 343, 346–52, 354, 355, 359, 365, 367, 368, 374, 375, 377, 379, 396, 430, 432, 447, 460, 469, 470, 518, 532, 547, 548
Temple of the Moon 282, 283, 288
temple-shrine 174
Ten Precepts 94
Tendai 84, 86, 172, 173, 175
tenno 169
Tenochtitlan 283–5
Tenrikyo 178
Teotihuacan 282–3, 284, 285
Terra Australis Incognita 248
terra nullius 249
Thailand 60, 61, 87–89, 91, 94, 95, 97, 99, 100, 104, 181
theism 19, 20, 25, 26, 32
theology 4, 544–6, 556, 559, 565, 566, 571, 656
theosis 405, 426
Theosophical Society 88, 521–2
Theravada 61, 71, 76–7, 78, 79, 81, 88, 90, 94, 96, 99–104
Third Wave of Confucianism 132
Thirst Dance 296, 309, 315, 318–20, 323, 329
Three Jewels 72, 98, 99, 101
Three Teachings, the 118, 129, 132, 154
Tibet 61, 73, 84, 87, 88, 90, 94, 96, 98, 101, 105–7, 132, 528

Tidalap 258
tikkun 357, 358, 360
tilak 45, 53
Time School 174
Tlaloc 283
tobacco 222, 276, 306, 308, 310, 315, 316, 318, 321, 323–9, 331, 489
Togo 213, 224
Tokugawa shogunate 88, 176–9, 181
Tokyo 173, 176, 179, 546, 553
Tonga 241, 251
Torah 337, 340–2, 349–51, 353, 355, 357–62, 364, 366–72, 374, 376, 381–3, 398, 464
Torah ark 337, 367, 368, 374
torii 185
totem 260, 554, 556, 558
Toxcatl, feast of 285
traditional types of change 521, 530
trance 105, 167, 178, 207, 233, 264, 315, 318, 321, 322, 325, 538, 551
transcendent x, 103, 170, 172, 213–15, 224, 256
Transcendental Meditation 53, 531, 571
transition 221–31, 232, 265, 331, 442, 443, 496
transubstantiation 413, 430
Tri-pitaka 72
trickster 216–7, 265, 300, 306, 307, 317, 559
trigrams 114, 140, 141
Trinity, the 244, 263, 417, 418, 422, 423, 425, 436
trishna 66
Trobriand Islands 262
trophy heads 289
true form and trace manifestation 172

True Light Supra-Religious Organization 520, 521
Tudi Gong 156, 157
Ture 217
Turkey 14, 81, 401, 408, 453, 473, 474, 476, 477, 492, 493, 500
Tuvalu 241, 251
Twelver Shiism 471, 498, 499
two-spirit people 321
Tylor, E.B. 207, 551–3, 554, 555, 562, 563
tzitzit 370, 381, 384

UFOs 533–4
Uganda 209, 213, 215, 234, 364, 422
Uighurs 117
Ukrainian Embassy of the Blessed Kingdom of God for All Nations 531
ulama 467, 473, 481, 482, 485, 497, 498, 500, 501
ultimate reality x, 5–7, 17, 19–21, 25, 32, 42, 66, 85, 92, 109, 133, 160, 213, 215, 216, 263, 267, 339, 513, 568
Ultra-Orthodox Judaism 341, 364, 377, 382
Uluru (Ayers Rock) 240
Uma 44
Umar, Caliph 262–4, 265
Umayyad dynasty 354, 465–6, 467, 471
Umbanda ix, 224, 226
ummah 160, 162, 165, 176, 478, 497
Unbounded One 357
uncarved block 124, 125
unconscious 557–9, 565
Unitarians 393, 417, 418, 521
United Arab Republic 478

United Nations Declaration on the Rights of Indigenous Peoples 244, 301
universities 91, 127, 130, 148, 183, 302, 341, 410, 411, 469, 543–4, 546–8, 550–3, 563, 564, 570–2
University of Berlin 546, 547, 550, 560
Untouchables 21, 31, 42, 90
Upanishads 17–19, 21, 29, 33, 513
Urban II, Pope 408
Uthman, Caliph 464–5, 495
Uthmanic Codex 465, 495

Vairocana Buddha 170
Vaishnavas 40, 42, 47, 56
vajra 80
Vajrayana 61, 80–82, 84, 87, 90, 93, 94, 98, 99, 101–3, 108
valley of Arafat 486, 488
Vanuatu 242, 253
Varieties of Religious Experience, The 564–7
Veda 15–17, 19, 21, 29, 30, 34, 35, 52, 554
Vedanta 17
Vessantara Jataka 105–6
vèvè 225
Vinaya-pitaka 60, 70, 72–74, 107
Viracocha 291
Vishnu 9, 22–27, 37–42, 44, 46, 50, 52, 56, 81, 88
vision quest 309, 315
visual arts, Islam 468–9
visual arts, Judaism 383
vital force 205, 210, 212, 215, 219, 220, 222, 223, 226, 229, 231, 232, 237, 256
vital matter (*qi*) 134
Vivekananda, Swami 531
vocation 235, 442–5, 560

Vodou ix, 205, 224, 225
Vorilhon, Claude (Raël) 533
votive tablets 198–9

Wa 169
Wahhabi reform movement 474, 477
Waiyaki, Virginia Wambui 230–31
Wang Yangming 129
Warramurrungundjui 257
Warring States period 175, 177
Weber, Max 560–62, 563
weddings *see* marriage
Western Paradise 83, 155
Western Wall 354
Wheel of Life 92, 93
Whirling Dervishes 506
Wicca 512, 525–7, 571
widow 29, 30, 490, 538
wine, Judaism 372–3
Wiredu, Kwasi 220
wish fulfillment 557, 558
witch and witchcraft 221, 223, 231, 233, 235, 236, 300, 317, 324–7, 362–3
wood henge 277
world axis 323, 568
World Divine Light Organization 520
World Parliament of Religions (Chicago, 1893) 89, 521, 553
Wovoka 299
wu wei 124–5

Xunzi 124

yakudoshi 190
Yakushi 169
Yamato court 168–70, 171
yang 122, 126, 134, 137–47 (*passim*), 150, 152, 154
yang qi 122, 134, 137

yangsheng 137
Yang Zhu 124
yantra 47
yarmulke 337, 369–70
Yaxchilan 281–2
Yellow Hat Sect 87, 103
Yemen 454, 458, 479, 499
YHWH 345, 359, 360
yidam 101
Yiddish 354, 361
yin 122, 126, 134, 137–47 (*passim*), 150, 152, 154
yin qi 122, 134, 137
yin-yang theory 127, 169
Yochai, Rabbi Simeon bar 357
yoga 47, 48, 53–55, 524, 567, 569, 571
Yogachara 76, 84
Yogananda, Swami Paramahansa 515
Yoga-Sutras 53–55
Yom Kippur 359, 373, 374
yoni 42, 43
Yoshida Kanetomo 176
Yuan dynasty 129, 158

zakat 483–4, 485, 493, 501
Zalman, Rabbi Shneur 362
Zambia 214
Zayidis 499
zazen 84, 175
Zedong, Mao 131, 156
Zen 84, 86, 89, 175, 184, 186, 515, 521 (*see also* Chan)
Zhang Daoling 127
Zhang Zai 129
Zhou dynasty 120, 122, 124, 125, 127, 145
Zhuangzi 124, 125, 127
Zimbabwe 207–9, 229, 231
Zionism 363–4, 365
Zohar 356–8
Zwingli, Ulrich 414